African American Women

A Biographical Dictionary

Garland Reference Library of the Social Sciences (Vol. 706)
Biographical Dictionaries of Minority Women, Volume 2

Biographical Dictionaries of Minority Women

Native American Women
A *Biographical Dictionary*
Gretchen M. Bataille
editor

African American Women
A *Biographical Dictionary*
Dorothy C. Salem
editor

Angela Howard Zophy
Series Editor

African American Women

A Biographical Dictionary

Dorothy C. Salem
editor

Garland Publishing
New York & London
1993

© 1993 Dorothy C. Salem

Library of Congress Cataloging-in-Publication Data

African American women : a biographical dictionary /
edited by Dorothy C. Salem.
    p.   cm. — (Garland reference library of social science ;
vol. 706)   (Biographical dictionaries of minority women ; v. 2)
    Includes index.
    ISBN 0-8240-9782-3 (alk. paper)
    1. Afro-American women—Biography—Dictionaries.
I. Salem, Dorothy C.   II. Series.   III. Series: Garland
reference library of social science ; v. 706.
E185.96A45   1993
920.72'089'96073—dc20
[B]   92-45727
                                                  CIP

Printed on acid-free, 250-year-life paper
Manufactured in the United States of America

Book design by Julia Threlkeld

Contents

Preface

I am very pleased to introduce Dorothy Salem's volume on African American women as an integral part of Garland's Biographical Dictionaries of Minority Women. Professor Salem has compiled a valuable and unique reference to facilitate research on African American women and to promote recognition of their many and varied contributions to our national culture.

African American Women: A Biographical Dictionary addresses the need for accessible general information on African American women and their contributions, a need that persists despite the increased visibility within contemporary U.S. society as well as among the disciplines of Women's Studies. I first confronted the disturbingly small number of basic reference sources on African American and other minority women when I began to edit the *Handbook of American Women's History* in the late 1980s. The most difficult task confronting me and the contributors was searching for elusive biographical information and bibliographical sources for women who were significant historical participants but who received only "honorable mention" in general historical monographs. When I lamented the dearth of sources for the most elementary information on the careers and works on minority women to my editor at Garland Publishing, Kennie Lyman, offered me the opportunity to coordinate the collection of such basic historical and historiographical data on these neglected women in this series.

We realized early on how fortunate we were that Dorothy Salem accepted my invitation to edit our volume on African American women. Her commitment to undertake this demanding assignment reflected her own assessment that this project was a long-overdue effort to restore to the historical record the names and contributions of African American women whose lives influenced the development of the history of the United States.

I congratulate Dr. Salem on her execution of our mission to render accessible fundamental information and research sources for this significant group of American women. Because of her completion of this volume so early in this series, we will cite her as an example to future editors: she undertook the challenge of the almost impossible task of restoring to public awareness women who have earned and deserve their place in U.S. history.

Although we lament that inevitably a few significant women still may not be found among the entries within each volume, we continue to strive to offer comprehensive coverage of minority women within this series. Therefore, I am very proud to be associated with this eagerly awaited reference work that is the result of the unstinting dedication of its editor and the contributors.

—Angela Howard Zophy
Series Editor
Associate Professor of History,
University of Houston—Clear Lake

Dedication and Acknowledgments

This volume is dedicated to all those who admire the tenacity and accomplishments of African American women. The authors, librarians, archivists, and technical staff who made this volume possible are greatly appreciated for their contributions and support to this effort for reconstructing and bringing to the forefront the lives of important African American women.

Introduction and Selected Bibliography

African American Women: A Biographical Dictionary introduces the student, librarian, teacher, scholar, and general reader to women who made meaningful, though largely unheralded, contributions to American history and culture. Even today most go unmentioned in Women's Studies, Black Studies, and specialized collections in the Humanities and the Sciences. Unfortunately, no single volume could include the innumerable African American women who have earned the right to be noted. *African American Women* is neither all inclusive nor solely a compilation of success stories. Rather it is a selection of biographies of women who have made significant contributions to social reform, politics, arts and entertainment, religion, business, education, and the professions from the Colonial era to the present.

Although the collection focuses on historical achievements, several women reflect contemporary accomplishments or historical "firsts." This collection, which contains biographies of nearly 300 women, displays a range in time from Colonial poet Lucy Terry (1730–1821) to Olympic runner Gail Devers (b. 1966). Most of these women were long-lived and remained active and committed to their ideals into their seventies and beyond. A few, such as Anna Cooper (1858–1964), Hallie Quinn Brown (1846–1949), and Rosina Tucker (1881–1987), became centenarians. Sadly, some left this world too soon, as did playwright Lorraine Hansberry (1930–1965), YWCA leader Juliette Derricotte (1897–1931), and civil rights activist Ruby Doris Smith Robinson (1942–1967). The stress of stardom coupled with the frustrations of racial barriers led still others to leave this life prematurely, as in the case of blues singer Billie Holiday (1915–1959) and actress/singer/dancer Dorothy Dandridge (1922–1965). Nonetheless, there are still many more who continue to shape the direction of the African American community through their writing, organizations, and leadership, as do Marian Wright Edelman of the Children's Defense Fund, Byllye Avery of the NBWHP, and filmmaker Julie Dash, creator of the highly acclaimed *Daughters of the Dust*.

Most of the women here are not limited to a single area of achievement. Several excel in divergent fields. May Chinn had developed a critical reputation as a pianist before becoming a physician. Jane Edna Hunter started out as a nurse, but due to racial discrimination in the North against black female nurses, she entered the field of social work and established the Phillis Wheatley Association, then a shelter and training center for young women. After receiving nationwide recognition for her settlement work, she went on to obtain a law degree to better enable her to maneuver through the political institutions of urban America. Alberta Hunter left the stage as a blues singer to become a practical nurse. Shirley Graham Du Bois was an ethnomusicologist before she became an advocate for racial justice. Rosina Tucker, a well-known composer and musician, became a major union organizer for the Brotherhood of Sleeping Car Porters and a community activist. Mary Ann Shadd went from teaching to editing an antislavery newspaper and then on to law school at Howard University. Catharine Lealtad entered community service through the YWCA, but racial discrimination led her to the NAACP and National Urban League before she eventually entered medical school to become a physician.

These women were not frivolously changing direction. Their intelligence and talent made them aware of other fields they could master that could better prepare them for service to the community. The majority of these women can be considered formal or informal educators because they sought to teach others their skills, whether in painting, singing, public speaking, fundraising, organizing, or campaigning for the presidency. Unlike many traditional male leaders who have sought to gain and maintain personal power, these African American women generally endeavored to pass on what they learned to future generations, and having shared those personal gifts, created an enduring legacy.

The stories of historic African American women reveal curious parallels with those of historic African American men, parallels often unknown even to educators in the disciplines of black history and Women's Studies. Educators inform students about the assassination of Malcolm X reputedly by representatives of the Nation of Islam, but how many students have heard about the assassination of Laura Adorkor Kofey, one of the most successful organizers in the Universal Negro Improvement Association (UNIA)? Her leadership attracted many of Marcus Garvey's followers, which in turn drew Garvey's criticisms and threats. As a result, Kofey formed her own organization, the African Universal Church and Commercial League. While delivering a sermon to her followers, she was shot. A UNIA member in the audience was beaten to death by her followers, and two other UNIA members were arrested for the crime.

The often-circulated story about the death of Dr. Charles Drew, the physician who developed plasma, is duplicated in fact, not rumor, by the death of Juliette Derricotte, the dean of women at Fisk University. Derricotte, seriously injured in a car accident in Dalton, Georgia, was refused treatment at the nearest white hospital, and had to wait for transport to Walden Hospital in Chattanooga, Tennessee, where she died, November 7, 1931, her short life of service sacrificed to the traditions of segregation.

Students can list the host of civil rights leaders from Martin Luther King, Jr., to Stokely Carmichael, but do they know about the multitudes of women who marched and who were beaten and jailed right alongside them? From the very beginning, women were leaders in activities from the Montgomery bus boycott

(Mary Fair Burks, Jo Ann Robinson, Rosa Parks) to the sit-ins (Diane Nash, Ruby Doris Smith Robinson), and were active in the the Mississippi Freedom Democratic Party (Fannie Lou Hamer) and the formation of the Student Nonviolent Coordinating Committee (Ella Baker, Eleanor Holmes Norton); others were educators in the Freedom Schools (Septima Clark) and nurturers of change (Queen Mother Audley Moore, Angela Davis). It is hoped that this collection will provide the educators and their students with information about these women, whose tireless efforts sought to better the world for us all.

Arranged alphabetically, the entries provide the reader with the necessary information to understand the woman and her place in history. The subjects' names head the entries in boldface type; following, if applicable, in brackets are the women's maiden names, first married names, slave names, and/or birth names (if the subject is better known by a pseudonym). The names are cross-referenced within the work, listed in categories of major influence, and indexed by occupations, organizations, regions, and related information. Through descriptions of family, education, and career background, the biographical entry places each woman in a specific time frame, as well as in locational, intellectual, and organizational contexts. The Appendix lists the women by career category. The extensive bibliographic information provides for scholars and students a trail that leads to primary sources and further discussion in secondary sources. Where such information is lacking, researchers are encouraged to provide greater delineation in their individual projects or future monographs. Given the necessary inquisitive motivation, much of the information of the details of these women's lives can be found.

Unlike many biographical dictionaries, these entries are neither biographical outlines nor general sketches, but are summaries and analytical descriptions of the woman, her significance, and her works. This volume becomes part of the informational matrix that explores the experiences of African American women as representatives of their race, gender, or area of specialization. *African American Women: A Biographical Dictionary* seeks to clarify, supplement, consolidate, and condense information that appears in limited form in the related biographical dictionaries, bibliographical indices, and almanacs.

The following related reference works provide information about African American women, but in limited, sporadic form, and often the information is diffuse and incomplete.

Dannett, Sylvia, ed. *Profiles of Negro Womanhood*. Chicago: Educational Heritage, 1964. Provides dates but only a few paragraphs of description.
James, Edward T., et al., eds. *Notable American Women: 1607–1950*. Cambridge, MA: Belknap, 1971. Contains entries for only 41 black women.
Kranz, Rachel. *Biographical Dictionary of Black Americans*. New York: Facts on File, 1992.

Logan, Rayford W., and Michael R. Winston, eds. *Dictionary of American Negro Biography*. New York: Norton, 1982. Contains biographical entries of black women deceased prior to 1970 but lacks an index to the alphabetical listing.

Ploski, Harry A., and James Williams. *The Negro Almanac: A Reference Work on the African American*. Detroit: Gale, 1989. Contains short biographies and information about contemporary and historical organizations and events.

Robinson, Wilhelmina S. *Historical African American Biography*. Cornwells Heights, PA: Association for the Study of Afro-American Life and History, 1967. Provides only a paragraph or two on each subject but does not include dates, sources, or other details.

Rush, Theressa G., et al. *Black American Writers Past and Present: A Biographical and Bibliographical Dictionary*. Metuchen, NJ: Scarecrow Press, 1975.

Shockley, Ann A., and Sue P. Chandler. *Living Black American Authors: A Biographical Directory*. New York: Bowker, 1973.

Sims, Janet. *The Progress of Afro-American Women: A Selected Bibliography and Resource Guide*. Westport, CT: Greenwood, 1980.

Southern, Eileen. *The Greenwood Encyclopedia of Black Music: Bibliographical Dictionary of Afro-American and African Musicians*. Westport, CT: Greenwood, 1981.

Turner, Darwin. *Afro-American Writers*. New York: Appleton-Century-Crofts, 1907.

Washington, Sarah M. *An Annotated Bibliography of Black Women's Biographies and Autobiographies for Secondary-School Students*. PhD dissertation. University of Illinois, Urbana-Champaign, 1980.

Williams, Ora. *American Black Women in Arts and Social Science: A Bibliographic Survey*. Metuchen, NJ: Scarecrow Press, 1978.

The following sources provide general information about many black women.

Arata, Esther, and Nicholas Rotoli. *Black American Playwrights*. Metuchen, NJ: Scarecrow Press, 1978.

Campbell, Dorothy W. *Index to Black American Writers in Collective Biographies*. Littleton, CO: Libraries Unlimited, 1983.

Cederholm, Theresa D. *Afro-American Artists: A Biographical Directory*. Boston: Trustees of the Boston Public Library, 1973.

Dictionary of Women's Biography. New York: Continuum, 1985.

Evans, Mari. *Black Women Writers, 1950–1980*. New York: Doubleday, 1984.

Glikin, Tonda. *Black American Women in Literature*. Jefferson, NC: McFarland, 1989.

Green, Mildred D. *Black Women Composers*. Boston: Twayne, 1983.

Hawkins, Walter L. *African American Biographies*. Jefferson, NC: McFarland, 1992.

Herman, Kali. *Women in Particular: An Index to American Women*. Phoenix, AZ: Oryx Press, 1984.

Ploski, Harry A., and Roscoe C. Brown, eds., *The Negro Almanac*. New York: Bellwether, 1967.

Yenser, T., ed. *Who's Who in Colored America*. New York: Who's Who in Colored America Corp. 1933+.

In the following reference works, which focus on careers, African American women are recognized for their specialized contributions in specific fields.

Mapp, Edward. *A Directory of Blacks in the Performing Arts*. Metuchen, NJ: Scarecrow Press, 1978.

Matney, William C. *Who's Who among Black Americans, 1990–1991*. Detroit: Gale, 1990.

Page, James. *Selected Black American Authors: An Illustrated Bio-Bibliography*. Boston: G.K. Hall, 1977.

Redfern, Bernice. *Women of Color in the United States*. New York: Garland, 1988.

Smith, Jessie Carney. *Notable Black American Women*. Detroit: Gale, 1992. Places greatest focus on contemporary women, with historical highlights.

Smythe, Mabel M. *The Black American Reference Book*. Englewood Cliffs, NJ: Prentice-Hall, 1966.

Some of the following books highlight the same selected women, which usually results in repetition of the same inaccuracies about the same women in each text.

Brawley, Benjamin. *Women of Achievement*. 1919.

Brown, Hallie Q. *Homespun Heroines and Other Women of Distinction*. Xenia, OH: Aldine, 1926. Reprinted, Freeport, NY: Books for Libraries, 1971, pp. 182–193.

Cherry, Gwendolyn. *Portraits in Color*. New York: Pageant, 1962. Offers more extensive biographical profiles with a select bibliography on each woman; however, only a limited number of women are profiled in each category (arts, professions, and a few others).

Davis, Marianna. *Contributions of Black Women in America*. Columbia, SC: Kenday, 1982. Provides a general narrative about contributions in categories of achievement. Individual women are described within the narrative, usually in a few lines to a few paragraphs. A full profile of each woman's background and career is absent.

Majors, Monroe A. *Noted Negro Women: Their Triumphs and Activities.* Donohue & Henneberry, 1893.

Mossell, Gertrude. *The Work of Afro-American Women.* Nashville: Fisk University Library Negro Collection, 1894.

Scruggs, L.A. *Women of Distinction.* Raleigh, NC: L.A. Scruggs, 1893.

African American Women is a creation of many contributors representing a variety of disciplines, backgrounds, and interests. The volume does not include everyone of significance, but it does include a range of women about whom little is known or published to this date. Because the focus is historical, the women who helped develop the history of African American women are specially featured, but profiles of African American women who excelled rapidly in their fields and achieved significance while young are also included.

Because the entire field of African American women's history is constantly evolving, a volume such as this is a work in progress. Therefore, it is the hope of this editor that readers will suggest other entries and additional information as the needs arise. Like the patchwork quilts made by African slave women, this work is the culmination of many patches connected by the common thread of African American women's experiences. I am confident that researchers will be aided by this volume in their quest for information and trust that they will continue to expand this quilt through their own contributions in the future.

—Dorothy Salem

A

ADAIR, CHRISTIA [DANIELS] (1893–1989), suffrage leader, civil rights activist, and educator, grew up in Edna, Texas, listening to her father discuss politics and helping her mother in church work. At an early age, she took on the responsibility of religious instruction at Edna Methodist Church. At age 16, she became the Sunday school superintendent. After graduating from Prairie View College in 1915, Adair taught for three years in the public schools in Edna. She married Elbert Adair, a brakeman for the Missouri-Pacific Railroad and moved to Kingsville, Texas in 1918. There, Adair organized the Sunday School for black children, led the campaign by black and white women's clubs to close down gambling establishments, and promoted petition drives for woman's suffrage. Her community work expanded as racial discrimination became more apparent: Although women won the right to vote in Texas primaries, black women experienced rejection when they attempted to vote; in 1919 presidential candidate Warren G. Harding refused to shake hands with her Sunday school students when he stopped at the train station during his campaign. In 1925, Adair moved to Houston.

After working as a volunteer for the NAACP, in 1943 she became a full-time worker for the organization, serving as the executive secretary of the Houston branch from 1949 to 1959, when she retired. In 1944, she tested the voting system by becoming one of the first black women in Texas to vote in the Democratic primary. Her leadership of the Houston NAACP branch led to the removal of "Whites Only" signs from the airport and libraries, the opening of public facilities to blacks, and the exposure of unfair treatment of black department store customers. In an attempt to ensure that black customers be treated with respect, Adair insisted on trying on an expensive girdle. She convinced the store's management to allow her to try on the garment, setting a precedent for other black women.

In 1950 Adair became the first black female precinct judge in Harris County, Texas, holding that position until 1972. In 1956, she refused to release the names of NAACP members to the Texas attorney general despite his official harassment. In her seventies, Adair participated in the sit-ins of the 1960s and served as the co-chair of the Commission on Christian Social Concern, Texas Methodist Conference.

Adair received many honors: in 1977 a Houston park was named after her; in 1984, she was recognized for her lifetime commitment to civic and volunteer involvement, one of twelve living women who were honored in ten areas of achievement by the Texas Women's Hall of Fame. She died in 1989.

—Dorothy C. Salem

Bibliography

Biographical and topical files on Christia Adair can best be found in the collection "Texas Women: A Celebration of History Exhibit Archives" housed in the Texas Woman's University Library, see: Ruthe Winegarten, ed. *Finder's Guide to the Texas Women: A Celebration of History Exhibit Archives* (Denton: Texas Woman's University Library, 1984). The interview with Christia Adair is part of the Black Women Oral History Project, Schlesinger Library, Radcliffe College. Other books that feature Adair's work include M.B. Rogers, et al. *We Can Fly* (Austin, Texas: E.C. Temple Texas Foundation for Women's Resources, 1983) and Ruthe Winegarten, *Texas Women: A Pictorial History* (Austin: Eakin Press, 1986).

ALBRIER, FRANCES (1898–1987), union organizer and civil rights activist, was born in Mt. Vernon, New York, and raised in Tuskegee, Alabama, by her grandmother, a former slave who was a midwife, African Methodist Episcopal Church activist, and friend to Harriet Tubman and Margaret Murray Washington. Frances Mary Albrier studied at Tuskegee Institute and Howard University, where she trained as a nurse and social worker. During the post–World War I era, she met Mary Church Terrell and joined the National Association of Colored Women. In 1920 she moved to Berkeley, California, and married an engineer who worked in construction because he was unable to secure work in his profession. Similarly, Albrier was unable to find employment in hospitals and became an assistant to an obstetrician who did home deliveries.

In 1921 after hearing Marcus Garvey speak in Oakland, Albrier joined Garvey's Universal Negro Improvement Association (UNIA) and became an instructor with the Black Cross Nurses, a UNIA auxiliary. Through her UNIA experiences she became involved in the Bay Area black community and learned organizational skills through work in homes, women's groups, and church groups. From 1926 to 1931 she worked as a maid for the Pullman Company and became involved in the Brotherhood of Sleeping Car Porters. Turning to union organizing, she became the president of the Women's Auxiliary of Dining Car Employees. She was laid off at the beginning of the Depression.

After working in a number of jobs in the early 1930s, she finally acquired a hospital nursing position. Her first husband died in 1930, and in 1934, she married William Albrier, a porter and fellow union activist. Albrier continued her activist work, lobbying the Works Progress Administration to hire married women and mothers, setting up food and clothing banks through churches, working to end racial discrimination in restaurants and hotels, organizing the East Bay Women's Welfare Club, and leading the successful fight for city schools to hire black teachers. By 1940 she was the president of the Citizens Employment Council, and led picketing of establishments that did not hire blacks.

During World War II, she trained as a welder, an action designed to force shipyards to hire blacks and unions to accept women members. Also during the war, she began the Department of Women in Industry within the Federation of

Colored Women's Clubs. After the war, she became a postal employee and organized black workers within the U.S. Postal Service. She was the first woman elected to the Alameda County Democratic Central Committee, and worked to organize women within the Democratic party and on the issues of day care and full employment for women. She was the president of the San Francisco chapter of the National Council of Negro Women. During the 1960s she was a member of the Women's International League for Peace and Freedom and protested the Vietnam War. She became a supporter of the women's movement and an advocate of the Equal Rights Amendment. Active in the NAACP and CORE, she was a member of a number of cultural and religious organizations, and an advocate for the teaching of black history in public schools. She died in 1987.

—Barbara Bair

Bibliography

Albrier's life and career have been documented in a long oral history conducted by Malca Chall in 1977–1978. This oral history was sponsored by the Schlesinger Library on the History of Women in America, Radcliffe College, Cambridge, Mass., Black Women Oral History Project, and by the Bancroft Library, University of California at Berkeley, Women in Politics Oral History Project. An article on Albrier, Raoul C. Peterson, "Garveyism in California: A Lady Remembers" *Core* (Fall/Winter 1973): 20–22, is reprinted within the oral history. Albrier's papers are available at the Bancroft Library. Albrier is also profiled in Charlotte Pointer and Pamela Valois, *Gifts of Age: Portraits and Essays of Thirty-Two Remarkable Women* (San Francisco: Chronicle Books, 1985), 46–49; and in *Women of Courage: An Exhibition of Photographs by Judith Sedgwick* ed. Ruth Edmonds Hill (Cambridge: Radcliffe College, 1984), p. 44.

ALEXANDER, SADIE [MOSSELL] (1898–1989), lawyer, civic leader, and social activist, was born in Philadelphia on January 2. She was the daughter of Aaron A. and Mary Louise (Tanner) Mossell, and the niece of Henry Ossawa Tanner, America's foremost African American artist of the late nineteenth and early twentieth centuries. Her maternal grandfather, Benjamin Tucker Tanner, was a bishop of the African Methodist Church in Philadelphia. She married Raymond Pace Alexander, a Harvard Law School graduate, in November 1923.

Education was both a tool and a path for achievement to Sadie Alexander, who attended the University of Pennsylvania, receiving a BS in education in 1918 and an MA in economics in 1919. In 1921 she became the first African American woman to earn a PhD from the University of Pennsylvania, and the second woman of African American descent to earn a PhD in the nation. In 1927 she became the first woman in the United States to earn a law degree. (Her father had been the first African American to graduate from the University of Pennsylvania Law School.) In the same year she became the first woman to be admitted to the bar in Pennsylvania.

Throughout her life, Alexander was active in numerous civic and cultural organizations. She was a founding member of the University of Pennsylvania chapter of the Delta Sigma Theta sorority a public service organization founded in 1913 at Howard University. She served five terms as president of Delta Sigma Theta from the organization's first national convention on December 27, 1919, at Howard University until 1923.

Alexander, an advocate for race history, was a good friend and associate of Carter G. Woodson, the founder of the Association for the Study of Negro Life and History (ASNLH). The Philadelphia chapter of ASNLH was founded in the Alexander home at 1708 West Jefferson Street in November 1929. She also belonged to the American Civil Liberties Union, Americans for Democratic Action, and served on the board of the National Urban League.

Alexander's civic commitment was demonstrated in professional and political activities. She and her husband ran a successful law practice in Philadelphia and founded the National Bar Association, an organization of African American attorneys. For the city of Philadelphia, Alexander was the first African American female assistant city solicitor, and she headed the Commission on Human Rights, serving on its interracial committee.

Through her involvement in the activities of Delta Sigma Theta sorority, ASNLH, and the National Bar Association, Alexander helped advance social justice issues, especially those relating to women and Americans of African descent.

She died of pneumonia on November 1, 1989, at Cathedral Village, a Philadelphia retirement community, survived by two daughters, Rae Alexander-Minter and Mary A. Brown.

—Regennia N. Williams

Bibliography

The papers of Sadie T.M. Alexander are housed in the Archives of the University of Pennsylvania in Philadelphia. Her interview is part of the Black Women Oral History Project, Schlesinger Library, Radcliffe College. A history of Delta Sigma Theta Sorority, *In Search of Sisterhood: Delta Sigma Theta and the Challenge of the Black Sorority Movement* by Paula Giddings (New York: William Morrow, 1988) chronicles much of Alexander's activism through her membership in this organization.

ALEXANDER, VIRGINIA M. (1900–1949), public health physician and peace activist, was born in Philadelphia. When she was four years old her mother died, leaving her with two brothers, one sister, and an unemployed father, who encouraged all his children to educate themselves. Later, Virginia and her brother Raymond Alexander attended the University of Pennsylvania on scholarship. She also attended the Woman's Medical College of Pennsylvania on scholarship; however, her support was limited, and while attending school she worked as a waitress, maid, and clerk prior to her graduation in 1925.

Dr. Alexander faced much discrimination in her nationwide search for an internship. One hospital president said, "If you were first among a thousand applicants you would still not be admitted." After completing her internship at Wheatley Provident Hospital in Kansas City, Missouri, she took an additional year at Kansas City General Hospital, where she was their first place woman physician. Dr. Alexander returned to Philadelphia in 1928 to establish an office of general medicine in the black community of North Philadelphia. Concerned about the mortality rate of black mothers and babies, Dr. Alexander established the Aspiranto Health Home, a lying-in hospital to provide maternity care for African American mothers and newborns. Dr. Alexander was known as the "guardian of the health of Negro women" for this clinic (founded in 1931) and the Well Baby Clinic she later founded. Both clinics were housed in her own three-story home.

Dr. Alexander stated:

If we can reduce the incidence of death at both ends of Negro life in the United States, we can add greatly to the overall contribution which our group can make to the Nation as a whole. To do this, we will have to send physicians into sections which have no bright lights and little social enterprise, take public health information across the railroad tracks and, above all, give knowledge to Negro women who are going to become mothers.

Her friends considered her a poor businesswoman because she often forgot to collect her fees or returned fees to poor patients. She furnished free medicine and worked endless hours maneuvering her little Ford through Philadelphia streets with hairraising accuracy. But other physicians and patients agreed that Virginia Alexander had answered the question as to whether a black woman could succeed in her profession. In 1937, she received her Masters in Public Health from Yale School of Medicine. Afterward, she travelled to Scandinavia to study public health. She was a member of the teaching staff of Howard University Medical School, was associated with Freedman's Hospital and maintained a practice in the District of Columbia. She left private practice for public health service and in 1941 she served as the public health physician for coal and iron mining communities in the hills of rural Alabama.

Affected by the horrors of World War II, Dr. Alexander became a pacifist and an active Quaker. She was the only African American member of the Philadelphia Yearly Meeting and was also chairperson of the "colored" Young Women's Christian Association (YWCA). She died of lupus at age 49.

—Janet Miller

Bibliography

Most of the information on Virginia Alexander can be found in the Virginia Alexander file, Black Women Physicians Project, Accession 178, Archives and

Special Collections on Women in Medicine, Medical College of Pennsylvania, and in the Virginia Alexander Alumnae folder, Accession 73, Archives and Special Collections on Women in Medicine, Medical College of Pennsylvania.

ALLEN, DEBORAH (DEBBIE) (b. 1950), dancer, choreographer, actress, vocalist, television director, producer, and writer

was born January 16 in Houston, Texas, to Vivian (Ayers) Allen, a Pulitzer prize nominee for poetry from South Carolina, and Dr. Arthur Allen, a dentist from Baton Rouge, Louisiana. Allen is the third of three children, all of whom have careers in the performing arts. Her sister, Phylicia Rashad, is an actress known for her role as Claire Huxtable on *The Cosby Show*; her brother, Andrew "Tex" Allen, is a jazz musician. Allen lives in California with her husband Norman Nixon, former Los Angeles Laker and Los Angeles Clippers basketball star, and their two children—Vivian Nicole, age seven, and Norman Ellard, Jr., age four.

Allen, the consummate performer, has made her mark on stage and in television and film, excelling as a choreographer, dancer, vocalist, television producer, and director. Allen began dance training at age three, and by age eight, she had already decided that her career would be in musical theater. Her mother encouraged her daughter's interest and talent in dance by attempting to enroll her in the segregated Houston Foundation for Ballet, to which she was denied entrance. Undeterred, she hired a former dancer from the Ballet Russe to teach Deborah privately. Later she moved herself, ten-year-old Deborah, and eleven-year-old Phylicia to Mexico, where Deborah continued ballet lessons at the Ballet Nacional de Mexico, attended performances of the Ballet Folklorico de Mexico, and became fluent in Spanish.

After approximately four years of study the three returned to Houston, where Deborah, now age fourteen, again attempted to enroll in the Houston Foundation for Ballet. This time she successfully integrated the Houston Foundation and received a full scholarship. This persistence inspired both daughters, who consider their mother as their mentor for achievement.

Allen again encountered racism when, after 11 years of ballet training, she was denied admission to the North Carolina School of the Arts in Winston-Salem, when the director stated that her body structure was inappropriate for ballet and suggested that she abandon dance as a career. Disheartened, Allen joined her sister Phylicia and enrolled in her parents' alma mater, Howard University in Washington, DC. At Howard University, Allen studied Greek classics, speech, and theater arts instead of dance. During the following year, she met Mike Malone, an accomplished choreographer, who persuaded her to join his dance troupe and encouraged her to perform in a production of *The Music Man* at a local dinner theater. With the added confidence inspired by this exposure, Allen resumed her dance study at the National Ballet School, accepted directorship of the Dance Department at the Duke Ellington School for the Performing Arts, and performed throughout Washington, DC, until she graduated from Howard University School of Fine Arts cum laude in 1971.

She then went to New York City, where in 1972 she made her Broadway debut in the chorus line of the musical *Purlie,* an adaptation of the drama by Ossie Davis. Subsequently, in 1973 she portrayed Beneatha in the Tony and Grammy award-winning musical *Raisin,* a musical version of the Lorraine Hansberry classic *A Raisin in the Sun.* Allen continued to star on Broadway in 1977 as Miss Adelaide with Leslie Uggams and Richard Roundtree in the National Company's revival of the musical *Guys and Dolls;* in 1980 she played Anita, in the Broadway revival of *West Side Story,* for which she won the Drama Desk Award and was nominated for the Antoinette Perry (Tony) Award. She sang, danced, and acted as Charity in the Broadway revival of *Sweet Charity* (1986), for which she received her second Tony nomination. Additional theater performances by Allen during the 1970s included *Anna Lucasta* (1978) with the New Federal Theatre at the Pilgrim Theatre, New York, and *Ain't Misbehavin'* (1979).

Allen has made her most notable entertainment contributions in television. Allen's first appearance on television was in a disposable diaper commercial with her sister, Phylicia. She has since accumulated an impressive list of television performance credits that include starring in the NBC pilot "Three Girls Three," a variety show that was canceled after 13 weeks irrespective of excellent reviews for Allen; appearances on *Good Times* (1976); *Love Boat;* and the lead in a short-lived disco version of *Alice in Wonderland* (1978). Allen gained fame when her bit part as Lydia Grant in the movie *Fame* was transformed into a major role in the NBC television series *Fame* (1982), for which she received two Emmy Awards for her choreography, one Golden Globe Award for Best Actress in a Series, and the opportunity to produce and direct several episodes. Although NBC canceled *Fame* after one season, it continued successfully for six seasons in first-run syndication.

Allen has also appeared in several television specials and made-for-television movies, which include Joseph Papp's television special *Alice at the Palace;* Alex Haley's television miniseries *Roots: The Next Generation* (1979), in which she played Haley's wife; *The Greatest Thing That Almost Happened,* with Jimmie Walker; *Ben Vereen: His Roots,* a television special; and *Women of San Quentin* (1983), in which she played a tough prison guard. She choreographed, co-wrote, and performed in the television production "Dancin' in the Wings" (1985); co-wrote, directed, produced, choreographed, and starred in *The Debbie Allen Special* (1988–1989 season) on ABC-TV, for which she won two Emmy nominations; she traced the roots of African American dance in her choreography and performance in "Motown 30: What's Goin' On Special" (1990); and was co-host with Spike Lee on PBS's *Great Performances,* "Spike Lee & Company: Do It A Cappella" (1990).

After Allen's directing debut on *Fame,* she continued her directorial activities for episodes of *Family Ties* (1986) and *The Bronx Zoo* (1986), eventually garnering a contract during the 1987–1988 season as producer-director of NBC-TV's faltering sitcom *A Different World*, for which her innovative directing and credible plots are attributed with reviving the show and maintaining the show's placement in the Nielsen Top 5 ratings. During the 1990–1991 television season Allen produced, directed, occasionally wrote, and appeared as a guest star on *A Different World*, during which she also directed episodes of *Quantum Leap* and of *The Fresh Prince of Bel Air*. Allen is the originator, co-executive producer, and director of the "The Boys" (1992), a musical comedy series featuring the vocal group of the same name. Allen's debut as a director of television movies began with *Polly* (1989), an NBC-TV black adaptation of the Disney classic "Pollyanna," for *The Wonderful World of Disney*, which Allen also choreographed. In 1992, she directed CBS-TV's made-for-television movie *Stompin' at the Savoy*.

Allen's performances in feature movies include her debut film, *The Fish That Saved Pittsburgh* (1979), which she choreographed behind the scenes and appeared as a cheerleader on camera. She played Sarah in *Ragtime* (1981), performing with a cast that included James Cagney, Moses Gunn, and Howard Rollins, Jr.; and starred as Michelle, one of Richard Pryor's wives in his "semi-autobiography" *Jo Jo Dancer, Your Life Is Calling* (1986).

Allen, an award-winning choreographer has choreographed the films *Under Fire* and *The Fish That Saved Pittsburgh* (1979); the television program *Midnight Special*; the musical theater version of *Carrie*, based on the book and horror movie (1988); and two Academy Awards Ceremonies, 1984 and 1992, starring in a dance sequence in 1984. In addition to her Emmy Awards, Allen has also received *Ebony's* Dramatic Award.

The indefatigable Allen recorded her first record album, "Special Look" (MCA), in 1989, and is presently embarking on a directing career in feature films. She has three projects underway: *Freedom Over Me*, recounts a story of the relationship between Seminole Indians and escaped slaves; *Paris Noir*, narrates the story of three black women vocalists working in Paris in the 1920s; and *Goodbye Papa*, inspired by the death of Allen's father, Dr. Arthur Allen.

—Elizabeth Hadley Freydberg

Bibliography

Since Debbie Allen is a contemporary performer, the resources of her life exist in contemporary materials and bibliographies of performing arts.

"The Black Entertainer in the Performing Arts," *Negro Almanac*, 5th edition. ed. Harry A. Ploski. Detroit: Gale, 1989: 1126–1127.

Bogle, Donald. *Blacks in American Films and Television: An Illustrated Encyclopedia*. New York: Garland, 1988.

Cohen-Strayner, Barbara Naomi. *Biographical Dictionary of Dance*. New York: Schirmer Books, 1982.

Contemporary Theatre, Film, and Television, Vol. 6. Detroit: Gale, 1989.

Crest, Sarah. *Notable Black American Women*, edited by Jessie Carney Smith. Detroit: Gale, 1992, pp. 10–12.

Current Biography Yearbook. New York: H.W. Wilson, 1987.

"Debbie Allen—Doing It All, Her Way!!" *Ebony* 45 (November 1989): 54–58.

Dunning, Jennifer. "Debbie Allen Chips Away at the Glass Ceiling," *New York Times* (March 29, 1992): H35+.

Koehler, Robert. "Allen Adds an American Accent," *Los Angeles Times/Calendar* (March 27, 1988): 51.

Mapp, Edward. *Directory of Blacks in the Performing Arts*. Metuchen, NJ: Scarecrow, 1978.

New York Theatre Critics' Reviews 34: 26 (1973): 218–221; 51: 3 (1980): 366–371.

Ploski, Harry A., and James Williams, eds. *Negro Almanac*. Detroit: Gale, 1989.

Randolph, Laura B. "Debbie Allen On Power, Pain, Passion and Prime Time," *Ebony* (March 1991).

Seibel, Deborah Starr. "Dynamo Debbie," *Chicago Tribune* (November 15, 1990): Section 5.

Terry, Wallace. "'Don't Be Afraid to Fail,'" *Parade Magazine* (November 17, 1991): 4–7.

Weaver, Maurice. "Allen Helps Turn Tide to a Brave New 'World,'" *Chicago Tribune*, "TV Week, Section 11 (December 23–29, 1990): 3+.

Weinstein, Steve. "A Pollyanna Sister Act," *Los Angeles Times* (July 25, 1989): Part VI, 1+.

Who's Who among Black Americans, 5th ed. Lake Forest, IL: Educational Communications, 1988.

ALLENSWORTH, JOSEPHINE [LEAVELL] (1855–1939), teacher and community leader, was born May 3 in Trenton, Kentucky. An accomplished pianist, she married the prominent Baptist minister Allen Allensworth (1842–1914), on September 20, 1877, at Bowling Green, Kentucky. They soon moved to the Union Baptist Church in Cincinnati, Ohio, where Allensworth assisted in her husband's pastorate by teaching church school and providing musical support; she also taught in the common schools. In 1886 Allen Allensworth, an active Republican, accepted a commission from President Grover Cleveland to become a chaplain in the United States Army to the 24th Infantry, a black regiment.

After he retired as a lieutenant colonel in 1906, they settled in Los Angeles, California. During her husband's 20-year military career, Josephine Allensworth accompanied him to various posts in the West, where she taught, helped with religious services, raised two daughters (Eva [Skanks] and Nella [Blodgett]), entertained families of other black soldiers, and on occasion assumed responsibility for the finances of the enlisted soldiers.

In 1908 she helped her husband and a few supporters establish the California Colony and Home Promotion Association, which aided blacks migrating to California and developed an all-black community in the San Joaquin Valley between Fresno and Bakersfield, which the promoters named for Allensworth. The town of Allensworth grew to become a market center for the area, with its citizens engaged in farming, dairying, and mercantile activities. Despite some setbacks as the growing scarcity of water, the souring of the soil, and growing opportunities in the San Francisco Bay shipyards, the area enjoyed growth until the Depression years of the 1930s. By 1966 only 34 residents remained. Today it exists only as a California State Park, designated the Allensworth State Historical Park.

In 1914 her husband died after being struck by a motorcycle. Allensworth continued her efforts for the town, however, although her primary residence was in Los Angeles. She spent a portion of the year in the all-black community and maintained an affiliation with it in a number of ways. An active clubwoman, she used her military experiences to help develop the Progressive Women's Improvement Association which initially provided a reading room and books for the community, and then a children's playground. She donated the land for the Mary Dickinson Memorial Library (dedicated to the memory of her mother), which opened on July 4, 1913. She also served as president of the school board at least through 1920. One commentator referred to her as a "gentle, refined, sweet-tempered" person. Allensworth died March 27, 1939, in Los Angeles.

—Bruce A. Glasrud

Bibliography

No repository of papers nor biographical sketch of Josephine Leavell Allensworth was discovered. Bits and pieces of her life can be gleaned from Charles Alexander, *The Battles and Victories of Allen Allensworth* (Boston: Sherman, French, 1914); Delilah Beasley, *Negro Trailblazers of California* (Los Angeles: privately printed, 1919); Elizabeth Davis, *Lifting as They Climb.* (Washington, DC: NACW, 1933); Edith Maureen Fisher, "Ethel Hall Norton and the Allensworth Colony," *American Libraries* XVIII (February, 1987): 140–141; Kenneth G. Goode, *California's Black Pioneers: A Brief Historical Survey* (Santa Barbara: McNally & Loftin, 1974); Kenneth Marvin Hamilton, "Allensworth," *Black Towns and Profit: Promotion and Development in the Trans-Appalachian West* (Urbana: University of Illinois Press, 1991), pp. 138–148; Eleanor Mason Ramsey, Allensworth, A Study in Social Change" (Unpublished PhD dissertation, University of California, Berkeley, 1977); Louis Robinson, "Death Threatens a Western Town," *Ebony XXII* (June, 1967): 60–66; W. Sherman Savage, *Blacks in the West,* (Westport, CT: Greenwood Press, 1976); Kathleen Edwards Small, *History of Tulare County II* (Chicago: S. J. Clarke, 1926), pp. 454–459; Frank N. Schubert, "Allen Allensworth," Dictionary of American Negro Biography, edited by Rayford W. Logan and Michael R. Winston (New York: Norton, 1982), pp. 13–14; and Octavia B. Vivian, *The Story of the Negro in Los Angeles County*, compiled by Federal Writers' Project of the Works Progress Administration (San Francisco: R and E Research Associates, 1970).

ANDERSON, MADELINE (b. 1936), television and film producer, was born in Lancaster, Pennsylvania, on December 28. Madeline Anderson loved to watch movies as a small child and yearned to be a filmmaker. She later attended Millersville State Teacher's College (Pennsylvania), New York University, and RCA Institute. From the very beginning, she sought to combine filmmaking and teaching in a creative way. Anderson's initial experience in filmmaking involved working with a group of individuals: Shirley Clarke, D.A. Pennebaker, and Richard Leacock. Later, Leacock and Anderson developed their own company, Andover Productions. Their first production was entitled *Berstein in Europe*. They also produced a science series for MIT (Massachusetts Institute of Technology).

Anderson's first film, *Integration Report I* (1961), was a short documentary on the civil rights struggle. From 1962 to 1964, Anderson worked as an assistant editor on the film *Cool World*, a controversial feature film exploring black male homosexuality. In the late 1960s (1964–1969), she worked for public television station in New York WNET as writer, film editor, associate producer, and producer/director. While employed at WNET, she also worked on *Black Journal*— a news program on black issues—under William Greaves. With many successful years of experience, Anderson embarked on a project to produce, direct, and edit a film for the Hospital Workers Union, Local 1199. The film, entitled *I Am Somebody* (1969), subsequently won national and international acclaim.

In the early 1970s, Anderson was employed at the Children's Television Workshop as the supervising film editor. Her responsibilities included film producer/director for both "Sesame Street" and "The Electric Company." In 1975, she started another independent film and video production company, Onyx Productions. Under the rubric of this company, she produced "The Walls Come Tumbling Down," a program delineating racial progress (Ford Foundation), and "Sesame Street Is Everywhere" in Portuguese. In addition, she continued to produce a number of shorts for "Sesame Street."

Building upon her interest in education, in the late 1970s, Anderson became executive producer for "Infinity Factory," a television series that taught children how to use math in their everyday interactions. The primary audience for this program was inner city African American and Latino children. The program was aired in over 250 PBS affiliate stations. Most importantly, with this accomplishment, Anderson became the first African American woman to serve as executive producer of a national television series.

In 1986–1987, Anderson worked as the senior producer on "Al Manaahil," an Arabic literacy series produced on location in Amman, Jordan. Children and women were the target audience. This award-winning television series also aired in Egypt, Morocco, and other Arabic-speaking, Middle East countries. Anderson taught at the Columbia Graduate School of the Arts and lectured at several prestigious universities. In addition, she has served as a film consultant and as a board member on the New York Film Council and Women Make Movies. Through the years, she has received numerous awards, including the Indie Award for Life Long Achievements and Contributions (Association of Independent Film and Video Makers). Currently, she is working on several film projects and is employed as the associate director of the Office of Black Ministry in the Diocese of Brooklyn.

—Gloria J. Gibson-Hudson

Bibliography

Few resources delineate achievements in televised film achievements. See: Spencer Moon, "Behind the Scenes: A Pioneer in Public TV," *Black Film Review*, 6:4 (1991): 27–30. *Who's Who in Black America*, 5th edition (1988), p. 17.

ANDERSON, MARIAN (1902–1993), internationally known opera singer, was born February 17 in Philadelphia, Pennsylvania, the daughter of John Berkely and Anna Anderson. At an early age she began singing in the Union Baptist Church choir, and by age 13 was a member of the adult choir. The public schools of Philadelphia provided further musical education, and black churches, colleges, and fraternal organizations provided opportunities for Anderson to develop her singing skills. With the support of the black community, she was able to study both in the United States and abroad under a number of teachers.

In 1924 Marian Anderson officially began her singing career. By the summer of 1925 she had acquired professional management and was becoming more and more popular. During the next decade she traveled abroad three times, performing extensively in the Scandinavian countries, France, and Austria. Anderson returned to the United States in 1935 as a renowned artist. Her popularity made it possible for her to overcome many racial barriers that faced African American performers, but it did not keep her from being prohibited from performing at Washington, DC's Constitution Hall in 1939. Public uproar over the decision was so great that the White House arranged an open air concert at the Lincoln Memorial. On Easter Sunday morning Anderson sang to an audience of 75,000. In 1940, after receiving the Bok Award of $10,000, she established the Marian Anderson Award for youth of all races possessing musical talent. In 1943 her performance before the Lincoln Memorial was immortalized in a mural at the Department of the Interior. That same year she became the first black woman to sing in the Metropolitan Opera House in New York City.

The 1950s were an exciting decade for Anderson. She appeared on the "Ed Sullivan Show" in 1952, made her first tour of Japan in 1953, and was honored, in 1955, as the first black artist to sing with the Metropolitan Opera Company. She sang to front line troops in Korea and spoke at the Gandhi Memorial in Delhi, India.

Marian Anderson was described by Italian conductor Arturo Toscanini to as having a voice "such as one hears once in a hundred years." During her 30-year career, she became known as one of the world's leading contraltos. She stood as a symbol of African American achievement, and she used her position not only to entertain but also to work for equal rights. Harold L. Ickes, the former Secretary of the Interior, called her "a symbol of American unity." Her farewell performance at Carnegie Hall attracted the rich and powerful on April 19, 1965.

Anderson represented her country not only as an entertainer but also as a U.S. delegate to the United Nations in 1955 and as a delegate to the thirteenth UN General Assembly. She was awarded the Congressional Medal of Honor in 1977, and has been given decorations and citations by numerous foreign governments. Anderson has received 23 honorary doctorates from institutions of higher education. On August 12, 1989, she was honored at the Charles Ives Center for the Arts in Danbury by performances of Jessye Norman, Isaac Stern, and Julius Rudel. Anderson retired to Danbury, Connecticut, and wrote her autobiography *My Lord What a Morning*.

Marian Anderson died April 8, 1993, following a stroke. She had sold her 105-acre Danbury, Connecticut, farm and moved to Portland, Oregon, during the summer of 1992 to be near her family members. She died at the home of her nephew, James DePriest, music director of the Oregon Symphony. She had no children from her marriage to architect Orpheus H. Fisher (married 1943 until his death in 1985).

—Christopher D. White

Bibliography

The information in this essay was taken primarily from Anderson's autobiography, *My Lord What a Morning*. Her collection of recorded works also provided additional information as did general biographical resources: *Who's Who Among Black Americans, 1990–91*; Eileen Southern, *Biographical Dictionary of Afro-American and African Musicians* (Westport, CT: Greenwood Press, 1981); Langston Hughes, *Famous American Music Makers* (New York: Dodd, 1973). Additional information was taken from a text adapted from "The Lady from Philadelphia," a television special, appearing on the cover of Marian Anderson's *He's Got the Whole World in His Hands*, a 1962 RCA release. Her social contributions are cited in Jessie P. Guzman's article "The Social Contributions of the Negro Woman since 1940," reprinted in *Black Women in United States History* VI, edited by Darlene Clark Hine (Brooklyn: Carlson, 1990), pp. 464–465. For specific information about the struggle for concert space see: *Esquire* (July 1939): 79, 160–161; *The Washington Evening Star* (March 7, 1939); and *the New York Times* (February 21, 1939). Other articles by or about Anderson include: "My Life in a White World," *Ladies Home Journal* 77:54 (September 1960); H. Schonberg, "Other Voices of Marian Anderson," *New York Times Magazine* (August 10, 1958); and "Philadelphia Lady," *Musical America* 78:18 (January 15, 1958).

ANGELOU, MAYA [MARGUERITE JOHNSON] (b. 1928), poet, writer, dancer, composer, producer, singer, lecturer, and civil rights activist, was born on April 4 in St. Louis, Missouri. She attended public school is Stamps, Arkansas, and in San Francisco. She studied music privately, later studied dance with Martha Graham, Pearl Primus, and Ann Halprin, and took drama lessons from Frank Silvera and Gene Frankel. Truly a Renaissance woman, Maya Angelou has written a series of autobiographical works published by Random House: *I Know Why the Caged Bird Sings* (1970); *Gather Together in My Name* (1974); *Singin' and Swingin' and Gettin Merry Like Christmas* (1976); and *All God's Children Need Traveling Shoes* (1986). Among her poetry collections are: *Just Give Me a Cool Drink of Water 'Fore I Diiie and The True Believers*. Maya Angelou, the playwright, has written "Cabaret for Freedom" (written with Godfrey Cambridge), "The

Least of These," "Ajaxl," and "Still I Rise." She has written two screenplays: "Georgia, Georgia" (Independent Cinema) and "All Day Long" (American Film Institute). She has also written and produced a ten-part television series on the African tradition in American life. She has a son, Guy Johnson.

As a performer, Maya Angelou appeared in *Porgy and Bess* on a 22-nation tour sponsored by the Department of State during 1954–1955. She has also appeared Off Broadway in *Calypso Heatwave*, Jean Genet's *The Blacks*, and *Cabaret for Freedom*. She made her Broadway debut in *Look Away* in 1973. She has also performed as a vocalist at the popular nightclubs Blue Angel and Village Vanguard in New York and at Mr. Kelly's in Chicago.

She has served in several other positions requiring understanding of other cultures. She was an associate editor for *The Arab Observer*, an English language newsweekly published in Cairo, Egypt. She served as assistant administrator at the School of Music and Drama, Institute of African Studies, University of Ghana and also was a freelance writer for *The Ghanaian Times*.

These trips abroad did not dampen her activism at home in the United States, however. Martin Luther King, Jr., appointed her as Northern Coordinator of the Southern Christian Leadership Conference due to her long-term commitment to civil rights activism.

She has received numerous awards. In 1975, she received *The Ladies Home Journal* Woman of the Year Award in Communications. She is also the recipient of honorary degrees from Smith College, Mills College, and Lawrence University. She currently serves as the Reynolds Professor of American Studies at Wake Forest University in Winston-Salem, North Carolina, and speaks to college campuses on various issues.

—Betty Plummer

Bibliography

Maya Angelou's *I Know Why the Caged Bird Sings* (New York: Random House, 1969) provides an excellent account of her early years and some of the most tragic aspects of her life. Further information is provided through her articles: "African Canvas," *American Visions* 5:6 (December 1990): 12–16; "Why Blacks Are Returning to Their Southern Roots," *Ebony* 45:6 (April 1990): 44–48. James A. Page's *Selected Black American Authors: An Illustrated Bio-Bibliography* (Boston: G.K. Hall), also provides some biographical data and a complete listing of Maya Angelou's writings. Other sources of valuable information include: Ann Allen Shockley and Sue P. Chandler, *Living Black American Authors* (New York: Bowker, 1973); and *Contemporary Authors*, edited by Jane A. Bowden (Detroit: Gale, 1977).

ASHFORD, EVELYN [EVELYN WASHINGTON] (b. 1957), Olympic and world record-setting track athlete, was born on April 15 in Shreveport, Louisiana. She is the oldest of five children of Samuel Ashford, a U.S. Air Force sergeant, and Vietta Ashford. She first started running at age 13 in Athens, Alabama.

Ashford attended Roseville High School near Sacramento, California, from 1973 to 1975. At Roseville, Ashford's math teacher noticed her speed in running and invited her to run matches against the school's star football player. Ashford repeatedly beat the player and also won her matches against members of the boys' track team. She joined the boys' team (one did not exist for girls) and won most of her races. Ashford became co-captain of the track team during her senior year at Roseville.

Ashford's high school success, including an appearance in a junior national meet, attracted the attention of the UCLA track coach. In 1975 she became one of the first women to receive an athletic scholarship to UCLA, where she majored in sociology. Ashford began a longtime association with UCLA's women's track coach, Pat Connolly, herself a former Olympic athlete.

Connolly coached and encouraged Ashford to qualification for the 1976 U.S. Olympic team. At the Olympic Games in Montreal, Canada, Ashford placed fifth in the 100-meter race. She continued her successful UCLA track career and earned All-American titles in 1977 and 1978. She also won the 1977 AIAW National Championships in the 100 meters, 200 meters, and the 800-meter relay. In 1978 Ashford dropped out of UCLA to train full time in hopes of qualifying for the 1980 Olympics. Connolly continued as her coach. In 1980 Ashford won the World Cup 100 meters and 200 meters. After looking forward to competing in the 1980 Olympics in Moscow, Ashford was dealt a heavy blow by President Jimmy Carter's decision to boycott the Games in protest of the former Soviet Union's invasion of Afghanistan. Later that year, she severely injured her right hamstring muscle at a track meet in Los Angeles.

Recovering from the injury, Ashford made a cross-country car trip with her husband, Ray Washington, whom she had married in 1978. She reassessed her goals and contemplated retirement but decided to continue as a track athlete, training for the 1984 Olympics. Ashford also entered California State University, Los Angeles, to pursue a degree in fashion design. By 1984 Ashford had repeated her double World Cup victories and had recorded 20 of the 23 fastest times for the 100 meters in U.S. history. In the 1984 Olympic Games in Los Angeles, she won a Gold Medal in the 100 meters, becoming the first woman to run the race in under 11 seconds in the Olympics. Ashford anchored the winning U.S. 400-meter relay team, clinching her second Gold Medal in the 1984 Olympic Games.

Ashford's next goal was to beat her biggest rival, Marlies Gohr of East Germany. Two weeks after winning the Olympic Gold, Ashford beat Gohr at a meet in Zurich, setting a new world record of 10.76 seconds in the 100 meters. In 1984 Ashford was chosen Track and Field Athlete of the Year. She took the 1985 season off to have daughter Raina Ashley.

Ashford now had the recognition needed to secure lucrative product endorsements. She became a reporter on ESPN's "World Class Women" and accepted speaking engagements. The combination of success and motherhood produced a more talkative and congenial Ashford, one different from the shy, media-avoiding competitor of her early track career. After a 17-month hiatus during which she lost 40 pounds and trained, Ashford returned to competition with her husband replacing Pat Connolly as her coach. She won the 55-meter run at the Vitalis/ USA Olympic meet in New Jersey. Ashford placed third in the 1986 U.S. Championships in Eugene, Oregon. At the Goodwill Games that year, she won the 100 meters and was part of the winning 400-meter relay team. In January 1987 Ashford received the Vitalis Award for excellence in track and field.

Although she had problems from the hamstring injury she had suffered in 1980, Ashford qualified for the 1988 U.S. Olympic team. This marked her fourth appearance on an Olympic track and field team. She carried the U.S. flag in the opening ceremonies in Seoul, Korea. Ashford won the Silver Medal in the 100 meters and the Gold Medal in the 400-meter relay, which she anchored for the U.S. team. She joined her role model Wilma Rudolph as a winner of three Gold Medals in an Olympic career.

In 1989 Ashford was awarded the Women's Sports Foundation's Flo Hyman Trophy. In 1991 she competed in the 100 meters at the U.S. nationals, placing third. She also qualified for the 1991 World Track and Field Championships in Tokyo, Japan. Although her records have been broken, Ashford will be remembered for having ranked as the world's fastest woman. Throughout her athletic career, she has been an outspoken critic of the use of performance-enhancing drugs in athletics. She now lives in California with her family.

—Heather Martin

Bibliography

Evelyn Ashford's life and accomplishments are covered in the following works: *Biographical Dictionary of American Sports*, Michael Davis's *Black American Women in Olympic Track and Field*, and Janet Woolum's *Outstanding Women Athletes*. Pat Connolly's *Coaching Evelyn: Fast, Faster, Fastest*, chronicles the relationship between athlete and coach. The *New York Times Biographical Service*, *Biography Index*, published by H.W. Wilson, and *In Black and White*, edited by Mary Mace Spradling, contain articles on Ashford's life and athletic career.

Secondary Sources

Avery, Mary. "Washington, Evelyn Ashford," in *Biographical Dictionary of American Sports. Outdoor Sports*, edited by David L. Porter. New York: Greenwood Press, 1988, pp. 557–558

Connolly, Pat. *Coaching Evelyn: Fast, Faster, Fastest Woman in the World*. New York: Harper Collins, 1991.

Davis, Michael D. *Black American Women in Olympic Track and Field: A Complete Illustrated Reference*. Jefferson, NC: McFarland, 1992.

New York Times Biographical Service. February 1983, July 1985, September 1988.

Spradling, Mary Mace, ed. *In Black and White*, 3rd ed., Supplement. Detroit: Gale, 1985.

Woolum, Janet. *Outstanding Women Athletes: Who They Are and How They Influenced Sports in America.* Phoenix: Oryx Press, 1992.

AUSTIN, LOVIE [CORA CALHOUN] (1887–1972), musician, composer,
and entertainer, was born September 19 in Chattanooga, Tennessee. Austin was a trained pianist who studied at Knoxville (Tennessee) College and Roger Williams College in Nashville. Along with her band, The Blues Serenaders, Austin accompanied many of the classic blues singers of the 1920s. Among these were Ida Cox, Alberta Hunter, Edmonia Lewis, Bertha "Chippie" Hill, Hattie McDaniel, Ethel Waters, and Ma Rainey. She accompanied Ma Rainey on her first Paramount session in 1923 and on eight other recordings in 1924 including her own compositions "Bad Luck Blues," "Barrel House Blues," "Jealous Hearted Blues," "Ya-Da-Do," and "Lucky Rock Blues" and "Walking Blues," for which she wrote the melodies. Austin and Alberta Hunter composed the song that catapulted Bessie Smith to fame, "Downhearted Blues," in 1923 for the Paramount label.

Described as a "shadow figure" on the blues scene because she accompanied and composed rather than sang, Austin is also credited with composing "'Bama Bound Blues" (with Ida Cox), "Chicago Bound Blues," "Experience Blues" (with Alberta Hunter), "Mistreating Daddy Blues," and "Traveling Blues" during her years in the music world.

During the 1920s Austin traveled on the Theater Owners Booking Association (TOBA) circuit as the pianist with the vaudeville team Austin and Delaney. She was a house pianist at the Monogram Theater in Chicago for a 20-year period spanning the 1920s and 1930s. Austin was also a studio musician for Paramount and Vocalion and also traveled with her own shows during this period. From the late 1940s into the 1960s, Austin worked as a resident pianist for the Jimmy Payne Dancing School in Chicago. She also appeared in a film, *The Great Blues Singers*, in 1961. Lovie Austin died in Chicago on July 10, 1972.

—Adrianne Andrews

Bibliography

Albertson, Chris. *Chicago: The Living Legends. Alberta Hunter with Lovie Austin and Her Blues Serenaders* (liner notes), Riverside LP 389/390; Stereo Riverside LP 9389/9390, September 1, 1961.

Harrison, Daphne Duval. *Black Pearls: Blues Queens of the 1920's.* New Brunswick: Rutgers University Press, 1988.

Lieb, Sandra. *Mother of the Blues: A Study of Ma Rainey.* Amherst: University of Massachusetts Press, 1981.

Southern, Eileen. *The Greenwood Encyclopedia of Black Music: Biographical Dictionary of Afro-American and African Musicians.* Westport, CT: Greenwood Press, 1982.

Steel, Suzanne. Personal communication. Columbia College, Center for Black Music Research, Chicago, Illinois, June 4, 1991.

AVERY, BYLLYE Y. (b. 1937), community activist, health care worker, and educator, was born in De Land, Florida, into the reserved family of a rural teacher. Byllye Y. Avery's early life followed a traditional path. After earning a master's degree in education, she became a teacher. Her early career years were devoted to teaching special education to emotionally disturbed students and to consulting on learning disabilities in public schools and universities throughout the southeastern United States.

When Avery's husband, Wesley, died suddenly of a massive heart attack at age 33, her commitment to whole health care in the black community was born. As she assumed her responsibility as single parent to her children, Wesley, Jr., and Sonja, Avery also assumed her responsibility as caretaker of an extended family of black women whose extreme stress she sought to help end. Avery initially formed small self-help groups of distressed black women who she felt were disabled by poverty, crime, violence, and racism. She then began to replicate this small group concept nationally and worldwide.

For Byllye Y. Avery, the incidents among black women of infant mortality and prenatal neglect, of sudden death from hypertension and of premature life from unplanned pregnancy, were problems that inspired her 1974 co-founding of the Gainesville (Florida) Women's Health Center. These same concerns led, in 1978, to her founding of Birthplace, an alternative birthing center also in Gainesville. Five years later in Atlanta, Georgia, she incorporated the internationally renowned National Black Women's Health Project (NBWHP). These innovative and important initiatives, along with 20 years as a selfless activist for responsive, holistic health care for women, were tangibly acknowledged in 1989. Byllye Y. Avery was awarded a Genius Grant of $310,000 for individual excellence by the John D. and Catherine T. MacArthur Foundation.

Avery's NBWHP remains headquartered in Atlanta. It has a network of more than 130 groups in 22 states and 6 foreign countries. Branch offices are located in New York City; Philadelphia, Pennsylvania; Oakland, California; the National Public Policy and Education Office is in Washington, DC. There is also an international network of 2,000 black women participants in this grassroots advocacy organization. Although Avery credits three white friends with showing her early on how to navigate institutional systems, NBWHP is run by and for black women.

Avery seeks to unify birth and death for black women by humanizing their lives. Through the self-help groups, self-esteem is developed within an environment fully supportive of black women. Moreover, a forum is provided for neutralizing the abusive and negative sexual, health, and family experiences of black women who participate in NBWHP.

Avery views black women's participation in NBWHP as a lifelong commitment, just as she views her own commitment as lifelong. She largely describes herself in terms of NBWHP's accomplishments. The organization sponsored the First National Conference on Black Women's Health Issues (1983); developed the first Center for Black Women's Wellness (1988); produced the first ever documentary film by black women to explore sexuality and reproduction from their perspective; pioneered the Avoidable Mortality Cancer Project jointly with Morehouse School of Medicine and the National Cancer Society; co-sponsored with the Children's Defense Fund a Health Center for Teen Parents in Bennettsville, South Carolina; and formed the Florida Healthy Mothers/Healthy Babies Coalition.

Avery serves on the boards of the New World Foundation, the Global Fund for Women, International Women's Health Coalition, Boston Women's Health Book Collective and the Advisory Committee for Kellogg International Fellowship Program. She continues to serve as the founding president of the NBWHP, and she lives out her understanding of sisterhood by being both blood kin and friend kin to the women whose lives she touches. Her work was recognized through the 1989 *Essence* award for community service.

—Yvonne Scruggs

Bibliography

Naylor, Gloria. "Power: Rx for Good Health," *Ms.* 56 (May 14, 1986).
Nelson, Liza, "Local Hero: Health Care for the Whole Woman," *McCalls* (December, 1990): 35.
Pinkney, Deborah S. "Power to Her People," *American Medical News*, December 15, 1989: 45–48.
Scruggs, Yvonne, "Byllye Y. Avery," *Sage* 2:2 (Fall 1985): 2.
———. "Byllye Y. Avery" in *Women of Distinction: Activists and Change Agents*, publication forthcoming.
Taylor, Susan L., "1989 *Essence* Award," *Essence* 20 (October 1989): 57–60.

AVERY, MARGARET (b. 1940?), an Oklahoma-born actress, is best known for her role as Shug Avery in the 1985 film *The Color Purple*. She was raised in San Diego, California, while her father was in the U.S. Navy. After her graduation from the University of California, Berkeley, she worked as a teacher in Oakland, California. She left teaching to begin her career as an actress in 1969.

Avery began her acting career in the theater. She and her (now former) husband, director Robert Gordon Hunt, formed the Zodiac Theater in Los Angeles. Avery's role in the Zodiac's *Does a Tiger Wear a Necktie?* won her the 1972 Los Angeles Drama Critics' Circle Award for Outstanding Performance by an Actress. In 1979 she was a member of the Potters Field Theatre Company in New York City. Avery continued her acting career with television commercials and then went on to land her first movie roles in several Blaxploitation films. Her movie appearances include *Hell Up in Harlem* (1973), *Magnum Force* (1973), and *The Fish That Saved Pittsburgh* (1979). She also played Belle Joplin opposite Billy Dee Williams in the television movie *Scott Joplin* (1977), for which she received an NAACP Image Award. She played Annie Mae, wife of Richard Pryor's character, in *Which Way Is Up?* (1977). During the 1970s and early 1980s, Avery guest starred on a number of television shows such as "Sanford and Son" and "Murder, She Wrote" and appeared in television movies including *Louis Armstrong—Chicago Style* (1976). In 1980 she received the Best Actress nomination from the Academy of Science Fiction, Fantasy, and Horror Films for her role in *The Lathe of Heaven* (1980), which appeared on PBS.

For almost five years before landing her role in *The Color Purple*, Avery's acting career was almost at a standstill. At one point she took typing lessons with the idea of becoming a court reporter. Instead of giving up, Avery set out to revitalize her career. She performed as a singer in Las Vegas and completed a six-month singing tour of Japan and Indonesia. On a return trip to Los Angeles, Avery sought and landed the role of Shug Avery in *The Color Purple* (1985). She received an Academy Award nomination as Best Supporting Actress in 1985 for her performance in the film.

After being in the spotlight for her critically acclaimed performance as Shug, Margaret Avery continued acting in movies and television. She also lectured at colleges around the country. However, the eminence she gained from her role in *The Color Purple* has eluded the veteran actress in her later performances. Described as "40ish" in 1986, Avery continues to live and work as an actress in California. She and former husband Hunt have one daughter, Aisha.

—Heather Martine

Bibliography

Margaret Avery is listed in a number of reference works on theater and film. Donald Bogle's *Blacks in American Films and Television*, Edward Mapp's *Directory of Blacks in the Performing Arts*, and *Contemporary Theatre Film, and Television*, edited by Owen O'Donnell, provide information on Avery's film credits and history as an actress. Articles in magazines should be consulted for more personal biographical information about Avery. Such articles are listed in Volume 15 of *Biography Index*, published by H.W. Wilson, and in *In Black and White*, edited by Mary Mace Spradling.

Secondary Sources

Bogle, Donald. *Blacks in American Films and Television: An Encyclopedia.* New York: Garland, 1988.

Collier, Aldore. "Margaret Avery Says She 'Couldn't Buy a Job' Before *The Color Purple.*" *Jet* 69 (March 10, 1986): 58–60.

Mapp, Edward. *Directory of Blacks in the Performing Arts.* Metuchen, NJ: Scarecrow, 1978.

O'Donnell, Owen, ed. *Contemporary Theatre, Film, and Television.* Vol. 8. Detroit: Gale, 1989.

Oliver, Stephanie Stokes. "Margaret 'Shug' Avery: Beyond *The Color Purple.*" *Essence* 17 (September 1986): 118–120+.

Spradling, Mary Mace, ed. *In Black and White*, 3rd ed., 2 vols. Detroit: Gale, 1980.

B

BAILEY, BERYL [LOFTMAN] (1920–1977), linguist and educator, was born in Black River, Jamaica, West Indies, on January 15. Her parents were both educators—her mother a teacher and her father an inspector of schools. Bailey was one of six children who grew up valuing education. She was an honor student at Wolmer's Girls' School in Jamaica and gained an almost perfect score on her Cambridge examinations. She came to the United States in 1948 to attend Columbia University, earning her bachelor's degree in 1952; her master's degree in linguistics in 1953, and her PhD in linguistics in 1964. Bailey married Neville Huntley Bailey, January 20, 1953. They had two daughters, Stephanie and Jennifer.

She remained in the United States, except to conduct fieldwork in Jamaica in 1956 and from 1960 to 1962. After completing college with distinction, she accepted an appointment to teach English literature and composition at the Bethlehem Training College in New York, a local institution run by the Moravian church for preparing women teachers. Bailey later became assistant professor in the Linguistics and Behavior Program at Yeshiva University, New York (1964–1968), then assistant professor of linguistics at Hunter College, New York (1968–1977), and finally founding chair of the Department of Black and Puerto Rican Studies, Hunter College (1969–1977).

Bailey grew up in a bidialectal environment, speaking both Jamaican Creole and Standard English. During her years as an English teacher in Jamaica from 1942 to 1948 she became acutely aware of the differences between native Jamaican speech and Standard English. That awareness eventually resulted in Bailey's becoming one of the scholars who played a major role in the debates that led to the development of Pidgin and Creole Studies as a respected field within linguistics beginning in the 1960s.

Bailey was a pioneer in the field of black linguistics, becoming one of the first black woman linguists in the United States and the first woman in the United States to claim the African background of Caribbean Creoles. Her master's thesis, "Creole Languages of the Caribbean Area: A Comparison of the Grammar of Jamaican Creole with Those of the Creole Languages of Haiti, the Antilles, the Guianas, the Virgin Islands, and the Dutch West Indies" (1953), was a breakthrough in several ways. First, Bailey maintained that the Caribbean Creoles covered in her thesis were all related, having as their African background the Niger Congo languages. Second, she classified them as having gained the vocabularies of either the Germanic languages, principally Dutch and English, or of the Romance languages, principally French and Spanish. Third, Bailey advocated abandoning the term "Creole" and utilizing instead "Afro-European languages" to describe those known to be comprised of both African and

European elements. Though the term "Afro-European" has never been adopted, many of Bailey's other ideas have been accepted in the field. Unfortunately, since her thesis has never been published, linguists are often unaware of how many seminal ideas are owed to her; in fact, some of her ideas have become associated with the works of others.

Bailey's second important contribution is the book *Jamaican Creole Syntax: A Transformational Approach* (1966), the first and only full-length grammar of a creole language to be written in the transformational grammatical format outlined by noted linguist Noam Chomsky in *Syntactic Structures* (1957). During her somewhat brief lifetime she wrote 14 books and articles, which focused on three related interests: (a) the study of Creole languages spoken by people of African ancestry in the Caribbean and the United States, (b) the implications of such studies for language teaching, and (c) the development of Black Studies to insure the preservation and perpetuation of data and understanding of the black experience.

She received many awards or honors during her lifetime, including Junior Research Fellowship, University of the West Indies (1960–1962) and Senior Graduate Fellowship, American Council of Learned Societies (1963–1964). She served as a consultant to the Department of Health, Education and Welfare; Brooklyn College; the Ford Foundation; the American Bible Society; and the National Council of Churches. She wrote *Jamaican Creole Language Course* (1966) for the Peace Corps. Malignant pulmonary disease caused her death on April 18, 1977, at age 57.

—Margaret Wade-Lewis

Bibliography

Works by Beryl Bailey

"A Note on Buckra," *American Speech*, 27 (1952), 143.

Creole Languages of the Caribbean Area: A Comparison of the Grammar of Jamaican Creole with That of the Creole Languages of Haiti, the Antilles, the Guianas, the Virgin Islands, and the Dutch West Indies. New York: Columbia University master's thesis, 1953.

A Language Guide to Jamaica. New York: Research Institute for the Study of Man, 1962.

"Language Studies in the Independent University," *Caribbean Quarterly* 8:1 (1962): 38–42.

"A Program for Teaching of English Noun-Verb Concord in Primary Schools in Jamaica," *Caribbean Quarterly* 9:4 (1963): 10–14.

A Proposal for the Study of the Grammar of Negro English in New York City. New York: Project Literacy Reports Number 2. Ithaca: Cornell University, 1964.

"Some Problems Involved in the Language Teaching Situation in Jamaica," in Roger Shuy, ed. *Social Dialects and Language Learning.* Champaign, IL: National Council of Teachers of English, 1964, pp. 105–111.

"Toward a New Perspective on Negro English Dialectology," *American Speech* 40 (1965): 171–177.

Jamaican Creole Language Course. Washington, DC: Peace Corps, 1966 (unpublished).

Jamaican Creole Syntax. Cambridge: Cambridge University Press, 1966.

"Some Problems Involved in the Language Teaching Situation in Jamaica," in Roger W. Shuy et al., eds. *Social Dialects and Language Learning.* Champaign, IL: National Council of Teachers of English, 1966, pp. 105–111.

"Some Aspects of the Impact of Linguistics on Language Teaching in Disadvantaged Communities," in A.L. David, ed. *On the Dialects of Children.* Champaign, IL: National Council of Teachers of English, 1968, pp. 15–24.

"Language and Communicative Styles of Afro-American Children in the United States," *Florida F.L. Reporter* 46 (1969): 53.

"Some Arguments Against the Use of Dialect Readers in the Teaching of Initial Reading," *Florida F.L. Reporter* 8:8 (1970): 47.

"Jamaican Creole: Can Dialect Boundaries Be Defined?" in Dell Hymes, ed. *Pidginization and Creolization of Languages.* London: Cambridge University Press. 1971, pp. 341–348.

Works about Beryl Bailey

Holm, John. "Focus on Creolists (3): Beryl Loftman Bailey," *The Carrier Pidgin* 10:3 (September, 1982): 1–2.

"Obituary: Dr. Beryl Loftman Bailey," *New York Times* (April 21, 1977): Section 4, Column 3, p. 21.

Wade-Lewis, Margaret. "Beryl Loftman Bailey: Africanist Woman Linguist in New York State," *Afro-Americans in New York Life and History* (Fall, 1992).

BAILEY, PEARL (1918–1990) was a singer and actress best remembered for her starring role in *Hello Dolly!*, a revamped production with an all-black cast based on the original Broadway musical hit. She won a special Tony Award in 1968 and was named Entertainer of the Year in 1967 by *Cue* magazine for her rendition of Dolly.

Pearl Mae Bailey, born on March 29 in Newport News, Virginia, was the youngest of four children born to the Reverend Joseph James Bailey and Ella Mae Bailey. Ancestors on both sides of the family included Creek Indians. After her parents divorced she lived in Philadelphia with her mother and stepfather and attended William Penn High School. At age 15, she won first prize for her song and dance routine at an amateur contest at a Philadelphia theater, where her famous tap-dancing brother, Bill Bailey, was a professional performer. After winning another amateur contest at Harlem's Apollo Theatre, she worked as a singer and dancer in small clubs in Pennsylvania's coal mining towns. Her talent led to nightclub engagements in Washington, DC, and Baltimore. She toured as a singer with jazz trumpeter Cootie Williams's orchestra between 1943 and 1944, winning acclaim and polishing her warm, earthy vocal style.

Success led to expanded engagements and to performance in varied media. In New York she obtained a booking at the prestigious Blue Angel nightclub and a theater tour with Cab Calloway's orchestra. Bailey made her New York stage debut as Butterfly in *St. Louis Woman*, an all-black musical comedy for which she won the Donaldson Award as Most Promising New Performer of 1946. Her first motion picture, *Variety Girl*, followed in 1947. Next she appeared in *Isn't It Romantic* in 1948. She returned to Broadway in 1950 in *Arms and the Girl*, followed by the Broadway musical revue *Bless You All* in 1950–1951, and *House of Flowers* in 1954. Other motion pictures include *Carmen Jones* (1954), *That Certain Feeling* (1956), *St. Louis Blues* (1958), *Porgy and Bess* (1959), and *All the Fine Young Cannibals* (1960).

In the early 1960s Bailey performed again in nightclubs in the United States and abroad. The peak of her career came in 1967 when she was chosen to star in *Hello Dolly!* Her performance charmed audiences and won the acclamation of critics.

Bailey was married to John Randolph Pinkett, Jr., from 1948 to 1952. She was married to drummer Louis Bellson, Jr., from 1952 until her death. She and Bellson adopted a son, Tom, and a daughter, DeeDee. Bailey wrote three autobiographical works and a children's fictional work, *Duey's Tale*, for which she won the American Library Association's Coretta Scott King Award in 1976. She recorded some of her best song renditions on various labels: "Tired" (her first single), "Row, Row, Row," "Toot Toot Tootsie, Goodbye," "That's Good Enough for Me," "Fifteen Years," "Legalize My Name," "A Woman's Prerogative," and a *Hello Dolly!* album. She also appeared on major television talk and variety shows. President Gerald Ford appointed Bailey a special advisor to the United States Mission of the UN General Assembly, thirtieth session (1975). Bailey died after collapsing at age 72 on August 17, 1990, and was buried in Philadelphia.

—Janet Owens

Bibliography

Pearl Bailey has chronicled her own life in three autobiographies: *Raw Pearl* (New York: Harcourt, Brace & World, 1968); *Talking to Myself* (New York: Harcourt Brace Jovanovich, 1971); and *Between You and Me: A Heartfelt Memoir on Learning, Loving, and Living.* (New York: Doubleday, 1989). A complete listing of her performances in films, theater, television, nightclubs, concerts, and recordings can be found in *Notable Names in the American Theatre* (Clifton, NJ: J.T. White, 1976).

Other works by Pearl Bailey

Duey's Tale. New York: Harcourt Brace Jovanovich, 1975.
Hurry Up America and Spit. New York: Harcourt Brace Jovanovich, 1976.

Pearl's Kitchen: An Extraordinary Cookbook. New York: Harcourt Brace Jovanovich, 1973.

Secondary Sources

Current Biography Yearbook (1969): 23–25.
Bogle, Donald. *Blacks in American Films and Television.* New York: Garland, 1988.
Mapp, Edward. *Directory of Blacks in the Performing Arts.* Metuchen, NJ: Scarecrow, 1978.
Wilson, John S. "Pearl Bailey, Musical Star and Humorist, Is Dead at 72," *New York Times Biographical Service* (August 1990): 758–759.

BAKER, ELLA (1903–1986), attacking civil rights issues at the grassroots in a career spanning five decades, developed a fundamental philosophy that inspired many civil rights activists. Often invisible in her behind-the-scenes organization, leadership, and thinking, Ella Jo Baker espoused her theory that "strong people don't need strong leaders," stressing that activists should strive to build strong people. She believed that by aiding others to acquire a sense of self-value and -ability, the civil rights movement would gain mass support. She emphasized that leaders should not singularly promote themselves through their charisma and social status in order to succeed; instead by empowering individuals Baker believed that group-centered leadership would achieve political goals.

Baker was born on December 13 at Norfolk, Virginia. Her parents, Blake and Georgianna Baker, insisted that their three children be well educated. Her father worked as a ferry waiter, and Baker's mother was a compassionate community helper. In 1911 they moved their family to Littleton, North Carolina, where Baker's grandparents owned the land they had worked as slaves. Her grandfather, a Baptist minister, preached sermons with Baker at his side. She attended local schools, and because of experiences in her wholesome farm life, religion, and family encouragement to share, she gained a strong sense of community. Realizing her social responsibilities, Baker dreamed of becoming a medical missionary, but costs were prohibitive, and instead she studied sociology at Shaw University in Raleigh, North Carolina, graduating as valedictorian in 1927.

Baker rejected a teaching career because she considered that an occupation traditionally expected of black women. Because graduate studies in sociology at the University of Chicago were too expensive, she moved to New York City, where she lived with cousins. She waited tables and held factory positions to pay her bills. Freed from the conservative environment of her southern home, Baker considered liberal political ideas she heard debated in Washington Square Park. She participated in discussion groups that examined theories to initiate social change and began writing essays for the black press as well as attending graduate courses at the New School for Social Research.

Baker joined the editorial staff of *American West Indian News* and *Negro National News* in the early 1930s. In addition to her employment, Baker organized and served as national director of the Young Negroes' Cooperative League. This group established consumer cooperatives that advocated group buying and cooperated with the New Deal Works Progress Administration to develop a consumer education project. This activity earned Baker renown for her organizational abilities, and in 1938 she began working for the NAACP as a field secretary, traveling throughout the South to enlist members, collect money, and publicize the inequalities of minorities in that region.

Her strategy was to convince people to identify with her, stressing that blacks should focus on their common needs, fears, and hopes and support each other, acquiring strength in numbers. She established a network of contacts in the Deep South that proved useful in her future work. By 1943 she returned North and became national director of the NAACP branches. She emphasized that job training was crucial to gain equal rights and held leadership conferences. Baker also recruited low-income members whom she felt the NAACP leadership ignored. In 1946 she became guardian to her niece, which restricted her ability to travel, and she resigned from the NAACP. Her resignation was also due to internal strife because the NAACP hindered her from obtaining her desired goals. Baker criticized the NAACP's priority of focusing on quantitative goals rather than on how members could participate within the organization. She also criticized the group's leaders catering to white interests.

She continued working for the local NAACP and raising funds for the National Urban League while she unsuccessfully campaigned for the New York State Assembly as the Liberal Party candidate in 1953. One year later she became president of the New York City branch of the NAACP and chaired its education committee. This position allowed her to focus on school desegregation because the city's schools resisted immediate integration after the federal ruling. She also served on the mayor's commission and received a salary from the New York Cancer Society. Baker, who had worked with Rosa Parks during her NAACP fieldwork in Alabama, organized In Freedom, a northern group of civil rights supporters, advocating the Montgomery Bus Boycott and other southern civil rights work.

In 1958 Baker, because of contacts made through In Freedom, actively participated in the creation of the Southern Christian Leadership Conference (SCLC), working with Martin Luther King, Jr. Somewhat reluctant to return to the South, Baker first served the organization as associate director. King requested that she establish the national office and organize meetings; Baker also performed the daily administrative work, distributed literature, and monitored direct action workshops, since she was more aware of the black community's sentiments regarding the work than her male peers. She endorsed the Crusade for Citizenship, in which churches affiliated with the SCLC encourage voter registration; Baker developed citizenship classes to aid blacks in passing literacy tests. In the spring of 1959 she became executive director.

Realizing that women were more actively involved in the routine aspects of civil rights work than men, she believed that more women and youth should be utilized in the SCLC. She wrote a column espousing her views in the *SCLC Newsletter*, but the male ministers who dominated the SCLC leadership rejected her ideas about this as well as suggestions to work closely with local organizations. Baker disliked the autocratic hierarchy of leadership in SCLC that emphasized specific "notables," instead of the ordinary people that were most important. She sought to democratize civil rights leadership and provide a legitimate role for women as leaders. Isolated within the SCLC, Baker resigned her position in the summer of 1960 shortly after becoming involved with student sit-ins.

She was intensely interested in organizing the students but cautiously advised them to remain separate of the SCLC, whom she feared would dominate the students. Autonomy, she believed, would enable the students to determine how to pursue civil rights without interference. She called a national conference of the youth at her alma mater in April 1960 and assisted the creation of the Student Nonviolent Coordinating Committee (SNCC). Establishing the office in Atlanta, she also earned wages from the Atlanta YWCA as a consultant in human relations. She instructed SNCC members how to organize Freedom Rides and voter registration efforts, which went into previously untapped rural regions. In 1961 when SNCC seemed destined to splinter, she suggested it form two wings, one for direct action and the other for voter registration. Baker served as advisor to SNCC until 1964.

She also organized workshops for civil rights activists at the Highlander Folk School with Septima P. Clark. Believing that leaders should empower others, Baker emphasized that the people, knowing what they needed and wanted, should be taught how to resolve their problems and help themselves. Through citizenship education and decentralized local leadership, Baker projected that national civil rights goals could be met.

After "Freedom Summer," a program initiated by the Council of Federated Organization (COFO) to increase black participation in voting, Baker helped organize an alternative to the all-white state Democratic Party, the Mississippi Freedom Democratic Party (MFDP) and was keynote speaker at its first convention at Jackson, Mississippi. She set up the MFDP office in Washington, DC, and canvassed for party support. In 1967 Baker joined the staff of the Southern Conference Educational Fund (SCEF) and sought racial cooperation. Five years later she moved to Harlem and served as vice chair of the Mass Party Organizing Committee and as a national board member of the Puerto Rican Solidarity Committee. She lectured and advised groups about human rights, especially regarding South Africa. Baker proclaimed that human rights work must never cease, hoping that future generations would understand her work and continue her struggle to liberate people unjustly restricted or abused.

Long suffering from asthma, Baker died on her eighty-third birthday, December 13, 1986. SNCC leaders served as her pall bearers at her funeral in Harlem.

Having influenced many prominent as well as local civil rights leaders, Baker's abilities as an organizer, philosopher, orator, and humanitarian enabled her grassroots "Power to the People" strategies to achieve an egalitarian method for civil rights. Throughout her life, Baker emphasized that people should try to better themselves and believe in their actions. She stressed that activists should be committed to their cause and well prepared to act. By listening to others' ideas and concerns to strengthen the individual, the group would ultimately benefit.

—Elizabeth D. Schafer

Bibliography

Examples of Ella Jo Baker's writing include "Bigger Than a Hamburger," *The Southern Patriot* (June 1960) (published by SCEF) and Ella Baker and Marvel Cooke, "The Bronx Slave Market," *The Crisis* 42 (November 1935): 330–331.

Several interviews with Baker are available to researchers: by Anne Romaine, March 25, 1967, in the Wisconsin State Historical Society, Madison, Wisconsin; by John Britton, June 19, 1968, held in the Civil Rights Documentation Project, Moorland-Spingarn Research Center, Howard University; by Gerda Lerner, December 1970, printed as "Developing Community Leadership," in Gerda Lerner, ed., *Black Women in White America* (New York: Vintage Books, 1973), pp. 345–352; by Eugene Walker, September 4, 1974, and by Sue Thrasher and Casey Hayden, April 19, 1977, in the Southern Oral History Collection, at the University of North Carolina, Chapel Hill; and by Lenore Hogan, March 4, 1979, in the archives at the Highlander Research and Education Center, New Market, Tennessee.

Correspondence with Baker is included in the National Association for the Advancement of Colored People Papers, Library of Congress, Washington, DC (also available on microfilm); the SCLC, SNCC, MFDP, and Martin Luther King. Jr., Papers, at the King Center in Atlanta, Georgia; the Howard Zinn Papers, Braden Papers, and Civil Rights Collection and the Wisconsin State Historical Society, Madison, Wisconsin; the Highlander Folk School Papers at both the Tennessee State Archives, Nashville, Tennessee, and the Wisconsin State Historical Society; and the Septima P. Clark Collection, Robert Scott Small Library. Baker's correspondence, administrative reports, memoranda, and writings in the *SCLC Newsletter* are available in the Martin Luther King, Jr., Collection, Special Collections, Mugar Memorial Library, Boston University. Additional archival and FBI sources are listed in David Garrow, *Bearing the Cross: Martin Luther King, Jr., and the Southern Christian Leadership Conference* (New York: William Morrow, 1986). The Schomburg Center for Research in Black Culture, New York Public Library, New York City, has photographs of Baker.

Several essays directly address Baker's civil rights work such as Carol Mueller, "Ella Baker and the Origins of 'Participatory Democracy,'" in Vicki L. Crawford, Jacqueline Anne Rouse, Barbara Woods, et al., eds., *Women in the Civil Rights Movement: Trailblazers and Torchbearers, 1941–1965* (Brooklyn: Carlson, 1990), 51–70; this volume contains other essays that mention Baker's role in the civil rights movement. Shyrlee Dallard's *Ella Baker* is part of the series published by Silver Burdett (Englewood Cliffs, NJ: Prentice-Hall, 1990). Ellen Cantarow and Susan G. O'Malley, "Ella Baker: Organizing for Civil Rights," in Darlene Clark Hine, ed., *Black Women in American History: The Twentieth Century* 1 (Brooklyn: Carlson, 1990), pp. 202–244, is based on an interview with Baker by the authors and includes annotated notes, a bibliography, and contemporary photographs: it was originally published in Ellen Cantarow, Susan O'Malley, and Sharon H. Strom, eds., *Moving the Mountain: Women Working for Social Change* (Old Westbury: Feminist Press, 1980).

Charles Payne, "'Strong People Don't Need Strong Leaders': Ella Baker and Models of Social Change," is an unpublished paper prepared for Northwestern University Department of African American Studies (1987); the author's published version is "Ella Baker and Models of Social Change," *Signs* 14 (Summer 1989): 885–899. Joanne Grant, "Mississippi Politics: A Day in the Life of Ella J. Baker," in Toni Cade, ed., *The Black Woman: An Anthology* (1970), pp. 56–62, concisely describes Baker's activism (and notes that Grant was preparing a biography of Baker). Jacqueline Trescott, "The Voice of Protest: Ella Baker, Civil Rights Legend," *Washington Post* (December 14, 1978), pp. C-1, 23, includes quotes from individuals such as Martin Luther King., Jr., and Marion Barry addressing Baker's work. Geraldine Wilson, "Essence Woman," *Essence* 38 (May 1985), focuses on Baker; and Jean Wiley, "On the Front Lines," *Essence* (February 1990) includes Baker in her discussion of women leaders in the civil rights movement. A contemporary article on Baker appeared in *Ebony* (August 1966): 27–37. Baker's obituary was printed in *Jet* 18 (January 19, 1987), and Madelyn A. Bonsignore, *American Visions* (February 1988): 10–11.

Joanne Grant, who was active in SNCC, produced the videocassette *Fundi: The Story of Ella Baker* ("Fundi" is a Swahili word that expresses the transfer of a craft or skill to the next generation). An audiotape, *A Salute to Ella Baker* is available at Pacifica Tape Library.

Several books depict the context for Baker's civil rights career. Howard Zinn, *SNCC: The New Abolitionists* (Westport, CT: Greenwood Press, 1964) dedicated his book to Baker, lauding her as the "most tireless, the most modest, and the wisest activist I know." James Forman, who was executive director of SNCC in the 1960s, devoted a chapter to Baker in *The Making of Black Revolutionaries* (Washington, DC: Open Hand Publishers, 1985), and Aldon D. Morris, *The Origins of the Civil Rights Movement: Black Communities Organizing for Change* (New York: Free Press, 1984) quotes her. For contextual histories that represent various phases of Baker's work see Sara Evans, *Personal Politics* (New York: Knopf, 1979); Clayborne Carson *In Struggle: SNCC and the Black Awakening of the 1960s* (Cambridge: Harvard University Press, 1981); Sally Belfrage, *Freedom Summer* (New York: Viking, 1968); Elizabeth Sutherland, ed., *Letters from Mississippi* (New York: McGraw-Hill, 1965); Anne Moody, *Coming of Age in Mississippi* (New York: Dial Press, 1968); Juan Williams, *Eyes on the Prize: America's Civil Rights Years, 1954–1964* (New York: Dial Press, 1987); Anne C. Romaine, "The MFDP Through August, 1964," M.A. thesis, University of Virginia (1970); and Leslie B. McLemore, "The MFDP: A Case Study of Grass-Roots Politics," PhD dissertation, University of Massachusetts (1971). The bibliographies in these treatises offer many additional sources to be consulted. Capus M. Waynick, John C. Brooks, and Elsie W. Pitts, eds., *North Carolina and the Negro* (Raleigh: North Carolina Mayor's Co-Operating Commission, 1964) briefly discusses Shaw University.

BAKER, JOSEPHINE (1906–1975), entertainer and social activist, was born June 3 in St. Louis, Missouri. The oldest child of Louis and Carrie (Smith) Baker, Josephine Baker lived most of her adult life in France because she could not adjust to the social, political, and economic injustices blacks faced in the United States. Trying to escape poverty, Baker, at age 16, joined a traveling theatrical company. In 1923 she appeared in the black Broadway musical "Shuffle Along." Afterward, Baker performed in theaters and nightclubs in New York City. Baker became widely known for her impeccable performance style in productions such as "Chocolate Dandies" on Broadway and the floor show of the Plantation Club in Harlem, singing and dancing her way to stardom. In 1925 Baker sang in "La Revue Negre" and introduced "le jazz hot" (hot jazz) to the French people. Baker found greater opportunities to perform in Europe, so she, along with other artists, joined the American community in Paris. During the late 1920s, she continued to perform in Paris, joining such magnificent productions as the "Folies Bergere." Baker sang professionally for the first time at Casino de Paris in 1930, made her screen debut as a singer in *La Creole* in 1934, and made several films such as *Black Shadows* (1923) and *Moulin Rouge* (1944) prior to World War II. She became a French citizen in 1937 to demonstrate her loyalty to her adopted land. During the following decades, Baker performed internationally despite intermittent periods of retirement that had to be cut short due to financial problems.

In addition to entertaining millions of people worldwide, Baker also supported significant causes. During the German occupation of France during World War II, she worked with the Red Cross and the Resistance. She was a member of the Free French Forces, and she entertained troops in Africa and the Middle East. For her contribution to the French war effort, Baker was awarded the Croix de Guerre and the Legion d'Honneur with the Rosette of the Resistance decorations.

After the war, Baker's humanitarian and political work continued. She arrived in the United States during the late 1940s to protest the unfair treatment of blacks. She refused to perform to segregated audiences, a stand that led to several cancellations of appearances. Taking a stand against racism and discrimination, Baker was initially well received, but whites reacted to her protest and attacked the entertainer/social activist. An incident occurred in New York's Stork Club that led to vicious attacks by columnist and radio commentator, Walter Winchell. When Josephine Baker overheard an employee of the restaurant complaining about having to serve "a nigger," she demanded an apology from the employee and management. Walter Winchell, eating in his favorite restaurant, overheard the argument and attacked Josephine Baker in his commentaries thereafter as a Communist and Nazi sympathizer. For her public denunciation of discrimination, she won the NAACP honor, Most Outstanding Woman of the Year, in 1951. By 1951, Baker was no longer popular and decided to leave the United States permanently. Her politics threatened her personal happiness and professional career. Baker returned to the United States during the 1960s to participate in the civil rights movement and the March on Washington in 1963. She gave many benefit performances for CORE, SNCC, and NAACP.

The rejection of Baker as "too controversial" by some blacks and the majority of whites in the United States did not cause the French people to regret her return home. Neither did the treatment Baker received in the United States prevent her from continuing to care about others. After purchasing a house (Les Milandes) in southwestern France, Baker, during the period 1954–1965, began "an experiment in brotherhood" by adopting many children of various ethnic backgrounds. Baker was unable to have children following an emergency hysterectomy in December 1941 in a Casablanca clinic following delivery of a stillborn child. They became her "Rainbow Family." This was Baker's way of showing that racism was taught and not inherited and that respect was necessary to improve race relations. While nursing her newly-adopted family, Baker retired from the stage in 1956. Due to financial hardships, however, this renowned entertainer was forced to work again. Her beloved mother, Carrie, died in 1959. She enjoyed triumphant appearances on Broadway in 1964 and in 1973 at Carnegie Hall in *Josephine*. She repeated her success on the Paris stage in a comeback April 1975.

During her lifetime, Josephine Baker married several times: Willie Wells (1919), Willie Williams (1921), Jean Lion (1942), and Jo Bouillon (1947). Her health declined following her first heart attack in Denmark in 1964. Her second heart attack in July 1974 was followed by a stroke. On April 12, 1975, Josephine Baker died in her sleep of a cerebral hemorrhage. Her life is not the story of an entertainer who became successful on stage as much as it is an example of the struggle of black people, particularly black women, to gain respect in the United States. Josephine Baker symbolized the beauty and vitality of the African American culture.

—Valerie Grim

Bibliography

Aloff, Mindy. "Josephine Baker's Naughty Jiggle Makes a Comeback: Jazz-age Princess," *Dance Magazine* 63 (July 1989): 32–34. This article examines the courage of a woman who, because of necessity, had to return to the stage. It shows how Baker overcame many struggles to become, once again, the world's most popular entertainer.

Baker, Josephine, and Jo Bouillon. *Josephine*. New York: Harper & Row, 1977. This autobiography provides valuable insight into the life and personality of one of the greatest entertainers.

Brown Sugar. German Educational Television Network. Transtel Productions. Written by Donald Bogle. Produced by Matthew Pook. New York, New York: Nexus Productions, 1985. This is a videorecording, hosted and narrated by Billy Dee Williams. It is based on the book *Brown Sugar: Eighty Years of America's Black Female Superstars*. The film examines the careers and influence of black women entertainers in America, using film clips, video clips, and interviews. Part one covers the early twentieth century through the 1920s, focusing on Josephine Baker and Bessie Smith. Part two examines the life of stars during the Depression years, including Billie Holiday, Hattie McDaniel, Freddie Washington, and Ethel Waters. Part three analyzes the 1940s and 1950s, with special attention given to the careers of Lena Horne, Hazel Scott, Eartha Kitt, and Dorothy Dandridge. Part four covers the 1960s through the 1980s by analyzing the careers of female groups such as the Supremes.

Davis, Thulani. "Baker's in the Oven," *American Film* 15 (October 1990): 15. This article discusses three films that analyze the life of Josephine Baker.

Gates, Henry L. "An Interview with Josephine Baker and James Baldwin," *The Southern Review* 21 (July 1985): 594–602. This article analyzes information taken from interviews conducted with Josephine Baker and James Baldwin. The information obtained from the interviews discusses Baldwin's and Baker's experiences, especially their lives in exile.

Guild, Leo. *Josephine Baker.* Los Angeles: Holloway House, 1976. This is another biography of Josephine Baker. It portrays Baker's life as interesting and exciting, especially her celebrated singing and dancing career.

Hammond, Bryan. *Josephine Baker.* London: Cape, 1988. This book is a compilation of stories based on the personal collections and recollections of Bryan Hammond. It also includes a theatrical biography by Patrick O'Connor.

Haney, Lynn. *Naked at the Feast: A Biography of Josephine Baker.* New York: Dodd, Mead, 1981. This biography describes Baker's life and her experiences as a dancer, living abroad in France.

Papich, Stephen. *Remembering Josephine.* Indianapolis: Bobbs-Merrill, 1976. This biography records in significant detail the whole life of Josephine Baker.

Rose, Phyllis. *Jazz Cleopatra: Josephine Baker in Her Time.* New York: Doubleday, 1989. This book depicts the life of Josephine Baker. Special attention is given to the contributions she made as an entertainer and the roles she played in trying to create better race relations among blacks and whites in France and the United States.

———."Josephine Baker's War on Racism," *American Visions* 4 (October 1989): 25–28. This research looks at the role Josephine Baker played in attacking racism in the United States.

"The Thirties Girls." Rare Radio Recordings of the Great Depression. Sandy Hook, CT: Sandy Hook Records: Distributed by Radiola, 1980. This is a sound disc, featuring popular song and dance arrangements, recorded between 1932 and 1936.

BALDWIN, MARIA LOUISE (1856–1922), educator, clubwoman, and civic worker in the Boston-Cambridge community, was the eldest of three children born to Baltimore native Mary (Blake) and Haitian emigrant Peter Baldwin. Maria Baldwin was born on September 13, and was educated in Cambridge, Massachusetts, attending Sargent Primary School and, later, the Allston Grammar School. She graduated from Cambridge High School in 1874.

After graduating in 1875 from the Cambridge Teachers' Training School, she taught for two years in Chestertown, Maryland, before returning in 1881 to Cambridge to teach in the Agassiz School, where she taught all seven grades to the children of Harvard professors. In 1879, she became the first woman to deliver the annual George Washington Birthday Memorial Address at the Brooklyn Institute. Her expertise and integrity led to higher positions, first as principal in 1889 and later as master of Agassiz School in 1916. This position made her one of two women and the only black to hold such an important position in the state of Massachusetts. She supervised a teaching staff of 12 white teachers and a student body numbering 500. Baldwin was known for her ability to motivate children to take on the responsibility of learning. As the first black female principal in Massachusetts, Baldwin served as a positive role model to young blacks and opened opportunities for black women in education throughout New England.

Baldwin continued her educator role in community activism. She helped improve the reading skills of black students attending Harvard University. For the poor blacks, she held classes at the Robert Gould Shaw Settlement House. Her dignity and beautiful voice impressed the community as Baldwin conducted public lectures throughout the United States on topics such as women's suffrage, poetry, history, and racial justice. She discussed social concerns in the many clubs and literary societies to which she belonged: the Twentieth Century Club of Boston, the Boston Ethical Society, League of Women for Community Service, Cantabriga Club, and Teacher's Association. Her Prospect Street home was the headquarters for many of these gatherings. She served on the Urban League of Greater Boston and in the local branch of the NAACP.

While addressing the council of the Robert Gould Shaw House, Baldwin collapsed and died from progressive heart disease. Funeral services were held in Arlington Street Church, the church of William E. Channing, one of the early abolitionists. The many avenues of reform brought honors to Baldwin. The memorial issue of *The Agassiz* contained tributes to her, and the Class of 1922 provided a memorial tablet, which was unveiled one year after her death. Educators and intellectuals in the Boston community held Baldwin in such high regard that the auditorium at Agassiz School was renamed Baldwin Hall, a scholarship was established, and a memorial library was dedicated in her honor. In 1950 a women's dormitory at Howard University was named Maria Baldwin Hall. Her ashes remain in the Forest Hills Cemetery in Boston.

—Dorothy C. Salem

Bibliography

Biographical accounts are available through local newpapers and the black press: *The Crisis* (April 1917): 281; W.E.B. Du Bois "Maria Baldwin," *The Crisis* (April 1922): 248–249; *Boston Herald*, March 18, 1922; and *Boston Transcript*, January 10, 19, 1922. Her photograph is in the Schlesinger Library, Radcliffe College. Mention of Baldwin's work in the Boston area is found in the Boston chapter of the NAACP records, NAACP Collection, Library of Congress.

Secondary Sources

Brawley, Benjamin. *Negro Builders and Heroes*. Chapel Hill: University of North Carolina Press, 1937.

Brown, Hallie Q. *Homespun Heroines and Other Women of Distinction*. Xenia, OH: Aldine Press, 1926; reprint ed., Freeport, NY: Books for Libraries Press, 1971 (pp. 182–193).

Daniels, John. *In Freedom's Birthplace: A Study of Boston Negros*. Boston: Houghton Mifflin, 1914.

Dannett, Sylvia, ed. *Profiles of Negroes Womanhood*. Chicago: Education Heritage, 1964.

Gibson, John W. *Progress of a Race*. Naperville, IL: J.L. Nichols, 1920.

Porter, Dorothy. "Maria Louise Baldwin, 1856–1922." *Journal of Negro Education* 21 (Winter 1952): 94–96.

Washington, Margaret Murray. "Club Work among Negro Women." In *Progress of a Race*, edited by John William Gibson. Naperville, IL: J.L. Nichols, 1920, pp. 186–189.

BARNETT, IDA B. WELLS. *See* Wells-Barnett, Ida B.

BARRETT, JANIE [PORTER] (1865–1948), social worker, teacher, and school founder, was the daughter of former slaves and was determined to improve the conditions and outlook for African American girls of the South. Born in Athens, Georgia, on August 9, Janie Porter received exposure to the finer things of life through her mother's employment. Julia Porter, a housekeeper and seamstress in the Macon, Georgia, home of the New York Skinner family, allowed her daughter to be raised as a "member of the family" within the Skinner household. Having her own room, Janie Porter played and studied with the Skinner's three children and came to love the refinement. Julia Porter became uncomfortable with this arrangement. She married a relatively prosperous railway worker by the name of Jackson and tried to get her daughter to move into her home. Mrs. Skinner prevailed, and Janie remained in the Skinner household. When Mrs. Skinner decided that Janie should attend school in the North, Julia Porter Jackson, fearing that the light-skinned Janie might lose her racial identity, sent Janie to Hampton Institute in 1880 at age 15.

Although she felt out of place during the initial months, she adjusted to the school and to the other students, most of whom came from rural areas of the South. She read a book by Walter Besant, *All Sorts and Conditions of Men*, in which the fictional character enters a life of social service. Following this fictional model, Janie Porter graduated in 1884 and entered her career of social service. She taught the sharecroppers in Dawson, Georgia, for the year after graduation. In 1886, she taught young women at Lucy Laney's Haines Normal and Industrial Institute in Augusta, Georgia. In 1889 she returned to Hampton as an instructor.

There she met and married (October 31, 1889) Harris Barrett, cashier of Hampton Institute.

Soon after the young couple settled in their home, Janie Porter Barrett invited neighborhood girls into her home for weekly meetings. She sought to expose the girls to a house furnished with quality and taste, her "Palace of Delight." Gradually, these meetings and discussions became the first settlement in Virginia and one of the first for African Americans, the Locust Street Social Settlement, officially founded in October 1890. Soon, with money they had saved for a luxurious bathroom tub and faucets, the Barretts built in 1902 a separate building on their property to serve as a practice house for the girls. Janie Porter Barrett raised money for furnishings, maintenance, and instruction from northern philanthropists. Hampton students received experience by interning at the settlement as instructors in cooking, sewing, gardening, teaching young children, and poultry raising.

These interests led to her participation in the national club movement while she raised her four children: May Porter, Harris, Julia Louise, and Catherine Barrett. In 1908 she became the first president of the Virginia State Federation of Colored Women's Clubs. The philanthropic work of the federation increasingly expanded to meet the social needs of the communities. When Janie Porter Barrett discovered an eight-year-old girl in a local jail, she brought this need for a juvenile reformatory to her federation. In 1914 their purchase of a 147-acre farm in Peake (also called Peakes Turnout), Virginia, was the culmination of several years' fundraising and organization to develop a reformatory for delinquent girls. By January 1915 the Virginia Industrial School for Colored Girls opened as a school, farm, and residence for delinquent girls. Residents of Peake protested the presence of the facility, which threatened the state appropriation for maintenance, upon which the women depended. To ease the tensions between the community and reformatory, Janie Porter Barrett, whose invalid husband had recently died, moved to the reformatory as the resident superintendent. She gave up her "pretty home to live in a dormitory and eat from thick plates with a tin fork," which was not easy for her. She refused an offer to become the dean of women at Tuskegee Institute and took on the responsibility for the reformatory in 1914.

Under her leadership, the reformatory became a model institution. She set up a biracial board, headed by white Hampton civic leader Mrs. Henry Lane Schmelz, to help with the fundraising and policymaking for the facility. She viewed the school as a "moral hospital" where each girl was given support, guidance, and instruction to reshape her life. The well-tended campus and cottages reflected a reformatory with minimum security barriers, since fences resembled those on neighboring farms. Instead, Barrett substituted personal interest and responsibility through the constant vigilance of teachers, the planned activities, and Barrett's personal concern for each girl. By the 1920s, the Virginia Industrial School for Colored Girls had become one of the five best reformatories in the country according to a major funder, the Russell Sage Foundation.

This recognition came as a result of Barrett's influence on shaping the philosophy and direction of the reformatory. Barrett felt that corporal punishment was counterproductive. If whipping produced virtue, she reasoned, then these children would be angels. Instead, Barrett consulted such social welfare experts as Hasting Hart. Her discipline came from the girls. She set up an honor system, a big sister plan, and an open forum where individuals could air their grievances and develop action plans for change. Individual responsibility enabled the girls to develop character to reshape their lives. The eighth-grade education coupled with training in sewing, laundry, and housekeeping prepared them for employment. The girls with a 2-year good behavior record were placed in state-approved homes until they reached age 21. Barrett monitored their progress and looked out for their wages, sleeping arrangements, clothing, and private time. Each graduate became a product of her institution and its philosophy; thus, she emphasized the importance of developing thoughtful, moral, and skilled women.

Barrett's influence was not limited to the reformatory. She served for four years as chairperson of the executive board of the National Association of Colored Women, on the executive boards of the Richmond Urban League and the Southern Commission on Interracial Cooperation, and on the White House Conference on Child Health and Protection. In 1929 she received the William E. Harmon Award for Distinguished Achievement for her years in social work. She continued her role with the reformatory until her retirement in 1940. She spent her final years in Hampton, where she died on August 27, 1948, of diabetes mellitus and arteriosclerosis. She was buried at Hampton's Elmerton Cemetery. In 1950 the reformatory was renamed the Janie Porter School for Girls.

—Kelle S. Taha

Bibliography

Janie Barrett received much recognition from her contemporaries for her achievements. Such works include: Mary White Ovington, *Portraits in Color* (New York: Viking Press, 1927); "Men of the Month" *The Crisis* (November 15, 1915): 13–14; Sadie I. Daniels, *Women Builders* (Washington, DC: Associated Publishers, 1931); Elizabeth L. Davis, *Lifting as They Climb* (Washington, DC: National Association of Colored Women, 1933); L.H. Hammond, *In the Vanguard of a Race* (New York: Council of Women Missions and Missionary Education Movement of the United States, 1922); Eleanor Sickels, *Twelve Daughters of Democracy* (New York: Octagon, 1969); and Irene McCoy Gaines, "Ten Living Negro Women Who Have Contributed Most to the Advancement of the Race," *Fisk News* 21 (May–June 1936): 10. She is cited in issues of *Southern Workman* (September 1912, November 1915, and August 1916). Her settlement is described in Robert A. Woods and Albert J. Kennedy, *Handbook of Settlements* (Philadelphia: William Fell, 1911).

For biographical information see entries on Barrett in Sylvia Dannett, ed., *Profiles of Negro Womanhood* (Chicago: Educational Heritage, 1964); Edward T. James, Janet Wilson, and Paul Boyer, eds., *Notable American Women, 1607–1950* (Cambridge: Belknap Press, 1971), pp. 96–97; Charles Wesley, *The History of the National*

Association of Colored Women's Clubs (Washington: NACW, 1984); Rayford Logan, *Dictionary of American Negro Biography* (New York: Norton, 1982); and *Who's Who in Colored America 1941–1944* (Detroit: Gale, 1945). The only major analysis is in Winona R. Hall, "Janie Porter Barrett, Her Life and Contributions to Social Welfare in Virginia," MA thesis, Howard University, 1954. Records of her work are included in the archives of Hampton Institute in Hampton, Virginia.

BASS, CHARLOTTA [SPEARS] (c. 1880–1969), editor of the *California Eagle* newspaper, civil rights and peace advocate, and the first black woman to run for the vice presidency of the United States, was born in October either in South Carolina or in Rhode Island, as sources disagree. Bass lived in Providence, Rhode Island, as a young woman and moved to Los Angeles in 1910; in 1912 she became the managing editor and publisher of the *California Eagle*, one of the oldest black newspapers in the West.

Throughout her life, Bass dedicated herself to political action on civil rights issues, including residential, resort, and school desegregation cases; opposition to discrimination in hiring and unionization; police and Ku Klux Klan violence; prisoners' rights; and "Don't Buy Where You Can't Work" campaigns. She was a member of the NAACP, the Council of African Affairs, the National Association of Negro Business and Professional Women's Clubs, the National Council of Negro Women, the Sojourners for Truth and Justice, and many other organizations. She and her husband, fellow journalist Joseph Bass, were founding members of the Los Angeles division of the Universal Negro Improvement Association, and Bass served briefly as the head of its women's wing.

Although she voted for both Democrats and Republicans, she was the director of the western regional campaign for Wendell Willkie's Republican presidential bid in 1940. She became the first black member of the Los Angeles County Grand Jury in 1943 and ran unsuccessfully for the Los Angeles City Council in 1945. She was a founding member of the Progressive Party in 1948 and co-chaired the "Women for (Henry) Wallace" aspect of the campaign. She ran as a Progressive candidate in the 14th California Congressional District in 1950. She was a delegate to the 1950 World Peace Congress in Prague and toured the USSR. She became the party's vice-presidential candidate in 1952, completing a presidential slate with leftist lawyer Vincent Hallinan. W.E.B. Du Bois gave the speech in support of her nomination, and Paul Robeson, a member of the nominating committee and a past Bass ally, became one of the major speakers for her campaign. Bass used the slogan "Guns or Butter" during the campaign to emphasize her support for domestic programs and social justice and her opposition to the Korean War. She was particularly critical of Republican vice-presidential candidate Richard Nixon's disregard for civil liberties.

She sold the *Eagle* in 1951. During the Joseph McCarthy era she was subjected to political repression; as a consequence, a black sorority revoked her honorary membership in 1956, stating that her name had been listed in a Report on Un-

American Activities in California. Bass, an active critic of the House Un-American Activities Committee's invasion of First Amendment rights, was deeply affronted by the sorority action. In the remaining years of her life she continued her local and international political work and wrote her memoirs. She died in Los Angeles following a long illness on April 29, 1969.

—Barbara Bair

Bibliography

Bass's autobiography, *Forty Years: Memoirs from the Pages of a Newspaper* (Los Angeles: author's publication, 1960), was written during the McCarthy era and contains material on the history of Los Angeles as well as about Bass's career. It is available at the Southern California Library of Social Studies and Research, Los Angeles, which is the repository of Bass's personal and political papers; the library also has a microfilm run of Bass's newspaper, the *California Eagle*. The *Eagle* and *Forty Years* are also available in Special Collections, University Research Library, University of California, Los Angeles. The Moorland-Spingarn Research Center, Howard University, and the Schomburg Center for Research in Black Culture, New York Public Library, have vertical files of clippings about Bass.

Biographical profiles and secondary sources that mention various aspects of Bass's career include: Harry A. Ploski and Roscoe C. Brown, Jr., eds., *The Negro Almanac* (New York: Bellwether, 1967); Andrew Buni and Carol Hurd Green, "Charlotta Bass," in *Notable American Women*, edited by Barbara Sicherman, Carol Hurd Green, et al. (Cambridge, MA: Belknap Press, 1980); Charles Wesley, *History of the National Association of Colored Women's Clubs* (NACWC, 1984); Martin Duberman, *Paul Robeson* (New York: Alfred Knopf, 1988); and Jill Watts, "Shout the Victory: The History of Father Divine and the Peace Mission Movement, 1879–1942" (PhD dissertation, University of California, Los Angeles, 1989).

Material about Bass and UNIA appears in Theodore Vincent, *Black Power and the Garvey Movement* (San Francisco: Ramparts Press, 1972): Emory J. Tolbert, *The UNIA and Black Los Angeles: Ideology and Community in the American Garvey Movement* (Los Angeles: Center for Afro-American Studies, 1980); and Volume 3 of the *Marcus Garvey and Universal Negro Improvement Association Papers*, edited by Robert A. Hill, et al. (Berkeley, Los Angeles, London: University of California Press, 1984).

For an excellent overview of Bass and the Progressive Party, see Gerald R. Gill, "Win or Lose—We Win: The 1952 Vice Presidential Campaign of Charlotta A. Bass," in *The Afro-American Woman: Struggles and Images*, edited by Sharon Harley and Rosalyn Terborg-Penn (Port Washington, NY: Kennikat Press, 1978). The University of Iowa Library, Iowa City, has press release copies of several of Bass's speeches from the 1952 campaign, including her nomination acceptance speech. A condensed version of that speech is reprinted as Charlotta Bass, "I Accept This Call," in *Black Women in White America: A Documentary History*, edited by Gerda Lerner (New York: Vintage, 1973), pp. 342–345.

BATES, DAISY [GATSON] (b. 1914), school desegregation leader, civil rights organizer, newspaper publisher, jounalist, and pilot, was the indominable spirit behind the integration of Central High School in Little Rock, Arkansas. She grew up in Huttig, Arkansas, a small saw mill town, in which everyone worked for the mill, lived in mill-owned houses, and traded at the mill's general store. Huttig's Main Street also defined the boundaries of "White Town" and "Negra Town." The Gatsons, like other black people in Huttig, lived in faded red "shotgun" houses, where "you could stand in the front yard and look straight through the front and back doors into the back yard."

Early in life, before age 5, Daisy Lee Gatson learned from a personal experience that an African American was different and that, though the two races seemed to co-exist peacefully, the attitudes of the community were in the tradition of the Old South. Her parents protected her from exposure to discrimination as long as they could.

One day, at age 7, Daisy was asked by her mother to go to the market to buy meat for dinner. Dressed in one of her prettiest dresses, she clutched the dollar bill and set forth to the market to purchase a pound of the center cut pork chops. She was forced to wait until all the butcher's white customers were waited on, and when she called attention to the fact that she had been waiting quite a while, the butcher ignored her. The butcher then said, "Niggers have to wait till the white people have all been served." He handed her a handful of fat chops and said, "Now take your meat and get out of here." She cried all the way home.

When she got home, her father painfully explained that in that Arkansas town a Negro had no rights that whites were obliged to respect. The following year, through a neighborhood boy, Daisy learned that the Gatsons were not her real parents; she had been orphaned because of racial prejudice. Her mother had been taken away late one afternoon by three white men, and the following morning her body had been found in the mill pond. She had been raped. Her father was so grief stricken that he had gone away, leaving her in the care of the Gatsons. He was never heard from again. This knowledge shaped her attitude toward whites, and she went looking for her mother's killers. When she found out that one of them was a drunk who slept outside the commissary, she walked by daily to stare and torment him with her resemblance to her biological mother.

Being told how her mother met her death neither destroyed nor marked Daisy Gatson. It gave her the courage and determination to do something about a world in which such a terrible thing could happen. To counteract the negative environment of the South, her adoptive parents sent her, while still a teenager, to the North and to Canada to observe the races living together harmoniously.

At age 15 Daisy Gatson was inspired by L.C. Bates, a visiting soft-spoken insurance agent, who became a frequent caller after the Gatsons had taken out a family policy. He often came laden with gifts, and on occasion would take the family to see the local movie. She grew to love and respect him and married Bates in 1932. The young couple moved and settled in Little Rock, Arkansas, where she attended Philander Smith and Shorter colleges.

During the Depression, her husband, who had majored in journalism at Wilberforce University, started the *Arkansas State Press* a newspaper for which Daisy Bates served as co-editor. During World War II, she became the only woman pilot in the Arkansas Civil Air Patrol. Following the war, Daisy Bates worked with 22 organizations in Little Rock to attack the barriers of discrimination. The newspaper fought the "Old Southern System" of segregation, police brutality, and all forms of inhumanity.

Daisy Lee Gatson Bates, the civil rights leader, became the moving spirit behind the integration of Central High School in Little Rock, Arkansas. In 1953 she was elected president of the Arkansas NAACP, placing her in an excellent position to engage in the fight against segregated schools. The 1954 Supreme Court decision *Brown* vs. *Board of Education* lent support to her struggle (1954–1958).

The struggle for school integration was long, hard and violent. In the face of continuing harassment and constant threat of bodily injury, Daisy Bates organized the Little Rock Nine, students who volunteered to enroll at Central High School to challenge the enforcement of the Supreme Court decision to desegregate public schools. The students completed the school term, but not without incident. Telephone threats, mob violence, individual acts of bigotry, cross-burnings and the bombing of homes accompanied the first year of integration. President Dwight D. Eisenhower had to send federal troops to bring order. The Bates home was bombed requiring thousands of dollars in repairs and the installation of protection devices. Their newspaper suffered economic reprisals and ceased publication in November 1959, one year after the NAACP awarded the Spingarn Medal to Daisy Bates and the Little Rock Nine for their pioneering role in upholding the basic ideals of American democracy.

The civil rights movement led Bates to a career as an author and a lecturer. She received several awards ranging from National Council of Negro Women and St. Louis NAACP; Woman of the Year; *Chicago Defender* Robert S. Abbott Award; the Spingarn Medal; honorary doctorates from Lincoln University, University of Arkansas, and Washington University. The *Arkansas State Press* was reestablished in 1985 with Daisy Bates as owner-operator.

—Olivia Pearl Stokes

Bibliography

For the account of her involvement in the civil rights movement see her autobiographical narrative,*The Long Shadow of Little Rock* (New York: David McKay, 1962). For biographical information see the following:
Cherry, Gwendolyn. *Portraits in Color*. New York: Pageant Press, 1962, pp. 181–187.
Dannett, Sylvia. *Profiles of Negro Womanhood*. Vol. II, Yonkers, NY: Educational Heritage, 1964, pp. 294–304.

Hampton, Henry, and Fayer, Steve, eds., *Voices of Freedom: An Oral History of the Civil Rights Movement from the 1950s through the 1980s*. New York: Bantam, 1990.

Lerner, Gerda, ed. *Black Women in White America*. New York: Random House, 1973, p. 306.

Robinson, Wilhelmina, ed. *Historical Negro Biographies*. New York: International Library of Negro Life and History, 1967–1969, pp. 162–163.

For several interviews with Daisy Bates see *Ebony* (February 19, 1972): 136–138; (October 1968): 142; (August 1966): 30; (September 1958): 17–24.

BEASLEY, DELILAH L. (1871–1934), journalist, historian, and clubwoman,

was born and raised in Cincinnati, Ohio. Her long career as a newspaper writer began at age 12, when she wrote articles for the *Cleveland Gazette*, a black newspaper edited by Harry C. Smith. By age 15, she was a regular columnist for the Sunday edition of her hometown paper, the *Cincinnati Enquirer*. Due to the death of both her parents, young Delilah Leontium Beasley worked as a domestic for a Cincinnati judge. From there, she went on to Chicago for training as a masseuse, an occupation she held in Chicago and then later in Springfield, Ohio. Following her interests in health therapies, Beasley took courses in gymnastics, hydrotherapy, and physical therapy and diagnosis. When this training had finished, she went to a family resort in Michigan to become the head supervisor of a bathhouse.

As Beasley earned her living with these occupations, she continued to study the history of her people. Always interested in the role of African Americans in the Far West, in 1910 Beasley took advantage of an opportunity to move to Berkeley, California, to serve as a nurse/therapist to a former patient. During her free time, she continued to do research on the role of African Americans in the West, interviewing leaders in the region and utilizing the Bancroft Library Archives of the University of California. The materials, though intended for a lecture series, became the basis for a book devoted to the black pioneers. When friend and minister David R. Wallace of Oakland heard her first lecture on San Francisco, her city of inspiration, he persuaded her to publish her findings to disseminate the information to a wider audience.

As she completed her investigation for the book *The Negro Trail Blazers of California*, she reentered her profession as a journalist. She wrote a series of articles in 1915 for the *Oakland Tribune* to protest the public showing of the movie *The Birth of a Nation*, which depicted vicious stereotypes of African Americans. Her articles stimulated a local movement to boycott the film and won her the recognition of the NAACP for her efforts. Contributing through her regular column "Activities among Negroes," Beasley campaigned against writers using such derogatory terms as "nigger," "darkie," and "coon." She attempted to raise the consciousness of journalists and newspaper editors to use greater discretion in their descriptions of race.

Her natural curiosity and skills in investigative reporting helped her compile and examine newspapers, tax records, hospital files, political journals, statutes, and land reports regarding African Americans in the West. Impressed by her commitment and tenaciousness, California scholars Charles Chapman, Herbert Priestley, and Theodore Hittell provided the historical information with which she could interpret the history of African Americans in the region. Finally in 1919, the book was finished and published. Immediately recognized by the United States Government, prominent libraries, and reputable historians, *The Negro Trail Blazers of California* became a genuine contribution to the scholarship of the period and region.

Divided into three parts, the book highlighted the achievements of the black middle class. Beginning with the Spanish exploration/settlement, Beasley followed the development of slavery up to California statehood. The second part delineated the history of the early black settlers, miners, and other pioneers in their struggle for civil rights and property accumulation. The third part celebrated the accomplishments of black individuals and institutions. Although her evaluations of the accomplishments were somewhat superficial, the book, nevertheless, is a significant contribution to the history of African Americans in California.

In 1925, as a representative of the Oakland *Tribune*, Beasley was the only black woman with press credentials at the National Convention of Women Voters in Richmond, Virginia. Later in the year, she was the only press delegate from a West Coast newspaper at the International Council of Women, held in Washington, DC.

When Beasley retired from the *Tribune* in 1925, she continued her concern about world peace as well as racial justice. She helped organize the National Association of Colored Women's biennial meeting in Oakland in 1926. She was a member of the League of Nations Association for Northern California and, later, the World's Forum. Advocating the entry of the United States to the World Court, Beasley circulated petitions that were later submitted to the United States Senate. She repeated a similar petition drive on behalf of the National League of Women Voters to the Disarmament Conference in Geneva, Switzerland. She brought the international issue to California when she led the campaign to support John D. Rockefeller's International House on the Berkeley campus, which was then opposed by groups objecting to black and Oriental students around the campus. Her persistence eventually lowered the resistance of local groups to the presence of minority students. Beasley died in Oakland in 1934.

—Dorothy C. Salem

Bibliography

The record of Delilah L. Beasley's work and opinions can be found in the newpapers for which she wrote and in several journal articles, including "Slavery in California," *Journal of Negro History* 3 (January 1918): 33–39; "Foreword," in Elizabeth L. Davis, *Lifting as They Climb* (Washington, DC: National Association of Colored Women, 1933).

Biographical information on Beasley can be found in the Davis book, *Lifting as They Climb*; Richard N. Dillon, *Humbugs and Heroes: A Gallery of California Pioneers* (1970); Charles Wesley, *The History of the National Association of Colored Women's Clubs, Inc.* (Washington, DC: NACW, 1984); Sylvia Dannett, *Profiles of Negro Womanhood* (Chicago: Educational Heritage, 1964); and Rayford Logan and M. Winston, *Dictionary of American Negro Biography* (New York: Norton, 1982), pp. 34–35.

BEAVERS, LOUISE

BEAVERS, LOUISE (1902–1962), actress and performer on stage, film, and television, was born in Cincinnati, Ohio, on March 8. Her family moved to Pasadena, California, in 1913. She completed high school at Pasadena High in 1918. After high school and prior to her acting career, Beavers worked as a dressing room attendant for a photographer and as a personal maid for film star Leatrice Joy. During the 1920s, she joined the Ladies' Minstrel Troupe, a group of 16 young women who put on local amateur shows.

There are two versions explaining how Louise Beavers was "discovered" as an actress. In one version, from an article she wrote for *Negro Digest*, Beavers claims that, while she was an aspiring concert singer, she signed up for an amateur show to sing "Pal of My Old Cradle Days." After competing, but not placing, Beavers received a phone call from film agent Charles Butler of Hollywood's Central Casting. He offered her a bit part in *Uncle Tom's Cabin*. In another version, a film agent saw Beavers perform at a show produced by the Ladies' Minstrel Troupe and he offered her a small role in *Uncle Tom's Cabin*. Beavers's first movie role usually is listed as *Uncle Tom's Cabin* in 1927, although some sources list her first screen appearance in the 1923 film *Gold Diggers*.

After *Uncle Tom's Cabin*, Beavers went on to appear in more than 125 movies, becoming perhaps the best known black actress of her time. Most of Beavers's roles were limited to such stereotypical figures as mammy, maid, cook, or housekeeper. Ironically, early in her career, Beavers supported herself working as a domestic between movie roles.

Only on a few occasions did she have the opportunity to step outside this role and demonstrate her acting ability. Of principal note are her roles as the mother of Jackie Robinson in *The Jackie Robinson Story* (1950); as Toinette, an ex-slave, in *Rainbow on the River* (1936); and as Nellie Silvers, the Harlem numbers queen, in *Bullets or Ballots* (1936).

Even in the stereotypical roles, Beavers managed to carve out a niche for herself. Based on Fannie Hurst's novel, the film *Imitation of Life* (1934) became the highlight of a movie career that spanned four decades. She received high praise from film critic Jimmie Fidler, who believed she deserved if not an Academy Award, then at least a nomination, for her performance. In the film Beavers portrayed Delilah, a maid who cared for the widowed Miss Bea (Claudette Colbert) and her daughter in addition to caring for her own daughter, Peola, played by Fredi Washington.

Many black critics criticized the negative characterizations of blacks in the film. Sterling Brown of the magazine *Opportunity*, criticized the film's portrayal of Delilah and her refusal to accept 20 percent interest in Miss Bea's profitable company—a company Delilah helped to establish by giving her family's secret pancake recipe to her employer. Another much criticized portrayal is that of Delilah's daughter Peola, a light-skinned young woman who left home in an attempt to pass as white and obtain the opportunities she would never obtain as a black woman. Her departure led to Delilah's death from a broken heart.

During her long career, Beavers appeared in films with a wide variety of stars, including *She Done Him Wrong* (1933) with Mae West, *Made for Each Other* (1939) with Carole Lombard and James Stewart, *Holiday Inn* (1942) with Bing Crosby, *Big Street* (1942) with Lucille Ball and Henry Fonda, and *Mr. Blanding Builds His Dream House* (1948) with Cary Grant. Beavers also played in two black-cast films produced by Million Dollar Productions: *Life Goes On* (1937) and *Reform School* (1939). Beavers's final film was *The Facts of Life* (1961).

Beavers branched into television when she replaced Ethel Waters as the black maid Beulah on the show "Beulah," which ran from 1950 to 1953. Beavers also made television appearances in "Cleopatra Collins" on "Star Stage" (March 9 , 1956); in "The Hostess with the Mostess" on "Playhouse 90" (March 27, 1957); in "Swamp Fox" on the "World of Disney Series" (1959) and on Groucho Marx's "You Bet Your Life" (1959).

Beavers's appearances on stage include a performance in New York City at the Roxy Theatre in February 1935, following the box-office success of *Imitation of Life*. She appeared again in New York at the State Theatre in 1944. In 1954 Beavers teamed up with old friend Mae West for two weeks in the Congo Room of the Sahara Hotel in Las Vegas. She even debuted on stage in *Praise House* in San Francisco's Alcazar Theatre on February 24, 1957.

Beavers lived with her mother until marrying LeRoy Moore in the late 1950s. During her career, Beavers served as a board member for the Screen Actors Guild, and when not acting, she spoke to young people at high schools within the black community. A diabetic, Beavers was hospitalized in late October 1962 and then died on October 26, 1962, of a heart attack, at the Cedars of Lebanon Hospital in Los Angeles. Beavers was inducted posthumously into the Black Filmmakers Hall of Fame in February 1976.

—Faye A. Chadwell

Bibliography

Three dictionaries provide standard biographical data on Beavers: *Dictionary of American Negro Biography*, *Dictionary of American Biography*, and *Notable Black American Women*. Donald Bogle's encyclopedia *Blacks in American Films and Television* is an excellent source for critical synopses of Beavers's films in addition to providing a good biography on Beavers. Bogle also provides commentary on Louise Beavers in *Brown Sugar*. The controversy surrounding *Imitation of Life* is covered in *Brown Sugar* as well as Daniel J. Leab's *From Sambo to Supershade* and Peter Noble's *The Negro in*

Films. Henry T. Sampson's *Blacks in Black and White: A Source Book on Black Films* provides an overview of blacks in films and black films with details on Beavers. Personal memories of Beavers by Leatrice Joy are recounted in *Hollywood Players: The Thirties,* by James Robert Parish and William T. Leonard. Finally, for contemporary profiles or insights, consult Beavers's article in *Negro Digest,* Chauncey Townsend's article in *The Crisis,* and the article "Sexiest Night Club Act," published in the November 1954 issue of *Ebony.* Comprehensive lists of Beavers's film credits may be found in Edward Mapp, *Directory of Blacks in the Performing Arts;* George Hill, et al., *Black Women in Television; The International Dictionary of Films* and *Filmmakers, Vol. III, Actors and Actresses;* and *Who Was Who on Screen.*

Article by Louise Beavers

Beavers, Louise. "My Biggest Break," *Negro Digest* 8 (December 1949): 21–22.

Secondary Sources

Bogle, Donald. *Blacks in American Films and Television: An Encyclopedia.* New York: Garland, 1988.
———. *Brown Sugar.* New York: Harmony Books, 1980.
Haba, Veroslav. "Beavers, Louise," in *International Dictionary of Films and Filmmakers, Vol. III, Actors and Actresses,* edited by James Vinson. Chicago, IL: St. James, 1986, pp. 61–62.
Hill, George, Lorraine Raglin, and Chas Floyd Johnson. *Black Women in Television.* New York: Garland, 1990.
Katz, Ephraim. *The Film Encyclopedia.* New York: Thomas Y. Crowell, 1979.
Leab, Daniel J. *From Sambo to Supershade: The Black Experience in Motion Pictures.* Boston: Houghton Mifflin, 1975.
Mack, Evelyn, ed. *Who Was Who on Screen,* 3rd ed. New York: Bowker, 1983.
Mapp, Edward. "Beavers, Louise," *Directory of Blacks in the Performing Arts.* Metuchen, NJ: Scarecrow, 1978.
Nelson, Elizabeth R. "Beavers, Louise," in *Dictionary of American Biography,* edited by John A. Garraty, Supplement 7, 1961–1965. New York: Scribner, 1981, pp. 43–45.
Noble, Peter. *The Negro in Films.* New York: Arno Press, 1970.
Parish, James Robert, and William T. Leonard. *Hollywood Players: The Thirties.* New Rochelle, NY: Arlington House, 1976.
Sampson, Henry. *Blacks in Black and White: A Source Book in Black Films.* Metuchen, NJ: Scarecrow Press, 1977.
"Sexiest Night Club Act," *Ebony* 10: 1 (November 1954): 103+.
Townsend, Chauncey. "Out of the Kitchen," *The Crisis* 42 (January 1939): 15–29.
Traylor, Eleanor R. "Beavers, Louise," in *Dictionary of American Negro Biography,* edited by Rayford W. Logan and Michael R. Winston. New York: Norton, 1982, pp. 35–36.
Warren, Nagueyalti. "Louise Beavers," in *Notable Black American Women,* edited by Jessie Carney Smith. Detroit: Gale, 1992, pp. 75–77.

BERRY, MARY (b. 1938), distinguished public servant, lawyer, academician, and administrator, was born in Nashville, Tennessee, on February 17 to George Ford Berry and Frances Southall (Wiggins) Berry. A multitalented woman, Mary Frances Berry has distinguished herself as a teacher, author, federal bureaucrat, and advocate of civil rights.

Berry received her introduction to black history from an inspiring high-school teacher in Nashville. She chose to attend a black college to major in philosophy. Her love for black history was reinforced by Rayford Logan and Elsie Lewis, her advisors at Howard University, the institution from which she received her BA (1961) and MA (1962). Their influence pushed Berry to take advantage of the opportunities opening to young black scholars. She accepted the position as a teaching fellow in American history at Howard University from 1962 to 1963, before going on to the predominately white campus of the University of Michigan, Ann Arbor (1965–1966) as a teaching assistant. Graduate study at the University of Michigan resulted in a PhD in constitutional history in 1966 followed by a law degree in 1970.

During these years of academic achievement, Berry held several positions within academic institutions. She held the position as an associate professor at the University of Maryland, College Park, from 1969 through 1976, during which time she served as acting director of Afro-American Studies (1970–1972) and as director (1972–1974) of Afro-American Studies at the University of Colorado, Boulder. Continuing in academia, she became chairman and later provost of the University of Maryland's Division of Behavioral and Social Sciences from 1973 to 1976. She became chancellor of University of Maryland in 1976 and served in that capacity until 1977. From 1980 through 1987, Berry became a professor of history and law and senior fellow in the Institute for the Study of Educational Policy at Howard University. In 1987 she was named the Geraldine A. Segal Professor of American Social Thought at the University of Pennsylvania.

During these years she served in many governmental positions. In 1977 Berry became the assistant secretary for education in the Department of Health, Education and Welfare and served in that capacity until 1980. She was appointed by President Jimmy Carter in 1980 to the U.S. Commission on Civil Rights and served as vice-chair. It is in this capacity that she gained renown for her outspoken advocacy of civil rights that led to her removal under the Ronald Reagan administration. Berry has authored several books: *Black Resistance/White Law* (1971); *A History of Constitutional Racism in America* (1971); *Military Necessity and Civil Rights Policy* (1977); *Stability, Security, and Continuity* (1978); *Blacks in the Year 2000* (1981); *Long Memory: The Black Experience in America* (1982) co-authored with John W. Blassingame; and *Why the ERA Failed: Women's Rights and the Amending Process of the Constitution* (1986). She served as associate editor of the *Journal of Negro History* from 1974 to 1978 and has authored numerous articles in various journals.

She was actively involved in numerous organizations such as the Organization of American Historians (executive board, 1974–1977), Association for the Study of Afro-American Life and History (executive board, 1973–1976), American Historical Association (vice president, 1980–1983), honorary member of Coalition 100 Black Women and Delta Sigma Theta. Her talents and credits to her profession are underlined by the numerous honorary degrees bestowed upon her. She has received honorary degrees from Howard University, Central Michigan University, the University of Akron, Benedict College, University of Maryland, Grambling State University, Bethune-Cookman College, Clark College, Delaware State College, Oberlin College, Langston University, Marian College, Haverford College, City College of the City University of New York, and DePaul University. Berry is further recognized for her excellence by the numerous awards granted her. She is the recepient of the Athena, or Distinguished Alumni, Award from the University of Michigan (1971), the Roy Wilkins Civil Rights Award from the NAACP (1983), Allard Lowenstein Award (1984), Women of the Year Award/National Capital Area YWCA (1985), Hubert Humphrey Civil Rights Award from the Leadership Conference on Civil Rights (1986), the Rosa Parks Award, Black Achievement Award from *Ebony* magazine, and Women of the Year Award from *Ms.* magazine (1986).

—Mary Hovanec

Bibliography

In addition to her own writings, many articles have been written on her public life; however, there has been no biography written about Berry. Her role in shaping perspectives in black history is noted in August Meier and Elliot Rudwick, *Black History and the Historical Profession, 1915–1980* (Urbana: University of Illinois Press, 1986). Numerous articles have been written in *Essence* (October, 1984); *Washington Weekly* (October, 1987); *Ms.* (January, 1987); *Jet* (October, 1984; August, 1986); *Time* (November, 1983); and *Scholastic Update* (May, 1987). Insight into Mary Berry can also be gained from articles she has written on pertinent topics.

BETHUNE, MARY McLEOD (1875–1955), educator, clubwoman, political advisor, and civil rights leader, is probably one of the most widely known African American women of the twentieth century. She was born on July 10, the fifteenth of 17 children born to former slaves Samuel and Patsy (McIntosh) McLeod. She grew up in a tightly knit extended family that included her grandmother Sophia. Their farm near Mayesville, South Carolina, provided model values for young Mary Jane McLeod. In this community that offered few opportunities to African Americans, she learned from her Methodist family the importance of hard work, planning, and moral standards. She remembered picking 250 pounds of cotton a day at age nine and pulling the plow after the death of their only mule.

Her parents recognized the importance of education for the new freeborn generation and sacrificed so that Mary Jane McLeod could attend the Trinity Presbyterian Mission School for Negroes. She received encouragement to pursue further education from the African American mission school founder Emma Wilson, who found a white patron, Mary Crissmon, to finance McLeod's education. This Quaker schoolteacher from Denver, Colorado, provided the scholarship to Scotia Seminary in Concord, North Carolina, which enabled McLeod to gain an excellent secondary education. At Scotia, she displayed talents in music and public speaking. She worked at various jobs to help pay for her education, which she completed in 1894.

Her education motivated her to serve her people. In preparation for a missionary career in Africa, she entered Moody Bible Institute in Chicago, Illinois. After graduation in 1895, she was deemed too young to secure a position as a missionary. Disappointed, she returned to the South to teach at Lucy Laney's Haines Institute in Augusta, Georgia. Laney demonstrated how Mary's new role was as important a mission as that in Africa. Both Emma Wilson and Lucy Laney were educators and school founders. These two role models taught Mary McLeod that African American women had a responsibility to uplift the race through education.

She left Haines Institute to teach at Kendall Institute in Sumter, South Carolina, where she met and later married Albertus Bethune, a tall, handsome dry goods employee in the Presbyterian Parsonage. In 1898, their only son, Albert McLeod Bethune, was born. The couple moved to Savannah, Georgia, where Albertus had been offered a teaching position. While her son was still an infant, Mary Bethune persuaded her husband to let her accept the teaching position at a missionary school in Palatka, Florida. There, she established a Presbyterian school in 1900, followed by an independent school in 1902.

A visit to Daytona Beach, Florida, brought her into contact with the problems faced by black railroad workers. Education could develop skills so that the children of these workers could have a better life. As did her mentors Wilson and Laney, Bethune decided to establish a school to help the children. In October 1904, she founded the Daytona Normal and Industrial Institute for Negro Girls in a small rented cabin using Scotia Seminary as a model. With five girls (and her own five-year-old son) ages 8 through 12 as pupils, $1.50 cash, and a firm faith in God, Bethune initiated fundraising techniques that included concerts, festivals, and lectures to purchase land, erect buildings, and pay for the educational services that expanded to 250 students and included boys 2 years later. Her marriage assumed a secondary position to her mission. The couple separated.

During the next two decades, Bethune struggled to build this school as an asset to the community. Through the day and night classes, students learned the rudiments of literacy and the work ethic. Her students served several turpentine camps (settlements of workers for the turpentine industry) in the region through mission schools. She enlisted the help of the two black churches in the area.

Bethune became a "good beggar" speaking to churches, lodges, clubs, and white philanthropists to solicit funds for the school. Her humility and dedication to her school developed supportive patrons among the wealthy visitors to Daytona Beach, which included Thomas H. White of White Sewing Machine Company, John D. Rockefeller of Standard Oil, and James M. Gamble of Proctor and Gamble Enterprises. Wealthy white women became a Ladies' Advisory Board to assist Bethune's efforts. Her students became part of a traveling singing troupe to raise money and provide entertainment at jails and hotels.

With this black and white support, the institution grew and responded to needs as they developed. When white hospitals denied service to black patients and training for black residents and nurses, Bethune organized McLeod Hospital in 1911 to serve the community and to provide training for black physicians and nurses. By 1914 the school offered a full high school course, as well as training for cooks, nurses, teachers, and homemakers. Combining academic, manual, and moral education, the school had over 300 students and a staff of 25 by 1922. A few years later, the school merged with a men's college to become the Bethune-Cookman College, whose motto was "Enter to Learn/Depart to Serve." By 1943 the college awarded its first bachelor of science degree in elementary education and was accredited with an "A" rating.

Education was only one of the fields in which Bethune excelled. Within the black women's club movement, Bethune served as the president of the Florida Federation of Colored Women's Clubs, as a Red Cross lecturer of the Potomac Division, and a founder of the Circle of Negro War Relief of New York City during World War I. Her long estranged husband died in 1918 during her flurry of patriotic service.

During the postwar era, she expanded her leadership. She gave impetus for Florida clubwomen to open a home for wayward and delinquent girls in Ocala in 1920. She helped southern clubwomen organize the Southeastern Association of Colored Women in the same year. As vice president of the Commission on Interracial Cooperation, she interpreted the perspective of African Americans to southern whites. She served as a founder and executive committee member of the National Association of Wage Earners and the International Council of Women of the Darker Races of the World, which were both formed in the 1920s reflecting concerns of black women. Bethune served as president for two terms in the National Association of Colored Women (1924–1928), during which time she established the national headquarters for the NACW and advised the Calvin Coolidge and Herbert Hoover administrations on African American educational issues through the National Child Welfare Commission.

Bethune was an activist for her race and gender. Her political advising raised her awareness about the need for black women to have a national coalition to effect political change. Thus, in 1935, she founded the National Council of Negro Women, an umbrella organization uniting various black women's groups to pressure the political system. She served as the president until 1949. She served as a life member and president (1936–1951) of the Association for the Study of Negro Life and History. Likewise, she served as the president of the National Association of Teachers in Colored Schools. She assisted several committees in the NAACP. For her efforts, she was awarded the Spingarn Medal in 1935, becoming the second African American woman to receive this honor. She also served as a vice president of the National Urban League during the 1920s. Bethune understood the need for organization and for political action. Bethune's club activities and interracial cooperation brought her into regular contact with Eleanor Roosevelt, another humanitarian who shared Bethune's concern for youth and for the oppressed minorities. They became good friends, a relationship that proved beneficial to Bethune for direct access to the President. When the New Deal revived the principle of federal auspices of racial equality, Bethune became the Director of Minority Affairs in the New Deal's National Youth Administration (1936–1943). In August 1936, she brought black leaders serving in the Franklin Roosevelt administration to her home to discuss strategies for improving racial status through the New Deal. This meeting led to the formation of the Federal Council on Negro Affairs, which came to be called the Black Cabinet. This group then organized two national conferences to explore problems facing the African Americans and to suggest means for their improvement. Their "Blue Book" on civil liberties was presented to the President and distributed throughout government departments. Her influence in the Roosevelt years led to greater numbers of black appointments and to a greater federal role in racial issues. During World War II, blacks received training in her National Youth Administration programs, gained employment in national defense plants, and sponsored the SS *Harriet Tubman*, the first ship to honor a black woman. Bethune endorsed A. Phillip Randolph's March on Washington Movement, served on the advisory committee of the Women's Interest Section (WIS) in the War Department's Bureau of Public Relations, and advised on racial situations as the Detroit Sojourner Truth Project.

During the war years, her chronic asthma worsened, forcing her to restrict her travels and to relinquish the presidency of Bethune-Cookman College in 1942. She was invited to serve as a second alternate for the NAACP to the San Francisco Conference charged with the writing of the charter of the United Nations. En route to California, she received news of President Roosevelt's death. She returned to Washington to appear on a memorial program as the speaker for minority groups. Eleanor Roosevelt presented his cane to Bethune in remembrance for her service and their friendship.

She retired from public life on her seventy-fifth birthday in 1950, settling in her home on the campus of Bethune-Cookman College. Although retired, Bethune handled the development of a black resort, Bethune-Volusia Beach; established the Bethune Foundation; and received 12 honorary degrees. She could not pass up a chance to serve as her country's representative; against the advice of her doctors, she traveled to Liberia in January 1952 as the U.S. delegate to the inauguration of President William Tubman.

Throughout her career, Bethune fought for civil rights and racial respect. She would not answer if addressed as "Mary" or "Auntie," common terms of the times. When preparing for a sinus operation at Johns Hopkins, she requested that black physicians be allowed to observe the operation, a request that broke the racial barriers at the prestigious hospital. She was part of a black protest against white domination of YWCA activities in the South that led to a greater role of black women within the YWCA.

For her efforts, she received numerous awards, honorary doctorates, and honors. In addition to the Spingarn Medal, Bethune won the Frances Drexel Award for Distinguished Service in 1937, the Thomas Jefferson Award in 1942, the Medal of Honor and Merit from Haiti in 1949, and the Star of Africa from Liberia in 1952. However, during the McCarthy era, she was denied the right to speak in Englewood, New Jersey, due to her being labeled as a communist subversive.

Bethune died of a heart attack on May 18, 1955. On July 10, 1974, the United States Government dedicated a statue at Lincoln Park in Washington, DC, the first such public monument dedicated to an African American or to a woman in the nation's capital.

—Dorothy C. Salem with Margaret Barron

Bibliography

Information on Mary McLeod Bethune is readily available in manuscript collections, periodical articles, and books. The National Black Women's History Archives is located in the Bethune home in Washington, DC, which has been declared a historical site. Much of her correspondence and papers can be found in the Washington area: National Council of Negro Women Papers, National Black Women's Archives; files of the Division of Negro Affairs, National Youth Administration Archives, National Archives; Moorland-Spingarn Research Center, Howard University; administrative files, NAACP Papers, Library of Congress; and Carter G. Woodson Papers, Library of Congress. Her other "home" in Daytona Beach, Florida, site of the Bethune-Cookman College, holds the Mary Bethune Papers, Bethune Foundation. Some correspondence exists in the Papers of W.E.B. Du Bois, University of Massachusetts, Amherst; the Schomburg Collection in the New York Public Library; the Eleanor Roosevelt Papers, Franklin D. Roosevelt Library; and the Amistad Research Center, Dillard University, New Orleans.

Her own writings appear in "Mary McLeod Bethune: Her Own Words of Inspiration" *Journal of Negro Education* 45 (Summer, 1976): 342–359; and in her columns appearing in the *Chicago Defender* and the *Pittsburgh Courier*. Articles appeared in *Opportunity, Ebony, Journal of Negro History*, and *The Crisis*. Anthologies containing her essays are Rayford Logan, *What the Negro Wants* (Chapel Hill, NC: University of North Carolina, 1944); Louis Finkelstein, *Thirteen Americans: Their Spiritual Autobiographies* (New York: Harper, 1953); and Gerda Lerner, *Black Women* in *White America* (New York: Random House, 1973). Her "Last Will and Testament" was first published in *Ebony* (August 1955): 105–110, as her legacy of racial pride.

Biographies about Bethune are many: Catherine Owen Peare's *Mary McLeod Bethune* (New York: Vanguard, 1951) is a partially definitive work about her background and career. Emma Gelders Sterne's *Mary McLeod Bethune* (New York: Alfred A. Knopf, 1957) and Rackham Holt's *Mary McLeod Bethune* (Garden City, NY: Doubleday, 1964) contain much of the same information about the educator and humanitarian. Few integrate Bethune's role in southern history; the comprehensive evaluation of Bethune is yet to be written.

She has consistently been included among lists of the top ten historical African-American women leaders from the 1920s to the present. Therefore, her biographical sketch and historical significance are evaluated in many diverse sources, such as Clement Richardson, ed., *The National Cyclopedia of the Colored Race* (Montgomery, AL: National Publishing, 1919); J.L. Nichols, *Progress of a Race* (Maperville, IL: J.L. Nichols and Co., 1920); Elizabeth L. Davis, *Lifting as They Climb* (Washington, DC: National Association of Colored Women, 1933); Benjamin Brawley, *Negro Builders and Heroes* (Chapel Hill: University of North Carolina Press, 1937); Gwendolyn Cherry, *Portraits in Color* (New York: Pageant Press, 1962); Wilhelmina S. Robinson, *Historical Negro Biographies* (New York: Publishers Company, Inc., 1967–1969); Sylvia Dannett, *Profiles of Negro Womanhood* (Chicago: Educational Heritage, 1964); William Brewer, "Personal: Mary McLeod Bethune," *Journal of Negro History* 40:3 (July 1955): 393–394; and several editions of *Who's Who of the Colored Race*.

Evaluative essays about her significance or career include the following: Irene McCoy Gaines, "Ten Living Negro Women Who Have Contributed Most to Advancement of the Race," *Fisk News* (ca. 1935/copy in the Mary Church Terrell Papers, Library of Congress): 10–13; Lerone Bennett, Jr., "No Crystal Stair: The Black Woman in History," *Ebony* 32 (August 1977): 167+; Benjamin Mays, "The Most Extraordinary Black Woman I Have Ever Known," *Ebony* 32 (August 1977): 139–140; Paula Giddings, "Anniversary Issue," *The Crisis* 87:10 (December 1980): 540–545; and B. Joyce Ross, "Mary McLeod Bethune and the National Youth Administration: A Case Study of Power Relationships in the Black Cabinet of Franklin D. Roosevelt," *Journal of Negro History* 60:1 (January 1975): 1–28. Elaine M. Smith criticizes Ross's interpretations of Bethune's role in the NYA in "Mary McLeod Bethune and the National Youth Administration," in *Clio Was a Woman: Studies in the History of American Women*, edited by Mabel E. Deutrich and Virginia C. Purdy (Washington, DC: Howard University Press, 1980), pp. 1093–1121. Dolores C. Leffall and Janet L. Sims have a more complete annotated bibliography of books and articles in "Mary McLeod Bethune—The Educator; Also Including a Selected Annotated Bibliography," *Journal of Negro Education* 45 (Summer 1976): 342–359.

For complete, concise summaries of biographical material see entries in Barbara Sicherman, ed., *Notable American Women* (Cambridge: Harvard University Press, 1980); Rayford Logan, *Dictionary of American Negro Biography* (New York: Norton, 1982); and Jessie Carney Smith, *Notable Black American Women* (Detroit: Gale, 1992).

BISHOP, ANNA [STEWARD] (b. 1916), educator and poet of African American culture, was born into a family of educators on August 31 in Wilberforce, Ohio. Her father, Gustavus Adolphus Steward, was a teacher at various schools including Tuskegee Institute during the presidency of Booker T. Washington; her stepgrandmother, Dr. Susan McKinney Steward, was one of the first female African American physicians in the country; her mother was a graduate of Wilberforce University; her grandmother, Anna Hughes Jones Coleman, was a graduate of Wilberforce University and a teacher for 49 years in the community's school. It was through Coleman that five-year-old Anna Bishop had her first contact with school, when she visited her grandmother's classes and ended up working with the first-graders. Bishop strongly believes that this initial contact with education propelled her into an impressive career as a teacher. She first attended the Eastwood Elementary School in Columbus, Ohio, but black children were transferred to Mt. Vernon Avenue School because school district boundary lines were redrawn. According to Bishop's father, the boundary lines were redrawn because the area had become predominantly black, which led to "visibility" since Eastwood School was close to an affluent white neighborhood. Bishop later graduated from Pilgrim Junior High School at age 13, and from East High School at age 16 (1932). She received her bachelor's degree in elementary education and drama education with a minor in music from Ohio State University in 1936. With this education, the dynamic Bishop not only taught for 35 years but also served as poet-in-residence in the Ohio Arts Museum from 1977 to 1982. This stimulated her desire for additional information about her culture. She reenrolled in the master's program of the Ohio State University, and four years later, in 1991, the 75-year-old Bishop graduated with a master of arts in Black Studies.

Bishop received many awards during these years, including the Christopher Columbus Award; Community Service Award; Inter-city Sertoma Club, Columbus; Doctor of Humane Letters from Wilmington College; and induction into the Black Hall of Respect at the Ohio State University Community Extension Center. She has also maintained and nurtured her music through the years, writing and performing "The Mayor" for *Afromation*, WOSU-TV. Bishop went on to act in four different movies, and has written several books and poems. Her most well known work is the four-volume *Beyond Poindexter Village*. She has volunteered in many capacities, including that of cultural activities director at the Black Studies Community Extension Center from 1975 to 1980. She currently works in the Columbus, Ohio, community, and participates in activities with her Alpha Kappa Alpha sorority sisters.

—Mary Ann Williams

Bibliography

Most of the information was obtained by the author through oral history interviews in 1989–1990 with Anna Bishop and community leaders in Columbus, Ohio.

BOWLES, EVA D. (1875–1943), YWCA administrator, was born on January 24 in Albany, Ohio, to a middle-class family. Her father was a postal clerk, and her grandfather was a Baptist minister and teacher in the Columbus, Ohio, public schools. Eva del Vakia Bowles's education included Columbus public schools, a business college, and courses at Ohio State University.

Bowles began her career as a teacher for the American Missionary Association and taught in schools in Kentucky, Virginia, Florida, and North Carolina. While teaching in Lawrenceville, Virginia, she met Addie W. Hunton, the wife of the secretary of the Bureau for Colored Work in the local Young Men's Christian Association, who recommended Bowles for a position at the Harlem Young Women's Christian Association (YWCA) in New York City, which she joined in 1905 as the first African American secretary of a YWCA branch.

After completing a training course in social work at the New York School of Philanthropy, she left the YWCA and, as one of the first black women to enter the relatively new field of social work, began casework for the Associated Charities of Columbus, Ohio. Four years later, in 1913, she returned to the YWCA and assumed the position of secretary of the newly formed Committee on Colored Work of the National Board, thus marking a new era in the history of the YWCA in which responsibility for black women's welfare became an integral part of the organization's work.

From 1905 to 1932, Bowles established the YWCA as an interracial organization. Her experience made her a significant member of a network of black women leaders. During and after World War I, black women migrated to the North, where the YWCA provided assistance for the homeless among them. In response to the need, and upon Bowles's recommendation, the YWCA established an Industrial Department to locate jobs for unemployed black women. The resulting increase in membership led Bowles to fear that a separate organization for blacks would emerge, following the example of the YWCA International Institute for foreign-born women. Believing that black women should be completely integrated into the YWCA, Bowles promoted interracial conferences with delegates from YWCAs throughout the country. However, conferences presented difficulties because of insistence upon equal accommodations for all delegates in the face of existing discrimination. Bowles continued to insist upon interracial conferences, and finally, in 1930, a national interracial convention was held in Detroit, which was free of discrimination. Despite the growing success of interracial conventions, Bowles knew there was a possibility for the national Y movement to change. During the 1920s, pressure was placed on the organization by some of the leaders in the white community to combine the YWCA and the YMCA into a single organization for blacks. Under this suggested plan, social activities for both men and women would be housed in one building for the purpose of economy. Bowles reminded board members of their commitment to an interracial policy, and the plan was abandoned.

As an organization pioneering in race relations, the YWCA Bureau of Colored Work accumulated a store of experience and information that was useful to other organizations and groups—the Federal Council of Churches, the American Interracial Peace Committee, the NAACP, the National Urban League, the National League of Women Voters, and the United States Department of Health. Therefore, a new research department was established with Eva D. Bowles, and Henrietta Roelofs from the YWCA Public Affairs Committee, selected to prepare a plan to make the Bureau an authority on black Americans and prepare bibliographies, course outlines, and a history.

During World War I, Eva Bowles tried to meet the needs of black women who were members of camp communities and those who visited enlisted men in army camps. She was delighted when the War Work Council of the YWCA allocated $200,000 for black women. Council work was directed by black leaders under the leadership of Eva Bowles. The women, all college graduates, established Hostess Houses as recreation centers near United States Army camps. Here, young women organized clubs and classes for recreation and self-improvement. The centers also provided a reception area for soldiers and their visiting wives, mothers, and friends. The War Work Council attracted national attention when Theodore Roosevelt sent $4,000 of a fund, awarded to him by a Special Act of Congress, to the Council for use by the Colored Work Committee. When he made the gift, Theodore Roosevelt stated that he had asked that "Miss Eva Bowles be consulted in the disbursement of this item . . . and that the money be used for the hostess houses for colored troops."

Bowles's objectives had been realized by 1932. The separate Bureau for Colored Work was dissolved by the National Board of the YWCA, and black girls and women were not considered a separate group, but were now an integral part of the organization. Bowles acknowledged that the YWCA had declined as a leading force in interracial affairs and now leadership among black women had passed to the Federation of Colored Women's Clubs.

There was an evolution in Eva D. Bowles's thoughts about African Americans over her lifetime. Early in her career she thought of women as YWCA workers first, and race was not a major issue. She hoped that women in the Y would work together toward solving the problems of women in general, and not those of a specific group. But as her experiences and contacts throughout the country expanded, she found that both black women and white women were not always ready for interracial work, and black women were not always ready to assume positions of leadership in the Y. It appeared that they were not aware of themselves as a group that could hold power.

She thought group consciousness would have to be awakened and developed before black women could assume their position of leadership without race consciousness. Therefore, the idea of "interracial readiness" appeared in her later writings. In 1926 she met with branch secretaries and chairmen of committees to talk over problems that were "intimate with us as colored women." These were not now interracial groups, but groups of black women formed to promote understanding of themselves. Bowles explained that it was "absolutely necessary to understand [ourselves] as a group before we can intelligently work interracially." In her later years, Bowles explained that she had a twofold job to do. As a black American she was committed to the uplift of the race as well as to an active role for blacks as members of an interracial society. Bowles died on June 14, 1943, in Richmond, Virginia.

—Lucille O'Connell

Bibliography

Eva D. Bowles's numerous committee reports and her extensive correspondence is in the YWCA Collection, Boxes 40, 41, and 42, in the Sophia Smith Collection, Smith College, Northampton, Massachusetts. Information also can be found in the Archives, National Board of the YWCA, New York City.

Works by Eva D. Bowles

"The Colored Girl in Our Midst," *The Association Monthly* (December 1917).
"The Young Women's Christian Association among Colored Women and Girls," *The Woman's Press* (January 1924).
"Race Relations in the Light of Social Research," *The Woman's Press* (February 1929).
"Negro Girls in Clerical Occupations," *The Woman's Press* (July 1929).

Works about Eva D. Bowles

Gladys Gilkey Calkins, "The Negro in the Young Women's Christian Association," MA thesis, George Washington University, 1960 (unpublished).
McCulloch, Rhoda E. "Eva D. Bowles," *The Woman's Press* (September 1943).
Olcott, Jane. *The Work of Colored Women.* New York, 1920.
YWCA. *Beginnings among Colored Women.* New York, 1913.
———. *A New Day for the Colored Woman Worker.* np, 1919.
———. War Work Council, Committee on Work among Colored Girls and Women. *Colored American Women in War Work.* New York, 1918.

BOWSER, ROSA [DIXON] (1855–1931), educator, clubwoman, and community activist, was born on January 7 to Henry and Augusta Dixon at the Clay Hill plantation in Amelia County, Virginia, southwest of Richmond. While she was still a child, her parents moved to Richmond, where she attended a private primary school. She graduated from the Richmond Normal School and received her certification to teach in 1872. She taught in the public school system of Richmond, Virginia. She was also active in educational and religious organizations and worked at the local, state, and national levels of the black women's club movement.

Her first teaching position was at the Navy Hill School in Jackson Ward, the black section of Richmond, where she taught from 1872 until her marriage in 1879. Her husband was James Herndon Bowser, a postal worker. The couple's only child, Oswald, was born in 1880. James Bowser died in 1881, and in 1883 Rosa Bowser returned to teach at the Navy Hill School. She transferred to the Baker Hill School the following year and taught there for almost 40 years until her retirement in 1923. She may also have taught at the Peabody Normal Institute.

For Rosa Bowser, teaching was never limited to the classroom. She created the first night class for black men in Richmond. She helped organize black teachers in the state, serving as the first president of the Virginia Teachers Association and later as president of the Women's Educational Convention of Virginia. Bowser was also an active member of the First African Baptist Church, where she taught Sunday school. Her religious commitments led her to be the first chairperson of the Women's Missionary and Educational Society of Virginia. For three years she headed a charity movement for black children named the Christmas Stocking Fund.

Like others of her generation, Bowser was instrumental in the organization and progress of the black women's club movement. In 1895 Bowser and other Richmond women organized the Richmond Women's League. Under her leadership, the group became the Mothers' Club, which had branches in three sections of Richmond and promoted night schools and day nurseries. The founding of the Hampton Negro Institute and its Women's Conference expanded Bowser's opportunities to work with other women who shared her goals. She spoke at the initial Women's Conference in 1897, and again in 1899, and in 1902, she chaired the section of the Hampton Negro Conference on Domestic Education. Bowser and the Richmond Mothers' Clubs became part of the Virginia State Federation of Colored Women's Clubs, which organized in 1907 and held its first meeting in 1908. Bowser also served as president of the Woman's Department of the Negro Reformatory Association of Virginia and on the Executive Board of the Southern Federation of Colored Women.

The creation of a national organization of black clubwomen was another of Bowser's interests. In 1895 she wrote for *The Women's Era*, the first monthly magazine published by black women. The following year she attended the National Federation of Afro-American Women's conference in Washington, DC, and served on the committee which united that organization with the National League of Colored Women. At the first annual meeting of the National Association of Colored Women in Nashville in 1897, Bowser spoke on women's need to order their households and to assist those whom she called their "weaker sisters." She also served as an organizer for the NACW.

A life-long resident of Richmond, Bowser died there on February 7, 1931. She is buried in the East End Cemetery. When Richmond opened its first library branch for black residents in 1925, its users chose to name it for Rosa D. Bowser.

In 1976, the National Biscuit Company named her in its Bicentennial Salute to 24 Outstanding Black Educators.

—Marilyn Dell Brady

Bibliography

Primary materials on Rosa Bowser can be found at Hampton University, where the archives hold materials on the Hampton Negro Conferences and the Virginia State Federation of Colored Women Clubs and the Peabody Room has a clipping collection on women's organizations that contains materials on her activities in Richmond.

The most useful source on Bowser's life is by an unidentified author, "Rosa D. Bowser: Talent to Spare, Talent to Share," *Richmond Literary and Historical Quarterly* 1 (Fall 1978): 45–46. Several scholars have noted Bowser's activities as a teacher, clubwoman, and speaker. For example, see Cynthia Neverdon-Morton, *Afro-American Women of the South and the Advancement of the Race, 1895–1925* (Knoxville: University of Tennessee Press, 1989); Dorothy Salem, *To Better Our World: Black Women in Organized Reform, 1890–1920* (Brooklyn: Carlson Press, 1990); Suzanne Lebsock, *Virginia Women, 1600–1945* (Richmond: Virginia State Library and Virginia Women's Cultural History Project, 1984); Elizabeth L. Davis, *Lifting as They Climb* (Washington, DC: NACW, 1933); and Charles Wesley, *The History of the National Association of Colored Women's Clubs* (Washington, DC: NACW, 1984).

Brief entries on Bowser appear in Harry A. Ploski and James Williams, eds., *The Negro Almanac*, 5th edition (Detroit: Gale, 1989) and Sylvia Dannett, *Profiles of Negro Womanhood* (New York: M.W. Lads, 1964), but both claim she was born in 1885. Given a variety of other sources on her activities before 1900, this is obviously an error.

Bowser's speech at the NACW Convention in 1897, "What Role Is the Educated Negro to Play in the Uplifting of Her Race?" was reprinted in D.W. Culp, *Twentieth Century Negro Literature* (Toronto: J.L. Nichols, 1902).

BRANCH, MARY ELIZABETH (1881–1944) was born on May 20 at Farmville, Virginia. Her father, Tazewell Branch, a former slave whose master had taught him to read and write, and mother, Harriett (Lacey) Branch, revered education and enrolled their six children in school and encouraged them to read books in their home library.

Mary Elizabeth Branch's father had been a member of the Virginia legislature in 1874 and 1876, but disgusted with political corruption, he retired and was employed as a shoemaker. To supplement his income, Branch's mother sought domestic jobs; teenaged Branch collected laundry from the State College at Farmville for her mother to wash. She also worked as a maid in the college's library, where access to multitudes of books inspired her to seek advanced education.

She finished high school at the normal school of Virginia State College in Petersburg. Concerned that the English language be used correctly, she taught that subject at an elementary school in Blackstone, Virginia, before beginning a 20-year tenure at Virginia State College, where Branch also assumed responsibility as director of the dormitories and counseled students. During the summers, she pursued undergraduate work at the University of Pennsylvania, Columbia University, and the University of Chicago, where she received her bachelor's degree in 1922. Three years later she completed her MA in English from the same university and began course work for a doctorate.

In 1925 she taught social studies at Sumner Junior College in Kansas City, Missouri, then became dean of girls at the St. Louis Vashon High School. Branch especially enjoyed being a role model for children in the impoverished neighborhood, realizing that she could improve their lives through education.

In 1930 the American Missionary Association asked Branch to be president of Tillotson College in Austin, Texas. She initially refused because the salary was less than what she earned at Vashon, but, realizing other teachers' sacrifices to help students, she accepted. When Branch arrived, Tillotson, suffering low enrollment because of the Depression, had been reduced to the status of junior college.

Branch considered the college's poor condition to be a challenge. She immediately designed a five-year plan to improve buildings and attract more students. She campaigned for library expansion and insisted that all faculty have a master's degree. She established scholarships to recruit outstanding students. Branch successfully increased enrollment from 140 students in 1930 to 502 in 1944, and Tillotson was merited higher accreditation rankings.

Although active in the African Methodist Episcopal church, Branch abolished mandatory chapel and permitted more social and extracurricular activity on campus. Branch enjoyed participating in her sorority, Alpha Kappa Alpha, and walking around campus, meeting people. She believed that students should work to pay for their education and oversaw work-study employment, personally pairing students with suitable jobs.

She encouraged the students and faculty to become active in the community. In 1943 Branch was president of the Austin chapter of the National Association for the Advancement of Colored People and advised the Tillotson chapter. She was also a member of the State Interracial Commission of Texas and boycotted segregationist businesses. In the New Deal National Youth Administration (NYA) she assisted with vocational training. In 1935 the NYA director in Texas, Lyndon B. Johnson, appointed her to the Texas NYA Negro Advisory Board. Dr. Frederick Patterson of Tuskegee Institute sought her counsel in creating the United Negro College Fund. Branch received two honorary degrees: Virginia State College gave her their first doctor of pedagogy, and Howard University honored her with a doctor of laws.

Unexpectedly, Branch suffered a painful goiter, and in summer 1944, she traveled to the Johns Hopkins University Hospital for consultation and treatment. She died on July 6, 1944, in a Camden, New Jersey, hospital while visiting her sisters. Before her death Branch had sought a merger of Tillotson with nearby Samuel Huston College, which occurred in 1952.

—Elizabeth D. Schafer

Bibliography

The Mary Branch Papers are located in the archives of Huston-Tillotson College at Austin. Archival records relating to her work with the National Youth Administration are included in the Lyndon B. Johnson Library in Austin.

Olive D. Brown, who was librarian at Tillotson while Branch was president, and Michael R. Heintze wrote a detailed profile of Branch, "Mary Branch: Private College Educator," in Alwyn Barr and Robert A. Calvert, eds., *Black Leaders: Texans for Their Times* (Austin: Texas State Historical, 1981). Branch's obituary, with several dates incorrectly listed, is featured in "Doctor Mary E. Branch," *Journal of Negro History* 29 (July 1944): 399–400. Her obituary is also in the *Austin American-Statesman* (July 7, 1944) and *Houston Informer* (July 15, 1944). Additional biographical sketches are included in Thomas Yenser, ed., *Who's Who in Colored America, A Biographical Dictionary of Notable Living Persons of African Descent in America, 1930–1932* (New York: Who's Who in Colored America Corp., 1933) and James McKeen Cattell, ed., *Leaders in American Education* (Lancaster, PA: Science Press, 1941). The *Tillotson College Bulletin, A Memorial Issue* (January 1945), as well as other issues and the *Catalogue of Tillotson College* provide information about Branch's career as university president. Other treatises dealing with Tillotson include Mabel Crayton Williams, "The History of Tillotson College, 1881–1952," MA thesis, Texas Southern University (1967); William H. Jones "Tillotson College, from 1930–1940: A Study of the Total Institution," mimeograph at Huston-Tillotson College (1940); and Chrystine I. Shackles, *Reminiscences of Huston-Tillotson College* (Austin: privately printed, 1973).

Branch is quoted in Mary Jenness, *Twelve Negro Americans* (New York: Friendship Press, 1936). Contemporary newspapers containing information about Branch include the *Austin American-Statesman, Houston Press, Negro Labor News* (Houston), *Houston Informer, Dallas Gazette,* and *San Antonio Register*. Alwyn Barr, *Black Texans: A History of Negroes in Texas, 1528–1971* (Austin: Jenkins, 1973) notes Branch's significance as an educational leader. Henry Bullock, *A History of Negro Education in the South* (Cambridge: Harvard University Press, 1967) and Ruthe Winegarten, *Texas Women: A Pictorial History* (Austin: Eakin, 1986) provide a context for Branch's career as an educator.

BRISCO-HOOKS, VALERIE (b. 1960), track and field athlete, a triple Gold Medalist at the 1984 Los Angeles Olympics, was the first American, male or female, to win both the 400-meter and 200-meter dash at the same Olympiad. She set Olympic records for both these events with a performance of 48.83 and 21.81 seconds, respectively. Capturing her third Gold Medal running the third leg of the 1,600-meter relay with another record-breaking 49.23 seconds, she became the first American woman since Wilma Rudolph in 1960 to win three Gold Medals at the same Olympiad.

Born on July 6 in Greenwood, Mississippi, Valerie Ann Brisco-Hooks was the sixth of ten children of Arguster and Guitherea Brisco. When Valerie was five years old the family moved to Los Angeles, where she attended Locke High School and excelled in 100-, 200-, and 400–meter races to become a 1978 High School All-American. She continued her training at California State University, Northridge, in 1979, where she was an AIAW Champion and AAU runner-up in the 200-meter title. She won a Gold Medal for her participation in the Pan-American Games in San Juan, Puerto Rico, on the U.S. 400-meter relay team.

In 1981 she married Alvin Hooks, a Philadelphia Eagles wide receiver (they divorced in 1984). Pregnancy prevented Brisco-Hooks from competing in 1982, but after her son, Alvin, Jr., was born, she resumed serious training with her former coach at Northridge, Bob Kersee. Like a significant number of female athletes, Brisco-Hooks credits pregnancy with improving her strength and performance. She joined Kersee's World Class Track Team in 1983 and trained with future champions Jackie Joyner-Kersee and Florence Griffith-Joyner. Brisco-Hooks ran in the Athletic Congress (TAC) track meet, winning the 400-meter title in 49.83 seconds, the first American woman under 50 seconds for that distance, just one week before her brilliant performance in the 1984 Los Angeles Olympics. During 1985, 1986, and 1987, Brisco-Hooks continued to set world and track records; the Metropolitan Track Writers Association named her the Outstanding Female Athlete of 1985. In the 1988 Olympics in Seoul, South Korea, she ran the third leg of the 1,600-meter relay, winning a Silver Medal as a team member. Although she trained for the 400-meter dash for the 1992 Olympics, a hamstring pull prevented her from making a comeback. She lives in California and continues to represent the World Class Athletic Congress.

—Janet Owens

Bibliography

Brownlee, Shannon. "Moms in the Fast Lane," *Sports Illustrated* (May 30, 1988): 57–60.

Castro, Tony. "After the Gold, Some Glitter," *Sports Illustrated* (June 3, 1985): 44–46.

Davis, Michael D., ed. *Black American Women in Olympic Track and Field*. Jefferson, NC: McFarland, 1992.

Hawkins, Walter L. *African American Biographies*. Jefferson, NC: McFarland, 1992.

Johnson, D. "Track and Field News Interview: Valerie Brisco-Hooks," *Track and Field News* (March 1985): 64–65.

Page, James A., ed. *Black Olympian Medalists*. Englewood, CO: Libraries Unlimited, 1991.

Porter, David L., ed. *Biographical Dictionary of American Sports. Outdoor Sports*. New York: Greenwood Press, 1988.

Track and Field News (June 1992): 34.

BROOKS, GWENDOLYN E. (b. 1917), writer and poet, the first African American to win the Pulitzer Prize for Poetry was born on June 7 in Topeka, Kansas. Gwendolyn Elizabeth Brooks graduated from Wilson Junior College in 1936. In 1939 she married Henry Lowington Blakely II, and they had two children: Henry, Jr., and Nora. She published A *Street in Bronzeville* in 1945 and wrote her Pulitzer Prize–winning volume *Annie Allen* in 1949. In 1950 Brooks won the Pulitzer Prize for Poetry. Prior to receiving the Pulitzer Prize, Brooks had won numerous awards, including two Guggenheim Fellowships in Creative Writing (1946 and 1947), became one of *Mademoiselle* magazine's Ten Women of 1945, and in 1949 received the Eunice Tietjens Memorial Prize from *Poetry* magazine.

Brooks continued to write poetry and teach at major American colleges and universities and since the 1960s has offered poetry and fiction-writing workshops across the country. In Chicago, she established a poetry workshop for some of South Chicago's street gangs, including one of the best known—the Blackstone Rangers. This encounter and that with activist writers and artists in the black arts movement gave Brooks, in her own estimation, other directions for her art and her life. She became, she said, "blackness"-conscious especially after the 1967 Fisk University Writer's Conference held in Nashville and attended by such movement writers as John Killens, John Henrik Clarke, Amiri Baraka (then known as LeRoi Jones), and Lerone Bennett, Jr.

Her poetry deals with the African American common man and woman, inter- and intraracism and -colorism, the black poor and particularly the plight and strength of the black woman, and urban ghetto living with a Third World focus. She has said that had she died before she was 50, she would have died a "Negro fraction." The summation of these experiences, in the 1960s, led her to leave mainstream publishing houses for black publishers and also to publish her own work.

During the 1970s she continued to win recognition. In 1976 she was appointed to the National Institute of Arts and Letters. In 1985–1986 she was Consultant to the Library of Congress, becoming the second African American and first African American woman to receive that honor. Brooks continues to live and write in Chicago and lectures to students throughout the country.

Among Gwendolyn Brooks's works are A *Street in Bronzeville* (1945), *Maud Martha* (1953), *The Bean Eaters* (1960), *In the Mecca* (1968), *Report from Part One* (1972) and *Beckonings* (1975).

—Nancy Elizabeth Fitch

Bibliography

Gwendolyn Brooks's *Report from Part One* (Detroit: Broadside Press, 1972) is an important autobiographical statement of the writer's life and career up to 1972 discussing a transforming event in her political perceptions and thoughts about black life that also changed her writing—namely the 1967 Fisk University Writer's Conference. Maria K. Mootry and Gary Smith's *A Life Distilled. Gwendolyn Brooks, Her Poetry and Fiction* (Urbana: University of Illinois Press, 1987) is a collection of critical essays assessing and analyzing Brooks's body of work, including her prose writing. In *Gwendolyn Brooks* (Boston: Twayne Publishers, 1980), Harry B. Shaw provides a biographical and critical treatment of Gwendolyn Brooks's life and her work by looking at the social themes that run consistently through her writing and how social concerns have affected her own life. In the *Washington Post* article "The 40-Year Quest of the Poet. Gwendolyn Brooks, a Light at the Library" (September 25, 1985: DI, D4), journalist Jacqueline Trescott talks with the writer about her career and her new appointment as the 29th Poet Consultant to the Library of Congress. Based on her discussion with Brooks, Trescott looks at her work in terms of her political awakening in 1967 and how her canon has affected the world of women's literature. See also Don L. Lee's article "The Achievement of Gwendolyn Brooks," *The Black Scholar* (Summer 1972): 32–41.

Editor's note: Brooks is also featured in Gwendolyn Cherry's *Portraits in Color* (New York: Pageant Press, 1962); *Famous Blacks Give Secrets of Success*, Vol. II of the *Ebony* Success Library (Nashville, TN: Southwestern Co., 1973): 22–27; Ann Allen Shockley and Sue P. Chandler, *Living Black American Authors: A Biographical Directory* (New York: Bowker, 1973); Michael Popkin, *Modern Black Writers* (New York: Frederick Ungar, 1978); and "The Negro Woman in American Literature," *Freedomways* 6 (Winter 1966): 8–25.

BROWN, CHARLOTTE HAWKINS (1883–1961), one of the South's best known educators and activists in the first half of the twentieth century, was born Lottie Hawkins on June 11 in Henderson, North Carolina. The daughter of Edmund H. Hight and Carrie Frances Hawkins, the family moved to Cambridge, Massachusetts, where Lottie Hawkins changed her name to Charlotte Eugenia Hawkins. She attended Massachusetts State Normal School at Salem and, later in life, Wellesley College, Harvard University, and Simmons College. She received several honorary degrees, including an MA from Livingstone College and from North Carolina Central University, an LLD from Wilberforce University and from Lincoln University. In 1944, Howard University awarded her the honorary EdD.

In 1901 Brown returned to North Carolina as an American Missionary Association teacher in Sedalia. After the AMA withdrew, Brown raised funds herself and renamed the school Palmer Memorial Institute in honor of Alice Freeman Palmer, the first woman president of Wellesley and a friend of Brown's. During the 1920s and 1930s, Brown added high school grades and formed a board of northern philanthropists and local prominent whites. By the 1940s, when state-funded high schools for blacks became more common, Palmer added a junior college, and gained renown as the premier southern preparatory school for African Americans.

In 1911, Charlotte Hawkins married Edward S. Brown, but they separated shortly thereafter. Although she had no children, Brown raised two of her nieces.

Brown's career as a social activist falls into two distinct periods. From her arrival in North Carolina until the late 1920s, she struggled at great personal risk against Jim Crow laws and the violence of white supremacy. During the 1930s and 1940s, as her reputation grew, she strove to force whites to recognize her and her students as members of the middle class. During the first period of activism, Brown was the second president of the North Carolina Federation of Colored Women's Clubs in 1912, a position that she held until 1936. In 1916 she became the recording secretary of the National Association of Colored Women's Clubs and reached the office of vice president. She attended the first interracial women's meeting in Memphis in 1920 and returned to the state to lead a campaign to register black women to vote. The same year she brought suit against the railroad for refusing her Pullman car service. She was a member of the regional and state Commission on Interracial Cooperation from 1921 until her death and persuaded the state to found the North Carolina Home for Delinquent Colored Girls in the 1920s.

Brown became the leading black spokesperson for a number of state organizations after 1930. She held the presidency of the North Carolina Teachers Association in 1935 and served on the North Carolina Defense Council during World War II. Regionally, she was on the executive board of the Southern Conference for Human Welfare and on the advisory board of the Southern Division of the Urban League. She was a member of Alpha Kappa Alpha sorority and of the Congregational Christian Church.

In 1928, as she acquired a national reputation, she became first black woman admitted to membership in Boston's prestigious Twentieth Century Club. She served on the national boards of the Progressive Education Association, the National Association of Teachers in Colored Schools, the YWCA, and the Council on Red Cross Home Nursing. Nominated for the Spingarn Medal in 1941, she was one of three black delegates from the U.S. to the International Woman's Congress in Paris in 1945.

In 1919 Brown published *Mammy*, a slim volume that appealed to white women for cooperation across racial lines. In 1940 she wrote *The Correct Thing To Do—To Say—To Wear*, a guide to etiquette and healthful living for teenagers. The contrast between her publications reveals her shifting civil rights strategies during her life. Due to ill health, Brown resigned as president of Palmer in 1952. She died in Greensboro in 1961.

—Glenda Elizabeth Gilmore

Bibliography

Charlotte Hawkins Brown's papers are at the Arthur and Elizabeth Schlesinger Library at Radcliffe College and are available on microfilm. Her work, *The Correct Thing to Do—To Say—To Wear*, has been reprinted in 1990 by the Charlotte

Hawkins Brown Historical Foundation. The Foundation, headquartered in Sedalia, North Carolina, oversees the Charlotte Hawkins Brown Memorial, a state historical site open to the public. Constance Hill Marteena's *The Lengthening Shadow of a Woman* (New York: Exposition Press, 1977) is the only full-length biography of Brown and is complemented by the following articles: Tera Hunter, "The Correct Thing: Charlotte Hawkins Brown and the Palmer Institute," *Southern Exposure* XI (September/October 1983): 1–15; Sandra N. Smith, "Charlotte Hawkins Brown," *Journal of Negro Education* 51 (1982): 191–206.

Works by Charlotte Hawkins Brown

Mammy. Boston: Pilgrim Press, 1919.

The Correct Thing To Do—To Say—To Wear. Boston: Christopher Publishing House, 1941; reprint edition, Sedalia, NC: Charlotte Hawkins Brown Historical Foundation, 1990.

Manuscript Collections

Charlotte Hawkins Brown Collection, Arthur and Elizabeth Schlesinger Library, Radcliffe College, Cambridge, MA.

Jesse Daniel Ames Papers and Commission on Interracial Cooperation, Southern Historical Collection, Wilson Library, University of North Carolina, Chapel Hill.

Nannie Helen Burroughs Papers, Manuscript Division, Library of Congress, Washington, DC.

North Carolina Commission on Interracial Cooperation Papers, Trevor Arnett Library, Atlanta University, Atlanta, GA.

Mary McLeod Bethune Papers, Amistad Research Center, Tulane University, New Orleans, LA.

The Moorland-Spingarn Research Center, Manuscript Division, Howard University, Washington, DC, houses the following collections with correspondence: Lucy D. Slowe Papers; Arthur B. Spingarn Papers; Mary Church Terrell Papers; and Washington Conservatory of Music Records.

Neighborhood Union Collection, Atlanta University Center, Woodruff Library, Atlanta University, Atlanta, Georgia.

Secondary Sources

Birmingham, Steven. *Certain People: America's Black Elite.* Boston: Little, Brown, 1977.

Brawley, Benjamin. *Negro Builders and Heroes.* Chapel Hill: University of North Carolina Press, 1937.

Brownlee, Fred L. "She Did It," *The American Missionary* (July 1927): 711.

Cherry, Gwendolyn. *Portraits in Color.* New York: Pageant Press, 1962.

Daniel, Sadie Iola. *Women Builders.* Washington, DC: Associated Publishers, 1931.

Dannett, Sylvia. *Profiles of Negro Womanhood.* New York: Educational Heritage, 1931.

Fleming, G. James, and Christian E. Burckel, eds. *Who's Who in Colored America.* Yonkers, NY: Christian E. Burckel and Associates, 1950.

Foster, M. Marie Booth. *Southern Black Creative Writers, 1829–1953.* New York: Greenwood Press, 1988.

Hall, Jacquelyn Dowd. *Revolt Against Chivalry: Jesse Daniel Ames and the Women's Campaign Against Lynching.* New York: Columbia University Press, 1974.

Hunter, Tera. "The Correct Thing: Charlotte Hawkins Brown and the Palmer Institute," *Southern Exposure* XI:5 (September/October 1983), 37–43.

Lerner, Gerda, ed. *Black Women in White America: A Documentary History.* New York: Random House, 1972.

Marteena, Constance Hill. *The Lengthening Shadow of a Woman.* Hicksville, NY: Exposition Press, 1977.

Neverdon-Morton, Cynthia. *Afro-American Women of the South and the Advancement of the Race, 1895–1920.* Knoxville: University of Tennessee Press, 1989.

Rouse, Jacqueline Anne. *Lugenia Burns Hope: Black Southern Reformer.* Athens: University of Georgia Press, 1989.

BROWN, CLARA (1803–1885),

known best for her pioneering activity in Colorado, was born in Virginia. She was sold with her mother in 1806 to an owner who migrated to Kentucky. Clara married and had three children. When her owner died in 1835, her family was auctioned to different owners. An agonized Brown, distraught at being separated from her family, tried to persuade a purchaser to buy her family as a unit but was unsuccessful. The separation upset her deeply, and her desire to be reunited with her family molded her life.

She decided to purchase her freedom in order to search for her family and collected sufficient funds by 1857. Hearing rumors that her daughter had been taken west, Brown traveled to St. Louis and, taking advantage of the Colorado gold rush, convinced gold prospectors to hire her as a cook. In 1859 she accompanied a thirty-wagon caravan to Denver, often walking on the eight-week trek.

In Denver the devoutly religious Brown helped two Methodist ministers create the Union Sunday School. She then relocated to Central City and organized the Methodist Episcopal Church, hosting prayer meetings in her home before the church was built. She established the city's first Sunday school and also served the community as a nurse and midwife. She welcomed destitute and hungry individuals, especially newly arrived pioneers—both white and black—into her home, feeding them, giving them money, and helping them locate employment. Her friendly, empathetic, and generous nature earned Brown the honorary title "Angel of the Rockies." The Colorado Pioneer Association selected Brown as one of their first black members.

Although she was charitable, Brown was also thrifty, saving money for her family. She established a laundry in Central City, washing flannel shirts for 50¢ each, in order to raise funds to transport her family west. She invested some of her earnings in shares in prospectors' mining claims, garnering approximately $10,000 by the end of the Civil War. Brown owned several gold mines, being one of the first African American women to own land.

In 1866 she initiated her quest to locate her family. She found approximately 34 friends and relatives and arranged for their passage by steamboat from Kentucky to Leavenworth, Kansas. She then sponsored black wagon trains to Denver and assisted their settlement into their new communities.

Brown moved to Denver in 1880 because its milder climate soothed her health ailments. Friends sought information about her children, locating her daughter Eliza Jane in Council Bluffs, Iowa. Brown and her daughter were reunited in 1882. Unfortunately her husband and other children were never found.

Clara Brown died in 1885 (although some sources claim she died two years earlier). The Colorado Pioneers Association buried her with honors, eulogizing Brown as a "kind old friend whose heart always responded to the cry of distress." The St. James Methodist Church erected a bronze plaque, noting her contributions to the Central City religious community, and an opera house chair was dedicated with her name.

—Elizabeth D. Schafer

Bibliography

Clara Brown's life is documented in a biography by Kathleen Bruyn, *Aunt Clara Brown: Story of a Black Pioneer* (Boulder, Pruett Publishing, 1970). The often published photograph of Brown was provided by the State Historical Society of Colorado, which, along with the Black American West and Heritage Center in Denver, contains information about Brown, mining, wagon trains, pioneers, and the communities in which she resided. George F. Jackson's *Black Women Makers of History: A Portrait* (Oakland, CA: GRT Book Printers, 1985) includes a profile of Brown that is somewhat emotional. William L. Katz's, *The Black West*, 3rd edition (Seattle: Open Hand Publishers, 1987) and W. Sherman Savage's *Blacks in the West* (Westport, CT: Greenwood, 1976) present a more scholarly approach to Brown's role as a pioneer. The *Denver Rocky Mountain News* (September 19, 1880) mentions Brown's work as a mine owner and philanthropist. Contemporary newspapers, including the *Denver Rocky Mountain News* and other midwestern periodicals, publicized Brown's reunion with her daughter. Kenneth W. Porter, ed., *The Negro on the American Frontier* (New York: Arno Press, 1971); James R. Harvey's "The Negro in Colorado" (MA thesis, University of Denver, 1941); James H. Baker and LeRoy R Hafen, eds., *History of Colorado* (Denver: Linderman Co., 1927); Susan Armitage, Theresa Banfield, and Sarah Jacobus, "Black Women and Their Communities in Colorado," *Frontiers* 2 (1977); and the 1969 series "Black Colorado" by Cary P. Stiff in the *Denver Post* provide secondary and primary sources as well as a context for Brown's life and work. Additional sources can be located in James de T. Abajian, *Blacks and Their Contribution to the American West: A Bibliography* (Boston: G.K. Hall, 1974).

BROWN, EMMA V. (1843–1902) was a distinguished teacher dedicated to educating African Americans. Brown taught the newly freed slaves through the American Missionary Association; became the first teacher in the newly created black public school system of Washington, DC; and, when her marital status prohibited her from teaching, Brown worked as the corresponding secretary for an industrial school.

Born Emmeline Victoria Brown in 1843 at Georgetown in Washington, DC, (exact birthdate unknown), she was the daughter of John Mifflin Brown, a bishop of the African Methodist Episcopal Church, and Emmeline Brown, a dressmaker. When Brown's father died, her mother worked to keep the family together. Emma Brown was educated at Miss Myrtilla Miner's School for Colored Girls, which opened in 1851 with the goal of training teachers for the Washington, DC, area. By 1859 Emma Brown already had her own school in Georgetown. An outstanding student, Brown was strongly encouraged to attend Oberlin College to enhance her teaching skills.

The college of choice for many African American women, Oberlin was founded by abolitionists and distinguished itself as the first coeducational and interracial college in the country. Arriving in February 1860 for the spring term, Emma Brown enrolled as a literary degree candidate. Her expectations at Oberlin were cut short due to health problems. Plagued by severe headaches followed by insomnia, Brown was compelled to leave in June 1861. On returning home she regained her health, and Brown was able to open her own school the following year.

Emma Brown continued to teach her own school until March 1, 1864, when the Board of Trustees of Public Schools in Washington, DC, opened a black school in Ebenezer Church on Capitol Hill and offered her the first teaching position at a annual salary of $400. Opening with an initial enrollment of 40 students, the count soared to 130 students by summer. Brown continued teaching until 1869, when she left to work as a clerk in the Washington, DC, Pension Office, and then moved on to teach for a term in South Carolina and Mississippi.

When Emma Brown returned to Washington she became principal of the John F. Cook School on Capitol Hill. In 1872 Brown received the most prestigious appointment in the Washington, DC, school district when she was named principal of the Sumner School at a starting annual salary of $900. A modern school with ten classrooms, offices, playrooms, and an auditorium, the appointment was the pinnacle of Brown's teaching career.

In 1879 Emma Brown married Henry P. Montgomery, the principal of the John F. Cook School, a former slave from Mississippi and ex–Union Army soldier. Since married women were barred from teaching, Emma Brown's career ended. She maintained her educational interests and worked as a secretary for the Manassas Industrial School. Suffering poor health in her later years, Emma Brown died in October 1902, three years after her husband's death.

—Thea Gallo Becker

Bibliography

Lawson, Ellen N., and Marlene Merrill. "Antebellum Black Coeds at Oberlin College," *Oberlin Alumni Magazine* (Jan.–Feb. 1980): 18–21. Reprinted in Hine, Darlene Clark. *Black Women in United States History*. Vol. 3. New York: Carlson Publishing, 1990. Provides a list of black women students at Oberlin up to 1865.

Oberlin College Archives. Record Group No. 28. Records of deceased non-graduates. Contains useful information on Emma V. Brown.

Sterling, Dorothy. *We Are Your Sisters: Black Women in the Nineteenth Century*. New York: Norton, 1984. Provides a history of Brown's life through correspondence from her days at Oberlin College and Georgetown.

BROWN, HALLIE QUINN (1846–1949), educator, clubwoman, and writer, was one of six children born in Pittsburgh, Pennsylvania, to Frances Jane (Scroggins) and Thomas Arthur Brown. During Brown's childhood the family moved to Chatham, Ontario, Canada. Several years later the family resettled in the United States at Wilberforce, Ohio, where Brown entered Wilberforce University in 1868. After graduating in 1873, she moved to the South to teach. Brown taught in South Carolina, in Mississippi on the Sonora plantation, and in Yazoo City. By 1885 she was dean of Allen University in Columbia, South Carolina. In 1887 she returned to Ohio and taught in Dayton public schools until becoming a dean of women at Tuskegee Institute in Tuskegee, Alabama, a post she held from 1892 to 1893. Brown then returned to her alma mater as a professor of elocution, a position she held for 30 years. Because of illness, she retired from teaching and became a professional lecturer. Throughout the United States and Europe, Brown gained national and international acclaim for her readings and lectures. This notoriety enabled her to solicit and raise funds for Wilberforce.

A champion of African American rights, her readings included the poetry of Paul Laurence Dunbar and her lectures dealt with topics such as education in the African American community, the status of African American women, and the leadership of Frederick Douglass. As a reformer and women's rights advocate, Brown held membership in the Women's Christian Temperance Union, the International Woman's Congress, and the Ohio State Federation Women's Clubs. She served as the president of the National Association of Colored Women from 1920 to 1924.

Brown was also a writer. Her works include *Bit and Odds: A Choice Selection of Recitations* (1900), *First Lessons in Public Speaking* (1920), *Tales My Father Told* (1925), and *Homespun Heroines and Other Women of Distinction* (1926).

Brown died of coronary thrombosis in 1949 in Wilberforce.

—Wanda A. Hendricks

Bibliography

Davis, Elizabeth Lindsay. *Lifting as They Climb*. Washington, DC: National Association of Colored Women, 1933.

Majors, M.A. *Noted Negro Women: Their Triumphs and Activities*. Chicago: Donohue & Henneberry, 1893.

McFarlin, A.S. "H.Q. Brown: Black Woman Elocutionist: 1845(?)–1949," PhD dissertation, Washington State University, 1975.

Sewall, Mary Wright, ed. *The World's Congress of Representative Women*. Chicago: Rand McNally, 1894.

BROWN, JILL (b. 1950), raised in an aviation-minded family, became the first black female pilot for the U.S. Navy and for a major commercial airline. Born in Millersville, Maryland, Brown, the daughter of Gilbert and Elaine Brown, grew up in Baltimore. She began flying at age 17, when her father, a U.S. Air Force instrument mechanic and building contractor, decided he wanted to purchase an airplane.

He bought a single-engine Piper Cherokee, and Brown soon began training at Lee Airport in Edgewater, Maryland; she first soloed in 1967. Referring to themselves as Browns' United Airline, they used their plane to travel in the United States and the Caribbean. Brown acquired 200 hours' flying time and earned her private pilot license.

She graduated from Arundel High School and attended the University of Maryland at College Park, earning a degree in home economics in 1973. Brown selected her major because she was a talented cook. Yet she desired to achieve greater goals such as pursuing a singing career, but her parents did not want her performing in night clubs. Brown continued flying, earning her instrument, commercial, and instructor licenses.

Her mother, an art resource teacher for Baltimore schools, encouraged her to be a teacher, and Brown accepted a position instructing home economics at Oakmont Regional High School in Boston. At a national conference for black pilots, she met Colonel Spann Watson, a veteran of the 99th Fighters Group, and he encouraged her to pursue a military aviation career, explaining that racial barriers were disappearing. She contacted a nearby U.S. Navy recruiter and became the first black woman accepted for military pilot training.

She began officers candidate school at Newport, Rhode Island, then attended naval flying school in Pensacola, Florida. Brown's military career was short-lived because her primary ambition was to accumulate flight hours so she could apply for a position with a major airline. She disliked the military protocol and quit after six months of training.

She returned to Baltimore and taught home economics. In spring 1976 she read an *Ebony* magazine article about Warren H. Wheeler, a Piedmont pilot who had operated a commuter line in Raleigh, North Carolina, since 1969. She wrote him, and he hired her. Brown's job required her to perform an odd assortment of tasks, from selling tickets, loading luggage, servicing the airplane, and being copilot. While flying for Wheeler Airlines, Brown accumulated 800 hours, applied to the major airlines, and was accepted by Texas International Airlines.

Brown graduated from officer training of Texas International Airlines with five other women and became a first officer in 1978. She flew a route from Albuquerque, New Mexico, to smaller cities within that state, aspiring to be the first black female captain. Since Brown was hired, the airline, as part of the Texas Air Corporation, underwent a series of mergers and acquisitions with other carriers, including Eastern, Trans World, and Continental airlines; it now operates under the latter's name.

—Elizabeth D. Schafer

Bibliography

Several articles discuss Brown's military and civilian aviation careers. See Simeon Booker, "Navy Trains First Black Woman Pilot," *Jet* 47 (November 28 1974): 20–25; "Jill Brown May Be First Black Woman Navy Pilot," *Jet* 47 (October 24, 1974): 19; and Michele Burgen, "Winging It at 25,000 Feet," *Ebony* 34 (August 1978): 58–62. W. Augustus Low and Virgil A. Clift, eds., *Encyclopedia of Black America* (New York: McGraw-Hill, 1981) has a photograph of Brown taken after her first solo flight in 1967. The George L. Lee feature of Brown is included in George L. Lee, *Interesting People: Black American History Makers* (Jefferson, NC: McFarland, 1976).

The transition from Texas International Airlines to Texas Air Corporation and its subsequent financial crises in the 1980s can be traced in national newspaper coverage, such as the *New York Times*, as well as aviation periodicals and in Roger Bilstein and Jay Miller, *Aviation in Texas* (Austin: Texas Monthly Press, 1985).

Although Von Hardesty and Dominick Pisano's, *Black Wings: The American Black in Aviation* (Washington: National Air and Space Museum, Smithsonian Institution, 1983) does not specifically mention Brown, it provides a historical context as does Judy Lomax, *Women of the Air* (New York: Dodd Mead, 1986). The Black Wings Collection and research files at the National Air and Space Museum has information about black aviators. The Library of the Ninety-Nines, in Oklahoma City, Oklahoma, maintains bibliographical sources concerning women aviators.

BROWN, WILLA B. (b. 1906), the first black woman to earn a commercial pilot license, promoted equal opportunities in aviation, by lobbying for the participation of blacks in military and civilian aerospace careers. Born in Glasgow, Kentucky, on January 21, to Eric and Hallie Mae (Carpenter) Brown, Willa Beatrice Brown earned a BA from Indiana State Teachers College in 1927; she was a member of Alpha Kappa Alpha sorority. She taught school in Gary, Indiana, where she read about the aviation accomplishments of Bessie Coleman. This sparked her interest in flying.

Realizing that she did not enjoy being a housewife or teacher, Brown divorced her husband Wilbur Hardaway and moved to Chicago in 1932. An avid automobile racer, she abruptly concluded that activity when she survived a dangerous crash. Black pilots John C. Robinson, who later commanded the Ethiopia Air Force, and Cornelius R. Coffey, an airplane mechanic, offered to teach her to fly.

Considering flying safer than automobile racing, in 1934 Brown began taking lessons at the Harlem Airport in Chicago, joining the Challenger Air Pilot's Association, a black flying club. Brown bought a plane and participated in the Chicago Girls Flight Club. She obtained a limited commercial license by 1937; at that time there were only about 200 black pilots in the United States. In that same year she received an MA from Northwestern University.

With the cooperation of Coffey and Enoch P. Waters, city editor of the *Chicago Defender*, Brown promoted and made Chicago the nucleus of black aviation. Brown initially approached Waters, requesting publicity for an air show in 1936. He agreed to sponsor the show, after seeking approval of newspaper owner Robert Abbott, who had encouraged Bessie Coleman to obtain a pilot's license in France. The air show was successful, and as a thankful gesture, Brown flew Waters over Chicago. He arranged for the show to become an annual event.

Waters suggested that Brown and Coffey create a national organization for black aviators that could disseminate information and promote black aviation, hoping to obtain racial equality in aviation. The National Airmen's Association of America (NAAA), with headquarters in the *Chicago Defender* office, was formed in 1937. Brown, a charter member, as executive secretary led the membership drive to expand the NAAA into a national organization, sending letters and flying to interested aviation clubs to establish chapters in the Midwest and East. The dramatic Brown inspired recruits; her confidence and determination aided the growth of the organization.

One year later Brown and Coffey founded the Coffey School of Aeronautics, of which Brown served as director. Between 1938 to 1945 the school trained approximately 200 pilots, both black and white. Brown married Coffey soon after the school was established. She aspired for Coffey and the school to achieve fame and recruited additional students with press releases, air shows, and flying visits.

Brown campaigned for additional integration of aviation so that blacks could participate in the Civilian Pilot Training Program (CPTP) and Army Air Corps, lobbying in Washington, DC, on this issue. She directed a test with 20 black pilots in 1940, and proved they were capable pilots and equal in ability to white flyers. As a result of proving their potential, some of these Coffey graduates eventually became instructors and members of the 99th Pursuit Squadron at Tuskegee Institute. Among Brown's supporters was Eleanor Roosevelt, and in 1941 Brown succeeded in gaining approval to become a Civil Aeronautics Administration training coordinator and CPTP instructor.

Receiving permission to teach noncollege CPTP participants, Brown recruited students and taught ground school in the Wendell Phillips High School basement and CPTP courses at the Coffey School, increasing the number of black pilots and providing pilots for segregated air squadrons in World War II. Through this work Brown persuaded national leaders to consider fully integrating the U.S. Air Force.

In 1942, Brown, with the rank of lieutenant, became the first black member and officer of the Civil Air Patrol. As part of her duties, she taught courses in aviation to Chicago high school students, organized a Civil Air Patrol squadron, and participated in the Chicago Board of Education and Illinois Vocational Association. She continued to promote aviation, talking on the "Wings Over Jordan" radio program with the Reverend Glenn Settles of Cleveland. Held in high esteem by the black community, Brown was welcomed with an elaborate reception at the airport.

In addition to her aviation activity, Brown, keenly interested in politics, was the first black woman to run for a seat in the Illinois House of Representatives. In 1972 she was invited to become a member of the Federal Aviation Agency's Women's Advisory Committee on Aviation, being the first black woman so appointed. The committee's task was to collect information and distribute educational material about recreational flying. Brown's third husband was J.H. Chappell. As a pioneer aviatrix and promoter of equal opportunity in the air, Brown accumulated approximately 1,000 hours of flying time.

—Elizabeth D. Schafer

Bibliography

"Willa B. Brown," *Who's Who in Aviation 1942–1943* (Chicago: Ziff-Davis Publishing, 1942) provides basic biographical information about Brown. Ted Watson, "Colored Aviation as it is Today in Chicago at Oak Hill's Harlem Airport," *Pittsburgh Courier* (January 13, 1940) discusses aviation at the Coffey School of Aeronautics, especially for black women, and includes photographs of Brown. "School for Willa," *Time* (September 25, 1939) profiles her wartime efforts for integration in military aviation. Luci Horton, "First Black Woman Commercial Pilot Joins FAA Panel," *Chicago Tribune* (February 27, 1972) notes Brown's post–World War II activity in aviation. Von Hardesty and Dominick Pisano, *Black Wings: The American Black in Aviation* (Washington, DC: National Air & Space Museum, Smithsonian Institution, 1983) also contains photographs as well as information about Brown and her peers in Chicago.

Interviews with Brown and articles about aviation activity in Chicago, efforts to integrate military aviation, and advertisements for air shows appear in the *Chicago Defender* and *Pittsburgh Courier*. Enoch P. Waters, *American Diary: A Personal History of the Black Press* (Chicago: Path Press, 1987) reflects on his friendship with Brown; Chauncey Spencer, *Who Is Chauncey Spencer?* (Detroit: Broadside, 1975) discusses the formation of the NAAA. Dempsey Travis, *An Autobiography of Black Chicago* (Chicago: Urban Research Institute, 1981) notes that Brown taught him aviation mechanics at Wendell Phillips High School.

The Robert H. Hinckley Papers located in special collections at the University of Utah Library, Salt Lake City, include material addressing the inclusion of blacks in the CPTP. The Federal Aviation Administration History Program Files, in Washington, DC, and records of the Civil Aeronautics Administration, Record Group 237, National Archives and Records Agency, also include documents about blacks participating in the CPTP. The records of the Secretary of War, Record Group 107, Civilian Aide to the Secretary of War Subject File, National Archives, has memorandums to Brown, fliers she distributed, and transcripts of a conversation with her.

Correspondence with Brown is in the Frederick Douglass Patterson Papers, Tuskegee University Archives. The United States Air Force Collection, USAF Historical Research Center, Maxwell Air Force Base, Montgomery, Alabama, contains information about Chicago aviation in the 1930s and 1940s as well as materials pertaining to the Civil Air Patrol. The Black Wings Collection and research files at the National Air and Space Museum have information about black aviators, and the Library of the Ninety-Nines, in Oklahoma City, Oklahoma, maintains bibliographical sources concerning women aviators. The Chicago Historical Society should be consulted for artifacts relating to aviation in that city.

Dominick A. Pisano, "The Civilian Pilot Training Program, 1939–1946: A Case Study of New Deal, War Preparedness-Mobilization Aviation Policy," PhD dissertation, George Washington University (1988), discusses the role of blacks in the CPTP, and Patricia Strickland, *The Putt-Putt Air Force: The Story of the Civilian Pilot Training Program and the War Training Service (1939–1944)* (Washington, DC: U.S. Department of Transportation, FAA, 1971) also examines the program. Robert Jefferson Jakeman, "Jim Crow Earns His Wings: The Establishment of Segregated Flight Training at Tuskegee, Alabama 1934–1942," PhD dissertation, Auburn University (1988), analyzes Brown's lobbying and its affect on integrating military aviation as does Jesse J. Johnson, ed., *Black Women in the Armed Forces 1942–1974* (Hampton, VA: Johnson Publishing, 1974). David Young and Neal Callahan, *Fill the Heavens with Commerce: Chicago Aviation, 1855–1926* (Chicago: Chicago Review Press, 1981) notes Brown's role in the Civil Air Patrol, and Robert E. Neprud, *Flying Minute Men: The Story of the Civil Air Patrol* (New York: Duell, Sloan and Pearce, 1948) is a contemporary account of the Civil Air Patrol but does not discuss the role of blacks or women.

William J. Powell, in his persuasive, contemporary, book *Black Wings* (Los Angeles: Ivan Deach, 1934), urges blacks to pursue aviation training as the key to achieving racial equality, and *Negro Aviators*, a bulletin published by the Division of Negro Affairs, Bureau of Air Commerce, lists the names of licensed black pilots. George L. Washington, who directed Tuskegee's aviation programs, describes the Coffey School in *The History of Military and Civilian Pilot Training of Negroes at Tuskegee, Alabama, 1939–1945* (Washington, DC: by author, 1972). Alan L. Gropman, *The Air Force Integrates, 1945–1964* (Washington, DC: Office of Air Force History, 1978) provides a historical context for integration in the military, including events in Chicago. Joseph J. Corn, *The Winged Gospel: America's Romance with Aviation, 1900–1950* (New York: Oxford, 1983) is a social history of aviation. Claudia M. Oakes, *United States Women in Aviation, 1930–1939* (Washington, DC: Smithsonian Institution Press, 1985); Charles P. May, *Women in Aeronautics* (New York: Nelson, 1962); and Charles E. Planck, *Women with Wings* (New York: Harper & Brothers, 1942) discuss women aviators, including Brown.

The *New York Times, American Aviation Daily,* and *American Aviation* included extensive coverage of the CPTP program, and additional articles about aviation in the black press can be located in the Tuskegee Clipping Files. The George L. Lee feature of Brown in "Interesting People" is included in George L. Lee, *Interesting People: Black American History Makers* (Santa Rosa, CA: Womens History Project, 1976).

BRUCE, JOSEPHINE BEALL [WILLSON] (c. 1840s–1923), clubwoman,

teacher, society leader, and race activist, was born in Philadelphia to Dr. Joseph Willson, a prominent dentist born in Georgia and educated in Boston, and his wife, a singer and musician. While in Philadelphia Joseph Willson authored a book on the black elite entitled *Sketches of the Higher Classes of Colored Society in Philadelphia* (1841). Willson moved his family to Cleveland, Ohio, in 1854, where they joined elite society. There Josephine Willson received her education and became the first black teacher in the public schools of Cleveland. Poised and well educated, she became an accomplished linguist and loved literature and classical music.

On June 24, 1878, she married Republican senator Blanche K. Bruce, a political leader and plantation owner from Mississippi and the only black United States senator. After an extensive tour of Europe they established their residence in Washington, DC. Josephine Bruce was a cultured and charming hostess, and the Bruce home soon became a center of Washington social life. Mary Church Terrell was one of many who commented on the Bruces' elite status in Washington society.

Elected senator in 1874, Blanche K. Bruce's term ended in 1880. He subsequently received political appointments such as register of the treasury and recorder of deeds for the District of Columbia, thus enabling the couple to remain active in social and community life. In 1886, during a Democratic administration, the Bruces and their son, Roscoe Conkling Bruce (born April 21, 1879), moved to Indianapolis, where her father had relocated. They returned to Washington in the spring of 1888.

After their return to Washington, Josephine B. Bruce became active in the emerging women's club movement. In 1892 she became one of the charter members of the Colored Woman's League of Washington, DC. As one of a small group of black women in the nation's capital who organized the National Organization of Afro-American Women, a group incorporated in 1894 to improve and promote the interests of black women, she spoke at the convention of the National Federation of Afro-American Women in 1896, which led to the merger of two national black women's organizations to form the National Association of Colored Women. This early leadership led to her election as first vice president of the National Association of Colored Women (NACW) at the 1899 convention. At that organization's 1906 meeting in Detroit she was an unsuccessful candidate for the presidency when her fair complexion was used against her. Although she reduced her involvement with the NACW, she continued her club activities. At a conference for Volunteers and Employed Workers in Colored YWCA's in Cities, which met in New York in 1912, she delivered an address, and she supported and worked for the fledgling NAACP's effort to begin a chapter in Washington, DC.

Former senator Blanche K. Bruce died in 1898. Josephine Bruce moved to Indianapolis to live with her two sisters. The following year, she accepted an offer to join the staff at Tuskegee Institute in the fall of 1899, becoming the dean of women. She remained there until 1902. In addition to the club and educational work, she wrote at least three articles, one in *The Crisis* and two for the *Voice of the Negro*. She served as editor of *National Notes*, the official organ of the National Association of Colored Women, which was published at Tuskegee Institute. Throughout this time, she managed extensive real estate holdings in the District of Columbia and a plantation in Mississippi.

She died on February 24, 1923, at the residence of her son in Kendall, West Virginia. Although sometimes criticized for being too insensitive toward the plight of lower-class blacks, she contributed greatly to the cause of black women's improvement and to that of the black race through her organizational and educational efforts.

—Bruce A. Glasrud

Bibliography

Some information can be found in the Blanche K. Bruce Papers and the Roscoe Conkling Bruce Papers at the Library of Congress and Moorland-Spingarn Research Center, Howard University. The only extant discussion of her life is in Willard B. Gatewood, *Aristocrats of Color: The Black Elite, 1880–1920* (Bloomington: Indiana University Press, 1990). Information about her activities can be found in issues of the *Washington Bee*; Josephine B. Bruce, "Colored Women's Clubs," *The Crisis* X (August 1915), p. 190; Josephine B. Bruce, "What Has Education Done for Colored Women," *Voice of the Negro* I (July 1904), pp. 294–298; Josephine B. Bruce, "Afterglow of the Women's Convention," *Voice of the Negro* I (November 1904), pp. 541–543; David A. Gerber, *Black Ohio and the Color Line, 1860–1915* (Urbana: University of Illinois Press, 1976); Constance Green, *The Secret City: A History of Race Relations in the Nation's Capital* (Princeton: Princeton University Press, 1967); Cynthia Neverdon-Morton, *Afro-American Women of the South and the Advancement of the Race, 1895–1925* (Knoxville: University of Tennessee Press, 1989); Dorothy Salem, *To Better Our World: Black Women in Organized Reform, 1890–1920* (Brooklyn: Carlson, 1990); William J. Simmons, "Hon. Blanche K. Bruce," *Men Of Mark: Eminent, Progressive and Rising* (New York: Arno Press, 1968), pp. 699–703; Sadie Daniel St. Clair, "The National Career of Blanche Kelso Bruce" (Unpublished PhD dissertation, New York University, 1947); Floris Cash, "Womanhood and Protest: the Club Movement among Black Women, 1892–1922" (Unpublished dissertation, State University of New York at Stony Brook, 1986); Frank E. Smith and Audrey Warren, "Blanche Kelso Bruce," *Mississippians All* (New Orleans: Pelican Publishing House, 1968), pp. 45–58; Joseph Willson, *Sketches of the Higher Classes of Colored Society in Philadelphia*

(Philadelphia: Merriheu and Thompson, 1841); and Mary Church Terrell, *A Colored Woman in a White World* (New York: Arno Press, 1980).

BRYANT, ELIZA [SIMMONS] (1827–1907),

founder of the first welfare institution supported by Cleveland's African American community, was born in North Carolina to Polly Simmons, a slave. In 1848 Polly Simmons and her three children were freed by their master, who was also the father of the children. The emancipation documents, signed by ten influential whites and North Carolina governor, David Reid, implied that Polly Simmons was also of mixed race heritage and described her request to leave North Carolina for a free state in the North. She left North Carolina in 1848 at age 40 with sufficient funds from her master to purchase a home in Cleveland, Ohio, on East 31st Street (then called New-ton). She allowed newcomers to stay there temporarily until they found work and could provide for themselves.

Eliza Simmons grew up in this home, which provided a model of community service. Hence, when she had married and established a home of her own, she continued to display the helping behavior of her mother. In 1893 Eliza Bryant became aware that, due to slavery, many aging African Americans had been left without family to care for them in their old age. She related the dilemmas of the black elders denied admission to white homes for the aged to a small group of her friends, many of whom were members of her church. The women sought to raise money to establish a home so that the aging African Americans could spend their last days in a secure atmosphere. The women tapped into the female networks in the churches and clubs in the Cleveland area. The black newpaper carried their story. Their appeals for humane treatment won supporters as volunteers and as contributors. In January 1895, the board of trustees was selected with Emma Ransom as president over the all-female trustees. They met in each other's homes to make plans for the future.

Incorporated on September 1, 1896, the Cleveland Home for Aged Colored People started official action in fundraising through benefit parties, socials, and fairs and in planning the purchase and operation of facilities. Purchased for $2,400, the Home opened on August 11, 1897, at 284 Giddings (East 71st) Street.

On September 2, 1897, the formal dedication took place, bringing out the leadership of black Cleveland. Over 500 took pride in celebrating the birth of this institution, which in the next six years went through various changes due either to its growth or to certain setbacks that it faced.

Eliza Bryant's dream had not only become a reality, but also developed into the most widely supported institution of the Cleveland black community. On May 13, 1907, Eliza Bryant died at age 80. Her Home continued to grow. In 1914, the Home moved again to a larger facility and became a participating member of the Cleveland Welfare Federation. In 1960, the name of the institution was changed to the Eliza Bryant Home to honor its founder. In September 1967, the Home moved again, and this facility continues to provide community services.

—Dorothy Salem with Mark Heppner

Bibliography

Most of the sources on Eliza Bryant can be found in the Eliza Bryant Home for Aged Colored People Collection in the Manuscript Division of the Western Reserve Historical Society, Cleveland, Ohio. See also Kenneth Kusmer, *The Making of a Ghetto: Black Cleveland, 1870–1920* (Urbana: University of Illinois Press, 1973); Russell Davis, "Memorable Negroes in Cleveland's Past," (Cleveland: Western Reserve Historical Society, 1969); Russell Davis, *Black Americans in Cleveland: 1796– 1969* (Washington, DC: Associated Publishers, 1972); "Blacks," in *The Encyclopedia of Cleveland History*, edited by David D. Van Tassel and John J. Grabowski (Bloomington: Indiana University Press, 1987), p. 1013; and Dorothy Salem, *To Better Our World: Black Women in Organized Reform, 1890–1920* (Brooklyn: Carlson, 1990).

BURKE, YVONNE BRATHWAITE [WATSON] (b. 1932) became in 1972 the first black woman from California elected to the United States House of Representatives. She was born in southeast Los Angeles on October 5 to James T. Watson, a janitor at Metro-Goldwyn-Mayer movie studios, and his wife, Lola (Moore), a real estate agent. Pearl Yvonne Watson attended the public schools of East Los Angeles and impressed her teachers with her intelligence. The principal urged her parents to transfer her to a model high school affiliated with the University of Southern California, which they did. As the only black pupil, Yvonne Watson was treated harshly by her classmates, but she nevertheless excelled. Her honors as an orator and as the vice president of her high school class led to her interest in the law profession. With a scholarship from her father's union, she attended the University of California at Berkeley in 1949, later transferring to the campus at Los Angeles, where she graduated in 1953 with a BA in political science. She became the first black female student in 30 years to enter the University of Southern California Law School. When she discovered discrimination in the women's law sorority, she joined with two Jewish women to form a rival law sorority. She received her JD degree, graduating in the top third of her class in 1956.

Following the bar examination, Yvonne Watson opened a private practice specializing in civil, probate, and real estate law. In 1957 she married a mathematician, Louis Brathwaite. They had no children, and the marriage ended in seven years. She became active in Democratic politics supporting Lyndon Johnson's campaign in 1964. In 1965 she became a defender of the rioters in Watts, which led to her serving on the McCone Commission investigation of the uprising. In 1966 she won a seat in the California legislature, a position she continued until 1972. In 1971, she became chair of the Urban Development and

Housing Commission. These positions at the state level won her national recognition.

In 1972 her personal and professional life ascended. She married businessman William A. Burke and went to Miami, where she served as the vice-chair of the Democratic National Convention. Within months she was elected to Congress from her district in southwest Los Angeles. In the House, she demonstrated a concern for the human condition and voted for better employment protections (minimum wage, unemployment benefits, mortgage protections for unemployed, and equal employment opportunity); funding for a West Coast mass transit system; aid to local governments to comply with court-ordered desegregation; and support to small businesses. Her "Burke Amendment" called for equal employment opportunity on the Alaska pipeline. When she gave birth to her daughter, Autumn, she became the first congressional representative to take maternity leave. She was reelected two more times, allowing her to chair the Congressional Black Caucus and to serve on the House Appropriations Committee and the Select Committee on Assassinations. She left Washington in 1978 to campaign unsuccessfully for the position of California's attorney general. She continued her activities in southern California, her law practice, and her family responsibilities.

During her career, she has combined many activities and won many honors for her commitment. She served on the John F. Kennedy School of Government at Harvard University, as a trustee for the University of California, on the board of directors for UCLA, the National Athletic Health Association, and the United Negro College Fund. She has won the Loren Miller Award from the NAACP, the Sojourner Truth Award from the Negro Business and Professional Women's Clubs, and awards from UCLA, *Time* magazine, Iota Phi Lambda, Yale University, and others.

—Kelle S. Taha

Bibliography

Most of the information on Burke can be found in biographical references or through her political career. These sources include Marianna Davis, *Contributions of Black Women to America* II (Columbia, SC: Kenday, 1982); Christopher Maurine, *Black Americans in Congress* (New York: Thomas Y. Crowell, 1976); *Who's Who Among Black Americans* (1980); both volumes of the *Ebony Success Library*, *1,000 Successful Blacks* and *Famous Blacks Give Secrets for Success* (Nashville: Southwestern, 1973); *Ebony* (March 1974/August 1977); *Current Biography* (1975); and *Contemporary Biography—Women* (Tuslin, CA: American Biographical Services, 1983).

BURKS, MARY FAIR (c. 1915–1991), one of the women who started the Montgomery bus boycott of 1955–1956, was a native Alabamian. She earned her bachelor's degree at Alabama State College in Montgomery. Pursuit of her master's degree took her out of the South to the University of Michigan. In 1934, she returned to teach at Alabama State Laboratory High School, where she married the principal. Later, she completed her doctorate at Columbia University. In addition, she studied at the Sorbonne, Oxford, the University of Nairobi (Kenya), Middlebury College, and Indiana University.

Throughout her life, Mary Fair Burks was committed to the struggle for equality and racial uplift. While serving as professor and head of the English Department at Alabama State University, she became involved in an altercation with a white woman. Her arrest incited her to wage her own personal war against racial injustices. After listening to Vernon Johns, the pastor of Dexter Avenue Baptist Church, attack his affluent congregation for their complacency, Burks called 50 women together to discuss ways to improve the situation in Mongomery. She sought membership in the League of Women Voters, but was refused by the chapter. Consequently, in 1946 she founded the Women's Political Council.

Primarily the WPC was designed to accomplish three goals: to serve as a vehicle for political action, to protest racial abuses, and to educate youth and community about the rights and responsibilities of democracy. Specifically, the women sought to inspire blacks "to live above mediocrity," to elevate thinking, to fight juvenile and adult delinquency, to encourage the use of the ballot and to improve the status of blacks. From 1946 to 1950 Mary Fair Burks served as president of this organization of primarily black professional women: teachers, principals, nurses, social workers, and community leaders, most of whom lived in the vicinity of the college. Under her leadership, they worked together and agreed to safeguard the "secrets" of the WPC.

These women, organized and inspired by Mary Fair Burks, coordinated the Montgomery bus boycott. Convinced that they could no longer ignore the atrocities committed against blacks on city buses, they started planning a boycott before the Rosa Parks incident. They did the critical work in mapping out a strategy, which made integrated bus service a reality in Montgomery. According to Burks, these women were trailblazers in the civil rights movement; Dr. Martin Luther King, Jr., was the torchbearer who came after the women opened the "trail." Mary Fair Burks said the arrest of Rosa Parks penetrated the indifference of the middle class and shook the passive masses to action. Mobilizing the community through the schools and churches, the women provided the foundation for a successful boycott.

In 1960 Mary Fair Burks resigned her position at Alabama State as she and other staunch supporters of the boycott were brought under investigation by a special state committee. She accepted a position in the English Department at Maryland State College (now the University of Maryland, Eastern Shore [UMES]) in Princess Anne, Maryland. In addition to her teaching activities at UMES, Burks was active in the American Association of University Women, the Links (a black women's community service organization), and several professional organizations. She retired in 1986, and was honored as professor emeritus. Mary Fair Burks died on July 21, 1991, after a brief illness.

—Betty Plummer

Bibliography

The best published source of information on the role of Mary Fair Burks and the WPC in the Montgomery bus boycott is found in Jo Ann Gibson Robinson's *The Montgomery Bus Boycott and the Women Who Started It: The Memoir of Jo Ann Gibson Robinson*, edited by David Garrow (Knoxville: University of Tennessee Press, 1987). Burks takes issue with several points in her recent article, "Trailblazers: Women in the Montgomery Bus Boycott," in *Women in the Civil Rights Movement*, edited by Vicki L. Crawford, Jacqueline Rouse, and Barbara Woods (Brooklyn: Carlson, 1990), pp. 71–83. Most of the male-written accounts of the civil rights movement mention the importance of women, yet the women remain nameless or sketchy in their delineation. There is a passing reference to Mary Fair Burks and the WPC in Martin Luther King, Jr., *Stride Toward Freedom: The Montgomery Story* (New York: Harper & Row, 1958). Her obituary appeared in the Salisbury *Daily Times* (July 22, 1991). Information also appears in *Who's Who in the East* (1985).

BURRILL, MARY POWELL (1879–1946) belonged to the group of black women playwrights who wrote in support of the National Association for the Advancement of Colored People's campaign for national legislation against lynching. She contributed *Aftermath* (1919) to the body of lynch plays produced between 1916 and 1929. A depiction of the reactions of a black World War I soldier to his father's lynching and the soldier's ensuing murder, *Aftermath* contributed to realism in the American theater through its graphic presentation of the brutality of lynching. Echoing the message of a W.E.B. Du Bois editorial in *The Crisis* for the returning black soldiers to marshal their courage to fight "the forces of hell at home," *Aftermath* became part of the effort to stop the rising tide of lynchings in the South and race riots in the North that followed World War I. The success of the play, produced by the Krigwa Players Little Negro Theatre in association with the Worker's Drama League (Manhattan) at the National Little Theater Tournament in New York (Frolic Theatre, May 8, 1928), enhanced Burrill's reputation as a playwright.

Lynching was not the only issue of social justice that Burrill attacked through her plays. She also wrote to support the Birth Control League's campaign to disseminate contraceptive information to women. In 1919 Burrill published a one-act play, *They That Sit in Darkness*, in Margaret Sanger's *Birth Control Review*, which also featured a short story by Angelina Grimké, "The Closing Door."

Little is known about Burrill's personal life. Born in Washington, DC, in 1879 to Clara and John Henry Burrill, Mary Burrill received her education in the local schools. In 1905 she graduated from the Emerson School of Oratory in Boston. Returning to Washington, DC, Burrill taught English and drama at Dunbar High School with teacher, playwright, and former companion Angelina Grimké. Critic Gloria Hull's examination of a February 1896 correspondence documents a clearly lesbian relationship between the two.

In 1912 Burrill began a 25-year companionship with Lucy Diggs Slowe, the dean of women at Howard University. At Slowe's death in 1937, Burrill received volumes of letters and telegrams of condolence from leaders in the black community such as Mary McLeod Bethune and Mordecai Johnson, Howard University president.

Burrill continued her work at Howard University. Her narration of the Christmas piece *The Other Wise Man*, with the Howard University choir, was performed at the university's Rankin Chapel for 15 years. Following her retirement in 1944, Burrill died in New York in 1946 after a long illness. She was returned to Washington DC's Woodlawn Cemetery for burial. She was survived by a sister, Clara Burrill Bruce, a member of the NAACP's Drama Committee. Burrill is remembered for her plays for social justice.

—Patricia A. Young

Bibliography

Primary source materials are located in the Moorland-Spingarn Research Center, Howard University, Washington, DC, in the following manuscript collections: Blanche K. Bruce Papers, Angelina Weld Grimké Collection, and Lucy Diggs Slowe Papers.

Secondary Sources

France, Rachel. *A Century of Plays by American Women*. New York: Richards Rosen Press, 1979. Places Burrill's play within American literature context and provides biographical information.

Hull, Gloria T. *Color, Sex, and Poetry: Three Women Writers of the Harlem Renaissance*. Indiana University Press, 1987. Addresses the Burrill-Grimké relationship and provides insight into Grimké's works.

————. "Under the Days: The Buried Life and Poetry of Angelina Weld Grimké." *Conditions Five* (Autumn 1979): 17–24.

Molette, Barbara. "Black Women Playwrights," *Black World* 25 (April 1976): 28–33.

Shine, Ted, and James Hatch. *Black Theatre USA*. New York: Macmillan, 1974. Devotes an entire chapter to women playwrights.

BURROUGHS, NANNIE (1879–1961), educator, reformer, and religious leader, was born on May 2 in Culpeper, Virginia, to John and Jennie (Poindexter) Burroughs. In 1883, after the death of her father, the family moved to Washington, DC. There Nannie Helen Burroughs graduated in 1896 from M Street High School. She moved to Louisville, Kentucky, where she became the bookkeeper and stenographer for the Foreign Mission Board of the National Baptist Convention, Philadelphia, Pennsylvania, a position she held until 1909. In 1900, she spoke at the organizational meeting of the Women's Convention

Auxiliary to the National Baptist Convention in Richmond Virginia. As one of the founders, Burroughs served as the group's corresponding secretary from 1900 to 1947 and as its president from 1948 to 1961.

She used this national women's religious auxiliary to mobilize forces and energies to develop an industrial school for black girls in the nation's capital. But first, she prepared herself for the task. In 1902 Burroughs took courses in a business college in Washington, DC. She attended the organization conference of the Baptist World Alliance in 1905. In the fall of 1909 she became the founder and president of the National Training School for Women and Girls, later (1934) renamed the National Trade and Professional School for Women and Girls. She remained the spiritual and administrative leader of the school throughout her life. The school motto, "Learn to do at least one thing extremely well," symbolized her belief. At the school, which attracted girls from throughout the United States and the Caribbean, basic principles of the three Bs—Bible, Bathtub, and Broom— were stressed.

From this position, Burroughs combined her religious, labor, and racial leadership interests to accomplish many goals. From 1934 until 1961, she edited *The Worker*, a publication of Trade School for the Women's Convention (for 48 years) that described racial conditions, church leadership, and women's issues. Since Burroughs never married and had no children, she used her powerful oratorical skills to speak at church meetings to raise funds to support the school. A strong believer in self-help, Burroughs sought first education, then character development, then a trade, and finally, home ownership. At one time, she turned to John D. Rockefeller for a contribution. He sent her one dollar with a note requesting how such a businesswoman might make use of the money. She bought a dollar's worth of peanuts, roasted them, and sent them to Rockefeller with the request that he autograph each peanut and return them to her for sale at one dollar a peanut. Rockefeller was thoroughly convinced that she was one of the most astute and remarkable businesspersons that he had ever met. Burroughs received an honorary doctorate from Shaw University in 1949 for her efforts to train young women. She brought the industrial conditions of black women to the forefront of the National Association of Colored Women and helped found the National Association of Wage Earners. She served (1950–1960) as a member-at-large on the executive committee of the Baptist World Alliance. On May 20, 1961, Burroughs died in the District of Columbia, from a stroke and severe arthritis. Her funeral at the 19th Street Baptist Church program stated, "Her worth cannot be measured in gold." In 1964 her school abandoned the trade school curriculum and became the Nannie Helen Burroughs School for elementary children.

—Olivia Pearl Stokes

Bibliography

The Nannie Burroughs Papers are located in the Manuscript Division of the Library of Congress, Washington, DC. See also Sadie Daniels, *Women Builders* (Washington, DC: Associated Press, 1931); Earl Harrison, *The Dream and the Dreamer* (Washington, DC: Nannie Burroughs Literature Foundation, 1956); Sylvia Dannett, *Profiles of Negro Womanhood* (Chicago: Educational Heritage Press, 1964); William Pickens, *Nannie Burroughs and the School of the Three B's* (New York: Negro Universities Press, 1921). The specialist on Burroughs is Evelyn Brooks Barnett. See her entry in Rayford Logan and Michael Winston's *The Dictionary of American Negro Biography* (New York: Norton, 1983) and her articles "Nannie Burroughs and the Education of Black Women," in Sharon Harley and Rosalyn Terborg-Penn, eds., *The Afro-American Woman* (Port Washington, NY: Kennikat Press, 1978); "Religion, Politics, and Gender: The Leadership of Nannie Helen Burroughs," *Journal of Religious Thought* 44 (Winter/Spring 1988): 7–22. Other sources include: Clement Richardson, ed., *The National Cyclopedia of the Colored Race* (Montgomery, AL: National Publishing, 1919); and Edward T. James, et al., eds., *Notable American Women* (Cambridge: Belknap Press, 1971).

BURROWS, VINIE (b. 1928), "Queen of Black Theater" and human rights activist, was born on November 15 to dentist Nelson Burrows and Phyllis (Smith) Burrows in New York City. There she and her brother, George Nelson Burrows, received their education. Vinie Burrows followed the example of her father by attending and finally graduating from New York University. Unlike her father's choice of dentistry, she graduated with a prelaw degree.

She started her dynamic career as a child actress with Helen Hayes. She went on to appear in several Broadway and Off-Broadway productions and international festivals, which include but are not limited to appearances with Ossie Davis, Mary Martin, James Earl Jones, and David Wayne. She appeared in Joshua Logan's *The Wisteria Trees* in 1950.

After these initial successes, Vinie Burrows came to the realization that the roles available for black women were too few and far between to sustain a career. She also observed, as have others, that the black poet/writer lacked adequate public exposure. Burrows solved this dilemma by creating her own one-woman show, *Walk Together Children*, an exploration of the black presence in America. Using the poetry, prose, and songs of well-known and lesser-known writers, *Walk Together Children* opened in New York on November 11, 1968. The critical acclaim was instant, unanimous, and ecstatic. The *New York Times* called her "a magnificent performer." In addition to *Walk Together Children*, there have been six other one-woman shows including *Sister! Sister!* and *Africa Fire!* In these one-woman shows, Burrows has appeared at over 900 college campuses.

The diminutive writer, producer, actress-manager, and active member of the Dramatists Guild has also gained honors in radio, television, and film. For three years, she conducted a two-hour live talk show, *More Than Half the World*, on the station WBAI in New York City. Her program included guests representing the arts, literature, international affairs, local politics, and grassroots leaders. In 1981 she also starred in a feature film that was shot on location in Douala, Cameroon. Burrows also served as an affiliate member of the Black Theater Alliance, formed from the cooperation of 13 of New York City's community-based theaters in the 1970s to produce black productions to community audiences.

Her lifetime concern for human rights, disarmament, and anti-apartheid has resulted in many awards and offices. In addition to the Black Theatre Recognition Award from Audience Development Co. (AUDELCO) in 1986, she received the prestigious Paul Robeson Award for her commitment to human rights and for her use of the arts to create understanding and respect for diversity from Actors Equity Association (AEA). In 1990 the National Alliance Against Racist and Political Repression gave her their Human Rights Award. She is a member of American Federation of Television and Radio Artists, Black Theatre Alliance, and Screen Actors Guild. Her concerns for political, economic, and social democracy found concrete expression in her leadership roles as founding member and vice president, Women for Racial and Economic Equality; chair, Sub-Committee on Southern Africa of the Non-Governmental Organization (NGO) Committee on Human Rights at the United Nations; and United Nations permanent representative of the Woman's International Democratic Federation. She was particularly active throughout the United Nations Decade for Women (1976–1985) and served as co-convenor for the Mid Decade NGO Forum held at the University of Amager in Copenhagen in 1980.

Burrows, the mother of two children, Gregory Brian Harrison and Sojourner Aletha Harrison, currently resides in the East Village in a book-lined cooperative apartment with a spectacular view of the New York City skyline. In the words of a Howard University workshop participant, Vinie Burrows is "the essence of a legend." She continues her work for women's rights and international human rights.

—Mary Ann Williams

Bibliography

Most of the information has been obtained from interviews with Burrows by Mary Ann Williams, recently deceased associate professor of Black Studies at Ohio State University. An interview with Burrows appeared in *Essence* 3 (May 1972): 76–77; and *Encore* (August 4, 1975): 48. Biographical and career information is available in *Encyclopedia of Black America*, edited by W. Augustus Low and Virgil A. Clift (New York: McGraw-Hill, 1981); *The Negro Almanac: A Reference Work on the African American*, edited by Harry A. Ploski and James Williams (Detroit: Gale Research, Inc. 1989); Raoul Abdul, *Famous Black Entertainers of Today* (New York: Dodd, Mead, 1974); and Edward Mapp, *A Directory of Blacks in the Performing Arts*. (Metuchen, NJ: Scarecrow Press, 1978).

BURTON, ANNIE LOUISE (c. 1850s–c. 1910), independent business-woman, was born to the slave Nancy, who cooked for Mr. and Mrs. William Farrin on their plantation about 23 miles from Clayton, Alabama. Her father, whom she never knew but saw several times during her childhood, was a white planter who was born in Liverpool, England, owned a plantation two miles from the Farrins, and died in Lewisville, Alabama, in 1875. Annie Louise Burton described her early years as "happy, care-free," largely because her owners were preoccupied with the Civil War; but she was aware of the hunger, sexual exploitation, whippings, hangings, and sale of slaves around her. Her own mother fled the Farrin plantation for three or four years after a severe beating.

After emancipation, Burton, her older sister Caroline and younger half-brother Henry supported themselves by gathering chips, picking cotton, washing, and babysitting, at first for the Farrins, and later with their mother in a log cabin on a nearby plantation. In 1866 Burton went to live in Clayton with Mrs. E.M. Williams, a music teacher and wife of a lawyer, to help care for the Williams's daughter. She began to attend Sunday school at the Methodist church and learned to read and write. She was engaged to be married, but her fiancé died before their wedding day.

During the next 10 years, Burton worked as cook and laundress, attended Lewis High School in Macon for six months, and, after the death of her mother, cared for her brother and two adoptive siblings. Around 1875, after two serious illnesses and a vision, Burton was baptized by the Reverend Dr. Pope and joined a church in Macon. In 1879 Burton moved to the North, where she worked as laundress, cook, chambermaid, and housekeeper, first in Boston and then in New York.

After her sister's death, she returned to the South to care for her young nephew, Lawrence, who later graduated from Hampton College, Virginia. Burton became an independent businesswoman, successfully running a restaurant first in Jacksonville, Florida, and then later in Boston. In 1888 she joined the Tremont Temple in Boston, where Dr. Lorimer was pastor, and married Samuel Burton. The two supported themselves alternately in service positions and business ventures. Over a six-year period beginning around 1900, Burton attended the Franklin Evening School in Boston, where Mr. Guild, the master, assigned all students to write the story of their lives. Although she did not graduate, she completed three such assignments as well as a "graduating composition" on Abraham Lincoln. The date of Burton's death is unknown.

—Rosalie Murphy Baum

Bibliography

Few resources exist about Annie Burton's life except her own. Burton wrote three autobiographical essays, "Recollections of a Happy Life," "Reminiscences," and "A Vision," as well as an essay on Abraham Lincoln and a poem, "The Creation." These works were published, along with her favorite poems and hymns and an essay by Dr. P. Thomas Stanford in *Memories of Childhood's Slavery Days* (Boston: Libraries of

American Civilization, 1909). They have been republished in William L. Andrews, *Six Women's Slave Narratives* (New York: Oxford, 1988), part of the Schomburg Library of Nineteenth-Century Black Women Writers.

BUSH, ANITA (1883–1974) was introduced into the world of drama at an early age. Her father, who worked as a tailor for a local theater in Brooklyn, gave his daughter the task of carrying costumes to the theater for him. From that initial contact backstage, her interest in the entertainment business blossomed and flourished.

By age 16, Bush was able to convince her apprehensive father to allow her to join the Williams and Walker Company. From 1903 to 1909 she performed in the chorus touring Europe in the production of *In Dahomey*. In 1909 the company disbanded, which forced her to seek employment elsewhere.

During the next few years, Bush was plagued by misfortune, including a serious bout of pneumonia. Her spirits were undaunted as she vowed to make a complete recovery and realize her dream of forming a dramatic stock company. Amazingly, even before she had completely recovered, Bush held a meeting with Eugene "Frenchy" Elmore, manager of the Lincoln Theater in Harlem, to discuss the formation of such a company. Because of Bush's confident air, Elmore was easily convinced.

Bush then scurried around Harlem to find performers to help transform her dream into reality. Besides Bush, the company included Charles Gilpin, Dooley Wilson, Carlotta Freeman, and Andrew Bishop. Billie Burke, a talented and highly respected white dramatist, was secured as director. On November 15, 1915, the Anita Bush Stock Company opened at the New Lincoln Theater with the production *The Girl at the Fort*, a comedy written by Burke. The *Amsterdam News* gave the play a favorable review, which successfully launched Bush into an exciting new career.

Because of a dispute with the owner, Bush soon moved to the Lafayette Theater. The Anita Bush Stock Company made its debut to rave reviews on December 27, 1915, with *Across the Footlights*. The Lafayette presented a new work every week, including *The Gambler's Sweetheart*, *The Girl of the Golden West*, and *The Octoroon*. Later, with Bush's approval, the name of the company changed to the Lafayette Stock Company.

During the 1920s Anita Bush also starred in movies. In her letter dated June 28, 1921, she explained to white, Florida-based filmmaker Richard E. Norman: "I can sew, drive, ride a wheel, sail a boat, dance, and do most anything required in pictures. I have lots of nerve and learn anything quickly." The letter was signed, "Anita Bush, The Mother of Drama in New York among Colored People."

Subsequent letters between Bush and Norman reveal a woman with highly refined negotiating skills. Not only was she able to secure a great salary for herself ($125 a week, plus expenses), but she also convinced Norman to hire Lawrence Chenault as the leading man ($80 a week, plus expenses). While filming in Boley,

Oklahoma, Norman decided to maximize his efforts and produce two films with Bush, *The Crimson Skull* (1921) and *The Bulldozer* (1922), both released in 1922. The latter work highlights the talents of black rodeo superstar Bill Pickett, while the former showcases Bush's remarkable acting talent. Neither film survives today—only posters and letters.

Anita Bush, without a doubt, was a trailblazer. After the film project, Bush returned to the vaudeville and theater circuits appearing in *Swing It* (1938) and *Androcles and the Lion* (1939). She was a member of Negro Actors Guild, serving as the executive secretary in 1971. Anita Bush proved to be a woman of extreme talent, intelligence, vision, and fortitude. She died on February 16, 1974, at age 91.

—Gloria J. Gibson-Hudson

Bibliography

Harry A. Ploski and James Williams's *The Negro Almanac: A Reference Work on the African American* (Detroit: Gale, 1989) and Edward Mapp's *Directory of Blacks in the Performing Arts* (Metuchen: Scarecrow Press, 1978) include a brief biographical information about Anita Bush. Sister M. Francesca Thompson, O.S.F., "The Lafayette Players, 1917–1932," in *The Theatre of Black Americans: A Collection of Critical Essays*, provides an in-depth history of Anita Bush and her relationship with the Lafayette Players. The Richard E. Norman Film Company Collection, Indiana University, includes personal correspondence, lobby cards, and posters pertaining to *The Bull-Dogger* and the *Crimson Skull*.

BUTCHER, MARGARET JUST (b. 1913), author and professor, is mentioned in a 1966 *Ebony* magazine article by poet Gwendolyn Brooks as one of five black women, along with Paule Marshall, Lorraine Hansberry, Era Bell Thompson, and Margaret Walker, deserving of the title "intellectual." Margaret Just was born in Washington, DC, on April 28 to Dr. Ernest Everett Just, a biologist and faculty member of Howard University, and Ethel (Highwarden) Just. Butcher taught English at Virginia Union University (1935–1936), various Washington, DC, public schools, and Minor Teachers' College (1940–1941). She married James W. Butcher in 1939. Butcher's daughter, Sheryl Everett, was born in 1949.

Butcher began teaching as an instructor at Howard University in 1943. She received her PhD from Boston University in 1947. By 1950 she was associate professor of English at Howard. She served as the Fulbright visiting professor in American literature at the Universities of Grenoble, Lyon, and Dijon in France between 1949 and 1950. While in the DC area, Butcher served on the DC Board of Education from 1953 to 1956. She was also a special consultant for the NAACP from 1954 to 1955. During this time, Butcher addressed many groups across the nation and spoke about desegregation.

In 1956 she became a delegate to the Democratic National Convention. That same year she completed *The Negro in American Culture*, a book based on materials left by Butcher's Howard University colleague, Dr. Alain Leroy Locke, who died before the work was complete. Since translated into Spanish and Portuguese among other languages, *The Negro in American Culture* was issued in a second edition in 1973.

Butcher served as lecturer at American University in 1959, and she left the United States again in the early 1970s to serve as director of the English program for the United States Information Service, based in Casablanca, Morocco.

As a Howard University faculty member, Butcher belonged to the American Association of University Women and the American Association of University Professors. She is retired from Howard University and resides in Washington, DC.

—Faye A. Chadwell

Bibliography

A full-length, up-to-date biographical sketch of Margaret Just Butcher has not been completed. Brief, albeit valuable, information on Margaret Just Butcher may be located in several sources: Ann Allen Shockley's *Living Black American Authors; A Biographical Dictionary* (New York: Bowker, 1973); *Who's Who of American Women* (1973); *Selected Black American Authors: An Illustrated Bio-Bibliography*, compiled by James A. Page (Boston: G.K. Hall, 1977); *In Black and White*, ed. Mary Mace Spradling (Detroit: Gale, 1980 and 1985); *Selected Black American, African, and Caribbean Authors*, compiled by James A. Page (Littleton, CO: Libraries Unlimited, 1985). Butcher is quoted in two *New York Times* articles (July 2, 1954, and July 6, 1955). The Howard University Library has a vertical file containing information about Margaret Butcher as well as some samples of her writings.

Works by Margaret Just Butcher

The Negro in American Culture. (Based on materials left by Alain Locke.) New York: New American Library, 1956.

Secondary Sources

"Bias Fight Discussed and Community Leadership Called Key to Pupil Integration." *New York Times* (July 6, 1955): 19.

Page, James. *Selected Black American, African, and Caribbean Authors: A Bio-Bibliography*. Littleton, CO: Libraries Unlimited, 1985.

———. *Selected Black American Authors: An Illustrated Bio-Bibliography*. Boston: G.K. Hall, 1977.

Pierce, Ponchitta. "Problems of the Negro Woman Intellectual." *Ebony* (August 1966): 144–149.

Popham, John H. "Shift in Opinion on Bias Stress." *New York Times* (July 2, 1954): 9.

Shockley, Ann Allen. *Living Black American Authors: A Biographical Dictionary*. New York: Bowker, 1973.

Spradling, Mary Mace. *In Black and White: A Guide to Magazine Articles, Newspaper Articles, and Books Concerning More Than 150,000 Black Individuals and Groups*. Detroit: Gale, 1980.

Who's Who of American Women and Women of Canada. Chicago: Marquis, 1972–1973.

C

CARROLL, DIAHANN (b. 1935), actress in television and films, was born Carol Dia(ha)nn Johnson in the Bronx, New York, on July 17 to Mabel (Faulk) and John Johnson. When she was ten years old she received a Metropolitan Opera scholarship for study at New York's High School of Music and Arts. While in high school Carroll competed on the popular television show "Arthur Godfrey's Talent Scouts." She won and performed for three weeks on Godfrey's daily radio show. Education was most important to Carroll's mother, a nurse who chose to remain at home to raise Diahann and a younger sister, Lydia, and her father, a subway conductor. To please them Carroll enrolled in New York University upon high school graduation. While she was a freshman, she competed on the television talent show "Chance of a Lifetime" and won for three straight weeks. She received $3,000 and the opportunity to sing at the Latin Quarter for one week. Carroll dropped out of the university and sang in nightclubs until she landed a role in the film *Carmen Jones* in 1954. That same year she got a coveted part in the musical *House of Flowers*, for which she received an Antoinette Perry (Tony) Award nomination.

In September 1956 Carroll married Monte Kay, and four years later gave birth to her only child, Suzanne Patricia Ottilie Kay. Carroll continued her film career appearing in *Porgy and Bess*, *Paris Blues*, and *Goodbye Again*. In 1962 Carroll performed in the musical *No Strings*, which Richard Rodgers tailored especially for her. She received a Tony for Best Female Performance in a Musical that same year. Carroll added television appearances to her growing list of credits. She guested on many shows, including Jack Paar's "The Tonight Show," "Hollywood Palace," the "Carol Burnett Show" and Dean Martin and Frank Sinatra specials. In 1968 she starred in "Julia," becoming the first black person to have her own situation comedy. Although the series and Carroll were criticized for failure to confront the racial issues of the day, the series was generally popular, and Carroll received the Golden Globe Award in 1969 for Best Female TV Star.

The 1970s brought opportunities and sorrow. Carroll married Freddie Glusman in 1972, but divorced him three months later. In 1974 she accepted the lead role in the film *Claudine* and was nominated for an Academy Award for Best Actress for her performance. In 1975 Carroll married Robert DeLeon, managing editor of *Jet* magazine, but was widowed two years later when he died in a car crash in 1977. Carroll immersed herself in the film project *Same Time Next Year* and then into a series of nightclub appearances.

In 1983 she filled in for the vacationing Elizabeth Ashley in the Broadway production of *Agnes of God*, becoming the first black actress to substitute for a white actress in a major role. In 1984 she was tapped to portray Dominique Deveraux in the popular television series "Dynasty" and became the first black woman to star in a nighttime soap opera. Carroll married singer Vic Damone in 1987. She performs solo and jointly with her husband and has continued to pursue her film and television career. She appeared in the television movie *Dead of Night* in 1989.

Among her many honors, she is a Patron Performer for the John F. Kennedy Center, has received the NAACP's Eighth Annual Image Award for Best Actress, and was inducted into the Black Filmmakers' Hall of Fame in 1976. She has also been the recipient of the *Cue* Entertainer of the Year Award and has received both Emmy and Grammy nominations. She is a member of Actors' Equity Association, the American Federation of Television and Radio Artists, and the Screen Actors Guild. Additional credits in television, film, and theater are too numerous to mention as are her recordings and club appearances.

—Linda Cannon-Huffman

Bibliography

Carroll's autobiography *Diahann* (Boston: Little, Brown, 1986), written with Ross Firestone, provides intimate details of Carroll's personal life and career. The entry on Carroll written by Carolyn R. Hodges in *Notable Black American Women* provides an excellent summation of Carroll's life and professional achievements. Donald Bogle's *Blacks in American Films and Television: An Encyclopedia* contains critical reviews of Carroll's major films plus a brief but informative biographical sketch.

Secondary Sources

Bogle, Donald. *Blacks in American Films and Television: An Encyclopedia*. New York: Garland, 1988.
———. *Black Arts Annual 1988/89* New York: Garland, 1990.
Feather, Leonard. "Carroll & Damone Having Wonderful Time," *Los Angeles Times* (January 27, 1989): Sec. VI, 11:1.
Moritz, Charles, ed. *Current Biography Yearbook 1962*. New York: Wilson, 1963.
O'Donnell, Monica M., ed. *Contemporary Theatre. Film and Television*, Vol. 3. Detroit: Gale, 1986.
Smith, Jessie Carney, ed. *Notable Black American Women*. Detroit: Gale, 1992.
Who's Who of American Women, 17th ed. Wilmette, IL: Marquis Who's Who, 1991.

CARTER, NELL (b. 1948), star of radio, television, and Broadway, has spent her life performing. When she was 11 years old, Nell Carter was singing on the radio program "The Y Teens" in her hometown of Birmingham, Alabama. Born on September 13 to Horace L. and Edna M. Hardy, Carter has been singing professionally ever since age 11. After appearing on many radio and television programs in Alabama, she was encouraged by a scout for NBC's "Today" show to leave Alabama for New York when she was age 19. There she sang in Manhattan clubs and played minor roles in a series of Broadway shows. Carter's career took off when she landed a part in *Ain't Misbehavin'* in 1978. The Fats Waller revue was the perfect vehicle to establish Carter as a singer who could move effortlessly from wistful to sizzling, from caressing lyrics softly to belting out notes in showstopping style. For her performance in *Ain't Misbehavin'*, she won the Antoinette Perry (Tony) Award for Best Featured Actress in a Musical in 1978. Other theatrical productions in which Carter has appeared include *I Can't Cope*, *Don't Bother Me*, *Hair*, *Jesus Christ Superstar*, *Blues Is a Woman*, *Dude*, *Bury the Dead*, *Rhapsody in Gershwin*, and *Black Broadway*. Recently, Carter starred in the Long Beach Civic Light Opera's production of *Hello Dolly!* As might be expected, Carter has made many concert appearances, including one with the Los Angeles Philharmonic.

The multitalented Carter is known for her acting ability as well. She has the distinction of being one of the few black females to star in a television series. "Gimme a Break" ran from 1981 to 1987 and is now in syndication. Although the series met with criticism for its portrayal of a black woman taking care of a white family, Carter won critical acclaim for her interpretation of the main character as a strong-willed, self-assured nanny and friend. Carter has been a member of the cast of numerous television specials such as "Baryshnikov on Broadway," "The Adventures of Sheriff Lobo," and the "Big Show," and she has hosted her own special, "Nell Carter, Never Too Old to Dream." In 1981 she won an Emmy for *Ain't Misbehavin'*, in a special class category, Outstanding Individual Achievement. In 1989, NBC aired a pilot, "Morton's by the Bay," which placed Nell Carter in a white cultural setting, for which she received criticism. Besides television and theater, Carter has had roles in the following films: *Hair*, *Quartet*, *Back Roads*, and *Modern Problems*.

Carter has received numerous other awards for excellence in her profession. Among them are an OBIE, the Drama Desk Award, and the Soho News Award, all for *Ain't Misbehavin'*. Married briefly while a teenager, Carter has a daughter, Tracey Jenniece, who grew up in Birmingham with Carter's sister. Carter wed Georg Krynicki, the son of a wealthy Austrian lumber tycoon, in May 1982. The marriage ended in divorce within two years. Carter lends personal and professional support to her community as evidenced by her memberships in the American Federation of Television and Radio Artists, Screen Actors Guild, Actors' Equity Association, and her lifetime membership in the National Association for the Advancement of Colored People.

—Linda Cannon-Huffman

Bibliography

Details of Nell Carter's life and career may be found in Volume 3 of *Contemporary Theatre, Film, and Television*, edited by Monica M. O'Donnell. *Blacks in American Films and Television*, written by Donald Bogle, is an excellent source for in-depth reviews of Carter's films and television appearances and for an informative biographical sketch of Carter. *The New York Times Biographical Service* 9:1 (January 1978) provides an interesting article on Carter's career through the late 1970s.

Secondary Sources

Adelson, Suzanne. "Feasting on TV Stardom and a New Marriage, Nell Carter Celebrates Life in Well, Fat City," *People Weekly* 17 (June 21, 1982): 100–102.

Bogle, Donald. *Blacks in American Films and Television: An Encyclopedia.* New York: Garland, 1988.

Bogle, Donald. *Black Arts Annual 1988/89.* New York: Garland, 1990.

Floyd, Iris, ed. *Who's Who among Black Americans 1990/91.* Detroit: Gale, 1986.

Hill, George. *Black Women in Television.* New York: Garland, 1990.

O'Donnell, Monica M., ed. *Contemporary Theatre, Film, and Television,* Vol. 3. Detroit: Gale, 1986.

Who's Who in America 1988–1989, 45th ed., Vol. 1. Wilmette, IL: Marquis Who's Who, 1988.

Wilson, John S. "Ain't Misbehavin', Just Yelling a Little," *New York Times Biographical Service* 9: 1 (January 1978): 167.

CARTER BROOKS, ELIZABETH (1867–1951), clubwoman, educator,

and community activist, was born to Martha D. Webb, a manumitted slave from President John Tyler's plantation in Virginia. Carter Brooks received her early education in the whaling city of New Bedford, Massachusetts. Upon graduating from New Bedford High School, she taught at the Howard Colored Orphanage in Brooklyn, New York, and served as the elected secretary of T. Thomas Fortune's Brooklyn Literary Union in 1883. She returned to New Bedford and became the first black woman to attend the city's Harrington Normal Training School. After completing the curriculum there, she became the first black woman to teach in the New Bedford Public School system, a position she held until she retired in 1929.

Carter Brooks is perhaps best remembered as the founder of the New Bedford Home for the Aged. Established in 1897, it is a shelter that houses both black and white elderly persons. During World War I she received a leave of absence from her teaching job to supervise the building of the Phillis Wheatley YWCA in Washington, DC. She was also very active in the women's club movement, having served as president of the National Association of Colored Women's Clubs (NACWC) from 1908 to 1912. According to NACWC historian Charles H. Wesley, one of Carter Brooks's greatest accomplishments as president was the establishment of a scholarship for young women at Mary McLeod Bethune's School in Daytona, Florida.

She married W. Sampson Brooks, a bishop in the African Methodist Episcopal church, in 1930. They resided in San Antonio, Texas, until his death in 1934. She returned to New Bedford, where she became president of the Women's Loyal Union, a sponsor of the New Bedford Home for the Aged. She held this position until she died.

Elizabeth Carter Brooks left a lasting legacy to her community. The New Bedford Home for the Aged still functions today. She also left a bequest that funds the Elizabeth Carter Brooks Scholarship, a $100 prize given annually to a high school senior in New Bedford, and a gift to Wilberforce University in Ohio, where she had earned an LLD.

—Frank W. Johnson

Bibliography

There are few primary sources on Elizabeth Carter Brooks. Most are obituaries that appeared in periodicals such as the *New Bedford Standard-Times* and the *Baltimore Afro-American*. There is some correspondence related to her clubwork in the Margaret Murray Washington Papers at Tuskegee University in Alabama.

All of the secondary sources provide brief sketches that credit her with the founding of the New Bedford Home for the Aged. These include Elizabeth Davis, *Lifting as They Climb* (Washington, DC: NACWC, 1933); Dorothy Salem, *To Better Our World: Black Women in Organized Reform, 1890–1920* (Brooklyn: Carlson, 1990); *New Bedford: A Pictorial History* (Donning Company Publishers, 1983); Sylvia Dannett, *Profiles of Negro Womanhood*, (Chicago: Educational Heritage, 1964); Jane C. Waters, *A Guide to New Bedford's Black Heritage Trail* (undated and unpublished); and Floris Cash, "Womanhood and Protest: The Club Movement among Black Women, 1892–1922" (unpublished dissertation, State University of New York at Stony Brook, 1986). The best source for Carter Brooks's activities in the club movement is Charles H. Wesley's *The History of the National Association of Colored Women's Clubs* (Washington, DC: National Association of Colored Women's Clubs, 1984).

CASH, ROSALIND (b. 1938), actress, was born December 31 in Atlantic City, New Jersey. She graduated from the City College of New York, where she became interested in the theater. Cash is a versatile actress who began performing on the stage. A veteran of the Negro Ensemble Company, Cash's stage credits include *Dark of the Moon* (1960), *No Strings* (1962), and *Daddy Goodness* (1967), by Richard Wright and Louis Sapin. Cash understudied Barbara McNair in *Song of the Lusitanian Bogey* (1968); *Ceremonies in Dark Old Men* (1968); and *God Is a Guess What?* (1968). An underrated actress, Cash has always given memorable performances, but often in easily forgotten film and television vehicles.

Cash co-starred with Charlton Heston in her debut film *Omega Man* (1971). This film was followed by *The New Centurions* (1972), *Hickey and Boggs* (1972), and *Melinda* (1972), in which Cash plays Terry Davis in a memorable bank scene that continues to be quoted by black woman. She continued in *The All American Boy* (1973); *Uptown Saturday Night* (1974), a comedy; and *Amazing Grace* (1974). In *Cornbread, Earl and Me* (1975), Cash portrayed Sarah Robinson, the mother of a traumatized child, the sole witness to the accidental shooting of a promising young teenager by the police. The next year, she appeared in *Dr. Black, Mr. Hyde*

(1976) and *The Monkey Hustle* (1976), in which she played Mama in a Chicago community that unites to keep the city government from building a freeway through their neighborhood. With a short time lapse between pictures, Cash again appeared in 1979 in *The Class of McMichael*. Later, she played a woman who becomes the first black female vice president in *Wrong Is Right* (1982).

Rosalind Cash made guest appearances on several television series, such as *The Mary Tyler Moore Show, Starsky and Hutch, Kojak, Police Woman, What's Happening* (1976), *Good Times* (1976), and more recently *The Cosby Show* (1986). She also rendered another classic performance as a Vodum Queen in *Franks Place*. Her television drama credits are "Ceremonies in Dark Old Men" (1975); "King Lear" (1975); "A Killing Affair" (CBS-TV, 1977), in which she plays Beverly York, wife of police officer Woodrow York, played by O.J. Simpson; "Up and Coming" (1980); "Special Bulletin" (1983); and "Go Tell It on the Mountain," an adaptation of James Baldwin's novel (1985).

Cash's versatility is further reflected in television movies ranging from tragedy as, *The Guyana Tragedy: The Story of Jim Jones* (1980), to *The Sophisticated Gents* (NBC-TV, 1981), in which she plays Christine Jackson, the unfaithful wife of Ezzard Jackson (Robert Hooks) in this story by Melvin Van Peebles, about the reunion of 9 black athletes in honor of their 70-year-old coach. In *Sister, Sister* (NBC-TV, 1982), Cash plays the errant, returning sister in this drama about three sisters sharing their rage at life in this Maya Angelou scripted drama.

Cash has a considerable following of black women because she projects "a resilient don't-mess-or-play-with-me toughness" in all of her performances. Still, Rosalind Cash appears to be a Hollywood enigma. She is a consummate artist who has garnered critical accolades, even for her outstanding performances in terrible movies, but she has yet to achieve the recognition that she deserves. Regarding Cash and the Hollywood scene, author Donald Bogle has accurately stated that "seldom in Hollywood's history was a black woman so repeatedly wasted, so thoroughly trashed by the industry" (Bogle, 1988).

—Elizabeth Hadley Freydberg

Bibliography

Bogle, Donald. *Blacks in American Films and Television: An Illustrated Encyclopedia.* New York: Garland, 1988.

————. *Brown Sugar: Eighty Years of America's Black Female Superstars.* New York: Harmony Books, 1980.

Mapp, Edward. *A Director of Blacks in the Performing Arts.* Metuchen, NJ: Scarecrow, 1978.

Parish, James Robert, and George H. Hill. *Black Action Films.* Jefferson, NC: McFarland, 1989.

CASS, MELNEA [JONES] (1896–1978), Boston civic leader and civil rights organizer, devoted her life to the community of Boston and to civil rights for blacks and women. Born in Richmond, Virginia, on June 16 to Albert Jones, a janitor, and Mary (Drew) Jones, a domestic worker, Melnea Agnes Jones was the eldest of three daughters. Her parents brought the family to the South End of Boston to improve their employment and the children's educational opportunities. In Boston, her mother cleaned homes and brought home laundry to supplement her father's income. Her mother died at age 32, when Melnea Jones was around 11 years old. At first, a neighbor lady watched the girls while the father worked. But soon, an aunt, Ella Drew, took the girls to Newburyport, Massachusetts, to attend school. When Melnea Jones completed grammar school, she attended a Catholic school in Rock Castle, Virginia, graduating as the valedictorian of her class in 1914. When she returned to Boston, the aunt had a home all established through financial help of their father, who never lived with his daughters. The aunt took on the responsibility for raising the family.

As a young woman, Melnea Jones worked at the Hyannis Inn in Cape Cod until she married Marshall Cass in 1917. She became a war bride during World War I and went to live with his mother, Rosa Brown. A son, Marshall Drew Cass, was born in 1919. After her husband returned from the service, they moved into their own house, where her two daughters were born. Melnea Cass initially entered community work through her mother-in-law's influence. Rosa Brown, a domestic worker, was a church leader and member of the NAACP, the Equal Rights League, and the Women's Service Club. Melnea Cass helped her raise money for printing William Monroe Trotter's *The Guardian*, a newspaper that raised Cass's awareness on justice issues. Melnea Cass followed the example of Rosa Brown and joined the NAACP and the club movement.

Through her involvement with her children, Melnea Cass began to initiate institutional services on her own. She helped establish a Kindergarten Mother's Club through her children's involvement at the Robert Gould Shaw House. Soon the need for expanded nursery school services, led the women to reorganize as the Friendship Club, which conducted all the fundraising, classes, athletics, choral groups, clubs, and so on, for the Robert Gould Shaw House.

As the years passed she increased her club activities to include the Harriet Tubman Mothers' Club, Sojourner Truth Club, Pansy Embroidery Club, all part of the the Massachusetts State Union of Women's Clubs and part of the National Association of Colored Women's Clubs. At St. Mark's Congregational Church, she served as chairperson of the Social Action Committee and belonged to the Pastor's Club and Missionary Guild, becoming a social leader of the community. Through other organizations, Cass worked for racial justice and civil rights. During the Depression, she helped A. Philip Randolph form the Brotherhood of Sleeping Car Porters in Boston. He called on her again in 1941 to help organize the national March on Washington for black jobs in defense industries. She became a member of the NAACP branch in her twenties, serving on almost every committee, until she became the president of the branch from 1962 to 1964, during the time of protest, sit-ins, and boycotts surrounding desegregation of the schools. She also attempted to broaden the practices of the YWCA, but finally resigned due to their discriminatory policies and behaviors.

All of these paths of community service produced myriad rewards and community recognition: a branch of the Boston YWCA bears her name; her community activity was celebrated in 1966 as Melnea Cass Day, proclaimed by the mayor of Boston; a few years later, a city swimming pool received her name; in 1970, the Eastern Chapter of the National Association of Social Workers awarded Cass for her "outstanding lay contribution to social welfare."

As society changed and Melnea Cass matured, her interests expanded to include the aged. She served several years on the Roxbury Council of Elders, which develops educational, nutritional, and social programs for the aged, representing many groups in the area. In the mid-1970s, she served as the chairperson of the Mayor's Advisory Committee for the City of Boston Elderly. These activities also put her on the National Council of Senior Citizens. A few years after her death in 1978, she was honored with a street in Boston bearing her name, Melnea Cass Boulevard (opened in 1981).

—Kelle S. Taha

Bibliography

The best published source on Melnea Cass's life is the oral history interview on February 1, 1977, as part of the Black Women Oral History Project, Schlesinger Library, Radcliffe College. Her community work can be found in the pages of the Boston newspapers, *The Guardian* and the *Bay State Banner*. The records of the Boston NAACP Branch can delineate her role, especially during the turbulent 1960s. Individual examination of the community organizations and club proceedings can produce some details, but most of the data exists in the memories of her contemporaries.

CATLETT, ELIZABETH (b. 1915), the foremost printmaker/sculptress among practicing artists of African American descent, throughout her career has been associated with the nonconformist, social protest school of art, focusing on the plight of women and the poor, especially among African and Latino peoples in the United States.

Catlett was born on April 15 in Washington, DC, to John and Mary (Carson) Catlett. Both parents were trained as teachers, and her father, who died six months before Elizabeth was born, served on the faculty of Tuskegee Institute. She attended Washington's Lucretia Mott Elementary School and graduated from Dunbar High School in 1933. She received a BS in art (cum laude) from Howard University and received her first MFA in sculpture from the University of Iowa in 1940, where she studied with the painter Grant Wood.

Her teaching career included work at Prairie View College in Texas, heading the Art Department at Dillard University, and faculty posts at Hampton University, and Universidad Nacional Autonoma de Mexico. While studying ceramics at the Art Institute of Chicago in 1941, Catlett met and married Charles White, a painter and printmaker. The couple moved to Hampton, Virginia, where she taught at Hampton Institute and he completed a mural commission. At Hampton, she was greatly influenced by the noted art educator Viktor Lowenfeld.

After moving to New York in 1942, she studied graphics and printmaking at the Art Students League with Ossip Zadkine from 1942 to 1943. The couple encountered other African American artists and intellectuals—including Langston Hughes and Jacob Lawrence—who shared their concern about defining the role of blacks in American art and culture. In these years, she continued to pursue her career as an independent artist of leftist-oriented political ideals while working at the George Washington Carver Evening School in Harlem, an alternative school, which brought her under the scrutiny of the House Un-American Activities Committee because it was a progressive school organized by intellectuals of varying political views. She received a Julius Rosenwald fellowship in 1945 to complete teaching and art production activities.

After Catlett and White divorced in 1947, she moved to Mexico to more freely express her cultural nationalism, and worked at Escuela de Pintura y Escultura, a government art school, and joined the Taller de Grafica Popular ("art school of the people"). In 1947 she met and married Mexican painter and printmaker Francisco Mora and became a nationalized citizen of Mexico in 1962. The couple has three sons: Francisco, Juan, and David. She served until her retirement in 1976 as the chair of the art department at the National University of Mexico's School of Fine Arts, where in 1966 she was the first woman to teach.

Catlett's political activities associating her art with support of grassroots reform movements seeking greater political and economic rights during the 1940s and 1960s resulted in her being declared an undesirable alien by the United States Government. It was not until 1974, following a protest mounted by members of the arts community and others, that the U.S. State Department granted her a visa.

Solo exhibitions in the United States include the New Orleans Museum of Art in 1983 and, more recently, the Malcolm Brown Gallery in Shaker Heights, Ohio, in 1991. Among her numerous awards are the first prize in sculpture at the American Negro Exposition, 1941; in the 1960s, the Xipe Totec Prize in Mexico's Sculpture Biennial, first prize in sculpture in Atlanta University's Annual Art Contest, and first prize in Mexico's National Print Salon; and special award of recognition from Harlem's Studio Museum, 1983.

Her commissioned works include a life-sized bronze bust of Phillis Wheatley for Jackson State College, Mississippi; a ten-foot bronze of Louis Armstrong for the city of New Orleans; a 24-foot bronze relief for the Chemical and Engineering

Building at Howard University; two life-sized bronzes for the Secretary of Education in Mexico. She lives in Cuernavaca, Mexico, and continues her work.
—Robin Chandler and Regennia N. Williams

Bibliography

Bontemps, Jacqueline, *Forever Free: Art by African American Women, 1862–1980*. Alexandria, VA: Stephenson, 1980.

Cederholm, Theresa D., ed. *Afro-American Artists: A Bibliographical Directory*. Boston: Trustees of the Boston Public Library, 1973.

City College of New York. *The Evolution of Afro-American Artists, 1800–1950*, Exhibition Catalog (1967).

Driskell, David. *Two Centuries of Black American Art*. New York: Alfred Knopf, 1976.

Gouma-Peterson, Thaliz. "Elizabeth Catlett," *Woman's Art Journal* (Spring/Summer 1983).

Harley, Ralph L., Jr. "A Checklist of Afro-American Art and Artists" *Serif* 7:4 (1970): 3–63.

Heller, Nancy G. *Women Artists: An Illustrated History*. New York: Abbeville Press, 1987.

Lewis, Samella. *Art: African American*. New York: Harcourt, Brace Jovanovich, 1978.

———. *The Art of Elizabeth Catlett*. Claremont, CA: Hancraft Studios, 1984.

———. "My Art Speaks for Both My Peoples," *Ebony* (February 1970).

Morrison, Allan. "(Black) Women in the Arts," *Ebony* (August 1966): 90–94.

Porter, James. *Modern Negro Art*. New York: Arno Press, 1969.

Studio Museum of Harlem. "Elizabeth Catlett," Exhibition Catalog, 1971–1972.

Tufts, Eleanor. *Our Hidden Heritage: Five Centuries of Women Artists*. New York: Paddington, 1974.

CHENZIRA, AYOKA (b. 1953), filmmaker and dancer, was born on November 8, educated in Philadelphia, and now resides in New York City. She attended the College of New Rochelle, where she studied film in the Department of Fine Arts. Later she transferred to New York University, where she received a bachelor's degree. Chenzira earned an EdM in communications from Columbia University/Teachers College.

While studying dance and film Ayoka Chenzira met and became very impressed by her dance teacher Syvilla Fort. They developed a close relationship. Fort became a role model and mentor to Chenzira. Subsequently, Chenzira decided to produce her senior film project on the life and accomplishments of Fort. *Syvilla: They Dance to Her Drum* (1979), a documentary, provides a concise overview of Syvilla Fort as a pioneering, first-generation black concert dancer. This film is representative of a number of films that African American women filmmakers are producing that chronicle the lives and accomplishments of African American women. Although Fort died before the film was finished, Chenzira completed the film as a tribute to the artist and became an accomplished dancer. In addition, she has conducted master classes and lectured on the history of African American dance.

Hair Piece: A Film for Nappy Headed People (1984) has become Chenzira's signature film. It premiered to rave reviews at the National Film Theatre in London. *Hair Piece*, an animated satire, blends a historical overview of black hairstyles with the cultural values and music that accompanied and influenced specific black hairstyles. *Secret Sounds Screaming: The Sexual Abuse of Children* (1986), a video documentary, examines the troubling issue of child abuse. *Zajota and the Boogie Spirit* (1989) is a short animated folktale that traces the journey of the mythical Zajota people from Africa to slavery in the United States. The film provides insight into the traumas of slavery and racism while celebrating African retentions in African American music and culture. Chenzira directed *Five Out of Five* (1987) and produced the animation for *On Becoming a Woman: Mothers and Daughters Talking Together* (1987). She has also produced Black History Month promos for the Public Broadcasting System. Currently, Chenzira is working on a full-length feature, *Ya So Dey So (Here to There)*.

Chenzira has traveled extensively with her work and won numerous awards and accolades, including a scholarship to the prestigious Sundance Institute (1984). She is currently teaching at City University of New York.

—Gloria J. Gibson-Hudson

Bibliography

Greg Tate, "Cinematic Sisterhood," *Village Voice* (June 4, 1991), a brief article on black women independent filmmakers, includes a discussion of Chenzira's work. Gloria J. Gibson, "The Cultural Significance of Music to the Black Independent Filmmaker," (doctoral dissertation, Indiana University, 1986) analyzes the music in *Hair Piece*. Gloria J. Gibson-Hudson, "African American Literary Criticism as a Model for the Analysis of Films by African American Women" *Wide Angle* 13: 3/4 (July/October 1991) discusses the similarities between African American literary and film criticism and includes a discussion of *Hair Piece*.

CHILDRESS, ALICE (b. 1920), whose childhood did not predict her success as a playwright, was born October 12 to a poor, uneducated family in Charleston, South Carolina. She was raised by her grandmother, Eliza Campbell. Unable to finish high school, Alice Childress nevertheless enjoyed writing. Her background made her interpret the experiences of ordinary people struggling to survive rather than the individual strivers and achievers that typically fill the pages of beginning writers. After living through the Depression, Childress started her career as a New York actress. Her first performance came through acting in *On Strivers Row* in 1940. As an actress and director of the American Negro Theatre for 12 years, Childress developed a reputation as an actress. She acted in several productions, such as *Natural Man* (1941), *Anna Lucasta* (1944), *The Candy Story, The*

Candy Story, *The World of Sholom Aleichem* (both 1953), *The Cool World* (1960) and *Emperor's Clothes*, which created respect for her performance abilities.

Her acting and directing received praise, but her historical significance is that of a playwright. Alice Childress became one of the first black female playwrights to attract attention during the turbulent decade leading to the emerging civil rights movement. *Just a Little Simple*, her adaptation of Langston Hughes's *Simple Speaks His Mind*, was deemed successful by critics. During the same evening of *Simple*, Childress presented her own one-act piece *Florence*, produced first in New York City by the American Negro Theatre in 1949. Buoyed by the reception of the theater piece about a mother trying to save her daughter from a theater career, Childress presented, two years later, *Gold Through the Trees* (1952), describing the struggles of South Africans and comparing the conditions to those of African Americans.

During the year of the Montgomery bus boycott, she released *Trouble in Mind*, which won an Obie Award for the best Off-Broadway production of the season in 1956. Based on the story of a black actress who refused to accept a stereotyped role in a play on a lynching in the South, *Trouble in Mind* reflected the collective experiences of black actresses of the time. *Trouble* brought Childress out of Harlem and into mainstream theater. Her first marriage ended leaving her with a daughter, Jean Lee; a second marriage to musician Nathan Woodard followed in 1957. From 1956 to 1958, she also wrote the column "Here's Mildred" in the *Baltimore Afro-American*.

The 1960s brought greater recognition from academic audiences. Alice Childress lectured to college audiences at the New School for Social Research (1965) and at Fisk University (1966) before she presented her next play, *The Wedding Band*, first produced in 1966 at the University of Michigan featuring Ruby Dee, Abbey Lincoln, and Clarice Taylor. Placed against the era of the First World War, the play focused on an interracial love affair between a white man and a black woman in South Carolina. From 1966 to 1968, she served as the scholar-writer at Radcliffe Institute for Independent Study at Harvard University and acted in the film *Uptight*.

Childress remained a prolific playwright. Her other works include *The World on a Hill*, a view of West Indian life from a white female perspective (1968); *Wine in the Wilderness*, a play that united inner-city and middle-class blacks brought together by a ghetto heroine, an uncultured black woman, who represented the answer to the cultural revolution (1969); *String*, a study in credibility of an aging eccentric man unjustly accused of theft (1969); *The Young Martin Luther King* (1969); and *The Freedom Drum*, a recounting of the trials of the Montgomery bus boycott (1970).

Although Childress won acclaim as a splendid playwright, her controversial themes provoked mixed reviews and therefore had difficulty getting her plays produced. *The Wedding Band*, though given rave reviews in 1966, did not make it to New York until 1972. In 1973 the New York stage embraced *The Wedding*

Band, for which lead actress Ruby Dee won the Drama Desk Award. Following *The Wedding Band,* she wrote *Mojo* (1970), recollections of a black couple who rediscovered each other following divorce; *When the Rattlesnake Sounds* (1975), a story about the conductor of the Underground Railroad, Harriet Tubman; *A Hero Ain't Nothin' But a Sandwich* (1977), a story about a drug addict, which became one of the *New York Times Book Review*'s Outstanding Books of the Year; *Straight Life of Fannie Lou Hamer* (1978 television production); and *Moms,* a play about Jackie "Moms" Mabley (1987).

In addition to her plays, Childress has written novels, such as *A Short Walk* (1979), and the children's story *Rainbow Jordan* (1980), which won the Coretta Scott King Award in 1982. For her achievements, she has received the Sojourner Truth Achievement Award (1975) from the National Negro Business and Professional Women's Clubs; the first Paul Robeson Medal of Distinction from the Black Filmmakers Association (1976); the Virgin Island Film Festival Award (1977); recognition in Alice Childress Week in Charleston and Columbia, South Carolina (1977); and the Audience Development Co. (AUDELCO) Pioneer Award (1986). She continues to live in New York City and belongs to the American Federation of Television and Radio Artists; Dramatists Guild; Actor's Equity Association; Harlem Writers Guild; and New Dramatists, Screen and Writers Guild. Her books have received numerous awards in young adult and children's literature categories. She continues to participate in conferences and contribute to anthologies and the journals *Masses and Mainstream, Black World, Negro Digest,* and *Freedomways.*

—Beth Schneider

Bibliography

The work of Alice Childress can be found in the following: "Florence" in *Masses and Mainstream* 3 (October 1950); "Trouble in Mind" in *Black Theater: A 20th Century Collection of the Work of Its Best Playwrights,* edited by Lindsay Patterson (New York: Dodd, Mead, 1971); *The World on a Hill* in *Plays to Remember* (New York: Macmillan, 1968); *The African Garden* in *Black Scenes,* edited by Alice Childress (Garden City, NY: Doubleday, 1971). *Wine in the Wilderness, Mojo,* and *String* are published by the Dramatists Play Service, New York.

Her views on her art are included in "The Negro Woman in American Literature," *Freedomways* 6 (Winter 1966): 8–25; and "Black Writers' Views on Literary Lions and Values," *Negro Digest* 17 (January 1968): 10–47. She is reviewed in articles: Gayle Austin, "Alice Childress: Black Woman Playwright as Feminist Critic," and Polly Holliday, "I Remember Alice Childress," both in *Southern Quarterly* 25:3 (Spring 1987): 52–62 and 63–65; and Elizabeth Brown-Guillory, "Alice Childress: a Pioneering Spirit," *Sage* 4:1 (Spring 1987): 66–68. Biographical information on Childress can be found in Darwin Turner, *Afro-American Writers* (New York: Appleton, Century, Crofts, 1970); Doris Abramson, *Negro Playwrights in the American Theatre: 1925–1959* (New York: Columbia University Press, 1969); Hal May and James Lesniak, eds., *Contemporary Authors* 26 (Detroit: Gale, 1990); Mari Evans, *Black Women Writers*

(New York: Doubleday, 1984); Edward Mapp, *A Directory of Blacks in the Performing Arts* (Metuchen, NJ: Scarecrow, 1978); Ann Shockley, *Living Black American Authors* (New York: Bowker, 1973). Her works are analyzed by Jeanne-Marie Miller, "Black Women Playwrights from Grimké to Shange," in *But Some of Us Are Brave*, edited by Gloria T. Hull, Patricia Bell Scott, and Barbara Smith (Old Westbury, NY: Feminist Press, 1982), pp. 280–296; and Mariana Davis, *Contributions of Black Women to America* (Columbia, SC: Kenday, 1982).

CHINN, MAY EDWARD (1896–1980), surgeon and pianist, was born in

Great Barrington, Massachusetts, on April 15, the only child of William Lafayette Chinn, a slave who had escaped to freedom at age 11 from the Chinn (Cheyne) plantation in Virginia, and his wife, Lulu Ann, who had been born on a Chickahominy Indian reservation near Norfolk, Virginia. When May was three years old, her family moved to New York City. Her mother, wishing to protect her from distress caused by her father's alcoholism, and determined that her daughter receive a good education, sent her to boarding school at the Bordentown Manual Training and Industrial School in New Jersey when she was five or six years old. She was obliged to leave school when she developed osteomyelitis, and, after a period of convalescence, went to live with her mother on the Tarrytown, New York, estate of jeweler Charles Tiffany. Though her mother was in service with the family, Dr. Chinn recalls having been raised as one of the Tiffany children—dining with them, studying the classics with them, and attending concerts with them as "just another child in the house."

It was through her exposure to foreign languages and music while living on the Tiffany estate that May Chinn's own musical gift was first nurtured. When she and her mother returned to New York after the Tiffany estate had been sold, May attended grammar school and took piano lessons. When she dropped out of high school because of "a disappointed love affair and a poor grade in Latin," she gave piano lessons to kindergarten children. Eventually, her mother's education ethic won out, and May took and passed a high school equivalency exam. She entered Teachers College of Columbia University as a fully matriculated student in 1917. After her first year, she changed her major from music to science, and graduated in 1921. While still in college, she played and sang in concerts around New York, accompanying such celebrated performers as Paul Robeson and Thomas W. Ennis and performed for soldiers under the auspices of the USO. As a surgeon and a pianist, she fully participated in the cultural scene of Harlem.

In 1926 May Chinn became the first "Negro" woman (the designation that she, herself, preferred) to obtain a medical degree from Bellevue Hospital Medical College. She went on to become the first Negro woman to hold an internship at Harlem Hospital, and the first woman physician to ride with the ambulance crew of the Harlem Hospital on emergency calls. In 1928 she joined the ranks of a group of black doctors who practiced in the Edgecombe Sanitarium, an alternative establishment to the predominantly white New York hospital system. She received a master's degree in public health from Columbia University in 1933. In an article in the *New York Times* (November 16, 1977), Dr. Chinn said of her work as an African American woman physician, "We were forced to practice medicine as doctors did 100 years before in rural Appalachia." She also noted that one black woman patient cried upon seeing Dr. Chinn because "she felt she had been denied the privilege of having a white doctor wait on her."

Known widely by the end of her career for her work in the early detection and diagnosis of cancer, she was on staff at the Strang Clinic, affiliated with Memorial and New York Infirmary hospitals, until her retirement in the early 1970s. Even after her retirement at the age of 81, she continued her work in three state-sponsored day care centers in Harlem. She was a member of the Surgeon General's Advisory Commission on Urban Affairs, and received an honorary doctor of science degree from Columbia University in 1980, the same year she was honored by the New York Urban League. In June 1980, New York University honored her with a doctor of science degree for her "long life service" to the profession. She collapsed and died while attending a dinner honoring her friend, John Wilson, at Columbia University on December 1, 1980.

—Janet Miller with Susan Shifrin

Bibliography

Manuscript collections and oral history sources can be found in "Interview with May Edward Chinn" (1979), Black Women Oral History Project, Schlesinger Library, Radcliffe College; and May Chinn file, Black Women Physicians Project, Accession 178, Archives and Special Collections on Women in Medicine, Medical College of Pennsylvania, Philadelphia.

Secondary sources and interviews can be found in Charlayne Hunter-Gault, "Black Women M.D.'s: Spirit and Endurance," *New York Times* (November 16, 1977); Brozan N. Day, *New York Times Biography* (May 1980), pp. 655–666; G. Davis, "Healing Hand in Harlem," *New York Times Magazine* (April 22, 1979), pp. 40–42; "Obituary," *New York Times* (December 3, 1980), B11.

CHISHOLM, SHIRLEY ANITA [ST. HILL] (b. 1924), the first black woman elected to the U.S. Congress, used her leadership to initiate opportunities for women and minorities. Born in Brooklyn, New York, on November 30, Shirley Anita Chisholm grew up in the Bedford-Stuyvesant section. Her parents, Charles and Ruby (Seale) St. Hill, were both immigrants from the Caribbean. Her father was born in British Guiana but grew up in Barbados, which was her mother's native country.

Chisholm's family was poor during her childhood. Her father worked in a burlap factory and admired Marcus Garvey. Realizing she was intelligent and perceptive, he encouraged Chisholm to read books in order to educate herself and learn about new ideas. He hoped to send his daughter to college so that she might realize her potential. Her mother was a seamstress and domestic who tended to be overprotective of and a stern disciplinarian to her four daughters.

When she was a toddler, Chisholm lived with her sisters on their grandmother's Barbados farm while their parents labored in New York to save money for their children's education. Chisholm attended schools in Barbados when her family could afford tuition, and she read voraciously, especially about women role models. She particularly admired Mary McLeod Bethune. She returned to New York when she was 11 years old and enrolled in school, which required extra work to catch up with her class. She quickly achieved academically and graduated from Girls' High School with several scholarship offers.

Chisholm studied sociology at Brooklyn College of the City University of New York, earning her BA in 1946. She minored in Spanish, becoming fluent. This skill enabled her to deliver speeches and communicate with Hispanic constituents. In 1949 she married Conrad Q. Chisholm, a private investigator and immigrant from Jamaica, who encouraged and supported her career.

Chisholm decided that the classroom was the only medium through which a black woman could achieve progress for herself and the community. Longing to improve conditions in New York City, Chisholm became involved politically on the local level in the Brooklyn NAACP and the Bedford-Stuyvesant Political League. She also volunteered at settlement houses for the Urban League.

Professionally she worked at the Mt. Calvary Child Care Center in Harlem and attended school at night, receiving her MA in elementary education from Columbia University in 1952. She also acquired education certificates for educational work beyond the master's and began course work for a PhD. From 1946 to 1953 Chisholm was a nursery school teacher in Brownsville, New York, and became director of a child care center in Manhattan, supervising ten day care centers. As a result, Chisholm became an established authority on education.

In 1959 Chisholm was selected as educational consultant to the division of day care of the New York City Bureau of Child Welfare, which increased her contact with politics. Well known as an independent thinker, excellent debater, and outspoken woman, Chisholm could also be trusted to reflect the needs of her peers. Chisholm, though not unique in advocating the need for social change in her neighborhood, stressed a long tradition of effort by local women constantly attempting to improve the community. In fact, she credits a welfare mother who relied on Chisholm's abilities to effect reform with convincing her to run for Congress.

In 1964 Chisholm won a seat as assemblywoman in the New York State Legislature, elected by a constituency comprised mostly of blacks and Puerto Ricans of her native Bedford-Stuyvesant. In the assembly she lobbied for interests close to her own professional and familial experiences that also reflected the needs of her community: laws for day care centers, the Search for Elevation, Education, and Knowledge (SEEK) program for disadvantaged students not meeting college entrance requirements, insurance for domestics, and consumer protection laws.

Although her neighborhood had been reapportioned as part of the new 12th Congressional District, Chisholm first won the Democratic primary then beat the Republican candidate to gain a seat in the 91st Congress. In the U.S. House of Representatives, Chisholm attracted attention when she protested being assigned to the Committee on Forests and Rural Villages, stating that it had no relation to her urban district. She issued an amendment and was reassigned to the Veterans Affairs Committee.

Chisholm earned a reputation as being a hard-working and opinionated legislator. Chisholm advocated pro-choice in the debate over abortion and criticized the Vietnam draft, favoring a voluntary military force that would not exploit a group of young citizens least represented by voters. She was reelected to the 92nd Congress in 1968 holding the Congressional seat for a total of seven terms until 1982. During this time she served as secretary of the Democratic Caucus and vice-chair of the Congressional Black Caucus.

Chisholm's diverse activities led to her conclusion that being a woman handicapped her more than being black. She lectured to college students around the nation who were enthralled by the vivacious Chisholm's speeches, which addressed pertinent issues that concerned and affected them and their communities, and they encouraged the verbose and insightful Chisholm to run for the presidency.

On January 25, 1972, Chisholm announced her candidacy for President at the Concord Baptist Church in Brooklyn. Although she was not the first woman to campaign actively for President (Maine senator Margaret Chase Smith won votes in the 1964 primaries and at the Republican National Convention), Chisholm was the first black woman to attempt to acquire that office. She realized that she lacked the necessary funds and support to win the race and acknowledged her true motivation was "to crack a little more of the ice which in recent years has congealed to nearly immobilize our political system and demoralize people." She wanted her candidacy to prove that she was determined to counter the status quo as well as to enable women to have more opportunities in politics. In order to mitigate obstacles, she established and chaired the National Political Congress of Black Women.

Since 1983 Chisholm has held the Purington Chair at Mount Holyoke College, South Hadley, Massachusetts. She teaches and gives lectures to schools and groups throughout the United States. She is active in the League of Women Voters, the National Organization for Women, and Delta Sigma Theta, and has received numerous honorary degrees and accolades. Her second husband is Arthur Hardwick, Jr.

—Elizabeth D. Schafer

Bibliography

Biographical sketches of Chisholm include: "Shirley Anita St. Hill Chisholm," in W. Augustus Low and Virgil A. Clift, eds., *Encyclopedia of Black America* (New York: McGraw-Hill, 1981); Edgar A. Toppin, *A Biographical History of Blacks in America since 1528* (New York: McKay, 1961); *Who's Who among Black Americans* (Northbrook, IL: Who's Who among Black Americans, 1991); George F. Jackson, *Black Women Makers of History: A Portrait* (Santa Rosa, CA: National Women's History Project, 1985); Carter Smith, ed., *American Historical Images on File: The Black Experience* (New York: Facts on File, 1990); and Brian Lanker, *I Dream a World: Portraits of Black Women Who Changed America*, edited by Barbara Summers (New York: Stewart, Tabori & Chang, 1989).

Shirley Chisholm wrote two books, *Unbought and Unbossed* (Boston: Houghton, Mifflin, 1970), an autobiographical account depicting Chisholm from her childhood to election as New York Congresswoman and *The Good Fight* (New York: Harper, 1973) about her presidential campaign, including several position papers and speeches.

Biographies of Chisholm include Joan Kuriansky and Catherine Smith, *Shirley Chisholm Democratic Representative from New York* (Washington, DC: Grossman, 1972); James Haskins, *Fighting Shirley Chisholm* (New York: Dial, 1975), which is a children's book but concisely provides information about her childhood, college years, and early political career; and Susan Brownmiller, *Shirley Chisholm: A Biography* (Garden City: Doubleday, 1971). Other biographies are listed in Susan Duffy, *Shirley Chisholm: A Bibliography of Writings by and about Her* (Metuchen, NJ: Scarecrow, 1988), which is an annotated bibliography of Chisholm's speeches, writings, and information about treatises examining her political career, newspaper articles reporting about Chisholm, and numerous articles from educational, black, and contemporary popular magazines and scholarly journals such as *Jet*, *Ebony*, and *Mount Holyoke Now*.

Her speeches are printed in the *Congressional Record*. Recorded and videotaped speeches, lectures, and filmstrips are kept at the Schomburg Center for Research in Black Culture, New York City, and numerous American universities. Other Chisholm correspondence is held in the Presbyterian Historical Society, Philadelphia, and the Schomburg Center for Research on Black Culture, New York Public Library, New York City, which also has typescripts, campaign material, press releases, and clippings. Published Chisholm letters are in *Negro History Bulletin* (May 1970): 128; and the *New York Times* (January 10, 1981). The Library of Congress contains photographs and papers, and current information about Chisholm is located at Mt. Holyoke.

Samples of Chisholm's speeches and writing include "The 51% Minority, 1970," in Gerda Lerner, ed., *Black Women in White America* (New York: Random House, 1973), pp. 352–357; also in Lerner is an essay "Facing the Abortion Question" (pp. 602–607), excerpted from *Unbought and Unbossed*. See also Chisholm, "Racism and Anti-Feminism," *The Black Scholar* 14 (September/October 1983): 2–7.

Chapters specifically addressing Chisholm's congressional activity are in Hope Chamberlin, *A Minority of Members: Women in the U.S. Congress* (New York: Praeger, 1974); Rudolf Engelbarts, *Women in the United States Congress, 1971–1972* (Littleton, CO: Libraries Unlimited, 1974); and Maurine Christopher, *Black Americans in*

Congress (New York: Crowell, 1976). Also see Margaret J. Hankle, "A Critical Analysis of Selected Speeches on Women's Rights by Representative Shirley Chisholm," MA thesis, California State University at Long Beach (1976), and Dorothy K. Williamson, "Rhetorical Analysis of Selected Modern Black Spokespersons on the Women's Liberation Movement," PhD dissertation, Ohio State University (1980), which includes information from an interview with Chisholm.

Herman D. Bloch, *The Circle of Discrimination: An Economic and Social Study of the Black Man in New York* (New York: New York University Press, 1969) has a chapter focusing on Bedford-Stuyvesant in the 1960s. Rita Seiden Miller, ed., *Brooklyn USA: The Fourth Largest City in America* (New York: Brooklyn College, 1979) also includes information about Bedford-Stuyvesant and provides a geographical context.

CLARK, SEPTIMA [POINSETTE] (1898–1987), teacher and unsung hero of the civil rights movement, was born on May 3 in Charleston, South Carolina. Her father, Peter Porcher Poinsette, was a former slave owned by South Carolina's Poinsette family, and her mother, Victoria Warren (Anderson), was freeborn. She was raised in the Methodist church and remained active in the church throughout her life. She married Nerie Clark, a sailor, in 1920 against her parents wishes. Clark's first child died within a month of birth. The couple then moved to Dayton, Ohio, where their second child, Nerie, was born. Shortly after this child's birth, the couple separated, and within the year, the elder Nerie died.

Clark taught for several years on Johns Island, South Carolina, and in the Charleston school system. In 1956 she was fired by the Charleston Board of Education for being a member of the National Association for the Advancement of Colored People (NAACP). At age 58, she began working at the Highlander Folk School in Tennessee. There, she specialized in teaching illiterate adults to read, who she then instructed to teach others to read once they returned to their communities. Barely at Highlander one year, Clark was jailed on a false moonshining charge fashioned by the prosecutor's plan to shut down the integrated school for social change.

Clark was put in charge of the citizenship school at the Highlander and for the Southern Christian Leadership Conference (SCLC) in Georgia. In one-week workshops, she turned sharecroppers and other unschooled blacks into potential voters with basic literacy skills and an understanding of their democratic rights. She also traveled by bus throughout the South testing the seating laws on the buses, visiting teachers, recruiting new teachers, and setting up citizenship schools. Clark had a gift for recognizing natural leaders among the poorly educated blacks with whom she worked. She instilled in them a sense of their self-worth, dignity, and confidence. She was known as SCLC's "Mother Conscience." Clark patiently worked with leading male figures such as John Lewis, Andrew Young, Ralph Abernathy, Wyatt Tee Walker, and Martin Luther King, Jr.

During the civil rights era she remained silent on the discrimination of women. In her later years she was vocal about the sexism in the movement and the role women played in the civil rights movement. She was a passionate advocate of women's ability to make significant contributions to social change movements.

Clark retired from SCLC in June 1970. She received the Race Relations Award from the National Education Association (1976) and a Living Legend Award in 1979. In her native Charleston, a day care center and an expressway are named in her honor. She belonged to the Alpha Kappa Alpha sorority and was the first black woman to serve on the Charleston Country School Board (1976–1983). She died December 15, 1987, on Johns Island at the age of 89.

—Emilie M. Townes

Bibliography

For primary sources see the Septima Clark Collection, Robert Scott Small Library, Charleston, South Carolina; Highlander Folk School files in State Historical Society of Wisconsin, Madison; Septima Clark, *Echo in My Soul* (New York: Dutton, 1962); Septima Clark, *Ready from Within* (Navarro, CA: Wild Tree Press, 1986). Secondary sources include Taylor Branch *Parting the Waters: America in the King Years, 1954–1963* (New York: Simon & Schuster, 1988); Gerda Lerner, *Black Women in White America: A Documentary History* (New York: Random House, 1973); Sandra Oldendorf, "The South Carolina Sea Island Citizenship Schools, 1957–1961," and Grace J. McFadden, "Septima P. Clark for Human Rights," in Vicki L. Crawford et al., eds., *Women in the Civil Rights Movement: Trailblazers and Torchbearers, 1941–1965* (Brooklyn: Carlson, 1990); and Aimee Horton, *The Highlander Folk School: A History of Its Major Programs, 1932–1961* (Brooklyn: Carlson, 1990); Grace Jordan McFadden, *Oral Recollections of Septima Poinsette Clark* (Columbia, SC: USC Instructional Services Center, 1980).

CLIFFORD, CARRIE WILLIAMS (1862–1934), a published poet and a noted public speaker, advocated women's suffrage and the advancement of her race. Her first volume of poetry, *Race Rhymes* (1911), was later included in her second volume, *The Widening Light* (1922). Also an activist, Clifford helped found the Ohio State Federation of Colored Women and served as its first president. Later, she helped organize the Washington, DC, chapter of the NAACP and held a variety of local and national positions within the association.

Clifford was born in September in Chillicothe, Ohio, and educated in Columbus, Ohio, where her mother ran a successful business. She taught school in Parkersburg, West Virginia, before her marriage in 1886 to William H. Clifford, a Republican member of the Ohio State Legislature. The couple lived in Cleveland, Ohio. William Clifford received a law degree in 1902. In 1908 he was appointed to a position in the War Department, and the family moved to Washington, DC. The Cliffords had two sons, Joshua and Maurice.

When Carrie Clifford helped create the Ohio State Federation of Colored Women around 1900, it was one of the first groups of its type, affiliated with the National Association of Colored Women (NACW). She served as the federation's first president and founded and edited the *Queen's Garden*, its official publication. Under the federation's auspices, she edited a compilation of essays on the advancement of women and blacks, entitled *Sowing for Others to Reap*. "The Forward Movement," her introduction to this slim volume, expands on her philosophy of the necessity of hard work, patience, and perseverance to obtain increased opportunity for blacks. A powerful orator, Clifford received national attention for a speech that she delivered before the National Negro Business League Convention in August 1905. She was a member of the female auxiliary of the Niagara Movement, the forerunner of the NAACP, in charge of involving black women in the movement. While in Cleveland, Clifford was the editor of the women's department for the Cleveland *Journal*, a publication geared toward black business interests.

In Washington, DC, Clifford opened her home weekly to black intellectuals from Howard University and elsewhere, and participated in the city's social and civic life. Beginning in 1910, she joined other prominent black women in founding a branch of the NAACP in the nation's capital. Clifford also took an active part in national NAACP efforts; for example, with Mary Church Terrell, she brought resolutions against lynching before President William Howard Taft. In 1910 she was elected to fill a vacancy on the organization's Committee of One Hundred. With the help of Addie Hunton, Clifford established a committee of women to assist the association in fundraising and public speaking. She headed the NAACP's Juvenile Department and created a card game to teach children about the accomplishments of blacks. *The Crisis*, NAACP's official publication, marketed the innovative teaching tool.

Clifford published short stories, articles, and poems in periodicals such as *Outlook*, *Opportunity*, and *The Crisis*. The most prevalent themes of her work were race harmony, the heritage of African Americans and their struggle for equal opportunity, and the contributions of all women to society. One of her poems, "We'll Die for Liberty," is a rewriting of "The Battle Hymn of the Republic."

Clifford died on November 10, 1934.

—Jimmy E.W. Meyer

Bibliography

Works by Carrie Clifford

"Cleveland and Its Colored People," *Colored American* 9:1 (July 1905): 365–380.
Race Rhymes. Washington, DC: R.L. Pendleton, 1911.
Sowing for Others to Reap: A Collection of Papers on Various Subjects of Vital Importance to the Race. (Edited by Carrie W. Clifford for the Ohio Federation of Colored Women). Boston: Charles Alexander, n.d.

"Votes for Children," *The Crisis* 10:58 (August 1915): 185.

The Widening Light. Boston: Walter Reid, 1922; new ed., with an introduction by Rosemary Clifford Wilson. New York: Crowell, 1971.

Works about Carrie Clifford

Davis, Russell H. *Black Americans in Cleveland.* Washington, DC: Association for the Study of Negro Life and History, 1972.

Kellogg, Charles Flint. *NAACP: A History of the National Association for the Advancement of Colored People, Vol. I, 1909–1920.* Baltimore: Johns Hopkins University Press, 1967.

"Robert C. Ogden Tells the Negroes to Work; A Colored Woman Orator Stirs the Business Men's Convention," *New York Times* (August 18, 1905): 4.

Roses, Lorraine Elena, and Ruth Elizabeth Randolph. *Harlem Renaissance and Beyond.* Boston: G.K. Hall, 1990.

Rush, Theressa Gunnels, et al. *Black American Writers Past and Present: A Biographical and Bibliographical Dictionary.* Metuchen, NJ: Scarecrow, 1975.

Salem, Dorothy, ed. *To Better Our World: Black Women in Organized Reform 1890–1920.* Brooklyn: Carlson, 1990.

Van Tassel, David D., and John Grabowski, eds. *Encyclopedia of Cleveland History.* Bloomington: Indiana University Press, 1987.

Williams, Ora. *American Black Women in the Arts and Social Sciences: A Bibliography.* Metuchen, NJ: Scarecrow, 1973.

COBB, JEWEL PLUMMER (b. 1924), scientist, educator, administrator, and specialist in cancer cell biology research, continues to serve as a living model of a lifetime commitment to attract more black students into science and technology. Her career experiences have demonstrated the importance of family and institutional support of career aspirations in scientific fields.

Born January 17 in Chicago, Illinois, Jewel Plummer grew up in a home that nurtured education and displayed the racial barriers of the era. Her mother was a physical education graduate of Sargeants College, a physical education college associated with Harvard University. As a physical education instructor in Washington, DC, and an admirer of Isadora Duncan, she taught children interpretive dance, an activity that combined her background in piano and dance with her educational preparation in physical education. This emphasis on physical education created an awareness in the Plummer household and led to Jewel's middle name, Isadora. Jewel's father, a 1923 graduate of Rush Medical College, was a staff physician at Provident Hospital and a specialist in dermatology. Provident Hospital provided black medical students and interns from the Medical School of the University of Chicago practical experiences with patients. Since black interns and medical students could not touch white patients, practice on their own people was the only alternative. Jewel's early years involved her in creative discussions with her father's scientific knowledge, her mother's teaching activities, and the realities of race.

Jewel Isadora Plummer attended the public schools during the time that school boards dealt with neighborhood transition by gerrymandering. At first she attended Sexton Elementary School in a largely white neighborhood, but after redistricting, she was forced to attend the overcrowded and dilapidated Betsy Ross Elementary School, where she spent her time in a portable classroom heated by a potbellied stove. She went on to Englewood High School under a double shift scheme that led to her attending from noon until dinner time. Due to the influence of her family, she took the college-preparatory track, which meant five years of science. A new world was opened to her by a high school biology teacher, who inspired her to become a biology teacher. She continued to take the necessary courses in botany, zoology, math, physics, and chemistry to graduate with honors.

She went on to college, choosing the University of Michigan in Ann Arbor, where she met black students from the South who had been denied admission to their own state universities. Plummer and the other black students, though admitted to the educational programs, were segregated in housing, in fraternities/sororities, and in campus social life. She joined the black sorority Alpha Kappa Alpha, lived in the black "official" residence, and started to consider transfer to another college. In 1942, the Plummers sent Jewel to Talladega College for its strong science program and supportive black environment. She graduated in 1944.

With the encouragement from a bacteriology professor, she entered New York University for graduate studies in cell physiology. As a graduate student, she did substitute teaching in high school biology classes, but the discipline problems presented by the age group detracted from her love of biology, hence, she chose to remain at New York University to gain her doctorate degree. She completed her doctoral dissertation on *in vitro* formation of melanin pigment granules and received the PhD in biology in 1950.

Her research specialization led to a postdoctoral fellowship from the National Cancer Institute to conduct research with Dr. Louis T. Wright at Harlem Hospital. In 1952 she received a faculty appointment to the Department of Anatomy at the University of Illinois Medical School, where she established the first tissue culture laboratory and a course in cell biology. She continued to conduct research on cancer cytology, receiving grants from the National Institutes of Health, the Damon Runyon Fund, and the American Cancer Society. She published data on human bladder cancer and melanomas. In 1954 she married Roy Raul Cobb and returned to the New York area to work for the Harlem Hospital Cancer Research Foundation, which affiliated with New York University Post-Graduate Medical School in 1955. While continuing to do research in cancer cytology, she moved through academic institutions in the New York area. From 1956 to 1960, Jewel Plummer Cobb served as an assistant professor of biology at Hunter College before becoming a full professor at Sarah Lawrence College in Bronxville, New York, from 1960 to 1969. In 1969 she became the dean of Connecticut College and professor of zoology. Divorced in 1967 with a son, Roy Jonathan Cobb, Dr. Cobb attempted to raise her son and to improve conditions for future black scientists. At Connecticut College, she established the Postgraduate Premedical and Predental Program for Minority Students. From 1974 to 1980, she served as the only minority member on the National Science Board, which formed the Women and Minorities in Science Committee to launch national programs for the creation of career awareness programs, refresher courses, and career facilitation grants to attract role models to high schools. While she served on the National Science Board, she moved on to Douglass College of Rutgers University before she became in 1981 the president of California State University, Fullerton. She retired in 1990, but continues to serve as president emeritus and trustee.

During her career, Jewel Plummer Cobb has received many honors. Her research has resulted in over 36 articles published in scholarly journals. She is the recipient of 16 honorary doctorate degrees from institutions such as the Medical College of Pennsylvania and Trinity College. Her awards include the Phelps Stokes Distinguished Visitors Program, NAACP's Woman of the Year, Scroll of Merit Award from the American Medical Association, and the Sojourner Truth Award. Her leadership has produced a generation of new scientists through her personal influence. She continues to live in Fullerton and to direct national attention to the preparation and motivation of minorities into the science and technology fields.

—Kelle S. Taha

Bibliography

Cobb has been recognized as a leader in scientific education since the early 1970s. Her personal papers are in the Schomburg Center for Research in Black Culture. Her biographical information is included in the various *Who's Who among Black Americans* (Northbrook, IL: Who's Who among Black Americans, 1980); *The Ebony Success Library: 1000 Successful Blacks* (Nashville: Southwestern Publishing, 1973); and Mariana Davis, *Contributions of Black Women to America* (Columbia, SC: Kenday, 1982). She is featured in several articles: Shirley Malcolm, "Increasing the Participation of Black Women in Science and Technology," Rosalyn Mitchell Patterson, "Black Women in the Biological Sciences," and Jewell Plummer Cobb, "A Life in Science: Research and Service," all in the special issue of *Sage* 6:2 (Fall 1989).

COFFEY, LILLIAN [BROOKS] (1896–1964), national supervisor of the Women's Department of the Church of God in Christ (COGIC), the highest position held by a woman in that denomination, was born in Paris, Tennessee. As a young girl, she moved to Memphis, and from there she migrated to Chicago in 1913. A devout woman, Coffey, like other COGIC women, developed a

dynamic lay ministry as she was denied ordination as an elder or minister. As an evangelist (nonordained preacher) she ministered to souls throughout Wisconsin, Ohio, Michigan, and Georgia. In 1951 she became national supervisor of the Women's Department, where she was one of the better known personalities among black women in civic and religious circles. As an ardent admirer of Mary McLeod Bethune, she too worked for the uplift of black women, and she had invited Bethune as her special guest when she was installed as supervisor of the COGIC Chicago District.

Concerned with the security and well-being of all Americans, Mother Coffey traveled thousands of miles to military bases and training centers during World War II and received a citation from the Women's Army Corps. In addition, her interest in social and welfare programs led to the establishment of the Lillian Brooks Coffey Rest Home in Detroit, dedicated as "a haven of rest" for evangelists, missionaries, and other retired COGIC women. Mother Lillian Brooks Coffey died in Chicago on June 9, 1964. More than 3,000 mourned at her final rites.

—Betty Plummer

Bibliography

Cheryl Townsend Gilkes is the best source for sociological studies on the women of the Church of God in Christ. Both of her articles are excellent sources: "The Role of Women in the Sanctified Church," *Journal of Religious Thought* 43:1 (1986) and "Together and in Harness: Women's Traditions in the Sanctified Church," *Signs* 10:41 (1985). Dr. Gilkes's article on the sanctified women in *Women & Religion in America, Volume 3, 1900–1968*, edited by Rosemary Radford Ruether and Rosemary Skinner Keller (New York: Harper & Row, 1990) is also quite helpful in understanding women's roles in a church that does not ordain women. Felton O. Best, a historian at Ohio State, is also pursuing studies on women in COGIC. Two publications of the Church of God in Christ are quite useful—*The Pioneer History of the Church of God in Christ* (Memphis: COGIC, 1975) and *History and Formative Years of the Church of God in Christ with Excerpts from the Life and Works of Its Founder—Bishop C.H. Mason* (Memphis: COGIC, 1969). Interesting information can also be found in the obituary appearing in the *Chicago Defender* (June 11, 1964).

COLEMAN, ELIZABETH (BESSIE) (1893–1926), aviatrix, barnstormer, parachutist, and activist, was born in Atlanta, Texas, on January 20, the twelfth of 13 children. Her mother, Susan Coleman, was an African American slave. Her father, George Coleman, was three-quarters Choctaw Indian and one-quarter African. While she was still a toddler, the Coleman family moved to Waxahachie, Texas, an agricultural region and trade center that produced cotton, grain, and cattle, about 30 miles south of Dallas. Here, the Coleman family made a living picking cotton. Coleman's father built a three-room house on a quarter-acre of land, but by the time Bessie was seven years old, he had returned to Choctaw

country in Oklahoma. Susan Coleman continued to raise nine children alone as she harvested the fields, picked cotton, and did domestic work to make ends meet. When the children became about eight years old, they too had to work in the cotton fields, except for Bessie, whose mother recognized that she was destined for something different in life. Bessie was assigned the responsibility of bookkeeping for the other cotton pickers in the family because of her excellent mathematical skills.

When Bessie Coleman was old enough to wash and iron for white people, her mother permitted her to save her earnings for her college education. Her mother enrolled her in the elementary division of the Colored Agricultural and Normal University, in Langston, Oklahoma. After graduating from high school, she attended Teachers College in Langston for one year, until her finances were depleted.

Sometime between 1915 and 1917, Coleman migrated to Chicago, where two brothers lived. She avoided seeking domestic and factory work, and instead, took some manicuring classes at the Burnham's School of Beauty Culture and later obtained a job as a manicurist in the White Sox Barbershop. Here, she listened to men who had returned from World War I, including her brother Johnny, discuss the war and the fledgling field of aviation. She developed an intense interest in aviation, quit her job as a manicurist, and focused her attention on becoming an aviator. She was rejected in her initial pursuit of a formal education in aviation because aviation schools conformed to Jim Crow laws, which stipulated separation between the races.

In 1920, with encouragement and financial support from two Chicago businessmen, Coleman registered in an aviation school located in France. She specialized in parachuting and stunt flying, and upon completion of her program of study on June 15, 1921, she received the first international pilot's license administered to an American aviator from the Federation Aeronautique Internationale. Armed with a license that allowed her to fly in any part of the world, she returned to the United States as a Barnstormer, a traveling aviation performer.

After Coleman received recognition as a top-flight barnstormer from predominantly white audiences and press in the northern and midwestern regional air shows, she concentrated her performances in the South toward primarily African American audiences. Many of her southern appearances were at circuses, carnivals, and county fairs on the Theatre Owners and Booking Association (TOBA) circuit that also included black theaters where documentary film footage of Coleman's achievements in Europe was shown between acts. She lectured at African American schools, churches, and recreation facilities in an attempt to encourage others to become involved in aviation, and to raise money to launch an aviation training school for African Americans in the United States.

She needed larger sums of money to establish her aviation school, but she would not compromise her racial integrity. She refused to perform at the

Waxachachie (Texas) Airport until the audience had been desegregated. She turned down the Orlando Chamber of Commerce in March 1926 when she learned that African Americans were not be allowed at her performance, so she would not agree to perform until "the Jim Crow order had been revoked and aviators had been sent up to drop placards letting the members of our Race know they could come into the field." Authorities relented. Shortly after this engagement, Coleman was hired by the Negro Welfare League in Jacksonville, Florida, to perform at their 1926 annual First of May Field Day.

Because dealers in Florida would not sell, rent, or loan an African American an airplane, Coleman had a plane flown to her in Jacksonville for the performance. During a dress rehearsal of the impending flight, Bessie Coleman was catapulted out of the airplane at about 2,000 feet when the plane somersaulted in several revolutions; she was not wearing a seatbelt or a parachute. Every bone in her body had been crushed by the impact.

In spite of her untimely death, Coleman had successfully persuaded other African Americans to pursue aviation as a profession, leaving a legacy for which African American pilots still honor her. An annual memorial service is held at Lincoln Cemetery in Southwest Chicago, during which a wreath is dropped onto her gravesite from an airplane. Today, there are engraved granite plaques next to two trees located in Atchison, Kansas, Amelia Earhart's birthplace. Each plaque is engraved with a name—one with Bessie Coleman, the other with Amelia Earhart—representing them in the International Forest of Friendship, the aviator's walk of fame, and commemorating their "exceptional contributions to aviation." In 1975, the Bessie Coleman Aviators Organization was formed. Coleman is one of two women featured in "Black Americans in Flight" a 51-foot mural by Spencer Taylor located at Lambert-St. Louis International Airport.

—Elizabeth Hadley Freydberg

Bibliography

The majority of information was gathered from personal interviews with Coleman family members, friends, and admiring aviators and from unindexed African American newspapers such as the *Chicago Defender*, *The Afro-American*, and the New York *Amsterdam News*. The Moorland-Spingarn Research Center, Howard University, has a photo of her and a copy of the magazine named after her, *Bessie Coleman Aero News* (1930). Coleman's contributions to American aviation are mentioned in "They Take to the Sky: Group of Midwest Women Follow Path Blazed by Pioneer Bessie Coleman," *Ebony* (May 1977); Marjorie Kriz, "Bessie Coleman, Aviation Pioneer," *U.S. Department of Transportation News* (n.d.); and "They Had Another Dream: Blacks Took to the Air Early," *U.S. Department of Transportation News*, reprinted from *FAA World* (January 1980). Coleman's name is mentioned in Enoch P. Waters, *American Diary: A Personal History of the Black Press* (Chicago: Path Press, 1987); "Bessie the Barnstormer," in *Sisters* (journal of the National Council of Negro Women) (Spring 1989); Valerie Moorlan, *Women Aloft* (New York: Time-Life Books, 1981); Von Hardesty and Dominick Pisano, *Black Wings: The American Black in*

Aviation (Washington, DC: National Air & Space Museum, Smithsonian Institution, 1983); Henry T. Sampson, *Blacks in Blackface: A Source Book on Early Black Musical Shows* (Metuchen, NJ: Scarecrow, 1980); and Marianna Davis, ed., *Contributions of Black Women to America* I (Columbia: Kenday, 1982). Coleman is also cited in the Smithsonian exhibit highlighting the history of blacks in aviation in the National Air and Space Museum in Washington, DC.

COLEMAN, NANNIE JUANITA (1885–?), serving with Tuskegee Institute's movable school, was the first black home demonstration agent in Alabama, which was the national leader in extension work for rural blacks. Born on August 5 in Temple, Texas, she attended and graduated from Temple City High School. She then attended Tuskegee Normal and Industrial Institute during the same time such luminaries as George Washington Carver taught agriculture. While she was a student, Booker T. Washington initiated the Jesup Agricultural Wagon donated by philanthropist Morris K. Jesup to disseminate progressive agricultural methods to isolated rural farmers.

After graduation in 1908 and with Margaret Murray Washington as a reference, Coleman taught at and served as the head of the Girl's Department of the Farmers' Improvement Society's Agricultural College established in 1906 at Ladonia, Texas. This association, founded by R.L. Smith in the 1890s, had a Women's Barnyard Auxiliary. Smith attended the annual farmers conferences at Tuskegee and affiliated his society with Tuskegee Institute.

In August 1915 Bradford Knapp, directing federal demonstration work, appointed Coleman to lead home demonstration work for black women in Alabama through increased funding from the 1914 Smith-Lever Act. Coleman moved to Tuskegee and began working with Thomas M. Campbell, who directed black extension work in coordination with the extension service at the Alabama Polytechnic Institute in Auburn.

Coleman demonstrated basic home economics projects to rural women and girls as she traveled with the movable school. She emphasized viewing the home as a business, teaching management techniques such as keeping record books of expenditures and income. Coleman told the women of money-making projects to earn extra income for their families through selling home-grown fruits and vegetables, poultry, and dairy products. She also taught them how to improve their houses to be comfortable. Practical household tasks such as cooking and canning were demonstrated to improve the quality of domestic life with nutritious meals and well-constructed clothes as well as to show potential income-earning activity, such as piecing quilts or sewing rag rugs. She showed women how to screen doors and windows, grow gardens to be self-sufficient, make soap, obtain a safe water supply, and drain wet areas to prevent insects, such as mosquitos indigenous to the region, from posing a health threat. She stressed sanitation, citizenship, hygiene, self-improvement, and enhanced self-esteem.

During World War I, Coleman used her role to aid the domestic war effort. She lectured in schools and community gatherings, persuading rural residents to increase food production to help win the war. Demonstrations were usually held in local residents' houses. Unfortunately, many rural residents were suspicious of Coleman: blacks thought she was an agent employed by whites to confiscate land, and whites believed she was hired by northern political groups to spread propaganda. In order to gain the trust of the women, Coleman selected a well-respected local woman to lead the demonstration. The participants accepted the demonstrations and learned practical skills such as making mattresses and curtains. Coleman also taught them games and showed them movies for recreation. Her work improving homes had more immediate impact than the agricultural demonstration work of male agents, which required several months for results.

Coleman was the only black home demonstration agent in the state of Alabama, even though white demonstration agents were hired for each county. Her travels throughout the state on wagon, train, and truck continued until 1917, when a second black home demonstration agent, Susan T. Whitfield, was hired to work in northern Alabama. Soon additional black agents were hired. During the 1920s Coleman served as the state black home demonstration agent to direct the work of the local black agents, a unique administrative position, since other states permitted supervision of black agents only by white state home demonstration agents. Between 1924 and 1928, Coleman was no longer employed by Tuskegee Institute, but she continued her role in the state home demonstration program. Little is known about her after the 1920s.

—Elizabeth D. Schafer

Bibliography

N. Juanita Coleman wrote of her experiences with the movable school in "Home Demonstration Work in Alabama," *Southern Workman* (September 1920): 412–414; Harry Simms and Coleman, "Movable Schools of Agriculture among Negroes in Alabama," *Alabama Polytechnic Institute Extension Service Circular* #39 (March 1920); and Coleman, "Extension Work in Agriculture and Home Economics in the State of Alabama, a Supplement to the Annual Report of the Agricultural Extension Service, Movable School for Women, for the Year Ending December 31, 1920," USDA, Records of the Federal Extension Service, Record Group 33, National Archives, which includes other significant documents about Coleman's work. Coleman's accounts are strictly professional; she does not include any personal information about herself.

Other archival sources concerning Coleman include the Alabama Extension Service Papers and Charles Coleman Thach Papers, Auburn University Archives, and Thomas Monroe Campbell Papers and Tuskegee Institute Extension Service Files, Tuskegee University Archives.

Thomas M. Campbell, *The Movable School Goes to the Negro Farmer* (New York: Ayer, 1936) does not mention Coleman by name. The *Tuskegee Student* (August 7,

1915) notes Coleman's appointment and provides some biographical data and "Lee County Has Movable School" in the October 2, 1915, issue discusses the demonstration work. See *Outlook* (March 31, 1900) and Alwyn Barr, *Black Texans: A History of Negroes in Texas 1528–1971* (Austin: Jenkins, 1973) for information about R.L. Smith and the Farmers' Improvement Society and Women's Barnyard Auxiliary. Cynthia Neverdon-Morton, *Afro-American Women of the South and the Advancement of the Race, 1895–1925* (Knoxville: University of Tennessee Press, 1989) notes Coleman's status as a high-level state extension administrator.

For the most part, Coleman has been ignored by historians of black county agents and the Tuskegee Institute Movable School. Authors refer to a female home demonstration agent, but Coleman's name is rarely cited and her publications utilized. See Gladys Baker, *The County Agent* (Chicago: University of Chicago Press, 1939); Earl W. Crosby, "Building the Country Home: The Black County Agent System, 1906–1940," PhD dissertation, Miami University (1977) and "The Roots of Black Agricultural Extension Work," *Historian* 39 (February 1977): 228–247; Felix James, "The Tuskegee Institute Movable School, 1906–1923," *Agricultural History* 45 (July 1971): 201–209; Lewis W. Jones, "The South's Negro Farm Agent," *Journal of Negro Education* 22 (Winter 1953): 38–45; and Charles W. Davis, "Early Demonstration Work in Alabama," *Alabama Review* 2 (July 1949): 176–188.

H.F. Wilson, "The Present Negro Extension Program," *Southern Workman* (October 1929): 469–472; and Clement Richardson, "Negro Farmers of Alabama: A Phase of Tuskegee's Extension Work," *Southern Workman* (July 1917): 383–390, are contemporary views. Also see government publications: J.A. Evans, "Extension Work among Negroes," USDA Department Circular 355 (1925) and O.B. Martin, "A Decade of Negro Extension Work, 1914–1924," USDA Miscellaneous Circular 72 (1926). *Agricultural Extension Work among Negroes in Alabama* began publication in October 1920 and is available at the National Agricultural Library, Beltsville, Maryland.

The Tuskegee Clipping File, available on microfilm, includes newspaper articles mentioning Coleman's work. Deborah Waldrop Austin, "Thomas Monroe Campbell and the Development of Negro Agriculture Extension Work, 1883–1956," MA thesis, Auburn University (1975) and Elizabeth Lynne Anderson, "Improving Rural Life in Alabama: The Home Demonstration Program, 1911–1972," MA thesis, Auburn University (1984) both note Coleman's unique role in demonstration work.

B.D. Mayberry, *The Role of Tuskegee University on the Origin, Growth and Development of the Negro Cooperative Extension System 1881–1990* (Tuskegee: Tuskegee University Cooperative Extension Program, 1989) and L. Albert Scipio II, *Pre-War Days at Tuskegee: Historical Essay on Tuskegee Institute (1881–1943)* (Silver Springs, MD: Roman Publications, 1987) include unidentified photographs of the movable wagon and truck and agents, possibly including Coleman. Other works on Tuskegee include Anson Phelps Stokes, *Tuskegee Institute: The First Fifty Years* (Tuskegee: Tuskegee Institute, 1931); Joseph F. Citro, "Booker T. Washington's Tuskegee Institute: Black School-Community, 1900–1915, EdD dissertation, University of Rochester (1973); Booker T. Washington, ed., *Tuskegee and Its People: Their Ideals and Achievements* (New York: Negro Universities Press, 1905; reprint edition 1969); and Max Bennett Thrasher, *Tuskegee: Its Story and Its Work* (Boston: Small, Maynard,

1901; reprint edition, New York: Ayer, 1969) which includes a chapter by Margaret Murray Washington, "What Girls Are Taught and How."

Roy V. Scott, *The Reluctant Farmer: The Rise of Agricultural Extension to 1914* (Freeport, NY: Books for Libraries Press, 1970) analyzes how farmers perceived extension workers, and Joel Schor and Cecil Harvey, *A List of References for the History of Black Americans in Agriculture, 1619–1974* (Davis: Agricultural History Center, University of California, 1975) lists additional secondary sources.

COLLINS (PRETTYMAN), KATHLEEN (1942–1988) was a multi-talented writer whose work explored the realities and ironies present in everyday life. As a trailblazer in cinema and a teacher at City College of New York, she became a role model and mentor to many younger African American women and men. Collins took her role as an artist seriously: "I'm beginning to think that real artists are basically religious figures. Real artists . . . are people who are compelled, are driven by their vision to produce creative work out of their souls. If you think of them as religious people, then they are driven by a need to enlighten man." In her work as in life, Collins's objective was to illuminate paradoxes and ultimately challenge the thinking of her viewers or readers and herself.

Kathleen Collins was born in Jersey City, New Jersey, but grew up in a place called Gouldtown. She attended Skidmore College and in 1963 received a bachelor's degree in philosophy and religion. She pursued her graduate education in France, where she received an advanced degree in French literature and cinema at Middlebury Graduate School. From 1967 to 1974, Collins worked as a film editor for various productions, including *Black Journal*.

Throughout her life Collins was passionately and profoundly involved in creative activity. She was a playwright, writer, song writer, and filmmaker. Her plays include *In the Midnight Hour*, *The Brothers*, *Remembrance*, and *Only the Sky Is Free*, which explores the life of black aviatrix Bessie Coleman. She also wrote many short stories and a novel, *Black and White Imagery*. Collins authored several screenplays: *Conversations with Julie*, *Madam Flor and Love*, *Summer Diary*, and *Women Sisters and Friends*. Collins produced two films: *The Cruz Brothers and Miss Malloy* (1980) and *Losing Ground* (1982). *The Cruz Brothers* explores the relationship between three Puerto Rican brothers and an elderly white woman as they attempt to help her realize a dream before dying. The film is an adaptation of *The Cruze Chronicle: A Novel of Adventure and Close Calls*. The central character in *Losing Ground*, Sara Rogers, an African American philosophy professor, searches for ecstasy and identity as she comes to terms with her life and destiny. At the time of her death, Collins was working on another film, *Gouldtown: A Mulatto Settlement*.

Throughout her life, Collins received numerous grants from funding agencies including the American Film Institute and the New York State Council on the Arts. She also won many awards for her work, including First Feature at the

Portuguese International Film Festival for *Losing Ground*. More than awards, however, students, friends, and associates remember Kathleen Collins Prettyman as a humanitarian striving for enlightenment through her creative energy.

—Gloria J. Gibson-Hudson

Bibliography

Gloria J. Gibson-Hudson, "The Cultural Significance of Music to the Black Independent Filmmaker," (PhD dissertation, Indiana University, 1986), analyzes the use of music in *Losing Ground*. Phyllis Klotman, *Screenplays of the African American Experience* (Bloomington: Indiana University Press, 1991), gives a brief biography of Collins's life and information about the screenplay *Losing Ground*. David Nicholson, "A Commitment to Writing a Conversation with Kathleen Collins Prettyman," *Black Film Review* 5:1 (Winter 1988–1989), is an in-depth interview with Kathleen Collins. Gloria J. Gibson-Hudson, "African American Literary Criticism as a Model for the Analysis of Films by African American Women," *Wide Angle* 13:3/4 (July/October 1991), analyzes the similarities between literary and film criticism and includes a discussion of Collins's *Losing Ground*.

COOK, CORALIE [FRANKLIN] (1861–1942), social reformer and educator, was born in Virginia, and is listed in the 1880 census as a mulatto living in Harpers Ferry, West Virginia, in a household consisting of herself and her mother, Mary C. Franklin. In Harpers Ferry, Coralie Franklin attended Storer College, graduating from the Academic Department in 1880 at age 19. Shortly thereafter, she secured a position as teacher of elocution at Storer, a position she held until around 1890. While teaching at Storer College, Coralie Franklin committed herself to the advancement of black women and children. In 1887 she began editing a column in the *Pioneer Press* of Martinsburg, West Virginia, a black newspaper edited by her brother-in-law, John Clifford. Her "Woman's Column" covered subjects varying from cleanliness and teasing children to books for the home, the girl graduate, and temperance issues. In June 1887 the Harpers Ferry chapter of the Women's Christian Temperance Union (WTCU) was organized with Coralie Franklin as president. She also served as superintendent of press for the Women's Christian Temperance Publishing Association. In March 1880 she attended the International Convention of Women's Rights, and in March 1888, she attended the Women's Jubilee, both held in Washington, DC. It was sometime in the next two years that she moved to Washington.

By June 1890 Coralie Franklin had taken up residence in Washington, occasionally writing letters to the *Pioneer Press*, and in later years maintained her relationship with Storer College as a member of the board of trustees. She continued her work for the black woman's cause in Washington, joining with Anna Julia Cooper and Mary Church Terrell in becoming a charter member of the Woman's League, founded in 1892 to promote causes dear to black women.

In 1894 the Woman's League became a national organization, and in 1896, its merger with the Federation of Women's Clubs gave birth to the National Association of Colored Women.

On August 31, 1899, Coralie Franklin married George W. Cook, a professor and future dean at Howard University. At that time she had been serving for a number of years as superintendent of the Colored Orphan Asylum of Washington. The couple had one child, George W. Cook, Jr. Only bits and pieces of information on Coralie Cook's life are available after her marriage to George Cook; her accomplishments were, no doubt, overshadowed by those of her husband.

While her husband served as dean of his department at Howard University, Coralie Cook became a member of the Washington, DC, Board of Education. At the time of George Cook's death in August 1931, Coralie Cook was described by Alaine Locke as her husband's "silent copartner. . . . For years an active and influential member of the Board of Education of the public school system of the District of Columbia." Although it is uncertain on what date Coralie Cook assumed her post, DC Board of Education correspondence indicates she was serving by 1916. She also became a member of the College Alumnae Club of Washington, DC, and joined the National Association for the Advancement of Colored People (NAACP), and participated in the organized actions against Jim Crow laws. In 1915 she attended a symposium on women's suffrage, where she delivered her address entitled "Votes for Mothers," which was published in the August 1915 issue of *The Crisis*.

After her husband's death, Coralie Cook apparently devoted much time to her hobby of writing fiction. A December 29, 1932, letter to Cook from the Palmer Photoplay Corporation in Hollywood, California, indicates that she had submitted for consideration a sample of her writing for enrollment in a writing course. In her letter to the corporation, she had apparently indicated her interest in writing a play about the pre–Civil War South. What came of this is not known.

Coralie Franklin Cook died in Washington, DC, on September 16, 1941, after a long illness. Her lifetime dedication as an educator and to the struggle for progress for black women embodies the directive she issued to "all lovers of fair play . . . to be actively engaged in some definite work on behalf of [those] folks who number only one in ten in the country and whose future is still insecure in the face of . . . bitter antagonism" to achieve the end of "Universal Brotherhood."

—Rama Ramakrishna

Bibliography

Some of the information in this article comes from the Cook Family Papers at Howard University's Moorland-Springarn Center and District of Columbia Board of Education records. Correspondence from Cook can be found in the NAACP Papers, Washington, DC, branch, Manuscript Division, Library of Congress; the Mary Church Terrell Papers, Manuscript Division, Library of Congress; and the W.E.B. Du

Bois Papers, University of Massachusetts, Amherst. The bulk of the references to materials containing information on Coralie Cook comes from a computerized index of newspapers and public documents compiled by the Historical Research Team at Harpers Ferry National Historical Park in Harpers Ferry, West Virginia. Additional information is available in Sharon Harley's, "Black Women in the District of Columbia and the Fight for Racial and Sexual Equality, 1890–1940," in *Women in the District of Columbia: A Contribution to Their History* (Washington, DC: DC International Women's Year Coordinating Committee, 1977). This article also cites Cook's only major published work, "Votes for Mothers," *The Crisis* 10:4 (August 1915): 7–8.

COOPER, ANNA J. [HAYWOOD] (1858–1964), educator, administrator, and social reformer, was born into slavery in Raleigh, North Carolina. Of mixed parentage as the daughter of Hannah (Stanley) Haywood, the slave hired out by her master as a nurse, Anna Julia Haywood decided at an early age that by becoming an educator she could best help her people. Around 1868 she benefited from the receipt of a scholarship to St. Augustine's Normal School and Collegiate Institute, a school supported by the Protestant Episcopal church. There she spent 14 years, fought to gain access to the Latin and Greek classes reserved for men, and graduated in 1877. A few years later she met and married the Reverend A.C. Cooper at St. Augustine's, where each was an instructor. After his death in 1881 she left Raleigh, and began the second phase of her education at Oberlin College in Ohio.

Anna Cooper joined a few African American women at Oberlin in 1881. She graduated with Mary Eliza Church (Terrell) and Ida A. Gibbs (Hunt)—the three became the first African American women to graduate with bachelor of arts degrees from an American college, and the only African American female members of the class of 1884. She later returned to Oberlin for a master of arts degree in Mathematics, which she received in 1887.

After college, Cooper returned to St. Augustine to teach, but the administration would not allow her to teach classical subjects. She, therefore, turned down the position and taught at Wilberforce University for a year before returning to St. Augustine to teach Latin and Greek under a new administration. There she became active in the North Carolina Teacher's Association and organized the community outreach program at St. Augustine's. Her outspoken leadership, however, led to the failure to get her teaching contract renewed despite excellent evaluations. She accepted a teaching position in the Preparatory Department of Washington, DC, Colored High School (known as the M Street School).

Anna Cooper is most known for her work in the educational arena initially with the public school system and later with a privately supported institution. In Washington, Anna Cooper became part of a cadre of African American educators, many of whom sacrificed their salaries in order to educate African American youth. During her tenure at the school as its principal from 1902 to 1906, she aligned herself with the Du Boisian side of a national struggle over what should be the focus of African American schools, intellectual or industrial/ practical knowledge. During this time, white philanthropy supported African American schools, many of which had white presidents and white-dominated boards. The vast majority of those presidents and boards unconditionally supported the Booker T. Washington philosophy. Cooper was constantly pressured by the school's board to accommodate the school's curriculum to reflect a Washingtonian analysis and acknowledge, rather than challenge, her white superiors. She left the M Street School in 1906, took a position at Lincoln Institute in Missouri, and, with the help of philanthropic whites and African American clergy, contributed to the development and organization of Frelinghuysen University, an interdenominational Bible college, on April 27, 1906. In 1910 she returned to the M Street School as a teacher.

During her years at the M Street School and before her Frelinghuysen years, Cooper was a trailblazer on all fronts representing her race and gender. Cooper wrote *A Voice from the South*, a feminist manifesto against the sexism of African American men and a plea for their help in placing women on an equal plane in the pursuit for racial and social justice. Cooper also worked through a variety of organizations to achieve this goal. She was a leader in the National Association of Colored Women, a speaker at feminist and educational conferences held in the United States, the only female member of the American Negro Academy (the "black think tank" of its day) and a participant at the Pan-African Conference in 1900 in London, England. In London, she presented her paper "Address to the Nations," calling for self-determination for African Americans and an end to colonialism in Africa and to apartheid in South Africa. Her participation was unique in that women then did not play dominant roles in national or international organizations. She served as a member of the executive committee of the Pan-African Congress Committee along with such other Pan-Africanists as Henry Sylvester Williams and W.E.B Du Bois. In addition to these national and international activities, Cooper worked to secure the benefits of progressive reform for the community. As a founder of the independent Colored Young Women's Christian Association, Cooper functioned as a mentor for young women. She served as a trustee of the Colored Settlement House in Washington, DC, and director of the summer programs.

During this time, she used herself as a model of achievement. She began work on her PhD in 1914 at Columbia University, battling time and financial contraints. Due to residency requirements for the doctorate and her full-time teaching load, Cooper transferred to the University of Paris. At the Sorbonne in 1925, she defended her thesis on French policies during slavery. Although it took her a decade to achieve, Cooper earned her PhD in 1925.

While teaching and studying, Cooper continued to shape Frelinghuysen. By 1919 the college had expanded to incorporate a college of liberal arts, a commercial college, a school of theology, a school of law, a pharmaceutical school, and a school of useful arts. Frelinghuysen University languished from a lack of financial support. Anna Cooper assumed the presidency of the university on June 15, 1930, at age 72, during the beginning of the Great Depression. After several moves, Cooper allowed her home at 201 T Street, NW, in Washington, DC, to become the final location of the school. Continued financial problems, licensing and accreditation changes, and attrition rates challenged the university's existence. She remained active in the school's affairs, but her last official report as registrar of the modified Frelinghuysen Group of Schools for Colored Working People was published in 1950.

Anna Julia Cooper's remaining years were spent raising her five foster children. She lived until February 27, 1964, and died in Washington, DC, at age 105. Her long life embodied her credo: "Education for Service."

—Debra Calhoun and Glenda Elizabeth Gilmore

Bibliography

The Anna Julia Cooper Papers are located in the Moorland-Spingarn Research Center, Howard University, Washington, DC. Cooper's papers are in the Manuscript Division of the Moorland-Spingarn Research Center. Some information can also be found in the Oberlin College Alumnae Records, Archives, Oberlin College. The most complete published work on Anna Julia Cooper is Louise Daniel Hutchinson's *Anna J. Cooper: A Voice from the South* (Washington: Smithsonian Institution Press, 1981). Mary Helen Washington has provided an excellent introduction to Cooper's life and work in her forward to the 1988 Oxford University press reprint edition of *A Voice from the South*. Also valuable are Sharon Harley, "Anna J. Cooper: A Voice for Black Women," in *The Afro-American Woman: Struggles and Images*, edited by Harley and Rosalyn Terborg-Penn (Port Washington, NY: Kennikat Press, 1968); Melinda Chateauvert, "The Third Step: Anna Julia Cooper and Black Education in the District of Columbia, 1910–1960," reprinted in Darlene Hine et al. eds., *Black Women in United States History* 5 (Brooklyn: Carlson, 1990), pp. 261–276; and Nancy Elizabeth Fitch, "Anna J. Cooper, Ph.D.: Community Leader and Educator" (June 1984), copy in Mary McLeod Bethune Historical Archives and Black Women's History Museum, Washington, DC.

Biographical sketches of Cooper are included in Sylvia G.L. Dannett, ed., *Profiles of Negro Womanhood* (Yonkers, NY: Educational Heritage Press, 1964); *Who's Who in the South and the Southwest* (Chicago: Marquis, 1950); and Lawson Andrew Scruggs, *Women of Distinction* (Raleigh, NC: Edwards and Broughton, 1900).

Cooper's major work is *A Voice from the South, by a Black Woman of the South* (Xenia, OH: Aldine Printing House, 1892), reprint edition, with introduction by Mary Helen Washington (New York: Oxford University Press, 1988). She wrote four privately printed pamphlets: *Legislative Measures Concerning Slavery in the United States; Personal Collections of the Grimke Family and the Life and Writings of Charlotte Forten Grimke; The Third Step: An Autobiography;* and *Equality of Races and the Democratic Movement.* Cooper was also the author of *The Social Settlement: What It Is, and What It Does* (Washington: Murray Brothers Press, 1913). She edited *The Southland,* a North Carolina periodical, and published an article in *The Crisis,* entitled "Angry Saxons and Negro Education" (November 1913).

COPPIN, FANNIE JACKSON (1837–1913) was born a slave in Washington, DC. Information concerning her early childhood is sketchy and inconclusive. Little is known of her mother, Lucy, who was the only one of six children not bought or freed by Jackson's successful mulatto grandfather John Orr of Washington. According to Jackson's autobiography in 1913, her mother's freedom was not purchased due to circumstances surrounding Jackson's birth. Her father's identity is unknown. A devoted aunt, Sarah Orr Clark, worked as a domestic for years to save the $250 needed to purchase Jackson's freedom.

Jackson moved to live with relatives in New Bedford, Massachusetts, and in 1851 she and her relatives moved to Newport, Rhode Island. In Newport, Jackson secured a position as a domestic in the home of George Henry Calvert, great-grandson of Lord Baltimore, settler of Maryland. Calvert's wife, Mary Stuart, was a descendant of Mary, Queen of Scots. With the money earned at the Calvert's, Jackson was able to hire a tutor for one hour a day for three days a week. Near the end of her six-year stay with the Calverts, she briefly attended the segregated public schools of Newport. In 1859 Jackson enrolled in the Rhode Island State Normal School in Bristol. In addition to the Normal course, Jackson studied French privately.

In 1860 Jackson enrolled in the Ladies Department of Oberlin College in Ohio with the financial assistance from her aunt Sarah Clark, a scholarship from Bishop Daniel Payne of the African Methodist Episcopal (AME) church and scholarship aid from Oberlin. Jackson also worked while a student at Oberlin. By 1861 Jackson transferred into the Collegiate Department at Oberlin and graduated in 1865 with a BA degree, the second African American woman to do so. Jackson distinguished herself at Oberlin and was active in all facets of student life. Her outstanding academic achievements resulted in Jackson being chosen as the first black student teacher of the Preparatory Department at Oberlin. At commencement she was chosen class poet.

After graduating from Oberlin in 1865, Jackson was appointed principal of the Female Department of the prestigious Institute for Colored Youth (ICY) in Philadelphia, a classical high school founded by the Society of Friends in 1837. ICY included a preparatory department, girls and boys high school departments, and a teacher training course. By 1869 Jackson was appointed principal of the entire school. She spent her entire career in this capacity until she retired 1902. Jackson enjoyed the reputation of being an outstanding teacher and an important leader within the Philadelphia black community. ICY was located within the heart of the Philadelphia black community, near the historic Mother Bethel AME Church.

In 1881 at the age of 44, Jackson married Levi Jenkins Coppin, an AME minister at least 15 years her junior. Her devotion to ICY was so great that she remained as principal throughout her marriage. In the first three years of her marriage, Levi Coppin pastored a church in Baltimore and commuted to Philadelphia. When it became apparent that Fanny Coppin would not leave the

ICY, he transferred to a smaller church in Philadelphia in 1884. After her marriage, Coppin joined the AME church. She was elected president of the local Women's MITE Missionary Society and later became national president of the Women's Home and Foreign Missionary Society of the AME church. In 1888 she represented the organization at the Centenary of Missions Conference in London. Her husband was appointed in 1888 editor of the AME *Review*, a prestigious position within the AME church. He maintained this position until 1896, when he was appointed senior pastor of Mother Bethel, where he remained until 1900, at which point he was elected bishop of the 14th Episcopal District in South Africa. After her retirement from ICY in 1902, Fanny Jackson Coppin accompanied Bishop Coppin to Capetown, South Africa. They returned to Philadelphia in the spring of 1904. Bishop Coppin was then appointed to the 7th Episcopal District, which encompassed South Carolina and Alabama. Fanny Coppin traveled some with her husband; however, the South African trip severely affected her health. By 1905 Coppin was so physically weak that the remaining eight years of her life were spent primarily confined to her Philadelphia home, where she died on January 21, 1913.

—Linda M. Perkins

Bibliography

Published materials on Coppin include Fanny Jackson Coppin, *Reminiscences of School Life, and Hints on Teaching* (Philadelphia: AME Book Concern, 1913); Levi Jenkins Coppin, *Unwritten History* (New York: Negro Universities Press, 1968, reprint edition); Linda M. Perkins, *Fanny Jackson Coppin and the Institute for Colored Youth, 1865–1902* (New York: Garland, 1987); Biographical entries include Dorothy Drinkard-Hawshawe, "Fannie Jackson Coppin," in *Dictionary of American Negro Biography*, edited by Rayford W. Logan and Michael Winston (New York: Norton, 1982), pp. 130–132; Leslie H. Fishel, Jr., "Fanny Jackson Coppin," in *Notable American Women 1607–1950* 1 (Cambridge: Harvard University Press, 1971), pp. 383–384.

Primary documents concerning Fanny Jackson Coppin's Oberlin years are available in the Oberlin College Archives. Documents of her years as principal at the Institute for Colored Youth are available at the Friend's Historical Library, Swarthmore College. The *Christian Recorder* carried articles by and about Coppin's community, school, and church activities from 1865 until her death in 1913.

COX, IDA [PRATHER] (1896–1967) (a.k.a. Velma Bradley/Kate Lewis/Julia Powers/Julius Powers/Jane Smith), billed as "the sepia Mae West" during the height of her career as a performer and a composer, and also known as the "Uncrowned Queen of the Blues," was born Ida Prather on February 25 in Toccoa, Georgia. She was raised in Cedartown, Georgia, where she sang in the choir of the local African Methodist Episcopal (AME) church. Cox ran away from home at age 14 and worked on the theater circuits. She toured with F.S.

Wolcott's Rabbit Foot Minstrels and the Silas Green from New Orleans Show during her teens. She was also a featured artist on the East Coast vaudeville circuit during the 1920s. Ida Cox also frequently worked with the King Oliver Band at the Plantation Club in Chicago during this period as well as playing the Grand Theater in Chicago during 1929. She also toured with her own road show, "Raisin' Cain," which played in theaters across the country from 1929 into the early 1930s. Another Ida Cox show that toured the country during the 1930s and 1940s was *Darktown Scandals*. Cox also worked with Bessie Smith in *Fan Waves Revue* at the Apollo Theater in Harlem in 1934. In the early 1940s, Cox toured the South with the Billie Pierce Revue and appeared in a film in 1945.

Cox was the first of the "classic" blues singers to record on the Paramount label, in June 1923, six months prior to Gertrude "Ma" Rainey's first Paramount recording. In addition to performing, Cox was also a prolific composer. She is credited with having written "Fogeyism," "Mean Papa Turn in Your Key," "Western Union Blues," and "Tree Top Tall Papa."

From 1945 until 1949 Ida Cox dropped out of the music scene and settled in Buffalo, New York. In 1949 she moved to Knoxville, Tennessee, where she owned a mansion and raised her only child, a daughter. Cox was known to have a keen business sense. She managed her own road shows, handling all accounting matters and payroll herself. She had a reputation for integrity, and performers gladly worked for her because they knew they could count on being paid—which was often not the case with other managers. In 1950 she played the Oshkosh Theater in Wisconsin, and in 1961 she made her final recording, *Blues for Rampart Street*, with the Coleman Hawkins Quintet on the Riverside label.

Ida Cox was married twice (a third marriage is unconfirmed). Her first marriage was to Adler Cox in the early 1920s. She later married Jesse Crump, a pianist who was her accompanist during a performance in Indianapolis. Crump also composed for Cox. Ida Cox died a wealthy woman on November 10, 1967, in Knoxville, Tennessee.

—Adrianne Andrews

Bibliography

Harris, Daphne Duval. *Black Pearls: Blues Queens of the 1920's*. New Brunswick: Rutgers University Press, 1988.

Harris, Sheldon. *Blues Who's Who: A Biographical Dictionary of Blues Singers*. New Rochelle, NY: Arlington House, 1979.

Lieb, Sandra. *Mother of the Blues: A Study of Ma Rainey*. Amherst: University of Massachusetts Press, 1981.

Oliver, Paul. *The Story of the Blues*. Philadelphia: Chilton, 1969.

Southern, Eileen. *The Greenwood Encyclopedia of Black Music: Biographical Dictionary of Afro-American and African Musicians*. Westport, CT: Greenwood Press, 1982.

Stewart-Baxter, Dexter. *Ma Rainey and the Classic Blues Singers*. New York: Stein and Day, 1970.

CRAFT, ELLEN [SMITH] (1826–1891) and her husband, William, were fugitive slaves whose daring escape from the Deep South brought them celebrity status as they toured the antislavery circuit. Their narrative, *Running a Thousand Miles for Freedom, or the Escape of William and Ellen Craft from Slavery*, told the story of their escape from Georgia. Oftentimes overshadowed by her husband, Ellen Craft's contributions toward their escape and her later work in aiding and educating runaway slaves cannot be minimized.

Ellen Craft was born in Clinton, Georgia, to a house servant, Maria Smith, and her master, Major James Smith, one of the wealthiest men in Georgia. Being the master's daughter brought no benefits to Ellen Craft, who was treated coldly by her father and cruelly by his wife. In 1837 Craft was given as a personal maid to her half-sister, Eliza, on her wedding day.

As Georgia law prohibited teaching slaves to read or write, Ellen Craft developed her talent as a seamstress and was rewarded for her work with a one-room cabin of her own behind her master's home in Macon, Georgia. It was here that Ellen Craft met the young slave and carpenter William Craft. In 1846 they were permitted to marry, but, like most slave marriages, it was done without legal or religious formality. Their masters merely permitted them to live together. After two years they accumulated what savings they could and devised a plan to run away.

Her talent as a seamstress worked well in preparing their disguise. Ellen Craft, who was light enough to pass for white, outfitted herself as a wealthy, yet sickly young gentleman named William Johnson, while William Craft, who was darker, posed as her slave. To mask her sex Ellen Craft fashioned a poultice to conceal her face and wore green eyeglasses. To mask her illiteracy she wore her right arm in a sling so she could excuse herself from giving a signature and allow her husband to sign when necessary.

Choosing the holiday season when discipline was lax and their absence would not quickly be noticed, the Crafts escaped on December 21, 1848. They traveled first on the railroad to Savannah, Georgia. There they boarded a steamer for Charleston, South Carolina, from where they traveled by boat to Wilmington, North Carolina and finally boarded a train for Philadelphia.

They arrived in Philadelphia on December 25, 1848, where they met black abolitionist William Wells Brown, who was so impressed with their 1,000-mile trek to freedom that he encouraged them to accompany him on an antislavery speaking tour. The Crafts spent the next year in Boston addressing abolitionist meetings, and then they embarked on a six-month speaking tour in Scotland and England. When the tour ended they returned to Boston, and on December 6, 1850, they were legally married.

Notoriety surrounding their escape attracted the attention of Ellen Craft's former master who hired slavehunters to return the pair to Georgia. Using the Fugitive Slave Law, two agents were dispatched with arrest warrants, forcing the Crafts into hiding. Extreme resistance and threatened violence forced the slavehunters to withdraw from the chase, and the Crafts decided to leave for England.

The Crafts spent 19 years in England, where they were received into the finest social circles. Settling in a small village just outside London, the Crafts were educated, started a family, and toured the antislavery circuit. Publishing their narrative in 1860, William Craft supported their family of five children as a lecturer while Ellen Craft divided her time between raising her children and working with the antislavery movement. With the changing social climate following the Civil War, the Crafts decided to return to the United States in 1879.

The Crafts settled first in South Carolina, where they leased a plantation. Here Ellen Craft opened a school to educate newly freed slaves, teaching children during the day and adults in the evening. She taught not only reading and writing but personal hygiene and housekeeping as well. The Crafts were driven out when the Ku Klux Klan burned their plantation. They moved near to Savannah, Georgia, where they bought Woodville, the only plantation in the area owned by African Americans, and it provided the only school for former slaves. From 1872 to 1890 Ellen Craft ran the plantation and continued teaching while her husband went on a lecture tour. In 1890 the Crafts left Woodville for Charleston, South Carolina, to live with their daughter's family. Ellen Craft died the following year in 1891 and was buried at Woodville.

—Thea Gallo Becker

Bibliography

Blockson, Charles G. *The Underground Railroad.* New York: Prentice-Hall, 1987. An excerpted collection of slave narratives, grouped together by states. An excellent, brief treatment of the Crafts.

Bontemps, Arna. *Great Slave Narratives.* Boston: Beacon Press, 1969. Contains Ellen and William Craft's narrative, *Running a Thousand Miles for Freedom, or the Escape of William and Ellen Craft from Slavery,* in its entirety, originally published in London in 1860. The first source to consult.

Daniel, John. *In Freedoms' Birthplace, A Study of the Boston Negroes.* Boston: Houghton Mifflin, 1914. New York: Johnson Reprint Corporation, 1968.

Horton, James Oliver, and Lois E. Horton. *Black Bostonians: Family Life and Community Struggle in the Antebellum North.* New York: Holmes & Meier, 1979. Outlines an unsuccessful attempt by slavehunters to return the Crafts from Massachusetts to their masters.

Sterling, Dorothy. *Black Foremothers: Three Lives.* New York: Feminist Press, 1979. Craft is one of three women featured; includes several photographs of Ellen and William Craft. Full of valuable information.

Sterling, Dorothy. *We Are Your Sisters: Black Women in the Nineteenth Century.* New York: Norton, 1984. Highlights the last stage of the Crafts' escape and includes an illustration of Craft in her escape outfit.

CRAFT, JUANITA (1902–1985) was a social reformer and activist whose efforts in the civil rights movement contributed to opening long-denied political, educational and socioeconomic opportunities to African Americans and other minority groups. Craft helped organize 182 chapters of the NAACP in Texas, was involved in numerous demonstrations and sit-ins, and during her later years, was an elected government official. She was the recipient of numerous awards and honors attesting to her years of dedicated service to others.

Born February 9, Juanita Jewel Craft was the only child of schoolteacher parents in Round Rock, Texas, 15 miles outside of Austin. Craft's father provided her elementary instruction. She then attended Anderson High School in Austin. Following her mother's death in 1918, Craft joined her father in Columbus, Texas, where she graduated from high school.

For two years Craft studied sewing, millinery, and business at the predecessor industrial school of Prairie View Agricultural and Mechanical University. Transferring to Samuel Houston College in Austin, Craft received a teaching certificate for the second grade, which she used for one year. In 1925 Craft moved to Dallas, where she worked as a hotel bell maid, and later, a dressmaker.

In 1935 Craft joined the NAACP, becoming a life member and attending all the conventions from 1944 until her death. Craft became instrumental in helping the organization open branches throughout Texas. Traveling intrastate by railroad, Craft would ride in cars designated for white people only and refuse to give up her seat. Craft also involved herself with the NAACP's Youth Department, seeking to instill pride, self-worth, and a hopeful purpose for the future in the young.

In an effort to open equal educational opportunities for African Americans, Craft joined demonstrations against the University of Texas at Austin, which resulted in the case of *Sweatt* vs. *Painter* (1950) and the admission of minorities to the university. In 1955 Craft assisted in filing a similar lawsuit against North Texas State University, again with successful results. Once admissions for minorities had been won, Craft worked to help prepare youths for higher education by opening a dropout preparation program in Dallas.

Craft first married in 1922, but separated from her husband three years later. In 1938 Craft remarried. Never having a job that paid a steady salary Craft lived modestly following her husband's death in 1950 on her social security benefits and by selling handmade arts and crafts. From 1975 to 1979 Craft served on the Dallas City Council, working especially to care for the needs and improve the status of Hispanic Americans and Native Americans.

Craft also served as a delegate to the White House Conference on Children and Youth, as a member of the Governor's Human Relations Committee, as a board member of the National Conference of Christians and Jews, and worked with the Urban League. Craft's involvement in numerous civic organizations dedicated to securing the rights and improving the quality of life of minorities brought her several invitations to the White House. In 1972 Dallas honored Craft with a park and recreation center in her name. She died in 1985.

—Thea Gallo Becker

Bibliography

Information about Craft's work with the NAACP can be found in the NAACP Papers, Manuscript Division, Library of Congress. Several local activities are covered in the Dallas newspapers. The best source is in the Black Women Oral History Project, Volume 3, edited by Ruth Edmonds Hill (Westport, CT: Meckler, 1991), which contains a lengthy interview with Craft by Mrs. Dorothy R. Robinson on January 20, 1977. This autobiographical memoir provides invaluable information and insights into Craft's life and career. Her achievements are also included in *Finder's Guide to the Texas Women: Celebration*, edited by Ruthe Winegarten (Denton, TX: Texas Woman's University Library, 1984), which is a concise summary of the highlights of Craft's life and career.

CRAIG, ELLEN [WALKER] (b. 1906), affectionately called Aunt Dolly or Mother Craig by those who know her, was the first black female elected mayor in the United States. Born June 5 in Franklin County, Ohio, she moved at the age of three months to Urbancrest, Ohio, where she became part of the community. Craig was the sixth of 11 children born to her mother, who died when Ellen was 11 years old. When her father remarried, three more siblings came into the family. Educated in Urbancrest and Columbus public schools, Ellen Walker married in 1923 at age 17 and built a stable commitment with her husband, James H. Craig. She gave birth to two children, James P. Craig and Esterleen Moore. She cared for those needing help in the community; her home was always open. She had a "God's Drawer," a drawer in her china cabinet in which she and her husband kept money for the needy. Every pay period something was put into the drawer, and whenever a family was burned out or someone lost his job "God's Drawer" was opened.

She lived the Christian principles that were instilled in her by her parents, both church deacons. Her mother served as Sunday school teacher and her father as director of the men's chorus at Union Baptist Church in Urbancrest. After her mother passed away, it was up to her father to raise and care for the children. He taught her that the world owes you nothing; you work for what you get. Faith, family, and hard work served as foundation blocks for her life. She did not graduate from high school until in her thirties. In 1953, a bout with cancer tested her faith. Her recovery strengthened her courage. Her marriage, which spanned over half a century, ended with the death of her husband. Again she endured.

As a former domestic worker, Craig's achievements demonstrated her commitment to Urbancrest and her dynamic leadership skills. She served on the Urbancrest City Council for 12 years prior to becoming mayor. She also prepared herself by serving on the board of trustees on the United Community Council, as chairperson of the board for the Manpower Advising Council, and as the first president of Columbus Metropolitan Area Community Action Organization (CMACAO) Federal Credit Union. Her list of accomplishments includes: member of Mid-Ohio Regional Planning Commission, Franklin County Mayor's Council, Black Women's Leadership Council, Ohio Black Politician's Assembly, Central Ohio Mayor's Council, State of Ohio Mayor's Council, CETA (Community Employment and Training Administration), and Urbancrest Community Recreation Board. Mayor Craig has been rewarded for her achievements, including: the Baptist Church Humanity Award, by CMACAO in 1972; the Outstanding Achievement Award by the Federation of Consumers Council in 1974; Ellen Walker Craig Day, proclaimed by Ohio governor John Gilligan in 1974; the Humanitarian Award, by the Ohio Black Politicians Assembly in 1974; the Service to Mankind Award, by Grove City Sertoma Club in 1975; Ellen Walker Craig Day, by the city of Springfield, Ohio, in 1975; the Merit Award, by the Affiliate Contractors of America in 1975; and the Mayor's Medal, by the city of Columbus, Ohio, and Mayor Tom Moody in 1978.

With all the stresses and tedium of politics behind, Craig now relaxes and enjoys retirement in her home in the village of Urbancrest, Ohio, a town four miles southeast of Columbus with approximately 730 citizens, including a very special one, herself.

—Mary Ann Williams

Bibliography

Much of the information was gathered in interviews with Mayor Craig over several years by Mary Ann Williams. Biographical information can be obtained through the governor's office, state of Ohio, and in featured articles in the press. Her biographical information can be found in William Matney, ed., *Who's Who among Black Americans* (Lake Forest, IL: Ann Krouse Publishing, 1980); and *Profiles of Black Mayors* (Chicago: Johnson Publishing, 1977).

CUNEY HARE, MAUD (1874–1936), playwright, folklorist, pianist, and author, was born in Galveston, Texas, and started life in a family of privilege. Her father, Norris Wright Cuney, was a leading Reconstruction Republican in Texas. Her mother, Adelina (Dowdy) Cuney, a music teacher, encouraged interest in music and the arts. Maud Cuney attended the public schools, graduating from Central High School in Galveston. She pursued her musical education at Boston's New England Conservatory, where she fought racial discrimination to stay in the dormitory. She also received private lessons from Emil Ludwig, a pupil of Rubenstein, and Edwin Klare, a pupil of Liszt.

She returned to Texas to become the director of music at the Deaf, Dumb, and Blind Institute of Texas, and Prairie View State College. Her study in Boston was influential in prompting her father to establish three free night schools in Galveston in 1893.

She returned to Boston in 1906 to marry William P. Hare, a member of a well-known elite Boston family. They established a home, Sunnyside, in Squantum, Massachusetts, which became a frequent visiting place for prominent black intellectuals. From this central point, Maud Cuney Hare branched out to write and to travel. In 1913 she published a laudatory biography of her father, *Norris Wright Cuney: A Tribune of the Black People*. In 1918 her anthology of poetry, *The Message of the Trees*, began with an introduction by her good friend William Stanley Braithwaite. She contributed articles to *Musical Observer*, the *Christian Science Monitor*, *Musical Quarterly*, and other periodicals catering to the musical public. She also edited a column for *The Crisis* for her close friend W.E.B. Du Bois. During the 1920s she worked with the Little Theatre movement, frequently corresponding with Du Bois for his advice. She wrote plays for the black community, the best known being, *Antar, Negro Poet of Arabia* (1924).

Her interests combined with her travels to such foreign countries as Mexico, the Virgin Islands, Puerto Rico, Cuba, and to areas of the United States with peculiar styles of music from the rural South and New Orleans. She believed that music embodied national characteristics in the form of expression, thus she collected songs from the countries and regions she visited. The first to bring Creole music to the American public, Cuney Hare's music was published by Carl Fischer and Company of New York City as *Creole Songs*. She wrote about African musical instruments and the secular and religious folk songs from her own people and those from the various countries she visited. During her trips, she collected photographs of people and instruments, information that has been invaluable to musicologists. She likewise wrote biographical sketches of prominent black musicians such as Robert Cole, Rosamond Johnson, Abbie Mitchell, Harriet Gibbs Marshall, E. Azalia Hackley, and Samuel Coleridge-Taylor. As a musical folklorist, Cuney Hare not only studied these musical styles but also brought them to the public as a concert and lecture pianist. She appeared with the noted baritone William Howard Richardson. A song recital in Boston was accompanied by a viola player, Arthur Fiedler, and Cuney-Hare as pianist.

She died of cancer in 1936 after completion of her book *Negro Musicians and Their Music* (1936).

—Kelle S. Taha

Bibliography

The information on the career of Maud Cuney Hare can be found in the various publications of her work, especially in her book *Negro Musicians and Their Music* (New York: Da Capo Press, 1936), in which Clarence Cameron White's "Introduction" contains biographical information on Cuney Hare. A limited biographical sketch is included in Rayford Logan's *Dictionary of Negro Biography* (New York: Norton, 1983), p. 152. She is also featured in Ruthe Winegarten's *Finder's Guide to the Texas Women:*

A Celebration of History Exhibit Archives (Denton, TX: Texas Woman's University, 1984), pp. 45–46; and *Texas Women: A Pictorial History from Indians to Astronauts* (Austin: Eakin Press, 1986), p. 80. Her articles are cited in Dorothy Porter, compiler, *Dictionary Catalog of the Jesse E. Moorland Collection of Negro Life and History* (Washington, DC: Howard University, 1970). Her activities and final illness are well documented in her correspondence with W.E.B. Du Bois in the Du Bois Papers, University of Massachusetts, Amherst.

D

DANDRIDGE, DOROTHY (1922–1965), vocalist, actress, and dancer, was born November 9 in Cleveland, Ohio, to Ruby and Cyril Dandridge. Her mother, an actress who continued to pursue her own career in films, stage, and television, started her daughter's career at age five touring vaudeville with her sister, Vivian, billed as the Wonder Children. Definitely a family affair, Dorothy Jean Dandridge was accompanied at the piano by their aunt, Geneva Williams. The children sang, danced, did acrobatics, and performed skits written by their mother. Etta Jones later joined the sisters, and the trio became known as the Dandridge Sisters. The Sisters performed with such renowned orchestras as those of Cab Calloway, Duke Ellington, and Jimmie Lunceford. Dandridge had gone solo by age 16, and was performing as a vocalist in nightclubs, including the celebrated Cotton Club in Harlem.

Dandridge's film career began at age 15 in an appearance with the Marx Brothers in A Day at the Races (1937); during the early 1940s she was cast in several "soundies," or "photovisions," precursors to today's music videos. Some of the "soundies" titles in which Dandridge appeared were "Yes Indeed," "Sing for My Supper," "Jungle Jig," "Easy Street," "Moo Cow Boogie," and "Paper Doll."

Although she possessed the prerequisites to achieve dramatic film stardom with her physical beauty and acting experience and ability, she nevertheless was cast in stereotypical black roles in feature films such as a maid in Lady from Louisiana (1941) starring John Wayne, a native in Bahama Passage (1942), Drums of the Congo (1942), and Jungle Queen (1946). Dandridge (as well as other notable African American entertainers) provided the specialty acts in 1940s films, including Sun Valley Serenade (1941) with the Nicholas Brothers and The Hit Parade of 1943 (1943) with Count Basie. Dandridge's early dramatic film endeavors consisted of lightweight fare such as Flamingo (1947), in which she starred with Herbert Jeffrey; Four Shall Die (1946); The Harlem Globetrotters (1951); Tarzan's Peril (1951); and Remains to Be Seen (1953).

During the early 1950s, Dandridge's film career appeared to be on the upswing beginning with her starring role as a schoolteacher in Bright Road (1953) with Harry Belafonte. Dandridge received critical acclaim for her portrayal of Carmen in the film Carmen Jones (1954), which propelled her to stardom. Newsweek magazine compared her performance in Bright Road with that of Carmen and concluded that "the range between the two parts suggests that she is one of the outstanding dramatic actresses of the screen." While a Time magazine critic wrote, "Actress Dandridge employs to perfection the method of coquette: by never giving more than she has to, she hints that she has more than she has given—and sometimes even more than she really has to give." This film was loosely based on Bizet's nineteenth-century opera, which was based on a work written by French novelist Prosper Merimee, about a Spanish Gypsy peasant girl (Carmen) who works in a tobacco factory in Seville, Spain. The setting for *Carmen Jones*, featuring an all-black cast, was changed to a parachute factory in Jacksonville, Florida, during 1943, with Dandridge portraying a captivating African American. Dandridge's performance won her an Academy Award nomination for Best Actress, making her the first African American woman to achieve this honor. She became the first African American woman to appear on the cover of *Life* magazine. As a result, she signed a three-year film contract with Darryl F. Zanuck, then head of 20th Century–Fox Studios, that guaranteed her star billing for one film a year at $75,000 per film.

The studio vacillated in their selection of film properties befitting Dandridge's talent because they lacked the commitment to cast her in roles that deviated from the archetypical stereotypes of African American women as licentious sexual beings. Her next several films displayed this reality. Dandridge starred with James Mason, Joan Fontaine, John Justin, and Harry Belefonte. Although the film *Island in the Sun* (1957) was supposed to present a romantic relationship between the characters of Dandridge and John Justin (the first black actress to co-star in a film with a white man as his romantic interest), the producers instead presented an ambiguous portrayal of their interracial relationship. This film was succeeded by *The Decks Ran Red* (1958), *Moment of Danger* (1959), and *Tamango* (1959, France)—all films that continued to typecast Dandridge as a wanton sex object. Dandridge earned $125,000 for *Tamango* in which she co-starred with German actor Curt Jurgens. Since the two kissed in the film, *Tamango* had limited distribution. While the French had no objections, the British and American movie moguls preferred to adhere to their tacit agreement of segregation in film as in the rest of society.

Dandridge did not receive further critical acclaim for her acting until she reunited with producer Otto Preminger and again appeared with an all-black cast in *Porgy and Bess* (1959), portraying the vamp Bess, for which she received 1959 Hollywood Foreign Press Association Golden Globe Award as Best Actress in a Musical. Even with the accolades for her acting, Dandridge received no offers to appear in serious dramatic films. Three years later Dandridge experienced frustration and controversy similar to those suffered on the sets of *Tamango* and *Island in the Sun* when she resurfaced in the British-produced film *Malaga* (1962) co-starring with Trevor Howard. Although typecast once again as the sex object, the film was discouraging for the stars because the producers remained indecisive with regard to whether the characters of Dandridge and Howard, who were in love, could kiss on screen.

Although Dandridge was designated as one of the world's five most beautiful women, Hollywood's first and only genuine African American "Love Goddess," she suffered several devastating disappointments in both her professional and private lives. Her earnings for each film in which she appeared were formidable (an attestation to her talent); she was the first African American entertainer to perform in the Waldorf Astoria's Empire Room (1955), but race restricted many roles. Although director Roubin Mamoulian suggested that she would be perfect for the role of Cleopatra, Elizabeth Taylor was cast instead. Although she studied acting for two years at the Actors Laboratory with classmates Marilyn Monroe, Anthony Quinn, and Morris Carnovsky, she was prohibited from performing in classical plays because, although she was considered an excellent actress, her instructors believed such roles could only be played publicly by whites.

Dandridge had settled happily into marriage with Harold Nicholas (one of the famed tap-dancing duo the Nicholas Brothers) about 1938. The marriage was blessed with baby Harolyn, born one year later. But her world began to disintegrate when she learned that her three-year-old child was retarded. Four years later she divorced her philandering husband and returned to nightclub entertainment, which she detested. Once describing herself as "a singer by necessity and an actress by choice," Dandridge studied psychology at UCLA to learn how to captivate her prospective audiences. She perfected her vocal skills enough to play some of the best clubs in the country and abroad (Hollywood's Mocambo, Manhattan's La Vie En Rose, and London's Cafe de Paris) to win critical acclaim for her nightclub act. Despite her many achievements, Dandridge continued to condemn herself for her child's condition and her failed marriage.

By 1960 film offers had ceased. In 1963 her second and final marriage to white restaurateur Jack Denison, whose imprudent investments had plummeted prudent Dandridge into bankruptcy, concluded in divorce. Two years later, Dorothy Jean Dandridge was found dead from an overdose of antidepressant pills. Dandridge died at approximately 2:27 P.M. on September 8, 1965, in her West Hollywood apartment. Although her career appeared to be on the upswing at the time of her death, she remained despondent because she was an accomplished, serious, dramatic actress with whom Hollywood had trifled.

—Elizabeth Hadley Freydberg

Bibliography

Dorothy Dandridge and Earl Conrad provide a candid and poignant account of Dandridge's life in the posthumously published autobiography *Everything and Nothing: The Dorothy Dandridge Tragedy* (New York: Abelard-Shuman, 1970); and in *Dorothy Dandridge* (Los Angeles: Holloway House, 1970) by her manager, Earl Mills. Donald Bogle provides an overview of Dandridge's life with a list of the majority of her film credits including synopses in *Toms, Coons, Mulattoes, Mammies and Bucks: An Interpretive History of Blacks in American Films* (New York: Continuum, 1989); Bogle also provides an overview of Dandridge's life in "Dorothy Dandridge: Tragic Venus" with photographs in *Brown Sugar: Eighty Years of America's Black Female Superstars* (New York: Harmony House, 1980) and in *Blacks in American Films and Television: An Illustrated Encyclopedia* (New York: Garland, 1988). Jim Haskins provides an account of the Dandridge Sisters' Cotton Club engagements and Dandridge's relationship with Harold Nicholas in Chapter Eight of *The Cotton Club* (New York: Random House, 1977). A brief account of Dandridge's contribution to the destruction of segregation in American hotels and nightclubs and a discussion of her significance to American culture from a feminist perspective is presented in "Diva under Glass" (1983) by Michelle Parkerson. One of the most provocative and empathetic accounts of Dandridge's life and death appears in the cover story "Dorothy Dandridge: Hollywood's Enigma" by longtime personal friend Louie Robinson in the March 1966 issue of *Ebony*; an intimate history of Dandridge's life in show business from age five is presented along with a pictorial spread of her opulent California home in "The Private World of Dorothy Dandridge" by Louie Robinson in the June 1962 issue of *Ebony*; an account of Dandridge's bankruptcy appears in an article entitled "Why the Stars Go Broke" in the July 1963 issue of *Ebony*; a description of Dandridge's marriage to Jack Denison with photographs appears in an article entitled "Simple Wedding Is Movieland Wonder" in the September 1959 issue of *Ebony*; an account of Dandridge's reception in London, England, appears in "Dandridge Gets Red Carpet Treatment" in the August 1956 issue of *Ebony*. Reference works in which Dandridge is cited include *The Film Encyclopedia* (New York: Crowell, 1990) by Ephraim Katz; Edward Mapp's *A Directory of Blacks in the Performing Arts* (Metuchen, NJ: Scarecrow, 1978); and *Who's Who in Hollywood 1900–1976* (Chicago: Marquis, 1976) by David Ragan.

DANDRIDGE, RUBY JEAN (1904–1987), movie and television actress,

was born March 3 in Memphis, Tennessee. Dandridge performed in secondary film roles throughout the 1930s and into the late 1950s.

Film credits include *Midnight Shadow* (1939), *Tish* (1942), *Cabin in the Sky* (1943), *Gallant Lady* (1943), *Melody Parade* (1943), *Junior Miss* (1945), *Three Little Girls in Blue* (1946), *My Wild Irish Rose* (1947), *The Arnelo Affair* (1947), and *A Hole in the Head* (1959). She also performed on radio and television. Dandridge played Geranium on "The Judy Canova Show" (1943), an NBC half-hour radio show; and Raindrop on "The Gene Autry Show," (1944).

Dandridge, with her high-pitched voice, easily made the transition from film and radio to television during the 1950s in mammy-type maid roles. Most notably she was the original dim-witted, giggling Oriole, the black maid and best friend to Beulah on the television series *Beulah*, when this series was transferred to television in 1952. This role led to her role as Belinda, the housekeeper in the CBS television series *Father of the Bride* (1961–1962). It seems that Ruby Dandridge's claim to fame is that she was the mother of and the inspiration behind the now legendary Dorothy Dandridge (1922–1965). She died in Los Angeles on October 29, 1987.

—Elizabeth Hadley Freydberg

Bibliography

Bogle, Donald. *Blacks in American Films and Television: An Illustrated Encyclopedia.* New York: Garland, 1988.

MacDonald, J. Fred. *Blacks and White: Afro-Americans in Television since 1948.* Chicago: Nelson-Hall, 1983.

Pomerance, Alan. *Repeal of the Blues: How Black Entertainers Influenced Civil Rights*. New York: Carol Publishing Group, 1991, pp. 145, 146.

Hill, George. *Black Women in Television*. New York: Garland, 1990.

McRae, F. Finley. "Ruby Dandridge Dies," *Los Angeles Sentinel* (October 29, 1987).

DASH, JULIE (b. 1951), a Georgia-based independent filmmaker, was raised in a housing project in Queens, New York. In the late 1960s she enrolled in a film workshop offered in Harlem. This experience provided the impetus for Dash to study and receive a degree in film from the David Picker Film Institute of City College of New York. During this time she also produced *Working Models for Success* (1974) for the New York Urban Coalition.

After her undergraduate experience, Dash relocated to Los Angeles, where she studied with notable scholars, including Jan Kadar at the American Film Institute. In 1977–1978, Dash finished two films: *Four Women* and *Diary of an African Nun*. The former is a dance film utilizing stylized movements and attire to express the metamorphosis of the black woman from Africa to a black woman in the United States struggling for survival. *Diary of an African Nun* is an adaptation of a short story by Alice Walker.

In 1982 Dash shot her master's thesis *Illusions* in ten days for under $30,000. The eradication of illusion and the presentation of authenticity regarding African American life and history is a dominant thread woven into the film. Its spiritual center communicates the power of self-awareness and maturation. *Illusions* won numerous awards including the Best Film of the Decade by the Black Filmmaker Foundation.

Dash, among the second generation of black graduates from the UCLA film school, also worked on films of her contemporaries. These positions (assistant sound/*Passing Through* [1973], production manager/*Sylvia* [1975], and first assistant director/*My Brother's Wedding* [1983]) not only provided bonding between Dash and other filmmakers, but also gave her specific experience in various aspects of film production.

When Dash relocated to Georgia, she produced two films for the National Black Women's Health Project entitled *Preventing Cancer* (producer, director, editor, 1987) and *Breaking the Silence: On Reproductive Rights* (director, 1987). She also produced *Relatives*, a dance film featuring Ishmael Houston Jones, and directed "Praise House" for the PBS series *Live from Off Center*. Dash wrote the original script for *Daughters of the Dust* in 1976 while at the American Film Institute. A few years later (1981), she was awarded a grant from the Guggenheim Foundation to conduct extensive research related to the Gullah culture. It was not until 1987 that Dash shot a ten-minute trailer for the film. The trailer, however, became a valuable asset. With this brief visual document, coupled with hard work and determination, Dash eventually secured funding from American Playhouse, the Fulton County Arts Council, the Georgia Endowment for the

Humanities, the Corporation for Public Broadcasting, and the Appalsop Southeast Fellowship Program.

Ostensibly, *Daughters of the Dust* (1991) recounts the story of a younger generation Gullah family preparing to leave the Georgia Sea Islands for the mainland at the turn of the twentieth century. On another level, the film unleashes the folklore and folk traditions and the memories and heritage of black women as they grapple with their destinies. The story is told in a style of African griots, people brought to special occasions to recount a family's oral history. This style produces a film with a dreamy and experimental outcome. Filmed in 35mm, critics have heralded the film as an unparalleled and unprecedented achievement in American cinema. With *Daughters of the Dust*, Dash became the first African American woman since Kathleen Prettyman to direct a 35mm feature film. Without a doubt, during the 1990s, Dash's talent will be recognized and celebrated by a wider audience of viewers, critics, and scholars.

—Gloria J. Gibson-Hudson

Bibliography

Gloria J. Gibson, "The Cultural Significance of Music to the Black Independent Filmmaker" (PhD dissertation, Indiana University, 1986), analyzes the historical and cultural significance of music in *Illusions* and *Four Women*. Phyllis Klotman, *Screenplays of the African American Experience*, gives a brief biography of Dash's life and the screenplay *Illusions*. Zeinabu Irene Davis, "Daughters of the Dust," *Black Film Review* 6:1 (1990), provides an in-depth interview with Dash regarding the film *Daughters of the Dust*. Greg Tate, "Of Homegirl Goddesses and Geechee Women: The Africentric Cinema of Julie Dash," *Village Voice* (June 4, 1991), is an overview article and interview with Julie Dash. Gloria J. Gibson-Hudson, "African American Literary Criticism as a Model for the Analysis of Films by African American Women," *Wide Angle* 13:3/4 (July/October 1991) discusses the similarities between African American literary and film criticism and includes a discussion of *Illusions*. Her work is analyzed in Ally Acker's article "Arts: Women Behind the Camera" in *Ms.* (March/April 1992): 64–67. An interview with Dash by Nick Charles appears in "A New Curtain Is Raised," Cleveland *Plain Dealer* (February 22, 1992): 1F–4F.

DAVIS, ANGELA (b. 1944), political activist, educator, and community organizer, was born January 26 to B. Frank Davis, a former teacher who owned a small business, and Sallye Davis, a teacher. Angela Yvonne Davis grew up in Birmingham, Alabama, the industrial center of the South, in a neighborhood that was called "Dynamite Hill" because of the racial violence perpetrated by white supremacists against black residents. There she attended school and witnessed the civil rights movement firsthand, as her activist mother took her along to demonstrations in the 1950s. She also spent time in New York City, where her mother was studying for a master's degree at New York University. She excelled in school and attended Parker High School in Birmingham. In her junior year, with the aid of a scholarship from the American Friends Service Committee, she transferred to the progressive Elizabeth Irwin School in Greenwich Village. While in New York she joined Advance, a Marxist-Leninist group, and was influenced by the teachings of Herbert Aptheker and the leadership of Bettina Aptheker.

She entered Brandeis University as a French literature major in 1961 and spent her junior year abroad studying at the Sorbonne. She met African students in Paris and became more aware of the impact of French colonialism in Africa. In September 1963, four girls that she knew were killed in the bombing of the Sixteenth Street Baptist Church in Birmingham, further strengthening her conviction in the principle of the personal responsibility to take action on social justice issues. In the following year Davis studied with the well-known philosopher Herbert Marcuse at Brandeis. She graduated magna cum laude in 1965 and went to Germany for two years to study philosophy at Goethe University in Frankfurt. She returned to the United States in 1967 and enrolled at the University of California, San Diego, where Marcuse had begun teaching. She earned her master's degree in philosophy in 1969 and advanced to ABD status in 1970. During this period she met Franklin and Kendra Alexander and became involved in the Student Nonviolent Coordinating Committee and the Black Panthers in Los Angeles. She joined the Communist Party on June 22, 1968.

In 1969 she started teaching at the University of California, Los Angeles, where she offered courses in political theory, philosophy, and literature. Her membership in the Communist Party was "leaked" to the student newspaper by an FBI informant who pointed out that under state law the state universities could not hire communists. Governor Ronald Reagan and the university regents called for her ouster. The law prohibiting the hire of members of the Communist Party was found unconstitutional, and Davis was reinstated to her position by court order. Despite excellence in teaching, her contract was not renewed by the UC Regents after the 1969–1970 academic year. As a result, the university was censured by the American Association of University Professors.

Davis's involvement in the Black Panthers led her to activist work in support of black political prisoners, who she argued were imprisoned as a consequence of their class status and racial discrimination. She became an outspoken advocate for the Soledad brothers and developed a close relationship with the imprisoned George Jackson. In August 1970 Jonathan Jackson, George Jackson's brother, took a judge and other court authorities hostage in a San Rafael courtroom. In subsequent gunfire, Jackson and Judge James Haley were among those killed. Davis was accused of having supplied the gun Jackson used in the incident and was placed on the FBI's Most Wanted List. She lived underground for two months and was arrested in New York in October 1970. Her trial, on conspiracy, kidnapping, and murder charges, lasted over ten months and became a cause célèbre. She was acquitted on all charges in June 1972.

After her acquittal the National United Committee to Free Angela Davis, which had worked for her release, evolved into the National Alliance Against Racist and Political Repression, an independent political group with a primarily black and Hispanic membership. Davis continued to serve in the leadership of the Communist Party and was the party's vice presidential candidate in 1980 and 1984. A productive writer, Davis has produced an autobiography (written when she was 28 and recently reprinted); two major texts on feminism, race, class, and culture; and other books. She has taught at a number of California universities in addition to UCLA, including Claremont College, Stanford University, the California College of the Arts and Crafts in Oakland, San Francisco State University, and the San Francisco Art Institute. She currently is a professor of history of consciousness at Oakes College, University of California, Santa Cruz, where she specializes in feminism, African American studies, popular music, culture and social consciousness, and the philosophy of punishment (women's jails and prisons). She is a member of the executive boards of the National Political Caucus of Black Women and the National Black Women's Health Project.

—Barbara Bair

Bibliography

For writings by Angela Davis, see her books *Angela Davis: An Autobiography* (New York: Random House, 1974); *If They Come in the Morning: Voices of Resistance* (New York: Third Press, 1971); *The Black Woman's Role in the Community of Slaves* (Somerville, MA: New England Free Press, 1971); *Women, Race and Class* (New York: Random House, 1981); *Violence Against Women and the Ongoing Challenge to Racism* (Latham, NY: Kitchen Table Press, 1985); *Women, Culture and Politics* (New York: Random House, 1989); and her article "Reflections on the Black Woman's Role in the Community of Slaves," *Black Scholar* 3 (December 1971): 2–15. She is the focus of many books and articles: *Angela Davis Case Collection*, edited by Ann Fagan Ginger (Berkeley: Meiklejohn Civil Liberties Institute, 1974); Mary Timothy, *Jury Woman* (Palo Alto: Emty Press, 1974); Bettina Aptheker, *The Morning Breaks: The Trial of Angela Davis* (New York: International Publishers, 1975); J.A. Parker, *Angela Davis: The Making of a Revolutionary* (New Rochelle, NY: Arlington, 1973); Reginald Major, *Justice in the Round: The Trial of Angela Davis* (New York: Third Press, 1973); Regina Nadelson, *Who Is Angela Davis?: The Biography of a Revolutionary* (New York: P.H. Wyden, 1972); Marc Olden, *Angela Davis* (New York: Lancer Books, 1973); R.A. Deleon, "A Look at Angela Davis from Another Angle, *Jet* 41 (February 24, 1972): 8–14; "In Defense of Angela," *Black Law Journal* 2 (Spring 1972): 45–53; C. Williams, "A Conversation with Angela," *Black Scholar* 3 (March-April 1972): 36–38; and "Angela Davis Eyes Her Future After 13-Week Trial," *Jet* 42 (June 22, 1972): 22–25. She also is interviewed by Joe Walker in the sound recording *Angela Davis Speaks*, for Folkways in 1971. Another sound recording, *Soul and Soledad/Angela Davis*, was produced by Flying Dutchman Productions (New York, 1971). An oral history with Davis is available in the Black Oral History Collection, Special Collections, Fisk

University Library. The National United Committee to Free Angela Davis Records, ca. 1970–1972, and the Mary Timothy records of the Angela Davis trial (four linear feet) are available in Special Collections, Stanford University. For secondary sources citing Angela Davis's significance see Jacqueline Jones, *Labor of Love, Labor of Sorrow* (New York: Basic Books, 1985); Paula Giddings, *When and Where I Enter* (New York: Morrow, 1984); Marianna Davis, *Contributions of Black Women to America, II* (Columbia, SC: Kenday, 1981); Bettina Aptheker, *The Academic Rebellion in the United States* (Secaucus, NJ: Citadel Press, 1972); and Sara Evans, *Personal Politics: The Roots of Women's Liberation in the Civil Rights Movement and the New Left* (New York: Knopf, 1979).

DAVIS, HENRIETTA VINTON (1860–1941), actress and elocutionist,

was one of the international leaders of the Universal Negro Improvement Association (UNIA). Born in Baltimore, she became a schoolteacher in Maryland and Louisiana, and in the 1880s was the assistant to Frederick Douglass in the Office of the Recorder of Deeds. Douglass strongly encouraged her to pursue a dramatic career and introduced her when she made her debut in a one-woman show in Washington, DC, in 1883. She embarked on the first of many tours, performing work by African American and other authors. She volunteered to lecture for the Populist Party in 1892 and established a black theater company in Chicago in 1893. She began a tour of the Caribbean in 1912, and over the next few years worked in Jamaica and Central America. She joined the Garvey movement in New York in 1919 and immediately rose to a position of official prominence unique for women in the movement. She was one of the directors of the Black Star Line.

The leading woman orator of the movement, she appeared regularly on platforms with Marcus Garvey at Liberty Hall, on organizational tours, and at UNIA conventions. She chaired the historic UNIA meeting at Carnegie Hall in August 1919, conducted nationwide tours of local UNIA divisions, and traveled as international organizer and ranking officer upon Black Star Line tours of the Caribbean in 1919–1920, 1921, and 1925. Garvey created the position of fourth assistant president general for her in 1922; it was one of the few positions in the top hierarchy of the movement that was occupied by a woman. She was the only woman member of the UNIA delegation to Liberia in 1923–1924 and of the UNIA delegation that presented African colonization petitions to President Calvin Coolidge in 1924. She continued to work under Garvey's close instruction during the UNIA leader's incarceration in 1925–1927, traveling to Belize to oversee UNIA financial dealings there. After Garvey's deportation, he left Davis in Jamaica in charge of UNIA affairs while he conducted an organizational tour of Europe.

Despite their long collaboration, relations between Garvey and Davis grew strained. In 1929 she reluctantly backed Garvey in the split in the movement between the original UNIA, Inc., in New York, and Garvey's newly declared

UNIA (August 1929) of the World, and was elected secretary general of the latter, which was based with Garvey in Jamaica. Having maintained strong ties with movement leaders in New York, Davis returned there, and in the early 1930s was elected first assistant president general of the rival UNIA, Inc. She became acting president general in 1934. Davis died in Washington, DC, in 1941.

—Barbara Bair

Bibliography

The best single source on Henrietta Vinton Davis's life is William Seraile, "Henrietta Vinton Davis and the Garvey Movement," in *Afro-Americans in New York Life and History* (July 1983): 7–24. Davis is briefly profiled in the following sources: Bettye Collier-Thomas, "Henrietta Vinton Davis, 1860–1941," in *Black Women in America: Contributions to Our Heritage* (Washington, DC: Bethune Museum & Archives, 1984); Errol Hill, "Henrietta Vinton Davis" in *Women in the American Theatre*, edited by Helen Chinoy and Linda Jenkins (New York: Crown, 1981); and *Shakespeare in Sable: A History of Black Shakespearean Actors* (Amherst: University of Massachusetts, 1984); Barbara Bair, "Henrietta Vinton Davis," in *Marcus Garvey: Life and Lessons*, edited by Robert A. Hill and Barbara Bair (Berkeley, Los Angeles, and London: University of California Press, 1987), pp. 375–376; and Barbara Bair, "True Women, Real Men: Gender, Ideology, and Social Roles in the Garvey Movement," in *Connected Domains: Beyond the Private/Public Dichotomy in Women's History*, edited by Susan Reverby and Dorothy O. Helly (Ithaca, NY: Cornell University Press, 1991). Davis's long career with the Garvey movement is extensively documented in the microfilm of the *Negro World* (available at the Schomburg Center for Research in Black Culture, New York Public Library, and at the University Research Library, University of California, Los Angeles) and in the first seven volumes of the *Marcus Garvey and Universal Negro Improvement Association Papers*, edited by Robert A. Hill et al. (Berkeley, Los Angeles, London: University of California Press, 1983–1990). A biographical annotation of her appears in Volume One of that series (pp. 419–420). The Schomburg Center for Research in Black Culture maintains archival materials on Davis's career, including correspondence in the John E. Bruce Collection.

DEE, RUBY (b. 1922), actress and political activist, was born Ruby Ann Wallace on October 27 in Cleveland, Ohio, to Emma (Benson) Wallace, a schoolteacher, and Marshall Edward Wallace, a porter and waiter on the Pennsylvania Railroad. The Wallaces moved their four children to Harlem, New York, when Dee was a baby. Emma Wallace encouraged the three girls and one boy to spend their idle time studying music and literature. All members of the family read poetry aloud to each other in the evenings. Dee married Ossie Davis on December 9, 1948, after they had co-starred in several plays since 1946. They have two daughters, Nora and LaVerne, and a son, Guy.

Dee decided to become an actress while attending Hunter High School after having received applause from her classmates for her reading of a play. She attended Hunter College, where she studied romance languages and graduated with a BA in 1945, after which she worked briefly as a French and Spanish translator for an import business. While attending Hunter College, Dee performed in radio plays; and throughout the period 1941–1944, she apprenticed with the American Negro Theatre along with Hilda Simms, Harry Belafonte, and Sidney Poitier, among others. Dee was completely involved in the theater on and off stage. In between performances in plays such as *Natural Man, Starlight, Three's a Family, Hard Walk*, and *On Striver's Row*, Dee mopped floors, ushered, sold tickets, and painted scenery.

Throughout her long, illustrious acting career, Dee has performed in white and black plays. This practice is evident from the beginning of her career. Dee's theater debut occurred in 1943 as Ruth, a native girl, a walk-on part in *South Pacific*. Her acting career in the theater escalated, and throughout the 1940s and into the 1950s she achieved recognition in such productions as *Jeb* (1946), in which she played Libby George opposite Ossie Davis; *Anna Lucasta* (1946), in which she played the title role in both the Broadway production and the national tour; *A Long Way from Home* (1946), an all-black production in which Dee played Marcy; *Alice in Wonder* (1952), a play written by her husband Ossie Davis; *Bontche Schweig* and *The World of Shalom Aleichem* (1955), which received greater acceptance from Jewish audiences, as the female lead than from black audiences, who remained skeptical; *Agamemnon* as Cassandra; presenting excerpts from *Antony and Cleopatra* at New York and Connecticut schools (1958); as the original Ruth Younger in Lorraine Hansberry's prize-winning play *A Raisin in the Sun* (1958–1959); as the co-star in *Purlie Victorious* (1962); Jean Genet's play *The Balcony* as a prostitute (1963); portraying Lutiebelle Gussie Mae Jenkins with Davis, the playwright; *The Imaginary Invalid* (1971); *Wedding Band* (1972), by Alice Childress; as Queen Gertrude in *Hamlet* (1975); portraying Mary Tyrone in an all-black version of Eugene O'Neill's *Long Day's Journey into Night"* (1982); and more recently as Amanda Wingfield in a 1989 all-black production of Tennessee Williams's *The Glass Menagerie* at Washington, DC's Arena Stage.

Although Dee's acting career began in theater, her film credits are equally as impressive and extensive. Her film credits include *The Jackie Robinson Story* (1950), in which she played the female lead opposite Robinson, who played himself; *No Way Out* (1950); *The Tall Target* (1951); *Go, Man, Go!* (1954); *Edge of the City* (1957), for which she received excellent reviews as Sidney Poitier's middle-class wife; *St. Louis Blues* (1958); *Virgin Island* (1960); *Take a Giant Step* (1961), for which she received excellent reviews for her rendition of the family maid in this adaptation of a play written by black playwright Louis Peterson; *A Raisin in the Sun* (1961), repeated stage role of Ruth Younger; *The Balcony* (1963), cast as a prostitute; *Gone Are the Days* (1963), the film version of *Purlie Victorious*, in which she repeated her stage role; *The Incident* (1967); *Uptight* (1968), which she co-wrote; *Boesman and Lena* (1970); *Buck & the Preacher* (1971); *Black Girl* (1972), a film about three generations of black women, by black playwright J.E.

Franklin; *Countdown at Kusini* (1976); *Cat People* (1982); and Spike Lee's *Do the Right Thing* (1989), in which Dee plays the memorable role of Mother Sister.

By 1960 Dee had begun to make television history beginning with her debut in "Actors Choice" on "Camera Three," presented on CBS. This appearance was succeeded by "Seven Times Monday," a Play of the Week on WNTA; "Black Monday" (1961); her role as Harriet Tubman in "Go Down, Moses," on the historical *Great Adventure* series (1963–1964 season); *Wedding Band,* a play by Alice Childress, in which Dee re-created the role she had first performed on stage (ABC Theater Showcase, 1974); *I Know Why the Caged Bird Sings* (1979), a television adaptation of Maya Angelou's autobiography; *Roots: The Next Generation* (1979); the Alcoa-funded PBS television series *With Ossie and Ruby* (1981– 1982); her portrayal of Mary Tyrone in *A Long Day's Journey into Night* in an all-black rendition of Eugene O'Neill's autobiographical play (PBS, 1982); *The Atlanta Child Murders* (1985), a five-hour docudrama; and her portrayal of the award-winning playwright Lorraine Hansberry in a PBS production of *To Be Young, Gifted and Black.*

Throughout her career Ruby Dee has made appearances in several television series, most notably *The Great Adventure* (CBS), *The Defenders* (CBS), *The Fugitive* (ABC), and *The Nurses* (CBS). Dee has also appeared with Davis on several National Educational Television programs, including the *History of the Negro People* series. And in 1955 she played the title role in "This is Norah Drake," a daytime radio serial.

In 1965 Dee played Kate in *The Taming of the Shrew* and Cordelia in *King Lear,* thus becoming the first black actress to appear in principal roles at the American Shakespeare Festival at Stratford, Connecticut. Dee continued to perform in traditionally white classical roles. For example, she starred in productions of the Ypsilanti Greek Theatre and the University of Michigan's professional theater program; she appeared with Bert Lahr in Aristophane's *The Birds* and played in Off-Broadway productions of *The Cherry Orchard* and *The Would-Be Gentleman.* Dee also became the first black actress to be featured in the popular ABC-TV series *Peyton Place,* in 1968 when she was cast as Alma Miles, the wife of a neurosurgeon.

In addition to her numerous film, stage, and television appearances, Dee has recorded, along with her husband, several talking albums for Caedmon Records, among them, *The Poetry of Langston Hughes.* The two continue to tour the United States together, presenting recitals of dramatic scenes, poems and stories. In 1964 they presented poetry readings against a jazz background at the Village Vanguard, a New York City nightclub; and in 1974 Dee and Davis produced *The Ruby Dee/ Ossie Davis Story Hour,* sponsored by Kraft Foods on more than 60 stations of the National Black Network.

Ruby Dee has written a musical satire entitled *Take It from the Top* (1979); edited a book of poetry, *Glowchild and Other Poems* (1972); and published "Tattered Queens" (1966) in *Negro Life and History,* an article in which she questions the stereotypical roles made available to black actresses, and states that the African American actress "faces double discrimination—that of sex and that of race," and that "we know best on stage and screen the prostitute. The Negro Maid (as a person rather than a stereotype), the Negro Mother, the Average Woman, and the Middle-Class Woman have for the most part yet to be dealt with in depth"; and has further taken time to write "Exciting Novel by Talented Story Teller," a review of *The Autobiography of Miss Jane Pittman,* by Ernest J. Gaines.

Dee has spent a considerable amount of time from her busy schedule providing for others. She has made recordings for the blind. She has established, with her husband, the Institute of New Cinema Artists to train youths for employment in films and television and the Recording Industry Training Program to generate occupations in the music industry for underprivileged youths. She instituted the Ruby Dee Scholarship in Dramatic Art to assist talented young black women to become established in the acting profession. Dee has performed in benefit shows and served on national committees to raise money for the Black Panthers, the Young Lords, and the legal defense of civil rights workers arrested in demonstrations. She has also raised money to combat drug addiction and has raised her voice in opposition to United States military involvement in Southeast Asia.

Dee has dedicated most of her life to ensuring racial equality. Her political affiliations include membership in the National Association for the Advancement of Colored People (NAACP), the Congress of Racial Equality (CORE), the Southern Christian Leadership Conference (SCLC), and the Student Nonviolent Coordinating Committee (SNCC).

Ruby Dee has received among her many accolades an Emmy nomination for her performance in an episode of the *East Side, West Side* series. The New York Urban League presented Dee and Davis with the Frederick Douglass Award in 1970 for bringing "a sense of fervor and pride to countless millions." She also received the 1971 Obie Award, the 1972 Martin Luther King Jr. Award from Operation PUSH, and a 1974 Drama Desk Award. In 1975 Actor's Equity presented both Dee and Davis with a Paul Robeson Citation "for outstanding creative contributions both in the performing arts and in society at large." In 1991 Dee won an Emmy for her performance in "Decoration Day" (NBC). Yale University named their African American Film Archives after Ruby Dee and Ossie Davis in April 1992. In March 1992, she returned to her hometown of Cleveland, Ohio, to perform in Adrienne Kennedy's play *The Ohio State Murders,* presented by the Great Lakes Theatre Festival at the Ohio Theatre.

—Elizabeth Hadley Freydberg

Bibliography

"The Black Entertainer in the Performing Arts." *Negro Almanac,* 5th edition, 1989: 1136–1137.

"Black Poetry," *Washington Post* (November 5, 1969): C1, 2.

Bogle, Donald. *Blacks in American Films and Television: An Illustrated Encyclopedia.* New York: Garland, 1988.

Champlin, Charles. "'Right Thing' Stars: A New Era for Blacks," *Los Angeles Times* (July 6, 1989): Part VI, 1+.

Current Biography. New York: Wilson, 1970.

Dannett, Sylvia G.L. *Profiles of Negro Womanhood*, Vol. 2. Chicago: Educational Heritage, 1966.

"Facts of (Ghetto) Life," *Commonweal* 116 (July 1989): 402–403.

Hill, George. *Black Women in Television.* New York: Garland, 1990.

Kaufmann, Stanley. "Books and the Arts," *New Republic* 201 (July 3, 1989): 24–26.

Kilian, Michael. "Dee-Parture," *Chicago Tribune* (November 19, 1989): Section 13, 24–25.

Landay, Eileen. "Ruby Dee," *Black Film Stars.* New York: Drake Publishers, 1973.

Lahmon, Jo Ann. *Notable Black American Women* (edited by Jessie Carney Smith). Detroit: Gale, 1992, pp. 260–262.

Norment, Lynn. "Three Great Love Stories," *Ebony* 43 (February 1988): 150, 152, 154, 156.

Rywell, Martin, comp. and ed. *Afro-American Encyclopedia*, Vol. 3. North Miami: Educational Book Publishers, 1974.

Smythe, Mabel M. "Black Influneces in American Theater: Part II, 1960 and After." *Black American Reference Book.* Englewood Cliffs, NJ: Prentice-Hall, 1976.

Sweeney, Louise. "Melting Stage Stereotypes: Ruby Dee Talks of Her Role as a Nonwhite Amanda in 'Glass Menagerie,'" *Christian Science Monitor* (November 21, 1989).

Turner, Renee. "My Happiest Moment," *Ebony* 43 (March 1988): 86, 88, 90.

Walker, Alice. "Black Sorority Bankrolls Action Film," *Ms.* 4 (June 1976): 45.

Who's Who among Black Americans, 6th edition. Detroit: Gale, 1990, p. 333.

DELANEY, LUCY A. (c. 1830–c. 1890s), ex-slave, author, and civic leader, was born to slave parents owned by Major and Mrs. Taylor Berry; but, during her childhood in St. Louis, she enjoyed, as she wrote in her autobiography, "a pleasant home and surroundings, . . . the same joyful freedom as the little white children." Upon the death of Major Berry in a duel and of his widow (who had become Mrs. Robert Wash), however, the family was not freed, as Major Berry had arranged. Instead, Delaney's father was sold, and her mother, who had been born free and kidnapped into slavery, began to encourage her two daughters to escape. Delaney's older sister, Nancy, escaped to Canada while accompanying Major Berry's daughter, Mary Cox, to Niagara Falls; and at age 12, Delaney herself began "to plan for freedom." Her mother also escaped to Chicago at this point but returned to St. Louis for fear of the consequences to her still-enslaved daughter; she then successfully sued for her freedom on the grounds that she had been kidnapped into slavery. Another of Major Berry's daughters, Martha Mitchell, angry both at Delaney's poor work and arrogant attitude (Delaney objected to being called a "nigger" and refused to be whipped), planned to sell Delaney; but Delaney escaped and hid with her free mother. Her mother then sued for Lucy Delaney's freedom on the grounds that she was born of a free black. Delaney remained in jail for 17 months until the courts, largely through the efforts of Judge Edward Bates, ruled in her favor in 1844. Delaney, "an expert seamstress," and her mother, "a first-class laundress," then established a comfortable living for themselves. They were able to save enough for Delaney's mother to visit Nancy in Toronto, where she had married a prosperous farmer and had several children. In 1845 Lucy Delaney married Frederick Turner, and she and her mother moved to Quincy, Illinois, where her husband was killed shortly afterward in an explosion on the steamboat *Edward Bates*, where he worked. She and her mother returned to St. Louis, where four years later she married Zachariah Delaney of Cincinnati. They had been married for 42 years at the time she wrote her autobiography. The couple had four children, all of whom died young, two in childhood and two in their early twenties. Delaney's only consolation was that "our children were born free and died free!" After her mother's death, Delaney searched for and found her father on a plantation 15 miles from Vicksburg, Mississippi. The date of her death is unknown.

Delaney's effort in her lifetime to make "the best of my time, and what few talents the Lord has bestowed on me" led her to be active in many religious and civic organizations. She joined the African Methodist Episcopal church in 1855. She became president of the Female Union, the first African American society organized exclusively for women; president of the Daughters of Zion; matron of Siloam Court, No. 2; most ancient matron of the Grand Court of Missouri, an organization of wives of masons; grand chief preceptress of the Daughters of the Tabernacle and Knights of Tabor; and secretary of Colonel Shaw Woman's Relief Corps, Grand Army of the Republic. Delaney concludes her autobiography with the hope that her account of her life will show that "the negro race [can] succeed, proportionately, as well as the whites, if given the same chance and an equal start."

—Rosalie Murphy Baum

Bibliography

Lucy A. Delaney's autobiography, *From the Darkness Cometh the Light or Struggles for Freedom*, was published around 1891. A reprint appears in the Schomburg Library of Nineteenth-Century Black Women Writers' volume entitled *Six Women's Slave Narratives*, with introduction by W.L. Andrews (New York: Oxford, 1988).

DELANY, CLARISSA [SCOTT] (1901–1927), poet and educator, was born in Tuskegee, Alabama, the daughter of Emmett J. Scott (secretary to Booker T. Washington) and, in her own words, spent her "early years in what is known as the 'Black Belt.'" She was educated at Tuskegee Institute and then spent seven years in New England (1916–1923)—three at Bradford Academy and four at Wellesley College. In New England, Delany explained, her "southern blood became tinged with something of the austerity of that section." Frequently described as "beautiful and talented," she was a magazine cover girl in 1923. Delany then taught for three years at Dunbar High School in Washington, DC, before deciding that, although "children were interesting, teaching was not my *metier.*"

She married Hubert Delany, a New York City domestic relations court judge, in 1926. Delany completed a study of "Delinquency and Neglect among Negro Children in New York City" before, in her words, devoting herself to her role as wife, a position that "as careers go . . . is an interesting and absorbing one." She continued to write occasionally. Among her known works are four poems, "Joy," "Solace," "Interim," and "The Mask," as well as a 1924 play, *Dixie to Broadway.* Delany died in 1927 following an illness.

—Rosalie Murphy Baum

Bibliography

Delany's most frequently anthologized poem, "Solace," appeared in *Opportunity* in November 1927. She also contributed to *The Crisis* and *Palms.* Her poems "Joy," "Solace," "Interim," and "The Mask" are anthologized in *Caroling Dusk,* edited by Countee Cullen (New York: Harper & Brothers, 1927), which also includes a brief autobiographical statement. Selections have appeared in many anthologies, including Langston Hughes, *The Poetry of the Negro* (Garden City, NY: Doubleday, 1949, 1970); Arna R. Bontemps, *American Negro Poetry* (New York: Hill & Wang, 1963); and Arnold Adoff, *The Poetry of Black America* (New York: Harper, 1973). A tribute in the November 1927 issue of *Opportunity* states, "With a well-trained and restlessly searching mind, a magnificent and sturdy idealism and all of the impetuous zeal of youth, she was superbly poised for life; and quietly she left it." "To Clarissa Scott Delany," a poem in her memory by Angelina W. Grimké, appeared in *Ebony and Topaz: A Collectanea,* edited by Charles S. Johnson (New York, Opportunity, National Urban League, 1927).

DERRICOTTE, JULIETTE [THOMAS] (1897–1931), national secretary of the YWCA, achieved much in her short life, both in her own education and in her support for increasing opportunities for young African American women, especially those in the South. Born in Athens, Georgia, the fifth child of Isaac and Laura (Hardwick) Thomas, Derricotte attended the public schools in Athens before going on to and graduating from Talladega College in 1918. She received her MA degree in religious education in 1927 from Columbia University and served as the only woman trustee at Talladega College (1929–1931).

Derricotte is remembered for her work with the YWCA. As a college student and one of the YWCA's first national secretaries, she began to address the needs of African American women. While at Talladega, she was active in the YWCA, visiting many colleges to recruit women to the organization. After graduation, Derricotte traveled to New York City to complete the summer course at the National YWCA Training School, one of the first efforts of the YWCA to expand its membership within black communities in cities and in southern colleges. Designed to prepare young black women as recruiters and branch developers throughout the country, the course pushed Derricotte into leadership as one of several secretaries who traveled throughout the country helping local chapters organize. These leadership positions helped Derricotte to influence the structure of the interracial Student YWCAs developing throughout the 1920s and the programs of the YWCA in the urban black communities of the North and South.

Derricotte left the YWCA in 1929 to become the dean of women at Fisk University. She continued to influence the direction of young people through this role until a tragic accident led to her death. While traveling with three students to her home in Athens, Georgia, she was in a car accident in Dalton, Georgia. There, blacks were not allowed to receive treatment at the only hospital in town. Derricotte, seriously injured, had to wait for transport to Walden Hospital in Chattanooga, Tennesee. She died there on November 7, 1931. After a short lifetime of service, Derricotte lost her life to traditions of segregation. Derricotte was widely eulogized and her death was decried in the press.

—Sharlene Voogd Cochrane

Bibliography

Three works highlight the life and career of Juliette Derricotte: Marion V. Cuthbert's *Juliette Derricotte* (New York: The Woman's Press, 1933); Delores Leffall's "Juliette Derricotte," in *Dictionary of American Negro Biography*, edited by Rayford Logan (New York: Norton, 1982); and Mary Jeanness's portrait in *Twelve Negro Americans* (Freeport, NY: Books for Libraries Press, 1936). For eulogies or commentaries about her death see W.E.B. Du Bois, "Juliette Derricotte; Dalton, Georgia," *The Crisis* (March 1932), and Walter White, "The Color Line: Even at Death's Door in the Case of Miss Derricotte," *New York Herald Tribune* (December 10, 1931).

DEVERS, GAIL (b. 1966) became an Olympic Track Gold Medalist at the Barcelona 1992 Summer Games after coming back from a life-threatening illness. Her triumph was not only one of the body but also one of the spirit. Her early years witnessed many awards for her physical achievements, but her future seemed bleak the few years before her feat in Barcelona.

Gail Yolanda Devers was born on November 19 in Seattle, Washington. Her family moved to National City, California, where Gail attended Sweetwater High School. She entered competitive track in high school. In 1984 Devers placed second in the National Junior Championships in the 100-meter dash and third in that event in the Pan-American Junior Games.

After graduating from high school, she attended UCLA, becoming a world-class athlete in hurdles, sprints, and the long jump, under the tutelage of coach Bob Kersee. Her outstanding track records led to her inclusion on the 1988 United States Olympic Team. She was eliminated in the 100 semifinals in Seoul, Korea, in 1988 due to poor health. While some questioned the veracity of her "ill health," Gail Devers entered a three-year nightmare. She experienced weight fluctuation by as much as 30 pounds. Migraine headaches, vision loss, blood clots, and muscle tears followed. Devers consulted 13 doctors before her final diagnosis of Graves' disease, a thyroid gland malfunction. Leaving goiters on her neck and pop eyes, Graves' disease disfigured her body and wracked her with convulsions, and led to menstrual cycles three to four times a month. By the time the disease was finally diagnosed, her thyroid was almost cancerous. Radiation therapy destroyed her thyroid and produced lesions on her feet that prevented her from walking. The beta-blocker prescribed for the radiation side effects was a banned substance for world-class athletics, so she declined the medication. Whenever she tried to work out, her skin broke out. The skin on both feet ulcerated. She developed psoriasis on her knees, under her arms, and between her legs. Her parents moved in with her to care for her. In the spring of 1991, she was finally hospitalized. Doctors discussed amputation of her infected feet.

Consultation with yet one more doctor, who prescribed a change in medication, started her on the road to recovery. In April 1991, Bob Kersee started her training. She quickly regained the speed to place second in the 100-meter hurdles in the Summer 1991 World Championships. In September 1991, she established a new U.S. record, breaking the record shared by her and Jackie Joyner-Kersee in the 100-meter hurdles with a time of 12.48 seconds at the track meet in Berlin, Germany. Similarly, Devers participated in the Snickers Millrose Games in Madison Square Garden, New York City, in February 1992 to win the women's 60-meter high hurdles with a time of 7.93 seconds, the fastest ever at the Millrose meet and at Madison Square Garden.

Her fight to reestablish control over her body culminated in her achievements at the Summer Olympics in Barcelona, Spain. The 25-year-old, five foot three inch, 115 pound Devers became the 1992 Olympic Gold Medalist for her time of 10.82 seconds in the women's 100-meter race. In the 100-meter hurdles, however, she tripped over the last hurdle, just seconds from the finish line. She responded, "It wasn't meant to be. . . . I can say I finished this time, so that's a step farther than I went in '88."

What was most remembered about Devers's performance at the 1992 Olympics was summed up in a description of her following the women's 100-meter run: "Seldom has the grand stage of the Olympics produced a winner who has won so much more than the medal she wore around her neck." She continues to live in the Los Angeles area and train with Bob Kersee for future events.

—Julieanne Phillips

Bibliography

The sources that are the most useful on the life of Gail Devers are recent newspaper and periodical articles. A biographical data sheet can be obtained from the Athletics Congress/USA and the Track and Field Writers of America (Indianapolis, Indiana). Devers's track career is related in William N. Wallace, "Unexpected Performances Steal Spotlight at Millrose," *New York Times* (February 9, 1992); Michael Jaffe, "Established" (For the Record), *Sports Illustrated* 75 (September 23, 1991): 80; Tenley Jackson Hawkins and Linda Villarose, "Solid Gold," *Essence* 23 (July 1992): 56; Michael Janofsky, "Devers Conquers All and Captures the 100," and "Last Hurdle Stops Devers from Gaining Second Gold," *New York Times* (August 2 and August 7, 1992); Bill Livingston, "Now They Believe It," *Cleveland Plain Dealer* (August 2, 1992).

DOBSON, TAMARA (b. 1947), a six foot two inch model and actress, was born in Baltimore, Maryland. She was one of four children in a family headed by two working parents. Her father, Melvin Dobson, worked for the Pennsylvania Railroad Company, while her mother, Evelyn Dobson, a beautician, owned two beauty shops. During her childhood, Tamara Dobson worked with her mother after school in the salons, and became a licensed beautician at age 16. Although money was tight in the Dobson household, her parents paved the way for Dobson's future career by providing her with piano, tap dancing, and ballet lessons. Dobson attended the Maryland Institute of Art, and in 1970 earned a bachelor of fine arts degree in fashion illustration.

Dissatisfied with both fashion illustration and cosmetology as career choices, Dobson decided to try her hand at modeling. In 1970 she traveled to New York City, and was signed her first day in the city by the Fashion and Film Agency. Within two weeks, she had landed a contract for a television commercial. Her modeling credits include *Vogue, Ebony, Harper's,* and *Essence.* She has appeared in over 25 television commercials. In 1978 she served as Faberge's model-representative for "Tigress" products. Although successful as a model, Dobson is most well known for her portrayal of the karate-chopping, narcotics agent heroine of the films *Cleopatra Jones* (1973) and *Cleopatra Jones and the Casino of Gold* (1975). In addition, Dobson appeared in small roles in several other films including *Fuzz* (1972), *Come Back Charleston Blue* (1972), *Norman? Is That You?* (1976), *Chained Heat* (1983), and in the made-for-television feature *Amazons* (1984).

—Ann M. Lindell

Bibliography

Brief biographical entries on Tamara Dobson appear in several editions of *Who's Who among Black Americans,* as well as in the *Directory of Blacks in the Performing Arts.* Donald Bogle includes information about Dobson's acting career and films in his two works *Brown Sugar* and *Blacks in American Films and Television: An Encyclopedia.* Helpful for personal information is an August 19, 1973, *New York Times* article

"Tamara Dobson—Not Super Fly But Super Woman," by Judy Klemesrud. Dobson's modeling career is chronicled in several short articles in popular publications such as *Ebony*, *Sepia*, and *Life*. References to these articles appear in *In Black and White: A Guide to Magazine Articles, Newspaper Articles, and Books Concerning More Than 15,000 Black Individuals and Groups.*

Secondary Sources

Bogle, Donald. *Brown Sugar*. New York: Harmony Books, 1980.
————. *Blacks in American Films and Television: An Encyclopedia*. New York: Garland, 1988.
Mapp, Edward. *Directory of Blacks in the Performing Arts*. Metuchen, NJ: Scarecrow, 1978.
Spradling, Mary Mace, ed. *In Black and White: A Guide to Magazine Articles, Newspaper Articles, and Books Concerning More Than 15,000 Black Individuals and Groups*, 3rd edition. Detroit: Gale, 1980.
Who's Who among Black Americans, 4th edition. Northbrook, IL: Who's Who Among Black Americans, 1985.

DOUGLASS, ANNA MURRAY (c. 1813–1882) was the first wife of abolitionist Frederick Douglass, whose successful career as orator and journalist was bolstered by his wife's constant support and loyalty. Her exemplary role as wife and mother allowed Frederick Douglass to realize his dream of an end to slavery. Behind this great man there stood, at every step of the way, Anna Murray Douglass.

Anna Murray Douglass was born in Denton, Maryland. She was the eighth of 12 children of former slaves Bambarra and Mary Murray, and the first of the family to be freeborn. Lacking a formal education, Anna Murray remained illiterate throughout her life. She left home at age 17 for Baltimore, where she found employment for 9 years as a domestic servant.

Joining the East Baltimore Improvement Society was a turning point in Anna Murray's life, for it was here, in 1838, that she met her future husband. Slaves were not ordinarily admitted as members to this small and exclusive group of free people, but an exception was made for the young slave Frederick Douglass. Although she was a few years older, the attraction between the two inspired Anna Murray to give Frederick Douglass part of her savings to aid his escape to New York on September 3, 1838. She joined him a week later and they married.

Beginning their life together in New Bedford, Massachusetts, the couple worked raising a family and building Frederick Douglass' career. To help support their five children, the eldest of whom was Rosetta M. Douglass Sprague, Anna Murray Douglass worked at a variety of jobs: domestic servant, shoe-binder, and launderer. And while Frederick Douglass spent months away from home touring the antislavery lecture circuit, it was his wife who kept the family together.

Anna Murray Douglass worked with various antislavery societies while contributing financially to the abolitionist cause. She was also one of the first agents of the Underground Railroad. When the family moved to Rochester, New York, in January 1848, they purchased a two-story, nine-room house, one room of which was reserved for runaway slaves en route to Canada via the railroad network. Anna Murray Douglass cared for the fugitives by providing food and clothing until they could be transported to freedom.

While the ideal housewife and mother, Anna Murray Douglass was not her husband's intellectual equal. An attempt by Frederick Douglass to have his wife tutored failed, and she felt uncomfortable mixing in his social circles. As his career achieved momentum, he spent less time with his family. In the later years of their 44-year marriage the couple grew apart and Anna Murray Douglass steadily became less involved in her husband's professional life.

In her later years, Anna Murray Douglass suffered from rheumatism and confined herself to home. After an illness lasting four weeks, she died of a stroke at Cedar Hill, their Anacostia home in Washington, DC, on August 4, 1882.

—Thea Gallo Becker

Bibliography

Blight, David W. *Frederick Douglass' Civil War*. Baton Rouge: Louisiana State University Press, 1989.

Foner, Philip S. *The Life and Writings of Frederick Douglass: Early Years, 1817–1849*. New York: International Publishers, 1950. Provides an informative outline of Anna Murray and Frederick Douglass's early years.

Quarles, Benjamin. *Frederick Douglass*. Washington, DC: Associated Publishers, 1948.

Render, Sylvia Lyons. "Afro-American Women: The Outstanding and the Obscure." *Quarterly Journal of the Library of Congress* 32 (October 1975): 307–319. Reprinted in Darlene Clark Hine. *Black Women in United States History: Theory and Practice* 2. New York: Carlson, 1990. More interpretive than factual; favorably portrays Anna Murray Douglass as one of the obscure who is deserving of her place in history. Excellent work, up to date.

Sprague, Rosetta Douglass. "Anna Murray Douglass—My Mother As I Recall Her," *Journal of Negro History* 8 (1923): 93–101. Cited most often by biographers, it highlights the positive aspects of her mother's life. The first source to consult on Anna Murray Douglass.

Sterling, Dorothy. *We Are Your Sisters; Black Women in the Nineteenth Century*. New York: Norton, 1984. Includes correspondence from Rosetta Douglass Sprague to her father, Frederick Douglass. Briefly addresses the gossip and innuendo surrounding the Douglass's marriage in later years.

DOUGLASS, GRACE [BUSTILL] (1782–1842), community organizer and abolitionist, was born in Philadelphia. Her father, Cyrus Bustill (1732–1806), an ex-slave, had purchased his freedom and prospered as a baker, brewer, and carter. Her mother, Elizabeth (Morey) (1743–1827), was the daughter of an Englishman

and a Delaware woman. Grace was one of eight children. After retiring from business Cyrus Bustill opened a school for black children, and it was probably there that his daughter received her formal education. She was also trained as a milliner.

Grace Bustill married Robert Douglass (1775–1849), an immigrant from St. Kitts who ran a successful barbershop in Philadelphia. The Douglasses had a comfortable income, and Grace Douglass recalled that in her new home at 54 Arch Street she entertained in style with the best wine and cake. It was not poverty that eventually induced her to economize but a desire to save money to assist the poorer members of her community. The Douglasses had five children: Sarah, Robert, Jr., Charles, James, and William, whose education posed a serious problem. The public schools for black children in Philadelphia were woefully inadequate, and private academies would not accept them. Eventually, Grace Douglass and a family friend, sailmaker James Forten, opened their own school.

Having been raised as a Quaker, Grace Douglass took her children to the Society of Friends Meeting. All the children, with the exception of Sarah, reacted against the coldness of white Quakers and so joined their father at the First African Presbyterian Church. Although she attended Meeting faithfully, and adopted Quaker dress and speech, Grace Douglass was advised not to apply for membership in the Society of Friends because she certainly would be denied.

Saddened by the treatment meted out to her by most white Quakers, Grace Douglass recognized that there were few whites who shared her commitment to abolition and racial equality. She and her daughter developed close friendships with Lucretia Mott and the Grimké sisters, Sarah and Angelina.

Over the years Grace Douglass worked tirelessly in the antislavery cause. In 1833 she and her daughter became founding members of the Philadelphia Female Anti-Slavery Society. In 1837 she served as one of the vice presidents of the first women's antislavery convention, and she took an active role in the third and final convention in 1839.

To the end of her life Grace Douglass continued to work for the betterment of her community. In 1841, with other elite black Philadelphians, she established the Gilbert Lyceum, a cultural and literary association. She was unswerving in her devotion to the antislavery cause. When she died, her co-workers in the Female Anti-Slavery Society praised her as having been "one of [their] . . . most self-denying members."

Grace Douglass died in March 1842 at age 59. She was survived by her husband and three of her children. Charles and William Douglass had died of tuberculosis in their early twenties. Of her surviving children, James went into business with his father; Sarah became a much respected teacher; and Robert achieved considerable success as an artist.

—Julie Winch

Bibliography

For information about Grace Douglass and her family see Anne Bustill Smith, "The Bustill Family," *Journal of Negro History* 10 (October 1925): 638–644. The records of the Philadelphia Female Anti-Slavery Society give insight into her abolitionist activities. The letter describing her decision to live simply so she can assist the poor is reprinted in William W. Catto, *A Semi-Centenary Discourse Delivered in the First African Presbyterian Church, Philadelphia, on the Fourth Sabbath of May, 1857* (Philadelphia, 1857). On her difficulties with white Quakers see Sarah Grimké, "Letter on the Subject of Prejudice Against Colour Amongst the Society of Friends," Antislavery Manuscripts, Department of Rare Books and Manuscripts, Boston Public Library.

DOUGLASS, SARAH MAPPS (1806–1882), a dedicated teacher and staunch abolitionist, was born September 9 to Robert and Grace Douglass of Philadelphia. Her mother and maternal grandfather, Cyrus Bustill, were Quakers. Bustill was an active member of the Free African Society, one of the first black benevolent organizations. Douglass's father was one of the founding members of the First African Presbyterian Church in Philadelphia. Sarah Douglass followed her grandfather and mother and became a devout Quaker.

In the 1820s Douglass opened a school for black children. When the school faltered, the Female Anti-Slavery Society of Philadelphia assumed administration and provided financial support. Douglass joined the Society, of which her mother was a charter member, soon after its founding in 1833 and served as corresponding secretary in 1838. In 1837 she was a delegate to the Society's first national convention. The Society was a racially mixed group, and it was through the meetings that Douglass met leading black and white abolitionists. She became close friends with Sarah and Angelina Grimké, white South Carolinians who had moved to Philadelphia and became Quakers.

Douglass found that even the Quakers were not exempt from racially discriminatory practices. There were the "Negro pews" where the blacks were to sit during meetings and the obvious snubbing of blacks by white Quakers. Douglass supplied the details of her experiences to William Bassett, a New England Quaker, and to Elizabeth Pease, an English Quaker, to aid them in their abolitionist activities. In 1837 the Grimké sisters, disgruntled with Quaker prejudice, sat between Sarah and Grace Douglass on the "colored bench" at a weekly meeting. For this they were censured.

In May 1838 Douglass and her mother were among black guests who attended the wedding of Angelina Grimké and Theodore Weld. The Philadelphia press coverage of the event was so inflammatory that it is believed to have provoked the riot that occurred two days later, which ended in physical violence and the burning of the Pennsylvania Hall. The second annual convention of the Female Anti-Slavery Society was being held at Pennsylvania Hall at that time and so had to move to a school room. At this convention Sarah Douglass was elected treasurer and was elected to remain in this office in 1839 at the third convention. Sarah and her mother continued to support the abolitionist movement. In 1839 the two were among the first to support publicly William Lloyd Garrison, who felt that women's rights should be of equal importance with the antislavery movement.

Douglass continued to teach throughout her adult life. In 1853 she was appointed the head of the Girls Primary Department of the Quaker-supported Institute for Colored Youth in Philadelphia. The Institute, which later became Cheyney State College, was known for the excellent preparation of public school teachers. Douglass remained there until she retired. Douglass continued her own education by attending the Ladies Institute of Pennsylvania Medical University and by starting the Sarah Mapps Douglass Literary Circle in 1859. Ever busy, she served after the Civil War as the assistant head of the Women's Pennsylvania Branch of the American Freedmen's Aid Commission.

On July 23, 1855, Sarah Douglass married the Reverend William Douglass. He was the rector of St. Thomas's Protestant Episcopal Church. After six years of marriage, William Douglass died. After her husband's death, Sarah Douglass taught 16 additional years and retired in 1877.

Sarah Mapps Douglass died in 1882 at age 76.

—Linda Cannon-Huffman

Bibliography

Many interesting sources exist that contain biographical data on Sarah Mapps Douglass. Among the best ones are Gerda Lerner, *The Grimké Sisters from South Carolina* (New York: Schocken, 1967); Anna Bustill Smith, "The Bustill Family," *Journal of Negro History* 10 (October 1925): 638–644; and Benjamin Quarles, *Black Abolitionists* (New York: Oxford University Press, 1977). Brief biographical sketches may be found in *Notable American Women 1607–1950*, Volume I, edited by Edward T. James (Cambridge: Belnap, 1971) and *American Reformers*, edited by Alden Whitman (New York: H.W. Wilson, 1985); and *Dictionary of American Negro Biography*, edited by Rayford Logan and Michael R. Winston (New York: Norton, 1982).

Correspondence of Sarah Mapps Douglass can be found in the manuscript collections Theodore Dwight Weld Collection, William Clements Library, University of Michigan; Sarah Grimké File, Library of Congress; and Minutes of Philadelphia Anti-Slavery Society, Historical Society of Pennsylvania.

Secondary Sources

Cadbury, Henry J. "Negro Membership in the Society of Friends." *Journal of Negro History* (April 1936).

Lerner, Gerda, ed. *Black Women in White America*. New York: Pantheon Books, 1972.

Logan, Rayford W., and Michael R. Winston, eds. *Dictionary of American Negro Biography*. New York: Norton, 1982.

DOZIER-CRENSHAW, DORIS [SCOTT] (b. 1943), civil rights orga-
nizer and community activist, now known as Doris Dozier-Crenshaw, was born
May 22 in Montgomery, Alabama, to Mary Belle (Banks) and John Scott. Her
mother remarried when Dozier was very young to Charlie Dozier who adopted
her. They had a good family life. Charlie Dozier, was a businessman who repaired
radios and played an instrument with the Erskine Hawkins band.

Doris Dozier learned at an early age the importance of a good education and
her responsibility to the community. She was always interested in the struggles of
her people. As a Girl Scout and later through the NAACP Youth Council, she
read black history books and was encouraged to do community work. Her
interests inspired her to work in the civil rights movement as an activist. In 1955,
as a member of the NAACP Youth Council in Montgomery, Alabama, Dozier
entered the organized civil rights movement to help the secretary of the NAACP,
Rosa Parks, in her protest against inhumane treatment on the segregated buses.

After Charlie Dozier died, Doris Dozier went to Alabama State College
Laboratory High School. She went to college in Atlanta, where she lived with her
biological father. Throughout her high school and college years, she participated
in sit-ins, voter education, and voter registration helping the Congress of Racial
Equality (CORE), the Southern Christian Leadership Conference (SCLC), and
Vernon Jordan of the National Urban League in Alabama and Louisiana. As soon
as she graduated from college, she went to Chicago to help with the open housing
campaign led by Dr. Martin Luther King, Jr., of SCLC. In this role, she worked
with community groups, religious groups, and college students.

Her professional career began in 1967 as the southern field representative for
the National Council of Negro Women. Traveling through the South, Dozier
designed programs ranging from establishing quilting bees to grocery stores and
credit unions to help the rural economic development of black communities. She
served on the national board of the YWCA. As a Ford Foundation fellow, she
worked in New York, Los Angeles, Mississippi, and South Carolina to develop
rural health delivery programs. Then she joined the Federation of Southern
Cooperatives as public relations director for the Office of Minority Business
Development Program, which served 14 southern states.

She entered politics with the 1976 presidential campaign of Jimmy Carter as
the deputy campaign manager for Alabama. With Carter's success, Dozier-
Crenshaw joined the Carter White House Domestic Policy staff for Small and
Minority Business, serving as director of minority affairs. In 1980 she served as the
deputy director for the South in Carter's unsuccessful presidential campaign.

Since 1980 Dozier-Crenshaw has served in many political and community
roles. She assisted Jesse Jackson from 1981 through 1983 as mobilization director
for special projects. She was consultant to Walter Mondale in 1983 and became
his national political director. Dozier-Crenshaw assisted the mobilization for the
First National Black Family Reunion, which attracted over 600,000 in August
1986 to Washington, DC. In 1987 she served as political consultant to Mayor
Harold Washington, who won reelection.

She currently serves as consultant to Coretta Scott King and to Southern Company Services and raises money for the archives of the Montgomery bus boycott. Dozier-Crenshaw is committed to ensuring that the many women involved in the boycott are remembered along with Rosa Parks.

—LaVerne Nickson

Bibliography

Much of the information was obtained in an interview with Doris Dozier-Crenshaw and materials sent to the author (October 4, 1991). For information about the role of women in the civil rights activities mentioned by Dozier, see Sara Evans, *Personal Politics* (New York: Random House, 1979); Juan Williams, *Eyes on the Prize* (New York: Viking Penguin, 1987, 1988); and *Women in the Civil Rights Movement: Trailblazers and Torchbearers, 1941–1965*, edited by Vicki Crawford, Jacqueline Rouse, and Barbara Woods (Brooklyn: Carlson, 1990).

DU BOIS, SHIRLEY GRAHAM (1907–1977), composer, musician, playwright, author, essayist, and peace and civil rights advocate, was born in Indianapolis, Indiana on November 11 to the Reverend David Andrew and Etta (Bell) Graham. Shirley Lola Graham married Shadrach T. McCanns in 1921, the year after she finished high school, and was widowed only a few years later in 1924. (While some biographical sources claim that Graham and McCanns divorced in 1929, Graham asserts in her 1971 biography of her second husband *His Day Is Marching On* that she was widowed). Her family helped her raise the two children from this marriage, Robert and David.

In 1926, with the child care support of her parents, she pursued higher education. Graham studied music in Paris both at the Sorbonne and privately. Graham then went on to head the Department of Music at Morgan State College in Baltimore, Maryland, from 1929 to 1931. To pursue a career in music and to support her two sons, Graham attended Oberlin College in Ohio in 1931 receiving her BA in 1934 and her MA, in music history and fine arts, in 1935. While at Oberlin, Graham wrote and composed *Tom Tom*, the first all–African American opera produced on a large scale with a professional cast. In addition, it was the first opera by an African American woman to be produced. After *Tom Tom*'s great success in 1932, Graham benefited from a full scholarship at Oberlin.

Although she had met W.E.B. Du Bois when she was 13 years old when he was a guest in her father's house, it was during her tenure at Oberlin that they began to correspond in earnest. Graham sought advice, solace, and guidance from the older leader.

In 1936 Graham won the position of director of the Chicago unit of the Federal Theatre Project (a subdivision of the Works Progress Administration); from then until 1938 Graham directed, wrote, designed, and composed musical scores, organized classes, and acted as general administrator. From 1938 until 1941, Graham concentrated on playwrighting as a Rosenwald fellow at Yale

University School of Drama. After this, she was appointed director of a YWCA-USO camp at Fort Huachuca, Arizona, where Graham started a camp magazine and directed productions.

The experiences at the camp and the discrimination against African American soldiers nurtured Graham's nascent activism. Graham repeatedly petitioned Washington, encouraged the reopening of cases, and frequently spoke out against racial injustices she witnessed. Not suprisingly, Graham was dismissed from her job in 1942. She went on to become the field secretary for the NAACP in New York City. The death of her son Robert in 1943 due to lack of medical treatment at a U.S. Army induction center in Indiana further galvanized Graham's activism against racial oppression. From this point on, her career shifted from music and drama to peace activism and "race work."

Graham contributed articles to the magazines *The Crisis*, *The Masses*, and *Harlem Quarterly* and later was a founding editor of *Freedomways*. In addition, she wrote widely acclaimed biographies of successful African Americans. In 1944, in collaboration with George Lipscomb, she wrote *Dr. George Washington Carver, Scientist*, a biography for young people. A year later she wrote *Paul Robeson, Citizen of the World*, and in 1949 completed *The Story of Phillis Wheatley*. Her other biographies treat Booker T. Washington, Benjamin Banneker, Frederick Douglass, W.E.B. Du Bois, Gamal Abdel Nasser, Pocahontas, Jean Baptiste Point Le Sable, and Julius Nyerere. In 1947 Graham received a Guggenheim grant, and in 1948 won the Julian Messner Award for *There Was Once a Slave*. In 1950 her *Your Most Humble Servant* won the Anisfield-Wolf Prize.

In 1951, after a long friendship forged through faithful letter writing, Graham married W.E.B. Du Bois. They each gave much of their time to various world peace and social justice organizations, and suffered recrimination from the U.S. Government during the "Red Scare," the anti-communist persecution of the McCarthy era. Despite Du Bois's advanced age, the couple traveled and lectured together until his death in 1963 in Ghana. Graham continued her activism for world peace until her death in Peking, China, on March 27, 1977.

—Thea S. Arnold

Bibliography

The best source of primary materials is in the W.E.B. Du Bois Papers, University of Massachusetts, Amherst, and an oral interview with W.E.B. Du Bois at Oral History Archives, Columbia University, New York City. These are published in Herbert Aptheker, ed., *The Correspondence of W.E.B. Du Bois* II and III (Amherst: University of Massachusetts Press, 1976). She posthumously published a pictorial biography of their life in *DuBois* (Chicago: Johnson Publishing, 1978).

Secondary and autobiographical sources include Kathy Perkins, "The Unknown Career of Shirley Graham," *Freedomways* 25:1 (1985): 6–17; Shirley Graham Du Bois, *His Day Is Marching On* (New York: Lippincott, 1971).

DUNBAR, MATILDA [MURPHY] (1844–1934), community leader and mother of poet Paul Laurence Dunbar, was born into slavery on the plantation of squire David Glass, Shelby County, Kentucky. As a slave child, at age 7 she was hired out to surrounding plantations for menial chores. At the Murphy plantation she met and married R. Weeks (Willis) Murphy. Two sons were born from the marriage: William T. and Robert S.

In the spring of 1866, when the slave laws were repealed in Kentucky, Willis Murphy sent Matilda and the two sons to live with her mother in Dayton, Ohio. Speculation has it that Willis Murphy died after joining the Union Army troops in regulating operations that followed the end of the Civil War. At that time, the women of Matilda's family had already settled in the Dayton area. Her grandmother, Becca Porter, had been purchased and manumitted by a Dayton abolitionist, Samuel Steele; and Matilda's mother had been "freed" when she was no longer able to work. With the support of the female network, Matilda Murphy proceeded to provide for her children.

In 1871 she married Joshua Dunbar, 20 years her senior. As a slave, he had been a plasterer and had learned to read and write. He had escaped from the South on the Underground Railroad, gone to Canada, returned to join the 55th Massachusetts Infantry and later the Cavalry. He had achieved the rank of sergeant and saw action in the Civil War. He moved to Ohio in 1863. Two children were born to Matilda and Joshua Dunbar: Elizabeth, who died before her second birthday, and Paul Laurence Dunbar (born June 27, 1872, in Dayton, Ohio).

The family attended the African Methodist Episcopal Church. At the time of Paul's birth, Matilda had acquired the ability to read. Several stories have described her as learning to read with the children of the slave owner, with Joshua at night, or with Paul "as she pieced together passages from the Bible which she propped over her washtubs." Joshua and Matilda were separated in 1873, when he went to live in the Old Soldier's Home, where he died in 1884 or 1885.

Matilda Dunbar dedicated her waking hours to her son. She worked as a laundress to pay for Paul Laurence Dunbar's schooling. Although she had wanted her son to be a minister, she (and Joshua) had encouraged the boy's writing of poetry. Both gave him firsthand knowledge of life in the South both before and immediately after the war. Throughout his career as poet and writer, she supported, encouraged, and helped him. She became a confidante of his wife, Alice Moore. When he became ill with tuberculosis, she nursed him. Paul Laurence Dunbar died in her house at 219 Summit Street, which has since been renamed Paul Laurence Dunbar Street.

During her life in Dayton, Matilda Dunbar was a member of various literary societies in Dayton. She was blind for the last four years of her life but was supported by friends and family, and especially by the Paul Laurence Dunbar Memorial Association, initiated by Langston Hughes, W.E.B. Du Bois, and Charles Higgins. She died on February 24, 1934.

—Mary Ann Williams

Bibliography

No biography exists for Matilda Dunbar, but the Paul Laurence Dunbar Museum in Dayton, Ohio, contains valuable information and has an extremely capable and friendly staff. Further information can be gleaned from the various biographies of Paul Laurence Dunbar and related works, such as Benjamin G. Brawley, *Paul Laurence Dunbar, Poet of the People* (Chapel Hill: University of North Carolina Press, 1936); Hallie Q. Brown, *Homespun Heroines and Other Women of Distinction* (Xenia, OH: Aldine Press, 1926); Ashley Bryan, "Introduction," *I Greet the Dawn. Paul Laurence Dunbar* (New York: Atheneum, 1978); Addison Gayle, Jr., *Oak and Ivy* (New York: Doubleday, 1971); R.W. Logan and M.R. Winston, *Dictionary of Negro Biography* (New York: Norton, 1982); Jay Martin and Gossie Hudson, *The Paul Laurence Reader* (New York: Dodd, Mead, 1975); Lida Keck Wiggins, *The Life and Works of Paul Laurence Dunbar* (New York: Kraus Reprint, 1971).

DUNBAR-NELSON, ALICE [MOORE] (1875–1935), teacher, author, and civic leader, was born on July 19 in New Orleans, the younger of two daughters of seamstress Patricia (Wright) Moore and seaman Joseph Moore. Alice Ruth Moore graduated from a public high school in 1889, completed a two-year teacher-training program at Straight University (now Dillard University), New Orleans, and earned an MA at Cornell University in addition to studying at the Pennsylvania School of Industrial Arts and the University of Pennsylvania.

Dunbar-Nelson devoted much of her life to teaching, her first position being at the Old Marigny Elementary School in New Orleans. From 1897 to 1898 she taught at Public School 83, Brooklyn, and Public School 66, Harlem, and helped to found the White Rose Mission (later the White Rose Home for Girls in Harlem). After an epistolary courtship that began in 1895, she married Paul Laurence Dunbar in 1898 and moved to Washington, DC. The Dunbars separated in 1902. Dunbar-Nelson moved to Delaware, where she taught at Howard High School, Wilmington, and taught at the State College for Colored Students (now Delaware State College), Dover. She taught at Hampton Institute during the summers. During this time, she lived with her mother, her sister (Leila Young, who was also divorced and teaching at Howard High School), and her sister's four children.

In 1910 she was secretly married to teacher Henry Arthur Callis, but the two divorced the next year. In 1916 she married Robert J. Nelson, a journalist and widower with two children. Failed marriages and participation in women's activities have led authors to assume her lesbian identity, but Dunbar-Nelson's only documented lesbian relationships occurred during the 1920s. From 1924 to 1928, Dunbar-Nelson was teacher and parole officer at the Industrial School for Colored Girls in Marshalltown, Delaware, which she had helped found in 1920. From 1928 to 1931 she was executive secretary of the American Friends Inter-Racial Peace Committee, a subsidiary of the American Friends Service Committee.

166   *Dunbar-Nelson, Alice*

During the Depression, Dunbar-Nelson and her husband moved to Philadelphia, when he was appointed to the Pennsylvania Athletic Boxing Commission. She died of heart disease at the University of Pennsylvania Hospital on September 18, 1935. Since no Philadelphia establishment would perform a cremation on a black person, she was returned to Wilmington for the service and her ashes "strewn to the four winds" as she requested in her will.

Dunbar-Nelson was an active journalist during her lifetime. From 1913 to 1914 she wrote for and helped edit the *A.M.E. Church Review*. From 1920 to 1922 she published and co-edited the Wilmington *Advocate*, a weekly newspaper. She wrote a column, "Une Femme Dit," for the Pittsburgh *Courier* in 1926; a column, "As in a Looking Glass," for the Washington *Eagle* from 1926 to 1930; and a column, "So It Seems to Alice Dunbar-Nelson," for the Pittsburgh *Courier* in 1930. Some of her work was syndicated by the Associated Negro Press.

Dunbar-Nelson was also very active in civic and political activities. After leaving New Orleans in 1896, she became secretary of the National Association of Colored Women and a member of the Woman's Era Club as well as of the Massachusetts Corps. In 1915 she was field organizer of the Middle Atlantic States in the struggle to pass state constitutional amendments to guarantee women's suffrage. She founded a local chapter of The Circle for Negro War Relief in 1918 and toured the South as a field representative of the Woman's Committee of the Council of National Defense to encourage African American women in the war effort. Dunbar-Nelson was the first African American woman in the United States to serve on the Republican State Committee of Delaware. She also served as chair of the League of Colored Republican Women. In 1922 she headed the Anti-Lynching Crusaders in Delaware fighting for the Dyer Anti-Lynching Bill.

—Rosalie Murphy Baum

Bibliography

Two invaluable sources of information about Dunbar-Nelson's life exist: the Diary that she kept from July 29 to December 31, 1921, and from November 1926 to December 1931 and the letters from her to Paul Laurence Dunbar that are in Special Collections, Morris Library, University of Delaware. Gloria T. Hull offers an excellent biography of Dunbar-Nelson in *Color, Sex, and Poetry: Three Women Writers of the Harlem Renaissance* (Bloomington: Indiana University Press, 1987). She has also edited the diary as *Give Us Each Day: The Diary of Alice Dunbar-Nelson* (New York: Norton, 1984). Hull's articles "Researching Alice Dunbar-Nelson: A Personal and Literary Perspective," in *All the Women Are White, All the Blacks Are Men, But Some of Us Are Brave*, edited by Patricia Scott Hull and Barbara Smith (Old Westbury, NY: Feminist Press, 1982); and "Alice Dunbar-Nelson: Delaware Writer and Woman of Affairs," in *Delaware History* XVII (Fall–Winter 1976): 87–103, provide further resources and photographs of the writer.

Dunbar-Nelson began publishing early, in 1895, with *Violets and Other Tales*, a collection of essays, poetry, reviews, short stories, and sketches that reveal her as a romanticist. In 1899 she published a collection of short stories, *The Goodness of St. Rocque and Other Stories*, intended as a companion piece to a special edition of Dunbar's work, *Poems of Cabin and Field*, and revealing her as a local colorist. Dunbar-Nelson also wrote two novels that have not been published, *This Lofty Oak* and *Confessions of a Lazy Woman*, and a number of plays, including *Mine Eyes Have Seen*, *Gone White*, *The Author's Evening at Home*, and *Love's Disguise*. Some of her work is available in *An Alice Dunbar-Nelson Reader*, edited by R. Ora Williams (New York: Oxford, 1979). Even more has been made available recently as a part of the Schomburg Library of Nineteenth-Century Black Women Writers in *The Works of Alice Dunbar-Nelson*, edited by Gloria T. Hull, in three volumes. Her unpublished writings are in Special Collections, Morris Library. Dunbar-Nelson also edited several collections of African American writing: *Masterpieces of Negro Eloquence: The Best Speeches Delivered by the Negro from the Days of Slavery to the Present Time* (New York: Bookery, 1914); and *The Dunbar Speaker and Entertainer* (Naperville, IL: Nichols, 1920). A valuable reference source is R. Ora Williams's "Works by and about Alice Ruth (Moore) Dunbar-Nelson: A Bibliography," in the *CLA Journal* 19 (March 1976).

DUNHAM, KATHERINE (b. 1912), born June 22 (another source, however, lists 1909 as her year of birth) in Glen Ellyn, Illinois, is best known as a dancer/choreographer, teacher, and anthropologist. Dunham earned her baccalaurete, master's, and doctoral degrees in anthropology from the University of Chicago with graduate study also at Northwestern University, where she studied with noted anthropologist Melville Herskovits. Under his guidance, she took a travel fellowship from the Julius Rosenwald Foundation to do anthropological fieldwork in the West Indies and the Caribbean. In 1935 she did research among the maroons of Accompong, Jamaica, which culminated in her book *Journey to Accompong* (New York: H. Holt, 1946). She married John Pratt on July 10, 1941, and adopted a daughter, Marie Christine.

Dunham's decision not to remain at Northwestern for her doctorate but to return to the University of Chicago was an important one. She said, if she had not returned to Chicago, she would not have continued her research in the field of dance and choreography as cultural and historical dimensions of African existence. Dunham had come to believe that an important foundation of African and African diasporic cultures would be seen through motion and that dance was one of the African "survivalisms" that scholars like Herskovits spoke about. While she excised and exposed the role of dance in the African American experience, she also made a major contribution to the theories of modern dance.

The 1960s brought Dunham both personal and professional gratification. She has returned her gifts to the community. Since the 1960s she has been based in East St. Louis, Illinois, directing the Katherine Dunham Center for Performing Arts of Southern Illinois University. She has worked with that city's young black militants in attempts to bring into their lives some semblance of social justice. In Brian Lanker's *I Dream a World: Portraits of Black Women Who Changed America*, she called this "socialization through the arts."

The decade also brought her many honors. In 1966 Katherine Dunham became the technical and cultural advisor to the president of Senegal. Part of her responsibilities included the training of that country's National Ballet. In 1968 she received the Professional Achievement Award from the University of Chicago Alumni Association.

Her honors continued. In 1983 Dunham received the Kennedy Center Honors Award. She received the Scripps American Dance Festival Award in 1986. Dunham is a mentor of the Women's Honorary Scientific Fraternity at the University of Chicago and a member of the Royal Society of Anthropologists in London.

Dunham is an honorary citizen of Haiti, where she has kept a home named "Habitation Leclerc." In 1961 she became a commander of their Legion of Honor. Dunham has written scholarly and autobiographical works including: *The Dances of Haiti* (1947), *A Touch of Innocence* (1950), *Island Possessed* (1969), and *Kasamance* (1974). Her choreographed works include "Tropics" (1937), "Haitian Suite" (1937), "Island Songs" (1938), "Plantation Dances" (1940), "Bal Negre" (1948), "Afrique" (1949), "Spirituals" (1951), "Jazz Finale" (1955), and "Diamond Thief" (1962).

—Nancy Elizabeth Fitch

Bibliography

Joyce Aschenbrenner wrote a very interesting book on Katherine Dunham for the Dance Research Annual XII, *Katherine Dunham: Reflections on the Social and Political Contexts of Afro-American Dance with Notations of the Dunham Method and Technique by Lavinia Williams*, edited by Patricia A. Rowe (New York: CORD Inc., 1981). As do several of the other monographs in this bibliography, Aschenbrenner looks at African American dance in its cultural and historical contexts. Ruth Beckford wrote an authorized biography of Katherine Dunham entitled *Katherine Dunham: A Biography* (New York: Marcel Dekker, 1979). Beckford is a colleague and former student of the choreographer-anthropologist and was asked by Dunham to write her story. It is an interesting insider's look at Dunham's life, interests, and achievements. Ruth Biemiller, *Dance: The Story of Katherine Dunham* (Garden City, NY: Doubleday, 1969); and Terry Harnan, *African Rhythm. American Dance: A Biography of Katherine Dunham* (New York: Alfred Knopf, 1974) incorporate ideas and connections Dunham made between African dance and motion and African cultural history and anthropology in the Western Hemisphere. Brian Lanker's section on Dunham in his photographic essays *I Dream a World: Portraits of Black Women Who Changed America* (New York: Stewart, Tabori, & Chang, 1989) provides a wonderful personal statement from Dunham reinforcing her idea of a nexus between motion and Africans wherever they are found.

E

EARLY, SARAH [WOODSON] (1825–1907), educator and moral reformer, was born in Chilicothe, Ohio, on November 15, the eleventh child of free black parents Thomas and Jemima Woodson. The Woodsons were members of the local Methodist church in Chilicothe, which, like many others during this time, forced black members to sit apart from white members, and receive communion separately. The Woodsons were among a group of black communicants who, objecting to these practices, left the church to form their own black Methodist church. The strong religious conviction of the Woodson family would have a significant impact on Sarah Jane Woodson's life.

In 1850 Sarah Woodson enrolled at the Albany Manual Labor Academy in southern Ohio. Two years later she enrolled in the collegiate program at Oberlin College, one of a few schools recommended by the African Methodist Episcopal (AME) church as a college sympathetic to the education of blacks, and where there was no racial discrimination in classrooms or living quarters. She graduated in 1856, the same year her brother, Lewis Woodson, was named a trustee of the newly established Wilberforce University in Xenia, Ohio. In 1858 Sarah Woodson secured a teaching position at Wilberforce, becoming one of the first black women on a college faculty.

Sarah Woodson remained at Wilberforce until 1868, when she joined the ranks of the teachers who headed to the South under the auspices of the Freedmen's Bureau. She taught at a girls' school in Hillsboro, North Carolina, until her marriage to AME church minister Jordan Winston Early. Although the couple had no children of their own, Early was a widower with several young children who became the charges of Sarah Woodson Early.

The couple were married 18 years, until Jordan Early's death in 1903. During this time, Sarah Woodson Early traveled to various cities in Tennessee in which her husband's churches were located, teaching in black schools until his retirement in 1888. In 1894 she wrote a biography of her husband, her only book. She was actively involved in her husband's ministry, and organized women church members to use their time, money, and influence for the good of the church. This work set the stage for her future involvement in the Women's Christian Temperance Union (WCTU).

From 1888 until 1892 Sarah Woodson Early served as superintendent of the Colored Division of the WTCU, and as a spokesperson for the Prohibition Party in Tennessee. Her efforts gained her entries in two books on important black women published in 1893. Maintaining that moral reform was key to self-improvement for the black races, Sarah Early carried on her reform activities with fervor and enthusiasm, traveling widely in the South, and encouraging women to extend their moral influence beyond the realm of the home. Expanding her interest beyond temperance reform, she encouraged women to form mutual aid societies, and fostered an organizational spirit, which would ultimately empower black women, and in turn, the race.

Sarah Woodson Early died at age 83 in 1907. Her career is evidence of her commitment to education, religion, and moral reform as the path to racial self-help, which she viewed as the key to the successful integration of African Americans into American society.

—Rama Ramakrishna

Bibliography

Information on Sarah Woodson Early is taken from Ellen NicKenzie Lawson's *The Three Sarahs: Documents of Antebellum Black Women* (New York: Edwin Mellen Press, 1984). Writings by Sarah Woodson Early referenced by Lawson include her 1894 biography of her husband, *Life and Labors of Rev. Jordan W. Early*; "The Great Part Taken by the Women of the West in the Development of the African Methodist Episcopal Church," published in Lawson Scruggs's work *Women of Distinction* (Raleigh, NC: L.A. Scruggs, 1893); and "The Effort of the Colored Women of the South to Improve Their Condition," which appears in the *National W.C.T.U. Annual Report* for 1894.

EDELMAN, MARIAN [WRIGHT] (b. 1939), civil rights activist and advocate for children, was born in Bennettsville, South Carolina, on June 6 to Arthur J. and Maggie (Bowen) Wright. Her father, a Baptist minister, felt that helping others was the basic duty of all people. Thus, service was an essential part of her life.

Her education emphasized international understanding. She attended Spelman College in Atlanta, when in her junior year, she received a Merrill scholarship to study at the University of Paris and in Geneva, Switzerland, during the academic year 1958–1959. That summer, she participated in a student exchange study tour of East Germany, Poland, Czechoslovakia, and the USSR. In 1960 she was the valedictorian of her class at Spelman College. Her achievements led to her receipt of another award as J.H. Whitney Fellow, 1960–1961. During the summer of 1962, she worked in Crossroads Africa, a work project in the area of the Ivory Coast of West Africa. She received an LLB from Yale University in 1963.

Armed with a law degree from Yale University, she became the first black woman admitted to the bar in Mississippi. She also became a member of the bar in Washington, DC, and Massachusetts. From 1963 to 1964, she served as the staff attorney for the NAACP Legal Defense and Educational Fund in New York City. From 1964 to 1968 she directed the NAACP Legal Defense and Educational Fund in Jackson, Mississippi, where she successfully defended the Head Start program from political attacks. Her advocacy for the poor of Mississippi led to testimony to the Senate and a liaison role between the Poor People's

Campaign and Congress. This role brought her to Peter Edelman, an assistant to Senator John F. Kennedy. Fifteen months after their meeting, she married Edelman on July 14, 1968. She continued her varied roles while raising three children: Joshua, Jonah, and Ezra.

Again in 1968, she toured Eastern Europe, India, Israel, East Africa, and Southeast Asia. From 1968 to 1973 Edelman was a partner for the Washington Research Project of the Southern Center for Public Policy, which became the parent organization of the Children's Defense Fund, which became incorporated in 1973. She also served as director of Harvard University's Center for Law and Education, 1971–1973. In 1973 Edelman became the president of the Children's Defense Fund. A lawyer by profession, she has addressed numerous legal and social issues. She has risen to prominence for her strong advocacy on children's issues. Edelman has spoken out on issues from prenatal care to early childhood to the prevention of teenage pregnancy. Through the Children's Defense Fund, Edelman seeks to make it "un-American" for any child to grow up poor, lacking adequate health care, food, shelter, child care, or education.

She has been a member on numerous committees addressing social, educational, and public policy: member of the advisory council of Martin Luther King Jr. Memorial Library; member of the advisory board of Hampshire College; member of the Presidential Committee on Missing in Action (1977); Presidential Committee on International Year of the Child (1979); and member of the board of directors of the Eleanor Roosevelt Institute, Carnegie Council on Children (1972–1977), and Martin Luther King Jr. Memorial Center. She has served as trustee for the March of Dimes, Joint Center for Political Science, Yale University Corporation (1971–1977) and the Aetna Center.

Her outstanding contributions have been recognized with many awards. Edelman has been the recipient of numerous honorary degrees, from such insitutions such as Smith College (1969), Columbia University, Swarthmore College, Rutgers University, Georgetown University, and Yale University. Named one of the Outstanding Young Women of America in 1966, Edelman has continued to be awarded for her outstanding achievements. She received the *Mademoiselle* magazine award (1965), the Louise Waterman Wise Award (1970), National Leadership Award from the National Women's Political Caucus (1980), Black Women's Forum Award (1980), Eliot Award from the American Public Health Association (1987), and the MacArthur Prize Fellow (1985). More recently Edelman has been honored with the Albert Schweitzer Humanitarian Prize from Johns Hopkins University (1987), Hubert Humphrey Civil Rights Award, and the AFL-CIO Humanitarian Award (1989).

—Mary Hovanec

Bibliography

No general biography has been written about Marian Edelman. However, biographical information does appear in various periodicals: Katherine Bouton,

"Marian Wright Edelman," Ms. 16 (July 1987): 1–2; Ellen Ruppel-Shell, "Edelman," Parenting (October 1990): 94; C. Thomkins, "Profiles," The New Yorker 65 (March 27, 1989): 48–50; and "Who's Behind the ABC?" Christianity Today 33 (March 17, 1989): 35. Edelman has written many articles to promote her causes for children: "Children's Crusade," Essence 7 (September 1980): 70; "Building Bridges," Black Collegian 20 (September/October 1989): 65+; "Children and Child Care," Journal of Negro Education 58:3 (Summer 1989): 288–296; "We Must Convey to Children That We Believe in Them," Ebony 43:10 (August 1988): 128–130; "How to Prevent Teenage Pregnancy," Ebony 42:9 (July 1987): 60–66; "Suffer the Little Children," Educational Record 68:4 (Fall 1987): 24–30; "An Agenda for Empowerment," Essence 19:1 (May 1988): 65–66+; and "Save the Children," Ebony 41:10 (August 1986): 53–58. Biographical information is included in Harry A. Ploski's The Negro Almanac (Detroit: Gale, 1989); The State of Black America (New York: National Urban League, 1989); and Who's Who (1990–1991). Her books include: Families in Peril (Cambridge: Harvard University Press, 1987) and The Measure of Our Success (New York: Random House, 1992).

EDMONDS, HELEN [GREY] (b. 1911), born on December 3 in Lawrenceville, Virginia, is a historian of the South and modern Europe and public servant in international relations for the U.S. Government. Dr. Edmonds attended Saint Paul's College from kindergarten through secondary school. She received her baccalaureate degree from Morgan State University in Baltimore, Maryland, and her master of arts from Ohio State University in Columbus. In 1946 she became the first black woman to receive a doctorate in history from Ohio State University.

Edmonds's first teaching experiences were at Virginia Theological Seminary and College in Lynchburg, Virginia, teaching Latin and Greek as well as history and at Saint Paul's College in Lawrenceville. She came to North Carolina Central University (NCCU) in Durham in 1941 and remained there until her retirement in 1977. While at NCCU she served as a professor of history, chairman of the History Department, dean of the Graduate School of Arts and Sciences, distinguished professor of history, and now as professsor emeritus. Since her retirement Dr. Edmonds has been visiting scholar at the Ford Foundation, University of Rochester, Harvard University, MIT, and Radcliffe College. While at Radcliffe's Mary Ingraham Bunting Institute, she worked on a monograph on the African American woman in American politics.

Edmonds published her first book in 1951, the classic The Negro and Fusion Politics in North Carolina. This book on North Carolinian politics discussed the disintegration of Democratic Party dominance from 1895 to 1901, an era called the "Fusion Period." In her Acknowledgments, she credits Dr. Henry H. Simms of Ohio State University for her interest in southern history. From 1954 to 1955 she did postdoctoral research at the University of Heidelberg in West Germany.

Most of her personal life has been spent within the Republican Party. Through this affiliation, Edmonds served as U.S. Alternate Delegate to the United

Nations, on various Department of State lecture tours, and on national advisory councils relating to American international affairs. In 1962 she published *Appropriate Directions for the Modern Liberal Arts College*, and in 1971, *Black Faces in High Places*.

During the past 20 years, Helen Edmonds has been honored by the academic community. She has served as the national president of the Links, Inc. (a black women's community organization that sponsors charitable activities and a grant-in-aid program), and has received honorary degrees from Ohio State University (1983) and Duke University (1983), and the Graduate Medallion from Radcliffe College (1989). In 1975 she received the Board of Governors Oliver Max Gardner Award from the University of North Carolina for her contributions "to the welfare of the human race," and in 1982, the Candace Award from the Coalition of 100 Black Women as well as the Hugh McEniry Award of the North Carolina Association of Colleges and Universities. In 1986 she was named a Distinguished Woman of North Carolina, and in 1988 the governing council of the American Historical Association unanimously elected her to receive its Award for Scholarly Distinction. In 1989 NCCU's history and social science building was dedicated in her honor. Dr. Edmonds currently resides in Durham, North Carolina.

—Nancy Elizabeth Fitch

Bibliography

Most of the information about Dr. Helen Grey Edmonds came from letters, newspaper articles, and other materials supplied by the Archives of the Library on the campus of North Carolina Central University in Durham. Those materials include Marney Rich, "Powerful Presence of Helen Edmonds," *News and Observer* (Raleigh, NC) (September 19, 1982): C1+; the *Quarterly* of the Ohio State University Department of History, May 1984, Vol. 11, No. 2, about her time as visiting professor on the OSU campus; Clinton Elliott, "Freedom House Gives Recognition Awards," *Bay State Banner* (May 3, 1986): 3+, about the keynote address given at Freedom House entitled "Excellence Without Excuses"; and documents, including the letter announcing the American Historical Association's (AHA) Award for Scholarly Distinction given at the AHA's annual meeting on December 28, 1988. She is profiled in *Black History and the Historical Profession, 1915–1980*, edited by August Meier and Elliot Rudwick (Urbana: University of Illinois, 1989).

ELAW, ZILPHA (c. 1790–1846), evangelist and visionary, was born to free parents in the Philadelphia, Pennsylvania, area. Her mother died in childbirth of her twenty-second child when Elaw was 12 years old. All but three died in infancy. Her father consigned her to a Quaker family, with whom she remained until she was 18 years old. Within six months of this arrangement, Elaw's father died.

Elaw had a pious upbringing by her parents. She began to have religious visions in her mid-teens and eventually converted and joined the Methodist society in 1808. Two years later she married Joseph Elaw, moved to Burlington, New Jersey, and gave birth to a daughter.

In 1817 Elaw attended her first camp meeting. There she fell into a trance and became convinced that her soul was sanctified by God. She began her public speaking by offering prayers for those attending the meeting. In 1819, at a second camp meeting, Elaw began to exhort and pursued an itinerant ministry. Many whites were supportive of her ministry, but black Methodists were not enthusiastic at first. Elaw's husband begged her to give up a public ministry, fearing she would be ridiculed. In 1823 Joseph Elaw died of consumption, and Zilpha Elaw and her daughter turned to domestic work to survive. Elaw opened a school in Burlington, which survived for two years. She left her daughter in the care of a relative in 1828, and went to Philadelphia to begin her preaching career.

Elaw ventured into the slaveholding states in 1828 for almost two years. In 1840 she traveled to London and preached more than 1,000 sermons before family gatherings, outdoor revivals, and worship services, where, as a female evangelist, she met great resistance. The last record of her life and activity is her spiritual autobiography, *Memoirs of the Life, Religious Experience, Ministerial Travels and Labours of Mrs. Zilpha Elaw* (1846). She was still in Great Britain. Few records exist of her life after this time.

—Emilie M. Townes

Bibliography

Andrews, William L., ed. *Sisters of the Spirit: Three Black Women's Autobiographies of the Nineteenth Century.* Bloomington: Indiana University Press, 1986.

Dodson, Jualynne. "Nineteenth-Century A.M.E. Preaching Women," in *Women in New Worlds*, H.F. Thomas and R.S. Keller, eds., Nashville: Abington, 1981.

Elaw, Zilpha. *Memoirs of the Life, Religious Experience, Ministerial Travels and Labours of Mrs. Zilpha Elaw.* London, 1846.

She is featured in Margaret Busby, ed., *Daughters of Africa.* New York: Pantheon, 1992.

EPPS, ROSELYN (b. 1930), a strong advocate of medical services for the poor, has been a practicing pediatrician, teacher, administrator, and organizational leader for nearly 40 years. The first black woman to serve as president of the American Medical Women's Association (1990–1991), she was born in Little Rock, Arkansas, and grew up in Savannah, Georgia. Her father was the president of Georgia's Savannah State College; her mother, the principal of an elementary school. She received her BS in 1951 and her medical degree in 1955, both from Howard University.

Dr. Epps served her internship and residency at Freedmen's Hospital, where she was chief resident. Later she obtained her MPH from Johns Hopkins University and her MA from the American University in 1981. During the 1970s she served in various capacities in the government of the District of Columbia. Since 1981 Dr. Epps has been professor of pediatrics and child health at Howard University Medical School, for which she is also director of the Howard University Child Development Center in Washington, DC. From 1981 to 1985 she was the project director for the Project to Consolidate Health Services for High Risk Young People, which brought together doctors from a variety of fields, representatives of community service organizations, and members of the private sector, to establish a community-based facility at Howard that would care for adolescents and young adults, many from inner-city neighborhoods where the incidence of health-related deaths among the youthful population is high. From 1985 to 1988 she was director of the Know Your Body Health Project. Epps commented in a 1988 interview in *Black Enterprise* magazine:

> Many of the problems we're facing with young people today are a result of our being so isolated. Years ago, it seemed as if everyone was involved in raising one another's children. . . . Everyone made sure you did what was right or expected and kids grew up feeling secure and supported, as if they were part of something. . . . What we really need now is human effort. . . . We need more black doctors to work in and serve the black community. We need more black professionals to take an interest in young people and to act as role models.

Dr. Epps has served as an international consultant for the World Bank, the UN Fund for Population, and the U.S. Department of Health and Human Services. She is a fellow of the American Academy of Pediatrics and has served as an officer of many organizations, including the National Medical Association, the American Public Health Association, and the American Medical Association.

—Janet Miller with Susan Shifrin

Bibliography

The most complete information exists in the Roselyn Epps File, Black Women Physicians Project, Accession 178, Archives and Special Collections on Women in Medicine, Medical College of Pennsylvania. Interviews with Epps are in *Black Enterprise, Jet,* and other periodicals.

EVANS, MATILDA (c. 1870s–1935), the first black woman native of South Carolina to practice medicine in her home state, was born in Aiken County, South Carolina. Matilda Arabella Evans studied at the Schofield Normal and Industrial School founded and managed by Miss Martha Schofield, a Pennsylvania Quaker. In 1868 Evans wrote a biography, *Martha Schofield, Pioneer Negro*

Educator, which was published in 1916. Evans worked her way through Oberlin College, later returning to Schofield as a teacher.

She attended the Women's Medical College in Philadelphia on a scholarship given by Alfred Jones of Philadelphia, Pennsylvania. There she was the only African American in her class. She received her MD degree in 1897, and then returned to South Carolina to open her practice in Columbia the following year. Her practice grew due both to the railroad company serving Columbia, which brought her their injured employees, and to black patient referrals from white doctors. Evans treated patients in her own home until she was able to rent a building with room for 30 people. There, she established a nurse's training school. Eventually, this treatment center grew into St. Luke Hospital, one of the first hospitals organized and operated for the black community in Columbia. In 1918 St. Luke Hospital had 14 rooms and 20 beds. She gave up her hospital in 1918, when she volunteered to serve with the Peace Corps.

In 1932 she organized a medical clinic in Harden Street in Columbia. Some years later she founded the Negro Health Association of South Carolina. She also introduced medical examinations into the public schools. She never married, but she adopted and raised eight children. After practicing medicine for 37 years, Matilda Evans died in 1935.

—Terri L. Jewell

Bibliography

Limited resources are available from the archives of the Women's Medical College of Pennsylvania and Oberlin College. Evans is briefly described in Marianna W. Davis, *Contributions of Black Women to America* (Columbia, SC: Kenday, 1981); Thomas L. Johnson and Phillip C. Dunn, *A True Likeness: The Black South of Richard Samuel Roberts: 1920–1936* (Chapel Hill: Algonquin Books, 1986); Dorothy Sterling, *We Are Your Sisters: Black Women in the Nineteenth Century* (New York: Norton, 1984); George Brown Tindall, *South Carolina Negroes* (Columbia: University of South Carolina Press, 1952); Bettina Aptheker, "Quest for Dignity: Black Women in the Professions, 1865–1900," in her book, *Woman's Legacy* (Amherst: University of Massachusetts Press, 1982), pp. 89–110; and Sara W. Brown, "Colored Women Physicians," *Southern Workman* 52 (1923): 580–593.

EVANTI, (MADAME) LILLIAN [EVANS, TIBBS] (1890–1967), the first professional African American opera singer and a composer, was born in Washington, DC, to a prominent family. Both parents were educators. Her mother, Anne (Brooks), was a public school music teacher, and her father, Wilson Bruce Evans, a physician, founded and served as the first principal of Armstrong Manual Training High School, which she later attended. Tibbs began her music education at age four with a solo at a Friendship Gardens concert. She studied piano at age five and by her early teenage years was an accomplished pianist. She graduated from Armstrong Technical High School in 1908 and took

a kindergarten training course at Miner Normal School to become a teacher in the District of Columbia public schools. After graduating from Howard University in 1917, she combined the teaching and music training as the director of music at Miner.

In 1918 Evans married Roy Wilfred Tibbs, her former teacher and music director at Howard University. They had a son, Thurlow. Prior to his death in 1944, Tibbs and her husband became estranged. For her professional career, Tibbs combined both names, Evans and Tibbs, to become the public figure Madame Evanti.

Tibbs went to Europe in the 1920s, where she became a lyric and coloratura soprano known as Madame Lillian Evanti, earning her reputation with a debut in Nice, France, in 1925. Continuing her music studies in Paris, Milan, and Munich, she also sang on a European tour that took her to Monte Carlo, Menton, Montpellier, Nimes, and Toulon. Her debut in Italy was in Genova in the opera *The Barber of Seville.*

Madame Evanti spoke 5 languages and had 24 operas in her repertoire including *La Traviata, Lakme, The Barber of Seville, Romeo and Juliet, La Boheme, Carmen,* and *The Magic Flute.* In concert, her programs also included Negro spirituals.

In 1932 Madame Evanti returned to the United States at the invitation of Giulio Gatti-Casazza, the general manager of the Metropolitan Opera Company in New York City, who had heard her perform in Italy and wanted her to audition for the company. Reportedly, the board of the Metropolitan Opera vetoed his idea to have Evanti break the color line. Undaunted by her exclusion, she performed in Washington, DC's Belasco Theatre to an integrated audience on March 20, 1932. She then returned to New York in April to perform at the Town Hall under the management of Arthur Judson. In February 1934, Evanti gave a command performance at the White House for President Franklin D. and Eleanor Roosevelt. From 1932 to 1935 she did concert and radio work in the United States. During early 1940, she toured Latin American countries, receiving diplomas and medals from appreciative leaders. The U.S. State Department sponsored her tour of Argentina with Toscanini and the NBC Orchestra. In 1941, inspired by her Latin American experiences, she composed "Himno Panamericano," to influence relations in that area. The piece was selected for the U.S. Office of Education's Latin American exhibition. Her performances at U.S. Army and Navy installations during World War II won her numerous citations.

In 1942 she initiated and became a principal member of the new Negro National Opera Company of Philadelphia and later served on its advisory board to encourage performance careers among African Americans. Howard University honored her in 1944 with its distinquished Alumni Award in Music.

Evanti, also composed patriotic songs, including "On Furlough Mana," for soldiers and their loved ones during World War II; "Hail to Fair Washington"; "Forward March to Victory," for the dedication of the United Nations; and a commissioned piece, "Salute to Ghana," under the auspices of the government-sponsored radio program Voice of America in 1957. She also wrote ten songs that were published by W.C. Handy, including "Twenty Third Psalm," "Beloved Mother," and "My Little Prayer."

During the 1950s she was again invited to the White House to perform for Presidents Harry Truman and Dwight Eisenhower. She toured Africa and received decorations for her cultural diplomacy. Madame Evanti returned to Miner Teacher's College to coach singers and give voice lessons. The U.S. Army chorus recorded her "Salute to Ghana" in 1957 for the country's Independence Day celebration.

Evanti lived in her parents' home, a nineteenth-century townhouse near Howard University, until she entered Ruth's Personal Care Home, a nursing home, where she died on December 6, 1967. In 1984 Washington, DC, mayor Marion Barry proclaimed July 9 Madame Lillian Evanti Day in the federal city. Her parents' home now houses an art gallery and is a historic landmark. On July 9, 1984, the National Portrait Gallery in Washington, DC, placed her photograph in the Hall of Notable Americans. Other honors include the Chevalier de l'Honneur et Merite, an honor bestowed by the government of Haiti, and the *Afro-American* Honor Roll for 1943.

Madame Evanti was a member of Zeta Phi Beta sorority and Pi Kappa Lambda national music sorority.

—Nancy Elizabeth Fitch and Christopher D. White

Bibliography

Materials about Madame Evanti are found in the vertical files of the Schomburg Center for Research in Black Culture, New York Public Library, and from the vertical file and card catalogue on Madame Lillian Evanti at the Moorland Spingarn Reading Room at Howard University. Included are not only newspaper clippings of her performances but also playbills and public relations materials. Specific articles of importance include Lula Jones Garrett, "Mme Evanti Says That as a Cook She's a Good Chess Player . . . But," *The Afro-American* (May 10, 1955); "Mme Evanti Wins Acclaim of Capital, Performed at a Home-Coming Concert at the Belasco," *Washington Post* (March 21, 1932); and Katherine S. Seigenthaler, in the "Limelight section," *Washington Post* (July 8, 1984). Obituaries included: *New York Times* (December 9, 1967): 47; *Washington Post* (December 8 and 10, 1967): E16; and the Baltimore *Afro-American* on December 8, 1967. News of her career appears in *Washington Sentinel, Times Herald,* and *Washington Tribune.* Magazines such as *Musical America* also feature her performances. A brief biographical sketch by Raymond Lemieux appears in Rayford Logan and Michael Winston's *Dictionary of American Negro Biography* (New York: Norton, 1982).

F

FAUSET, CRYSTAL DREDA BIRD (1893–1965), whose life proves that tragic beginnings do not necessarily produce human beings incapable of surmounting great obstacles, was the first black woman elected to a state legislature in the United States. She was born Crystal Dreda Bird in Princess Anne, Maryland, on June 27, the second-youngest daughter of nine children born to Benjamin Bird, the first principal of Princess Anne Academy, and Portia E. (Lovett). Her father's leadership of the school for black youths ended in 1897 with his death. Her mother continued to serve as principal of the school until her own death in 1900.

Crystal went to live with her mother's sister in Boston, attending the public schools, and graduating from the Boston Normal School in 1914. She taught school for three years before becoming the field secretary for the national board of the YWCA. As a field secretary, Bird was responsible for organizing local programs for young black women.

The Interracial Section of the American Friends Service Committee hired her to develop human relations programs intended to enhance interracial understanding. She accepted the challenge with extraordinary energy and commitment. In a single year, she gave 210 speeches to 50,000 people.

Continuing her education, she graduated in 1931 with a BS from Teachers College at Columbia University. She married school principal Arthur Fauset that same year. With race relations as her field, she helped develop the Swarthmore College Institute of Race Relations and served as the joint executive secretary of the summer seminars from 1933 to 1935. These seminars brought her into contact with such influential white women committed to racial justice as Eleanor Roosevelt. Her abilities as a public speaker and her involvements in civic affairs led to her appointment to the Philadelphia Works Progress Administration (WPA) as the assistant director. The appointment led to active involvement in party politics. She organized the Philadelphia Democratic Women's League and served as the director of colored women for the Democratic National Committee in 1936. Party leaders recognized her organizational skills and prodded her to run for office.

In 1938 Crystal Bird Fauset won election in a white majority voting district that brought her to the Pennsylvania state legislature to join five black males. Her race relations leadership helped her to succeed in her telephone campaign that highlighted social issues. She worked for slum clearance, low-cost housing, enforcement of fair employment practices, and racial justice. Her national recognition created a larger stage from which to display her talents. By the end of 1939 she resigned from the state assembly to take over as assistant state director of the Education and Recreation Program of the Works Progress Administration and as race relations advisor to the state WPA.

Her relationship with Eleanor Roosevelt enabled racial concerns to penetrate the White House. Before American official entrance into World War II, Fauset received appointment to the Office of Civilian Defense to monitor black domestic programs, advising New York City mayor Fiorello La Guardia on race relations. When she resigned this position to work with the Democratic National Committee in 1944, conflict with new leadership led to her endorsement of the Republican presidential candidate, Thomas E. Dewey. This decision led to her political demise within the Democratic Party. During that same year her husband initiated divorce proceedings to end their marriage; they had separated years earlier.

The end of World War II symbolized a new direction for Fauset. She emphasized world affairs and international issues. As one of the founders of Philadelphia's United Nations Council, Fauset sought to bring together people from all cultural backgrounds to enhance mutual understanding. She attended the founding of the United Nations in San Francisco. She started a lengthy tour of international travel to the Middle East, Africa, and India as guest of Madame Pandit of the United Nations. Her travels led to her seeking a diplomatic post in Africa and to a call for greater representation on the U.S. delegation attending Ghanaian celebration of independence in 1957. She continued to seek intercultural understanding, but was regularly disappointed by people's attitudes.

Crystal Bird Fauset received much recognition for her efforts in intercultural relations. In 1939 Pennsylvania governor George Earle recognized her with the Meritorious Service Medal. A second award came in 1955 for her work with the American-Korean Foundation from Pennsylvania governor John S. Fione. Although Pennsylvania was her source of strength and support, her later years were spent in New York City. She died while visiting Philadelphia on March 28, 1965. The Lincoln Dames, a charitable political and social club, held a memorial service for their honorary member on May 23, 1965.

—Beth Schneider

Bibliography

Searching records of the organizations through which Crystal Bird Fauset worked for social change is the most productive. The archives of the national board of the YWCA contain much information about her early days as field secretary. The Moorland-Spingarn Research Center at Howard University has a clippings file on Fauset. Several articles highlight her career: Pittsburgh Courier (April 1, 1939, and January 29, 1955); Philadelphia Tribune (June 2, 1938); Philadelphia Record (November 13, 1938); and Washington Post (December 26, 1938). Her obituary in the New York Times (March 30, 1965) was helpful in citing achievements. Ruth Bogin's article in Notable American Women, edited by Barbara Sicherman and Carol Hurd (Cambridge: Belnap, 1980), pp. 224–225, provides greater detail and primary source locations.

FAUSET, JESSIE REDMON (c. 1882–1961), essayist, editor, and novelist,

displayed in her work the complexities of life for literary artists during the Harlem Renaissance and the Great Depression. Her career as a teacher, first at Washington, DC's M Street High School, then De Witt Clinton High School in New York City, and later, Hampton Institute, provided the stability of income and permanence that allowed her to write her novels and essays.

Born on April 26, 1882 (although other sources vary as to the exact date), as the seventh child to Ann (Seamon) and Redmon Fauset, Jessie Redmon Fauset received educational encouragement from her family, whose name was well known in Philadelphia because it stood for a large, freeborn, cultured, and respected clan. The Fausets moved around quite a bit during Jessie's childhood because of the pastoral responsibilities of her father's ministry in the African Methodist Episcopal church. Her father became extremely close to his young daughter after the death of his wife. The marriage of her father to the widow Belle Huff gave Jessie two half-brothers and a half-sister. She developed characterizations from her family experiences that reflected Philadelphia's "Talented Tenth" in her novels *Plum Bun* and *There Is Confusion.*

Fauset attended the public schools of Philadelphia, graduating with honors as the only black student from the High School for Girls in 1900. Instead of attending her selected college, Bryn Mawr College, Jessie Fauset received aid to attend Cornell University. There, she completed the challenging language program of Greek, French, English, and German; joined the Delta Sigma Theta sorority; and became the first black woman selected for Phi Beta Kappa. After receiving her BA from Cornell in 1905, she taught French and Latin at the M Street High School in Washington, DC, from the fall of 1906 to the summer of 1919.

As a college student, she had started corresponding with W.E.B. Du Bois, hoping his connections with black colleges might produce summer employment. This relationship became more meaningful following the creation of the NAACP and its journal, *The Crisis* (1911). She continued her teaching job but completed her workday schedule by writing and submitting articles to *The Crisis.*

These writings impressed *The Crisis* editor Du Bois, and he invited her to become a member of his staff. After resigning her position at the M Street School in 1919 she completed a year's work at the University of Pennsylvania for her master of arts degree in French. She then became the literary editor of *The Crisis,* a position she held until December 1923, after which she became managing editor until 1926. Working closely with Du Bois, Fauset not only assumed greater responsibility for *The Crisis* but also aided Du Bois in his Pan-African movement, a role that relied upon her facility with the French language. During this time she developed, edited, and managed *The Brownies' Book,* a monthly publication for children, that lasted from 1920 to 1921.

Jessie Fauset's role as literary midwife at *The Crisis* nurtured new black talent and thereby influenced the literary productivity of the Harlem Renaissance. New authors such as Langston Hughes and Nella Larson were frequent visitors to her home. Claude McKay, Countee Cullen, Jean Toomer, and many others received her encouragement to submit articles, poems, and short stories ranging in topics from international movements to "passing" to racial identity.

As both a foster mother to and a product of the Harlem Renaissance, Fauset wrote more novels than any other black writer from 1924 to 1933. Jessie Fauset felt motivated to write about black life after reading an unrealistic novel about black life by the white author T.S. Stribling. The black characters in her novels reflect the "Talented Tenth" and her own experiences with the hard-working, self-repecting black middle class. William Stanley Braithwaite, a contemporary of Fauset, felt that her novels differed from the other black writers of her time. In theme and milieu, her novels approached the conflict of will and passion comparable to Greek tragedies and comedies. Her essays reflected an interest in international cultures and realities that remained below the surface of superficial impressions.

After receiving a certificate from the Sorbonne, she left *The Crisis* in 1927 to achieve a more ordered life as a French teacher at De Witt Clinton High School. As an effective teacher, she could again influence the direction of many youths. In 1929 she married Herbert Harris, an insurance agent and businessman operating in the New Jersey/New York regions. They lived with her sister, Helen Lanning, in a Harlem cooperative apartment on Seventh Avenue. Following a brief separation (1931–1932) and Lanning's death (1936), the couple moved to Montclair, New Jersey, which lessened her literary influence. They had no children. She continued to teach in New York until 1944. She taught as a visiting professor in the English Department at Hampton Institute in 1949. Herbert Harris died in 1958. Jessie Fauset returned to live with her half-brother, Earl Huff, until her death on April 30, 1961, following a long illness.

—Dorothy C. Salem

Bibliography

Fauset's novels include *The Chinaberry Tree* (1931); *Comedy, American Style* (1933), *Plum Bun* (1929) (all published by Frederick A. Stokes of New York); and *There Is Confusion* (New York: Boni and Liveright, 1924). Her articles in *The Crisis* demonstrate her wide range of interests and competencies. A more personal nature is reflected in the correspondence with colleagues involved in the NAACP. The Du Bois Papers, University of Massachusetts, Amherst, are extremely enlightening about her roles with *The Crisis* and her friendship with Du Bois and other literati. The NAACP Papers, Library of Congress, Washington, DC, contain correspondence and copies of articles and reports as do the James Weldon Johnson Papers, Yale University, and Moorland-Spingarn Research Collection, Howard University.

Literary commentary and criticism of Jessie Fauset can be found in Nick Aaron Ford, *Contemporary Negro Novel* (Boston: Meador, 1936); Arthur P. Davis and Saunders Redding, eds., *Cavalcade* (Boston: Houghton Mifflin, 1971); Hugh Gloster, *Negro Voices in American Fiction* (Chapel Hill: University of North Carolina Press,

1948); Robert Bone, *The Negro Novel in America* (New Haven: Yale University Press, 1958); Nathan Huggins, *The Harlem Renaissance* (New York: Oxford University Press, 1971); Addison Gayle, *The Way of the New World: The Black American Novel in America* (Garden City, NY: Doubleday, 1975); Arthur Davis, *From the Dark Tower* (Washington, DC: Howard University Press, 1974); Langston Hughes, *The Big Sea* (New York: Hill and Wang, 1940); Amritjit Singh, *The Novels of the Harlem Renaissance* (University Park: Pennsylvania State University Press, 1976); Esther Arata, Carol Myers, and Theressa Rush, eds., *Black American Writers: Past and Present* (Metuchen, NJ: Scarecrow Press, 1975); Thomas Inge, Maurice Duke, and Jackson Bryer, eds., *Black American Writers: Bibliographic Essays* (New York: St. Martin's Press, 1978); Marianna Davis, *Contributions of Black Women in America* (Columbia, SC: Kenday, 1982).

Articles dealing with literary criticism include William Stanley Braithwaite, "The Novels of Jessie Fauset," *Opportunity* 12 (January 1934): 24–28; Joseph J. Feeney, "Greek Tragic Patterns in a Black Novel," *CLA Journal* 18 (December 1974): 211–215; Marion L. Starkey, "Jessie Fauset," *Southern Workman* 61 (1932): 217–220; Hiroko Sato, "Under the Harlem Shadow," in *The Harlem Renaissance Remembered*, edited by Arna Bontemps (New York: Dodd, Mead, 1972); Marion L. Starkey, "Jessie Fauset," in *Lifting as They Climb*, edited by Elizabeth Davis (Washington, DC: National Association of Colored Women, 1933), pp. 272–275; Joseph Feeney, "Jessie Fauset of *The Crisis*: Novelist, Feminist, and Centenarian," *The Crisis* 90:6 (June–July 1983): 20, 22; Abby Arthur Johnson. "Literary Midwife: Jessie Redmon Fauset and the Harlem Renaissance," *Phylon* 39:2 (Summer 1978): 143–153. There are a few dissertations that cover Fauset's life or contributions to literary production. The best is Carolyn Sylvander, "Jessie R. Fauset, Black American Writer: Her Relationships, Biographical and Literary, with Black and White Writers, 1910–1935," PhD dissertation, University of Wisconsin, 1976.

FEREBEE, DOROTHY [BOULDING] (1898–1980), a physician noted for

her work with women, blacks, and the disadvantaged, was born in Norfolk, Virginia. Although her family included seven lawyers, no family members were in the medical profession to support her efforts. Within a strong, supportive network of women, Dorothy Boulding tended to the injuries of birds and animals in her rural environment. At a young age she moved to Boston, where members of her family, including her great aunt Josephine St. Pierre Ruffin, president of the Woman's Era Club, had distinguished themselves. In 1923 she graduated from Simmons College and in 1927 she was awarded a medical degree from Tufts University. Although she was among the top five graduates in her class, hospitals rejected her application to intern on the basis of her race. Consequently, she interned at the predominantly black Freedmen's Hospital (now Howard University) in Washington, DC.

By the early 1930s Ferebee was a respected physician in the District of Columbia. However, she chose to devote a considerable amount of her time to providing health services to disadvantaged blacks in the rural South. In 1934 she and her sorority sister Ida Johnson drafted a proposal for Alpha Kappa Alpha sorority's Mississippi Health Project. Their plan provided medical services and instructions in hygiene in an area where public health services were sorely lacking. During her first year as medical director of the project in 1937, 2,000 persons received smallpox and diphtheria immunizations. During its second year, the project, with its headquarters in the black settlement of Mound Bayou, Mississippi, rendered services to 3,500 patients during a 2-week period. In addition numerous persons sought treatment at the Delta Pine Land Company in Scott, Mississippi, at the Project 5 Mobile Clinic. Dorothy Ferebee continued as medical director until 1941, when services were expanded to include dental operations, venereal disease screening, prenatal care, and self-help through diet and hygiene.

Through the efforts of Dr. Ferebee and her sorority sisters, the Mississippi Health Project became Alpha Kappa Alpha's first widely publicized social welfare project, which affected the lives of approximately 15,000 rural Mississippi blacks. Not surprisingly, this endeavor was acclaimed by the U.S. Public Health Service as one of the finest examples of volunteer medical services.

Besides her interest in the well-being of rural blacks, Dorothy Ferebee was concerned with the plight of the urban disadvantaged. In 1929 she helped to found Washington, DC's Southeast Settlement House and served as its president for 13 years. In addition to her obvious concern with health services for the needy, Dr. Ferebee played a vital role in women's organizations. She was the tenth national president of the Alpha Kappa Alpha sorority. In 1949 she also became the president of the National Council of Negro Women. She also worked with the Meridian House Foundation for International Visitors, the YWCA, and the National Girl Scouts of America. She spoke before the World Health Organization Assembly in Geneva, Switzerland, in 1967.

Ferebee was also well known for her long association with Howard University. In 1935 she joined the faculty of the Medical College as a clinical instructor in obstetrics. Moreover, she served as director of the university's Health Service from 1949 until her retirement in 1968. She served as a lecturer in preventive medicine at Tufts University School of Medicine in Medford, Massachusetts, shortly before her retirement from Howard.

Dorothy Ferebee was married to Claude Ferebee, a dentist, and was the mother of twins—a son and a daughter. She died in Washington, DC, on September 14, 1980, at age 83.

—Betty Plummer

Bibliography

The papers of Dorothy B. Ferebee are located in the Moorland-Spingarn Manuscript Collection at Howard University and are invaluable to anyone researching Ferebee. She is also included in the Black Women Oral History Project, Schlesinger Library, Radcliffe College.

Articles of interest can be found in the *Journal of the National Medical Association* 62 (1970): 177; *Bulletin of the Medical Chirurgical Society of the District of Columbia* 6:8 (November 1949): 12; and *Ebony* 3:4 (February 1948): 19; Alpha Kappa Alpha Sorority Heritage Series #4, *Women in Medicine* (1971); and Marianna Davis, *Contributions of Black Women to America* II (Columbia, SC: Kenday, 1981). Ferebee's obituary contains a wealth of biographical information—*Washington Post* (September 16, 1980).

FERGUSON, CATHERINE (c. 1779–1854), founder of a home for unwed

mothers and a Sunday school in New York City, was born into slavery at a time that slavery was still legal in the state of New York. Her mother, a slave from Virginia, was sold when Catherine (Katy) was seven years old. Her religious training came through accompanying her mistress to church services. At age 16 she became free when a white woman purchased her freedom for $200. At age 18, Katy had married. Two children born to this marriage died as children. Little information has been passed on about her husband, who died within two years of the marriage.

Emerging from these tragedies, the 20-year-old Ferguson initiated religious instruction of 20 white and 28 black children in her home on Warren Street in Manhattan. Around 1814, Dr. Mason offered his church basement to her for the continuation of her classes. From this church on Murray Street in Manhattan evolved the modern-day Sunday school. Black and white children, many from poorhouses, came to Ferguson for religious instruction. When confronted by a number of unwed mothers in this group of youths, Ferguson began to bring them into her home for care. Ferguson's life might have been forgotten in history following her death from cholera on July 11, 1854, but her example of Christian charity led to the founding of the Ferguson Home for Unwed Mothers in 1920. Funded by private donations, the Katy Ferguson Home provided care and instruction for unwed mothers as a memorial to her lifetime of service.

—Dorothy C. Salem

Bibliography

An undated publication of the American Tract Society entitled *Katy Ferguson* is the primary source for most of the information about Catherine "Katy" Ferguson. Many other sources have repeated the information with few additional details. These in-clude W.E.B. Du Bois, *Darkwater* (New York: Schocken Books, 1920), pp. 177–178; Wilhelmina S. Robinson, *Historical Negro Biographies* (Cornwells Heights, PA: Association for the Study of Afro-American Life and History, 1967), pp. 79–80; Hallie Q. Brown, *Homespun Heroines* (Freeport, NY: Books for Libraries Press, 1971 reported); Catherine A. Latimer, "Catherine Ferguson," *The Negro History Bulletin* (November 1941): 38–39; Linda Grant DePauu, *Four Traditions: Women of New York During the American Revolution* (Albany: New York State Bicentennial Committee, 1974); and Rayford Logan, *Dictionary of American Negro Biography* (New York: Norton, 1982).

FITZGERALD, ELLA (b. 1918), the "First Lady of Song," became known throughout the world as one of the greatest voices in contemporary jazz/swing. This contralto commanded the widest range of music of any instrumentalist or vocalist in history. Born April 25 in Newport News, Virginia, little information is currently available on Fitzgerald's childhood or early influences until 1934. At age 16, while competing in the Amateur Hour at Harlem's Apollo Theatre, her phenomenal talent was recognized by altoist Benny Carter. Through his urging, she became a vocalist with bandleader Chuck Webb at the Savoy Ballroom. There she rose to fame with the playful and sassy song "A-Tisket, A-Tasket," winning her the 1937 *Down Beat* Poll and a contract with Decca Records. Fitzgerald, a member of the American Society of Composers, Authors and Publishers, conducted Chuck Webb's orchestra after his death in 1937, arranging most of the songs herself. Some of her most famous of these included "You Showed Me the Way," "I Found My Yellow Basket," and "Into Each Life Some Rain Must Fall."

In 1941 she married her first husband, Bennie Kornegay, and embarked on a solo career to become the star attraction with such famous hits as "How High the Moon" and "Lady Be Good," mastering the core of modern scat-bebop, originally introduced and made famous by Louis Armstrong. This marriage lasted only two years, but Fitzgerald soon remarried to Ray Brown in 1949. This marriage produced a son, Ray Brown, Jr., and ended in divorce four years later in 1953. By the mid-1950s, Fitzgerald had developed her singing style into a mature, classical ballad voice, astounding the world with her mastery of yet another vocal technique. In 1956, after producing such memorable albums as "Ella Sings Gershwin," "Ella—Songs in a Mellow Mood," "Lullabies of Birdland," and "Sweet and Hot," Fitzgerald severed her 20-year relationship with Decca Records and joined the new Norman Granz recording company, Verve Records. In June 1956 she released her new "Cole Porter Song Book," listed by *Down Beat* as the second-best–selling album in the nation. She also produced her large, 19-volume record series, preserving well over 250 songs from the world's greatest composers, such as Duke Ellington, George Gershwin, Cole Porter, Richard Rodgers, Jerome Kern, and Johnny Mercer. With this series, she became the best-selling recording artist in history. Norman Granz soon became Fitzgerald's personal manager, and the two frequently traveled throughout Europe and Japan. She often sang with Granz's band at the famous New York Philharmonic.

Throughout Fitzgerald's remarkable career, she won numerous popularity awards and honors. She has gained worldwide respect as one of the most outstanding vocal artists in history. She appeared in several feature films, one of which was *Pete Kelly's Blues*. Over the past decade, Fitzgerald has undergone several cataract operations, and in 1987 she had to cancel her European tour due to exhaustion. Nevertheless, at her seemingly youthful age of 72, Fitzgerald has given no indication that she will retire. In February 1991, at the 33rd Annual

Grammy Awards ceremony, Fitzgerald won the Female Jazz Award for "All That Jazz," her 13th Grammy.

—Vivian Gartley-Hindrew

Bibliography

Information on Ella Fitzgerald can be found in Bud Kliment's book *Ella Fitzgerald* (New York: Chelsea House, 1988); Berendt E. Joachim, *The Jazz Book: From Ragtime to Fusion and Beyond* (Westport, CT: Lawrence Hill, 1981); Dan Morgenstern, *Jazz People* (New York: Harry N. Abrams, 1976); and *Current Biography* (New York: Wilson, 1956).

FLEMING, LETHIA [COUSINS] (1876–1963) served as director of the National Association of Republican Colored Women, led the women's activities in Cleveland's 11th Ward for about ten years, and directed national campaign efforts among black women for three Republican presidential candidates— Warren G. Harding, Herbert Hoover, and Alfred M. Landon. Fleming partici- pated actively in local, state, and national politics, led several major civic and charitable fundraising campaigns, and served in local and national leadership positions in fraternal and social service organizations.

Born in Tazewell, Virginia, on November 7, Lethia Henrietta Elizebeth Cousins attended high school in Ironton, Ohio, and Morristown College in Morristown, Tennessee. Fleming taught school in Virginia for one year and in West Virginia for about 20 years.

On February 21, 1912, Lethia Cousins married lawyer Thomas Wallace (Tom) Fleming and moved with him to Cleveland, Ohio. Tom Fleming was the first black city councilman in Cleveland. By 1914 Lethia Fleming chaired the board of lady managers of the Cleveland Home for Aged Colored People (later called the Eliza Bryant Home) and also chaired the home's committee to raise money to build a new facility. Another of Fleming's fundraising efforts focused on furnishing the first home of the Phillis Wheatley Association. Fleming also participated in the city's early community chest drives.

Fleming's political involvement began with her suffrage activity in West Virginia and Ohio. In 1920, Fleming, women's leader of Cleveland's 11th Republican Ward, was asked by the Republican National Committee to be the national director of the National Association of Republican Colored Women. Working from a Chicago office, she directed the campaign activities for Warren G. Harding among the women of her race. Mary Church Terrell assisted her in this effort. Fleming performed the same task later for Hoover and for Landon.

In 1929 her husband was imprisoned for allegedly accepting a bribe, so Fleming announced her candidacy for his council seat; however, she later withdrew from the race. Following this election, Lethia Fleming was ousted from her ward leadership position, which she had held for a decade, due to the scandal involving her husband.

From 1931 until 1951 Fleming worked as a visiting agent with the Cuyahoga County Child Welfare Board and continued her political activities. In 1936 and again in 1940 she left the Welfare Board to perform organizational work for the Republican National Committee. Her husband was paroled in 1933 and readmitted to the bar in 1934. Incapacitated by a cerebral hemorrhage in 1936 and a fractured hip in 1937, Tom Fleming died on January 18, 1948.

Lethia Fleming was a life member of the IBPOEW (Improved Benevolent Protective Order of Elks of the World). From 1928 until 1949 she was daughter ruler of the Glenara Temple #21 of the Daughter Elks. She was also active at the national level, serving as the first grand commissioner of education and in the Department of Civil Liberties. In 1949 Fleming was made grand directress of public relations of the IBPOE.

The Flemings owned and rented property throughout Cleveland and traveled to Europe early in their marriage. Lethia Fleming was a charter member of many service organizations, such as the Travelers' Aid Society, the Cleveland branch of the NAACP, and the Phillis Wheatley Association. She served on the first board of directors of the Negro Welfare Association, which later became the Cleveland Urban League. In addition, Fleming held life memberships in the National Association of Colored Women, the National Council of Negro Women, and the Frederick Douglass Memorial Association. She belonged to the National Negro History Association. Fleming was active in the Mt. Zion Congregational Church, serving as its first woman trustee, yet she maintained a lifelong interest in the Baha'i movement. Lethia Cousins Fleming died on September 22, 1963. She is buried in Lake View Cemetery, Cleveland, Ohio.

—Jimmy E.W. Meyer

Bibliography

Fleming, Lethia Cousins. Manuscript Collection. Cleveland: Western Reserve Historical Society (WRHS).

Fleming, Lethia Cousins. Vertical file. Cleveland: WRHS.

Fleming, Thomas W. "My Rise and Persecution." Typewritten ms. Cleveland: WRHS, [1932?].

Fleming, Thomas W., and Lethia Cousins Fleming. *Cleveland Press* Clipping Files. Cleveland: Cleveland State University, 1929–1963.

Salem, Dorothy. *To Better Our World: Black Women in Organized Reform 1890–1920.* Brooklyn: Carlson, 1990.

Van Tassel, David D., and John Grabowski. *Encyclopedia of Cleveland History.* Bloomington: Indiana University Press, 1987.

Wesley, Charles H. *History of the Improved Benevolent and Protective Order of Elks of the World, 1889–1954.* Washington, DC: Association of the Study of Negro Life, 1955.

FORTEN, CHARLOTTE [VANDINE] (1785–1884), antislavery leader

and social reformer, was born in Pennsylvania on January 2. Little is known of her background except that she was freeborn and of mixed African, European, and Native American ancestry. There were several black families by the name of Vandine in the Delaware Valley—the legacy of an early Dutch presence in the region.

On December 10, 1805, at St. Thomas's African Episcopal Church in Philadelphia, Charlotte Vandine married James Forten, a childless widower 18 years her senior. She moved into her husband's home at 50 Shippen Street, close to his sail loft. The home was shared with Forten's mother, his widowed sister, and her children. Within a year, his mother died, Forten purchased a house for his sister, and he and his wife moved to a comfortable three-story house on Lombard Street, one of Philadelphia's main thoroughfares. This would be Charlotte Forten's home for the rest of her life. She eventually managed a household that included herself and her husband; their eight children; assorted nieces, nephews, and wards; domestic servants; and journeymen and apprentices from her husband's sail loft.

James Forten's wealth grew steadily as he diversified his interests to include not only sailmaking but lending money, and investments in real estate and bank stock. As his wealth increased so did his prominence in the abolitionist movement. His wife found herself entertaining visiting reformers, black and white, from the United States and Europe. Guests at the Forten home included the English novelist Harriet Martineau, New England businessman Paul Cuffe, and abolitionists William Lloyd Garrison, Samuel J. May, Lucretia Mott, George Thompson, Arthur Tappan, and Sarah and Angelina Grimké.

Charlotte Forten shared her husband's devotion to the antislavery cause. She and her daughters were among the earliest members of the Philadelphia Female Anti-Slavery Society, an interracial organization established in 1833.

When he died in 1842 James Forten left his wife a life interest in the family home and one-third of his estate. The family business was taken over by their two eldest sons, James and Robert. They soon ran into difficulties, and James fled to New York to escape his creditors. However, Charlotte Forten weathered the financial crisis and invested successfully in real estate on her own account.

After the Civil War, her youngest son, William, emerged as a major figure in Republican Party politics in Philadelphia, and the house on Lombard Street again became a center of activity. Forten's daughter Margaretta, the principal of a private school, boarded some of her students in the house she shared with her mother and brother.

Despite the personal tragedies that beset her—including the deaths of four of her children and the permanent estrangement of a fifth, Charlotte Forten enjoyed a vigorous old age. In 1880 her son-in-law, Robert Purvis, wrote to a friend: "My Mother-in-law . . . in her 95th year, holds to life, in the enjoyment of excellent health, & unimpaired mental faculties." Charlotte Forten died on

December 29, 1884, and was buried in Philadelphia's Lebanon Cemetery on January 2, 1885, on what would have been her 100th birthday.

—Julie Winch

Bibliography

The source material on Charlotte Vandine Forten is limited and diffuse. In writing this short account of her life, the author depended on Philadelphia city directories, property deeds, Board of Health records, wills, the records of the Philadelphia Female Anti-Slavery Society, and files of the following newspapers: *The Liberator*, the *Public Ledger*, and *Poulson's American Daily Advertiser*. Some information can be found in the Grimké Family Papers, located in the Moorland-Spingarn Research Center at Howard University, Washington, DC.

Secondary Sources

Billington, Ray, ed. *The Journal of Charlotte Forten: A Free Negro in the Slave Era*. New York: Norton, 1981.

Birney, Catherine. *The Grimké Sisters: Sarah and Angelina Grimké, the First Women Advocates of Abolition and Woman's Rights*. Boston: Lee and Shepard, 1885.

Braxton, Joanne M. *Charlotte Forten Grimké (1837–1914) and the Search for a Public Voice*. Wellesley, MA: Wellesley College, Center for Research on Women, 1985.

Douty, Esther M. *Charlotte Forten. Free Black Teacher*. Champaign, IL: Garrard, 1971.

————. *Forten the Sailmaker: Pioneer Champion of Negro Rights*. New York: Rand McNally, 1968.

Giddings, Paula. *When and Where I Enter . . . The Impact of Black Women on Race and Sex in America*. New York: Morrow, 1984.

Hull, Gloria, Patricia Bell Scott, and Barbara Smith, eds. *All the Women Are White, All the Blacks Are Men, But Some of Us Are Brave: Black Women's Studies*. Old Westbury, NY: Feminist Press, 1982.

Lerner, Gerda. *The Grimké Sisters from South Carolina: Rebels Against Slavery*. New York: Schocken, 1967.

Loewenberg, Bert James, and Ruth Bogin, eds. *Black Women in Nineteenth Century American Life*. University Park: Pennsylvania State Press, 1976.

Sterling, Dorothy. *We Are Your Sisters: Black Women in the Nineteenth Century*. New York: Norton, 1984.

FORTEN, MARGARETTA (1808–1875), women's rights advocate and abolitionist, was one of eight children born to the famous African American sailmaker and abolitionist James Forten (1766–1842) and his wife, Charlotte Forten (1785–1884). The Forten family resided at 92 Lombard Street in Philadelphia, which served as a meeting place for renowned persons such as Harriet Martineau, William Lloyd Garrison, and the poet John Greenleaf Whittier, who dedicated the poem "To the Daughters of James Forten" in *The*

Liberator because of their antislavery struggles. Four of the eight Forten siblings, Margaretta, Sarah Louise, Harriet, and Robert, were most active in abolitionist and women's rights causes.

Along with her mother and sisters, Margaretta Forten became a charter member of the Philadelphia Female Anti-Slavery Society in 1833 and supported the cause until the Society's dissolution in 1870. She was initially elected to the position of recording secretary. This organization, also supported by men, particularly the Forten family, gave women the opportunity to publicly address civil rights issues regarding race and womanhood and the political advantages of alignment with white sympathizers.

Margaretta Forten served as a teacher and administrator of a school for black children in Philadelphia. Her special interest in education led her to serve on the educational board of the Philadelphia Female Anti-Slavery Society. She received much of her own education from home tutoring because her parents refused to allow their children to be hindered by the segregated school system.

Margaretta Forten remained the close confidante of her niece, Charlotte Forten Grimké, whose mother died at an early age. Grimké's diaries show that correspondence between the two was filled with affection. Margaretta Forten never married, so her special relationship with her famous niece gave meaning to her reform career until her death in 1875.

—Jacqueline D. Carr-Hamilton

Bibliography

The Grimké Family Papers, located in the Moorland-Spingarn Research Center, Howard University, Washington, DC, includes correspondence and references to Margaretta Forten. These journals have been edited by Brenda Stevenson. *The Journals of Charlotte Forten Grimké* (New York: Oxford University Press, 1988).

Secondary Sources

Billington, Ray, ed. *The Journal of Charlotte Forten: A Free Negro in the Slave Era*. New York: Norton, 1981.

Birney, Catherine. *The Grimké Sisters: Sarah and Angelina Grimké, the First Women Advocates of Abolition and Woman's Rights*. Boston: Lee and Shepard, 1885.

Braxton, Joanne M. *Charlotte Forten Grimké (1837–1914) and the Search for a Public Voice*. Wellesley, MA: Wellesley College, Center for Research on Women, 1985.

Douty, Esther M. *Charlotte Forten. Free Black Teacher*. Champaign, IL: Garrard, 1971.

———. *Forten the Sailmaker: Pioneer Champion of Negro Rights*. New York: Rand McNally, 1968.

Giddings, Paula. *When and Where I Enter . . . The Impact of Black Women on Race and Sex in America*. New York: William Morrow, 1984.

Hull, Gloria, Patricia Bell Scott, and Barbara Smith, eds. *All the Women Are White, All the Blacks Are Men, But Some of Us Are Brave: Black Women's Studies*. Old Westbury, NY: Feminist Press, 1982.

Lerner, Gerda. *The Grimké Sisters from South Carolina: Rebels Against Slavery*. New York: Schocken, 1967.

Loewenberg, Bert James, and Ruth Bogin, eds. *Black Women in Nineteenth Century American Life*. University Park: Pennsylvania State Press, 1976.

Sterling, Dorothy. *We Are Your Sisters: Black Women in the Nineteenth Century*. New York: Norton, 1984.

FRANKLIN, ARETHA (b. 1942), "Lady Soul" or "Queen of Soul," grew up
on the east side of Detroit, Michigan, the same humble turf that had produced Smokey Robinson and then the Supremes. But the home of Aretha Franklin was different. It rested on a tree-lined street and was large. The Reverend Clarence L. Franklin, her father, was one of the most respected and famous African American ministers in the nation.

Franklin was born in Memphis, Tennessee, on March 25. One of five children, the family migrated northward when the future "Lady Soul" was only two years old. The first stop was Buffalo, New York, and from there on to Detroit, where the Reverend Franklin became the pastor of the New Bethel Baptist Church. Aretha Franklin was only six years old when her mother, Barbara (Siggers), abandoned her family. Her mother died in 1952.

Like so many African American performers, the musical career of Franklin began in church—in this case her father's. In fact, some maintain that Franklin drew on a musical lineage. Reportedly, her mother was a great gospel singer in her own right. Other likely musical influences included Mahalia Jackson, Clara Ward, and James Cleveland, all fellow travelers and gospel singers on the same evangelical circuit.

Franklin sang solo in church at age 12; she cut her first recordings with JVP Records, and with her father's assistance, released two singles with Chess Records at age 14. Her real professional start commenced when she broke off singing in church and set out on her own performing in the Flame Show Bar in Detroit and eventually moved to New York City. It was there that she secured a contract with Columbia Records and worked under the direction of John Hammond. The relationship was less than successful, and by 1966, Franklin was in debt to Columbia.

Yet the Columbia years taught Franklin many valuable things, and she was ready to begin anew when Jerry Wexler, the vice president of Atlantic Records, signed her. By 1967 she had become the most successful singer in the entire country. Her first album on the Atlantic label, *I Never Loved a Man the Way I Love You*, and the single by the same name, which became a Top 10 hit in 1967, was the prelude to Franklin's five-year reign as the preeminent African American vocalist. In 1968 she even opened the Democratic National Convention by singing the national anthem.

Her vocal style has been characterized as chaotic and unpredictable. Yet clearly, however described, Franklin deployed more melisma than any other black artist except perhaps Bobby Blue Bland. Furthermore, she epitomized the close stylistic ties between blues singers and preachers. This she achieved with the broken phrase and repetition that are the functional equivalents of an intentional hang-up or intended stutter.

The early 1970s continued to be professionally successful with the release of *Spirit in the Dark* (1970), followed by *Live at the Fillmore West* (1971), and *Young, Gifted and Black* (1972)—often regarded as the last soul-baring look back on her tormented marriage to Ted White. Later she recorded the gospel track "Amazing Grace." In the late 1970s her professional career began to decline and did not pick up again until Luther Vandross provided her with a hit with the title track of "Jump to It" in 1982. She made additional new fans with *Get It Right* in 1983. Later she had a hit single with "Freeway of Love," made a new version of the Rolling Stones' "Jumping Jack Flash" and had a hit duet with George Michaels on "I Know You Were Waiting." Yet none of these came close to the self-produced 1987 double album of gospel music, *One Lord, One Faith, One Baptism*.

Home life was always more problematic. Her first marriage to Ted White, a physically abusive man, ended in divorce in 1969. In 1978 Franklin married again, this time to actor Glynn Turman. This, too, ended in divorce. Most tragically, her beloved father was shot by burglars and left in a coma in 1979. He subsequently died. Still residing in Detroit, Aretha Franklin is the devoted mother of four sons.

—Donna Van Raaphorst

Bibliography

A fine overall history of rock and roll, although now somewhat dated, is that edited by Jim Miller, *The Rolling Stone Illustrated History of Rock & Roll*, Revised edition (New York: Random House, Rolling Stone Press Book, 1980). A fine discography is also provided. Ralph Cooper provides the reader with the framework of amateur night at the Apollo Theatre and the various contributions of Franklin as an entertainer and to the theater's preservation. See Ralph Cooper and Steve Dougherty, *Amateur Night at the Apollo: Ralph Cooper Presents Five Decades of Great Entertainment* (New York: Harper, Collins, 1990). An excellent and up-to-date account of rock entertainers can be found in Timothy White, *Rock Lives: Profiles and Interviews* (New York: Henry Holt, 1990). One of the very best works to examine urban African American culture is found in Charles Keil's *Urban Blues* (Chicago: University of Chicago Press, 1966).

FULLER, META WARRICK (1877–1968), as most young sculptors working in the early part of the nineteenth century, was influenced by Auguste Rodin. Along with May Howard Jackson and Edmonia Lewis, Meta Warrick Fuller's prominence as a Philadelphia-born sculptor and the emotional realism that characterized her work, earned her both the title "Sculptor of Horrors" and an eventual meeting with Rodin.

Born to a middle-class family on June 9, Meta Warrick studied for five years at the Pennsylvania School of Industrial Art, where she completed *Head of Medusa*, a student work that prefigured her absorption with heroic themes of sacrifice, slavery, anguish, and suffering. In 1899 Meta Warrick studied in Paris at the Academie Colarossi and the Ecole des Beaux Arts, where she studied with Rodin. She returned to the United States in 1903. By 1907 the sculptor refined her skills at the Pennsylvania Academy of Fine Arts.

After her marriage to Liberian physician Dr. Solomon Carter Fuller in 1909, she spent most of her career in Framingham, Massachusetts. In her self-constructed studio, Meta Warrick Fuller continued her sculpting while raising a family. A suspicious fire in 1910 destroyed much of her work, a setback that failed to arrest her spirit of creativity. Inspired by W.E.B. Du Bois's Pan-African ideology, she emphasized the common African heritage in her works while she provided a social and political indictment of American race relations.

Her work appeared in the Paris Salon, the Jamestown Exposition (1907), and the New York Emancipation Exhibit (1913). Fuller was awarded Second Prize by the post–World War I Women's Peace Party for her group *Peace Halting the Ruthlessness of War*. By 1922 the sculptor presented one of her most compelling works, *Ethiopian Awakening*, at the New York "Making of America" Exposition. Working primarily in plaster and bronze, Fuller's genre paid tribute to William Monroe Trotter, Samuel Coleridge Taylor, Frederick Douglass, and Sojourner Truth. Her most notable exhibitions following this time include those of the Harmon Foundation, the Boston Art Club, Howard University, and the American Negro Exposition. James Porter, a historian, refers to her sculptures as "saturnalian conceptions," which confronted both pathetic and noble themes through her art. This was especially evident in the 1919 protest piece against lynching, *Mary Turner (A Silent Protest Against Mob Violence)*.

A longtime resident of Framingham, Massachusetts, Meta Fuller remained active in local community and civic affairs, including the American Federation of Arts, the Framingham Civic League, the Framingham Women's Club, the Arista Club (Boston), and Alpha Kappa Alpha sorority. She died in 1968.

Fuller has been cited and referenced in numerous texts and anthologies, all of which praise her compositional power and aesthetic drive and consider her one of the most important precursors of the Harlem Renaissance. In 1984 the Fuller family provided the Danforth Museum of Art with much of the work for the first retrospective exhibition of Fuller's pieces. This exhibition established her rank as one of America's most expressive and evocative artists, whose career greatly enriched the African American art tradition.

—Robin Chandler

Bibliography

Cederholm, Theresa, ed. *Afro-American Artists: A Bibliographical Directory*. Boston: Trustees of the Boston Public Library, 1973.

City College of New York. *The Evolution of Afro-American Artists, 1800–1950.* Exhibition Catalog (1967).

Driskell, David. "The Flowering of the Harlem Renaissance," in Mary Schmidt Campbell, ed. *Harlem Renaissance: Art of Black America.* New York: Harry N. Abrams, 1987.

———. *Two Centuries of Black American Art.* New York: Alfred Knopf, 1976.

Fax, Elton. *Seventeen Black Artists.* New York: Dodd, Mead, 1971.

Harley, Ralph L., Jr. "A Checklist of Afro-American Art and Artists" *Serif* 7:4 (1970): 3–63.

Heller, Nancy G. *Women Artists: An Illustrated History.* New York: Abbeville Press, 1987.

Lewis, Samella. *Art: African American.* New York: Harcourt, Brace Jovanovich, 1978.

Morrison, Allan. "(Black) Women in the Arts," *Ebony* (August 1966): 90–94.

Porter, James. *Modern Negro Art.* New York: Arno Press, 1969.

———. *Ten Afro-American Artists of the Nineteenth Century.* Exhibition Catalog, 1967.

Taft, Lorado. *The History of American Sculpture.* New York: Macmillan, 1903.

Tuckerman, Henry T. *American Artist Life.* New York: G.P. Putnam, 1867.

Tufts, Eleanor. *Our Hidden Heritage: Five Centuries of Women Artists.* New York: Paddington, 1974.

G

GARNET, SARAH [SMITH, THOMPSON] (1831–1911), educator, clubwoman, and suffragist, served as a principal in the New York City public school system for almost 40 years. She was born Sarah J. Smith in Brooklyn, the oldest of 11 children. Her sister, Susan Maria Smith, became Susan McKinney Steward [1847–1918], a physician. Her parents, Sylvanus and Annie (Springstead) Smith, were both of African-American and Native American descent. They owned a large farm on Long Island, New York.

At age 14, Smith began attending normal school in New York and teaching at the African Free School run by the Manumission Society of Williamsburg in what is now Brooklyn. Her career as an educator spanned 56 years. In 1863 she was named the principal of a grammar school in Manhattan, the first black woman in the city to be given this responsibility. As principal, she stressed both vocational and literary pursuits. Maritcha Lyons, public school teacher and founder of Woman's Loyal Union, a New York City club, and Florence T. Ray, a social reformer, were her students. When black teachers in New York City were faced with discrimination, she and two male leaders went to the state legislature in Albany and argued for justice, thereby correcting the situation. In addition to teaching, she ran a seamstress shop from her home on Hancock Street in Brooklyn in the 1880s. She retired from the New York City school system in 1900.

Smith's first husband, the Reverend James Thompson, was the rector of St. Matthews Episcopal Church in Brooklyn. The couple had two children, both of whom died young. The Reverend Thompson died in the 1860s. In 1879, Smith married the Reverend Henry Highland Garnet, a Presbyterian minister well known before the Civil War as an abolitionist. He died in 1882 while serving as U.S. ambassador to Liberia.

Concerned with both racial and gender equality, Sarah Thompson Garnet organized the only black Equal Suffrage League in Brooklyn. She was also a founder of the Woman's Loyal Union, a Brooklyn women's club that honored journalist Ida B. Wells, an event that stimulated the formation of a national club movement among black women. As an early member of the National Association of Colored Women, she served as the superintendent of its Suffrage Department. Sarah Garnet remained an Episcopalian all her life. On August 31, 1911, her eightieth birthday, she was the guest of honor at a London reception hosted by the Equal Suffrage League during the first Universal Races Congress in London. Shortly after returning home, she died of arteriosclerosis on September 17, 1911, at her Brooklyn home. At the time of her death, she was still actively working for women's suffrage. She was buried in Brooklyn's Greenwood Cemetery.

—Marilyn Dell Brady

Bibliography

The major information on Sarah Garnet comes from Hallie Q. Brown, *Homespun Heroines and Other Women of Distinction* (Xenia, OH: Aldine, 1926). Books that delineate the activities of the black club movement have information about Garnet: Elizabeth L. Davis, *Lifting as They Climb* (Washington, DC: NACW, 1933); and Charles H. Wesley, *The History of the National Association of Colored Women's Clubs* (Washington, DC: NACW, 1984). Entries by Rayford Logan in *Dictionary of American Negro Biography* (New York: Norton, 1982) and Leedell W. Neyland in *Notable American Women* (Cambridge: Harvard University Press, 1971) both rely heavily on Brown. A loving obituary written by Addie W. Hunton appeared in *The Crisis* 1 (October 1911). For official records of her teaching and her death, see the files of the New York City Board of Education and Department of Health.

GARVEY, AMY JACQUES (1896–1973), the second wife of Marcus Garvey, leader of the Universal Negro Improvement Association (UNIA), participated in the struggle to achieve the organization's goal: self-determination for black people around the world based on the doctrines of Pan-Africanism. Born in Kingston, Jamaica, and educated at Deaconess Home School, Colment's Girls School, and Wolmers Girl's School, Amy Euphemia Jacques' family's heritage was rooted in the Jamaican middle class. Her mother, Charlotte Jacques, received a formal education and her father, George Samuel Jacques, was a well-educated manager of a tobacco plant and property owner. Often in ill health with recurring bouts of malaria, Amy Jacques needed a cooler climate. Her health concerns led to a new life.

In 1917, after her father's death, she migrated to the United States. She immediately became affiliated with the UNIA, and by 1918 she was Marcus Garvey's private secretary and office manager at the UNIA general headquarters in New York. In 1922 she married Marcus Garvey in a private ceremony. During Marcus Garvey's incarceration for mail fraud, Amy J. Garvey's skills as a writer, spokesperson, archivist, and political/race activist developed. She served as the editor of the "Our Women and What They Think" section in the newspaper *Negro World*, and of the two volumes of *Philosophy and Opinions* by Marcus Garvey (1923, 1925).

As a liaison between Marcus Garvey and UNIA officials and treasurer of the Marcus Garvey Defense Fund, Amy J. Garvey traveled across the country and spoke on his behalf at rallies and public meetings. In the midst of this turmoil, Amy Jacques Garvey kept meticulous records on Marcus Garvey and the activities of the UNIA. In spite of her poor health, she enabled the UNIA to keep functioning during Marcus Garvey's incarceration. Following Marcus Garvey's deportation from the United States, they traveled to France, England, and Germany, but she eventually returned to her native Jamaica, where she gave birth to Marcus Garvey, Jr. (1930), and Julius Winston Garvey (1933).

Following Marcus Garvey's death in 1940, she was left alone to raise their two sons. Her inheritance of property provided the base of her income through rental of her property. She also earned a meager income by writing articles for journals like the *African* published in Harlem, New York. Nonetheless, Amy Jacques Garvey did not live in luxury and was often in need of financial assistance. Primarily because of her archival records documenting the activities of Marcus Garvey and the UNIA, along with her books *Garvey and Garveyism* (1964), and *black Power in America* (1968), a rebirth of interest focusing on the activities of Marcus Garvey and the UNIA has become evident. As a female nationalist Amy Jacques Garvey was not simply a symbol within a movement but an active participant advocating the philosophy of the organization and soliciting support for the UNIA. On July 25, 1973, Amy Jacques died at the University Hospital of the West Indies in Jamaica.

—Ula Y. Taylor

Bibliography

Amy Jacques Garvey's private papers are included in the Marcus Garvey Memorial Collection, located at Fisk University, Special Collections Unit, Nashville, Tennessee. The collection includes 18 boxes of letters and correspondence between Amy Garvey, Marcus Garvey, and others. To date, there have been no books published with a focus on Amy Jacques Garvey's activism. One must rely upon articles to provide a base for secondary sources. See the following works: Rupert Lewis and Maureen Warner-Lewis, "Amy Jacques Garvey," *Jamaica Journal* 20:3 (1987): 39–43; Mark Matthews, "Our Women and What They Think: Amy Garvey and the *Negro World*," *The Black Scholar* 10:8/9 (May–June 1979): 2–13; Ida Lewis, "Mrs. Marcus Garvey Talks with Ida Lewis," *Encore* (May 1973): 66–68; Beverly Reed, "Amy Garvey—Black, Beautiful and Free," *Ebony* (June 1971): 46–54; Terry Smith, "Amy Jacques Garvey—Portrait of a Courageous Woman," *The Jamaican Housewife* (Winter 1964): 22–25; Honor Ford-Smith, "Women and the Garvey Movement in Jamaica," *Garvey: His Work and Impact*, edited by Rupert Lewis and Patrick Bryan (Mona, Jamaica: Institute of Social and Economic Research, 1988), pp. 73–83; Barbara Bair, "Amy Jacques Garvey," *Marcus Garvey: Life and Lessons*, edited by Robert A. Hill and Barbara Bair (Berkeley, Los Angeles, London: University of California Press, 1987), pp. 396–397; Barbara Bair, "True Women, Real Men: Gender, Ideology and Social Roles in the Garvey Movement," *Connected Domains: Beyond the Private/Public Dichotomy in Women's History*, edited by Susan Reveby and Dorothy O. Helly (Ithaca, NY: Cornell University Press, 1991). Finally, Robert A. Hill serves as the general editor of the *Marcus Garvey and Universal Negro Improvement Association Papers* (Berkeley, Los Angeles, London: University of California Press, 1983, 1984, 1986, 1989). The published six volumes all include annotation on Amy Jacques Garvey and citations on her published works.

GEORGE, ZELMA [WATSON] (b. 1903), educator, singer and actress, diplomat, and civic servant, is a woman of a variety of accomplishments. George has performed on Broadway, toured as an unofficial ambassador for the United States, served as an alternate to the U.S. delegation to the United Nations (UN), directed local and national social service efforts, and held administrative and teaching positions in colleges and universities.

Zelma Mary Elizabeth Watson was born in Hearne, Texas, on December 8, the eldest of the six children of Lena (Thomas) and Samuel E.J. Watson. Both parents were college educated: her mother was a former teacher, and her father, an educator and a prominent Baptist minister. The family lived in various communities in the South and Midwest until George was in her teens, when they moved to Chicago. George graduated from the University of Chicago with a sociology major in 1924. She received a certificate in voice from the American Conservatory of Music in Chicago in 1928 and studied organ at Northwestern University. George received both a master's degree in personnel administration (1944) and a doctorate in sociology (1954) from New York University, researching African-American folk and art songs.

George first worked as a social caseworker in Evanston, Illinois (1924–1925), and later as a juvenile court probation officer in Chicago (1925–1932). After her father's sudden death in 1925, she helped to support the family and to send her siblings to college. From 1932 to 1937, George served as dean of women and director of personnel administration at Tennessee Agricultural and Industrial State University. She married her first husband and moved to California in 1937, where she founded and directed the Avalon Community Center, a multicultural, church-related, social service facility in Los Angeles. The community center was a success; the marriage was not. In 1942 George left California to pursue her research with a fellowship from the Rockefeller Foundation.

On a research trip to Cleveland, Ohio, George met widower Clayborne George, attorney and president of the city's Civil Service Commission. The couple married on September 2, 1944. Zelma George immediately became involved in social service in Cleveland, participating and holding board positions in such organizations as the Antioch Baptist Church, the YWCA, the Girl Scouts, the National Conference of Christians and Jews, the Phillis Wheatley Association, the NAACP, Karamu House, and the Cleveland Council on World Affairs.

In 1949 George had the opportunity to utilize her talent and love for singing. She played the title role of Madame Flora in Gian-Carlo Menotti's opera *The Medium*, first in Cleveland's Karamu Theater and the next year for 13 weeks at the Arena Theater on Broadway. The National Association of Negro Musicians presented George with a Merit Award, recognizing her pioneering performance in a Broadway leading role not specifically written for a black. Critics praised George's performance highly; producers offered her the chance to continue this new-found career in other roles. But George declined all offers. Her future acting took place in her home city, on the boards of the Cleveland Play House (Menotti's *The Consul*, 1951) and Karamu (Brecht/Weill's *The Threepenny Opera*, 1955).

Zelma George undertook her first national governmental responsibility in 1955 when Secretary of Defense Charles E. Wilson appointed her to the Defense Advisory Committee on Women in the Services. She served four years on this committee, touring military installations and studying and evaluating women's job conditions. In 1959 George embarked on a six-month worldwide lecture tour, as an unofficial goodwill ambassador for the U.S. State Department. The trip was an element of President Dwight Eisenhower's People-to-People program for furthering cross-cultural understanding. During this tour, George attended the Pan-Pacific and Southeast Asian Women's Conference in Singapore as a delegate, and in Accra, Ghana, addressed 3,000 women at the one hundredth anniversary of the founding of the Women's Society of the Presbyterian Church of Ghana.

In June 1960 the U.S. Senate approved the selection of Zelma George as an alternate delegate for the United States to the 15th General Assembly of the United Nations. She served a one-year term in this capacity. George attracted international attention on December 14, 1960, when she—alone among the U.S. delegates—rose and joined African nations in applauding the passage of a UN resolution recommending an end to colonialism. The United States and eight other nations had abstained from voting on the resolution.

In 1962 the government of Ghana invited George to speak and lead a workshop at the Accra Assembly, on the study of disarmament.

From 1966 to 1974 George was director of the Job Corps Center for Women of Cleveland. Cleveland's Job Corps Center, one of the first in the country, was unique in that it was sponsored by a black organization, the Alpha Kappa Alpha (AKA) sorority. George had long been active in AKA. In 1967 George testified before the House Education and Labor Committee on behalf of continued funding for the Job Corps. During this time, she also cared for her husband, ill with a lung ailment. Clayborne George died December 24, 1970.

In 1971 President Richard Nixon nominated George to the board of the Corporation for Public Broadcasting, a position she held for one year. From 1981 until about 1987 George—now "retired"—taught senior citizens at the elders campus of Cuyahoga Community College in Cleveland.

George has received numerous awards, including the following: honorary degrees from Baldwin Wallace College (1961), Heidelberg College (1961), and Cleveland State University (1974); Alumnus of the Year at both the University of Chicago (1969), and New York University (1973); the Dag Hammerskjold Award (1961) from the Mayor's United Nations Committee of Cleveland; and the Edwin T. Dahlberg Peace Award (1969) from the American Baptist Church. In 1991, from her Cleveland home, Zelma Watson George continued to pursue her wide interests, including the hobbies of collecting Bibles and portrayals of human hands.

—Jimmy E.W. Meyer

Bibliography

The most complete source of information about Zelma George is the interview in the black Women Oral History Project, Arthur and Elizabeth Schlesinger Library, Radcliffe College.

Secondary Sources

Afro-American Encyclopedia 4. North Miami, FL: Educational Book Publishers, 1974.

Christmas, Walter, ed. *Negroes in Public Affairs and Government I.* Yonkers, NY: Educational Heritage, 1966.

Current Biography Yearbook. New York: Wilson, 1961.

Feron, James. "UN Urges Steps to Free Colonies," *New York Times* (December 15, 1960): 1, 21.

Gard, Connie Schultz. "It's a Wonderful Life," *The Plain Dealer Magazine* (July 22, 1990): 6–15.

Garland, Phyl. "The Miracle on Ansel Road," *Ebony* 23:7 (May 1968): 90–100.

"George, Clayborne and Zelma Watson George," *Cleveland Press* Clipping Files. Cleveland: Cleveland State University, 1949–1981.

George, Zelma Watson. "A Guide to Negro Music: An Annotated Bibliography of Negro Folk Music, and Art Music by Negro Composers or Based on Negro Thematic Material," PhD dissertation, New York University, 1953.

———. "Negro Music in American Life," in *The American Negro Reference Book*, John P. Davis, ed. Englewood Cliffs, NJ: Prentice-Hall, 1966, pp. 731–758.

Here's Zelma. Pamphlet written by Rowena Jeliffe. Cleveland: n.p., 1971.

Kelly, Patrice A. "An Extraordinary Life in Profile." *Renaissance Magazine* (February 1991): 30–32.

Klyver, Richard D. *They Also Serve: Twelve Biographies of Notable Cleveland Women.* Solon, OH: Evans Printing Company, 1986.

"Medium in the Round." *Newsweek* 36:5 (July 31, 1950): 76.

Ploski, Harry A., and Warren Marr II, compilers. *The Negro Almanac*, 3rd ed. New York: Bellwether, 1976.

Van Tassel, David D., and John Grabowski, eds. *Encyclopedia of Cleveland History.* Bloomington: Indiana University Press, 1987.

Who's Who among Black Americans 1990–91, 6th ed. Detroit: Gale, 1991.

Who's Who of American Women. Chicago: Marquis, 1958–1959.

"Zelma George." *The Crisis* 57:9 (October 1950): cover, 548.

GIBSON, ALTHEA (b. 1927) rose to fame as a tennis player and golfer during a time when both sports reflected the affluence of the private club circuit. She went on to become the first member of her race to win a Wimbledon Championship.

Althea Gibson was born in Silver, South Carolina, on August 27, but was raised in Harlem, New York City. She was the eldest of five children of Anna (Washington) and Daniel Gibson. She had three sisters—Millie, Annie, and Lillian—and one brother Daniel. In Harlem, Gibson learned to play "paddle tennis" on the street. She started on the road to tennis greatness when she won the Department of Parks, Manhattan (NY) Girl's Tennis Championship. Buddy Walker, a Police Athletic League supervisor and bandleader, introduced her to the interracial Cosmopolitan Tennis Club. He also bought her the first "gut" tennis racket, and showed her how to practice against the wall at Mt. Morris Park. Fred Johnson, a one-armed professional, took her under his wing and taught her the essentials of tennis footwork and court strategy in 1942.

By 1943 Althea Gibson, a tall, wiry maverick, won the New York State Negro Girl's Single Title. In 1945–1946 she went on to win the National Negro Girl's Championship, and attend Industrial High School at Williston, North Carolina, while a guest of Dr. R.W. Johnson, a tennis enthusiast and physician. Her earlier schooling at Yorkville Trade School and working as a Chock Full O'Nuts restaurant counter girl, a mail clerk, and an elevator operator had left her unmotivated.

Dr. Hubert A. Eaton, another black physician and tennis enthusiast, took her under his supervision, coaching her very carefully. As a result, in 1948 she won the National Negro Women's Championship, and dominated this competition for over nine years. From 1949 to 1952 Althea Gibson attended Florida Agricultural & Mechanical University, playing tennis and basketball. In 1950 she won the USLTA Eastern Orange Lawn Tennis Indoor Championship (Orange Lawn Tennis Club, South Orange, NJ), was runner-up to Mrs. Ralph Kiner (nee Nanoy Chaffee) for the National Indoor Championship, and became the first black to appear on the Forest Hills, New York, courts. Gibson's unique talents and aggressive ability soon made her a star athlete, which allowed her to erase some of the color lines in the sport.

In 1951 she became the first African American to play in the All-England Championships at Wimbledon, losing to Beverly Baker in the quarter finals. Alhough she had won at Dortmund, Germany (July), and at Jamaica, in the British West Indies (February), she was in a slump and her ratings and rankings fell to eighth place. She became discouraged and seriously considered retiring from competition and joining the Women's Army Corps.

After college graduation, Gibson became an athletic instructor at Lincoln University in Jefferson City, Missouri. In the autumn of 1955 the U.S. State Department sponsored her for a "Good Will" tour of Asia. She received a commendation of praise from the Foreign Service as one of their best goodwill ambassadors. Her game began to improve as she won the Indian National and Asiatic Women's Single championships. In 1956–1957 she won several victories in France and in the United States. She continued to play at Forest Hills and even at Wimbledon, where she was defeated by Shirley Fry.

Althea Gibson had learned how to handle defeat and had learned from these setbacks. Finally on July 6, 1957, she defeated Darlene Hard in an all-American finals contest at Wimbledon in 100-degree heat, with a game that was a combination of power and deftness. Her return home to New York City was greeted with the traditional ticker-tape parade and a presentation of the Key to the City from Mayor Robert F. Wagner. On September 8, 1957, she finally defeated Louise Brough, National Clay Courts Championship, and won the U.S. Open Women's Singles Championship. When Vice President Richard M. Nixon presented her with the trophy she said, "There is nothing like winning the championship of your own country!" Gibson, both a national and international champion, was the best woman tennis player in the entire world.

Gibson was in fine physical shape, so she was ready for other challenges. She began a career in public relations, working with a bakery firm; had a happy marriage and home life; and started a career as a professional golfer. Regardless of what field she entered, she brought to it the same fierce energy that she did to tennis.

—Nicholas C. Polos

Bibliography

Most of the resources on Althea Gibson are autobiographical or secondary biographical sources. These include the books by Althea Gibson, *I Always Wanted to Be Somebody* (New York: Harper, 1958); and *So Much to Live For* (New York: Putnam, 1968).

Secondary Sources

Dannett, Sylvia G. *Profiles of Negro Womanhood.* Chicago: Educational Heritage, 1964.

Who's Who of American Women. Chicago: Marquis, 1988.

Who's Who in Colored America. New York: Who's Who in Colored America, Corp., 1950.

Davis, Mariana W. *The Contributions of black Women to America* II. Columbia, SC: Kenday, 1982.

Ploski, Harry A., and Brown, Roscoe C., Jr. *The Negro Almanac.* New York: Bellwether, 1967.

Information about Gibson's career is included in several magazines and newspapers:

Life 28:32 (April 3, 1950); 41:88 (July 2, 1956); 49:110 (October 17, 1960).

Time 56:74 (July 17, 1950); 67:64 (June 4, 1958); 70:44 (August 26, 1957); 76:74 (September 15, 1960).

New York Post Magazine (July 22, 1956).

New York Times (June 24, 1956): 3; (July 7, 1957): 4; (July 9, 1957): 33.

GIDDINGS, PAULA (b. 1947), journalist and author, is perhaps best known for her landmark history of black women in the United States, *When and Where I Enter: The Impact of Black Women on Race and Sex in America.* Born November 16, Giddings grew up as the only child of a New York City school teacher/guidance counselor and the first black fireman in a predominantly white neighborhood in Yonkers, New York. Carrying on his family's activist tradition, her father helped found the Yonkers branch of the Congress of Racial Equality (CORE). Paula Giddings remembers wanting to join the Freedom Riders at age 13, when she saw them for the first time on television in 1961. After entering Howard University in 1965, she became editor of its literary magazine and participated in the emerging black poetry movement, one of her early consciousness-raising experiences.

After graduation, Giddings worked at Random House and then as an editor at Howard University Press. She was Paris bureau chief for *Encore American and Worldwide News,* and was part of the press corps accompanying President Jimmy Carter on his 1976 trip to India, Poland, Saudi Arabia, and Egypt. She has written extensively for *The Nation,* the *New York Times Book Review,* the *Philadelphia Inquirer,* the *Washington Post,* the *International Herald Tribune, Jeune Afrique* (in Paris), and is a contributing editor at *Essence* magazine.

A grant from the Ford Foundation in 1982 enabled Giddings to complete *When and Where I Enter,* her critically acclaimed first book. The first comprehensive history of black women's experience in the United States, it has been translated into Japanese and Dutch, and is used extensively in undergraduate and graduate courses. Written from a black feminist perspective, the book is analytical, yet accessible to popular audiences, and was released as a Bantam paperback in 1985. William Morrow and Co. published her second book, *In Search of Sisterhood: Delta Sigma Theta and the Challenge of the Black Sorority Movement,* in 1988. In 1989 she was selected as a nonfiction judge for the National Book Awards.

An articulate chronicler of the black woman's experience in the United States, Giddings often shares her knowledge through teaching, lectures, and other public appearances. She was a United Negro College Fund Distinguished Scholar at Spelman College (1986–1987), and from September 1989 to June 1991 was the fourth occupant of the endowed Blanche, Edith, and Irving Laurie New Jersey Chair in Women's Studies at Douglass College, Rutgers University. The Laurie Chair, previously occupied by feminist philosopher Alison Jaggar, psychologist Carol Gilligan, and feminist theorist Charlotte Bunch, conducts two interdisciplinary seminars with distinguished scholars and graduate students from the Northeast. In 1990 Giddings's seminar examined "Pluralism and Women's Lives: Autobiographies of Race, Class, and Ethnicity." The 1991 seminar, "Women, Race and Reform," focused on activist collaborations between black and white women during the Progressive era.

Giddings, who resides in New York City, is working on her next book, a biography of antilynching activist/journalist Ida B. Wells-Barnett. In May 1990 Bennett College, one of three historically black women's colleges, awarded Paula Giddings an honorary doctorate in humane letters.

—Debra L. Schultz

Bibliography

The primary source for this biographical portrait is an oral history interview this author conducted with Paula Giddings on December 4, 1989. Additional information comes from the Rutgers University News Service, Bennett College President's Office, and Giddings's writings. Her books are *When and Where I Enter: The Impact of Black Women on Race and Sex in America* (New York: Morrow, 1984) and *In Search of Sisterhood: Delta Sigma Theta and the Challenge of the Black Sorority Movement* (New York: Morrow, 1988).

GIOVANNI, NIKKI (b. 1943), poet, activist, and lecturer, was named after her mother, Yolande Cornelis Giovanni. Born in Knoxville, Tennessee, on June 7, she moved to Ohio at a young age and grew up in a suburb of Cincinnati. In 1967 Nikki Giovanni graduated with honors, receiving a bachelor's degree from Fisk University, where she had fought to reinstate the campus chapter of the Student Nonviolent Coordinating Committee. She also pursued additional studies at the University of Pennsylvania and Columbia University.

Nikki Giovanni is one of the most successful black poets in America. Among her collections of poems are *Black Feeling Black Talk* (1969), *Re-Creation* (1970), and *Black Feeling Black Talk Black Judgment* (1970). She also has two significant works with other authors—*A Dialogue: James Baldwin and Nikki Giovanni* (1972) and *A Poetic Equation: Conversations Between Margaret Walker and Nikki Giovanni* (1974). She has also written an autobiographical work, *Gemini: An Extended Autobiographical Statement on My First Twenty-Five Years of Being a Black Poet* (1971). Although some of Giovanni's poetry includes black revolutionary sentiments characteristic of the black poets of the 1960s and 1970s, her work is usually concerned with love, life, and the individual's fight for survival.

Giovanni has taught and lectured in several institutions. She has held appointments at Queens College of the City University of New York and at Livingston College of Rutgers University in New Brunswick, New Jersey. She has also received honorary degrees from the University of Maryland, Eastern Shore; Ripon College; Wilberforce University; and Smith College. Among the numerous awards she has received are Woman of the Year in the category of youth leadership, *Ladies Home Journal* (1972); *Mademoiselle*'s Award for Outstanding Achievement (1971); and one of the Ten Most Admired black Women by the *Amsterdam News* (1969).

She currently combines writing with teaching as an English professor at Virginia Tech in Blacksburg, Virginia. She has a son, Thomas Watson. Giovanni continues to be a popular lecturer on the campus circuit and a frequent contributor to national magazines and scholarly journals.

—Betty Plummer

Bibliography

An excellent source of information on Nikki Giovanni's early life and young adulthood is her autobiographical work, *Gemini: An Extended Autobiographical Statement of My First Twenty-Five Years of Being a Black Poet* (New York: Penguin Books, 1976). James A. Page's *Selected Black American Authors: Illustrated Bio-Bibliography* (Boston: G.H. Hall, 1977) analyzes Giovanni's style and works. Biographical information is included in Ann Shockley, *Living Black American Authors* (New York: Bowker, 1973). A listing of her works is also found in *Contemporary Authors*, edited by Jane A. Bowden (Detroit: Gale, 1977). Works that include an analysis of her work are Claudia Tate, *Black Women Writers at Work* (New York: Continuum, 1983); *Sturdy Black Bridges: Visions of Black Women in Literature*, edited by Roseann Bell, Bettye Parker and Beverly Guy-Sheftall (Garden City, NY: Anchor Books, 1979); and Don Lee, "The Poets and Their Poetry: There Is a Tradition," *Dynamite Voices: Black Poets of the 1960's* (Detroit: Broadside Press, 1971). Giovanni's work is discussed in Peter Bailey, "Nikki Giovanni: 'I Am Black, Female, Polite.'" *Ebony* 27 (February 1972): 48–56; Russell Brooks, "The Motifs of Dynamic Change in Black Revolutionary Poetry," *CLA Journal* 15 (September 1971): 7–17; and Roderick R. Palmer, "The Poetry of Three Revolutionists," *CLA Journal* 15 (September 1971): 25–36. She is featured in Margaret Busby, *Daughters of Africa* (New York: Pantheon, 1992).

GOLDBERG, WHOOPI (b. 1955), comedienne, actress, and writer, had

a long and difficult struggle to get to the pinnacle of her craft, making history for the entertainment industry and African Americans. Although she received her first Academy Award nomination in her debut movie role as Celie in *The Color Purple* (1985), a movie adaptation of Alice Walker's novel of the same title, it was *Ghost*, the top-grossing money-maker of 1990, that garnered her the Oscar for Best Supporting Actress. In so doing, Goldberg became the second African-American actress in 52 years to receive the honor. In fact, in the 63-year history of the Academy Awards, only Hattie McDaniel shared the honor in 1939 for her role in *Gone with the Wind*.

Born Caryn Johnson on November 13, she grew up in a housing project in New York City. She began acting at age eight with the Children's Program at the Hudson Guild and the Helena Rubenstein Children's Theatre. She dropped out of school at age 17, discovering years later she was dyslexic. She experimented with drugs, which led her to become an outspoken leader in the antidrug movement. Her own drug rehabilitation brought her into a relationship with her drug counselor, who became her first husband. The marriage was short-lived, but produced Goldberg's only child, a daughter, Alexandrea.

At age 19 in 1974, she left New York to resettle in California to begin a new life. Believing in her own abilities, she joined the San Diego Repertory Company and worked at odd jobs at a funeral home or bricklaying to pay the bills. Unable to make ends meet, she was forced to go on welfare. Goldberg ranks getting off welfare as one of her greatest triumphs.

It was also in San Diego that she adopted the name Whoopi Goldberg. Her colleagues at the San Diego Rep dubbed her "Whoopi" for her flatulence, and she chose Goldberg, a family name from her mother's side. She later moved to the Bay Area and joined the Black Street Hawkeyes Theatre in Berkeley, California, partnered with David Schein. Moving shortly into solo performances, Goldberg created *The Spook Show*, which first played in San Francisco and then toured the United States and Europe.

It was at a 1983 performance of that show, performed at the Dance Theatre Workshop in New York, that Goldberg attracted the attention of producer Mike Nichols, who offered to present her in a new Broadway show. An evening of original material, written and created by Goldberg, the show opened at the Lyceum Theatre to critical acclaim. She later taped the show as an HBO special, *Whoopi Goldberg: Direct from Broadway*. The record album of her Broadway show won a Grammy Award as Best Comedy Recording of the Year in 1985.

Her Broadway show also turned out to be an audition to filmmaker Steven Spielberg, who cast her in *The Color Purple*. Prior to beginning the film, Goldberg briefly returned to San Francisco to star as the legendary Moms Mabley in *Moms*, a one-person show that she also co-wrote, based on the late comedienne's original material.

The Color Purple launched Whoopi Goldberg's film career and, in addition to her first Oscar nomination, earned her the 1985 Golden Globe Award for Best Performance by an Actress in a Dramatic Motion Picture, as well as the NAACP's Image Award for Best Actress in a Motion Picture. In 1986, she married Dutch cameraman David Claessen, whom she met while working on a documentary on the homeless. The marriage lasted less than two years.

Since *The Color Purple*, Goldberg has starred in such motion pictures as *Jumpin' Jack Flash* (1986), *Burglar* (1987), *Fatal Beauty* (1987), *Clara's Heart* (1988), *Ghost* (1990), *The Long Walk Home* (1990), *Soapdish* (1991), *The Player* (1992), the box office hit *Sister Act* (1992), *Sarafina!* (1992), and *Made in America* (1993).

On television, her appearance on an episode of *Moonlighting* in 1986 earned her an Emmy Award nomination as Best Guest Performer in a Dramatic Series. Goldberg starred with Jean Stapleton in CBS's *Bagdad Cafe*, and she has appeared for five seasons on the hit syndicated series *Star Trek: The Next Generation*. Goldberg also appeared in the CBS Schoolbreak Special *My Past Is My Own*, for which she was nominated for a Daytime Emmy Award, and she starred in the

CBS telefilm *Kiss Shot* with Dorian Harewood. In 1991, Goldberg guest-starred on the NBC series *A Different World*, and was nominated once again for a Prime-Time Emmy Award, as Best Guest Actress on a Comedy Series. She also starred in "Dead Wait," an episode of HBO's horror anthology series *Tales from the Crypt*.

She is the voice of Gaia, the spirit of Earth, on *Captain Planet and the Planeteers*, an animated environmental action-adventure series and another performance that garnered her a Daytime Emmy Award nomination. She also provides the voice of Mrs. Megawatt in George Lucas's animated series *Defenders of Dynatron City*, for the Fox Children's Network. Among her recordings is *Koi and Kola Nuts*, an African folktale narrated by Goldberg, with a score by Herbie Hancock for Rabbit Ears's international collection for children, *We All Have Tales*. Goldberg has been honored four times with Nickelodeon's Kid's Choice Award for Favorite Movie Actress.

Goldberg has appeared on a variety of television specials, including *Scared Straight: 10 Years Later*; *Carol, Carl, Whoopi and Robin* (Burnett, Reiner, Goldberg, and Williams, respectively); Marlo Thomas's *Free to Be . . . A Family*; *FreedomFest: Nelson Mandela's 70th Birthday Special* (co-host); and "The Truth about Teachers," which she hosted as part of a four-part series of specials entitled *Raising Good Kids in Bad Times*, *Rock the Vote*, and *Back to School '92*. She co-produced the syndicated special *A Laugh, A Tear*, and appeared in a co-produced "Hot Rod Brown," a "Tales from the Whoop" special for Nickelodeon, for which she earned another Daytime Emmy Award nomination. In February 1992, Goldberg hosted *The 34th Annual Grammy Awards* telecast.

In 1987, Goldberg, Billy Crystal, and Robin Williams co-hosted HBO's "Comic Relief" benefit for the nation's homeless. Following the equally successful "Comic Relief II" a year later, the three hosted "Comic Relief III," which raised more money than the first two combined, as did "Comic Relief IV." Additional funds were raised in November 1991, when HBO broadcast "The Greatest Hits of Comic Relief," and in 1992, Goldberg, Billy, and Robin reunited for "Comic Relief V."

Goldberg toured her one-woman show *Living on the Edge of Chaos* throughout the United States, Canada, and Australia, and in August 1988, she performed a television special for HBO Comedy Hour, titled *Whoopi Goldberg's Fontaine . . . Why Am I Straight?* Her second comedy album, *Fontaine . . . Why Am I Straight?*, was nominated for a Grammy Award. In 1990, prior to embarking on her SRO six-week tour of Australia and New Zealand, Goldberg hosted yet another special for HBO Comedy Hour, *Whoopi Goldberg and Billy Connolly in Performance*. Her most recent special for HBO, *Whoopi Goldberg: Chez Whoopi*, debuted in August 1991. In the summer of 1991, Goldberg returned to the legitimate stage to co-star with Timothy Dalton in A.R. Gurney's two-person play *Love Letters*.

Goldberg is well known for her tireless humanitarian efforts on behalf of children, the homeless, human rights, substance abuse, and the battle against

AIDS, as well as many other worthwhile causes and charities. In 1989, her daughter became pregant and gave Goldberg her first grandchild. September 1992 marked Goldberg's debut as a talk show host with *The Whoopi Goldberg Show*, her own syndicated half-hour late-night talk show. Goldberg has also published her first children's book, *Alice* (Bantam Books).

—Donna Van Raaphorst

Bibliography

To date there is no biography on Whoopi Goldberg. The best place to begin is in periodical literature from 1984 to the present. *Jet* magazine seems to have taken a proprietary interest in Goldberg's career from the beginning. Most entries are small, but helpful in re-creating her rise to stardom. Of particular value is "Whoopi Goldberg: Second black Actress to Win an Oscar in 52 Years," *Jet* 22 (April 22, 1991): 54–57. Other articles include: Pamela Noel, "Who Is Whoopi Goldberg and What Is She Doing on Broadway???" *Ebony* (March 1985): 55–57; "Whoopi Goldberg Leads Comics to HBO Benefit," *Jet* 69 (March 3, 1986): 20; S. Erickson, "Whoopi Goldberg," *Rolling Stone* (May 8, 1986): 24–25; "Whoopi to Star in Upcoming Comic Movie," *Jet* 70 (July 21, 1986): 59; "Whoopi Goldberg Weds Dutch Cinematographer," *Jet* 71 (September 22, 1986): 59; "Whoopi Goldberg Talks About New Movie, New Husband," *Jet* 71 (November 3, 1986): 58–59; "Whoopi Sounds Off on Sex, Drugs, Race," *Jet* 72 (June 15, 1987): 24; "Fatal Beauty Love Scene Cut: Goldberg Cites Racism," *Jet* 73 (October 5, 1987): 63; "Whoopi Goldberg and Sam Elliott Star in Fatal Beauty," *Jet* 73 (November 16, 1987): 58–60; P. Chulkow, "Remaking Whoopi," *Vogue* 181 (January 1991): 178–181+; Laura B. Randolph, "The Whoopi Goldberg Nobody Knows," *Ebony* (March 1991): 34–36+; and "Goldberg, Williams Make Historic Wins at Oscars," *Jet* 79 (April 15, 1991): 54–55.

Books on African Americans in the entertainment field are also helpful: Donald Bogle, *Blacks in American Films and Television: An Illustrated Encyclopedia.* New York: Simon & Schuster, 1988; and *Black Arts Annual 1988/89* New York: Garland, 1990; and George Hill, *Black Women in Television: An Illustrated History and Bibliography* New York: Garland, 1990. Sources that provides conflicting dates of her birth include: *Almanac of Famous People.* Detroit: Gale, 1989; *Who's Who in Entertainment 1992–1993.* Chicago: Marquis, 1992; *Who's Who among Black Americans 1992/1993.* Northbrook, IL: and *Current Biography.* New York: Wilson, 1992. The most recent interview is by Patrick E. Cole, "The Joy of Being Whoopi," *Time* (September 21, 1992): 58–60. She can be contacted through Creative Artists Agency of Beverly Hills, California.

GRAY, IDA (1867–1953), the first black woman to receive the doctor of dental surgery degree in the United States, was born March 4 in Clarksville, Tennessee to Jennie Gray John. Her parents moved to Cincinnati, Ohio, when she was still quite young. She attended Gaines Public High School in Cincinnati until graduation in 1887. The influence of Dr. Jonathan Taft, the founding dean of the University of Michigan Dental School, brought Ida Gray into the program.

As the only dentist in Cincinnati at the time, Dr. Taft supported the unpopular idea of female dentists. In 1859, he accepted a female apprentice, Lucy Hobbs, in his office. She was refused admission to the Ohio College of Dentistry in 1861, but gained admission finally in 1865 to become the first professional female dentist in the world in 1866. This personal and professional victory influenced Ida Gray, who worked in Taft's office before she entered the University of Michigan Dental School in October 1887, with Dr. Taft as her preceptor. She received her doctor of dental surgery degree in 1890 to become one of the dental school's twenty-two graduates, one of 1,337 women in the American dental profession, and the first African-American woman to earn the degree in the United States.

She practiced privately in Cincinnati for five years. Apparently, she was well respected in the community, as a newspaper editor said of Dr. Gray, "Her blushing, winning ways makes [sic] you feel like finding an extra tooth anyway to allow her to pull." In 1895 she married James S. Nelson, a quartermaster of the Eighth Regiment of Chicago, who fought in the Spanish-American War. He became an accountant and lawyer, and the couple moved to Chicago, where she became the first African-American female dentist. The couple resided on State Street while Ida Gray Nelson established her dental practice at 35th and Armour Avenue. She moved her practice to 3558 South State Street in 1898 and changed her residence to Wabash Avenue in 1903. Inspired by Gray's example, a patient, Olive M. Henderson, became the second African-American women dentist in Chicago opening her practice around 1912. Her husband died in 1926. In 1929 she married William A. Rollins, changed her professional name to Ida N. Rollins, D.D.S. and remained in Chicago the rest of her life. Her husband died in 1938. Neither marriage produced children. She died in 1953. On her gravestone is this epitaph: "Dr. Ida Gray Nelson Rollins, First Negro Woman Dentist in America."

—Dorothy C. Salem and Terri L. Jewell

Bibliography

Few sources describe the career of Ida Gray beyond the general information above. The best sources are in the University of Michigan, School of Dentistry, Alumnae Files, and from the Society for the Research and Study of the Negro in Dentistry, Inc. The best printed sources come from these files: Charles Kelsey, "Ida Gray: Class of 1890" in the University of Michigan, School of Dentistry *Alumni Bulletin* (1977–1978): 50–52; and Claude Evans Driskell, *History of Chicago Black Dental Professionals, 1850–1983* (Chicago: C.E. Driskell, 1983–1984), 22–23. For brief repetitions of the general information, see biographical sketches in Marianna W. Davis, ed., *Contributions of Black Women to America* (Columbia, SC: Kenday, 1981); Dorothy M. Love, *A Salute To Historic Black Women* (Chicago: Empak Enterprises, 1984); and Sylvia Dannett, *Profiles of Negro Womanhood* (Yonkers, NY: 1964), pp. 261.

GREENFIELD, ELIZABETH [TAYLOR] (c. 1824–1876), the celebrated

singer, was born into slavery in Natchez, Mississippi. Greenfield's owner, Mrs.
Jesse Greenfield, freed her slaves sometime in the late 1820s and moved to
Philadelphia, taking the young Greenfield with her. Mrs. Jesse Greenfield acted
as guardian and patroness to her ward until her death in 1844. A sizable portion
of Mrs. Greenfield's estate was left to Greenfield, but the will was contested and
the intended recipient never realized her bequest. Nevertheless, in honor of Mrs.
Greenfield's generosity and companionship, Greenfield assumed the surname of
her benefactress.

Greenfield's musical gifts became apparent at a young age, and instruction in
piano and voice were provided by her guardian. In the late 1840s, Greenfield
traveled to Buffalo, New York, and later returned to make her debut in 1851 in
a recital sponsored by the Buffalo Musical Association. A glowing review in the
Buffalo *Commercial Advertiser* compared her favorably with other renowned
singers and earned her the sobriquet "Black Swan." During the next two years she
toured extensively throughout the northern United States under the sponsorship
of the impresario Colonel J.H. Wood. Greenfield's repertoire included opera
arias, spirituals, and popular songs that exploited her unusual tessitura of three
and one-half octaves.

In 1853 Greenfield announced her intention to tour England, and a fundraising
concert was arranged by enthusiastic supporters. The Duchess of Sutherland
became her sponsor and arranged for her presentation to the elite of London in
a private concert given at Stafford House. On May 10, 1854, Greenfield was
invited to perform for Queen Victoria at Buckingham Palace, accompanied by Sir
George Smart, organist and composer to Her Majesty's Chapel Royal. Accounts
of Greenfield's highly acclaimed tour appeared in numerous London reviews and
in memoirs of Harriet Beecher Stowe, who was in London following the
publication of her first novel, *Uncle Tom's Cabin*. In her travelogue, *Sunny
Memories of Foreign Lands*, Stowe extolled Greenfield's "most astonishing voice,"
her "gentleness of manner and self-possession," and her "quietness and good
sense."

Greenfield returned to the United States in 1854 and resettled in Philadelphia, where she continued to concertize. For the next two decades Greenfield
taught voice, and during the 1860s, she directed productions of the Philadelphia
Opera Troupe. Greenfield died in Philadelphia in 1876, reportedly of paralysis.
Greenfield is remembered as a consummate concert artist, and the first black
American musician to win critical acclaim on both sides of the Atlantic. Her
legacy inspired W.C. Handy and Harry H. Pace to name their fledgling recording
company black Swan in her honor. Founded in 1921 it was the first such company
owned by black Americans. More recently, Greenfield's sobriquet and career
served as the artistic impetus of the black Swan Quartet, an improvising string
ensemble that launched its concertizing and recording career in the late 1980s.

—Juanita Karpf

Bibliography

A full-length account of Elizabeth Greenfield's life and career is to be found in *The Black Swan* (Detroit: n.p., 1969) by noted black music historian Arthur LaBrew. The most useful biographical sketches are included in the following: James M. Trotter, *Music and Some Highly Musical People* (Chicago: Afro American, 1878); Monroe A. Majors, *Noted Negro Women* (Chicago: Donohue & Henneberry, 1893); Maud Cuney-Hare, *Negro Musicians and Their Music* (New York: De Capo Press, 1936); Wilhelmina S. Robinson, "Historical Negro Biographies" (New York: Publishers Co., 1967); *Theatre Arts Monthly* (June 1931); and Eileen Southern, *Biographical Dictionary of Afro-American and African Musicians* (Westport, CT: Greenwood, 1982). Dictionaries that contain valuable information about Greenfield include articles by Samuel R. Spencer, Jr., in *Notable American Women, 1607–1950*, edited by Edward T. James (Cambridge: Belknap, 1971); and by William W. Austin, *The New Grove Dictionary of American Music* (New York: Groves Dictionaries of Music, 1980). Contemporaneous information about Greenfield is contained in the biographical pamphlet "The Black Swan at Home and Abroad" (Chicago: privately published, 1855), and Martin Robinson Delany, *The Condition, Elevation, Emigration, and Destiny of the Colored People of the United States* (1852, reprint ed. in *American Negro: His History and Literature* (New York: Arno, 1968). Harriet Beecher Stowe's *Sunny Memories of Foreign Lands* (Boston: Phillips & Sampson, 1854) provides valuable information about Greenfield's activities in London. Greenfield is also discussed in the writings of Benjamin Brawley, including *The Negro in Literature and Art in the United States* (Alexandria, VA: Chadwick-Healy, 1918) and *The Negro Genius* (Chapel Hill, NC: University of North Carolina Press, 1937). Greenfield's obituary appeared on April 2, 1876, in the *New York Times* and on April 3, 1876, in the *Philadelphia Public Ledger*. Reference to Greenfield is made in Hale Smith, "Black Swan Quartet in Conversation," *Strings* 3:3 (Winter 1989).

GRIER, ELIZA (1864–1902), physician persevered remarkably in the pursuit of her goals. Her desire to practice medicine among poor blacks in the South led her to write to the Woman's Medical College of Pennsylvania, "How much does it take to put one through a year in your school? Is there any possible chance to do any work that would not interfere with one's studies?" An emancipated slave, she took seven years to complete her college education at Fisk University, where she graduated in 1891. It took her another seven years to earn a medical degree from Woman's Medical College of Pennsylvania in 1897. The dean of the college later wrote that Eliza Grier had a "respectable standing" as a student, but "how much better she would have done had she not been constantly harassed by want of adequate means of support it is difficult to say." Whatever assistance Dr. Grier may have received was insufficient, for she had to put herself through medical school by attending for one year, then returning home to pick cotton in order to earn money.

Eliza Anna Grier was born in North Carolina. After completing her medical education, she set up practice in Greenville, South Carolina. Her practice was not financially successful as evidenced by a 1901 appeal she made to Susan B. Anthony, "I am a young Negro woman . . . engaged in the practice of medicine. . . . I have made a pretty good practice, but mostly among the very poor & in neglected areas. By & by I hope to get something from that source. I have been quite ill for six weeks with La Grippe. I have not been able to make a single dollar. . . . Please help me in this my time of severe trial & want."

In an attempt to better her circumstances, Dr. Grier moved from Greenville, South Carolina, to Thomasville, Georgia, in 1901. She was the first black woman to apply to the State Board of Physicians. On April 14, 1902, Dr. Grier died of a stroke. She was buried in Charlotte, North Carolina.

—Janet Miller

Bibliography

Information on Eliza Grier can be found in the Eliza Grier Alumnae Folder, Accession 73, Archives and Special Collections on Women in Medicine, Medical College of Pennsylvania; and the Eliza Grier file, black Women Physicians Project, Accession 178, Archives and Special Collections on Women in Medicine, Medical College of Pennsylvania.

Small amounts of information are included in Dorothy Sterling, *We Are Your Sisters* (New York: Norton, 1984), pp. 445–448; Margaret Jerrido, "Black Woman Physician: A Triple Burden," *Alumnae News*, Medical College of Pennsylvania (Spring 1979): 2.

GRIMKÉ, ANGELINA WELD (1880–1958) was part of the core of black women authors who participated in the theater's protest against the lynching of African Americans during the early twentieth century. She contributed *Rachel* to the body of lynch plays these writers produced between 1916 and 1929, the years encompassing the Harlem Renaissance, the black women's club movement, and the antilynching campaign. *Rachel* was first produced in 1916 by the National Association for the Advancement of Colored People in Washington DC, and became the means by which the organization officially denounced the lynching and the subjugation of African Americans. *Rachel* is important to African-American literature as "an early full-length black authored piece," and is important to American literature because it is one of the earliest American dramas to refute black stereotypes, using characters from the black middle class to protest racism. *Rachel* represents Grimké's unique contributions to the effacement of the disparaging black images as mammies, buffoons, darkies, and degenerates that were paraded in nineteenth-century American literature.

Angelina Grimké was a member of the renowned interracial Grimké family. She was born in Boston in 1880 to Sarah E. Stanley, a white woman, and Archibald Grimké, a mulatto former slave and nephew of sisters, Sarah and Angelina Grimké (Weld), fighters for abolition and women's rights. A lawyer, race leader, and diplomat, Archibald Grimké sent his daughter to prestigious

Massachusetts schools, including Fairmount School in Hyde Park, the Cushing Academy in Ashurnham, the Boston Normal School of Gymnastics, and the Carleton Academy at Northfield, Minnesota. After her 1902 graduation from the Boston Normal School, Angelina Grimké became an educator at Dunbar High School, the prestigious black college preparatory school in Washington DC, until her resignation in 1926.

Given her heritage of social activism and class elitism, Grimké probably lived a prescribed life, obligated to fulfill civic responsibilities. In the protest play *Rachel*, Grimké continued her family's participation in the civil rights campaign and became among the first to use the American stage to denounce social injustice. Grimké's fiction, however, not only reflects the legacy of race consciousness that her distinquished forebears passed down to her, but also reflects her resentment of being rejected by her mother at age seven. In 1887 her mother shipped Angelina back to her father saying, "It is for the best good and happiness of little Nana that she should go to you at once. . . . She needs that love and sympathy of one of her own race." Sarah Stanley Grimké was frustrated with the problems of facing a white world with her black daughter, and so she returned her child to the husband she had deserted five years earlier. Grimké never seemed to have forgiven her mother for rejecting her. Yet, Grimké assigned all her female protagonists loving mothers or mother surrogates, attempting perhaps to repress her own abandonment.

In addition to *Rachel*, published by Cornhill Company in 1920, Grimké's other publications include poems, articles, and short stories. Writing verse since the turn of the century, Grimké suppressed publication of much of it due to the homosexual themes. At Grimké's death in 1958, she left behind 20 woman-identified poems written in holograph. They can be found with her other unpublished works of drama, poetry, and short stories in the manuscript collection of the Moorland-Spingarn Research Center, Howard University, Washington DC.

—Patricia A. Young

Bibliography

The best collection of Angelina Grimké's correspondence and writings is her manuscript collection in the Moorland-Spingarn Research Center, Howard University, Washington, DC.

Secondary Sources

Drake, William. *The First Wave; Women Poets in America 1915–1945.* New York: Macmillan, 1987. Provides interesting detail about her parents and her resentment of her mother.

Ellington, Mary Davis. "Plays by Negro Authors with Special Emphasis upon the Period from 1916–1934." PhD dissertation, Fisk University, 1934. Summarizes

Rachel and shows how the play articulates the principal themes treated by other early twentieth-century playwrights.

Hull, Gloria T. *Color, Sex, and Poetry: Three Women Writers of the Harlem Renaissance.* Bloomington: Indiana University Press, 1987. Provides insight into the life and literature.

————. "Under the Days: The Buried Life and Poetry of Angelina Weld Grimké." *Conditions Five* (Autumn 1979): 17–24. Contends that her lesbianism explains the paucity of her published works and the scanty recognition accorded her.

McKay, Nellie, "What Were They Saying? Black Women Playwrights of the Harlem Renaissance." Manuscript. Contextualizes the place of *Rachel* within black literary history.

Miller, Jeanne-Marie A. "Angelina Weld Grimké: Playwright and Poet." *CLA Journal* 21 (June 1978): 514–519. Examines a revised four-act lynch play, *Mara*, still in manuscript.

Molette, Barbara. "Black Women Playwrights," *Black World* 25 (April 1976): 28+.

Shine, Ted, and James Hatch. *Black Theatre USA.* New York: Macmillan, 1974. Devotes an entire chapter to black women playwrights.

Stubbs, Carolyn A. "Angelina Weld Grimké: Washington Poet and Playwright." PhD dissertation, George Washington University, 1978. Examines the woman and her work.

GRIMKÉ, CHARLOTTE L. FORTEN (1837–1914) was a writer (poet,

essayist, translator, diarist), educator, abolitionist, and reformer whose life personifies the varying levels of activism by a free black woman in antebellum America. Born August 17 in Philadelphia, Charlotte Forten was part of a famous abolitionist family. Her grandparents were James and Charlotte Forten; paternal aunts were Margaretta Forten and Sarah Louise Forten Purvis. Her mother, Mary Virginia (Woods) Forten (1816–1840), died when Charlotte was three years old; thus, her father, Robert Bridges Forten (1813–1864), was instrumental in directing her early life.

As an abolitionist and a "race man," Robert Forten was committed to racial uplift. Having served as a member of the Young Men's Anti-Slavery Society of Philadelphia, the Philadelphia Vigilance Committee, the New England Anti-Slavery Society, and in the 43rd Colored Infantry, he held high standards for his children. He traveled to Canada in 1855 and England in 1858 considering escape from racism in the United States.

Her father was especially concerned about his daughter's education. She was privately tutored in Philadelphia until age 16 because her father refused to send her to segregated schools. She frequently resided in Byberry with her uncle Robert Purvis. She was very close to her aunt, Margaretta. Her education brought her exposure to many prominent reformers at an early age. In 1853 she was sent to live with a family friend, the abolitionist Charles Lenox Remond, in Salem, Massachusetts, to attend the integrated Higginson Grammar School (1855) and later Salem Normal School (1856). Charlotte Forten befriended William Lloyd Garrison, Lucretia Mott, John Greenleaf Whittier, and others while living at the Remond home. After graduation, she taught at the segregated (white) Epes Grammar School during 1856, 1860, and 1861, largely through the efforts of her teacher Mary Shephard. During periods in which her health failed her, Charlotte Forten returned to Philadelphia to teach at the school of her aunt, Margaretta Forten, with whom she frequently corresponded. This was the beginning of Forten's dedication to intellectual endeavors. In Salem, she journalized her feelings about racism and developed her life-long commitment to justice for black people in the United States.

She abandoned her journals for over a year until President Abraham Lincoln declared the seaport islands of Port Royal under protective blockade for the Union, an action that produced 10,000 slaves held as war contraband. They needed education and military training to remain free. Through the efforts of the Educational Commission, the Freedmen's Relief Association, and the Port Royal Relief Association, Charlotte Forten was commissioned to teach at St. Helena Island in 1862 upon the recommendation of family friend John Greenleaf Whittier. She proved that African Americans were as capable of self-improvement as whites during her tenure from 1862 to 1864. She instructed the slaves in basic education, providing abolitionist history to their curriculum, and worked cooperatively with the military regime, particularly with Colonel Higginson. One of the highlights of her adventures was meeting with the leader of the Underground Railroad, Harriet Tubman, at Tubman's home in Beaufort, South Carolina, on January 31, 1863. Although she taught at Lombard Street School in Philadelphia, Shaw Memorial School in Charleston, South Carolina, and a black preparatory high school in Washington, DC, her instruction of the ex-slaves in the Port Royal experiment was her most noteworthy accomplishment in a life dedicated to reform.

Following the Civil War, Charlotte Forten worked for the New England Freedmen's Union Commission (1865–1871) and Shaw Memorial School in South Carolina. In 1873, she received the appointment from 500 applicants to serve as a clerk in the Treasury Department. She married the Reverend Francis J. Grimké, pastor of the Fifth Street Presbyterian Church and nephew of Sarah and Angelina Grimké, in December 1878, she was age 41 and he was 28. Their one daughter, Cornelia, died in infancy (1879–1880). In addition to her role as an educator, she was also an active member of the Salem Anti-Slavery Society and a founding member of the National Association of Colored Women. Charlotte Forten Grimké died after recurring illness on July 23, 1914, in Washington, DC, at age 77.

—Ula Y. Taylor and Jacqueline D. Carr-Hamilton

Bibliography

Charlotte Forten Grimké's writings provide a window to her view of personal and public transitions in her lifetime. Her written publications in the form of poems, essays, and articles are located in the following magazines and journals: *The Liberator*, *Christian Recorder*, *National Anti-Slavery Standard*, *Anglo-African Magazine*, *New England Magazine*, and *Atlantic Monthly*. She also translated the French novel *Madame Therese; or The Volunteers of '92* by Emile Erckmann and Alexandre Chatrain. As a diarist, Charlotte Forten left five private journals spanning the period 1854–1892, tentatively recorded in her journals: Journal One (Salem: May 24, 1854–December 31, 1856); Journal Two (Salem: January 1, 1857–January 27, 1858); Journal Three (Salem: January 28, 1858–February 14, 1863); Journal Four (St. Helena Island: February 15, 1863–May 15, 1864); and Journal Five (Jacksonville: November 1885–July 1892). During the course of her writings, she addressed her journals affectionately to"Dear 'A'."

Charlotte Forten's manuscript diaries are located at the Moorland-Spingarn Research Center, Howard University, Washington DC. These journals have been edited by Brenda Stevenson. *The Journals of Charlotte Forten Grimké* (New York: Oxford University Press, 1988).

Secondary Sources

Billington, Ray, ed. *The Journal of Charlotte Forten: A Free Negro in the Slave Era*. New York: Norton, 1981.

Birney, Catherine. *The Grimké Sisters: Sarah and Angelina Grimké, the First Women Advocates of Abolition and Woman's Rights*. Boston: Lee and Shepard, 1885.

Braxton, Joanne M. *Charlotte Forten Grimké (1837–1914) and the Search for a Public Voice*. Wellesley, MA: Wellesley College, Center for Research on Women, 1985.

Douty, Esther M. *Charlotte Forten. Free Black Teacher*. Champaign, IL: Garrard, 1971.

————. *Forten the Sailmaker: Pioneer Champion of Negro Rights*. New York: Rand McNally, 1968.

Giddings, Paula. *When and Where I Enter: The Impact of Black Women on Race and Sex in America*. New York: William Morrow, 1984.

Hull, Gloria, Patricia Bell Scott, and Barbara Smith, eds. *All the Women Are White, All the Blacks Are Men, But Some of Us Are Brave: Black Women's Studies*. Old Westbury, NY: Feminist Press, 1982.

Lerner, Gerda. *The Grimké Sisters from South Carolina: Rebels Against Slavery*. New York: Schocken, 1967.

Loewenberg, Bert James, and Ruth Bogin, eds. *Black Women in Nineteenth Century American Life*. University Park: Pennsylvania State Press, 1976.

Sterling, Dorothy. *We Are Your Sisters: Black Women in the Nineteenth Century*. New York: Norton, 1984.

For a complete citation of Charlotte Forten's published writings see Brenda Stevenson, *The Journals of Charlotte Forten Grimké* (New York: Oxford University Press, 1988).

H

HACKLEY, EMMA AZALIA H. [SMITH] (1867–1922), singer, educator, humanitarian, and philanthropist, was born on June 29 in Murfreesboro, Tennessee. Racial hostilities forced the family to move, and in 1870 they resettled in Detroit. As a child Emma Azalia Smith studied piano, voice, and violin. In 1883 she was the first black student to graduate from Detroit Central High School, and that fall, she was the first black ever admitted to Washington Normal School, a teacher training institution.

On January 29, 1894, Hackley eloped with Denver attorney and journalist Edwin Henry Hackley. She entered the University of Denver School of Music as its first black student and completed her bachelor's degree sometime around 1901. While in Denver, she became active in the struggle for racial equality, and with her husband founded the Imperial Order of Libyans. She also organized a local branch of the Colored Women's League and assisted her husband as clerk and journalist with his fledgling black newspaper, the *Denver Statesman*.

Late in 1901 Hackley began an extended concert tour. She settled in Philadelphia rather than returning to Denver and founded the critically acclaimed People's Chorus. Hackley's programming consisted of a mixture of traditional classical works and black spirituals. In 1905 Hackley sought additional training as a singer and conductor in Europe. She spent a year in Paris studying with the well-known tenor and pedagogue Jean de Reszke. Upon her return to the United States, she formed the Hackley Foreign Scholarship Fund, a program she maintained through strenuous fundraising campaigns so that others of her race might reap the benefits of foreign study.

After a second trip abroad, Hackley's efforts turned increasingly toward vocal teaching, the art of what she called "voice culture." By 1910 she had abandoned her concert career in favor of recitals to large audiences, which included lectures and voice lessons. According to one critic, Hackley aided her race musically in the same spirit that Booker T. Washington promoted industry. Her audiences often numbered in the thousands.

By 1915 Hackley had become permanently separated from her husband and had settled in Chicago. Their childless marriage was never legally dissolved. In Chicago Hackley founded the Normal Vocal Institute to provide others of her race the opportunity to pursue a career in music education. Throughout her career, Hackley wrote books and articles that were intended to encourage African Americans to develop their musical talents, poise, and self-esteem, and to obtain an education.

Hackley's health began to deteriorate before 1920 when a severe ear ailment caused dizziness and impaired hearing. She was hospitalized in 1921 after a trip to Japan, and a tour in California planned for 1922 was canceled because of ill health. Her final emotional and physical collapse came that same year, and on December 13 she died of a cerebral hermorrhage.

In recognition of Hackley's immeasurable contributions to the cause of racial equality, the E. Azalia Hackley Memorial Collection of Negro Music, Dance, and Drama was established at the Detroit Public Library in 1943. During the mid-1930s Hackley's esteemed People's Chorus was renamed the Hackley Choral Society. The Detroit chapter of the National Association of Negro Musicians was named the Hackley Chapter in 1935, and a building at Hampton Institute in Virginia is named after Hackley.

—Juanita Karpf

Bibliography

Hackley published two books: *A Guide in Voice Culture* (Philadelphia: the Author, 1909), and *The Colored Girl Beautiful* (Kansas City, MO: Burton, 1916). She puplished one musical composition, a work for voice and piano, entitled "Carola: Spanish Serenade" (Detroit: the Author, 1918). Her series of 12 articles, "Hints to Young Colored Artists," appeared in the *New York Age*, 1914–1915. Hackley also published articles in the *Indianapolis Freeman* and wrote a regular column for the *Denver Statesman*.

Though replete with inaccuracies, the only full-length biography written about Hackley is M. Margarite Davenport, *Azalia: The Life of Madame E. Azalia Hackley* (Boston: Chapman and Grimes, 1947). Shorter biographical articles can be found in Hallie Q. Brown, *Homespun Heroines and Other Women of Distinction* (New York: Oxford University Press, reprint ed., 1988); Maud Cuney-Hare, *Negro Musicians and Their Music* (New York: Da Capo Press, reprint ed., 1972); and Ellistine Perkins Lewis Holly, "The E. Azalia Hackley Memorial Collection of Negro Music, Dance, and Drama: A Cataloque of Selected Afro-American Materials" (PhD dissertation, University of Michigan, 1978). Other useful and essential essays include the entries by Josephine Harreld Love about Hackley in *Notable American Women, 1607–1950*, edited by Edward T. Jones (Cambridge, MA: Belknap Press, 1973), and Eileen Southern, *Biographical Dictionary of Afro-American and African Musicians* (Westport, CT: Greenwood Press, 1982).

HAMER, FANNIE LOU [TOWNSEND] (1917–1977), born October 6, started life from a foundation of deprivation, yet developed into a giving adult. Fannie Lou Hamer was a charismatic, powerful grassroots civil rights leader whose 15 years as a social activist underscored the role women and grassroots organizers played in the civil rights movement of the 1960s and 1970s. She lived all her life in Mississippi, struggling for the rights of the dispossessed. Hamer became one of the most successful leaders of the movement. In addition to her organizing ability, she possessed an ability to lead rousing freedom songs and to create powerful extemporaneous orations.

Hamer was born the last of 20 children—14 boys and 6 girls—to sharecropping parents in Ruleville, Mississippi, a small town in Sunflower County. Her family worked hard to end the cycle of sharecropping by laboring from sun to sun. Eventually the family had picked enough cotton to afford several mules, a car, a cultivator, and 60 acres of rented land. After hostile white neighbors poisoned their mules and cows, the family slid back into sharecropping.

Hamer began work in the fields at age six. For four months of the year she attended school, but by grade six she was compelled to leave school to assist in supporting the family full time. In 1942 she married Perry Hamer, whom she called "Pap." He, too, was a sharecropper, but supplemented the family income with the proceeds from a small nightclub. Unable to have children, the Hamers adopted two daughters, one of whom, Dorothy Jean, died as a young adult in 1967. The Hamers subsequently fostered several children.

Hamer worked as a weigher and record keeper of the cotton, one of the "better" jobs on the cotton plantation. She and her husband lived on the Marlow Plantation until 1962, at which time her political involvement changed her life and the life of Sunflower County, where over 70 percent of blacks were disenfranchised. Hamer was age 45. She attended a mass meeting called by the Student Nonviolent Coordinating Committee. On that occasion Hamer met Bob Moses, Reggie Robinson, James Bevel, and James Forman. When they requested that local residents go to the courthouse the next day to register to vote, Hamer volunteered.

Such voluntary action carried a high price for Hamer. As one of 18 citizens who attempted to vote, Hamer received a literacy test. Having failed to copy and interpret a portion of the Mississippi Constitution, Hamer and the others boarded the bus to return to Ruleville. A highway patrolman stopped the bus and arrested the driver for operating a vehicle that was colored too much like a school bus. The group refused separation, which resulted in Hamer's arrest and imprisonment. After bail was made, Hamer returned to the Marlow Plantation to learn that she and her husband were being expelled. Medgar Evers, head of the state's National Association for the Advancement of Colored People, was murdered that same evening. Ten days later, someone fired 21 shots into the Tucker house, where the Hamers were staying. Work became more difficult to find, yet the Hamers decided that the human rights cause was one for which they were willing to make the ultimate sacrifice.

Until Hamer's death in March 1977, she faced many difficult circumstances. In her autobiography, *To Praise Our Bridges*, Hamer states, "I reckon the most horrible experience I've had was in June of 1963. . . . I was carried to a cell and locked up" [in Winona, Mississippi]. On June 3, as she and others were returning from a voter workshop in Charleston, South Carolina, Hamer stepped off the bus to see what had become of five blacks who had attempted to utilize the bus station rest room. Hamer and the men were arrested. On that occasion two black male prisoners were forced to beat her with a blackjack. Hamer almost died. For the rest of her life she walked with assistance of crutches or a cane as her right foot became partially paralyzed from the beating.

Having survived these experiences, she became more involved in community organizing. After unsuccessful attempts to participate in the Democratic Party of Mississippi, she became active in the Mississippi Freedom Democratic Party (MFDP) in the spring of 1964. Soon she became the vice-chairperson and ran for the Second Congressional District of Mississippi. Hamer gained national attention during the 1964 Democratic National Convention in Atlantic City, New Jersey. Her testimony recounting the violence and horrors of voter registration before the Credentials Committee appeared on national television. Although the MFDP refused the political compromise offered by the Democrats, Hamer did not give up the good fight. In 1964, the MFDP had registered 63,000 voters. She continued political work serving as a member of Democratic National Committee for Mississippi (1968–1971) and the Policy Council of the National Women's Political Caucus (1971–1977).

She returned to Mississippi and continued supporting causes for human rights. She worked to end the war in Vietnam and to end poverty in the United States. She helped to build up community services as well as criticize policy. She helped develop the Head Start program and the Freedom Farm Cooperative to aid farmers displaced by mechanization. She raised money and worked with a low-income housing project through Young World Developers. She helped establish a day care center and attract a garment factory to the region for jobs. In 1969 she founded Freedom Farm to raise food for hungry families on 640 acres.

During her years as voter registration organizer and political leader, she was relentless in her efforts to improve the lot of poor Mississippians. Over time she received many threatening telephone calls, abusive letters, and arrests. She also received recognition for her efforts through honorary doctoral degrees and the opportunity to teach a course at Shaw University. By the time of her illness and death of diabetes, breast cancer, and heart trouble on March 15, 1977, blacks in Mississippi had experienced better housing, more job security, and new dignity as a result of the good works of Fannie Lou Hamer.

—Margaret Wade-Lewis

Bibliography

The primary sources about Fannie Lou Hamer are included in the Fannie Lou Hamer Papers, Manuscript Division, Moorland-Spingarn Research Center, Howard University, Washington, DC; the Fannie Lou Hamer Collection in Special Collections, Coleman Library, Tougaloo College; and Fannie Lou Hamer Papers in the Amistad Research Center, Tulane University. Her testimonies are in the SNCC Papers, James Forman Collection, Martin Luther King, Jr. Center for Nonviolent Social Change, Atlanta. Oral histories are available at both Fisk and Howard universities and in the Mississippi Oral History Collection, University of Southern Mississippi.

Works by Fannie Lou Hamer

To Praise Our Bridges: An Autobiography, Julius Lester and Maria Varela, eds. Jackson, MS: Kipco, 1967.

"Sick and Tired of Being Sick and Tired," *Katallagete* (Fall 1968): 26.

"Black Voices of the South," *Ebony* 26 (August 1971): 51.

"It's in Your Hands: Speech for the NAACP Legal Defense Fund Institute" (New York City, May 7, 1971), in *Black Women in White America: A Documentary History*, Gerda Lerner, ed. New York: Random House, 1972, pp. 609–614.

Works about Fannie Lou Hamer

Bond, Julian. "The Most Extraordinary Black Woman I Have Ever Known," *Ebony* 31 (August 1977): 140.

Bramlett-Solomon, Sharon. "Civil Rights Vanguard in the Deep South: Newspaper Portrayal of Fannie Lou Hamer, 1964–1977," *Journalism Quarterly* 68: 3 (August 1991): 515–521.

Carroll, Kenneth. "New Seasons," *Black American Literature Forum* 24:3: 544. Poem in memory of Fannie Lou Hamer.

Carson, Clayborne et al., eds. "To Praise Our Bridges," in *The Eyes on the Prize Civil Rights Reader*. New York: Penguin, 1991. Excerpt from autobiography.

The Civil Rights Struggle: Leaders in Profile. New York: Facts on File, 1979.

Crawford, Vicki. "Beyond the Human Self: Grassroots Activists in the Mississippi Civil Rights Movement," in *Women in the Civil Rights Movement: Trailblazers and Torchbearers, 1941–1945*, edited by Vicki L. Crawford, Jacqueline Rouse, and Barbara Woods. Brooklyn: Carlson, 1990.

Egerton, John. "Fannie Lou Hamer," *The Progressive* (May 1977): 17.

Garland, Phyl. "Negro Heroines of Dixie Play Major Role in Challenging Racist Traditions," *Ebony* 21 (August 1966): 27–29.

Giddings, Paula. *When and Where I Enter*. New York: Morrow, 1984.

Grant, Jacqueline. "Civil Rights Women: A Source for Doing Womanist Theology," in *Women in the Civil Rights Movement: Trailblazers and Torchbearers, 1941–1945*, edited by Vicki L. Crawford, Jacqueline Rouse, and Barbara Woods. Brooklyn: Carlson, 1990.

Johnson, Thomas. "Young Eulogizes Fannie Lou Hamer, Mississippi Civil Rights Champion," *New York Times* (March 21, 1977): 30.

Jones, Jacqueline. *Labor of Love: Labor of Sorrow*. New York: Basic Books, 1985.

Jordan, June. *Fannie Lou Hamer: A Biography for Youth*. New York: Crowell, 1972.

Ladner, Joyce, "Fannie Lou Hamer in Memorial," *Black Enterprise* (May 1977): 56.

Locke, Mamie E. "Is This America? Fannie Lou Hamer and the Mississippi Freedom Democratic Party," in *Women in the Civil Rights Movement: Trailblazers and Torchbearers, 1941–1945*, edited by Vicki L. Crawford, Jacqueline Rouse, and Barbara Woods. Brooklyn: Carlson, 1990.

Mills, Kay. "Three Women Who Dared the House to Eject Five Colleagues on Principle," *Los Angeles Times* 109 (October 14, 1990): M4, Column 1.

New York Times, Obituary (March 21, 1977): 30.

Norton, Eleanor Holmes, "A Memory of Fannie Lou Hamer," *Ms.* (July 1977): 56.

Sanders, Charles, ed. "Fannie Lou Hamer: Success for Her Is Measured by the Strides She Has Helped Blacks Make," *Ebony Success Library* II. Nashville: Southwestern Company, 1973, pp. 96–99. See also Vol. I.

Williams, Juan. *Eyes on the Prize: America's Civil Rights Years, 1954–1965.* New York: Viking Penguin, 1987.

HANSBERRY, LORRAINE (1930–1965) was a celebrated playwright who had lived the life of an activist artist. When she died of cancer in New York at age 34, her testimonial was demonstrated in the number of eulogies published and by the cards and telegrams sent to her family by prominent figures in government, the arts, the civil rights movement, and ordinary people. Her life of commitment to social change and her involvement in the world of the artist earned her the title of "Warrior Intellectual." The locus of Hansberry's activism and of her artistic achievements originated in her family and in her early childhood on the Southside of Chicago.

Born May 20 into an affluent family in Chicago, Lorraine Hansberry was the fourth and last child of Carl Augustus and Nanny (Perry) Hansberry. Her parents' roots were southern: her father moved to Chicago from Mississippi following his completion of a technical course at Alcorn College, and her mother's move to the North came after she had finished teacher training at Tennessee Agricultural and Industrial University. By the time of Lorraine Hansberry's birth, Carl Hansberry was a successful and prominent real estate businessman. He was active in politics and social causes, contributing large sums of money to programs of both the NAACP and the Urban League. He worked continuously for improvements in the conditions of black people in Chicago in the areas of employment, housing, restaurants, and other public accommodations. In 1940 he ran unsuccessfully for Congress on the Republican ticket. He brought suit against restrictive covenants in Chicago, taking his case all the way to the Supreme Court, where he won the case. To initiate the challenge, he had moved his family to an all-white neighborhood. This revolutionary incident from her childhood formed the backdrop for her play *A Raisin in the Sun.* Hansberry's mother, a schoolteacher and later a ward committeewoman, was also active in community issues.

Lorraine Hansberry later wrote that much of her informal education was gained through growing up in a middle-class family at the center of Chicago's black social life. Such celebrated and political figures as Paul Robeson, Duke Ellington, Walter White, Joe Louis, and Jesse Owens were guests in the Hansberry home as were students from various parts of Africa—acquaintances of Hansberry's uncle, Leo Hansberry, professor of African history at Howard University.

Hansberry's formal education came through the public schools of Chicago. She attended and graduated from Betsy Ross Elementary School and from Englewood High School in 1947. For two years she attended on the University of Wisconsin at Madison, which provided the supportive environment through which her political and artistic views gained shape. She worked in the Henry Wallace presidential campaign and participated in activities of the Young Progressive League. During her last semester at Wisconsin, she became this organization's president. While at the university, Hansberry witnessed a production of Sean O'Casey's *Juno and the Paycock* and was struck by the manner in which the playwright captured the universality of suffering. This sparked her interest in theater and its potential to give a universal voice to the suffering of a particular people without loss of specificity. She captured this universality and the specificity of suffering in the voice of her own people in *A Raisin in the Sun*.

Hansberry became disillusioned with college and in 1950 moved to New York to pursue, in her words, "an education of a different sort." She worked as a writer for *Freedom*, Paul Robeson's radical black newspaper, and covered such issues as colonial freedom, equal rights for blacks, the conditions of Harlem schools, and variants of racial discriminations. She married Robert Nemiroff, a white student and aspiring songwriter whom she met on the picket line at New York University, where he was a student. During this period she was involved in peace and freedom movements and later traveled to the Intercontinential Peace Congress in Montevideo, Uruguay, as associate editor of *Freedom*. When she left *Freedom* in 1953, she sought to concentrate on her playwriting. She worked at a series of odd jobs while working on three plays. One of these, *A Raisin in the Sun*, was produced in 1959.

Lorraine Hansberry earned her position in American letters with the production of *A Raisin in the Sun*. Though not all reviews and evaluations of the play over the years have been positive, it was both a critical and a popular success. Much has been written about its influence on the black theater movement, and about its significance to American theater in general. Taking a theme from a poem by Langston Hughes, the play asked the question "What happens to a dream deferred. . . . Does it dry up like a raisin in the sun?" It focused on the lives of the Youngers, a downtrodden working-class black family trying to survive in a hostile environment filled with poverty, racism, and other problems. Using the dramatic form of social realism, Hansberry addressed several contemporary social issues: restrictive covenants, racism, segregation, abortion, women's liberation, humanism, black nationalism, materialism, and integration.

With the production of *A Raisin in the Sun*, Hansberry became the first black woman to have a play on Broadway and the youngest and first African American to win the New York Drama Critics Circle Award for Best Play. Her success revitalized black theater, enabling other blacks to get their plays produced. Columbia Pictures bought the rights to the play, and commissioned Hansberry to write the screenplay. Hansberry expanded the play to include several scenes that heightened the social significance of the drama, but Columbia Pictures rejected most of these scenes. The stellar cast included Sidney Poitier, Ruby Dee, Claudia McNeil, and several others from the Broadway production. Although not a box-office success, the movie captured the essence of Hansberry's drama.

As a testament to her political commitment and to her status among artists and the politically aware, Hansberry was invited in 1963 to speak at a rally to abolish the House Un-American Activities Committee. She denounced HUAC in one of her most popular speeches, "A Challenge to Artists." Hansberry was active in the civil rights movement conducting fundraisers and writing on the movement's behalf. She wrote the text for a photographic journal, *The Movement: A Documentary of a Struggle for Equality* (1964), for the Student Nonviolent Coordinating Committee (SNCC). When novelist James Baldwin was putting together a panel of prominent blacks and whites to discuss the racial crisis with Attorney General Robert Kennedy in 1963, Hansberry was among the first invited to participate.

Although most critics locate Hansberry's greatest artistic achievement in her play *A Raisin in the Sun*, she is the author of other works. Hansberry had early developed an opinionated voice, and so she wrote letters to newspapers and magazines on various political and often controversial subjects. Her published and unpublished essays are on black art, the Cuban missile crisis, black feminism, existentialism, the civil rights movement, world literature, and many other subjects. She also wrote several letters of support to *The Ladder*, a lesbian publication. Between 1960 and 1962, Hansberry completed her post-atomic play, *What Use Are Flowers?*; *The Drinking Gourd*, a teleplay about slavery; the screenplay for *A Raisin in the Sun*, and her play about intellectuals and social change, *The Sign in Sidney Brustein's Window*; she also made considerable progress on *Les Blancs*, an anticolonialist play set in Africa, which was completed by Robert Nemiroff after her death. Divorced from Nemiroff in Mexico in 1964, they remained close friends and collaborators, and in her will, he was named executor of Hansberry's estate.

Lorraine Hansberry died on January 12, 1965. Among the many who eulogized the playwright was Dr. Martin Luther King, Jr., who said, "Her commitment of spirit, . . . her creative ability and her profound grasp of the deep social issues confronting the world today will remain an inspiration to generations yet unborn."

—Mary Frances Stubbs

Bibliography

Lorraine Hansberry's play *A Raisin in the Sun* is widely anthologized and it as well as her other published works have been translated into French, German, Japanese, and other languages. A player's edition is available from Samuel French Publishers, New York, 1971. Robert Nemiroff edited a reprint (New York: New American Library, 1987) of *A Raisin in the Sun and The Sign in Sidney Brustein's Window*, restoring material in both plays that had been cut when they were originally produced. The PBS production (1989) starring Danny Glover in the role of Walter Lee used the restored version of the play. The uncompleted *Toussaint* is anthologized in *Nine Plays by Black Women*, edited by Margaret B. Wilkerson (New York: New American

Libraries, 1968). *To Be Young, Gifted and Black: Lorraine Hansberry in Her Own Words*, adapted by Robert Nemiroff (New York: Caedmon, 1969), is arranged chronologically and provides insight into Hansberry's life and philosophy, as does the biography *Lorraine Hansberry* by Anne Cheney (New York: Twayne, 1984). The most thorough Hansberry bibliography to date is "Lorraine Hansberry: Art of Thunder, Vision of Light," *Freedomways* (Special Volume, Fourth Quarter 1979).

Hansberry published articles and speeches covering a range of issues as indicated by the titles. Among her published works are "The American Theater Needs Desegregating, Too," *Negro Digest* (June 1961); "A Challenge to Artists," *Freedomways* (Winter 1963); "Genet, Mailer and the New Paternalism," *Village Voice* (June 1, 1961); "The Legacy of W.E.B. Du Bois," *Freedomways* (Winter 1965); "Willie Loman, Walter Younger, and He Who Must Live," *Village Voice* (August 12, 1969); "What Could Happen Didn't: Lorraine Hansberry Writes about Her Film," *New York Herald-Tribune* (March 26, 1961). Audiovisual materials on Hansberry's life and work include the film *A Raisin in the Sun* (Columbia Pictures, 1961, distributed by Swann fllms); *To Be Young, Gifted, and Black* (NET film, 1972, distributed by Indiana University Audiovisual Center); *Lorraine Hansberry: The Black Experience in the Creation of Drama* (Princeton, NJ: Films for the Humanities, 1971).

Hansberry has been the subject of several dissertations: Robert Grant, "Lorraine Hansberry: The Playwright as Warrior-Intellectual" (dissertation, Harvard University, 1982; Ann Arbor: University Microfilms); Frances Stubbs, "Lorraine Hansberry and Lillian Hellman: A Comparison of Social and Political Issues in Their Plays and Screen Adaptations" (dissertation, Indiana University, 1990; Ann Arbor: University Microfilms).

A selection of the wide range of reference works in which Hansberry is discussed includes *American Women Writers, Vol. II* (New York: Garland, 1980); Michael Anderson, et al., *Crowell's Handbook of Contemporary Drama* (New York: Crowell, 1971); C.W.E. Bigsby, *Confrontation and Commitment: A Study of Contemporary American Drama 1959–1960* (Deland, FL: Everett Edwards, 1969); *The Biographical Encyclopedia and Who's Who of the American Theatre* (Chicago: Marquis Who's Who, 1966); *Current Biography, 1959–1960* (New York: Wilson, 1960); *Contemporary Literary Criticism, Vol. 17* (Detroit: Gale, 1981); *Dictionary of Literary Biography, Vol 7; Twentieth-Century American Dramatist, Part I* (Detroit: Gale, 1981); *Dictionary of Literary Biography, Vol. 38. Afro-American Writers after 1955* (Detroit: Gale, 1985); *McGraw-Hill Encyclopedia of World Drama* (New York: McGraw-Hill, 1972); Myron Matlaw, *Modern World Drama: An Encyclopedia* (New York: Dutton, 1972); Robin May, *A Companion to the Theatre: The Anglo-American Stage from 1920* (New York: Hippocrene, 1973); Loften Mitchell, *Black Drama: The Story of the American Negro in the Theatre* (New York: Hawthorne, 1967); James A. Page, *Selected Black American Authors* (Boston: G.K. Hall, 1977); Alice M. Robinson, et al., *Notables in the American Theatre: A Biographical Dictionary* (New York: Greenwood, 1989); *Twentieth Century American Literature—Great Writers Library* (New York: Chelsea House, 1980); *Who Was Who in America, Vol. 4, 1961–1968* (Chicago: Marquis Who's Who, 1968); and *Who's Who of American Women, 1964–1965* (Chicago: Marquis Who's Who, 1963).

HARLEY, SHARON (b. 1948) has been a major contributor to the field of African-American women's history. Harley was born on August 16, in Washington, DC, to William E. and Grace M. Harley. She has one daughter, Ashley Kershaw.

Harley responded to the idealism that motivated young people to participate in social change through the movements for civil rights and women's rights. She sold newspapers for the Black Panthers during the 1960s. She graduated from St. Mary-of-the-Woods College in 1970 and immediately sought and achieved a MAT in education from Antioch College in 1971. She served as a social studies teacher in the Washington, DC, public school system (1970–1973) and held faculty positions at the University of the District of Columbia (1976–1979). As she taught, she noticed the black women's role absent or distorted in existing materials.

While pursuing her doctorate in history at Howard University, she became active in the systematic recovery of black women's history. As one of the founders and early officers of the Association of Black Women Historians (ABWH) in 1978, she worked closely with another student at Howard University, Rosalyn Terborg-Penn, who had recently completed her dissertation, "Afro-Americans in the Struggle for Women's Suffrage, 1830–1920." The two women decided to rectify the absence of black women in history by co-editing the anthology *The Afro-American Woman: Struggles and Images* (1978). She completed her dissertation, "Black Women in the District of Columbia, 1890–1920," and received her PhD in American history from Howard University in 1981.

Harley has continued her leadership in the field of black women's history through her professional organizations and in her research. She currently serves as the national vice-director of the Association of Black Women Historians and as editor of *Truth: The Newsletter of the Association of Black Women Historians*. While she served as acting director and professor of history and African-American studies at the University of Maryland at College Park, she and Terborg-Penn co-edited another contribution to the field, *Women in Africa and the African Diaspora*, published in 1987. She also had an impact on the shaping of undergraduate education when she served as the associate dean of undergraduate studies at the University of Maryland during the academic year 1991–1992.

Her honors and awards include a Certificate of Appreciation for Service to the ABWH and the Historical Profession (1984); an Outstanding Achievement Award from the University of Maryland, College Park (1985); the Fellowship for Minority Group Scholars from the Rockefeller Foundation (1986–1987); and a postdoctoral fellowship from the division of political history of the National Museum of American History, the Smithsonian Institution.

—Regennia N. Williams

Bibliography

Harley is best known for her co-edited volumes with Rosalyn Terborg-Penn:

The Afro-American Woman: Struggles and Images. Port Washington, NY: Kennikat Press, 1978.

Women in Africa and the African Diaspora. Washington, DC: Howard University Press, 1987.

Two articles are reprinted in the Black Women in American History *series, edited by Darlene Clark Hine (Brooklyn: Carlson, 1990):*

"Beyond the Classroom: Organizational Lives of Black Female Educators in the District of Columbia, 1890–1930."

"Black Women in a Southern City: Washington, DC, 1890–1920."

HARPER, FRANCES E. [WATKINS] (1825–1911), novelist, poet, journalist, orator, and activist for the abolition, temperance, and women's rights movements, was born September 24 to free parents in Baltimore, Maryland. Frances E.W. Harper has been called the best-known African-American writer of the nineteenth century, a journalistic "foremother," and an eloquent and persuasive lecturer who achieved a national stature rare for African-American women of the period.

Frances Watkins became an orphan at age 3, was raised by an aunt and uncle, and received her education in her uncle's school, the William Watkins Academy for Negro Youth, until age 13. Under her uncle's tutelage, the young Watkins obtained a classical education and received exposure to social reform and abolitionist actitivities. At age 14 she worked as a live-in seamstress and housekeeper, continuing her studies on her own. At this time, she started to write poetry, which culminated in the publication of her first collection, *Forest Leaves*, around 1854.

Education was one of her lifelong concerns. When she moved to Ohio in 1850 for a job as a sewing instructor, she started her teaching career and became the first female faculty member at Union Seminary, founded by the African Methodist Episcopal church. Two years later she took a second position in Little York, Pennsylvania. Increasingly politicized during this period due to the increased persecution of African Americans following the passage of the Fugitive Slave Act of 1850, she dedicated herself to the abolitionist movement by 1854. She moved to Philadelphia, where she lived in an Underground Railroad station, and began contributing to abolitionist newspapers. She launched a career on the lecture circuit with "Education and the Elevation of the Colored Race," presented to an antislavery gathering in New Bedford, Massachusetts, in August 1854. Hired as a traveling lecturer by the Maine Anti-Slavery Society, she became their first female orator and subsequently traveled across the North to give speeches.

These abolitionist concerns were a central theme in her writing, which included *Poems on Miscellaneous Subjects*, published in 1854. This book became a success, going through several reprintings and selling as many as 12,000 copies. Thus, Frances Watkins had become a widely read author by her mid-twenties. When she returned to Philadelphia in 1857, she served as a lecturer for the Pennsylvania Anti-Slavery Society and published another volume of poetry, simply titled *Poems*. In 1859 she wrote "The Two Offers" in *Anglo-African Magazine*, which may be the first short story published by an African American. Within months she married Fenton Harper, a widower from Cincinnati, on November 22, 1860. They settled on a farm near Columbus, Ohio. For a time she raised Harper's three children and their own daughter, Mary. Although she briefly limited her public activities, she continued to write and publish her work in a number of abolitionist newspapers and magazines.

Following the death of her husband in 1864, Harper resumed her public lecturing career. She published a narrative poem, *Moses: A Story of the Nile*, in 1869. At that time she became active in the women's suffrage movement through the American Woman Suffrage Association, actively criticizing movement leaders Elizabeth Cady Stanton and Susan B. Anthony for their opposition to black suffrage. Harper traveled extensively through the South, leading to her publication of *Sketches of Southern Life* in 1872. She expanded her reform activities to include leadership in the Women's Christian Temperance Union, the Colored Women's Congress (1895, 1897), and the National Association of Colored Women.

Her later work included several collections of poetry and the novel *Iola Leroy, or Shadows Uplifted* (1892), which was published in three editions and criticized as lacking artistic merit. Recently, the novel has been resurrected as an important historical document reflecting Harper's views on black women's experiences and racism at the end of the nineteenth century. Harper died in 1911 at age 85.

—Jane Rhodes

Bibliography

The most often cited biography of Frances E.W. Harper appears in William Still, *The Underground Railroad* (Philadelphia: Porters and Coates, 1872). A thorough contemporary overview of her life is found in the introduction to *A Brighter Coming Day: A Frances Ellen Watkins Harper Reader*, edited by Frances Smith Foster (New York: Feminist Press, 1990). See also Hallie Q. Brown, *Homespun Heroines and Other Women of Distinction.* Xenia, OH: Aldine, 1926; biographical entry by Daniel Walden, *Dictionary of American Negro Biography*, edited by Rayford W. Logan and Michael R. Winston (New York: Norton, 1982); and biographical entry by Louis Filler, *Notable American Women: 1607–1950*, edited by Edward T. James (Cambridge, MA: Harvard University Press, 1971).

There have been numerous analyses of Harper's work: Hazel Carby, *Reconstructing Womanhood* (New York: Oxford University Press, 1987); Barbara Christian, *Black Feminist Criticism* (New York: Pergamon Press, 1985), and *Black Women Novelists: The*

Development of a Tradition, 1892–1976 (Westport, CT: Greenwood, 1980); and Mary Helen Washington, *Invented Lives* (New York: Anchor Press, 1987).

HARRIS, BARBARA C. (b. 1930) was elected the first female bishop in the Episcopal church in 1988, breaking down a 2,000-year barrier to ascension of women in the Christian church and a 400-year tradition in the Anglican Communion, the international family of 28 autonomous churches tied to the Church of England. The issue of ordaining women was settled in principle at the 1976 General Convention of the Episcopal Church, which allowed women into the three orders of the clergy: deacons, priests, and bishops. Since Episcopalians traditionally expected priests to have ten years' experience before becoming bishops, the controversy over the ordination of a female bishop was not expected until the mid-1980s, when the initial group of women priests had served a decade of service. In 1986, as expected, a bishop's daughter, the Reverend Mary Chotard Doll, was nominated to the Washington, DC, post of suffragan bishop, but received second place in the voting. On September 24, 1988, however, Barbara C. Harris received the highest number of votes on the eighth ballot at the diocesan convention in Boston, making her the first woman and twenty-ninth black bishop.

The election of this Christian social activist was the culmination of her spiritual growth and her personal quest to make the church more responsive to social justice issues. Born into a steelworker family headed by Walter and Beatrice (Price) Harris, Barbara Harris began life in the Germantown section of Philadelphia on June 12, 1930. The life of the Harris children—Josephine, Thomas, and Barbara—concentrated on education and religion. The parents raised the children with a respect for human dignity. Barbara attended the public schools, received baptism and confirmation at St. Barnabas Church, played piano for the Sunday school, and organized the Young Adults Group, which soon became the largest youth group in the city. She graduated in 1948 from the Philadelphia High School for Girls, described in their yearbook as "slim, spirited, happy-go-lucky."

After graduation, Harris quickly gained employment with the black public relations firm Joe Baker Associates, named after the first permanent black writer on the *Philadelphia Inquirer*. Although she was told that she would probably not be worth her pay, she excelled at Baker Associates, where she served as the editor of a publication promoting black colleges. As her career developed, so too did the civil rights movement. She enjoyed jazz at the Showboat club and met other black professionals at the Postal Card, a South Philadelphia pub, to engage in animated debate over the movement's tactics, ideologies, and leadership styles. She helped the NAACP in picketing the city for jobs.

During the early 1960s, the mounting violence experienced by civil rights workers in the South drew "Babs" Harris into active participation outside her community. She spent her summer vacation helping in the drives to educate and register black voters in Greenville, Mississippi. In 1965, she participated in the

Selma to Montgomery march led by Dr. Martin Luther King, Jr., the same year her three-year marriage, which produced no children, ended in divorce. Her career progressed as she became the president of Baker Associates, experience that led to her new job as a top public relations executive for Sun Oil Company in 1968.

Increasingly, her spiritual roots merged with the era's spirit of social justice. In 1968 when St. Barnabas Church merged with the mostly white St. Luke's Church, Harris transferred her membership to the less staid North Philadelphia Church of the Advocate. Encouraged by her rector, the Reverend Canon Charles L.L. Poindexter, Harris became a volunteer with the St. Dismas Society, which held Sunday services at prisons and provided counseling and support to prisoners. Her service on the vestry and volunteer work proved fulfilling. When the 1976 General Convention opened all orders to women, she discussed a more permanent role in the church with her rector, the Reverend Paul Washington, who advised her to think about her calling and pray for guidance during the next year. At the end of that year, her sense of mission had not diminished. The Reverend Washington strongly recommended Harris for leadership positions in the church.

While Harris prayed for guidance, she also pursued the educational and theological preparation for leadership in the church. She attended the Metropolitan Collegiate Center in Philadelphia in 1976, and Villanova University from 1977 to 1979, during which time she was ordained a deacon at the Church of the Advocate. There, she served as a deacon-in-training until October 1980, when she was ordained to the priesthood. During mid-career, Harris received special training for clergy at Geneva, New York's Hobart and William Smith College, where she received an honorary doctorate in sacred theology in 1981. She served as priest-in-charge at the Norristown, Pennsylvania, St. Augustine-of-Hippo, from 1980 to 1984 and as interim rector at the Church of the Advocate, thereafter.

The special training she received at these institutions and her experienced church activism did not provide the conventional qualifications for the office of bishop. Although she was divorced, lacked a college degree, and had never been a full-time rector of her own parish, Harris was well known as an articulate activist and had scored higher on exams for the positions than those with seminary degrees. Best known as the executive director of the Episcopal Church Publishing Company (ECPC) and contributor to the *Witness*, an independent magazine representing views of the church liberals, Harris confronted the church's insensitivity to minorities, the poor, women, and homosexuals. As the author of the column "A Luta Continua" (Portuguese for "The struggle continues"), Harris criticized church attention to "non-issues" of homosexuality and ordination of women, while ignoring real issues of racism, sexism, class discrimination, and imperialism. In addition to her editorial position, Harris drew support from Consultation, a coalition of nine Episcopal groups concerned with social justice issues in the church, and from the Union of Black Episcopalians, a group formed in 1968 to encourage more black participation while simultaneously lessening the racism in church and society. These sources of support and general changes in the overall society helped Harris win the election as bishop, which made her the second-in-charge of the 96,000-member, Boston-based diocese. She continues to pursue her interests by serving on diocesan commissions handling pastoral care, social justice, and prison ministries.

—Beth Schneider

Bibliography

Most of the sources dealing with the church career of Barbara Harris can be found in church publications available through the Diocesan Press Service. For Harris's own views, one should consult her columns in the *Witness*, the independent magazine edited by Harris. Other Christian publications carrying the story include: J.L. Franklin, "Harris's Credentials Are Scrutinized," *The Christian Century* (December 21–28, 1988); M.R. Lawrence, "Helping the Holy Spirit Elect a Bishop," *The Christian Century* (October 19, 1988); R. Walker, "Episcopalians List Lambeth Ruling," *Christianity Today* (October 21, 1988). The newly published book edited by Catherine M. Prelinger, *Episcopal Women: Gender, Spirituality and Commitment in an American Mainline Denomination*, New York: Oxford University Press, 1992, emphasizes the centrality of women in today's church and addresses the specific information about the rise of Barbara Harris within the church.

The controversy over her election (September 1988) and ordination (February 1989) as bishop appears in the popular press throughout 1988 and 1989. The most informative pieces include: Richard N. Ostling, "The Bishop Is a Lady," *Time* (December 26, 1988); Lynn Rosellini, "The First of the 'Mitered Mamas'," and Joseph Carey, "A Denominational Gender Gap," *U.S. News and World Report* (June 19, 1989); James Barron, "Episcopal Diocese Chooses First Woman to Be a Bishop," *New York Times* (September 25, 1988); Peter Steinfels, "Advocate of Equality," *New York Times* (September 26, 1988); Kenneth Woodward, "Feminism and the Churches," *Newsweek* (February 13, 1989); "That New Time Religion," *National Review* 41 (March 10, 1989); and J. Redmont, "When the Spirit Leads," *Commonweal* 116 (March 10, 1989). *USA Today* carries several columns devoted to the issue on September 26 and 30, 1988. *Tennessean* covers the story on September 25, 26, 1988; and February 5, 13, 17, and 25, 1989.

The significance of race and gender are explored in various issues of *Jet* (October 10, 1988; February 13 and 29, 1989); Renee D. Turner, "The First Woman Episcopal Bishop," *Ebony* 44 (May 1989); Susan L. Taylor, "The 1989 Essence Awards," *Essence* 20 (October 1989). Photographic coverage appears in *Esquire* (August 1989).

Despite her achievements, Harris is still missing from most biographical reference works dealing with religion, women or African Americans as *Who's Who in Religion*, *Who's Who in Emerging Leaders*, and so on. For biographical material on Harris, consult Aleathia Dolores Nicholson's article in Jessie Carney Smith's *Notable Black American Women* (Detroit: Gale, 1992).

HARRIS, BLANCHE V. (1844–1918) was an educator whose career was dedicated to the education of African Americans. Harris began by teaching newly freed slaves in schools sponsored by the American Missionary Association. After distinguishing herself early in her career, Harris became one of the first five women selected by AMA to assist in the massive educational efforts in the South. Later, as part of the educational program sponsored by the Society of Friends, Harris continued her work of bringing long-denied educational opportunities to African Americans.

Born on January 21, she was the eldest daughter and third of five children of Beverly and Rebecca E. Harris, of Monroe, Michigan, where she spent her early years and attended the public school system. When she was denied admission to an all-white young ladies' seminary, her father, a carpenter, moved his family to Oberlin, Ohio, so that Blanche could receive a better education.

Founded by abolitionists, Oberlin College was the first coeducational and interracial college in the country. Blanche Harris entered the Preparatory Department at Oberlin in 1855 and, upon satisfying those requirements, enrolled in the College Department in 1857 as a literary degree candidate. Harris graduated from the Ladies' Department in 1860 with a bachelor of letters degree.

Founded by abolitionists, the AMA provided Blanche Harris with invaluable teaching experience. After a brief period of teaching in Columbus, Ohio, during 1863–1864, Harris was one of a select group chosen to aid in the massive educational efforts in the South. From Norfolk, Virginia, Harris moved to Natchez, Mississippi, in 1865, where she was struck by the difference in treatment accorded white teachers and teachers of color. In addition to racial slurs, Harris found that she was not assigned her own school and was obliged to live with AMA servants rather than in the teachers' quarters.

In 1868 Blanche Harris moved to North Carolina to teach for the Society of Friends, a Quaker organization. Moving on to Knoxville, Tennessee, Harris married William L. Brooks, also an Oberlin graduate, on October 26, 1871. The marriage produced one daughter, Maud Rebecca Harris Cotton, and lasted until her husband's death in 1897. Harris remained in Knoxville until 1893, teaching in the Knoxville city schools and remaining active in her mission work as well as organizations such as the Women's Christian Temperance Union.

On August 12, 1893, Blanche Harris married Elias Toussaint Jones, also of Oberlin, where they lived most of the time until Jones's death on May 13, 1917. Between 1903 and 1905 Harris accepted a teaching assignment in Henderson, North Carolina, where her daughter lived. Even after retiring in 1915 Harris never stopped studying and pursuing a variety of interests including membership in the Second Congregational Church.

The Oberlin College Annual Report of 1917–1918 reported that Blanche Harris Jones died of Bright's disease and arteriosclerosis on August 23, 1918, at her daughter's home in Henderson, North Carolina, where she spent the last months of her life. However, an obituary in the *Oberlin News* cited place of death as Oberlin with internment in Westwood Cemetery.

—Thea Gallo Becker

Bibliography

Hine, Darlene Clark. *Black Women in United States History*. Vol. 3. Brooklyn: Carlson, 1990. Discusses Blanche Harris's life from her early years in Michigan to her teaching career. Excellent work; up-to-date discussion of the subject.

Lawson, Ellen N., and Marlene Merrill. The Women's History Project. Oberlin College Archives, Record Group No. 30-157. The collection consists largely of photocopies of extensive handwritten correspondence, which are very difficult to read.

Lawson, Ellen N., and Marlene Merrill. "Antebellum Black Coeds at Oberlin College." *Oberlin Alumni Magazine* (Jan.–Feb. 1980): 18–21. Reprinted in Hine, Darlene Clark. *Black Women in United States History*, Vol. 3. Brooklyn: Carlson, 1990. Excellent source of information; very well written.

Oberlin College Archives. Record Group No. 28. Records of deceased graduates. Contains the most abundant information on Harris, particularly for her latter years. Files in the Oberlin College registrar's office were destroyed by fire in 1903. Harris's college records were among those destroyed, but annual reports, alumni records, and newspaper articles from the *Oberlin News* provide biographical data on Harris. (*Oberlin News* cites Harris's year of birth as 1847 while the 1915 Quinquennial Catalogue lists her year of birth as 1844.)

Sterling, Dorothy. *We Are Your Sisters: Black Women in the Nineteenth Century*. New York: Norton, 1984. A letter by Harris shows the racism and segregation she confronted as a teacher in post-bellum Mississippi.

HARRIS, PATRICIA [ROBERTS] (1924–1985), lawyer, educator, diplomat, and Cabinet officer,

was born on May 31 in Mattoon, Illinois, the daughter of Pullman porter Bert Fitzgerald and Hildren Brodie (Johnson) Roberts. She attended the public schools of Chicago and graduated summa cum laude with a bachelor's degree in political science and economics from Howard University in 1945. She undertook graduate studies in industrial relations at the University of Chicago from 1945 to 1947 and at the American University from 1949 to 1950, where she concentrated on public policy. In 1960 she earned the juris doctor degree with honors from George Washington University. More than 32 institutions of higher learning awarded Harris honorary doctorate degrees, including Johns Hopkins University, Williams College, Brown University, and the University of Maryland.

Harris was associated with humanitarian causes through her choice of employment as well as her volunteer activities. In 1946 Patricia Roberts was program director of the Chicago YWCA, a position that allowed her to design programs to fit the postwar needs of its constituents. Harris later was appointed to the national board of the YWCA. She also served as executive director of Delta Sigma Theta, a national African-American public service sorority founded at Howard University in 1913; she served in this capacity from 1953 to 1959. On September 1, 1955, Roberts married Washington, DC, attorney William Beasley Harris; this union did not produce children.

Harris entered public service through her law career. The U.S. Department of Justice hired Harris as a trial attorney in its Criminal Division for two years (1960–1961). From 1961 to 1967 Patricia Roberts Harris taught law at the Howard University School of Law, renowned for its civil rights victories before the Supreme Court; she also was appointed associate dean of students. In 1969 she was named dean of the Law School, but resigned precipitously following a controversy over student empowerment. Harris also was a partner in the prestigious District of Columbia law firm Fried, Frank, Harris, Shriver and Kampelman (1970–1977).

She combined her law career with appointments to national committees. President John F. Kennedy appointed Patricia Harris co-chair of the National Women's Committee for Civil Rights in 1963. From 1964 to 1966 she served President Lyndon Johnson on the Commission on the Status of Puerto Rico. Harris was on the board of directors of the NAACP Legal Defense Fund (1967–1977) and was assistant director on human rights for the District of Columbia. She also served on the Carnegie Commission on Education. President Johnson appointed Harris to the Commission on the Causes and Prevention of Violence, which was disbanded on December 10, 1969, after it submitted to the President its report "To Establish Justice, To Insure Domestic Tranquility." In 1972 Harris chaired the Democratic National Convention and was elected permanent chair. Her other board appointments include the American Civil Liberties Union and the National Educational Television. Patricia Harris was elected to the board of directors of a number of major corporations, including International Business Machines, the Twentieth Century Fund, and the Chase Manhattan Bank.

Serving on these commissions and boards marked her entry into national politics. President Johnson appointed her U.S. ambassador to Luxembourg (1965–1967), the first African-American woman to hold this diplomatic rank in the nation's history. Harris was Secretary of Housing and Urban Development from 1977 to 1979 during the Jimmy Carter administration, the highest position in government to which an African-American woman had acceded. Patricia Roberts Harris had built a reputation as a talented administrator and loyal team player. President Jimmy Carter nominated her to head the Department of Health and Human Services on July 20, the Senate confirming her appointment a week later. Supreme Court Justice Thurgood Marshall swore her in to head her second Cabinet post on August 3, 1979. During her tenure, the division was renamed Health and Human Services, with a separate Department of Education to provide the attention that this critical issue mandated.

After the defeat of Jimmy Carter in the 1980 presidential election, Patricia Harris terminated her service to the federal government and turned her attention once more to local politics in Washington, DC. Her 1982 bid to unseat District of Columbia mayor Marion S. Barry was unsuccessful. She succumbed to the effects of breast cancer on March 23, 1985, in Washington, DC.

—Lillian S. Williams

Bibliography

The Patricia Roberts Harris Papers are in the Manuscript Division of the Library of Congress, Washington, DC. They consist of 151.2 linear feet and contain 113,400 items. They span the years 1950–1983 and chronicle her tenure as secretary of HUD, secretary of HHS, and ambassador to Luxembourg, as well as her service on national government commissions. Papers pertaining to her civil rights activities are located in the Manuscript Division of the Moorland-Spingarn Research Center, Howard University, Washington, DC. These papers have not been processed. Harris's work with the YWCA is included in that organization's archives. The records of the YWCA of Chicago, 1876–1960, are located in the Manuscript Division of the University of Illinois Library, Chicago Circle. The National YWCA Papers are housed in the Sophia Smith Collection at Smith College, Northampton, Massachusetts.

Oral memoirs on her participation in the 1972 Democratic National Convention can be found in the American Jewish Committee papers at the William E. Wiener Oral History Library, New York.

The records of the Leadership Conference on Civil Rights, 1963–1974, include correspondence with Harris. These records are located in the Manuscript Division of the Library of Congress. Other records pertaining to Patricia Roberts Harris and government service can be found in the National Archives in Washington, DC. A useful guide is Debra L. Newman, *Black History: A Guide to Civilian Records in the National Archives*. (Washington, DC: National Archives Trust Fund Board, GSA, 1984).

Archival Source

Vertical File, Moorland-Spingarn Research Center, Howard University, Washington, DC.

Secondary Sources

Baskin, Wade, and Richard Runes. *Dictionary of Black Culture*. New York: Philosophical Library, 1973, p. 493.

Davis, Marianna, ed. *Contributions of Black Women to America*, Vol. I, Columbia, SC: Kenday, 1982, p. 447.

Dannett, Sylvia. *Profiles of Negro Womanhood*, Vol. II. New York: National Heritage, 1966, pp. 328–333.

Ebony Success Library. Vol. I. Chicago: Johnson Publishing, 1973, p. 144.

Fuller, Thomas O. *Pictorial History of the American Negro*. Memphis: Pictorial History Publishers, rev. ed., 1987, p. 295.

Low, Augustus, and Virgil A. Clift. *Encyclopedia of Black America*. New York: McGraw-Hill, 1981, p. 420.

Matney, William C., ed. *Who's Who among Black Americans*, Vol. I: 1975–1976. Northbrook, IL: Who's Who Among Black Americans, 1976, p. 271.

"Minority Opportunity Fellowships and Patricia Roberts Harris Memorial." *Black Issues in Higher Education* 3 (November 1, 1986): 2.

Pike, David F. "Washington's Lawyers: Rise of the Power Brokers," *U.S. News and World Report* 88 (March 10, 1980): 52.

Pinderhughes, Dianne. "Black Women and National Education Policy," *Journal of Negro Education* 51 (Summer 1982): 301–308.

Ploski, Harry, and Warren Marr II, eds. *Negro Almanac*. 3rd rev. ed., New York: Bellwether, 1976, p. 350.

Poinsett, Alex. "Patricia Roberts Harris: HUD Velvet-Gloved Ironedhand," *Ebony* 34 (July 1979): 33–34.

Smith, S. Clay, Jr., "Patricia Roberts Harris: A Champion in Pursuit of Excellence." *Howard Law Journal* 29:3 (1986): 437–455.

Stineman, Esther. *American Political Women: Contemporary and Historical Profiles*. Littleton, CO: Libraries Unlimited, 1980, pp. 61–65.

Webb, Dorothy. "Harris Promises Urban Focus in Human Services Delivery at HHS," *Nation's Cities Weekly* 3 (March 24, 1980): 6.

Wesley, Charles Harris. *The History of the National Association of Colored Women's Clubs: A Legacy of Service*. Washington, DC: NACWC, pp. 158–159.

Williams, Juan. "Blacker than Thou," *New Republic* 187 (September 20, 1982): 13.

HAYNES, ELIZABETH ROSS

(1883–1953) had a multifaceted career as a teacher, social worker, labor scholar, and committed activist. Involved in a myriad of black self-help and intergroup relations organizations, she is best known for her work with the YWCA and the U.S. Department of Labor.

She was born July 30 in Mt. Willing, Lowndes County, Alabama. Her parents, Henry and Mary Ross, were former slaves. Their relative success as farmers enabled their daughter to acquire an education and move beyond this rural milieu. She graduated from the Alabama State Normal School in Montgomery, and earned a BA from Fisk University in 1903 and an MA in sociology from Columbia University in 1923. She also studied at the University of Chicago during the summers between 1905 and 1907.

Haynes's first professional work was teaching, followed by social work. She taught in high schools in Galveston, Texas, St. Louis, and then as head teacher at her alma mater, the Alabama Normal School, from 1905 to 1908. She was then recruited by the YWCA and became the first full-time black national secretary. For two years she organized black college students.

Elizabeth Ross married George Edmund Haynes, a Fisk sociologist, on December 14, 1910. They had one son, George E. Haynes, Jr. An early "two career couple," they worked together to improve the socioeconomic status of

African Americans. When her husband became the director of the Negro Economic Division in the U.S. Department of Labor, Haynes began various roles within the federal government. Initially she worked as his assistant at $1.00 per year in his department. In 1919 she was employed in the Women in Industry Service (later the Women's Bureau), and from 1920 to 1922, became the Domestic Service Employment Secretary and a minimum wage consultant. In the above positions she used data from her master's thesis, "Negroes in Domestic Service in the United States" (a.k.a., "Two Million Negro Women at Work"). This work chronicled the difficulties black women workers faced when employers deserted them following World War I. It is still considered the first and most thorough study of domestic workers in the United States. Other efforts to help women workers include her participation in the first International Congress of Working Women. Providing testimony to Congress, they sought union representation for black women workers.

Haynes's volunteer commitments were wide ranging. She served as the first black woman on the YWCA national board from 1924 to 1934. With her husband, she worked with the race relations panel of the Federal Council of Churches (later, the National Council of Churches). She also participated in the National Association of Colored Women, Alpha Kappa Alpha sorority, the Adam Clayton Powell Home for the Aged, the National Association for the Advancement of Colored People, the National Health Circle for Colored People, the New York Fisk University Club, and the Abyssinian Baptist church.

During and after World War II she worked with the Emergency Committee to Save the Jewish People of Europe. Haynes also worked to improve the schools and hospitals within Harlem and integrate the staffs in these facilities.

Later in her life she became active in politics. In 1935 she was named Democratic co-leader of the 21st Assembly District in Harlem. Two years later New York governor Herbert Lehman appointed her, the only woman, to the New York State Temporary Commission on the Condition of the Urban Colored Population.

Her writings reflect her general interest in black advancement and special concern about black women workers in particular. Her major works include the above noted "Negroes in Domestic Service in the United States," *Unsung Heroes*, and *The Black Boy of Atlanta*, a work about black educator and banker Major Richard Robert Wright. Several additional articles stem from her thesis, as well as an article about Margaret Murray Washington.

Elizabeth Ross Haynes died October 26, 1953, in New York City.

—Susan Borchert

Bibliography

The early career of Elizabeth Ross is delineated in the archives of the YWCA National Board, New York City. Secondary sources that provide information on Elizabeth Ross Haynes include the following:

Giddings, Paula. *When and Where I Enter*. New York: Bantam Books, 1985. Written by a journalist: a very readable text on black women in U.S. history.

Haynes, Elizabeth Ross. "Negroes in Domestic Service in the U.S." *Journal of Negro History*, Association for the Study of Negro Life and History, Vol. 8, 1923. A well-written academic study that both describes and analyzes the women's employment problems and is considered a landmark work.

New York Times. Obituary. October 27, 1953.

Sicherman, Barbara, and Carol Green, eds. *Notable American Women: The Modern Period*. Cambridge, MA: Belknap Press, 1980. Interesting biographies of American women written in essay form.

Who Was Who in America. 1951–1960. Chicago: Marquis. Tersely written, but vital information regarding Americans no longer living.

HEDGEMAN, ANNA ARNOLD (1899–1990), born in Marshalltown, Iowa, on July 5 to William James Arnold II and Marie Ellen (Parker) Arnold, dedicated her life to civil rights.

She was raised in Anoke, Minnesota, by a family of devout Methodists that stressed religious service and educational achievement—both her father and grandfather had attended college. While in college she heard W.E.B. Du Bois speak, which inspired her to succeed as an educator. Hedgeman earned a BA in English from Hamline University, St. Paul, Minnesota, in 1922. She later pursued postgraduate studies at the University of Minnesota and the New York School of Social Work.

For two years, Hedgeman was professor of English at Rust College in Mississippi, where she experienced segregation for the first time while riding the train south. The intense segregation, especially in education and in denial of human rights, appalled Hedgeman, who wanted to organize northern whites and blacks to help southern blacks. She returned north in the fall of 1924 but was unable to secure a teaching position. Having previously volunteered at the YWCA in St. Paul, she applied for an executive position, beginning a ten-year tenure with the YWCA.

She first served as executive director of the black YWCA branch in Springfield, Ohio. She was shocked that the branch was segregated from white YWCA facilities, which were superior in quality. In the summer of 1926, she transferred to New York City and became aware that the segregation problem existed nationally, not solely confined to regional branches. She directed a branch in Jersey City, New Jersey. The continued segregation and discrimination that she faced convinced her that whites would never respect blacks' needs and problems.

In the fall of 1928, angry at whites who financed the YWCA and excluded blacks from facilities, Hedgeman accepted a position in the Harlem branch where segregation was not strictly enforced. In Brooklyn, Hedgeman supervised a picket of a store that refused to employ blacks; with the cooperation of white customers, the boycott enabled black sales clerks to be hired. Hedgeman believed that

YWCA members should have a voice in the selection of their leadership. Warned by executives not to interfere, Hedgeman changed the officer election procedure to become more democratic and to reflect membership interests. After instituting these changes, she resigned.

During the Depression she assisted the New York State Employment Service and was the first consultant on racial problems for the New York City commissioner. In this position she learned about the problems faced by such other minorities as Puerto Ricans. In 1933 she married Merritt A. Hedgeman, an interpreter of black folk music and opera, a union that lasted 54 years.

In 1944 A. Philip Randolph named Hedgeman executive secretary of the National Council for a Permanent Fair Employment Practices Commission (FEPC), established in Washington, DC, to lobby for the FEPC bill. She organized a national bipartisan educational program and also endorsed equal rights for women, focusing on the issue of total discrimination. Financial troubles plagued the council. Hedgeman, who considered Randolph's unequal treatment of his own female employees discriminatory (he paid them less than men), resigned in 1948. In 1946 Hedgeman served as assistant dean of women at Howard University. She received honorary degrees from Howard and Hamline universities

Hedgeman directed the national presidential fundraising campaign for Harry Truman, and after his election was appointed to the Federal Security Agency as assistant to its administrator, Oscar R. Ewing, from 1949 to 1953. She was a member of the National Advisory Council for the agency's Department of Health, Education, and Welfare. In 1953 Chester Bowles, U.S. ambassador to India, asked her to travel as a Department of State exchange leader to India. She toured India for three months, listening to Mahatma Gandhi speak.

The next year she became the first black woman cabinet member of a New York City mayor. In Mayor Robert F. Wagner's cabinet, Hedgeman was the liaison for eight city departments, advocating civil rights and education. She was able to establish contact with influential figures such as Lyndon B. Johnson and Martin Luther King, Jr. Destined to collect numerous honors and citations during her life, Hedgeman received the first Human Relations Award from the National Conference of Christians and Jews in 1955. After concluding her mayoral employment, she served as an editor and columnist for *New York Age* from 1958 to 1961.

Hedgeman was the keynote speaker at the First Conference of the Women of Africa and African Descent in Ghana in 1960. She attended and spoke at international conferences in Europe, Asia, and the Middle East. In 1960 she made an unsuccessful bid for the democratic congressional seat. Three years later she joined the staff of the Commission on Religion and Race of the National Council of Churches to battle racial injustice. As a consultant for the division of higher education of the United Church of Christ's American Missionary Association, she traveled to Africa and lectured throughout the United States, especially in black schools and colleges, as an example of a black hero. She stressed to students the importance of understanding history as a basis to achieve equality.

Hedgeman was a vocal leader in the March on Washington Movement, stressing that women speakers should be included on the rostrum, and for civil rights legislation. She unsuccessfully ran on the ticket of Representative William Fitts Ryan in 1965 for New York City Council president. She retired from the National Council of Churches in 1968, and, with her husband, formed Hedgeman Consultant Service. She devoted her time to research and travel, developing programs in Black Studies for schools.

Hedgeman died on January 17, 1990, in Harlem Hospital. Her career is highlighted by numerous awards and accolades such as her selection in 1978 by the National Conference of Christians and Jews as one of New York City's most extraordinary women of achievement.

—Elizabeth D. Schafer

Bibliography

"Anna Arnold Hedgeman," in *Encyclopedia of Black America*, edited by W. Augustus Low and Virgil A. Clift (New York: McGraw-Hill, 1981) is a brief biographical essay. Anna Arnold Hedgeman wrote two books, *The Gift of Chaos: Decades of American Discontent* (New York: Oxford, 1977) and *The Trumpet Sounds: A Memoir of Negro Leadership* (New York: Holt, Rinehart, Winston, 1964). An excerpt from the latter treatise is reprinted as "Reminiscences of a YWCA Worker," in *Black Women in White America*, edited by Gerda Lerner (New York: Random House, 1972). A profile of Hedgemen is included in Brian Lanker, *I Dream a World: Portraits of Black Women Who Changed America*, edited by Barbara Summers (New York: Stewart, Tabori, & Chang, 1989). For Hedgeman's obituary see Joan Cook, "Anna Hedgeman Is Dead at 90; Aide to Mayor Wagner in 1950s," *New York Times* (January 26, 1990) and a retraction concerning the spelling of Representative William Fitts Ryan's name in the *New York Times* (February 8, 1990).

Correspondence with Hedgeman is included in the A. Philip Randolph Files at the A. Philip Randolph Institute, New York City, some of which recently has been transferred to the Library of Congress, Washington, DC; National Association for the Advancement of Colored People Papers, Library of Congress, Washington, DC; B.F. McLaurin Papers, Schomburg Collection, New York Public Library; National Urban League Papers, Library of Congress; and Harry S. Truman Papers, Harry S. Truman Library, Independence, Missouri.

For information regarding Hedgeman's work as a YWCA branch director, see YWCA National Board Archives, New York City; Catherine D. Lealtad, "The National YWCA and the Negro," *The Crisis* 14 (October 1917): 317–318; two works sponsored by the YWCA, Jane Olcott-Walters, *History of Colored Work, 1907–1920* (New York: National Board of YWCA [NBYWCA], 1920) and *The Work of Colored Women* (New York: NBYWCA, 1919); and Gladys G. Calkins, "The Negro in the Young Women's Christian Association: A Study of the Development of YWCA Interracial Policies and Practices in Their Historical Setting," MA thesis, George Washington University (1960).

Paula F. Pfeffer, *A. Philip Randolph, Pioneer of the Civil Rights Movement* (Baton Rouge: Louisiana University Press, 1990) includes insights on Hedgeman's work as executive secretary of the National Council for a Permanent Fair Employment Practices Commission and her leadership in the March on Washington movement and notes that her books contain some factual errors. Louis Kesselman, *The Social Politics of FEPC: A Study in Reform Pressure Movements* (Chapel Hill: University of North Carolina Press, 1948) and Guichard Parris and Lester Brooks, *Blacks in the City: A History of the National Urban League* (Boston: Little Brown, 1971) provide historical context for Hedgeman's work.

Robert F. Wagner Papers are held by Georgetown University. J. Joseph Huthmacher, *Senator Robert F. Wagner and the Rise of Urban Liberalism* (New York: Atheneum, 1968) does not mention Hedgeman but provides a context for her political position in New York City. This is supplemented with focus on racial issues by Edwin R. Lewinson, *Black Politics in New York City* (New York: Twayne, 1974); Jervis Anderson, *This Was Harlem: A Cultural Portrait, 1900–1950* (New York: Farrar Strauss Giroux, 1982); Seth M. Scheiner, *Negro Mecca: A History of the Negro in New York City, 1865–1920* (New York: University Press, 1965); and Roi Ottley and William Weatherby, eds., *The Negro in New York* (New York: New York Public Library, 1967).

HEIGHT, DOROTHY (b. 1912), president of the National Council of Negro Women and head of the Department of Racial Justice of the YWCA, was raised with the philosophy of community service. Born in Richmond, Virginia, to James Edward and Fannie (Burroughs) Height on March 24, Dorothy Irene Height watched her parents help others. Her father, a building contractor, was a leader in the local Baptist church in Rankin, Pennsylvania, a small town outside of Pittsburgh, where they moved in 1916. Her mother, a nurse, cared for homebound cancer patients. Her job kept her away from the family on holidays and special occasions. The Height home provided aid to blacks coming to Pittsburgh for jobs in the steel mills.

Her parents encouraged active community participation in the children. During her primary school years, she suffered from severe asthma, but never missed a day of school. The condition produced a shyness and love for reading, an activity that required little movement. As a teen, her health improved and she played basketball, a game that rewarded the tall players. By age 11, she had already reached a stature of 5 feet, 9 inches tall. She volunteered at the Rankin Christian Center, which usually allowed participation of blacks only on Thursdays. Dorothy's Bible story classes took place throughout the week, making her the only black girl at the facility. At age 14, Dorothy had achieved the presidency of the Pennsylvania Federation of Girls' Clubs.

She attended the public schools, graduating from high school in 1926, finishing early due to two promotions. She went to New York City to live with her older sister in Harlem while she attended New York University on an Elks scholarship supplemented by employment waiting tables, working in a factory, ironing, writing obituaries, and other miscellaneous jobs. During the early years of the Great Depression, she completed both the bachelor's degree and the master's degree in educational psychology within four years, graduating in 1933. Although she was working primarily with whites, she organized a group of black students called the Rameses Club, which sponsored lectures by W.E.B. Du Bois and Paul Robeson. Although she was rushed by two sororities, she was never accepted. The social requirements did not suit the active Height. Not until 1939 did Height join a sorority. The commitment of the Delta Sigma Theta sorority to community service appealed to Height. Persuaded by the leadership to join, Height went on to become the president of the organization (1947–1958).

She was always combining activities with service and religion. While still in school, she completed an internship at the Brownsville Community Center in Brooklyn, which led to her first job as the assistant director of the center. There she helped organize the Christian Center and started a church there, the Universal Baptist Church. Through this position she worked with the Bureau of Charities, working out of a mission center without any real salary. In 1934 she became one of the first leaders of the United Christian Youth Movement.

All of these early jobs combined work, community service, and the teaching/learning process. Height was always teaching something and continuing her own learning simultaneously with her employment. While she was teaching courses at both the Friends' Seminary at the Fort Greene Training School for Religious Education and at Columbia University in religious education, financial realities led to her first salaried position as an investigator in Brooklyn with the New York City Department of Welfare. During this time she took courses at the New York School of Social Work doing research on the philosophy of social work. The Harlem riots of 1935 demanded black representation in the Department of Welfare. Both Anna A. Hedgeman and Dorothy Height received positions in response to these demands, Hedgeman as the minority representative in the Department of Welfare and Height as the personnel supervisor. She took courses at the Labor Temple to learn about economics and the relationship to social institutions and continued to apply her learning to her jobs. She remained at this position until she accepted a position with the Greater New York Council of Churches as the director of youth services in 1937 while spending evenings and weekends with her community religious activities.

Still the president of the Christian Youth Council of the State of New York and the vice-chair of the United Christian Youth Movement of North America, Height received in 1937 the opportunity to represent American youth in the World Conference on Life and Work of the Church in Oxford, England. Of the ten Americans, Height not only took part in the conference with representatives from 35 countries, but also remained behind to take a special seminar in international relations. During the fall of 1937 she made her first contact with the National Council of Negro Women (NCNW) as a member of the Resolutions Committee.

After her return to the United States, she received a letter from Cecelia Cabaniss Saunders, the YWCA's executive director of the Harlem branch, to join her as the assistant at the Emma Ransom House. She left her job at the welfare department and accepted the YWCA position, since it gave her greater flexibility to achieve her goals of community activism combined with religion. From this position, she worked with local groups and city council to lessen the human degradation of the "slave market," where the unemployed domestic workers stood on the corners waiting for hiring by potential employers driving by during the mornings. She did much to promote positive race relations. She organized "reconciliation tours" involving the branch with students from Smith College in visits to Harlem, Chinatown, and other ethnic enclaves. She brought black and white leaders such as Langston Hughes, Eleanor Roosevelt, and Countee Cullen to lecture at the branch. In 1938, she became the director of the Emma Ransom House when the director left, and was called by T. Arnold Hill, director of the National Urban League, to participate as a "non-organizational youth" in the National Council of Negro Women's convention dinner representing Mary McLeod Bethune at the Department of Labor in Washington, DC.

These contacts with the NCNW and Mary McLeod Bethune increased with her move to Washington. In 1939 she accepted the offer of the YWCA to become the executive director of the Phillis Wheatley YWCA in Washington, DC after her return from the World Conference of Christian Youth in Amsterdam. Bethune had Height working as the registrar with the NCNW. Height's natural shyness lessened under Bethune's guidance. Height admired Bethune's quality of leadership that enabled her to assess each woman's special skills and to push the individual into active use of these skills. While serving as the YWCA's director of the Phillis Wheatley YWCA on Ninth and Rhode Island, Bethune convinced Height to serve as the executive secretary of the NCNW. Since Bethune's home on Ninth Street was close to the YWCA, Height often worked on NCNW assignments at Bethune's home at night. Bethune did not try to make Height over into a shadow of her own leadership style, but instead nurtured her natural abilities.

At the Washington YWCA, Height developed programs to handle the flood of women entering the city in pursuit of federal employment during World War II. She started 24-hour programs providing courses in language, work skills, and appearance. She worked for housing and recreational programs. She continued to work with Bethune with the NCNW and with her sorority, Delta Sigma Theta.

In 1944 she returned to New York as the national board of the YWCA's secretary for interracial education, a position that required extensive travel and political negotiations at the national level. In 1946, due to her extensive work in interracial education, the YWCA adopted an interracial charter. In 1949 she served as the director for training. As the United States entered the 1950s era of domesticity and McCarthyism, Dorothy Height continued her emphasis on international issues and intercultural communications. She taught a semester at the Delhi School of Social Work in 1952, served as a member on the Defense Department's Advisory Committee on Women in the Services, and was elected president of the NCNW in 1957. From 1958 to 1968 she served on the New York State Social Welfare Board. In 1959 she went to South America as part of the 35-member American delegation under the International Seminars followed by a 4-month study tour of women's organizations in Africa in 1960, experiences that led to her serving as a consultant to the State Department on African affairs and as a future organizer for the Negro Leadership Conference on Africa and for the 1975 International Women's Year conference in Nairobi, Kenya.

The 1960s brought her into active leadership within the civil rights and women's rights movements. Under the leadership of Eleanor Roosevelt, Height became part of President John F. Kennedy's Commission to Study the Status of Women, during which time she gathered data on the problems facing American women. She also used her organizational insights to make suggestions about possible solutions to many of these problems. As president of the NCNW, Height became a member of the Council for United Civil Rights Leadership, a distinguished group of black leaders formed by the Taconic Foundation under the leadership of Stephen Currier in the early 1960s to assess and prepare the direction of blacks in the United States. The Council helped organized the 1963 March on Washington. The civil rights movement in turn brought the NCNW into the mainstream of community action, one of Height's lifetime values. Height brought the NCNW into Selma, Alabama, in October 1963 to help the Student Nonviolent Coordinating Committee's efforts to register voters. Later that year, women of all races and religions met in Atlanta to form new coalitions for change in their communities. The establishment of Women in Community Service (WICS) helped to recruit poor women into the Job Corps for occupational training, to establish enrichment programs called "Wednesdays" for the Freedom Schools in Mississippi, and to promote many other self-help projects to address needs in housing, schools, child care, and employment. She continued to break down barriers for women and for the race. Height became the first black woman to lecture at the University of Mississippi for a two-week Institute for Desegregation of Schools. She became the head of the Department of Racial Justice in 1963.

Today, the never-married Height has remained at the helm of the National Council of Negro Women longer than any major civil rights leader, including the founder, Mary McLeod Bethune. Her plans to retire as president and chief executive officer are being prepared for by management consultants to help coordinate the 30-member groups and over 100,000 dues-paying members. Despite her plans to step down, she continues to provide leadership for the Council's programs dealing with issues such as teen pregnancy, child care, and black women's history, the latter through the institution of the NCNW's Bethune Museum and Archives. Dorothy Height's legacy lives through such institutionalized programs within the YWCA, the Delta Sigma Theta sorority, and the National Council of Negro Women.

—Dorothy C. Salem

Bibliography

The primary sources related to Height's career can be found through her organizations. The Archives of the National Board of the YWCA in New York City can shed light on her branch and national leadership. The Washington, DC, Phillis Wheatley records have been processed at the Moorland-Spingarn Research Center, Howard University. The National Council of Negro Women records have been housed at the National Black Women's History Archives (Bethune Museum) in Washington, DC. Her oral history interviews are collected as part of the Black Women's Oral History Collection, Schlesinger Library, Radcliffe College. These 66 interviews are available in 10 volumes published in 1990 by Meckler Publishing of Westport, Connecticut.

Although she has been the leader of one of the largest coordinating groups of women, Height is seldom featured in most biographical dictionaries. She receives brief mention for her role in civil rights in Marianna Davis, *Contributions of Black Women to American History* (Columbia, SC: Kenday, 1981), but is overlooked in most histories of the civil rights movement. Height is the focus of many articles appearing in such periodicals as *Ebony, Essence, Ms., Jet,* and *American Visions*. Recent information about the transformation of the NCNW appear in Drew Jubera, "A Reign to Reckon with Nears the End," Cleveland *Plain Dealer* October 11, 1990.

HEMINGS, SALLY (1773–1835), the youngest daughter of John Wayles, the father-in-law of Thomas Jefferson, and Elizabeth Hemings, daughter of an African slave and a British sea captain, was the alleged mistress of Thomas Jefferson. When Wayles died in 1773, the year of Sally's birth, the entire family became the property of Martha Wayles Jefferson. As she grew up on Monticello, she was described by other slaves as a light-skinned beauty with long straight hair. She accompanied Jefferson's daughter, Mary, on a trip to Paris in 1785. She and her brother, James, Jefferson's valet, received tutoring in French and were given modest salaries. It is said that Jefferson fell in love with the half-sister of his dead wife in 1788, while still in France. Of free status in France, she reputedly refused to return to the United States until Jefferson promised to free all her children when they reached age 21. The agreement is unknown, but she returned to Monticello in late 1789.

Information about the relationship was first published in the *Richmond Recorder* on September 1, 1802, by a rumor-spinning journalist, James Thomson Callender, who said Hemings had produced five children by Jefferson. Such scandal did not influence the elections. Jefferson won all but two states in 1804. Sally Hemings stayed at Monticello, where she lived in the great house with her children, who did only light work until they learned a trade at age 14. The memoirs of Madison Hemings, the third son of Sally Hemings, recount the passing of his siblings into white society. Jefferson arranged to free two of her sons, Madison and Eston, in his will. Jefferson's daughter, Martha Randolph, arranged for the freedom of Sally Hemings in 1828 after her father's death in 1826. She lived the remainder of her days with her son and his family, listed as white in the census documents. She died in 1835 at age 62.

—Kelle S. Taha

Bibliography

Several accounts provide information about Sally Hemings. Fawn Brodie's *Thomas Jefferson, an Intimate History* (New York: Norton, 1974) gives information about her life and includes a section of reproductions of important documents: Madison Hemings's memoir, a corroborating slave's memoir, and an interview with Thomas Jefferson Randolph. She also provides geneological information in her article "Thomas Jefferson's Unknown Grandchildren," *American Heritage* 27 (October 1976): 96–98. A similar perspective is in Barbara Chase-Riboud's novel, *Sally Hemings* (New York: Viking Press, 1979). A rebuttal is offered in Virginia Dabney's *The Jefferson Scandals: A Rebuttal* (New York: Dodd, Mead, 1981). *The Papers of Thomas Jefferson*, edited by Julian Boyd, et al. (Princeton: Princeton University Press, 1950) have several references to Hemings. Her biographical sketch is included in Rayford Logan, *Dictionary of American Negro Biography* (New York: Norton, 1982). Articles about the family include James A. Bear, Jr., "The Hemings Family at Monticello," *Virginia Cavalcade* 80:2 (Autumn 1979): 78–87; Pearl M. Graham, "Thomas Jefferson and Sally Hemings," *Journal of Negro History* 44:2 (April 1961): 89–103; and Ellen N. Lawson, "Sarah Woodson Early," *UMOJA* 2 (Summer 1891): 16.

HINE, DARLENE CLARK (b. 1947) has become one of the leading historians in the field of black women's history, specializing in black women's organized reform roles and participation in the professions. Born to Levester and Lottie May (Thompson) Clark in Morely, Missouri, on February 7, Hine attended Roosevelt University for her BA in American history (1968). She then went to Kent State University to earn her MA in American history and to write her master's thesis on the American Colonization Society's efforts to convince blacks to immigrate to Africa (1970). While working on her PhD under August Meier, Hine served as a teaching assistant at Kent State (1968–1970), as assistant professor of history and coordinator of black studies at South Carolina State University (1972–1974), and as assistant professor of history at Purdue University (1974–1979). She received her PhD from Kent State University in 1975. Her dissertation focused on the NAACP and the demise of the Democratic white primary. This research culminated in *Black Victory: The Rise and Fall of the White Primary in Texas* (1979), a book that has inspired her to develop a forthcoming major work on black lawyers.

In the early 1980s Hine was asked by a group of women in Indiana to do a history on the women in the state. Her subsequent research produced *When the Truth Is Told: A History of Black Women's Culture and Community in Indiana*. This became her first monograph dealing with women's history and awakened a profound interest in black women's history that she developed in later works funded by research grants and fellowships.

Hine then embarked upon a major study of blacks in the professions: law, medicine, nursing, science, and education. She has to date published in only one of these fields. The wealth of information she uncovered produced eight years of articles and a book, *Black Women in White: Racial Conflict and Cooperation in the Nursing Profession, 1890–1950* (1989). While involved in this study, she received a $150,000 grant from the National Endowment for the Humanities as project director of the Black Women in the Midwest Project. She and other researchers collected manuscript and photographic records of black women in Indiana and Illinois. With research completed in 1986, these records were marketed to regional historical societies and libraries.

Hine has produced some of the most informative works dealing with black women in history. Among these are *The State of Afro-American History: Past, Present and Future* (1986), *Black Women in the Nursing Profession: A Documentary History*, and *Black Women in United States History: From Colonial Times to the Present*, a 16-volume series for which she served as general editor. She is a member of the Association for the Study of Afro-American Life and History, Organization of American Historians, Southern Association of Women Historians, Association of Black Women Historians, Phi Alpha Theta, American Historical Association, and others. Twice married, Hine is the mother of Robbie Davine.

Until recently, Hine was associate professor of history and vice provost at Purdue University. She is currently the John A. Hanna professor of American history at Michigan State University. Last year she served as a visiting professor of women's studies at the University of Delaware. She is currently working on a monograph, "The Joint Center for Political and Economic Studies, 1970–1990: A Catalyst for Change," and is beginning a project on black doctors in World War II.

—Christopher D. White

Bibliography

The most helpful sources of information about Darlene Clark Hine include *Who's Who among Black Americans, 1990–1991* (Northbrook, IL: Who's Who Among Black Americans) and August Meier and Elliott Radwick, *Black History and the Historical Profession, 1915–1980* (Urbana: Unversity of Illinois Press). The forewords to Hine's own works are also helpful. For an overview of the subjects she has researched see her article "Lifting the Veil, Shattering the Silence: Black Women's History in Slavery and Freedom," in *The State of Afro-American History: Past, Present, and Future* and *Black Women in White: Racial Conflict and Cooperation in the Nursing Profession, 1890–1950* (Bloomington: Indiana University Press, 1989). Much of the information about current and future projects was obtained through a phone interview with Darlene Clark Hine on May 4, 1991.

HINTON, JANE (b. 1920?) was one of the first two black women veterinary graduates, receiving her DVM from the University of Pennsylvania School of Veterinary Medicine in 1949, the same year Alfreda Johnson graduated from the Tuskegee Institute Veterinary School.

Hinton's father was Chicago native William Augustus Hinton, the son of former slaves, the first black Harvard professor, and a renowned medical researcher who developed an accurate serological test for syphilis at Harvard's Wassermann Laboratory. The Hinton Test was used in mass screenings to promote public health. He married Ada Hawes, of Macon, Georgia, in 1909, and finished medical school in 1912. They established their home in Canton, Massachusetts, where Hinton and her older sister, Ann Hinton Jones, grew up. Since William Augustus Hinton advocated technical training for underprivileged women during the 1930s, he sought higher education for his daughters. Ann Hinton Jones became a social worker, while Jane Hinton pursued veterinary medicine.

Hinton was a World War II technician, stationed in Arizona. After the war, she attended the University of Pennsylvania School of Veterinary Medicine, which developed a veterinary curriculum in 1884, and welcomed talented minority students. The first black male graduate in 1884 preceded Hinton's graduation by 50 years.

After graduation, Hinton returned to Canton, Massachusetts. As a member of the American Veterinary Medical Association, she was employed as a practitioner for small animals in Framingham, Massachusetts, by 1956. Eight years later, in addition to her veterinary practice, she also worked as a federal government inspector in Framingham Center, Massachusetts, performing regulatory veterinary work, a position she continued to hold in the 1980s. It is unknown if she has retired or continues in this role.

—Elizabeth D. Schafer

Bibliography

"Most Veterinarian Schools Do Not Maintain Color Line," *Ebony* 5 (August 1949): cites Hinton as being one of the first two black women to graduate from veterinary school. For information about Hinton's family see James E. Teele, "William Augustus Hinton," in *Dictionary of American Negro Biography*, edited by Rayford W. Logan and Michael R. Winston (New York: Norton, 1982), pp. 315–316, and Herbert M. Morais, *The History of the Afro-American in Medicine* (Cornwells Heights, PA: ASALH, 1976). The *American Veterinary Medical Association Directory* (Schaumburg, IL: AVMA, published annually), lists the educational affiliation, geographic location, and professional activity of Hinton.

For information about black veterinarians and a photograph of Hinton see William H. Waddell IV, *The Black Man in Veterinary Medicine* (Fargo, ND: Author, 1982). Waddell as well as Bert W. Bierer, *American Veterinary History* (Fort Dodge, IA: National Museum of Veterinary Medicine, 1940) briefly comment about women entering the veterinary profession. For veterinary medicine in Pennsylvania, see Ray

Thompson, *After 1883: One Hundred Years of Organized Veterinary Medicine in Pennsylvania* (Philadelphia: W.B. Saunders, 1982) and William H. Waddell IV, who graduated from the University of Pennsylvania School of Veterinary Medicine, *People Are the Funniest Animals* (Philadelphia: Dorrance & Co., 1978). J. Frederick Smithcors, *The Veterinarian in America, 1625–1975* (Santa Barbara, CA: American Veterinary Publications, 1975) is a historical overview.

Marvin P. Lyon, Jr., "Blacks at Penn, Then and Now," in *A Pennsylvania Album: Undergraduate Essays on the 250th Anniversary of the University of Pennsylvania*, edited by Richard S. Dunn and Mark F. Lloyd (Philadelphia: University of Pennsylvania, 1990) and Martin Meyerson and Dilys P. Winegrad, *Gladly Learn and Gladly Teach: Franklin and His Heirs at the University of Pennsylvania, 1740–1976* (Philadelphia: University of Pennsylvania, 1978) reveal historical information on black students at the University of Pennsylvania.

HOLIDAY, BILLIE (1915–1959), often referred to as the most influential jazz singer of all time, lived a life that embraced fame and infamy, triumph and tragedy. Though she is celebrated as a hometown celebrity in Baltimore, she was actually born in Philadelphia on April 7. Born to 13-year-old Sadie Fagan and 18-year-old Clarence Holiday, Billie Holiday started life as Eleanora Fagan. When her parents married three years after her birth, she assumed the Holiday name. Her first name evolved from that of her screen idol, Billie Dove. Since her father was on tour as a musician with the jazz band of Fletcher Henderson, and her mother worked as a maid, young Holiday lived a solitary childhood. Soon the father abandoned the family, leaving the mother struggling to make a living. She left young Holiday with relatives in Baltimore, while she went to New York. At age ten, she was sent to the House of Good Shepherd, a Catholic home for black girls. Records indicate that she had no guardian and was on the streets at this time. Her autobiography, *Lady Sings the Blues*, recounted these early years extreme poverty. Holiday remembered working at age six as a babysitter and a stepscrubber. Despite the poverty and separation, Holiday wanted to be with her mother. She finished the fifth grade in the Baltimore schools, and in 1927, she joined her mother in New York to work as a maid. From this time, she and her mother remained close throughout her lifetime.

In New York, Holiday became familiar with jazz, while performing household chores for Alice Dean, a brothel owner. In 1930, desperate to avert eviction from the apartment she shared with her mother, Holiday was forced to take a job as a vocalist at Pod's and Jerry's, a Harlem speakeasy. From that point on, Holiday enjoyed recognition. In 1933 jazz enthusiast John Hammond organized her first recording which launched her public career. She toured with Fletcher Henderson, Count Basie, and Artie Shaw. During this time, tenor Lester Young labeled her "Lady Day."

Holiday's unique blues-inspired jazz singing took subtle liberties with melodies, changing them much the way jazz musicians improvise on instruments. Moreover, Holiday sang simple, mundane lyrics, making them sound significant and urgent. Her sophisticated approach to singing yielded a novel effect. While earlier popular singers only entertained audiences, Holiday both entertained and communicated with her listeners. She conveyed to them in song what she knew about life. Holiday invested her music with a blues feeling that contained not only sadness but also an honesty and a directness of expression. Like the best blues artists, she transformed misery into something apart from trouble and pain. With the release of "Strange Fruit" in 1939, Holiday became a celebrity. Her record was based, on Lewis Allen's poem recounting lynchings in the South. The "strange fruit" was the bodies of the lynched blacks hanging from the branches of the trees. "Strange Fruit" as sang by Holiday became both one of the most powerful pleas for civil rights and her signature song.

In 1941 Holiday married James N. Monroe, a nightclub manager. When her mother died in 1945, Holiday felt alone. Although Holiday enjoyed fame—Jazz Critics Poll (1944), the Metronome Vocalist of the Year (1946), and a film role in *New Orleans* (1946) in which she was cast as a maid—she was handicapped by her drug addiction. Arrested several times, by 1949, she had divorced. New York denied her a license to perform. She married Louis McKay, her manager, and in 1956, Doubleday published Holiday's autobiography, *Lady Sings the Blues*, which included the singer's account of her abusive, impoverished childhood and her experiences with racism and drug addiction. Ultimately, the drug and alcohol addiction took their toll. Her last arrest was in her hospital bed for drug possession. She died on July 17, 1959.

—Patricia A. Young

Bibliography

Many published accounts of Holiday's life illuminate the various facets of her personality and career. Her autobiography prepared by William Duffy, *Lady Sings the Blues* (New York: Doubleday), provides details, but the chronology and many factual items cannot be trusted. The first major film on the life of a black woman, *Lady Sings the Blues*, was based on Holiday's life. Bud Kliment's *Billie Holiday* (New York: Chelsea House, 1990), looks at the development of her career as a singer. John Chilton's *Billie's Blues: Billie Holiday's Story, 1933–1959* (New York: Stein and Day, 1975) includes an extensive bibliography and discography. The most recent book by Robert O'Meally, *Lady Day: The Many Faces of Billie Holiday* (New York: Arcade, 1991) corrects many of the errors of previous works. Other standard works include James Burnett's *Billie Holiday* (Spellmount, NY: Hippocrene, 1984) and John White's *Billie Holiday: Her Life and Times* (New York: Neal, 1987). A short biographical sketch and annotated bibliography by George A. Ryder is included in *Notable American Women: The Modern Period*, edited by Barbara Sicherman, Carol H. Green, et al. (Cambridge: Harvard University Press, 1980), pp. 346–348.

HOPE, LUGENIA BURNS (1871–1947), community organizer and
proponent of racial justice, was born in Mississippi, where her grandparents had
moved from Canada during the nineteenth century. Her parents as free blacks
migrated to Cincinnati and then to St. Louis, seeking better employment and
educational opportunities. When her father died, the family moved to Chicago,
where Hope helped to support her deaf mother and younger siblings.

Hope developed charity and reform interests during a time when Chicago
blossomed with reform potential during the 1880s and 1890s. As the first and only
black member of the Cook County board of King's Daughters, Hope became
acquainted with intellectuals from the University of Chicago, worked with Jane
Addams, and met black intellectuals like Paul Laurence Dunbar. At the Chicago
Columbian Exposition in 1893, her beauty led to her title of "Genie with the
Light Brown Hair."

When she met John Hope, a student at Brown University, she found a person
with whom she could share similar interests in urban reform. In 1897 they married
and moved to Nashville, where he taught at Roger Williams University. They
became friends with the families of nationally known black business and
education leaders, such as John Napier and W.E.B. Du Bois.

Her husband's career in education brought the young couple to Atlanta
Baptist College (later renamed Morehouse College) in 1898. As she raised their
two sons, Edward Swain and John, Jr., she extended her concern into the
community by organizing the Atlanta Neighborhood Union in 1908. Under the
motto "And Thy Neighbor as Thyself," the black women of the community
developed lecture courses, fresh-air work, cleanup campaigns, probation and
employment services, reading rooms, clubs, classes, and health and recreation
campaigns. Applying the techniques of scientific reform, they conducted me-
thodical investigations of schools, sanitation, and vice to improve community life
and stimulate community responsibility. In cooperation with professionals in the
Sociology Department at Morehouse College, Hope improved the efficiency and
efficacy of black social work. The techniques developed through the Atlanta
Neighborhood Union influenced other communities through Hope's position as
the director of neighborhood work in the National Association of Colored
Women. As an affiliate of the National Urban League, the Neighborhood Union
became the model for urban reform recommended by the league.

Hope did not limit her activities to the Atlanta community. During World
War I she served as the director of the YWCA-sponsored Hostess House at Camp
Upton in New York. She hoped that the efforts of blacks during World War I
merited improved conditions in postwar America. When worsening race relations followed the war, Hope was instrumental in organizing black women to
pressure the YWCA to become more interracial in its policies and leadership.
Hope continued pressing for racial justice after the Neighborhood Union became
part of the community chest, thereby institutionalizing her programs for future

generations. Hope continued her work with the Neighborhood Union, YWCA, National Urban League and club movement.

Hope survived her husband (d. 1936) by almost a decade. She died on August 14, 1947, at the Riverside Sanitarium in Nashville, Tennessee.

—Dorothy C. Salem

Bibliography

Much of the information about Lugenia Burns Hope can be found in the Neighborhood Union Papers, Woodruff Library, Atlanta University Center. Interviews with her son, Edward, in 1984–1985 provided further personal insights into her life and personality. Hope has been overlooked in most biographical collections, but will gain deserved recognition since the publication of the first major biography on Hope's reform career: Jacqueline Rouse, *Lugenia Burns Hope: Black Southern Reformer* (Athens: University of Georgia Press, 1989). A shorter summary of her career appeared in the November 1947 issue of the *Morehouse College Alumnus*.

Secondary Sources

Chivers, Walter. "Neighborhood Union: An Effort of Community Organization," *Opportunity* 3 (June 1925): 178–179.

Hall, Jacqueline Dowd. "Revolt Against Chivalry: Jessie Daniel Ames and the Women's Campaign Against Lynching." Dissertation, Columbia University, 1974.

Johnson, Georgia D. "Frederick Douglass and Paul Laurence Dunbar at the World's Fair," *National Notes* 49 (January–February 1947): 10, 29

Torrence, Fred Ridgely. *The Story of John Hope*. New York: Macmillan, 1948.

HOPKINS, PAULINE (1859–1930), journalist, fiction writer, editor, publisher, and musician, was born in Portland, Maine. Her parents, Northrup and Sarah (Allen) Hopkins, raised her in Boston, where Pauline Elizabeth Hopkins spent most of her life. She attended Boston's public schools and graduated from Girl's High School, where she achieved her first literary success by writing a prizewinning essay, "The Evils of Intemperance and Their Remedies." In her early twenties, Hopkins wrote and produced two musical dramas in the Boston area: *Colored Aristocracy* in 1877 and *Slaves' Escape; or the Underground Railroad* in 1879, which featured Hopkins as a soprano. A talented and versatile woman, she was trained as a stenographer, a profession that supported her throughout her life.

Hopkins's literary career was launched with the publication in 1900 of her first novel, *Contending Forces, A Romance Illustrative of Negro Life North and South*, by the black-owned Colored Co-Operative Publishing Company in Boston. In the same year, the company also began publication of the *Colored American Magazine*, an African-American literary journal for which Hopkins was hired to edit the magazine's women's section. In an early issue of the magazine, Hopkins was described as having the ambition "to become a writer of fiction, in which the wrongs of her race shall be so handled as to enlist the sympathy of all classes of citizens, in this way reaching those who never read history or biography."

Hopkins quickly became one of the magazine's chief writers, although it took three years for her name to appear on the masthead as literary editor. She wrote short stories, essays, editorials, and biographical sketches. Three of her novels were serialized under the pen name Sarah A. Allen, her mother's maiden name. Her magazine novels, "Hagar's Daughter's: A Story of Southern Caste Prejudice," "Winona, a Tale of Negro Life in the South and Southwest," and "Of One Blood; or the Hidden Self," appeared between 1901 and 1903. She is also known to have paid the magazine's contributors for their work, a rare practice among black publications of the time.

Today's scholars view Hopkins's writing as a significant contribution to the development of black culture and literature in the early twentieth century. Her stories focused on such complex social and political issues as lynching and racial violence, disfranchisement, miscegenation, sexuality, changing gender roles, and the emergence of a black middle class—problems confronting African Americans of the period. Her influence at the *Colored American Magazine* ended in 1904 when Booker T. Washington started to subsidize the magazine and its offices were moved to New York City.

Hopkins continued her journalistic career as a contributor for the *Voice of the Negro*, a black magazine based in Atlanta. In 1905 she founded the short-lived publishing house, P.E. Hopkins and Company. She attempted another publishing venture in 1916 with Walter Wallace, a former owner of the *Colored American Magazine*, when they founded the *New Era Magazine: An Illustrated Monthly Devoted to the World-Wide Interests of the Colored Race*. Despite her efforts at writing for and editing the magazine, it too failed. Her literary career fell into obscurity, and she supported herself as a stenographer for the remainder of her life. Pauline Hopkins died on August 13, 1930, from burns sustained in a fire.

—Jane Rhodes

Bibliography

A more detailed biography by Dorothy Porter is listed in the *Dictionary of American Negro Biography*, edited by Rayford Logan and Michael Winston (New York: Norton, 1982), pp. 325–326. A brief sketch appears in "The Story of Our Magazine," *The Colored American Magazine* (May 1901): 47. An extensive analysis of Hopkins's work appears in Hazel Carby, *Reconstructing Womanhood* (New York: Oxford University Press, 1987), and in Carby's "Introduction," in *The Magazine Novels of Pauline Hopkins* (New York: Oxford University Press, 1988) (part of the Schomburg Library of Nineteenth-Century Black Women Writers). Other sources include Ann Allen Shockley, "Pauline Elizabeth Hopkins: A Biographical Excursion into Obscurity," *Phylon* 33 (1972): 22–26; Claudia Tate, "Pauline Hopkins: Our Literary Foremother," in *Conjuring Black Women, Fiction, and Literary Tradition*, edited by Marjorie Pryse and Hortense Spillers (Bloomington: Indiana University Press, 1985); Penelope L.

Bullock, *The Afro-American Periodical Press, 1838–1909* (Baton Rouge: Louisiana State University Press, 1981); and Mary Helen Washington, ed., *Invented Lives: Narratives of Black Women, 1860–1960* (Garden City, NY: Anchor Press, 1987).

HORNE, LENA (b. 1917), actress and singer, was born in a Brooklyn, New York, hospital on June 30. Edna (Scottron) Horne, her mother, was accompanied by her husband, Teddy Horne, and her mother-in-law. This copper-colored child was the product of a fiercely insular, and close-knit African-American middle-class family from the Bedford-Stuyvesant section of Brooklyn.

Her father was a numbers banker and her mother was a not-so-successful actress who pushed her daughter into show business, having early on recognized the exceptional beauty of her child. The father remained largely removed from the child's day-to-day existence; the most dominant force in Horne's early life was her paternal grandmother.

Horne's professional career began at age 16 in Harlem's Cotton Club. Subsequently, she toured as a singer with a variety of dance bands, including Noble Sissle and the integrated Charlie Barnet band in 1940, her first big break. By this time, Horne had already carved out a fairly substantial career for herself as an African-American entertainer. In addition to the Cotton Club and singing with a major black orchestra, she had appeared twice on Broadway in *Dance with Your Gods* (1934) and *Blackbirds* (1939), and made a Hollywood film. In January 1937, she married Louis Jones. At age 23 she found herself legally separated from her husband and the mother of two children—Teddy and Gail.

She went on to make a number of films and became the first African-American to sign a contract with a major Hollywood studio (MGM). Some of her best known movies include *Panama Hattie* (1942), *Cabin in the Sky* (1943), *Stormy Weather* (1943), *Swing Fever* (1943), *Broadway Rhythm* (1944), *Ziegfeld Follies* (1946), and *Till the Clouds Roll By* (1946). Thereafter, Horne was primarily active as a nightclub entertainer throughout the United States and Europe.

In 1947 her marriage to Lennie Hayton, a white musician, created considerable controversy because of its interracial character. It proved to be both a happy and professionally productive relationship. Horne spent many years learning from her musician husband, as well as from all the marvelous musicians she met through her husband. Their marriage lasted for 24 years, until Hayton's death of a heart attack on April 24, 1971.

Throughout her long and active life, Lena Horne has been involved in community and charity work along with civil rights. Because she was a member of the NAACP since age two (her grandmother enrolled her), a friend of Paul Robeson (she had been called his female counterpart), and a member of the Hollywood Independent Citizens Committee of the Arts, Sciences, and Professions made it was all but inevitable that Horne would become a victim of the 1950s Red Scare. She was drummed out of the Screen Actor's Guild and blacklisted.

Nonetheless, she returned to Broadway in *Jamaica* in 1957 and continued to have a productive recording career. Horne published two biographies—*In Person: Lena Horne* (1950) and *Lena* (1965). She received a Tony Award for her hit *Lena Horne: The Lady and Her Music* in 1981 and was the recipient of a Kennedy Center Honor in 1984 and then a New York Governor's Arts Award in 1985.

—Donna Van Raaphorst

Bibliography

Accounts on Lena Horne must begin with her own autobiographies. Consult *In Person: Lena Horne as Told to Helen R. Stein and Carleton Moss* (New York: Greenberg, 1950) and Lena Horne and Richard Schickel, *Lena* (Garden City, NY: Doubleday, 1965). Equally insightful is the history of the Horne family as told by Horne's daughter. See Gail Lumet Buckley, *The Hornes: An American Family* (New York: Knopf, 1986). Of additional value is the work by James Haskins and Kathleen Benson, *Lena: A Personal and Professional Biography of Lena Horne* (New York: Stein and Day, 1984). She is included in Gwendolyn Cherry's *Portraits in Color* (New York: Pageant Press, 1962); and Langston Hughes's *Famous Negro Music Makers* (New York: Dodd, 1955).

Accounts of Horne's contributions to music may be found in Leslie Gourse, *Louis's Children: American Jazz Singers* (New York: William Morrow, 1984); Grover Sales, *Jazz: America's Classical Music* (Englewood Cliffs, NJ: Prentice-Hall, 1984); and Dave Gelly, *The Giants of Jazz* (New York: Macmillan, Schirmer Books, 1986).

HUNT, IDA [GIBBS] (1862–1957), educator, civil rights leader, and Pan-Africanist, was born on November 16 in Victoria, British Columbia. Her father, Judge Mifflin Wistar Gibbs (1823–1903), was a social reformer and successful businessman in California and in British Columbia. In the 1860s the middle-class family moved to Oberlin, Ohio, where her mother, Maria Ann (Alexander) (d. 1904), had attended Oberlin College. Her father briefly studied in the Law Department of the Oberlin Business College. There Ida Gibbs studied in the Conservatory of Music (1872–1876), attended the Oberlin Public Schools (1876–c. 1879), and joined the First Congregational Church in Oberlin in 1878. Subsequently, after completing her senior year of high school in Oberlin College's Preparatory Department, as a boarding student Ida earned a bachelor of arts degree in English in 1884. To supplement her classical and scientific course of study in the Department of Philosophy and the Arts, Ida stayed on one additional year to pursue her musical interests in the Conservatory of Music. In 1892 she received an MA degree.

Compelled to do "something good" after graduation, in 1885 she returned to Little Rock, Arkansas, where her father practiced law, to do missionary work. From there she went on to Huntsville, Alabama, to teach Latin and mathematics in the State Normal School for two years, only to return to Oberlin in 1889 due to ill health. Between 1892 and 1895 she apparently served as principal of the

Preparatory Department in the State Normal School (now Florida A & M College) in Tallahassee, Florida. In 1895, at age 33, Ida Gibbs went to Washington, DC, to teach English in the old M Street High School (later Dunbar Senior High) until her marriage in 1904 to William Henry Hunt (1869–1951), the U.S. consul at Tamatave, Madagascar. This union produced no children.

After having retired from teaching in 1904, for the following 27 years Ida Gibbs Hunt accompanied her husband on his assignments as a U.S. consul. These included three years at Tamatave (1904–1906), twenty years at St. Etienne, France (1906–1926), two years in Guadeloupe, West Indies (1927–1928), a year in St. Michaels, the Azores (1929), and two years at Monrovia, Liberia (1931–1932). The Hunts returned to Washington in late 1932, following reassignment and retirement from the State Department, where they lived for the remainder of their lives. He died on December 19, 1951, and she died, at age 96, on December 19, 1957.

Over a half-century, Ida Gibbs Hunt pursued her interests in literature and remained active in civic affairs. She published several essays and reviews on literary and general cultural themes as well as read papers or lectured before literary societies, teacher associations, and other audiences. Her published articles include "The Price of Peace" (1938), "Civilization and the Darker Races" (n.d.), and a number of pieces appearing in the newspapers. Growing out of her international experience and her admiration for France, Ida Hunt supported organizations promoting racial justice, civil rights, peace, and women's suffrage through the Red Cross, YWCA, Croix Rough Francaise, Femmes de France, Club Franco-Etranger, Women's International League for Peace and Freedom, and the National Association for the Advancement of Colored People.

Ida Hunt, committed in the service of civil rights for African Americans, is listed among the 1905 incorporators of the Colored Young Women Christian Association (later YWCA of the District of Columbia). She served as assistant secretary of the First Pan-African Congress, in Paris (1919), attended the Paris session of the Second Pan-African Congress (1921), and delivered the paper "The Coloured Races and the League of Nations" at the London session of the Third Congress (1923). She is also remembered as the co-chair with W.E.B. Du Bois of the executive committee that planned the London session. Five years before her death, in 1952, Ida Hunt and two of her Oberlin College classmates, Dr. Anna J. Cooper and Mary Church Terrell, held a reunion in Washington. "They agreed," as reported in the *Washington Post* (April 4, 1952), "that the difficulties they encountered as mere female members of a recently freed race only made their triumphs sweeter."

—Roland Baumann

Bibliography

Sources used include documents contained in the Alumni File of Ida Alexander Gibbs (Mrs. William H. Hunt), Alumni and Development Office Records (28/2); Hunt Papers, in the Moorland-Spingarn Research Center, Howard University, Washington, DC; W.E.B. Du Bois Papers, University of Massachusetts, Amherst; Louise Daniel Hutchenson, *Anna J. Cooper, A Voice from the South* (Washington, DC: Smithsonian Institution Press, 1981), pp. 36–37, 124; and the sketch by Allison Blakely in *Dictionary of American Negro Biography*, edited by Rayford W. Logan and Michael R. Winston (New York: Norton, 1982), pp. 336–337.

HUNTER, ALBERTA (1895–1984), blues singer, was born in Memphis, Tennessee, on April 1. There were times when, under contract to one recording company while singing for another, she used the pseudonyms May Alix and Josephine Beatty, the name of her half-sister.

Hunter was a blues/jazz cabaret singer in the 1920s and 1930s, and she used the terms "blues" and "jazz" interchangeably. She was accompanied by such jazz musicians as Fletcher Henderson, Louis Armstrong, Fats Waller, and Sidney Bechet and spent those two decades performing mainly in Europe. In the 1930s Hunter also co-starred with Paul Robeson in the musical *Showboat* at the Drury Theatre. During World War II she toured with the USO in Europe, Korea, Burma, and India.

In the 1950s, after touring Britain and Canada, Hunter retired from music. Though she had little prior formal education, she started a career in nursing after graduating from the Harlem YWCA Nursing School in 1956. She earned her cap as a licensed practical nurse and continued in this work until she was forced to retire because of her age.

After this second retirement, Alberta Hunter returned full time to her music in 1977. She made quite an impression upon her return, at age 82, with her debut at Carnegie Hall on June 27, 1978. She was called a "national treasure" by the American press, and the highlight of her singing career came when she performed on December 3, 1978, at the White House for President and Mrs. Jimmy Carter. From then until her death, she performed regularly at the Greenwich Village Cookery in New York City.

Hunter was married briefly to Willard Saxby Townsend, who would later become the first black on the executive council of the AFL-CIO. Alberta Hunter received many accolades during her life. In 1952 she would become one of the few women to be elected to the American Society of Composers, Authors, and Publishers. She received the 1980 Handy Award as Traditional Female Blues Artist of the Year given by the Blues Foundation of Memphis, and in 1983, the New York City Mayor's Award of Honor for Arts and Culture and the B'nai B'rith Humanitarian Award. Alberta Hunter died in New York City on October 17, 1984.

—Nancy Elizabeth Fitch

Bibliography

Information about Alberta Hunter can be found in books about the blues era and its singers. These include Daphne Duval Harrison, *Black Pearls: Blues Queens of the 1920s* (New Brunswick, NJ: Rutgers University Press, 1988), pp. 198–217, which is an interesting collection of historical and critical vignettes of black women who were blues divas of the 1920s. The biography *Alberta Hunter: A Celebration in Blues* (New York: McGraw-Hill, 1987) is important due to the authors: journalist Frank C. Taylor writing with Gerald Cook, who not only was Hunter's accompanist for seven years, but also had accompanied cabaret singer "Bricktop" Smith and blues/jazz singer and actress Ethel Waters. Cook knew the people in the blues/jazz field and therefore was able to put Hunter's career and talent into context for the reader and for Cook as well. Hunter collaborated on the book.

HUNTER, CLEMENTINE [RUBEN, DUPREE] (c. 1885–1988), often referred to as the "Black Grandma Moses," was a painter from rural Louisiana who began her artistic career after years of agricultural and domestic work. In addition to its importance as folk art, Hunter's work documents the life of African Americans on Louisiana plantations.

Clementine Rubin was the oldest child of John Ruben, a Frenchman, and Mary Antoinette (Adams) Ruben. Her birth occurred in December 1885, or earlier, on the Hidden Plantation near Cloutierville, in the Cane Region of Louisiana. Her grandparents included an Irish horse trader, a Native American, and an ex-slave from Virginia. She grew up in a Creole culture speaking French and learned English only after her second marriage.

Unhappy at a school in Cloutierville, she quit school at an early age to work in the cotton fields and as a teenager moved to the Melrose Plantation near Natchitoches, where she resided the rest of her life. Her first husband was Charlie Dupree, with whom she had two children, Joseph and Cora. After his death in 1914, she married Emanuel Hunter in 1924 and had five more children, three who lived—Agnes, King, and Mary. Emanuel Hunter died in 1944.

Most of her life Clementine Hunter worked as a field laborer. Eventually, she became maid and cook for Mrs. Cammie Henry of Melrose Plantation. Since Mrs. Henry was particularly interested in local arts and crafts, she hired the French writer Francois Mignon as the curator of the plantation and collections. In the 1940s Alberta Kensey, a New Orleans artist visiting Melrose, left behind some brushes and oil paints. Hunter, in her sixties and ready to retire, used Kensey's supplies and taught herself to paint. She first painted on cardboard and brown paper and gave her pictures away. But soon, her paintings were discovered by Mignon and James Register, a writer and painter from Oklahoma visiting Melrose, who encouraged and publicized her work.

In 1949 Hunter held her first public exhibition at the New Orleans Arts and Crafts Gallery. Since then her paintings have been widely shown in galleries such as the Museum of American Folk Art, the New Orleans Museum of Art, the

Anderson-Hopkins Gallery, the Smithsonian Institution, and the Cleveland Museum of Art. Discussion of her work has been featured in popular magazines, and one of her paintings hangs in the Louisiana State Capitol. In 1986, Hunter received an honorary doctor of fine arts from Northwestern State University in Natchitoches, where her work had been displayed over 30 years earlier.

Hunter's paintings are stylized depictions of black rural life in Louisiana. She painted pictures of daily tasks such as picking cotton and washing clothes and of communal ceremonies such as baptisms and funerals. Rather than paint people and objects she knew, Hunter relied on her imagination and on the pictures she felt God gave her to paint.

Hunter died near her birthplace on January 1, 1988.

—Marilyn Dell Brady

Bibliography

The most extensive discussion of Hunter's life and work is James Wilson, *Clementine Hunter: American Folk Artist* (Grentna, LA: Pelican Publishing, 1988). This volume includes extensive information about Melrose Plantation and Hunter's early supporters plus an extensive bibliography of publications of and about her paintings. Numerous color plates of her paintings, photographs of Hunter, and her comments on her life and works make this book an extremely important source for understanding Hunter as a person and an artist. Hunter was interviewed by Radcliffe College for *The Black Women: Oral History Project* (Westport, CT: Meckler, 1990), edited by Ruth Edmonds Hill.

Discussion of Hunter and her paintings appears in Diana Petterson, "Clementine Hunter," *American Visions Magazine* 3 (1988): pp. 26–29; A.H. Jones, "The Centennial of Clementine Hunter," *Women's Art Journal* 8 (1987): 23–27; C. Kurt Dewhurst, Betty MacDowell, and Marsha MacDowell, *Artists in Aprons: Folk Art by American Women* (New York: Dutton for the Museum of American Folk Art, 1979); and Guy C. McElroy, Richard Powell, and Sharon Patton, *African-American Artists, 1880–1987* (Washington, DC: Smithsonian Institution Traveling Exhibition Service and the University of Washington Press, 1989).

HUNTER, JANE EDNA [HARRIS] (1882–1971), community center founder, was born on the Woodburn Plantation near Pendleton, South Carolina on December 13. She was the second of four children (Winston, Jane, Rosa, and Rebecca) born to Edward and Harriet (Milner) Harris. Edward, the son of a slave woman and the plantation overseer, named his first daughter for his English grandmother, Jane McCrary. The young Jane resembled her father, with light complexion and keen features.

During her childhood, Jane Harris had little opportunity for an education. Her father's death, when she was ten years old, forced the family to break up. She was sent away to become a domestic servant for a family of six. In 1896 she had the opportunity to work and attend school at Ferguson Academy in Abbeville, South

Carolina. Within a year following her graduation in 1900, she married Edward Hunter, a man 40 years her senior, a marriage that lasted only 15 months. Jane Hunter then moved to Charleston, South Carolina, where she attended the Cannon Street Hospital and Training School for Nurses. She received further training at Dixie Hospital and Training at Hampton Institute.

Hunter moved to Cleveland, Ohio, in 1905 and discovered that, in spite of her training, black nurses were not welcome. Furthermore, there was no decent place for single black women to live. This experience helped to determine the course of her life's work. She pledged to find a way to help young women like herself, who were flooding into the city to find work and a better way of life.

The Phillis Wheatley Association Home opened in a 23-room house in Cleveland's Central Area in 1913, with Jane Hunter as secretary of the board and manager. The home was mostly financed with contributions from wealthy white philanthropists, even though the effort to raise funds began with a small group of black women domestic workers. In return for their large contributions, Hunter promised white donors that the home would not only be a place of lodging, but would serve as a training school and referral service for domestic workers. In addition, she was forced to concede control over the composition of the board of trustees. Thus, for many years, although the Phillis Wheatley Association was maintained as an independent institution for black women, leaders of the all-white Young Women's Christian Association dominated the interracial board.

Jane Hunter served as director of the Association until 1946, when she retired. During her tenure she led the Association from its original site to a renovated building for 75 women in 1918, and finally into an all-new, $500,000, 11-story building in 1927. Services expanded to include a nursery school, music school, beauty school, two homemaking cottages, three extension branch facilities, a summer camp, gymnasium, and numerous classes and clubs. Beginning with the first home, the Phillis Wheatley dining room was a favorite meeting place for black professionals, as well as serving as one of the few eating establishments where interracial groups could meet. Further, Hunter used the Association as a model for self-help institutions and clubs for black women nationwide, under the auspices of the National Association of Colored Women, for which she served as a national and state officer.

Hunter received a law degree from Cleveland Law College and passed the Ohio Bar in 1925. She also received honorary degrees from Fisk, Allen, and Wilberforce universities, and Tuskegee Institute. In December 1947, she had reached the age of retirement. To conform to the Welfare Federation guidelines for eligible retirement benefits, she reluctantly submitted her resignation. In 1960, Hunter was confined to a rest home. At her death on January 18, 1971, she left the bulk of her estate of nearly a half-million dollars to the Phillis Wheatley Foundation to be used for scholarships for women. To date, the fund is still awarding monies.

—Adrienne Lash Jones

Bibliography

A *Nickel and a Prayer* (Cleveland: Eli Kani Press, 1940) is Jane Edna Hunter's autobiography. A biography entitled *Jane Edna Hunter: A Case Study of Black Leadership, 1905–1950*, by Adrienne Lash Jones is included as Volume 12, in Black Women in United States History Series (Brooklyn: Carlson, 1990).

Articles on Hunter can be found in Sadie Iola Daniels, *Women Builders*. (Washington, DC: Associated Press, 1931) Ruth Neely, *Women of Ohio* Vol. III (Columbus: S.J. Clarke, 1967); and Russell Davis, *Memorable Negroes in Cleveland's Past* (Cleveland: Western Reserve Historical Society, 1964). The Manuscript Collection at Western Reserve Historical Society has papers of both the Phillis Wheatley Association and Jane Edna Hunter. Additional information on Cleveland's black community is found in Kenneth Kusmer's *A Ghetto Takes Shape: Black Cleveland, 1870–1930* (Urbana: University of Illinois Press, 1978).

HUNTON, ADDIE WAITES (1875–1943), clubwoman, author, and
community organizer, was born June 11 in Norfolk, Virginia, the eldest child of Jesse and Adelina (Waites) Hunton. Her father owned a wholesale oyster and shipping business, co-owned a black amusement park, and co-founded the Negro Elks Improved Benevolent Protection Order of Elks of the World (IBPOEW). Hunton's mother died when Hunton was a child. Following her mother's death, Hunton went to Boston, where a maternal aunt reared her. In Boston, Hunton attended the Boston Girls Latin School. After finishing high school, she attended a Spencerian business college in Philadelphia. Next, Hunton took a teaching job in Normal, Alabama, at a vocational school, which would later become Alabama Agricultural and Mechanical College.

In 1893 Hunton married William Alphaeus Hunton in Norfolk, Virginia. Her husband, who descended from a Virginia slave/emigrant, had come to Norfolk in 1888 to serve as secretary of the YMCA for black youth. He had lived previously in Chatham, Ontario. In 1891, when invited by the International Committee of the YMCA, William Alphaeus Hunton became administrative secretary of the Colored Men's Department of the International Committee.

The couple moved to Atlanta in 1899 and then to Brooklyn in 1906. The Huntons had four children. The first son, named William Alphaeus Hunton, Jr., and the first daughter both died as children. Their second son, also named William Alphaeus Hunton, Jr., became the major founder and secretary of the Council on African Affairs, an organization established to help black Americans seek clarity about their African heritage and understand the similar struggles of African Americans and Africans. The Huntons' second daughter was named Eunice Hunton Carter.

Because her husband traveled frequently to YMCA conferences, Addie Hunton was well known among YMCA and YWCA members. In 1907 the national board of YWCA appointed her secretary for work among black students. Serving in this capacity, she toured the South as well as the Midwest in the winter of 1907–1908. She later traveled to Switzerland and Strasbourg with her children. While in Europe, she attended classes at Kaiser Wilhelm University. She returned to the United States in 1910.

Brooklyn remained the family's home, except for Hunton's sojourns to Europe in 1910 and during World War I and a brief move to Saranac, New York, in 1914, when Hunton's husband was suffering from tuberculosis. The family returned to Brooklyn in 1916 following Mr. Hunton's death. Hunton later authored the book *William Alphaeus Hunton* (1938) in honor of her husband.

At the onset of World War I, Hunton volunteered for the YMCA. She traveled to France in June 1918 as one of 3 black women to work with 200,000 black men. Her assignment at St. Nazaire, a supply and transport center, challenged her to offer more than the standard canteen and movies offered at most YMCA huts. Hunton met this challenge by adding a literacy course and a popular Sunday evening discussion program for the black servicemen.

Her second assignment in France, following a serious illness, took Hunton to Aix-les-Bains in southern France in January 1919. At this new post, Hunton aided in establishing a complete range of activities, including religious, educational, athletic, and cultural events, for black troops who came through for weeklong breaks from the war.

In May 1919 Hunton began working at the Romagne Military Cemetery near Verdun. This assignment proved the most trying, as Hunton had to assist black troops already enduring racial discrimination and undertaking the task of burying American soldiers killed in action at the Meuse-Argonne. Working with troops on their eventual trip home, Hunton completed her final six weeks for the YMCA in Brest in the fall of 1919.

Upon returning to the United States, Hunton co-authored *Two Colored Women with the American Expeditionary Forces* (1920) with another YMCA volunteer, Kathryn M. Johnson. Their book exposes not only the racial discrimination endured by black troops during World War I, but also the discrimination perpetrated by white YMCA workers against Hunton and Johnson.

Following her career as a YMCA volunteer, Hunton went on to serve, sometimes as an officer, on several national boards, councils, and organizations: the Council on Colored Work of the YWCA National Board, the International Council of the Women of Darker Races (president), the Empire State Federation of Women's Clubs, the NAACP (vice president and field secretary). She also served as parliamentarian for the National Association of Colored Women. As a delegate from the Women's League of Richmond, Virginia, she attended the NACW's founding convention in Boston in 1895. She served as a national organizer for the NACW from 1906 to 1910.

In 1926 Hunton traveled to Haiti to observe the U.S. occupation of this country. Hunton did so as a member of a six-woman committee for the Women's International League for Peace and Freedom. The committee's observations and findings were published in the book *Occupied Haiti*, which called for the U.S. Government to withdraw from Haiti and reestablish the country's self-governance. Hunton co-authored a chapter on race relations for this source with the book's editor Emily Greene Balch.

In 1927 Hunton served as an organizer for the Fourth Pan-African Congress held in New York. She was also president of Circle for Peace, a supporter of women's rights, a suffragette, and a noted speaker. Her last public speaking engagement was at the New York World's Fair, where Hunton presided over a ceremony honoring important black women.

Hunton died as a result of diabetes in Brooklyn on June 21, 1943. She is buried in Brooklyn's Cypress Hills Cemetery.

—Faye A. Chadwell

Bibliography

Addie Hunton's books *Two Colored Women with the American Expeditionary Forces* and *William Alphaeus Hunton* are excellent chronicles of her work and career. Two other sources for information on Hunton are Jean Blackwell Hutson's articles in *The Dictionary of American Negro Biography* and in *Notable American Women, 1607–1950*. In addition Anna V. Rice's *History of the World's YWCA* is a source to be consulted as are *Lifting as They Climb*, edited by Elizabeth Davis; *Fifty Years of Association Work among Young Women*, edited by Elizabeth Wilson; *Who's Who of the Colored Race*, edited by Frank Lincoln Mather. A final source is the article "William Alphaeus Hunton: His Roots in Black America," about Hunton's son. Authored by George B. Murphy, Jr., this article is in *Freedomways*.

Works by Addie D. Waites Hunton

William Alphaeus Hunton: A Pioneer Prophet of Young Men. New York: Association Press, 1938.

With Kathryn Johnson. *Two Colored Women with the American Expeditionary Forces*. Brooklyn: Brooklyn Eagle Press, 1920.

With Emily Greene Balch. "Racial Relations," in *Occupied Haiti*, edited by Emily Greene Balch, pp. 113–121. New York: Writers Publishing Co., 1927.

Secondary Sources

Davis, Elizabeth L., ed. *Lifting as They Climb*. Washington: NACW, 1933.

Hutson, Jean Blackwell. "Addie D. Waites Hunton," in *Dictionary of American Negro Biography*, edited by Rayford W. Logan and Michael R. Winston, pp. 337–338. New York: Norton, 1982.

———. "Addie D. Waites Hunton," in *Notable American Women, 1607–1950: A Biographical Dictionary*, edited by Edward T. James, pp. 240–241. Cambridge, MA: Belknap Press, 1971.

Malther, Frank Lincoln. *Who's Who of the Colored Race*. Chicago, 1915.

Murphy, George B. "William Alphaeus Hunton: His Roots in Black America," *Freedomways* 10:3 (1970): 249–253.

Rice, Anna V. *History of the World's YWCA.* New York: Woman's Press, 1948.

Wilson, Elizabeth. *Fifty Years of Association Work among Young Women.* New York: National Board of the YWCA, 1916.

HURSTON, ZORA NEALE (1891–1960), born in the small all-black town of Eatonville, Florida, was to become, for 30 years, the most prolific African-American female author in the United States. Despite this, Hurston and her work drifted into obscurity for almost 30 years until her rediscovery in the 1970s. Much of this neglect can be attributed to the controversy that always seemed to surround this independent and free-spirited woman.

Although her birth year has often been given as 1901, it now seems indubitable that the correct date was January 7, 1891. Two crucial forces were to have an early and profound affect on Hurston's life and work. The first was Eatonville, a town populated and governed by African Americans. Eatonville was a most unusual town; an idyllically sheltered world where Hurston was both protected from racial prejudice and nourished in rich sources for African-American cultural traditions. According to many, the most significant force during her childhood was her mother, Lucy, a woman who encouraged the indomitable spirit of her favorite offspring. Lucy Hurston died when her daughter was nine years old

Both of these forces combined to produce a controversial, independent, outspoken, eccentric, and racially proud woman. One who, throughout her career, chose to write about the positive side of black Americans. If Zora Neale Hurston never depicted that experience as tragic, it was because she did not perceive it that way. Instead she celebrated the great distinctiveness of black cultural life and saw it as clearly superior to the pallid accomplishments of white society. This was expressed most vividly in her controversial essay "How It Feels to Be Colored Me." Here was a woman determined to write about black life apart from Jim Crow laws and their injustices. American racism was simply not her concern. Instead she focused on the world of her people—a people unaware of being a problem. By the 1940s this was terribly out of vogue.

In a way her career began with her father's remarriage. Hurston and her stepmother never got along, and she lived with other relatives for awhile in Jacksonville, Florida. After working as a domestic, she joined a Gilbert and Sullivan traveling dramatic troupe and labored as a maid and wardrobe girl. She left this employment at age 26 and began attending classes at Morgan Academy, a division of what today is Morgan State University in Baltimore. Hurston relocated to Washington, DC, where, for the next seven years, she attended Howard University. Supporting herself in a variety of menial occupations, she became part of a group of young artists/intellectuals who centered around Alain Locke and Montgomery Gregory, exponents of the Harlem Renaissance. Accepted as a member of Stylus, the campus literary club, Hurston published for the first time—a short story entitled "John Redding Goes to Sea"—in 1921.

Hurston moved to New York City in 1925. *Opportunity* magazine had just published her short story "Drenched in Light." The editor, Charles S. Johnson, helped her and other promising young African-American writers. Very quickly Hurston became one of the members of the Harlem Renaissance. She was able to attend Barnard College on a scholarship and became the favorite student of the nation's foremost anthropologist, Franz Boas. She completed her undergraduate work at Barnard in 1927, and in February, returned to Florida to collect black folklore. In May she married Herbert Sheen, the second of her believed three husbands. This, like all of her marriages, ended in divorce.

Hurston was awarded a Julius Rosenwald Fellowship in 1934 for the further collection of folklore. Her efforts were concentrated on Florida, New Orleans, Jamaica, Haiti, and the Bahamas. The research resulted in two articles and eventually two books of folklore, *Mules and Men* (1935) and *Tell My Horse* (1938).

During the 1930s her two best novels, *Jonah's Gourd Vine* (1934) and, her masterpiece, *Their Eyes Were Watching God* (1937), were published. Her career produced seven books and more than fifty shorter works ranging from autobiography to folklore to music and mythology.

From the outbreak of World War II, her fortunes deteriorated until her death of heart disease (January 18, 1960) as a penniless inmate at the Saint Lucie County Welfare Home. Perhaps her most controversial act was a public disavowal of the 1954 *Brown vs. Topeka Board of Education* decision. True to her cultural philosophy, she believed the decision implied the inferiority of black students, teachers, and the schools of the South. Proud to the end, she died alone, and her grave remained unmarked until novelist Alice Walker located it in an overgrown Fort Pierce, Florida, cemetery. Thereafter, Walker's 1975 article "In Search of Zora Neale Hurston," in *Ms.* magazine revived interest in one of the foremost writers of the Harlem Renaissance.

—Donna Van Raaphorst

Bibliography

To date the single most important volume on Hurston is Robert E. Hemenway's *Zora Neale Hurston: A Literary Biography* (Urbana, IL: University of Illinois Press, 1978), which contains the most definitive bibliography on Hurston and her collected works. Of great value is S.P. Fullinwider's provocative interpretation of twentieth-century African-American thought, including a chapter on Hurston and other writers of the Harlem Renaissance, *The Mind and Mood of Black America* (Homewood, IL: Dorsey Press, 1969); Martin Fletcher's *Our Great Americans* (New York: Gamma Corporation, 1953); and Harry Warfel's *American Novelists of Today* (New York: American Book, 1951). Her autobiography, *Dust Tracks on a Road*, has recently been reissued by Harper Perennial in the paperback series edited by Henry Louis Gates, Jr., who has also included Hurston in his book, *Bearing Witness* (New York: Pantheon,

1991). Gwendolyn Cherry's *Portraits in Color* (New York: Pageant, 1962) includes a biographical sketch and bibliography.

All of the following contain extremely worthwhile introductory sections on the author and her respective work: Zora Neale Hurston, *The Sanctified Church: The Folklore Writings of Zora Neale Hurston*, Introduction by Toni Cade Bambara (Berkeley, CA: Turtle Island, 1981); Zora Neale Hurston, *Jonah's Gourd Vine: A Novel*, Introduction by Rita Dove (Philadelphia: Lippincott, 1934). Zora Neale Hurston, *Moses Man of the Mountain*, Introduction by Blyden Jackson (Philadelphia: Lippincott, 1939. Reprint. Urbana: University of Illinois Press, 1984); Alice Walker, ed., *I Love Myself When I Am Laughing*, Introduction by Mary Helen Washington (New York: Feminist Press, 1979); Zora Neale Hurston, *Their Eyes Were Watching God*, Introduction by Shirley Anne Williams (Philadelphia: Lippincott, 1937. Reprint. Urbana: University of Illinois Press, 1978).

J

JACKSON, ELIZA BELLE [MITCHELL] (1848–1942) spent most of her life in educational, club, and business leadership roles among African-American women. Though born during slavery, she overcame its oppression and earned herself a respected position among many of Kentucky's outstanding African Americans.

Eliza Belle Mitchell was born in Danville, Kentucky, on December 31. She has been described as being European in appearance, with straight hair and light skin. Some discrepancy exists regarding her racial heritage. According to Burnside (1988), E. Belle had a white father and an African-American mother who were married. Her great granddaughter Myrtle Mitchell, however, indicated in an interview (1991) that both E. Belle's parents were black, even though her father was the son of the plantation owner and her mother was his slave. E. Belle's parents, Mary and Monroe Mitchell, provided her a strong religious foundation in the Methodist church. She received her early education from free blacks in a school in Danville. Her parents instilled within her the desire to use her abilities to improve life for herself and other African Americans.

E. Belle first attracted public attention in 1865 when only age 18. During the Civil War, John G. Fee invited E. Belle to assist him in teaching the thousands of black soldiers and their families who had gathered at Camp Nelson seeking their freedom. (Fee 1891). The American Missionary Association had employed Fee as superintendent of the Union Army's training station. In hiring E. Belle, Fee underestimated the limits of the missionaries, Christianity as his experiment in interracial cooperation did not go as intended. While Fee was away from the camp, E. Belle was fired. The white missionaries responsible for her dismissal indicated that they did not mind her teaching, but objected to her eating and living in the same area with them (Burnside 1988; Sears 1988).

Upon leaving Camp Nelson, E. Belle Mitchell went to Lexington, Kentucky, where she taught in a school organized by the American Missionary Association. In 1867 she entered Berea College, which was founded by Fee. She left Berea before graduating to marry a prominent Lexington businessman, Jordan C. Jackson, in 1873.

According to Booker T. Washington (Washington 1907), Jordan owned the best livery stable in Lexington. In addition, Jordan owned a funeral business, had been a banker, a politician, an author, and an advocate for education. He also was a spokesman for the committee that secured funding from the legislature to establish the State Normal School for Negroes (now called Kentucky State University) and was elected trustee at Wilberforce University and Berea College. They had two children, a daughter, Minnie, and an adopted son, Henry Mitchell. E. Belle Jackson was also a businesswoman, co-owning a millinery business in downtown Lexington and supporting her husband in his business enterprises. (Benjamin 1899; Harris 1908; Johnson 1897).

During the late 1800s and early 1900s, Jackson was actively involved in the colored women's club movement. The women's clubs focused on raising the cultural, intellectual, and educational status of the black family. Jackson was elected honorary president of the Kentucky Association of Colored Women. The focus of all of her philanthropic activities was the elevation of her race, especially through the proper home training of children.

Her most notable contributions were in the area of education. She was certainly one of the earliest black teachers documented in Kentucky and was a member of the Kentucky Negro Education Association. She served as a charter member of the Ladies Hall, a colored educational center in downtown Lexington, and was instrumental in establishing the Phillis Wheatley branch of the YWCA (Fouse 1918; Harris 1908).

Her most enduring contribution, however, was the founding of the Colored Orphans Industrial Home. The history of the Home is truly a story of remarkable achievements despite almost insurmountable obstacles. Purchased in 1892 for $4,000 by a small group of African-American women led by Jackson, the Home served as a monument to the colored race. In addition to providing food, shelter, and clothing to hundreds of destitute children, the Home had a reputable educational program. The educational program was modeled after that of Tuskegee Institute and included training in areas such as cooking, sewing, chair caning, shoemaking, and blacksmithing. During its early development, the Home also existed to meet the diverse needs of the African-American community and served as an "old folks home," a hospital, and a lending institution. The facility still serves the community almost 100 years after its founding as a testimonial to their labors.

Jackson's death in October 1942 marked the end of a life of service to others. Jackson lies in an unmarked grave in Lexington, Kentucky, beside the husband she dearly loved, who preceded her in death. The community lost a zealous, enthusiastic, hard-working, woman filled with missionary spirit. More important, her life and contributions reflect what black women have always had to do— remove obstacles to open opportunities for the race.

—Lauretta F. Byars

Bibliography

Primary sources on E. Belle Mitchell Jackson are in the Special Collections Division of the University of Kentucky. Some of these sources include:

Benjamin, R.C.O. *Negro Business Directory Fair Souvenir for Lexington, Ky*. Lexington, KY: n.p., 1899.

Burnside, Jacqueline Grisby. "Black Symbols: Extraordinary Achievements by Ordinary Women," in *Appalachian Heritage, A Magazine of Southern Appalachian Life and Culture* (Summer, 1987). Article discusses three Berea College Alumnae who made extraordinary achievements during early the 1890s.

———— "Philanthropists and Politicians: A Sociological Profile of Berea College, 1855–1908. Doctoral dissertation, Yale University, 1988. A sociological analysis of Berea College's early history.

Colored Orphan Industrial Home. 1892–1980s. Special Collections University of Kentucky. Collection contains minutes records, annual reports, letters, and other correspondence. Most thorough account of the Home available.

Fee, John G. *Autobiography of John G. Fee, Berea, Kentucky*. Chicago: National Christian Association, 1891.

Fouse Family Papers. Special Collections, University of Kentucky, Lexington. Contains photographs, programs, minutes and notes of social and educational activities involving African Americans, 1918–1951.

Harris, Lawrence. *The Negro Population of Lexington in the Professions, Business, Education and Religion*. Lexington, KY: L. Harris, 1908. (1908 is crossed out and 1907 is written in ink.)

Johnson, W.D. *Biographical Sketches of Prominent Negro Men and Women in Kentucky*. Lexington, KY: Standard Printing, 1987. Fascinating sketches of selected African Americans during late 1890s documenting their background, education employment, and community service.

Mitchell, Myrtle Y. Interview with great granddaughter. Lexington, Kentucky, March, 1991.

Sears, Richard. *Practical Recognition of the Brotherhood of Man*. Berea: Berea College Press, 1986. A history of Berea College.

Washington, Booker T. *The Negro in Business*. Boston: Hertel, Jenkins and Co., 1907. Provides biographical information on selected African Americans who had established businesses. Jordan C. Jackson, E. Belle's husband, is included.

JACKSON, MAHALIA (1911–1972), the "Queen of the Gospel Song," was responsible for popularizing religious/gospel music worldwide. Born to deeply religious parents on October 26 in New Orleans, Louisiana, Mahalia Jackson was the third of six children. Her father, a stevedore, porter, and Sunday preacher, discouraged his children from becoming entertainers, and often forbade them from listening to anything but "sacred music." Jackson, however, already had sisters in vaudeville and the theater, and was heavily influenced by Bessie Smith and Ida Cox, whose performance she would clandestinely attend. She often went to houses of friends to listen to popular singers' music.

Although restricted in her access to the blues, Jackson gained singing experience as a child singing in her father's church choir. She left school after the eighth grade to work as a laundress and maid. In 1928, at age 16, Jackson moved to Chicago, where she worked as a maid and date packer, saving her money in hopes of fulfilling her dream of becoming a nurse or starting her own beauty school. She joined the Salem Baptist Church and sang in the choir. Soon Jackson earned enough money to study cosmetology, and open up her beauty school, and later a flower shop.

In the mid-1930s she began what became a 14-year association with Thomas A. Dorsey, touring and promoting her songs. Her big break came in 1934, after signing with Decca Records. She recorded "God Gonna Separate the Wheat from the Tares," and later in 1945, "Move on up a Little Higher," on the Apollo label, which catapulted her to national fame—selling over a million copies. Though Jackson, a woman of great piety, later became very critical of being identified with secular music, it was difficult for her to hide the Bessie Smith influence in her songs. Many in the jazz world began to take note of what Langston Hughes called a "new kind of rhythmical Negro singing."

Her fame spread as far as Europe, where she was praised as being the greatest gospel singer the world had ever known. In 1949 her "Let the Power of the Holy Ghost Fall on Me" won her the French Academy's Grand Prix du Disque. In 1950 her first concert at Carnegie Hall sold out. She appeared in concert halls throughout Europe, taking Denmark by storm with "Silent Night," rated as a phenomenal success. In September 1954 Jackson began her own weekly radio program called "Mahalia," where she was heard every Sunday evening over the CBS radio network. She also began a recording contract with Columbia Records. Some of her most memorable albums were *Mahalia Jackson*, *Sweet Little Jesus Boy*, *Bless This House*, and *The World's Greatest Gospel Singer*, saving Columbia Records from sure bankruptcy.

Besides numerous awards, honors, and sold out performances, Jackson appeared singing gospel music in the movie *Jazz on a Summer's Day*. During the later years of Jackson's life, she became inseparable from the ongoing civil rights movement, often using her voice as a means of bridging the bitter world between blacks and whites. On January 27, 1972, Mahalia Jackson died in Chicago of heart failure, but is still loved by millions.

—Vivian Gartley-Hindrew

Bibliography

Berendt, E. Joachim. *The Jazz Book: From Ragtime and Beyond*. Westport, CT: Lawrence Hill, 1981.

"Born to Sing," *Newsweek* 43:98 (February 22, 1954).

Case, Brian, and Stan Britt. *The Illustrated Encyclopedia of Jazz*. New York: Harmony Books, 1978.

Current Biography. New York: Wilson, 1957.

Ellison, Ralph. "As the Spirit Moves Mahalia," *Saturday Review* 41:41 (September 27, 1958).

"Gospel Queen Mahalia," *Life* 37 (November 29, 1954): 63–66.

Hentoff, Nat. "You Can Still Hear Her Voice When the Music Stops," *Reporter* 16 (June 27, 1957): 34–36.

JACKSON, MAY [HOWARD] (1877–1931), teacher and sculptor, was born in Philadelphia, Pennsylvania, to Floarda Howard and Sallie Durham.

Jackson began her education in the public schools of Philadelphia. She later graduated from Professor J. Liberty Tadd's Art School. She then became the first black woman to win a scholarship to the Pennsylvania Academy of Fine Arts, where she studied for four years and graduated in 1899.

In 1902 May Howard married William T.S. Jackson of Washington, DC. She then moved to Washington, where her husband was a mathematics teacher and, eventually, a high school principal. They lived at 1816 Sixteenth Street, NW, for many years, where Jackson had her own studio.

As a teacher, May Howard Jackson contributed much to the field of sculpture. In Washington, DC, Jackson was asked to join Howard University's Art Department, where she taught modeling for many years. Additionally, Sargent Johnson, her husband's orphaned nephew, spent part of his youth in Jackson's household; he may first have been introduced to art through her. He later became one of the twentieth century's most important sculptors.

Artistically, May Howard Jackson was naturally talented and a gifted sculptor. Yet, she faced some severe drawbacks. First, she chose to rely solely on her American training as a sculptor rather than pursue her training in Europe. In this, she was well ahead of her time. Second, Jackson suffered from the severe lack of exhibition outlets for black artists in her time. Third, after 1914 Jackson turned her skills from portrait busts to thematic sculptures that focused on portraying mulattos and the individual differences among black people. This helped to overcome many of the stereotypical portrayals of black people in art. Her use of these racial themes resulted in the general rejection of her work though, and she became withdrawn and cynical.

May Howard Jackson's sculpture is a lasting tribute to her talent. Portrait busts were Jackson's forte. Among her most famous works are busts of Dean Kelly Miller of Howard University, Paul Laurence Dunbar, W.E.B. Du Bois, and the Reverend Francis J. Grimké. Although Jackson was never recognized as a great thematic sculptor, *Mulatto Mother and Her Child*, *Head of a Child*, and *Bust of a Young Woman* are three of her best known thematic works.

Jackson's work was exhibited and did win praise. In 1912 her bust of the Reverend Francis J. Grimké was exhibited and highly praised at the Veerhoff Gallery in Washington DC. She had subsequent exhibitions in 1913 at the Emancipation Exhibition, in 1915 at the Corcoran Art Gallery, and in 1916 at the National Academy of Design. Jackson's *Mulatto Mother and Her Child* and *Head of a Child* were shown in a solo exhibition in 1916 at the Veerhoff Gallery and also won much critical attention. In 1928 Jackson won the Harmon Foundation's bronze award for her bust of Dean Kelly Miller.

Although May Howard Jackson never achieved complete success, her death in Long Beach on Long Island, New York, on July 12, 1931, ended the career of one of the most gifted woman sculptors.

—Lisa M. Reynolds Abu-Raad

Bibliography

Contemporary writings on May Howard Jackson can be found in *The Crisis* 4:67 (June 1912), 34:231 (September 1927), and 38:351 (October 1931). May Howard Jackson's life has also been examined in Harry A. Ploski and James Williams, eds., *The Negro Almanac: A Reference Work on the Afro-American* (New York: Wiley, 1983). Other biographical citations are contained in Marianna W. Davis, ed., *Contributions of Black Women to America* (Columbia, SC: Kenday, 1982); in Charlotte Streifer Rubinstein, *American Women Sculptors: A History of Women Working in Three Dimensions* (Boston: G.K. Hall, 1990); and in Jessie Carney Smith, ed., *Notable Black American Women* (Detroit: Gale, 1992).

JACKSON, REBECCA [COX] (1795–1871), preacher, Shaker eldress, and founder of a black Shaker community, was born just outside of Philadelphia, Pennsylvania, a free woman. Nothing is known of her father. Her mother was married at least twice and died in 1808. Jackson was a seamstress and married when she began her public speaking career.

There are no details of Jackson's life between 1808 and 1830. However, it is known that during this period she married Samuel S. Jackson and apparently had no children. The couple lived in her brother's (the Reverend Joseph Cox) house. The Reverend Cox was an active participant in the affairs of Bethel African Methodist Episcopal (AME) Church of Philadelphia. As an active participant in the life of the church, Jackson participated in Holiness praying bands and her visionary and supernatural gifts emerged.

Jackson experienced a spiritual conversion during a thunderstorm in July 1830 at age 35. She eventually turned to celibacy and separated from her husband in 1836. Jackson led a covenant meeting with her spiritual sister Mary Peterson, wife of AME preacher Daniel Peterson. These meetings drew large crowds and led to the charge that she was acting improperly for a woman. In 1837, when she was charged with heresy, Jackson demanded a formal, interdenominational trial in her home. She was refused the trial and apparently broke all ties with her brother and the AME church.

By 1840 she was associated with a group of predominantly white religious Perfectionists in the Albany, New York, area. This group eventually joined the Shaker community at nearby Watervliet. From 1843 on, Jackson was completely committed to the Shakers. She was recognized as a prophet and formally joined the Watervliet community in 1847 with Rebecca Perot, another black woman. They became known as "the two Rebeccas" in Shaker documents.

Jackson became dissatisfied with Shaker efforts to reach out to blacks. Jackson and Perot, estranged from the Watervliet community, left in 1851 to found a Shaker community among the blacks in Philadelphia. Jackson participated in spiritualistic circles and trained herself to act as a medium.

She ended her exile from Watervliet and returned when the mission to Philadelphia failed. Jackson remained there for one year and eventually secured the blessing of the eldress to attempt another mission to Philadelphia in 1858. She held her first solemn meeting as a Shaker eldress in April 1859. Little is known of what happened to Jackson, Perot, or the small black Shaker community after 1858. After her death in 1871, the Philadelphia Shaker community survived for nearly 40 years, which were headed by Perot, who took the name Mother Rebecca Jackson.

—Emilie M. Townes

Bibliography

Few sources detail the life of Rebecca Jackson. Those that provide biographical detail include the following:

Humez, Jean McMahon, ed. *Gifts of Power: The Writings of Rebecca Jackson, Black Visionary, Shaker Eldress.* Amherst: University of Massachusetts, 1981.

Walker, Alice. "Gifts of Power: The Writings of Rebecca Jackson," in *In Search of Our Mothers' Gardens: Womanist Prose.* New York: Harcourt, Brace, Jovanovich, 1984.

JACOBS, HARRIET [LINDA BRENT, PSEUD.] (1813–1897), slave narrator, reformer, antislavery activist, and Civil War and Reconstruction relief worker, was born into slavery in Edenton, North Carolina. Harriet Ann Jacobs's major contribution is her narrative *Incidents in the Life of a Slave Girl: Written by Herself* (1861), the most comprehensive antebellum autobiography by an African-American woman. *Incidents* is a first-person account of the sexual oppression and struggle for freedom of Jacobs's pseudonymous narrator Linda Brent. Jacobs is also important for her relief work with black Civil War refugees in Alexandria, Virginia, and Savannah, Georgia.

In *Incidents*, Jacobs tells the story of her life in the South as slave and as fugitive, and of her life as a fugitive slave in the North; she explains that, at age six, she was taught to sew and to read by her first mistress; then, breaking the taboos forbidding women to discuss their sexuality, describes the abuse by her licentious master and of becoming sexually involved with a neighboring white man in an attempt to prevent her master from forcing her into concubinage. This involvement produced her two children, Joseph (b. 1829?) and Louisa Matilda (b. 1833). Also in *Incidents* her 1835 runaway from her master and her seven years in hiding in a tiny crawlspace in her grandmother's Edenton home is described. Further, she describes her 1842 escape north, her reunion with her children in New York City, her move to Rochester, New York, her friendships with the antislavery circle around Frederick Douglass's newspaper *The North Star*, the efforts of slave hunters to seize her after passage of the 1850 Fugitive Slave Law, and finally, the purchase by her employer that freed her and her children.

While she was producing this text, Jacobs wrote a series of informal letters to her Quaker feminist-abolitionist friend Amy Post. Readers of these letters can follow the history of her slave narrative from its inception through its composition and completion to its publication.

Although *Incidents* appeared anonymously, from the first, Jacobs's name was connected with her book; only in the twentieth century were its authorship and its autobiographical status disputed. *Incidents* made Jacobs's name known among northern abolitionists. After the firing on Fort Sumter, she used her new-found celebrity to collect money and supplies for the "contraband"—black refugees crowding behind the lines of the Union Army in Washington, DC, Alexandria, Virginia, and Savannah, Georgia.

With the support of northern groups, Jacobs now launched a new career working among the refugees. In 1863 she and her daughter moved to Alexandria, where they supplied emergency relief, organized primary medical care, and established the Jacobs Free School—black led and black taught—for the black refugees. In 1865 the mother and daughter moved to Savannah, where they continued their work. In 1868 they sailed to England (where her book had appeared as *The Deeper Wrong: Incidents in the Life of a Slave Girl Written by Herself* (1862), and successfully raised money for a home for Savannah's black orphans and aged.

In the face of the increasing antiblack violence in the South, however, Jacobs and her daughter retreated north. They lived in Massachusetts, then in Washington, DC, where Jacobs continued to work among the destitute freed people and her daughter worked in the newly established "colored schools" and, later, at Howard University. In 1896 when the National Association of Colored Women held its organizing meetings in Washington, apparently, Louisa M. Jacobs was present. The following spring, Harriet Jacobs died at her Washington home. She is buried in Mount Auburn Cemetery, Cambridge, Massachusetts.

—Jean Fagan Yellin

Bibliography

In the United States, Harriet Jacobs's slave narrative was entitled *Incidents in the Life of a Slave Girl: Written by Herself* (1861); in England, it was called *The Deeper Wrong: Incidents in the Life of a Slave Girl Written by Herself* (1862). The standard edition of *Incidents*, edited by Jean Fagan Yellin, was published by Harvard University Press in 1987; this edition, which includes a scholarly introduction, annotates Jacobs's text with information about the people, places, and events she describes pseudonymously. In addition, it includes some of Jacobs's correspondence, both published and unpublished, as well as her portrait and maps and diagrams of geographical settings she describes. Manuscript sources for the study of Harriet Jacobs include materials among the Isaac and Amy Post Family Papers, Department of Rare Books, Manuscripts, and Archives, University of Rochester Library; the Boston Public Library; the Sydney Howard Gay Papers, Rare Book and Manuscript Library, Columbia University; the Sophia Smith Collection, Smith College; and the Norcom Family Papers, North Carolina State Archives.

Commentaries on Jacobs include William C. Andrews, *To Tell a Free Story: The First Century of Afro-American Autobiography* (Bloomington: Indiana University Press, 1986); Joanne Braxton, "Harriet Jacobs' Incidents in the Life of a Slave Girl: The Re-Definition of the Slave Narrative Genre," *Massachusetts Review* 27 (1986): 379–387; Hazel Carby, *Reconstructing Womanhood: The Emergence of the Afro-American Woman Novelist* (New York: Oxford University Press, 1987); Charles T. Davis and Henry Louis Gates, Jr., eds., *The Slave's Narrative* (New York: Oxford University Press, 1985); Frances Smith Foster, "In Respect to Females: Differences in the Portrayals of Women by Male and Female Narrators," *Black American Literature Forum* 15 (1981): 66–70; Frances Smith Foster, *Witnessing Slavery: The Development of Ante-Bellum Slave Narratives* (Westport, CT: Greenwood, 1979); Elizabeth Fox-Genovese, *Within the Plantation Household: Black and White Women of the Old South* (Chapel Hill: University of North Carolina Press, 1988); Bell Hooks, *Feminist Theory: From Margin to Center* (Boston: South End Press, 1984); John Sekora and Darwin T. Turner, eds., *The Art of Slave Narrative* (Macomb: Western Illinois University Press, 1982); Valerie Smith, *Narrative Authority in Modern Afro-American Fiction* (Cambridge: Harvard University Press, 1979); Mary Helen Washington, "Meditation on History: The Slave Narrative of Linda Brent," in *Invented Lives: Narratives of Black Women, 1860–1960* (New York: Doubleday, 1987). The documentary materials on Jacobs's authorship and on her experiences are presented in Jean Fagan Yellin's "Introduction" and "Notes" of the standard edition of *Incidents*, and in her "Text and Contexts of Harriet Jacobs's *Incidents in the Life of a Slave Girl: Written by Herself*," in Davis and Gates; her "Profile: Harriet Ann Jacobs" in *Legacy* 5 (1988): 55–61; her "Written by Herself: Harriet Jacobs's Slave Narrative," *American Literature* 53 (1981): 479–486.

JAMISON, JUDITH (b. 1944), dancer and choreographer, was born in Philadelphia on May 10 to John Jamison, a steelworker, and Tessie Jamison, a teacher and homemaker. Judith Jamison began dance lessons at age six at the Judimar School of Dance studying tap, acrobatic, jazz and primitive styles, and ballet. Her childhood was rich with a variety of other activities including piano lessons, theater work, and membership in the Bethel African Methodist Episcopal Church.

After graduating from high school, Jamison enrolled as a psychology major at Fisk University in Nashville, but, having decided to pursue a career in dance, transferred to the Philadelphia Dance Academy (now the University of the Arts). She supplemented her classes with studies in dance history, the Lester Horton technique, and Labanotation (a system of dance symbols based on movement of specific body parts).

In 1964 Jamison was invited by Agnes de Mille to dance in the premiere of her new ballet *The Four Marys* at New York's Lincoln Center. She made her debut, in 1965, with the Alvin Ailey Dance Company (now the Alvin Ailey American Dance Theater), the most successful racially integrated professional dance company in the world. She became Ailey's leading dancer, as well as appearing as guest artist with numerous other American and European companies. In 1980 Jamison starred in the Broadway musical *Sophisticated Ladies*. She began to experiment with choreography, premiering her first work, *Divining*, in 1984. Her own 12-member company, the Jamison Project, made its debut in 1988. With Ailey's death in 1989, Jamison assumed the position of director and choreographer of his company and its school of over 3,000 students.

The many honors and awards received by Jamison include *Dance* Magazine Citation, 1972; Key to New York City, 1976; Harvard University Distinguished Service Award, 1982; and Mayor of New York City Distinguished Service Award, 1982.

—Juanita Karpf

Bibliography

Detailed information about Jamison's life and career through 1981 can be found in Olga Maynards, *Judith Jamison, Aspects of a Dancer* (New York: Doubleday, 1982).

The history of black Philadelphia's dance companies, such as the Judimar School of Dance where Jamison studied as a child, receives thorough coverage in Melanye White-Dixon, "Marion Cuyet: Visionary of Dance Education in Black Philadelphia," PhD dissertation, Temple University (1987); and in the article by the same author representing a continuation of her research, "The Legacy of Black Philadelphia's Dance Institutions and the Educators Who Built the Tradition," *Dance Research Journal* 23:1 (Spring 1991): 25–30.

Other important sources include numerous periodical and journal articles: Zita Allen, "Majesty in Motion: Judith Jamison," *Encore* 4 (December 22, 1975): 27–28; "Creative Woman," *Ebony* 32 (August 1977): 135; Nancy Vreeland Dalva, "The Jamison Project, Joyce Theatre, November 15–20, 1988," *Dance* 63:2 (February 1989): 91–92; "Entertainment," *Connoisseur* 220 (December 1990): 52; Valerie Gladstone, "Judith Jamison Leaps Forward," *Ms.* 11:3 (November/December 1991): 80–81; Jessica Harris, "Judith Jamison," *Essence* 9 (May 1978): 62; Charlayne Hunter-Gault, "Interview with Judith Jamison," *A Mind Is* 1 (Winter 1991): 4–8; Robert Johnson, "Ailey Season Opens at City Center," *Dance* 64:12 (December 1990): 12; Robert Johnson, "New Doors Open for Ailey Company," *Dance* 64:8 (August 1990): 12; Robert Johnson, "Two Debuts Highlight Ailey Season," *Dance* 65:12 (December 1991): 13; "Judith Jamison: Extending the Alvin Ailey Dance Legacy," *Ebony* 46 (December 1990): 132–136; Ellen Sherman, "Bringing Dance Home Again," *Essence* 4 (February 1975): 34; "The Best Christmas I Ever Had," *Ebony* 47: 2 (December 1991): 58; Tobi Tobias, "Beauty and the Beast," *New York* 25:1 (January 6, 1992): 57–58; Tobi Tobias, "Multiple Choice," *New York* 23:6 (February 12, 1990): 59–60; Tobi Tobias, "Rites of Passage," *New York* (January 7, 1991): 55–56; Tobi Tobias,

"Standing Tall," *New York* (December 24, 1990): 106; Bert Wechsler, "Jamison Project, Joyce Theater, January 23–28, 1989," *Dance* 64:4 (April 1990): 93; Edward Willinger, "Come and Get the Beauty of It Hot," *New Dance Review* 3:3 (January–March 1991): 11–13.

Jamison is also the subject of articles and entries in major biographical references including Virgil A. Clift and W. Augustus Low, eds., "Jamison, Judith," in *Encyclopedia of Black America* (New York: McGraw-Hill, 1981), p. 469; *Current Biography Yearbook* (New York: Wilson, 1973), pp. 202–205; Kali Herman, ed., "Jamison, Judith," *Women in Particular: An Index to American Women* (Phoenix, AZ: Oryx Press, 1984), p. 50; Roy L. Hill, "Judith Jamison (1944–), Dancer, Dance Company Director," in *Notable Black American Women*, edited by Jessie Carney Smith (Detroit: Gale, 1992), pp. 568–570; "Jamison, Judith," in *Who's Who in Entertainment* (Wilmette, IL: Macmillan Directory Div., 1988), p. 315; *One Thousand Successful Blacks* (Chicago: Johnson, 1973), p. 173; Harry A. Ploski and James Williams, eds., "Judith Jamison, Dancer," in *The Negro Almanac: A Reference Work on the African American*, 5th ed. (Detroit: Gale, 1989), pp. 1146–1147; Sharon Rose, "Judith Jamison," in *Newsmakers, 1990*, edited by Louise Mooney (Detroit: Gale, 1990), pp. 228–229.

Many major newspapers and news magazines have carried articles and reviews about Jamison: *Detroit Free Press* (March 18, 1990), *Detroit News* (March 17, 1990), *Newsweek* (September 18, 1989), *New York Times* (November 15, 17, 1988; December 7, 15, 23, 1990; December 12, 21,1991); and *Time* (July 15, 1991).

JEMISON, MAE C. (b. 1956), astronaut and physician, was born October 17 in Decatur, Alabama, the youngest of three children of Charlie and Dorothy Jemison, a maintenance worker and a schoolteacher. As a child, she knew she wanted to be a scientist. She ran goldfish through mazes, discussed the qualities of stars with her Uncle Louis, and used the hospital lab to complete her high school science project. Raised in Chicago, Illinois, she graduated from Morgan Park High School in 1973. She went on to earn a bachelor of science degree in chemical engineering from Stanford University in 1977, also fulfilling the requirements for a bachelor of arts degree in African-American studies. She continued her education at Cornell University, where she was awarded a doctor of medicine degree in 1981. While in medical school, she traveled to Cuba, Kenya, and Thailand, providing primary medical care to individuals living in those countries.

Dr. Jemison's travels during medical school readied her for service in the Peace Corps from January 1983 to June 1985. She served in Sierra Leone and Liberia in West Africa as the area Peace Corps medical officer, supervising the pharmacy, laboratory, and medical staff, providing medical care, instructing in personal health care, writing self-care manuals, and developing and implementing guidelines for health and safety issues. She also worked in conjunction with the Centers for Disease Control on research for various vaccines.

Upon her return to the United States in 1985, Dr. Jemison secured a position with CIGNA Health Plans of California as a general practitioner in Los Angeles, began attending graduate classes in engineering, and applied to the National Aeronautics and Space Administration (NASA) for admission to the astronaut program. It was after submitting her second application in 1987 that she was selected as an astronaut candidate, one of 15 in some 2,000 applicants to the program.

Dr. Jemison successfully completed her astronaut training program in August 1988, becoming the fifth black astronaut and the first black female astronaut in NASA history. She is outspoken about the impact of technological advances on the black population, and encourages African Americans to pursue careers in the space program. Dr. Jemison, who is unmarried, is based at NASA's Lyndon B. Johnson Space Center in Houston, Texas. She is currently assigned to a cooperative mission between the Unites States and Japan in which she will conduct experiments in materials processing and life sciences. In August 1992, SPACELAB J, was a successful U.S./Japanese science mission, making Jemison the first black woman in space.

—Rama Ramakrishna

Bibliography

Information on Mae Jemison is in Walter L. Hawkins, *African American Biographies* (Jefferson, NC: McFarland, 1992), a January 1991 biographical data sheet issued by NASA headquarters in Washington, DC; an interview by Karen R. Long in the Cleveland *Plain Dealer* (December 12, 1991); and an article by Marilyn Marshall entitled "Child of the '60s Set to Become First Black Woman in Space," which appears in *Ebony* 44 (August 1989): 50ff.

JOHNSON, GEORGIA DOUGLAS [CAMP] (1877–1966), one of the most productive and respected writers of the Harlem Renaissance, was a poet, playwright, and story writer whose work reflected her family background, her musical training, and her era. Born to Laura (Jackson) and George Camp in Atlanta, Georgia, on September 10, Georgia Blanche Douglas Camp's physical appearance revealed a mixed heritage from English, Native American, and African grandparents. Her mother, a giving and shy woman, had to work the entire day, which left Georgia on her own much of the time. Growing up in Rome, Georgia, was a lonely experience that led to increased withdrawal during her childhood. Her schooling started in Rome and continued in Atlanta, where she attended the Normal School at Atlanta University. Here, she developed self-taught talents in music, which eventually led her to the Cleveland College of Music and the Oberlin Conservatory of Music, where she studied harmony, violin, piano, and voice.

Georgia utilized her normal school training to find suitable employment. She taught school in Marietta, Georgia, and then became an Atlanta school principal. Marriage to Atlanta attorney Henry Lincoln Johnson, on September 28, 1903, provided her with the leisure time to nurture her music and her writing. She started to submit stories and poems to magazines. In the summer of 1905 her poem "Omnipresence" appeared in the *Voice of the Negro*. By 1906 she gave birth to her first son, Henry Lincoln Johnson, and by the following year, a second son, Peter Douglas Johnson, joined the family. With these added responsibilities, Henry Johnson admonished his wife to focus on family rather than writing. Her husband's leadership in the Republican Party led first to Washington, DC, in 1910, and then to an appointment as the recorder of deeds in 1912 by William Howard Taft.

These family responsibilities and the attitude of her husband led to less focus on her writing, the intellectual climate of Washington rose to support Georgia Douglas Johnson, the writer. Dean Kelly Miller of Howard University, an admirer of her poetry, introduced Johnson to poet and critic William Stanley Braithwaite. Encouraged by his comments, Johnson renewed her writing, submitting many poems to *The Crisis* and *Opportunity*. In 1916 *The Crisis* published "My Little One," "Gossamer," and "Fame." Supported by Jessie Fauset, a writer and the literary editor of *The Crisis*, Johnson collected 62 poems for her first book, *The Heart of a Woman* (1918), which included an eloquent introduction by Braithwaite. A second collection of poems followed in 1922, *Bronze: A Book of Verse*, but this time her themes had changed from a focus on the female perspective to a focus on race pride. Her poetry reflected universal themes, integrationist perspectives, and conventional forms, rhythms, and rhymes, all characteristics of the "Genteel School."

In the 1920s, influenced by black female playwrights Angelina Grimké and Mary Burrill, who wrote dramas protesting lynching, and by Zona Gale, a white writer, motivated Johnson to begin writing plays. Johnson's plays *A Bill to Be Passed* and *And Still They Paused* became part of the antilynching propaganda developed in support of the Dyer Anti-Lynching Bill. She continued the lynching theme in *A Sunday Morning in the South* (ca. 1925), *Blue Blood* (1926), and later in the Federal Theatre Project's *Blue-Eyed Black Boy* and *Safe* (1935–1939).

With her developing literary reputation, Johnson had to face tragedy and financial responsibilities brought on by the death of her husband on September 10, 1925. At this time, since her writing could not support her sons' educational goals, she accepted a political appointment from President Calvin Coolidge as the Commissioner of Conciliation in the Labor Department. From 1925 through 1934, Georgia Douglas Johnson worked in this position and tried to continue her writing. She ventured into black folklore in her play *Plumes* (1927), in which the character Charity Brown makes a choice about her daughter's care between advice given by a physician and a friend reading coffee grounds. In 1928 she completed *An Autumn Love Cycle,* her third poetry collection, a chronicle through 58 poems of a love affair. She submitted plays to the Federal Theatre Project between 1935 and 1939.

Through her three books of poetry and her antilynching plays, Johnson's reputation was established, yet she continued to struggle for publication. The war years revived her enthusiasm, creating in her patriotic poems and songs images of social justice. "To Gallant France," "A Soldier's Letter," "Whose Son," and "Tomorrow's World" echo the conflicts of being an African American during World War II. Johnson utilized her earlier musical training in her collaborations with Lillian Evanti on the songs "Dedication" (1948), "Beloved Mother" (1952), and "Hail to Fair Washington" (1953). Harry Burleigh recorded her musical poem "I Want to Die While You Love Me," on Victor Records.

The postwar era with its repressive milieu for writers did not stop Johnson's literary efforts. She wrote two novels, *White Men's Children* and *The Black Cabinet,* but neither was published; however, this did not stop her productivity. She continued to write poetry, plays, and short stories, remembering that Balzac had died with 40 books left unpublished and hoping her own work might meet a similar fate. That legacy went unrealized. On May 14, 1966, she died in Freedmen's Hospital from a stroke suffered earlier that month. She was buried in Lincoln Cemetery. The volumes of writing that she left in various stages of completion were discarded on the day of her funeral.

—Dorothy C. Salem with Beth Schneider

Bibliography

When Georgia Douglas Johnson died in 1966, her papers and manuscripts were thrown away. For insight into her writing and her feelings, one can consult correspondence of Georgia Douglas Johnson with W.E.B. Du Bois in the W.E.B. Du Bois Papers, University of Massachusetts, Amherst; and with Jessie Fauset in the NAACP Papers, Library of Congress, Washington, DC.

Her own work includes three collections of poetry: *The Heart of a Woman* (Boston: Cornhill, 1918); *Bronze: A Book of Verse* (New York: Brimmer, 1922); and *An Autumn Love Cycle* (New York: Neal, 1928). Her plays include: *A Bill to Be Passed* and *And Still They Paused* (1922); *A Sunday Morning in the South* (1925); *Blue Blood* (1926); and *Plumes* (1927). Her plays are included in anthologies: *Fifty More Contemporary One-Act Plays,* edited by Frank Shay (New York: Appleton, 1928); *The New Negro Renaissance,* edited by Arthur P. Davis and Michael Peplow (New York: Holt Rinehart and Winston, 1975); and *Black Theatre, U.S.A.,* edited by James W. Hatch and Ted Shine (New York: Free Press, 1974). Her plays *Frederick Douglass* and *William and Ellen Craft* are included in Willis Richardson and May Miller, eds., *Negro History in Thirteen Plays* (Washington, DC: Associated Publishers, 1930). She submitted plays to the Federal Theatre Project, including *Blue-eyed Black Boy* and *Safe.* She also wrote the words for Lillian Evanti's "Hail to Fair Washington," "Beloved Mother," and "Dedication," for solo voice and piano published in New York by Handy Brothers in 1951, 1952, and 1958.

Contemporaries that include Johnson in critical or literary discussions are Benjamin Brawley, *The Negro Genius* (New York: Dodd, Mead, 1937); and Countee Cullen, *Caroling Dusk: An Anthology of Verse by Negro Poets* (New York: Harper, 1927). She is featured in articles appearing in black newpapers and periodicals: Calvin Floyd, "Georgia Douglas Johnson Fears She Won't Have Time to Complete All the Work She Has Planned," *Pittsburgh Courier* (July 7, 1928); Cedric Dover, "The Importance of Georgia Douglas Johnson," *The Crisis* 59 (December 1952): 633–636, and 674; and "Contest Spotlight," *Opportunity* 5 (July 1927): 204. Her poems appeared in these and in the Baltimore *Afro-American* and in *Negro Digest* during the 1920s.

The most complete analysis of Johnson is Gloria T. Hull's *Color, Sex, and Poetry: Three Women Writers of the Harlem Renaissance* (Bloomington: Indiana University Press, 1987). For biographical and critical information on Johnson and her writings see Winona Fletcher, "Georgia Douglas Johnson," in *Afro-American Writers from the Harlem Renaissance to 1940*, edited by Trudier Harris (Detroit: Gale, 1987); *Afro-American Writers after 1955: Dramatists and Prose Writers*, edited by Trudier Harris (Detroit: Gale, 1985); Lorraine E. Roses, *Harlem Renaissance and Beyond: Literary Biographies of 100 Black Women Writers, 1900–1945* (Boston: G.K. Hall, 1990); Jessie Carney Smith, *Notable Black American Women* (Detroit: Gale, 1992); Ora Williams, *American Black Women in Arts and Social Science* (Metuchen, NJ: Scarecrow Press, 1978); Darwin Turner, *Afro-American Writers* (New York: Appleton-Century-Crofts, 1970); Esther Arata and Nicholas Rotoli, *Black American Playwrights* (Metuchen, NJ: Scarecrow, 1978); James Page, *Selected Black American Authors* (Boston: G.K. Hall, 1977); and Jeanne-Marie Miller, "Black Women Playwrights from Grimké to Shange" and Ora T. Williams, "American Black Women Composers," both in *But Some of Us Are Brave*, edited by Gloria T. Hull, Patricia Bell Scott, and Barbara Smith (Old Westbury, NY: Feminist Press, 1982).

JOHNSON, HALLE [TANNER, DILLON] (1864–1901), the first African-

American woman and first woman to practice medicine in Alabama, was born on October 17, and received the benefits of a warm, supportive family of achievers. Her father, Benjamin Tucker Tanner (1835–1923), was born of free parents in in Pittsburgh, Pennsylvania. He worked as a barber to pay for his college education at Avery College. Her mother, Sarah Elizabeth (Miller) Tanner (1804–1914), was born in Virginia. She met Benjamin in Pittsburgh, where she taught school. After their marriage in 1858, Benjamin studied at Western Theological Seminary, was ordained first as a deacon and then as an elder in the African Methodist Episcopal church. Before the birth of his daughter, Halle, he became a minister in the African Methodist Episcopal church, served as pastor for churches in Georgetown and Baltimore, and administered the AME Conference School in Frederick, Maryland. During her childhood, he began editing the *Christian Recorder* and *AME Church Review*. In 1888 he achieved the position of bishop in the AME church in Philadelphia. Sarah raised a family of seven children, taught in Sunday school, and served as president of the Parent Mite Missionary Society. Three of these children went on to achieve fame: Henry Ossawa Tanner (1859–1937) became an internationally known artist of biblical, landscape, and genre subjects; Carlton Tanner entered the ministry; and their eldest daughter, Halle Tanner Johnson, became a physician.

From this nurturing home in Philadelphia, Halle Tanner received her education. Records or memoirs about her childhood are not available or are overshadowed by information about her parents. Records indicate a marriage in 1886 to a man from Trenton, New Jersey. Although they had a child, the information about the fate of this child and the death date of her husband, Charles E. Dillon, is lacking.

Halle Tanner Dillon entered the Woman's Medical College of Pennsylvania at age 24, completed a 3-year course, and graduated with high honors in May 1891. As a graduate of the Woman's Medical College, she received a copy of Booker T. Washington's letter to the college inquiring about potential African-American graduates. She responded to his offer to become the resident physician for Tuskegee Institute.

Arriving there in late summer of 1891, she acquainted herself with the campus, the facilities, and the town. She went to Montgomery to study with Dr. Cornelius Corsette, a black physician and the first black to pass the state medical examination. Within a few weeks, Booker T. Washington accompanied her to the Alabama Capitol Building for the examination. On September 22, 1891, the *New York Times* featured a small article on the front page detailing the certification of a black female doctor after a ten-day examination covering ten subjects, and all major newspapers in Alabama noted her achievement.

As the resident physician at Tuskegee from 1891 to 1894, her duties were extensive. She provided care for 450 students. She received extra pay for administering to Tuskegee's 30 officers, faculty, and families. To save money for Tuskegee Institute, she made her own medicines, established and managed the Lafayette Dispensary, established a Nurses' Training School, and taught one to two classes each term. For this effort, she received an annual salary of $600, one month's vacation, and board for the year.

In 1894 she married the Reverend John Quincy Johnson, a mathematics teacher at Tuskegee Institute, and began her short career of wife and mother. The couple moved to Columbia, South Carolina, when he accepted the presidency of Allen University. In 1900 they moved to Nashville to enable her husband to accept the religious post as pastor of St. Paul AME Church. Ironically, Halle Tanner Dillon Johnson died in a manner similar to many women of her era. The Johnsons had three sons: John Quincy, Jr., Benjamin T., and Henry Tanner. During the birth of her last child, Halle Tanner Dillon Johnson died in her Nashville home on April 26, 1901, due to childbirth complicated by dysentery. This thirty-seven year old woman was listed as a housekeeper on the death certificate. She was buried in Greenwood Cemetery. Her family later moved to Princeton, New Jersey.

—Beth Schneider

Bibliography

Manuscript collections containing information about Halle Tanner Dillon Johnson's education and career include the Archives and Special Collections on Women in Medicine, Medical College of Pennsylvania; correspondence between Booker T. Washington and Halle Tanner Dillon are in *The Booker T. Washington Papers* 3, edited by Louis R. Harlan, 1889–1895 (Urbana: University of Illinois Press, 1974).

As with many African-American women, Johnson's birthdate is disputed in several sources. Her death certificate lists 1865 as her birthdate. Gerri Major lists 1863 as the birthdate in *Black Society* (Chicago: Johnson, 1976).

Resources detailing the struggles of African-American women in the medical profession include Margaret Jerrido, "Black Woman Physicians: A Triple Burden," *Alumna News*, Medical College of Pennsylvania (Spring 1979): 1–5; Herbert Morais, *History of the Afro-American in Medicine* (Cornell Heights, PA: Publishers Agency, 1976); and Mary Roth Walsh, *"Doctors Wanted: No Women Need Apply:" Sexual Barriers in the Medical Profession, 1835–1975* (New Haven: Yale University Press, 1977). Brief discussions of African-American female physicians are in Dorothy Sterling, *We Are Your Sisters: Black Women in the Nineteenth Century* (New York: Norton, 1984); Bettina Aptheker, *Woman's Legacy* (Amherst: University of Massachusetts, 1982); and Marianna W. Davis, *Contributions of Black Women to America* (Columbia, SC: Kenday, 1982).

Biographical information is provided on Tanner's family in Hallie Q. Brown, *Homespun Heroines and Other Women of Distinction* (Xenia, OH: Aldine Press, 1926); Monroe Majors, *Noted Negro Women* (Chicago: Donahue and Henneberry, 1893); Sylvia Dannett, *Profiles of Negro Womanhood* (Yonkers, NY: Educational Heritage, 1964); and Jessie Carney Smith, *Notable Black American Women* (Detroit: Gale, 1992).

JOHNSON, PAMELA [McCALLISTER] (b. 1945), journalist, educator, and newspaper publisher, was born in McAlester, Oklahoma, on April 14, and grew up in Evanston, Illinois. She was the oldest of five children born to Elmer Reuben and Esther Queen (Crump) McAllister. Johnson was encouraged by a grade-school teacher and her husband, a journalist, to study communications at the University of Wisconsin at Madison. Johnson completed a dual undergraduate degree in journalism and education in 1967, and was one of a handful of African-American students in the school. She remembered her undergraduate education as a mixture of positive and discouraging experiences, some of which had racial overtones. "In one of my classes, the professor went around the room and asked the students what we wanted to do in our careers," recalled Johnson. "I said I wanted to be in television news. Well, he looked around the room and, of course, I was the only black there, and then he said, 'My friend teaches the course in television, and I'm sure he'd like some color in his class.'"

Following graduation Johnson landed a coveted reporting job at the *Chicago Tribune*, where she worked for a year until returning to Madison to marry a college friend. She wed Donald Nathanial Johnson, a psychologist, in 1968. Job prospects were limited in the smaller city, and she struggled to continue her journalistic career. Eventually Johnson got her foot in the door; she worked as a radio news reporter and interview show host, as a television news reporter, as a reporter for the CBS bureau in Chicago, as a free-lance writer, and as an editor of *Wisconsin Magazine*. She returned to the University of Wisconsin journalism program to complete a master's degree in 1971 and a doctorate in 1977. Her doctoral dissertation focused on audience reactions to the television miniseries "Roots." During this period Johnson also had two children, Dawn and Jason.

In 1971 Johnson became the University of Wisconsin's first black female faculty member in the School of Journalism, where she taught for seven years. Johnson states that she helped increase the black student population of the school tenfold in just two years. In 1979 she joined the faculty of Norfolk State University, where she played a central role in building the school's journalism program. Johnson was developing an interest in media management, and while she taught at Norfolk State, she participated in a summer executive training internship sponsored by the Gannett Corporation at the *Patriot-Ledger*, a newspaper in Quincy, Massachusetts. With this experience, Johnson found her niche, and when Gannett offered her a change to enter a publishing trainee program, she seized the opportunity.

Johnson left teaching in 1981 to work as a general executive at the *Courier-News*, another Gannett paper in Bridgewater, New Jersey. A few months later she was transferred to the *Ithaca Journal* in New York State to serve as assistant to the publisher. When the publisher left a month later, Johnson became the first black woman to head a white-owned daily newspaper in the United States. The *Journal*, the second-oldest newspaper in the Gannett chain, has a circulation of 20,000 and serves a university community in the heart of upstate New York's Finger Lakes region. Johnson today remains the only black female newspaper publisher in the nation, a fact she finds discouraging. Johnson has been active in national organizations established to encourage minorities to consider the media business.

—Jane Rhodes

Bibliography

This profile is based on two interviews with Pamela Johnson: December 1981 and February 1992. See also Jane Rhodes, "A Page One Story," *Syracuse New Times* (January 20, 1982).

JONES, CLAUDIA [CUMBERBATCH] (1915–1964), journalist and political activist, was born February 21 in Port of Spain, Trinidad. The Cumberbatch family resided in Belmont, the northern region of the city. In 1924 her family immigrated to New York City on the SS *Voltaire* to settle in Harlem. Three years later, her mother, a garment worker, died at work. As a result, young Claudia Cumberbatch had to leave school to begin work as a factory worker and salesperson.

The Great Depression combined with the racism in the United States led her to join the youth section of the Communist Party of the USA (CPUSA) in 1934. She had been working as a journalist and studying acting at the Urban League. Torn between the two, she walked away from a promising acting career to take a job in 1934 with the party paper, the *Daily Worker*. She continued this role as a full-time political activist until her death 30 years later.

Harlem was her base of operations. She rose quickly in the hierarchy of the Young Communist League. A brief marriage in the 1930s led to the surname for which she is better known (Jones). By 1940 she became the chair of their national council. When she applied for citizenship in the United States in 1940, the year that Congress debated the Smith Act, which forbade the teaching of Marxism-Leninism, she was denied. During World War II, the alliance of the United States and the USSR eroded the notion that the CPUSA was a tool of Moscow, a belief that had slowed the party's growth and acceptance. As the party gained acceptance, Claudia Jones became recognized as the major spokesperson for the party and for African-American women. Her writings gained wide circulation in the party press and black press. She played a key organizing role when her comrade Ben Davis became the first black Communist to win elective office to the New York City Council, representing Harlem in 1943 and 1945.

This situation changed with the end of the war and the onset of the Cold War. Again the party assumed the role as a presumed tool of the antagonist, the Soviet Union. Soon, Claudia Jones was arrested on a deportation warrant and taken to Ellis Island, where she had landed years earlier. Able to make bail, Jones had to organize a defense committee to stall deportation orders. The Red Scare hampered the support from old allies such as the NAACP, but she was able to gain the support from the international Caribbean trade union movement. On December 22, 1950, she was found guilty of being an alien and a member of the Communist Party. Paid witnesses testified. Though technically a legal organization, CPUSA affiliation was the prime reason for her legal difficulties.

As if this were not enough, on June 20, 1951, she and 16 other party leaders were arrested by the FBI in New York for violating the Smith Act. In February 1953 she was convicted and sentenced to serve one year and a day in prison and was ordered to pay a fine of $2,000. The Supreme Court refused to hear her appeal in January 1955, leading to her rearrest, transport to the Women's House of Detention in New York, and transfer to the Federal Reformatory for Women in West Virginia. Since she suffered from heart trouble, her condition worsened in prison. An international campaign made sure she received proper medical treatment from the unwilling authorities, but could not free her. After her release in December 1955, the government deported her.

Because of her medical needs, Jones moved to London using her British citizenship via her birth in Trinidad. There she quickly became a leader of the expanding black British population through her writing and editing of the influential newspaper *West Indian Gazette*. She coordinated the first West Indian festival in London and became a leader of the British Communist Party. Traveling to the Soviet Union and China, she led the campaign to free the recently jailed South African anti-apartheid leader Nelson Mandela in 1962. This campaign became the most significant outside of South Africa itself.

Poor health eventually took its toll. Having contracted tuberculosis in Harlem at age 17, complicated by an asthmatic condition and other lung and heart problems, Jones died alone in her North London flat on Christmas Day 1964. Her passing was mourned and noted in the United States and by Communist parties on every continent.

—Gerald Horne

Bibliography

References to Claudia Jones are quite sparse. The best sources exist in the monthly journals of the Communist Party, *Political Affairs* and the *Daily Worker*.

JONES, LOIS MAILOU (b. 1905) is known throughout the world as the first important and recognized African-American female painter. She has exhibited in over 45 shows, including a 1972 retrospective at Howard Univeristy. Today she is professor emeritus at Howard University after a lifetime of teaching, painting, designing, and promoting black art: "I believe it is the duty of every Black artist to participate in the current movement which aims to establish recognition of works by 'Black Artists.' I am and will continue to exhibit in 'Black Art Shows' and others which express my sincere creative feelings."

Jones is a painter of amazing versatility whose work includes landscape oil paintings, subjects dealing with American social injustice, and more abstract design pieces done in acrylic. Her artistic style has been enriched by her contact with and love for French, Haitian, and African cultures.

Lois Mailou Jones was born in Boston on November 3 to Carolyn D. Jones and Thomas Vreeland Jones. Her family, which included a brother, John Wesley Jones, nine years her senior, descended from African, Scotch, Dutch, and Native American heritage. As a young girl she heard her parents speaking Dutch in the home.

She started drawing at age three or four and has continued throughout her life. She attended Bowdoin School in a Jewish neighborhood in the West End of Boston and then was referred to the predominantly white High School of

Practical Arts, which gave her the opportunity to do special study in art. There, Laura Wentworth, advisor for the students, took a great interest in her. She founded and participated for more than a decade in the Pierrette Club, a group of 30 girls organized at the League of Women for Community Serivice in Boston. In 1927, as one of the first black graduates of the Boston Museum School of Fine Arts, Jones, a drawing and design major, received a special graduate scholarship to study at the Designers' Art School at the special invitation of Ludwig Frank, a famous textile designer from Germany. In the 1920s design companies in New York and Boston printed and sold her work.

Although her education and most of her time was spent in Boston, her summers were spent on Martha's Vineyard, where she fell in love with nature. There she met Harry T. Burleigh, composer of spirituals, and sculptor Meta Warrick Fuller of Framingham, Massachusetts, who filled her with stories about studying in Paris with French sculptor Auguste Rodin. Both artists discussed life in Paris, the work of Henry O. Tanner, the pioneer of black artists, and the importance of strength from within.

Filled with a desire to be an artist and to study and travel in Europe, Jones had to accept reality. After graduation, she experienced firsthand racial discrimination when the museum director rejected her application for an assistantship, telling her instead to go to the South and teach at an all-black college. Instead, Jones worked as a textile designer, took courses at Harvard, Columbia, and Howard universities. She taught at Palmer Memorial Institute from 1928 to 1930, and then in 1930, became a professor of design and watercolor painting in the College of Fine Arts at Howard University, where she taught until her retirement in 1977. Elizabeth Catlett and Alma Thomas, two leading artists, studied with Jones.

In 1937 she was awarded a fellowship to study at the Academie Julien in Paris. She was exhilarated by the liberating experience of being in a city that was not prejudiced against blacks. Her landscapes and portraits in this period showed the unmistaken influence of Paul Cézanne and the Impressionistic style. She soon found work in a Montparnasse studio and found a mentor, the "father" of French symbolism, Émile Bernard.

When she returned to the United States, she was shocked at the virulence of racism, so at the urging of Alain Locke, also at Howard University, she painted *Mob Victim* (1944); the model for this painting had actually witnessed a lynching. She exhibited her early Impressionistic work at the Vose Galleries in Boston and the newly emerging paintings in the African genre at the Harmon Foundation and Atlanta University, which featured the work of African-American artists in exhibitions and permanent collections. Her landscapes and seascapes reflect the influence of Martha's Vineyard, a her favorite retreat since childhood.

In 1941 Jones won the Corcoran Gallery Robert Woods Bliss Prize for the landscape painting *Indian Shops, Gay Head*. However, knowing that museums and galleries refused to exhibit works by black artists, Jones had asked a white friend to submit the piece and to pick up the award. Two years later, Jones claimed the credit. Her other works from this period include *Dans Un Cafe a Paris* (1939), *Les Fetiches* (1938), *Ville d'Houdain* (1949), and *Place Du Tertre, Paris* (1938).

In 1953 Jones married the Haitian artist Louis Vergniaud Pierre-Noel in Cabris, southern France, and the home of her lifelong friend and colleague Celine Tabary. Since her husband was a known graphic designer for the World Health Organization, from 1962 onward, the couple conducted student study tours of Europe and Africa. They made frequent visits to Haiti, and her work in the 1950s shows the influences of Cubism and Haitian culture. Inspired by the ve-ve designs in her vou-dou series, Jones painted *Ubi Girl from the Tai Region* (1972) as an exciting combination of Cubism, realism, and passion for African art and cultures. The painting hangs in the Boston Museum of Fine Arts, the very place that once discouraged her efforts. *Vendeuses de Tissus* (1964) also celebrates this period of abstract expressionism.

Among her many honors, Jones was decorated in 1954 by President Magliore of Haiti with the Diplome et decoration De l'Ordre National Honneur et Merite au Grade de Chevalier. She has received many honorary doctorate degrees from such institutions as Suffolk University, Howard University, and Massachusetts College of Art. In 1962 she was elected a fellow of the Royal Society of the Arts in London and to the Women's Caucus for the Art Hall of Fame. Her work can be seen in the collections of the Metropolitan Museum of Art, the Hirshhorn Museum and Sculpture Garden, the Phillips Collection, the Brooklyn Museum, the National Portrait Gallery, the Boston Museum of Fine Arts, the Palais National (Haiti), the Johnson Publishing Company, the University of Punjab (Pakistan), the American embassy in Luxembourg, and the Rosenwald Foundation among others.

Retrospectives of her work began in 1972 and 1973 at Howard University and the Boston Museum of Fine Arts. In 1980 Jones received an award for international achievement in art presented by President Jimmy Carter. In 1990 another retrospective of her work was held at Meridien House in Washington, DC. Jones continues to work at Howard University.

—Barbara Winslow and Robin Chandler

Bibliography

The oral history interview with Jones is part of the Black Women's Oral History Collection, Radcliffe College. The most complete bibliography and catalogue of Jones's work is found in Lynn Moody Igoe with James Igoe, *250 Years of Afro-American Art: An Annotated Bibliography* (New York, London: Bowker, 1981) and William Matney, *Who's Who among Black Americans*, 6th ed. 1990/1 (Detroit: Gale, 1991). There is no biography of Jones. Photographs of Jones at work are included in the biographical sketches in *Famous Blacks Give Secrets of Success*, Volume II of the *Ebony Success Library* (Nashville: Southwestern Co., 1973), pp. 188–191. For other works that treat Jones's art or her position in the arts community, see the following:

Chandler, Robin. Taped interview with Lois M. Jones (1973).

Fine, Elsa Honig. *The Afro-American Artist: The Search for Identity*. New York: Hacker Art Books, 1982.

Gauther, Edmund Berry. *Reflective Moments: Lois Mailou Jones, Retrospective 1930–1972*. Boston: Museum of the National Center of Afro-American Artists and the Boston Museum of Fine Arts, 1973. Exhibition Catalogue.

LaDuke, Betty. "Lois Mailou Jones: The Grande Dame of African-American Art," *Woman's Art Journal* VIII/2 (Fall–Winter 1987–1988): 28–32.

Lewis, Samella. *Art: African American*. New York: Harcourt Brace Jovanovich, 1978.

Rubinstein, Charlotte Streifer. *American Women Artists: From Early Indian Times to Present*. New York: Avon, 1982.

Striar, Margurite. "Artist in Transition," *Essence* (November 1972): 22–23.

JONES, PEARL [WILLIAMS] (1931–1991), gospel music performer, composer and scholar, was born in July in Washington, DC. There, she attended the public schools and received her BA (cum laude) and MA degrees in music from Howard University. Although trained as a classical pianist, Jones grew up with gospel music. Her father, Bishop Smallwood E. Williams, founded and was the pastor of the Bible Way Church of Our Lord Jesus Christ World Wide for 64 years. Her mother, Verna Williams, was a music teacher and founder of the church's well-known radio choir. According to Verna Williams, her daughter Pearl "was born to play," and learned early to sing gospel and play the piano—becoming a familiar voice to many who listened to the church's weekly radio broadcasts.

Described as "a woman of gospel," Pearl Verna Williams Jones believed that gospel was a legitimate American art form. She popularized this view, in lectures, workshops, articles, and as a professor of music at the University of the District of Columbia, where she directed the gospel studies program. A well-rounded music scholar, Jones also taught jazz history and music appreciation. Despite her scholarly endeavors, she devoted considerable time and effort to her duties as minister of music at the Bible Way Temple, one of Washington's largest churches. There, she was responsible for all the choirs, but personally directed the radio and television choir. At the time of her death, Pearl Williams Jones was the artistic director of "Women of the Gospel," a radio program sponsored by the Washington Performing Arts Society and that performed at the Kennedy Center in Washington, DC, which focused on locally and nationally known female gospel artists.

She died after a long struggle with cancer on February 4, 1991, at her home in Washigton, DC.

—Betty Plummer

Bibliography

Most of the information about Pearl Williams Jones is from two interviews by the author, one with her father and one with her mother, during August 1986 through 1989. An interesting and valuable article about her work with gospel music in Washington, DC, appeared in the *Washington Post* (February 9, 1991). The University of the District of Columbia has a variety of sources spanning her career.

JONES, SISSIERETTA [JOYNER] (1869–1933) is best remembered for her outstanding vocal repertoire and as a pioneer in the black music profession who prepared the world to accept talented blacks as serious artists. Jones, also known as "Black Patti," in reference to the Italian soprano Adelina Patti, was born Matilda Sissieretta Joyner in Portsmouth, Virginia, on January 5 to the Reverend Jeremiah Malachi Joyner and Henrietta Joyner. She went to Providence, Rhode Island, as a young woman to start formal voice training at the Providence Academy of Music. After completing her education at the Academy, she studied at the New England Conservatory in Boston, Massachusetts, and went on to launch her professional career in New York City in 1888 as the first black singer to appear on the stage of Wallack's Theater. Her dynamic soprano voice and her poise and commanding presence made Jones a popular and succesful vanguard for black vocalists.

On September 4, 1883, Jones married Richard Jones, who became her business manager, but by 1898 she filed for divorce, charging her husband with drunkeness. Jones's career continued as she toured the United States, Europe, the West Indies, and South America. Three of her greatest performances came in 1892 when she performed at Madison Square Garden's "Grand African Jubilee," at the White House for President William Henry Harrison, and for the Prince of Wales in London. Jones continually sang in vaudeville and in opera houses throughout her life and was hailed as the best black singer ever.

The last part of Jones's career, from 1896 to 1916, she starred in an all-black troupe known as Black Patti's Troubadours. The Troubadours were a company of black singers and entertainers who toured the major cities of the western and southern United States. After the Troubadours disbanded, she retired to her home in Providence, where she died of cancer on June 24, 1933.

—Julieanne Phillips

Bibliography

Sissieretta Jones's scrapbook and other papers were placed in the Moorland-Spingarn Collection, Howard University, Washington, DC, by Dr. Carl R. Gross of Providence, Rhode Island. Willia E. Daughtry, a descendent of the singer, completed a dissertation on Jones, "A Study of the Negro's Contribution to the 19th Century Concert and Theatrical Life" in 1968 at Syracuse University. Secondary sources written by her contemporaries often containing minor inaccuracies include Benjamin

Brawley, *The Negro Genius* (Chapel Hill: University of North Carolina Press, 1937); F.C. Terry, "The Closing Chapters of the Life of 'Black Patti,'" in the *Providence Sunday Journal* (July 16, 1933). Biographical articles are in Sylvia Dannett, *Profiles of Negro Womanhood, 1619–1900*, Volume I (New York/Philadelphia: M.W. Lads, 1964); and William Lichtenwanger, *Notable American Women 1607–1950: A Biographical Dictionary II* (Cambridge: Belknap Press, 1971), p. 288. Lichtenwanger's extensive bibliography is based upon interviews with family members as well as written sources.

JORDAN, BARBARA (b. 1936), lawyer, politician, and legal educator, was born in Houston, Texas, on February 21, the youngest of three children of Benjamin and Arlyne (Patten) Jordan. A dynamic, intelligent, talented woman, Barbara Charline Jordan has become a champion for many causes, specifically those involving women, blacks, and the poor. Strong willed and outspoken, Jordan grew up in a strict Baptist environment. Religion was central to the Jordan family. They lived in the modest home of her paternal grandfather, who served as the chairman of the deacon's board, Good Hope Missionary Baptist Church. A typical Sunday involved an early prayer service in their home followed by a trip to the Good Hope Missionary Baptist Church for church service. It is there that her parents met and later married. Called to the Baptist religious ministry, her father administered to churches in the rural areas of Thompsons and Kendleton, Texas. He became pastor of his own church, the Greater Pleasant Hill Baptist Church, and supplemented his income with a job as a warehouse clerk. He held high expectations for his daughter in education, giving her biographies of successful individuals, including many black role models. He encouraged her to strive to achieve her own personal goals. He also taught her through example and instilled in her the belief that she could do nearly anything she believed she could do.

Both her grandfathers were important to Barbara Jordan. Although she lived in the home of her paternal grandfather, she became the favorite of her maternal grandfather, John Ed Patten, the victim of "racial justice." Her grandfather was found guilty of shooting a white policeman, while protecting his store in an attempted robbery. He served six years in prison before being released by Texas governor Miriam "Ma" Ferguson. The time spent with Grandfather Patten was spent reading and conversing. He read to her from the Bible, the dictionary, and the book *Songs for the Bloodwashed*. His role in Jordan's life was that of wise guide and teacher.

During a career day at Phyllis Wheatley High School, Barbara Jordan heard Edith Spurlock Sampson, a black female lawyer from Chicago, speak, and decided to pursue a career in law following that speech. She graduated from high school in the top 5 percent of her class and went on to attend Texas Southern University in Houston. With an excellent mastery of the English language from her extensive reading, the exposure to her father's preaching, and her mother, who was also known as an orator, Jordan became a member of her college debate team. At the Southern Intercollegiate Forensic Conference at Baylor University in 1954, she led her team to a tie with the Harvard debate team. Jordan completed her undergraduate degree in government, graduating magna cum laude in 1956, having served in a wide range of student leadership positions. Jordan continued her education at Boston University Law School graduating with an LLD in 1959. She passed the bar exam in Texas on her first attempt. She joined the American Bar Association and the Houston Lawyers Association in 1960. At age 26, she was elected president of the black, all-male Houston Lawyers Association in 1962 as the only female member. This marked the beginning of many firsts for this remarkable woman.

Her career continued to spiral upward as her talents and interests propelled her into the world of politics. Jordan strongly believed that the only way to move things along was to get into a position to make the laws. Jordan became the first black woman elected to the Texas Legislature in the South since the Reconstruction. The experience in the all-white, all-male Texas State Senate helped her to develop talents and abilities that aided her successful entry into the U.S. Congress as the first black woman elected to the Congress from the South and the first to represent a southern state in the House of Representatives from 1966 to 1972.

Her career in politics went untarnished. She served on the House Committee on Government Operations and on the Subcommittee on Monopolies and Commercial Law. She sponsored several bills protecting the rights of the poor regarding food stamps, emergency housing, health programs, and civil rights enforcement. Jordan earned a reputation beyond the world of politics. In 1976 she was the first woman and first black to give the keynote address at the Democratic National Convention. As a member of the Judiciary Committee, she was a strong and important voice in the proceedings to impeach President Richard Nixon.

After leaving politics due to health limitations, she continued to serve in numerous capacities in academic life, holding the Lyndon B. Johnson professorship at the University of Texas at Austin from 1979 to 1982 and the university's endowed Centennial Chair in National Policy in 1982. She continued to serve on a number of public service committees and as a member of the United Nations panel of multinational corps in South Africa and Namibia.

Jordan has received many honors and numerous awards. She was selected as one of the Ten Most Influential Women of Texas; she was named as Democratic Woman of the Year by the Women's National Democratic Club; and she was chosen by Harper's Bazaar as one of the 100 Women in Touch with Our Time. She received the Eleanor Roosevelt Humanities Award in 1984. As a tribute to her talents and achievements, a Barbara Jordan Fund was established in her honor at the Lyndon B. Johnson School of Public Affairs. Her autobiography, Barbara

Jordan: Self Portrait, depicts the personal triumphs and challenges still awaiting this dynamic, outspoken leader.

—Mary Hovanec

Bibliography

Due to the prominence of this individual, information is readily available. Her autobiography, Barbara Jordan: A Self-Portrait (Garden City, NY: Doubleday, 1979), written with Shelby Hearon, provides an honest perspective of Jordan's career and life. Jordan's career is also highlighted in Hope Chamberlain's A Minority of Members: Women in the United States Congress (New York: Praeger, 1973); Texas: Its Government and Politics (Englewood Cliffs, NJ: Prentice-Hall, 1976); Hearings of the Committee on the Judiciary, House of Representatives, Impeachment of Richard Nixon, President of the United States (Washington, DC: U.S. Government Printing Office, 1974); and Margaret Young's Black American Leaders (New York: Franklin Watts, 1969). The basics are included in Who's Who in Black America (Detroit: Gale, 1976); and Maurine Christopher's Black Americans in Congress (New York: Crowell, 1976).

Some of the best articles are in periodicals: "Women Lawmakers on the Move," Ebony (October 1972): 48–56; "Barbara Jordan: Texan Is a New Power on Capitol Hill,"Ebony (February 1975): 136–142; "Recognizing the Gentleladies of the Judiciary Committee," Ms. (November 1974): 70–73; "Barbara Jordan: Rising Political Star," U.S. News and World Report (February 9, 1976): 43–44; " How I Got There: Staying Power," Atlantic (March 1975): 38–39; "Impact on Congress," Christian Science Monitor (March 18, 1974): 6; and "Jordan: Seeking the Power Points," Newsweek (November 4, 1974): 22.

Newspaper articles include information on issues during the years specified. See New York Times (1971–1977); Chicago Daily News (October 24, 1975); Washington Post (October 22, 1972 and July 1974); Wall Street Journal February 1975; and the Houston Chronicle (1962–1976).

JOSEPH-GAUDET, FRANCES (1861–1934), school founder, temperance leader, and prison reformer, was born in Pike County, Mississippi, but moved to New Orleans as a young girl. Her maternal grandfather, Squire Yancey, was a slave freed by the Civil War, who became a preacher for the African Methodist Episcopal church and founder of the first black church in Summit, Mississippi. His church became the black school where Frances Joseph received her early education. Her father left for the Civil War and never returned. Her move to New Orleans from Mississippi was sudden, as her mother and grandparents left to accompany her uncle, who had killed a white overseer over the rape of her aunt.

In New Orleans, the eight-year-old girl attended the public schools and started to attend Straight University when she and her brother had to help their mother support the family. She soon married but, after ten years of her husband's alcoholic rages, sought a legal separation in 1894. This separation led to a lifetime of community service. After witnessing the imprisonment of poor blacks for vagrancy and other minor offenses, she visited the prisons for prayer meetings. There, she saw young boys placed with criminals until their trials came up—usually in a month or more. To rescue these children, she took them into her home. Likewise, she found the conditions of the indigent insane needing reform. Hence, she sought the support of the mayor and the city commissioners, and when that failed, she used the press to gain the support of white clubwomen of the Era Club. As a result, she initiated the juvenile court system in the city. At the 1899 biennial meeting of the National Association of Colored Women, members heard reports about the first kindergarten for black children in New Orleans, established by Joseph, the Women's Christian Temperance Union (WCTU) superintendent of prison reform.

She carried her mission abroad as she traveled for the Louisiana Negro Chapter of the WCTU, for which she served as president. As a delegate to the International WCTU Convention in Edinburgh, Scotland (1900), she toured England, Ireland, and Europe visiting prisons and giving speeches to raise money for her child welfare and prison reforms. Shortly after her return from Europe, she put the money to good use by purchasing 105 acres of farmland to build a school on Gentilly Avenue in New Orleans.

Joseph mustered community support for her school by gaining the help of the New Orleans *Times-Democrat* in raising money to pay off the mortgage and by acquiring the support of Ida A. Richardson, wife of the dean of the Louisiana State University Medical School, Tobias G. Richardson. Ida Richardson organized the Louisiana Episcopal Diocesan Women's Auxiliary in assisting the work of the school and in fundraising for construction of a school building and dormitory. One of the members of the advisory board was Adolphe P. Gaudet, whom Frances Joseph married.

Founded in 1902, the Colored Industrial and Normal School served as both an orphanage and as an academic institution based on the industrial education model of Booker T. Washington. Students received academic instruction mixed with training in gardening, domestic science, care of livestock, mattress-making, and other skills needed in the southern economy. Expansion of the school was demonstrated by the addition of a girls' dormitory named after Richardson in 1911 and three more buildings by 1913. By 1921 the school served around 100 boarding students with a program known for academic excellence. The building and land was worth $100,000 and attracted even students wealthy enough to pay for tuition and board. Her role as principal had achieved success for her reform interests.

Her age and failing eyesight led Frances Joseph-Gaudet to seek institutional sponsorship from the Episcopal church in 1919. In 1921 the offer was officially accepted by the Diocesan Convention. When the church accepted the responsibility, the fundamental test of Christianity was achieved in the embracing of believers of all colors. With additional funds from the American Church Institute for Negroes, the New Orleans Community Chest, the city of New Orleans, and the American Church Institute, the school continued to grow. She remained as principal until her eyesight failed. She moved to Chicago to live with relatives, but returned to monitor the school's progress. She died on December 24, 1934. The school was closed in 1955 as a result of expanding opportunities for blacks to receive education. In October 1955, the diocese opened the Gaudet Episcopal Home for boys and girls from 4 to 16 years of age as a shelter, care, and supervisory institution. Today, Episcopal Community Services administers programs that carry on her spirit of reform from funds of the Gaudet Fund. The Gaudet Center of St. Luke's Episcopal Church in New Orleans and St. Michael's in Baton Rouge administer programs for community youth, hunger centers, and senior citizens. Her message of community outreach lives on.

—Beth Schneider

Bibliography

Frances Joseph-Gaudet's autobiography, *He Leadeth Me* (New Orleans: Amistad Research Center, 1913), provides much of the information about her early life and the motivations leading to her prison, temperance, and child welfare work. She is also cited in Elizabeth L. Davis, *Lifting as We Climb* (Washington: NACW, 1933). Her reforms are noted in "Mrs. Frances A. Joseph," *Colored American* 4 (December 1903): 218–221. Much of the information about the school can be found in the records of the Episcopal Diocese of New Orleans, Special Collections, Howard-Tilton Library, Tulane University. The most concise summary of her life is in Violet Harrington Bryan's article, "Frances Joseph-Gaudet: Black Philanthropist," *Sage* III:1 (Spring 1986): 46–49.

JOYNER, FLORENCE [GRIFFITH] (b. 1959), athlete and Olympic Gold Medal runner, was the seventh of 11 children born to Robert, an electronics technician, and Florence Griffith, a seamstress, on December 21. At age four, when her parents divorced, she moved from the Mohave Desert to Jordan Downs housing project in the Watts area of Los Angeles. Though she never went hungry, she ate oatmeal for breakfast, lunch, and dinner on several occasions.

Known as "Dee Dee" to distinguish her from her mother, she started to run and win races at age seven. When she visited her father in the Mohave Desert, she honed her running skill by chasing rabbits. She competed in Los Angeles under the auspices of the Sugar Ray Robinson Youth Foundation. At age 14, she won the annual Jesse Owens National Youth Games and was awarded an all-expenses-paid trip to a meet in San Francisco. While a teenager, she kept a pet boa constrictor, whose skin she saved after shedding for painting. She studied the Bible and became an expert in crocheting, knitting, styling hair, and decorating fingernails.

In 1978 she graduated from Jordan High School in Los Angeles, where she had set records in the long jump and sprinting. In 1979 she enrolled at California

State University, Northridge (CSUN), where she majored in business. Due to lack of funds, she had to leave after her first year and obtain employment as a bank teller. Bob Kersee, the assistant track coach at CSUN, helped her obtain financial aid and suggested that she concentrate her track career on the 200-meter dash. When Kersee accepted a coaching position at the University of California, Los Angeles, Griffith-Joyner decided to follow him there in 1980. During the trials for the 1980 Olympics, she narrowly missed making the team that would never compete due to the U.S. boycott of the Moscow Olympics over the Soviet Union's intervention in Afghanistan.

She continued to improve and won the 400-meter dash in the National Collegiate Athletic Association (NCAA) championships in 1983 and placed second in the 200-meter dash. Training with Kersee and his World Class Track Club, though she no longer studied at UCLA, she was catapulted into prominence in 1984 during the Los Angeles Olympics for her performance winning the silver medal in the 200-meter and her lengthy fingernails painted red, white, and blue. Disappointed, she returned to Union Bank in Los Angeles as a customer service representative and worked nights braiding hair. She gained weight, ended her engagement to sprinter Greg Foster, and went into semiretirement.

As the Seoul Olympics approached, she asked Kersee to help her train. A new friend and coach, Al Joyner, a triple jumper who had won the 1984 Olympic Gold Medal, encouraged her. They married in Las Vegas in October 1987. She went on to win the silver medal in the 200-meter race at the World Championship Games in Rome. On the advice of Ben Johnson, a world record holder in the 100-meter race, she started a lengthy weightlifting regimen. In July 1988 at the U.S. Olympic team trials in Indianapolis, she set a world record clocking 10.60 seconds in the 100 meters, but high tail winds prevented this time from being accepted. In the next preliminary round she again broke the record at 10.49 seconds. Later that week, she set a U.S. record in the 200-meter dash with a time of 21.77 seconds. All through these competitions she sported flamboyant running outfits that attracted as much attention as her record times.

Also attracting attention was her broken relationship with Kersee, who was replaced as coach by her husband, Al Joyner. She charged that the World Class Track Club had cultish overtones. These allegations did not prevent her from appearing on the covers of Newsweek, Sports Illustrated, Ebony, and others in the United States and major publications in Germany, Japan, and France. By that point she was receiving $25,000 per race, compared to her earlier rate of $1,500.

At the Summer Olympics in Seoul, she continued to break records and attract attention. Still her accomplishments were clouded by allegations of steroid use that accelerated after her friend Ben Johnson was found to have ingested these banned substances. Unsubstantiated allegations did not bar "Flo-Jo" from attracting so many offers for endorsements that some suggested her nickname should be "Cash Flo." She began writing children's fiction and a novel. She signed a contract with IBM to give promotional talks. On February 25, 1989, she retired from track to devote full-time effort to her commercial ventures. Her daughter, Mary Ruth, born on November 13, 1990, has already received offers for scholarships from colleges impressed by her genetic background. Flo Jo today combines motherhood with her business interests.

—Gerald Horne

Bibliography

References on Florence Griffith Joyner are voluminous, especially during the period of the Olympics. A book by Nathan Aaseng entitled *Florence Griffith Joyner* (Minneapolis: Lerner Publications, 1989) provides the details of her life and career as does Michael Davis, *Black American Women in Olympic Track and Field* (Jefferson, NC: McFarland, 1992); and Allen Guttmann, *The Olympics* (Urbana: University of Illinois Press, 1992). Articles include: *USA Today* (September 7, 1988); *Washington Post* (July 22, 1988); *People* (August 29, 1988); *New York Times* (August 4, 1988); and *New York Newsday* (July 24, 1988).

JOYNER-KERSEE, JACKIE (b. 1962), the first woman to win the heptathlon in two Olympics, was born March 3 in East St. Louis, Illinois, a city with high unemployment, poverty, and crime. She was the second of four children born to Alfred, Sr., and Mary Joyner. Her siblings include Alfred, Jr., an Olympic Gold Medalist in the triple jump (1984), Angela, and Debra. Named for Jacqueline Kennedy because her grandmother knew she would be the "first lady of something," Joyner-Kersee began competing in track at age nine. By age 12 she was long jumping more than 16 feet. Taking a coach's advice to try multiple events, she began participating in the long jump and the pentathlon, an event later replaced by the heptathlon, featuring these events: 100-meter hurdles, high jump, shot put, 200-meter dash, long jump, javelin, and 800-meter run.

Joyner-Kersee spent her grade school years at John Robinson Elementary School and attended Lincoln High School, where she excelled in volleyball, basketball, and track and field. The Lincoln High girls' basketball team beat opponents by an average of 52.8 points, compiling a 62–2 record her last 2 seasons. In her junior year, Joyner-Kersee set the state high school record for the long jump, and in her senior year she made the All-State Basketball Team. At age 14 she won her first of four National Junior Championships in the pentathlon, and in 1979, she won the long jump at the Pan-American Junior Games. At the Olympic trials in 1980, she jumped 20 feet, 9 3/4 inches, a personal best. Unfortunately, the U.S. boycott kept her from participating in the 1980 Summer Olympics in Moscow.

Joyner-Kersee also performed well in the classroom, graduating in the top 10 percent of her class in 1980. She received a scholarship to attend UCLA in basketball and in track and field. In January 1981, the beginning of the second semester of her freshman year, Joyner-Kersee's mother died suddenly at age 38 from spinal meningitis. Joyner sought comfort from a new assistant coach, Bob Kersee. Noticing that she had lots of potential, Kersee asked to coach her. Presently the head coach for women's track and field at UCLA, Kersee has continued to coach Joyner-Kersee; the couple eventually married January 11, 1986.

At UCLA Joyner-Kersee began demonstrating her enormous athletic ability in basketball and in track and field in spite of her being diagnosed as an asthmatic. A star forward, Joyner-Kersee helped the Lady Bruins to a 20–10 record her senior year, a season she averaged 12.7 points per game and 9.3 rebounds. When she had finished her basketball career, Joyner-Kersee had placed on the top ten all-time lists in rebounding (fourth), scoring (eighth), and assists (tenth). Continuing her outstanding performance in the heptathlon and long jump, Joyner-Kersee led the Lady Bruins to the 1982 NCAA Championships in track and field, scoring 32 of the team's 153 points. While competing in the World Track and Field Championships in Helsinki in 1983, she pulled a hamstring and was forced to withdraw. In the 1984 Summer Olympics in Los Angeles, she finished second behind Australian Glynis Nunn in the heptathlon and settled for a Silver Medal. Again a hamstring injury hampered Joyner-Kersee, who, as a result of this disappointment, decided to take a year off from basketball to train for the 1988 Olympics.

The decision paid off enormously, and Joyner-Kersee started down a path that has earned her the unofficial title of the "World's Greatest Woman Athlete." Joyner-Kersee broke the American record for the long jump at Zurich, Switzerland, in 1985. She also established the collegiate long jump record (22 feet, 11 3/4 inches) and the collegiate heptathlon record (6,718 points). In July 1986 at the Moscow Goodwill Games, she broke the world record in the heptathlon, scoring 7,148 and eclipsing the older mark by 200 points. Just 26 days later at the U.S. Olympic Festival in Houston, she placed first in every heptathlon event and again broke the world record by scoring 7,161 points. In 1987 Joyner-Kersee tied the world record in the long jump at the Pan-American Games in Indianapolis, won in both the long jump and heptathlon at the U.S. Olympic Track and Field Trials, once again setting the heptathlon world record at 7,215 points, and set the indoor 55-meter hurdles world record. Finally, in the 1988 Summer Olympics in Seoul, Korea, Joyner-Kersee obtained two well-deserved Gold Medals in the long jump and the heptathlon, along the way setting the world record for the heptathlon with 7,291 points. On August 25, 1991, at the World Track and Field Championships in Tokyo, she twisted her ankle during a long-jump takeoff, but still won a Gold Medal. Later, however, she pulled her hamstring while running the 200 meters and had to withdraw from the heptathlon. Because of this injury she had to take nearly five months off for recuperation, but came back to set a long jump record at the 85th Millrose Games at Madison Square Garden on February 7, 1992. Joyner-Kersee competed and won in the long jump and heptathlon at the 1992 Olympic Trials in New Orleans. Her achievements in the

1992 Summer Olympics in Barcelona, Spain, in July 1992 made her the first woman to win the heptathlon in two Olympics.

These performances and others have earned her many awards including American Athletic Federation (AAF) World Trophy recipient (1989); University of Missouri honorary doctorate (1989); *Essence* Award Winner (1988), *Sporting News* Female Athlete of the Year (1988), MacDonald's Amateur Sportswoman Award (1987), the Associated Press Female Athlete of the Year (1987), Women's Sports Foundation Amateur Sportswoman of the Year (1987), the Sullivan Award for the Best U.S. Athlete (1986), the *Track and Field News* Athlete of the Year (1986, 1987), the Jesse Owens Award (1986, 1987), the Broderick Cup for Collegiate Woman Athlete of the Year (1986), the UCLA Most Valuable Player in basketball and track and field (1986), and UCLA Scholar Athlete (1985).

Joyner-Kersee graduated from UCLA in 1986 with a BA in history and a minor in communications. She started the Jackie Joyner-Kersee Foundation, serves on the advisory board of the track club Athletics Congress, which was organized by Bob Kersee, and is a member of the board of directors for the St. Louis Girls Club. She and her husband live in Long Beach, California.

—Faye A. Chadwell

Bibliography

Several standard biographical sources offer current biographical data on Jackie Joyner-Kersee, including *Who's Who among Black Americans, Who's Who of American Women,* and *Who's Who of America.* Joe Morgenstern's entry on Joyner-Kersee in *New York Times Biographical Service,* Janet Woolum's entry in *Outstanding Women Athletes,* and *Current Biography Yearbook's* entry all offer interesting details about Joyner-Kersee's life. For specifics about her performances, consult appropriate issues of *Track and Field News.* Additionally there is wide coverage of Joyner-Kersee in most large daily newspapers and popular magazines. All of these are too numerous to list but may be accessed in appropriate indexes like *Reader's Guide* or *Biography Index.*

Secondary Sources

Cloyd, Iris, ed. *Who's Who among Black Americans,* 6th ed. Detroit: Gale, 1990–1991, pp. 723–724.

Collier, Aldore. "The World's Greatest Woman Athlete," *Ebony* 41 (October 1986): 77–78.

Davis, Michael. *Black American Women in Olympic Track and Field.* Jefferson, NC: McFarland, 1992.

Dunaway, Jim. "JJK Sails to Second Gold," *Track and Field News* 41:11 (November 1988): 69.

Guttmann, Allen. *The Olympics.* Urbana: University of Illinois Press, 1992.

Hendershott, Jon. "*Track and Field News* Interview: Jackie Joyner Kersee," *Track and Field News* 43:9 (September 1990): 38–39.

"Jackie in Her Own Zone," *Track and Field News* 41:2 (February 1988): 35.

"JJ Matched World Record," *Track and Field News* 41:2 (February 1988): 30.

"Joyner-Kersee, Jackie," in *Current Biography Yearbook*, edited by Charles Moritz. New York: Wilson, 1987, pp. 293–296.

Kort, Michele. "Go, Jackie, Go," *Ms.* 17 (October 1988): 31–33.

———. "Picture Perfect," *Runner's World* 23:10 (October 1988): 28–30.

Lee, Yvonne. "Women's Athlete of the Year: Joyner-Kersee Ubiquitous Again," *Track and Field News* 41:2 (February 1988): 6–7.

Morgenstern, Joe. "Olympic Athlete Jackie Joyner-Kerseee: Worldbeater," *New York Times Biographical Service* 19:7 (July 1988): 857–860.

Moore, Kenny. "Ties That Bind," *Sports Illustrated* 66 (April 27, 1987): 76–80+.

Nelson, Bert. "Jackie Rings up WR No. 4," *Track and Field News* 41:11 (November 1988): 74.

Page, James. *Black Olympian Medalists.* Englewood, CO: Libraries Unlimited, 1991.

Reid, Tony. "Cason, Dees Run Millrose Show," *New York Times* (February 8, 1992): Sec. H, 1:1.

Who's Who of America, 17th ed. Wilmette, IL: Marquis Who's Who, 1991–1992, p. 510.

Who's Who of American Women, 16th ed. Wilmette, IL: Marquis Who's Who, 1989–1990, p. 459.

Willman, Howard. "*Track and Field News* Interview: Jackie Joyner," *Track and Field News* 39:9 (September 1986).

Woolum, Janet. *Outstanding Women Athletes: Who They Are and How They Influenced Sports in America.* Phoenix, AZ: Oryx Press, 1992.

K

KECKLEY, ELIZABETH [HOBBS] (1818–1907),

born a slave at Dinwiddie Court-House, Virginia, became a national figure as a result of her employment by Mary Todd Lincoln. Her slave parents, Agnes and George Pleasant Hobbs, who had different owners, were separated because her father's master moved west. Elizabeth soon was separated from her mother too, loaned at age 14 by her master to his son. Four years later Elizabeth was sold to a couple in North Carolina. Her new master and his wife abused her; Keckley was raped by her master and bore a son she named George. She returned to Virginia to serve her original master's daughter and her husband, who relocated to St. Louis, Missouri, hoping to improve their economic woes.

The family's debts grew, and Keckley's master stated he would send Keckley's mother to work. Keckley, delighted to be reunited with her frail mother, volunteered to earn wages instead. Talented with needle and thread, Keckley became a respected dressmaker, accumulating ample funds. She desired to buy freedom for herself and George, attempting to save some of her earnings for that purpose. With the help of her patrons, Keckley paid the $1,200 price in 1855.

She married James Keckley but realized he was a slave, not a freeman as he claimed. She learned to read and write and departed Missouri on a train to Baltimore in 1860. Keckley taught black women how to cut and fit dresses and then moved to Washington, DC, where Varina Davis hired her to construct garments for her family. They adored Keckley and invited her to move south with them as sectional tensions grew, but she elected to remain in Washington, DC, where she had many clients, including such luminaries as Stephen Douglas's wife.

Mary Lincoln admired a dress Keckley made and arranged an introduction. Keckley designed Lincoln's inaugural ball gown and, because of her loyalty and industriousness, became Lincoln's modiste and confidante. Lincoln clipped designs from *Godey's Lady's Book* for Keckley to construct and built a large wardrobe. Mary Lincoln confided to Keckley about her debts as well as her opinions of generals and politicians. Keckley often conversed with President Abraham Lincoln, and her presence helped shape his opinion of blacks and policy toward them. He invited Keckley to be present at family and political functions such as touring Richmond after its capture in 1865.

Keckley's son attended Wilberforce University in Xenia, Ohio, and enlisted in the Union Army; he was killed at the Battle of Wilson's Creek in August 1861. She hired spiritualists to communicate with his spirit and encouraged Mary Lincoln to seek similar help when her son and husband died.

In 1862 Keckley founded the Contraband Relief Association, of which she was the first president, to assist freedmen; she also established the Home for Destitute Women and Children. She garnered support from black churches in the capital and also traveled to New York and Boston with Mary Lincoln to establish branches and acquire funds.

After Lincoln's assassination, Keckley consoled his widow. Mary Lincoln gave Keckley some of her husband's personal belongings for Keckley to donate to Wilberforce University. Keckley accompanied Lincoln on her move to Chicago, but when Lincoln ran out of funds, Keckley returned to the capital. She was hired by President Andrew Johnson's daughters to make dresses. She corresponded frequently with Mary Lincoln, especially about financial concerns. Lincoln believed that Congress would give her funds to reimburse Keckley's services. However, these funds were not readily granted.

In March 1867 Lincoln wrote Keckley about her lack of adequate funds and her scheme to sell her clothes and jewelry in New York City that fall. She insisted Keckley join her, but their efforts were fruitless. Keckley decided to stage an exhibit of the clothes, asking for patron donations. She asked Frederick Douglass and Henry Highland Garnet to donate proceeds from their lectures, but Lincoln refused to accept this plan and Keckley's suggestion to sell the clothes in Europe.

Soon thereafter, Keckley wrote her book, perhaps with the help of writer James Redpath, about her experiences in the White House and her friendship with Mary Lincoln. Keckley published the book to raise funds to alleviate Lincoln's financial woes and to compensate herself for the unpaid services rendered Lincoln. Mary Lincoln was outraged to find the text included confidential letters. Robert Lincoln immediately had the book pulled from store shelves or purchased in bulk by Lincoln allies. Mary Lincoln denounced Keckley, who suffered client boycotts and received minimal profits from the book. Many blacks felt that she had betrayed the Lincolns and that her actions adversely affected other black seamstresses.

Keckley received a small pension from her son's death. She visited her former masters and taught domestic science at Wilberforce University from 1892 to 1893. For the remainder of her life, she lived in obscurity, ironically, at the Home for Destitute Women and Children that she had created. Devoutly attending the Fifteenth Street Presbyterian Church, Keckley clung to her memories and trinkets, such as strands of President Lincoln's hair, from her days in the White House. She died on May 26, 1907, of a paralytic stroke and was buried in Harmony Cemetery in Washington, DC.

In the 1930s controversy emerged concerning the authorship of her book. Detractors claimed that journalist Jane Grey Swisshelm actually penned the text since Keckley was not capable of writing the volume. Her friends refuted the claims, defending Keckley's capability and presence at the time of the writing.

—Elizabeth D. Schafer

Bibliography

Elizabeth Keckley, *Behind the Scenes: Or, Thirty Years a Slave and Four Years in the White House* (New York: Arno Press, 1868) is Keckley's intimate account of her life and relationship with the Lincolns. Materials relating to Keckley's receipt of her son's pension are contained in the National Archives. A letter from Keckley to Jesse Weik, dated April 2, 1889, about Lincoln artifacts she owned is included in the Herndon-Weik Papers at the Library of Congress.

Rayford W. Logan, "Elizabeth Keckley," in *Dictionary of American Negro Biography*, edited by Rayford W. Logan and Michael R. Winston (New York: Norton, 1982), 375–376; Benjamin Quarles, "Elizabeth Keckley," in *Notable American Women, 1607–1959: A Biographical Dictionary* 2, edited by Edward T. James, Janet Wilson James, and Paul S. Boyer (Cambridge: Belknap, 1971), pp. 310–311; Sylvia G.L. Dannett, *Profiles of Negro Womanhood 1619–1900*, Volume 1 (Chicago: Educational Heritage Press, 1964); and Bert James Loewenberg and Ruth Bogin, eds., *Black Women in Nineteenth-Century American Life: Their Words, Their Thoughts, Their Feelings* (University Park: Pennsylvania State University Press, 1976) are biographical profiles of Keckley's activities.

Jean H. Baker, *Mary Todd Lincoln: A Biography* (New York: Norton, 1987); Jeannie James and Wayne Temple, "Mrs. Lincoln's Clothing," *Lincoln Herald* 62 (Summer 1960): 54–65; Hallie Q. Brown, *Homespun Heroines and Other Women of Distinction* (Xenia, OH: Aldine Press, 1926); and Smith D. Fry, "Lincoln Liked Her," *Minneapolis Register* (July 6, 1901) note Keckley's role in the Lincoln White House. Ruth Painter Randall, *Mary Lincoln: A Biography of a Marriage* (Boston: Little, Brown, 1953) comments on the reliability of Keckley's book.

Charles S. Wesley and Patricia W. Romero, *Negro Americans in the Civil War: From Slavery to Citizenship* (New York: Publishers Co., 1967) and Benjamin Quarles, *The Negro in the Civil War* (New York: Russell, 1952) comment on Keckley's influence on President Lincoln's attitudes toward African Americans. John E. Washington, *They Knew Lincoln* (New York: Dutton, 1942) expresses admiration of Keckley. C. Percy Powell, *Lincoln Day by Day, 1809–1865* (Washington, DC: U.S. Sesquicentennial Commission, 1960) contains comments on Keckley in contemporary newspapers such as the *Anglo-African* (New York). The *First Annual Report of the Contraband Relief Association of D.C.* (1863) notes her work with aiding freed slaves adjust to new roles, responsibilities, and lifestyles.

The *Washington Star* (November 11 and 15, 1935) contains some controversial correspondence addressing the authorship of Keckley's book. Letters from Francis J. Grimké, Keckley's minister, as well as individuals supporting and denying Keckley's authorship, are included in the *Journal of Negro History* (January 1936): 56–57 and 313–317. Carter G. Woodson, ed., *The Works of Francis J. Grimké* 4 (Washington: Associated Publishers, 1942), pp. 545–549, reiterates Grimké's belief that Keckley wrote her book.

KELLY, LEONTINE [TURPEAU, CURRENT] (b. 1920), the first woman of African-American descent to be elected to the episcopacy of the United Methodist church, was born on March 5 in Washington, DC, and reared in Cincinnati, Ohio. Her parents served as models for her career in the ministry and community activism. Her father, Dr. David D. Turpeau, was both a pastor and a member of the Ohio Legislature. Her mother, Ila M., was active in the

community and helped organize the National Association for the Advancement of Colored People (NAACP) and Urban League chapters in Cincinnati.

Kelly attended West Virginia State College through her junior year. She then married her first husband, Gloster Current. The couple divorced 15 years later. After marriage to her second husband, the Reverend David Kelly, she returned to school and graduated from Virginia Union in 1960 at age 40. The mother of four became a social studies teacher in the public school system. At her husband's urging, Kelly also became a lay speaker in the church.

Kelly did not enter the ordained ministry until 1970, one year after her husband's death. She attended Union Theological Seminary in Richmond, Virginia, graduated with a master of divinity degree at age 56. She pastored two churches, served as the associate director of the Virginia Conference (United Methodist) Council on Ministries, and was director of a cooperative urban ministry and outreach program at her second church, Asbury–Church Hill United Methodist Church of Richmond. Kelly then served as the evangelism executive for the board of discipleship of the United Methodist church, and was the first woman to preach on the national radio pulpit in 1984.

In 1983 Kelly became the first African-American woman to be elected to the episcopacy of the United Methodist church. Until her retirement in 1988, she served as bishop of the San Francisco area. She currently resides in San Mateo, California, and maintains a rigorous speaking schedule.

—Emilie M. Townes

Bibliography

Marshall, Marilyn. "First Black Woman Bishop," *Ebony* (November 1984): 164–168.
Weidman, Judith L., ed. *Women Ministers: How Women Are Redefining Traditional Roles.* San Francisco: Harper & Row, 1984.

KEMP, MAIDA [STEWART, SPRINGER] (b. 1910), a leader in the trade union movement since the 1930s, has contibuted to worker education, women's health, and the organization of African workers through her efforts at the local, national, and international levels of the union movement. Born in Panama on January 12 to Harold and Adina (Forrest) Stewart, Maida Stewart lived with her father, an Englishman working on the construction of the Panama Canal. At age seven, she immigrated to New York City, where her mother supported herself and her daughter by working a variety of jobs, eventually becoming a licensed beautician. Her mother was a follower of Marcus Garvey, leader of the Universal Negro Improvement Association and advocate of black pride. Maida Stewart attended public school in New York City and a black boarding school in New Jersey. She later claimed that her mother's involvement in the Garvey movement, the black church, and the boarding school prepared her for labor activism.

After boarding school, she returned to New York to receive training as a beautician. Instead of practicing those skills, she served as a receptionist for Poro College, which was part of the Malone College of Beauty Culture. In 1928 she quit her job to marry Owen W. Springer, also a West Indian. He worked on equipment for dentists before employment at a shipyard during World War II. The couple had one child, Eric.

In 1932 the Depression forced Springer to take a position in the garment industry, where she continued to work for about a decade. Faced with poor working conditions, she joined Local 22 of the Dressmakers Union of the AFL. When the International Ladies Garment Workers Union (ILGWU) went on strike in 1933, she was active on a strike committee. As Springer moved into leadership positions in her own union, she received training at the Educational Department of ILGWU, Wellesley Institute, the Hudson Shore Labor School, and the Rand School of Social Sciences. She became a captain in the Women's Health Brigade and served as its business agent. In 1942 she became an education director for the Plastic Button and Novelty Workers' Union, where she worked with groups entering trade unions for the first time during World War II. She was the only black women chosen by the AFL to go to Great Britain in 1945 to meet with working women there.

After World War II, Springer's responsibilities expanded. Working for A. Philip Randolph, she directed a major rally in Madison Square Garden in support of a permanent Fair Employment Practices Commission. She also created the Midwestern Regional Office of the A. Philip Randolph Institute (1969–1972). In addition she was an organizer for ILGWU in the southwestern United States in the 1960s.

Springer expanded her involvement in the international labor movement, studying worker education in Sweden and Denmark and at Oxford University in England. She served as a representative of the AFL-CIO Department of International Affairs from 1959 to 1965. After visiting Africa as a representive of the AFL-CIO at the International Confederation of Free Trade Unions, she became particularly interested in African workers and was involved in a variety of projects there. In the 1980s she was on the international staff of ILGWU and was a consultant for the African Labor History Center.

In addition to her trade union work, Springer was vice president of the National Council of Negro Women, and a member of the board of the DuSable History Museum in Chicago. She worked against segregation in the armed forces and for the Neighborhood Day Nursery School. Her memberships include NAACP, Urban League, National Organization for Women, and the Coalition of Labor Union Women.

Her labor activism brought Springer her second husband, James Kemp, a labor activist in Illinois. An Episcopalian, Maida Springer Kemp continues to make Chicago her home.

—Marilyn Dell Brady

Bibliography

Maida Kemp was among the black women interviewed by the Black Women's Oral History Project, Radcliffe College. Ruth Edmonds Hill, ed., *The Black Women: Oral History Project* (Westport, CT: Meckler, 1990) includes biographical notes putting Kemp's life in historical context and the transcript from her 1977 interview in which Kemp gives her own perspective on her life. Standard reference works are useful in establishing her various memberships and positions. For example, see Harry A. Ploski and James Williams, ed., *The Negro Almanac* (Detroit: Gale, 1989, 5th ed.); and *Who's Who in Colored America* (New York: Burchell, Christain E. & Associates, 1950, 7th ed.). A description of her World War II activities can be found in the Schomburg Clipping Collection, New York Public Library.

Articles by Kemp have appeared in the publications of the Hudson Shore Labor School, *Opportunity* magazine, and *Justice* magazine.

KENNEDY, ADRIENNE (LITA) [HAWKINS] (b. 1931), playwright and lecturer, was born September 13 in Pittsburgh, Pennsylvania, to Cornell W., a social worker and member of the NAACP, and Etta Hawkins, a schoolteacher. She grew up in this cultured, middle-class family, which relocated to the integrated community of Mount Pleasant and Glenville in Cleveland, Ohio. Although Cleveland had its problems, Kennedy did not become aware of racial prejudice until she went to college at Ohio State University. There, in a dormitory of over 600 girls, the dozen black women experienced a silent type of persecution. Some of the feelings stirred up by her years at Ohio State University, from which she received her BA in 1952, became the basis for her recent play, *The Ohio State Murders*, which examines the awakening of intellectual curiosity within a young black student who resents the white faculty initiating that growth. Commissioned by the Great Lakes Theater Festival in 1990, the play was first presented to the Yale Drama School's Winterfest of works in progress before coming to the Ohio Theatre in Cleveland in March 1992. With this most recent play, Adrienne Kennedy has come full circle in her return and examination of her own roots.

Following her graduation from Ohio State, Adrienne Hawkins married Joseph C. Kennedy on May 15, 1953; had a son, Joseph C. Adam; and went on to graduate study at Columbia University (1954–1956). She became a member of a playwriting unit at Actors Studio in New York following her trip to Africa in 1960, a cultural awakening that profoundly influenced her perspective on the continent and of the people. The playwriting unit nurtured her inner voice, and the playwright emerged. *Funnyhouse of a Negro*, an examination of the experience of being black in America, was first produced Off Broadway at the Circle in the Square Theatre in 1962, for which she won an Obie Award in 1964. In 1963 her one-act theatre piece *The Owl Answers* was first produced in Westport, Connecticut. Again, identity is the crux of the play in which a mulatto girl struggles with the dominant symbol—hair. The kinky hair of the black mother is contrasted with the long, silky hair of her white father, as are the symbolic birds the dove and the owl. By 1969, the play received good reviews in an Off-Broadway production at the Public Theatre in New York City.

These and other early plays were neglected by her contemporaries, who felt they were not sufficiently "political" for the times. It is not that the plays lacked political content, rather they presented themes in subtle imagery. Instead of using the conventional techniques of her predecessors, Kennedy chose to use metaphor, surreal illusions, and other devices of the poet. Most of her plays are one-act pieces that display semi-autobiographical introspections on identity and self-knowledge. This theme appears throughout works such as *Boats* (1969), *Sun: A Poem for Malcolm X* (1970), *A Movie Star Has to Star in Black and White* (1976), and *Black Children's Day* (1980).

While continuing to write her plays, Kennedy has supported herself through teaching college and obtaining grants. She won the coveted Guggenheim Fellowship in 1967; Rockefeller grants in 1967–1969, 1974, and 1976; National Endowment for the Humanities Grant in 1973; CBS Fellowship in 1973; Creative Artists Public Service Grant in 1974; and Yale Fellowship in 1974–1975. She added to her formal study with work at the New School for Social Research, American Theatre Wing, Circle in the Square Theatre School, and Edward Albee's workshop.

These experiences and her life as a playwright led to her 1987 publication of *People Who Led to My Plays*, an autobiographical memoir. The three plays *The Ohio State Murders*, *She Talks to Beethoven*, and *The Film Club* were published as *Deadly Triplets* in 1992 by the University of Minnesota Press. She continues to teach as a member of the Afro-American Studies Department at Princeton University.

—Beth Schneider

Bibliography

Much of the information was obtained from interviews with Adrienne Kennedy during the Adrienne Kennedy Festival, January–March 1992, Cleveland, Ohio. Critical perspectives of her work are included in *But Some of Us Are Brave*, edited by Gloria T. Hull, Patricia Bell Scott, and Barbara Smith (Old Westbury, NY: Feminist Press, 1982); and Marianna Davis, *Contributions of Black Women to America* (Columbia, SC: Kenday, 1982). Biographical information can be found in Esther Arata, *Black American Playwrights* (Metuchen, NJ: Scarecrow, 1978); *Contemporary Authors* 26, edited by Hal May and James Lesniak (Detroit: Gale, 1989); and Mari Evans, *Black Women Writers, 1950–1980* (New York: Doubleday, 1984).

KENNEDY, FLORYNCE (FLO) (b. 1916), feminist, political activist, and lawyer, was born in Kansas City, Missouri, the third of five daughters of Zella and Wiley Kennedy. She graduated at the top of her high school class, but could not afford to go to college, so she worked cleaning houses and then opened a hat shop with her sisters, with whom she always remained close. After their mother's death in 1942, she and her sister Grayce moved to New York City. Ignoring the advice of those who tried to steer her toward City College and a career in teaching or nursing, Flo Kennedy took pre-law evening courses at Columbia University, working during the day to support herself. When the dean of Columbia Law School explained that she was denied admission in 1948 because she was a woman, she suggested that racism was the real reason and talked her way into being admitted.

Intensely political in her consciousness from the 1940s onward, Kennedy saw in law school how the law helped maintain the status quo, and she vowed to use her profession to fight for change. As a lawyer for the Billie Holiday and Charlie Parker estates in the 1950s, she attempted to make the recording and publishing industry accountable for their exploitation of jazz musicians and set a precedent for protecting artists' rights. In 1957 she married Charlie Dye, a Welsh writer ten years her junior, who died of alcoholism not long after their marriage.

In the 1960s Kennedy's professional skills, militancy, and verbal acuity enabled her to play a more visible role than that allowed most black women in either the black power movement or the early women's movement. She represented black activist H. Rap Brown on several occasions and was an original member of the National Organization for Women (NOW), founded in 1966. Frustrated with what she viewed as NOW's conservatism, in 1970 she joined The Feminists, a radical feminist group that had splintered from NOW in October 1968. In 1971 Kennedy formed her own group, the Feminist Party, and also published the book *Abortion Rap*, a book delineating perspectives on abortion, with Diane Shulder.

Throughout the 1970s and 1980s, Flo Kennedy spoke at many public forums, using such terms as "pathology of the oppressed" and "horizontal hostility" (within and among oppressed groups) to reinforce her key theme—that no pervasive system of oppression can exist without the consent of the oppressed. Much of her outrageous public behavior and colorful use of language can be interpreted as psychological decolonization.

Kennedy co-authored the 1981 book *Sex Discrimination in Employment* with William Pepper. Although health problems have mostly confined Kennedy to her New York apartment in recent years, she is working on a guide for young women on how to organize.

—Debra L. Schultz

Bibliography

The main source of biographical information for this essay is Flo Kennedy's autobiography, *Color Me Flo: My Hard Life and Good Times* (Englewood Cliffs, NJ: Prentice-Hall, 1976). See also two other publications co-authored by Kennedy, with Diane Shulder, *Abortion Rap* (New York: McGraw-Hill, 1971), and with William Pepper, *Sex Discrimination in Employment* (Charlottesville, NC: Michie Company,

1981). A characteristic essay by Kennedy is "Institutionalized Oppression vs. the Female," in *Sisterhood Is Powerful: An Anthology of Writings from the Women's Liberation Movement*, edited by Robin Morgan (New York: Vintage Books, 1970). Kennedy's friend, Irene Davall, described Kennedy's current situation to the author at the Women, Men, and Media Conference at Columbia University in October 1990. As part of its current project on the founding of the National Organization for Women, the Schlesinger Library on the History of Women in America at Radcliffe College completed an oral history interview with Flo Kennedy in late 1992.

KING, CORETTA SCOTT (b. 1927), civil rights activist and music educator, has continued to nurture the seed of nonviolence and human rights associated with her late husband, Dr. Martin Luther King, Jr., through her public roles and private life. Born in Marion, Alabama on April 27 to Obadiah (Obie) and Bernice (McMurray) Scott, Coretta Scott grew up in a secure, middle-class family that valued education. She graduated from Lincoln High School in Marion, Alabama, before leaving the South to attend Antioch College in Yellow Springs, Ohio. Her father had opened a general store in 1946 that afforded the family a greater degree of independence. At Antioch College, she functioned within a white world very different from the South. Since the college required students to alternate work experience with academic study, Coretta Scott received exposure to Karamu Camp, where she worked as a counselor and dining room worker. The camp was operated by Cleveland's Karamu House, a social settlement that brought people of both races together through arts and music. She also worked for five months with the poor populations served by the Friendly Inn Settlement House in Cleveland. These experiences gave her greater understanding about common human problems and about the techniques to improve interracial communications. The college granted her work experience for helping her father set up accounting methods, inventories, and merchandising at the family's general store. She graduated with a bachelor's degree in music and elementary education in 1951.

Her lifelong dream of attending a music conservatory was fulfilled through her training at the New England Conservatory of Music. Aided by a grant from the Jessie Smith Noyes Foundation, Coretta Scott began her studies and was soon introduced to a seminary student from Atlanta attending Boston University for his doctorate degree, Martin Luther King, Jr. Within a year, his parents had visited Boston to meet Coretta Scott, who became Mrs. Martin Luther King, Jr., on June 18, 1953, in Marion, Alabama. The young couple returned to Boston to complete their educational programs. She completed the Mus. B. degree in voice in June 1954, while her husband, having completed his residency requirements and comprehensive examinations, accepted a position as pastor to Dexter Avenue Baptist Church in Montgomery, Alabama. His predecessor, the Reverend Vernon Johns, a well-respected advocate for civil rights, had prepared the ground for the young couple's entrance to the city. She established a home while her husband completed his dissertation and served the congregation as the assistant pastor.

The Montgomery bus boycott brought both Kings into the center of the civil rights movement. From the arrest of Rosa Parks on December 1, 1955, Coretta Scott King became involved. When her husband wavered about accepting the position as the head of the Montgomery Improvement Association, she provided the support and guidance for his positive response. She had recently given birth to her first child, Yolanda Denise, but both became directly involved when the King home was bombed. No injuries resulted, but the King family's commitment to nonviolence was tested. As the boycott continued, Coretta Scott King had to buoy her husband's spirits many times before victory came through a federal order to desegregate the buses in December 1956.

As her family roles expanded with three more children (Marty, Dexter, and Bernice), Coretta Scott King continued an active role within the civil rights movement through the campaigns of Birmingham, Selma, and Chicago. As the FBI intensified its efforts to discredit Dr. King's leadership, she was again tested as a wife, exposed to information about her husband's liaisons. Her support continued throughout the years until her husband's assassination in 1968. She expanded his legacy by fighting for recognition of a national holiday honoring her husband and his goals and by establishing the Martin Luther King, Jr., Center for Nonviolent Social Change in Atlanta, Georgia. Declared a National Historic Site by the National Park Service, the center is situated on a 23-acre area around King's birthplace on historic Auburn Avenue. She served as the symbolic leader of the twentieth anniversary celebration of the March on Washington in 1983 and coordinated the first legal celebration of the King national holiday in 1986 and the annual events thereafter.

For her commitment to human rights throughout the world, she has received many honors. President Jimmy Carter appointed her as an alternate delegate of the United Nations. Over 100 colleges have presented her with honorary doctorates. She is a frequent speaker at national and international conferences, and a weekly contributor to newpapers. Her support of the anti-apartheid movement has brought her into the international spotlight with such leaders as Nelson Mandela.

Domestic issues continue to hold her attention as she serves on the Full Employment Action Council, the Black Leadership Roundtable, and the Black Leadership Forum. Conscious of her responsibility to future generations, Coretta Scott King perseveres in the King legacy as she furthers the goals of the Martin Luther King, Jr. Center for Nonviolent Social Change by abiding as its founding president and chief executive officer.

—Kelle S. Taha

Bibliography

Much of the information about Coretta Scott King is found in the materials written about and by her husband. As the wife of such a famous leader, she is often left out of biographical dictionaries due to this connection. Of the works written about Martin Luther King, Jr., that discuss the role of Coretta Scott King, see Lerone Bennett, Jr., *What Manner of Man: A Biography of Martin Luther King, Jr.* (Chicago: Johnson Publishing, 1976); Stephen B. Oates, *Let the Trumpet Sound* (New York: Harper & Row, 1982); David L. Lewis, *King: A Biography* (Urbana: University of Illinois Press, 1970); and David J. Garrow, *The FBI and Martin Luther King, Jr.* (New York: Norton, 1981), and David Garrow, *Bearing the Cross* (New York: Morrow, 1986).

Books by Martin Luther King, Jr. contain references to her: *Stride Toward Freedom* (New York: Harper & Row, 1958); *Strength to Love* (New York: Pocket Books, 1964); *Why We Can't Wait* (New York: Harper and Row, 1964); *Where Do We Go from Here: Chaos or Community?* (New York: Bantam, 1968); and *Trumpet of Conscience* (New York: Harper & Row, 1968).

The Martin Luther King, Jr. Center for Nonviolent Social Change in Atlanta, Georgia, contains much of the primary sources of Coretta Scott King's life and roles. Other collections that have some information are the Martin Luther King, Jr. Collection, Mugar Memorial Library, Boston University; Horace Mann Bond Center for Equal Education, University of Massachusetts Library, Amherst; and the John F. Kennedy Library, Boston. Perspectives of her life are in her autobiography, *My Life with Martin Luther King, Jr.* (New York: Holt, 1969). She is featured in Brian Lanker, *I Dream a World* (New York: Stewart, Tabori and Chang, 1989); Jessie Carney Smith, *Notable Black American Women* (Detroit: Gale, 1992); *Encyclopedia of Black America,* edited by W. Augustus Low and Virgil Clift (New York: A Da Capo, 1990); and *Who's Who among Black Americans, 1990–91* (Detroit: Gale, 1990). Some information can be found in articles about the movement appearing in the *New York Times* and in interviews in *Essence, Ebony,* and other periodicals.

KITT, EARTHA (b. 1928), actress and singer, was born on January 26 in North, South Carolina, to William and Anna Mae (Riley) Kitt, poverty-stricken sharecroppers. As the oldest of two girls, Eartha Kitt took on the role of protector to her younger sister, Anna Pearl, especially after her father disappeared and her mother abandoned them to live with a man who had eight children. Kitt related her early abandonment in her autobiography, *Thursday's Child,* in which she tells of her mother's death from voodoo. At age eight, her aunt, Mamie Lue Riley, brought the girls to New York to live with her, supported by her wages as a domestic in New York City. They lived in a Puerto Rican–Italian section of New York, where Kitt developed an ear for languages and a love for singing and dancing. Frequently alone as she grew up, she was able to practice these skills on the streets and at home with little interference. At the New York School of the Performing Arts, her speech class performances produced audiences commanded by her voice. Although these experiences combined with success at such sports as baseball and track and field (she became a champion pole vaulter), she left school at age 14 to work in a sweatshop sewing uniforms for the U.S. Army. She did not forget her love of music and saved some of her earnings for piano lessons.

At age 16, a friend introduced Kitt to Katherine Dunham, dancer and choreographer. Dunham helped Kitt secure a dance training scholarship. Her stage debut was at New York's Belasco Theatre on May 21, 1945, as a member of Dunham's Dance Group in the revue "Blue Holiday." Her achievements led Dunham to select her for the Katherine Dunham Dance Group to tour the United States, Mexico, South America, and Europe as a featured soloist with that group performing Bal Negre. This experience brought confidence and more offers. She appeared in a dance sequence in the film *Casbah* (1947). She appeared in front of the Royal Family in London and toured Paris in 1948. When the Dunham troupe returned to the United States in 1948, Kitt stayed in Paris, finding a room in a hotel that looked out on the Seine River. She started singing at one of the popular nightclubs, Carroll's, and became a popular sensation in Paris. Her career took her to many European cities as well as the Mediterranean and Egypt, where her reception was acclaimed by audiences and critics alike. Her gowns and language abilities garnered rave reviews.

In 1951 her aunt died. Kitt flew home for the funeral. Returning to Paris brought an offer from the acclaimed producer Orson Welles to play Helen of Troy in *Faust*, a performance that won her critical acclaim, even though she had only two days to learn her part. When producer Leonard Sillman saw her performance of "C'est Si Bon" at the New York City nightclub the Village Vanguard in 1952, he invited her to become part of "New Faces," his revue. She received acclaim for her performance and broke all-time attendance records for her singing at the after-dinner show at the Blue Angel nightclub in New York City. She recorded the *Eartha Kitt Album* for RCA Victor, and Twentieth Century Fox produced *New Faces*, a film version of the Sillman revue.

Following the tour of *New Faces* in 1954, she met with her old friend Leonard Sillman, who was producing a play, *Mrs. Patterson*, for Broadway. She agreed to star as Teddy Hicks in the Broadway production. Appearances on television programs, *Toast of the Town*, *The Colgate Comedy Hour*, *Your Show of Shows*, and Edward R. Murrow's *Person to Person*, produced a national reputation. After 101 performances in *Mrs. Patterson*, the show closed in February 1955. She took a hiatus from performing to write her autobiography in 1956. After that she appeared in another Broadway production as Mehitabel in *Shinbone Alley* (1957). In 1958 she appeared in the film *St. Louis Blues* and in the title role of the film *Anna Lucasta*. She ended the decade with another Broadway performance as Jolly in *Jolly's Progress* (1959).

The 1960s brought personal relationships and change in her career. She married William McDonald on June 9, 1960; had a daughter, Kitt, in 1962; and was divorced in 1965. She received the Golden Rose of Montreux, an award for the Swedish television production "Kaskade" in 1962. In the mid-1960s she toured as Doris W in *The Owl and the Pussycat* (1965–1966). When she attended a White House lucheon in January 1968, she openly voiced her views against the war in Vietnam when asked a question about the increased juvenile delinquency in America, which Kitt attributed to the escalating poverty caused by the war. Her statements led to curtailed employment potential. She was investigated by the CIA. Although she won the Woman of the Year award from the National Association of Negro Musicians in 1968, her career was at a standstill for her words at the White House. She again turned to writing and produced a second book, *Alone with Me* (1976).

She returned to Broadway as Sahleem-La-Lume in *Kismet, Timbuktu* in 1978. She returned with her daughter, Kitt McDonald, to the White House as guests of President Jimmy Carter in February 1978. With her career achievement of two Tony nominations and one Grammy Award, Kitt expressed no resentment about the ups and downs of her career. One of her last public appearances on national television was her interview on CBS's *Sixty Minutes* (December 3, 1989).

—Beth Schneider

Bibliography

Kitt's life and career can best be retraced through her autobiographical writings, the periodicals, and reference books on the entertainment field. Her biographical information appears in Jessie Carney Smith, ed., *Notable Black American Women* (Detroit: Gale, 1992); *Current Biography* (New York: Wilson, 1955); *Who's Who in Entertainment* (Chicago: Marquis, 1968); Eileen Landay, *Black Film Stars* (New York: Drake, 1973); Donald Bogle, *Toms, Coons, Mulattoes, Mammies and Bucks: An Interpretive History of Blacks in American Films* (New York: Viking, 1973); Charlemae Rollins, *Famous Negro Entertainers of Stage, Screen, and TV* (New York: Dodd, Mead, 1967); *Who's Who among Black Americans 1991/1992* (Northbrook, IL: Who's Who among Black Americans, 1992); George Hill, *Black Women in Television* (New York: Garland, 1990); Ann Shockley, *Living Black American Authors* (New York: Bowker, 1973); and *Who's Who in the Theatre* (Detroit: Gale, 1981). Her autobiographies include: *Thursday's Child* (New York: Duell, Sloan and Pierce, 1956) and *Alone with Me* (Chicago: Regnery, 1976).

Articles about her appear in *Collier's* (June 11, 1954); *Cue* (November 27, 1954); *Negro History Bulletin* 19 (October 1955): 10; "Eartha Kitts Takes Off," *Ebony* (March 1956): 24; Eartha Kitt, "Fame Can Be Lonely," *Ebony* (December 1957): 83–92; *Time* (January 26, 1968); *Afro-American* (June 17, 1976); *Detroit Free Press* (September 17, 1978); *Washington Post* (January 19, 1978); and Jack Hawn, "Eartha Kitt on Survival," *Los Angeles Times* (March 20, 1986).

KOFEY, LAURA (c. 1893–1928) was perhaps one of the most successful mass organizers of the Universal Negro Improvement Association next to founder Marcus Garvey himself. Her origins are mysterious. Laura Adorkor Kofey claimed

to be an African princess from the Gold Coast (Ghana) who migrated to the United States in 1926 to support the UNIA program for the commercial development of, and repatriation to, Africa. UNIA critics claimed that her real name was Laura Champion; that she was born in Athens, Georgia; and that she lived in Detroit in the early 1920s, where she aspired to be a preacher and joined the Garvey movement. She began to tour widely in the South as a UNIA organizer in 1926, speaking in camp meeting style in several cities in Louisiana, Alabama, and Florida. Her extraordinary charisma reportedly drew thousands of new members into the Garvey movement. She presented herself as an apostle of Marcus Garvey, and in August 1927 she visited the imprisoned UNIA leader at Atlanta Federal Penitentiary.

Her great success and enthusiastic personal following, however, soon drew Garvey's ire, and he took measures to suppress her activities and discredit her reputation. He denounced Kofey in announcements in the UNIA organ, the *Negro World*, urged her arrest by white authorities, and expelled UNIA members who supported her. As a response, she formed her own rival organization, the African Universal Church and Commercial League, based in Miami. AUCCL meetings were regularly disrupted by UNIA hecklers loyal to Garvey. Local black clergy also opposed her because her well-attended Sunday sermons drew away congregants from their own churches.

Kofey was assassinated by a gunman on the evening of March 8, 1928, as she read from the Bible at the beginning of an AUCCL sermon. A UNIA member who was a known opponent of Kofey's and who was present in the audience at the time of the shooting was beaten to death by enraged congregation members who had just witnessed her death because they believed him to be the murderer. Two other UNIA members were soon arrested for the crime, but later released for lack of evidence. The murder was never solved, but was widely believed to have been UNIA instigated. Kofey's body lay in state in several Florida cities and was viewed by mourners who lined the streets. The AUCCL was continued after her death, with members supporting Kofey's vision of Pan-African identification, education in African history, and black nationalist religious convictions. An AUCCL commune, named Adorkaville in Kofey's memory, was established on the outskirts of Jacksonville, Florida, in the 1940s.

—Barbara Bair

Bibliography

The best single source on Kofey's life is Richard Newman, "'Warrior Mother of Africa's Warriors of the Most High God': Laura Adorkor Kofey and the African Universal Church," in *Black Power and Black Religion: Essays and Reviews*, edited by Richard Newman (West Cornwall, CT: Locust Hill Press, 1987), pp. 131–135. Newman conducted interviews and consulted primary sources from within the AUCCL. Kofey's UNIA career and the furor that erupted over the circumstances of her death are documented in Volumes 6 and 7 of *The Marcus Garvey and Universal*

Negro Improvement Association Papers, edited by Robert A. Hill et al. (Berkeley, Los Angeles, London: University of California Press, 1989, 1990) and in *Negro World* microfilm, available at the Schomburg Center for Research in Black Culture, New York Public Library, and at the University Research Library, University of California, Los Angeles. Kofey is also discussed in Barbara Bair, "True Women, Real Men: Gender, Ideology, and Social Roles in the Garvey Movement," in *Connected Domains: Beyond the Private/Public Dichotomy in Women's History*, edited by Susan Reverby and Dorothy O. Helly (Ithaca, NY: Cornell University Press, 1991).

L

LAMPKIN, DAISY [ADAMS] (1888–1965) was a prominent activist for civil rights, especially for African Americans. Her dedicated work for the National Association for the Advancement of Colored People (NAACP) is her best known and most successful. Between the 1930s and the 1940s, she held key marketing positions within the NAACP—first as a regional field secretary (1930–1935) and then as the national field secretary (1935–1947). Her final service was as a member of the board of directors (1947–1965).

Lampkin was born Daisy Elizabeth Adams in Reading, Pennsylvania, on August 9, the only child of George S. Adams, a porter, and Rosa (Proctor). Her mother married John Temple after her father died. The family continued to live in Reading, where Daisy Adams attended the public schools. After graduation, she left for Pittsburgh, where she married William Lampkin in 1912, and started her career in motivational speaking by organizing housewives into consumer protest groups. Through the Lucy Stone Woman Suffrage League, Lampkin promoted the woman suffrage issue among black women's groups, raised money for scholarships, and went on to become a national organizer and board chairman for the National Association of Colored Women (NACW). Although they had no children of their own, Lampkin did help raise the daughter of a deceased friend. This young woman, Romaine Childs, became Lampkin's only heir.

Lampkin's service with the NAACP spanned three administrations: James Weldon Johnson's (ended in 1930); Walter White's (1930–1955); and Roy Wilkins's (1955–1977). She died before the end of Wilkins's directorship. Lampkin also served on several of the NAACP's committees during her long career. Her hard work within the Pittsburgh community and the NAACP as well are still fondly remembered by those in that community, who called her "Aunt Daisy."

Lampkin's work for the NAACP required constant travel to establish or revitalize branches across the country. In 1944 she was able to increase the NAACP's membership more than any other NAACP executive. In 1945 the NAACP named her Woman of the Year due to her many successes with fundraising and membership intakes. A 1947 leaflet published by the *Pittsburgh Courier* reported that Lampkin had raised over $1 million for the NAACP.

In addition to her work with the NAACP, the NACW, and the Lucy Stone Woman Suffrage League, Lampkin was also active in other organizations. These roles include the vice-chair of the Colored Voters' Division of the Republican National Committee, chair for the Allegheny County Negro Women's Republican League, vice-chair of the Negro Voters League of Pennsylvania, board member of the Pittsburgh Urban League, and charter member of the National Council of Negro Women (NCNW). She also served as vice president of the

Pittsburgh Courier from 1925 to 1965 and was an elder of Grace Memorial Presbyterian Church.

Lampkin suffered from many health problems, including hypertension and severe arthritis. Despite these recurring illnesses, Lampkin continued to work hard—even after resigning as the national field secretary in 1947 in order to limit her travels. Her election to the NAACP National Board proved to be very demanding as well.

During a membership drive in Camden, New Jersey, in October 1964, Lampkin suffered a stroke. A few months later, the National Council of Negro Women awarded her the first Eleanor Roosevelt–Mary McLeod Bethune World Citizenship Award in December 1964. But due to her weakened condition, Lampkin was unable to attend and died in Pittsburgh on March 10, 1965. That day's edition of the *Pittsburgh Courier* declared, "Mrs. Lampkin was herself an institution. There was no line of separation between herself and the NAACP. She was truly 'Mrs. NAACP.'"

—Lisa Beth Hill

Bibliography

Primary sources include manuscript collections and oral history interviews. The "Biographical Sketch of Mrs. Daisy E. Lampkin," NAACP Papers, Board of Directors Files III and Branch Files, Library of Congress, Manuscript Division, Madison Building, Washington, DC. Oral history resources include an interview with Romaine Childs, November 12, 1990, Pittsburgh, Pennsylvania; Conversation with attorney Wendell G. Freeland, September 10, 1990, at the Joint Center for Political and Economic Studies, Washington, DC. Mr. Freeland is a lifetime resident of Pittsburgh, Pennsylvania, and is also a close acquaintance of Romaine Childs. Freeland still resides in Pittsburgh. Telephone interview with Dr. Edna B. McKenzie, January 4, 1991, Roanoke, Pennsylvania.

Many of Lampkin's papers are in the possession of Edna B. McKenzie, who is currently writing a biography of Daisy Lampkin. For publications, see her article "Daisy Lampkin: A Life of Love and Service," *Pennsylvania Heritage* IX:3 (Summer 1983): 12. Dr. McKenzie is largely responsible for having a historical marker placed on Lampkin's home, August 9, 1983. Lampkin is the first black woman to be so honored in the state of Pennsylvania. See Sylvia Sachs, "Historical Marker in Hill to Honor Late NAACP Organizer," *Pittsburgh Press* (June 30, 1983): B4.

Secondary Sources

Giddings, Paula. *In Search of Sisterhood: Delta Sigma Theta and the Challenge of the Black Sorority Movement.* New York: William Morrow, 1988. Lampkin was the first honorary member of the Delta Sigma Theta sorority in 20 years when she was inducted on February, 3, 1947. The sorority leaders knew of Lampkin's extraordinary fundraising abilities. The sorority placed Lampkin in charge of their campaign to purchase a national headquarters (p. 227).

————. *When and Where I Enter: The Impact of Race and Sex on Black Women in America.* New York: Bantam Books, 1985, pp. 208-209, 258. Giddings discusses black women's work in the NAACP and similar organizations in Chapters 12 and 14, especially. Lampkin is mentioned as having been an indispensable part of building up and maintaining the NAACP. Giddings says Lampkin and others like her "performed much of the nuts-and-bolts work of their organizations, yet were hardly expected to gain public recognition or even to be in on major policy decisions.

McKenzie, Edna B. "Daisy Lampkin: A Life of Love and Service," *Pennsylvania Heritage* IX:3 (Summer 1983): 12. McKenzie highlights the many contributions Lampkin made to the NAACP and other organizations with which she was affiliated. This is probably the most detailed account of Lampkin's life to date.

Pittsburgh Courier, "Mrs. Daisy Lampkin to Be Delta Honorary Soror: NAACP Executive Is the First Honorary Member in Twenty Years" (February 3, 1947): 8.

————. "NAACP Pioneer: Mrs. Daisy Lampkin Buried in Pittsburgh," (March 20, 1965): front page. This article briefly chronicles the life and service of Lampkin as an executive officer of both the NAACP and the *Pittsburgh Courier* in addition to several other organizations she joined.

Rouse, Jacqueline A. *Lugenia Burns Hope: Black Southern Reformer.* Athens: University of Georgia Press, 1989. Rouse's account of Lugenia Hope chronicles the community and social service of Hope and her contemporaries including Daisy Lampkin. The notion of "ancestral mission" as an inherited responsibility to the uplift of the race as it applied particularly to black women activists is also developed in this biography of Hope.

Salem, Dorothy. *To Better Our World: Black Women in Organized Reform, 1890–1920.* New York: Carlson, 1990. Salem chronicles the activities of black women in the organization of the NAACP from its inception in 1909 until 1920 in Chapter 5 of this book. The contributions of black women particularly and their branch organization efforts were vital to the shaping and continued existence of the NAACP. Although Lampkin's tenure with the NAACP actually began after 1920, Salem provides a detailed history of the original and subsequent work of black women in the organization. Salem asserts, "Black women played a prominent and often overlooked role in the development of the NAACP's branches, black membership, finances, and leadership" (p. 145).

Zangrando, Robert. *The NAACP Crusade Against Lynching, 1909–1950.* Philadelphia: Temple University Press, 1980, pp. vii, viii, and 140. Zangrando provides a history of the NAACP in its early years, focusing on its efforts to stop lynching activities, which had reached significant proportions in the early part of the twentieth century. Daisy Lampkin directed the NAACP antilynching button-selling campaign in 1944, which proved to be quite successful.

LANEY, LUCY (1854–1933), educator and community activist, was born in Macon, Georgia, on April 13. During her lifetime, Lucy Craft Laney's personality was shaped by a variety of experiences. First, she was the daughter of former slaves. Her father, David Laney, was born a slave in South Carolina during the early nineteenth century. Her mother, Louisa Laney, belonged to the Campbell family in Macon. Second, Lucy Laney was a member of a household where education was strongly advocated. David Laney was a well-read and respected Presbyterian preacher. He, along with his wife, encouraged their daughter to read widely. Third, Lucy Laney lived in a community where people cared for others' needs as their own. Fourth, Lucy Laney was privileged, having obtained an education at a time when public education for blacks was not encouraged. She attended Lewis High School (later Ballard Normal School). At age 15, Lucy Laney graduated and was among the first group of students selected by the American Missionary Association to attend its newly opened Atlanta University. Finally, Lucy Laney lived during a time when blacks lacked social, political, and economic rights. These experiences influenced the roles she played as practitioner and organizer, and they formed the attitude she adopted in becoming one of America's greatest educators.

As an educator, Lucy Laney taught in the public schools of Macon, Milledgeville, Augusta, and Savannah until 1885. Aware of the need to establish a school that addressed specific problems confronting black children, Laney, in 1883, opened a school in a rented room in the basement of Christ Presbyterian Church in Augusta. Three years later, in January 1886, the school received a charter from the state of Georgia. In 1887 this concerned educator traveled to Minneapolis to secure financial support from the general assembly of the Presbyterian church, which primarily pledged moral support. Due largely to contributions from Francina Haines and a Mrs. Marshall, Lucy Laney gained popular support for her school, which was later named Haines Normal and Industrial Institute. Financial gifts over the years made it possible for Lucy Laney to erect several brick buildings. Since both a classical and industrial education were strongly emphasized, the enrollment at Lucy Laney's school increased from 5 to 234.

Haines Institute continued to grow as the program attracted outstanding students such as Mary McLeod Bethune. By 1917 the school had a faculty of more than 25 teachers and a student body of at least 900 pupils. At Haines Normal and Industrial Institute, Lucy Laney also implemented programs that emphasized kindergarten education and health care. She founded Augusta's first kindergarten and a nurses training department, which evolved into the School of Nursing at Augusta's University Hospital. Lucy Laney's school was successful because she was austere, strict, and beloved by generations of students for her concern for humankind and for emphasizing service, character, and scholarship. To honor this great educator, a Lucy Laney League was organized in 1900 in New York City.

Lucy Laney, at age 80, died of nephritis and hypertension in Augusta, Georgia, on October 23, 1933. Yet, her legacy continued to influence lives. In 1949 the Haines Normal Institute was replaced with a school that bears her name, Lucy Laney High School.

—Valerie Grim

Bibliography

Beard, Mary R., ed. *America Through Women's Eyes*. New York: Macmillan, 1933. This collection of essays examines women's perceptions of their status, contributions, and progress in the United States.

Brawley, Benjamin. *Negro Builders and Heroes*. Chapel Hill: University of North Carolina Press, 1937. This book describes the most notable African Americans who, during that time, made significant contributions to the development of an African-American history and culture.

Dannett, Sylvia. *Profiles of Negro Womanhood*. New York: M.W. Lads, 1964. This work describes the life and contributions of significant black women in the United States.

Daniel, Sadie I. *Women Builders*. Washington, DC: Associated Publishers, 1970. This book lists the outstanding contributions of black women in the United States.

Death Certificate. Georgia Department of Public Health. Atlanta, GA. This certificate documents the time and place of Lucy Laney's death.

Derricotte, Elise P. *Word Pictures of Great Negroes*. Washington, DC: Associated Press, 1964. This work contains brief biographies of 28 black men and women who gained prominence in a variety of fields.

Griggs, Augustus. "Lucy Craft Laney," *Journal of Negro History* 13 (January 1934): 97–102. This article examines the life of Lucy Craft Laney; it shows that she made significant contributions to the black community in the field of education.

Lerner, Gerda. *Black Women in White America: A Documentary History*. New York: Vintage Books, 1973. This is a documentary history of the contributions made by women in the United States.

Lowenberg, Bert James, and Ruth Bogin, eds. *Black Women in Nineteenth Century America: Their Words, Their Thoughts, Their Feelings*. University Park: Pennsylvania State University Press, 1976. This volume presents a variety of life experiences of some articulate black women of the nineteenth century. The study is designed to bring historical understanding of the American life as it related to black women.

Miller, Kelly, and Joseph R. Gay. *Progress and Achievements of the Colored People*. Washington, DC: Jenkins Press, 1917. This is a detailed book that contains descriptions of the advancements made by black Americans.

Ovington, Mary W. *Portraits in Color*. New York: Viking Press, 1927. This book provides detailed descriptions of African Americans who have made outstanding contributions to the black community, in particular, and the American society in general.

Ploski, Harry A., and James Williams, eds. *The Negro Almanac: A Reference Work on Afro-Americans*, 4th edition. New York: Wiley, 1983. This is a reference book that documents the contributions of African Americans in the United States.

Presbyterian Board of Missions for Freedmen. *Annual Reports, 1886*. Philadelphia: Presbyterian Historical Society, 1886. These reports document Lucy Laney's efforts to secure moral support and financial assistance from the Presbyterian church to support her school.

Who's Who in Colored America. New York: Who's Who in Colored America Corporation, 1927–1928. This is a biographical dictionary of notable living persons of African-American descent in the United States.

LEALTAD, CATHARINE (1886–1989), teacher, social worker, and pediatrician, gained renown providing medical care for poor children and adults in Harlem, Europe, China, Puerto Rico, and Mexico. In her pursuit of medical training and practice, she both fought discrimination and followed family tradition. Her aunt, Dr. Verina Morton Jones, had practiced medicine and social work in Brooklyn as the head of the Lincoln Settlement, leader in the social hygiene movement in the YWCA and board member of the NAACP.

Catharine Deaver Lealtad was raised in St. Paul, Minnesota. Her father, the Reverend Alfred Lealtad, was rector of St. Philip's Episcopal Church. After graduating from the Mechanical Arts High School in St. Paul, she continued her education at Macalester College and became the first black graduate of the college in 1915, majoring in history and chemistry.

Her first jobs were in education and social work. She taught for a short period in Columbus, Ohio. She then became a national secretary for the YWCA involved with organizing black college students. She fought discrimination directly. When she and other African-American women were denied accommodations at a hotel in Des Moines in 1919 during a Y convention, she demanded the Y authorities assist the female staff as the YMCA had recently done for the black men. When the leadership refused, Lealtad resigned her position. She worked briefly as the associate secretary for the New York Urban League, followed in 1920 as the assistant national director for the NAACP branches.

Tiring of the social services, Lealtad pursued the medical science field in the 1930s. She worked as a laboratory technician for three years, until she decided to become a doctor. She spent one year at Cornell Medical School, until an anatomy professor (allegedly) vowed that no black person would pass his course. A French professor, Dr. Phoebe Du Bois, helped her raise enough money to continue her medical education in Europe. She completed training in Lyon and Berlin. She returned to the United States as World War II approached. Following specialized training in pediatrics, Lealtad interned in Chicago and then established a medical practice in Harlem. She worked in various public health clinics.

As World War II was ending, the army sought her services. Commissioned as a major and sent to Germany in 1945, Lealtad aided children in displaced persons' camps. Completing this assignment, the U.S. Public Health Service sent her to China in 1946 to aid victims of the civil war and cholera epidemic in Shantung Province.

She returned to the United States to work for interracial cooperation. She bought a home in a Quaker-sponsored, multiracial cooperative in Connecticut and joined the staff of Sydenham Hospital, the first interracial hospital in New York.

In semiretirement, Lealtad continued to provide medical care for poor children. In 1968 she worked at a church-related mission hospital in Puerto Rico and then volunteered at a free clinic in Mexico City for seven years. Lealtad lived her last nine years in a Veterans Administration retirement home in Queens, New York, where she died on January 30, 1989.

—Susan Borchert

Bibliography

For primary sources on Catharine Lealtad's various careers, consult the collections in the various organizations: Archives of the National Board of the YWCA, New York City; NAACP Papers, Manuscript Division, Library of Congress, Washington, DC; National Urban League Papers, Manuscript Division, Library of Congress; and the Macalester College Archives, Macalester College, St. Paul, Minnesota.

Secondary Sources

Baker, Ann. "Black Woman Doctor Has Fought Prejudice," *St. Paul Dispatch* (June 18, 1979). Probably the best single source of information on Lealtad in this interview by a reporter.
Lealtad, Catharine. "The National YWCA and the Negro," *The Crisis* (April 1920): 317–318. Explains the crises within the YWCA.
New York Daily News. "Obituary" (February 3, 1989).
Salem, Dorothy. *To Better Our World.* Brooklyn: Carlson, 1990. Provides Lealtad's experiences in social work and correspondence about racial conflict.

LEE, JARENA (1783–c. 1849), itinerant preacher, was born on February 11 in Cape May, New Jersey, to free parents. In 1804 Lee converted to Christianity and joined Philadelphia's Bethel African Methodist Episcopal (AME) church. Around 1811 Lee began to feel a call to preach, which was rebuffed by the Reverend Richard Allen, founder of the AME church. In this same year she married the Reverend Joseph Lee, who died in 1817. The couple had two children.

Lee approached Richard Allen again in 1818. Allen, now bishop of the AME church, gave her permission to hold prayer meetings in her home. In 1819 Lee interrupted a sermon in Bethel Church and exhorted extemporaneously from the text chosen by the minister.

Shortly thereafter, Lee began an itinerant preaching career that stretched across the Middle Atlantic and Northeastern states and as far west as Dayton, Ohio. In 1827 Lee traveled 2,325 miles alone mostly on foot and delivered 178 sermons. She was never licensed as a preacher, but was an official traveling exhorter. Lee met Zilpha Elaw in 1839, and for a time they were a preaching team. In 1840 Lee joined the Antislavery Society believing that abolitionism was the best vehicle for the propagation of the gospel.

Lee published her autobiography, *The Life and Religious Experience of Jarena Lee, A Coloured Lady*. This religious autobiography was published in 1836 and distributed at camp meetings, at quarterly meetings of the AME church, and on street corners. The book was reprinted in 1839, and in 1849 Lee retitled it *Religious Experience and Journal of Mrs. Jarena Lee, Giving an Account of Her Call to Preach the Gospel*. Her activities after 1849 are unknown.

—Emilie M. Townes

Bibliography

Very little information exists on Jarena Lee. The limited resources that provide general information about her life include: Jarena Lee, *Religious Experience and Journal of Mrs. Jarena Lee, Giving an Account of Her Call to Preach the Gospel* (Philadelphia: AME, 1849); Bert James Loewenberg, and Ruth Bogin, eds., *Black Women in Nineteenth-Century American Life: Their Words, Their Thoughts, Their Feelings* (University Park: Pennsylvania State University Press, 1976); Jualynne Dodson, "Nineteenth-Century A.M.E. Preaching Women: Cutting Edge of Women's Inclusion in Church Polity," in *Women in New Worlds*, edited by Hilah F. Thomas and Rosemary Skinner Keller (Nashville: Abington, 1981).

LEE, REBECCA (c. 1833–?), the first African American to obtain the title doctor of medicine, had moved from a slave state to the Yankee bastion of the antislavery movement, when in 1859, the 26-year-old from Richmond, Virginia, was accepted into the medical program at the New England Female Medical College in Boston. But her achievement was fraught with obstacles, the most prominent of which was the outbreak of the Civil War in 1861, when Dr. Lee was forced to quit her studies and seems to have been deported to the Confederacy. Upon returning to college in 1863, she discovered that her financial aid had been forfeited. However, she won a tuition award from the Wade Scholarship Fund (established by Ohio abolitionist Benjamin Wade), which enabled her to complete her final examinations by February 1864.

The faculty of the college, oblivious to Dr. Lee's extraordinary struggles, cited her "slow progress," and grudgingly awarded her a medical degree. In the faculty minutes, the dean noted, "Some of us have hesitated very seriously in recommending her . . . and do so only out of deference to what we understand to be the wishes of the Trustees and the present state of public feeling."

There is scant information about Dr. Lee before or after her battle to receive a medical education. She appears to have been married and to have established her practice in Richmond after the war.

—Janet Miller with F. Michael Angelo

Bibliography

Although Rebecca Lee is frequently cited as the first black woman doctor in the United States, little else is known about her life after the Civil War. The best source of information is the Rebecca Lee File, Black Women Physicians Project, Accession 178, Archives and Special Collections on Women in Medicine, Medical College of Pennsylvania.

LEWIS, (MARY) EDMONIA (1845–1909), considered the first African-American and female sculptor of prominence, was born on July 14 in Greenbush, New York (near Albany), of maternal Chippewa and paternal freedman of African heritage. Very little factual material has emerged on her early years, although there are several versions of her childhood in print. The printed sources indicate she was raised by the Chippewa under her Indian name, Wildfire, and soon became an orphan. She attended New York Central College, founded by the American Baptist Free Mission Society in McGraw, New York, from 1856 to 1858.

In 1859, through the efforts of her brother and other abolitionists, Lewis entered the Preparatory School of Oberlin College, which opened admission to African Americans in 1835. She resided in the home of the Reverend John Keep with a dozen other girls. With 30 other African-American students enrolled at Oberlin, Lewis worked diligently at her studies until 1862, when she was accused of poisoning two white female classmates with cantharides (Spanish Fly) in a "spiced wine" incident. White vigilantes abducted and beat Lewis as a result of the charges. The hearing lasted two days and resulted in Lewis's acquittal through the adept defense of John Mercer Langston, who battled two prosecuting attorneys to achieve dismissal of the case based on insufficient evidence.

She had developed rudimentary drawing skills at Oberlin, where her earliest known work is an untitled drawing, now in the Oberlin College Archives, executed in her last year at Oberlin. Depicting a classical figure, the drawing was a wedding gift to a classmate. She left Oberlin during the summer of 1862 to study in Boston with the sculptor Edmund Brackett. One of her first works was a medallion of John Brown, and she offered plaster copies of it to the public through an advertisement in William Lloyd Garrison's *The Liberator*. Specializing in portrait busts, she executed a bust of Colonel Robert Gould Shaw, who had died leading the Union Army's first regiment of soldiers, the Massachusetts 54th Black Infantry Regiment. These works were exhibited in the Boston Fair for the Soldier's Aid Fund in 1864, thus establishing her career in art. Proceeds from the sale of photographs of the work and the patronage from the Story family enabled her to travel to Rome in 1865.

Rome was then a magnet for sculptors, as the city was filled with antique and Renaissance art to study and copy and because the much-favored material marble and the craftsmen to work it were readily available. She was one of a group of women pursuing what seemed at the time an unusual career for their sex. It was a phenomenon noted by, among others, the writer Henry James, who dubbed them the "white, marmorean flock," a reference to their output of white marble sculpture. A few extant letters, art reviews, and mention of her by contemporaries, such as the artist Anne Whitney, the writer Lydia Maria Child, and the actress Charlotte Cushman, reveal a little of Lewis's life and work in this period. She adopted the neoclassical idiom along with her associates Harriet Hosmer, Emma Stebbins, and Charlotte Cushman.

Some of her sculpture reflected her heritage as both black and Indian—themes from Hiawatha and those marking emancipation. Though showing anatomical weakness, they are, perhaps, her most successful in originality and substance. Other works are more typical products of the prevailing neoclassicism or are of religious subjects. At some point, Lewis converted to Catholicism.

By the 1870s she was a celebrated figure on two continents. The Philadelphia Centennial Exposition of 1876, which featured other such African-American artists as Robert Duncanson and Edmund Bannister (his painting "Under the Oaks" received a medal), exhibited six examples of Lewis's works including the award-winning "Death of Cleopatra," her most provocative and controversial work. Other famous works include "Forever Free" (1867), "Hagar in the Wilderness" (1868), "Hiawatha" (1868), and "Old Indian Arrowmaker and His Daughter" (1872).

In a relatively short time, the artist could count on wealthy patrons in the United States, England, and Italy: Henry Tuckerman, Ulysses S. Grant, William Wells Brown, Ida Wells Barnett, Lorado Taft, Laura Curtis Bullard, Pope Pius IX, and William Lloyd Garrison. Edmonia Lewis's legacy of freedom in the cultural expression of her Native American, African-American, and female identities gained her an international reputation.

Where and exactly when she died has not been determined. According to several Catholic publications, she was still living in Rome in the first decade of this century. Her innate gifts as a sculptor and social innovator survived the obscurity of her death in 1909. Some of her sculptures are now in the National Museum of American Art, Howard University, Harvard University, San Jose Public Library, and several private collections.

—Robin Chandler

Bibliography

The letters of Edmonia Lewis to Maria Weston Chapman and William Lloyd Garrison from Rome are in the Boston Public Library, Boston, Massachusetts. Other letters include: Lydia Maria Child to Sarah Shaw, New York Public Library; Anne Whitney to her sister Sarah, Wellesley College Library. Information also exists in the student records of Oberlin College; *The Liberator*, January 29, 1864; December 9, 1864; January 20, 1865.

Secondary Sources

Blodgett, Geoffrey. "Spiced Wine: An Oberlin Scandal of 1862," *Journal of Negro History* (July 1968): 201–218.

Cedarholm, Theresa. *Afro American Artists, A Bio-bibliographic Directory.* Boston Public Library, 1973.

Chandler, Robin. "Early Dreams," in *Black Women Artists: Lessons in Struggle and Liberation.* Unpublished manuscript, 1973.

City College of New York. *The Evolution of Afro-American Artists, 1800–1950,* Exhibition Catalog (1967).

Craven, Wayne. *Sculpture in America.* New York: Crowell, 1968.

Driskell, David. *Two Centuries of Black American Art.* New York: Alfred Knopf, 1976.

Goldberg, Marcia, and William Bigglestone. "A Wedding Gift of 1862," *Oberlin Alumni Magazine* (January–February 1977).

Harley, Ralph L., Jr. "A Checklist of Afro-American Art and Artists," *Serif* 7:4 (1970): 3–63.

Heller, Nancy G. *Women Artists: An Illustrated History.* New York: Abbeville Press, 1987.

Igoe, Lynn Moody, with James Igoe. *250 Years of Afro American Art.* New York: Bowker, 1981.

James, Edward T., and Janet W., eds. *Notable American Women.* Cambridge: Harvard University Press, 1971.

Leach, Joseph. *Bright Particular Star; The Life and Times of Charlotte Cushman.* New Haven: Yale University Press, 1970.

Lewis, Samella. *Art: African American.* Claremont, CA: Hancraft Studios, 1977.

Morrison, Allan. "(Black) Women in the Arts," *Ebony* (August 1966): 90–94.

Porter, James. *Modern Negro Art.* New York: Arno Press, 1969.

———. *Ten Afro-American Artists of the Nineteenth Century.* New York City College: Exhibition Catalog, 1967.

Taft, Lorado. *The History of American Sculpture.* New York: Macmillan, 1903.

Tuckerman, Henry T. *American Artist Life.* New York: G.P. Putnam and Son, 1867.

Tufts, Eleanor. *Our Hidden Heritage: Five Centuries of Women Artists.* New York: Paddington, 1974.

LOGAN, ADELLA [HUNT] (1863–1915), educator and social reformer,

was born February 10 in Hancock County, Georgia, to white planter Henry Hunt and his wife, Mariah Hunt, the daughter of white judge and legislator Nathan C. Sayre, and Susan Hunt of mixed black and Indian parentage. As the fourth of eight children, Adella Hunt mirrored similar achievements of her siblings. Her brother Henry A. Hunt became the president of Fort Valley State College. A sister, Sarah Leigh Hunt, became a social worker in Newark, New Jersey, after the breakup of her romance with George Washington Carver. Like her siblings, Adella Hunt was privately educated. She attended Atlanta University, where she graduated from the Normal School as a teacher in 1881. She taught for two years in an American Missionary School in Albany, Georgia, before she joined the Tuskegee Institute faculty in Alabama in 1883. On the personal recommendation of Edmund Ware, the president of Atlanta University, she became the assistant to Olivia Davidson, lady principal of the Normal College and Model School and second wife of Booker T. Washington.

On December 27, 1888, Adella Hunt married the treasurer of the Tuskegee Institute, Warren Logan, and resigned her post. Eight children were born from the marriage from 1890 to 1909: Ruth Mackie, Warren Hunt, Ralph Walter, Helen, Paul Howland, Louise Thrasher, Myra Adele, and Arthur Courtney. Family responsibilities did not quench her reform interests. She was a founder/ charter member of the Tuskegee Women's Club (founded 1895). As the leader of the suffrage committee, she kept a large library on the matter and named her youngest child after Isabel and Emily Howland, noted suffragists. In 1901 the National American Woman Suffrage Association listed her as the only life member in Alabama. Given the discriminatory practices of the NAWSA, Logan carried on much of her suffrage activities by passing as white. She voted under a Louisiana Taxpayers' Franchise in 1912 and campaigned for the Ohio suffrage amendment in 1912—both while passing as white. She worked with the Women's Christian Temperance Union at Tuskegee but was not a member.

While devoting her time to community and reform interests, she expanded her education through completion of the Chautauqua Course and an MA degree from Atlanta University in 1903. During these years she wrote articles on health and reform issues. Her article on prenatal hereditary influences was presented at the Atlanta University Conference (1897), while her discussion of urban mortality among blacks appeared in D.W. Culp's, *Twentieth Century Negro Literature*. Her articles about woman's suffrage appeared both in *The Colored American* (1905) and *The Crisis*, "Colored Women as Voters" (September 4, 1912): 242–243. From 1910 to 1913 Logan headed the departments on suffrage and rural issues in the National Association of Colored Women.

Given her interest in reforms considered unpopular in the Deep South and within the Booker T. Washington household at Tuskegee, Adella Hunt Logan was pulled in many directions. As an academic, idealist, and friend of W.E.B. Du Bois, during the time of increasing antagonism to the "radical" concerns, she must have experienced many frustrations and criticism for her activism. These negative influences led to her commitment in October 1915 to a sanatorium at Battle Creek, Michigan, for treatment of nervous disorders. She returned to Alabama where she died before the year was out by jumping from the top floor of the academic building at Tuskegee Institute on December 10, 1915. The event so traumatized the family that very little was discussed about her thereafter.

—Mary Ann Williams

Bibliography

Exhaustive searching by both the compiler of this biography and the staff of the Atlanta University Center produced very little on Adella Logan's life. Besides Logan's own writings in Culp, *Twentieth Century Negro Literature*, *The Colored American* (Naperville, IL: J.L. Nichols, 1902), and *The Crisis*, pieces of information can be found in Sylvia G.L. Dannett's *Profiles of Negro Womanhood* 1 (New York: M.W. Lads, 1964); Louis R. Harlan and Raymond W. Smock, eds., *The Booker T. Washington Papers* (Chicago: University of Illinois Press, 1981); and Dorothy Salem, *To Better Our World: Black Women in Organized Reform, 1890–1920* (Brooklyn: Carlson, 1990).

Much of the detailed information was obtained through the 1982–1983 correspondence of editor Dorothy C. Salem with Logan's granddaughter, Adele Logan Alexander, who is completing her own biography on Adella Hunt Logan. Alexander's article "How I Discovered My Grandmother," which appeared in *Ms.* (November 1983): 29–37, summarizes her quest for information.

LORDE, AUDRE

LORDE, AUDRE (1934–1992), poet and writer, was born of West Indian parents in New York City on February 18. She worked as a nurse's aide and factory worker. Her marriage to Edwin Ashley Rollins produced two children, Elizabeth and Jonno.

At first she attended the University of Mexico (1954–1955), then she transferred to and graduated from Hunter College (1959). In 1961 she earned a MLS degree (master's in library science) from Columbia University. For several years, she worked as a librarian in the New York Public Library system, Town School Library, and at the library at City College in New York. In 1968 she became a lecturer in creative writing at City University of New York. During the same year, she served as the poet-in-residence at Tougaloo College in Jackson, Mississippi. She later taught at Herbert Lehman College, John Jay College of Criminal Justice, and Hunter College. Lorde served as a distinguished professor at Atlanta University and was an English professor at Hunter College.

Lorde began writing poetry when she was a preteen. Her first poem was published in *Seventeen* magazine while she was still a high school student. Her poetry includes "The First Cities" (1968), "Cables to Rage" (1970), "Coal" (1978), and "The Black Unicorn" (1978).

She also enjoyed success as a prose writer. In *The Cancer Journals* (1980) she recounts her bouts and struggles with breast cancer. She has also written a fictionalized account of her coming of age as a lesbian entitled *Zami: A New Spelling of My Name* (1982), a work that she calls "biomythography." Lorde's works reveal her fascination with matriarchal myths and goddesses of Africa and of the West Indian island Carriacou, her mother's birthplace. Her writings also reflect her anger with racism and sexism in the United States.

Lorde died November 17, 1992, in St. Croix after a 14 year battle against cancer. In August 1993 her last collection of poetry, *The Marvelous Arithmetic of Distance*, was published by W. W. Norton.

—Betty Plummer

Bibliography

Audre Lorde's books include *Coal* (New York: Norton, 1968); *The First Cities* (New York: Poets Press, 1968); *Cables to Rage* (London: Paul Breman, 1970); *From a Land Where Other People Live* (Detroit: Broadside Press, 1973); *The New York Head Shop and Museum* (Detroit: Broadside Press, 1974); *Between Ourselves* (Point Reyes, CA: Eidolon Editions, 1976); *Black Unicorn* (New York: Norton, 1978); and *I Am Your Sister: Black Women Organizing Across Sexualities* (New York: Kitchentable, Women of Color Press, 1985).

Interviews with Lorde appear in Claudia Tate, *Black Women Writers at Work* (New York: Continuum, 1983); and *Sturdy Black Bridges*, edited by Roseann Bell, Bettye Parker, and Beverly Guy-Sheftall (Garden City, NY: Doubleday, 1979). *Contemporary Authors*, edited by Hal May and James G. Lesniak (Detroit: Gale, 1989) contains biographical information and a list of her work as does James A. Page, *Selected Black American Authors: An Illustrated Bio-Bibliography* (Boston: G.K. Hall, 1977). See also Arna Bontemps, *American Negro Poetry* (New York: Hill & Wang, 1963); Darwin Turner, *Afro-American Writers* (New York: Appleton-Century-Crofts, 1970); Carol F. Myers, et al., *Black American Writers: Past and Present* (Metuchen, NJ: Scarecrow, 1975); Ann A. Shockley, *Living Black American Authors* (New York: Bowker, 1973). Articles by or about Lorde appear in *Ebony* (March 1974): 100+; *Freedomways* (February 1972): 31–33; and *The Black Scholar* 10 (April 1979): 19.

Christia Adair
Photo courtesy of Houston Metropolitan Research Center, Houston, TX

Debbie Allen, Fifth Annual Essence Awards Ceremony, 1992

Maya Angelou
Photo courtesy of Cuyahoga Community College

Byllye Avery
*Photo courtesy of the National Black
Women's Health Project*

Maria Baldwin
*Photo reproduced by permission of the
Schlesinger Library, Radcliffe College*

Mrs. Harris Barrett and a club of the Locust Street Settlement
Photo courtesy of Hampton University Archives

Mary McLeod Bethune
Photo reproduced by permission of the
Library of Congress

Mary Branch
Photo reproduced by permission of the
Special Collections Library,
Texas Woman's University

Valerie Brisco-Hooks and
Florence Griffith

© Steve Powell, All-Sport

Clara Brown
Photo reproduced by permission of the
Colorado Historical Society

Playbill from "The Crimson Skull,"
co-starring Anita Bush

Anna Cooper
*Photo courtesy of
Oberlin College Archives*

Fannie Jackson Coppin
*Photo courtesy of
Oberlin College Archives*

Maud Cuney-Hare
*Photo reproduced by permission of the
Special Collections Library,
Texas Woman's University*

© Mike Powell, All-Sport

Gail Devers

Julie Dash

Photo by Arthur Jafa

Anna Douglass
Photo courtesy of the
National Park Service

Shirley Graham Du Bois and William Edward Burghardt
Photo courtesy of the personal collection of Shirley Graham Du Bois

Marian Edelman

Photo by Jonathan Levine

Roselyn Epps, M.D.
*Photo courtesy of the Archives
and Special Collections on Women
in Medicine, Medical College
of Pennsylvania*

Matilda Arabelle Evans, M.D. (1897)
*Photo courtesy of the Archives and Special
Collections on Women in Medicine,
Medical College of Pennsylvania*

Lethia Fleming
*Photo reproduced by permission of the
Allen Cole Collection,
Western Reserve Historical Society*

Ella Fitzgerald
*Photo collage courtesy of the Graphic Designers in
Technical & Creative Services,
Cuyahoga Community College*

Zelma Watson George,
with Marlene Dietrich
*Photo courtesy of Dr. Zelma W. George,
Personal Collection*

Whoopi Goldberg
Photo courtesy of Brad Cafarelli

Charlotte Forten Grimké
*Photo reproduced by permission of the
Schomburg Center for Research in Black
Culture, New York Public Library*

Barbara Harris
Photo courtesy of AP/Wide World

Ida Gibbs Hunt
Photo courtesy of
Oberlin College Archives

Jane Hunter
Photo courtesy of the Phillis Wheatley
Association, Cleveland, OH

Photo by Max Waldman

Judith Jamison performing in "Cry,"
a production of the Alvin City Center Dance Theatre

Mae Jemison, astronaut candidate
Photo courtesy of NASA

Mae Jemison
Photo courtesy of
Cuyahoga Community College

Halle Tanner Dillon Johnson, M.D. (1891)
Photo reproduced by permission of the
Archives and Special Collections on Women in Medicine,
Medical College of Pennsylvania

Left to right, top row: Mrs. M.S. Davage, Mrs. Charles Johnson, Mrs. Amos, Mrs. T.H. Slater, Mrs. H.A. Rucker, Mrs. W.F. Penn; bottom row: Mrs. Walter Thomas, Mrs. A.M. Wilkins, Mrs. H.R. Bailer, Mrs. John (Lugenia) Hope, Mrs. George White
Photo courtesy of Atlanta Neighborhood Union Papers, Atlanta University Center, Woodruff Library

Photo by Alex Gotfryd

Barbara Jordan
Photo reproduced by permission of the Special Collections Library, Texas Woman's University

© Tony Duffy, All-Sport

Florence Joyner
1988 Seoul Olympics

Jackie Joyner-Kersee
Gold Heptathlon,
1992 Barcelona Games

Elizabeth Keckley
Photo courtesy of Anacostia Museum,
Smithsonian Institution,
Washington, DC

© Tony Duffy, All-Sport

Photo by Virginia Sexton

Coretta Scott King
Photo courtesy of Cuyahoga Community College

Catharine Lealtad
(1915 Macalester College Yearbook)
*Photo courtesy of
Macalester College Archives*

Audre Lorde
Photo courtesy of Ms. magazine

Victoria Earle Matthews
*Photo reproduced by permission of the
New York Public Library*

Toni Morrison with Nikki Giovanni
*Photo courtesy of
Cleveland State University*

Photo by Liz Malby

"Queen Mother" Audley Moore

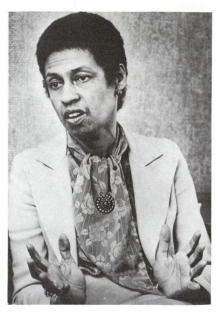

Eleanor Holmes Norton
Photo reproduced by permission of
The Plain Dealer, *Cleveland, OH*

Lucy Parsons
Photo reproduced by permission of the
Labadie Collection,
University of Michigan Library

Lucy Parsons
Photo reproduced by permission of the
University of Illinois at Chicago,
The University Library, Department of
Special Collections Archives

Mary Jane Patterson
Photo courtesy of Oberlin College

Composite of five YWCA
staff members.

*Photo reproduced by permission
of YWCA of the USA,
National Board Archives*

Wilma Rudolph
*Photo reproduced by permission of the
Library of Congress,
General Collection*

Wilma Rudolph (USA)
100-200M Champion at the
1960 Rome Olympics

Sonia Sanchez

Rosetta Douglass Sprague

Betty Shabazz

The Fisk Jubilee Singers.
Ella Sheppard is seated at front left by table.
Photo courtesy of Fisk University Library

Meeting of the National Association for the Advancement of Colored People (c. 1916). Middle row includes Addie Waites Hunton (far left), Mary Church Terrell (third from left), and Mary B. Talbert (fourth from left).
Photo reproduced by permission of the Library of Congress

Mary B. Talbert
Photo courtesy of Oberlin College Archives

Harriet Tubman
*Photo reproduced by permission of the
Library of Congress*

Photo by Jim Marshall

Alice Walker
Photo from Walker's book
Temple of My Familiar

Photo by Ron Slenzak

Dr. Mary Ann Williams
Photo courtesy of her husband,
Ko Jo Kamau

Oprah Winfrey
Photo reproduced by permission
of Harpo/King World

Meeting of the National Association of Teachers in Colored Schools, Hampton Institute. From left to right: John Hope, Lugenia Hope, unknown, Margaret M. Washington, Mary McLeod Bethune, unknown, unknown.

M

MABLEY, JACKIE ("MOMS") [AIKEN] (1894–1975), the rubber-faced comedienne with a toothless grin and baggy clothes, was a gravel-voiced, sharp-tongued entertainer of vaudeville, stage, television, and film. Born March 19 in Brevard, North Carolina, as one of 12 children of mixed African, Cherokee, and Irish ancestry, Loretta Mary Aiken started life with a father, Jim Aiken, who owned several businesses, including the town grocery store. Her early life is not well documented. She related that the religious inspiration learned from her great grandmother, Harriet Smith, a former slave, kept her strong during a long and hectic career. She also described a forced marriage instigated by a tyrannical stepfather to a man who was so old and weak that "somebody threw one grain of rice and it knocked him out."

She spent her early years in the Anacostia area of Washington, DC, and also in Cleveland, Ohio, both referred to as her hometowns. She entered show business as a teenager because she "was pretty and did not want to become a prostitute." She started by entertaining at church functions and fundraising events, soon graduating to the segregated vaudeville circuit, the Theatre Owners and Booking Association (TOBA). She had a bit part in the vaudeville skit "Rich Aunt from Utah," with the team of Buck and Bubbles. She played every state in the Union except Mississippi, saying, "I won't go there. They ain't ready."

She adopted the stage name Jackie Mabley from one of her early boyfriends and the nickname "Moms" from her maternal behavior to fellow entertainers and audiences. Similar to Charlie Chaplin's hat and cane, Mabley was clearly defined by her run-over shoes as she tottered on stage wearing her crushed hat and sloppy dress. The dance team of Butterbeans and Suzie saw that she had a rare talent to make people laugh, so they urged her to come to New York City in the early 1920s as the Harlem Renaissance was flourishing. With the help of comedienne Bonnie Bell Drew, Mabley developed her sharp monologue that later included singing and some dancing. Her sassy folk-wisdom and sly insights became a hit when she made her debut at Connie's Inn in 1923. She drew her material from daily life including the battle of the sexes, race relations, domestic strife, and government. She became a steady performer at the Apollo Theatre in Harlem, the Cotton Club (Harlem), the Club Harlem in Atlantic City, and others. She appeared regularly with such entertainment giants as Count Basie, Redd Foxx, Louis Armstrong, Cab Calloway, Duke Ellington, Pearl Bailey, Bill "Bojangles" Robinson, and even Benny Goodman, as well as such lesser known greats as Pigmeat Markham, Tim "Kingfish" Moore, "Peg Leg" Bates, and "Dusty" Richard Fletcher.

During her career, Mabley had some small parts in films. Her first role was in *Boarding House Blues* (RKO, 1929), which was distributed under the title, *Jazz Heaven*. She appeared in *Emperor Jones* (United Artists, 1933) to "make my children and great grand-children proud of me, like all mothers do." Her last movie role was in the film *Amazing Grace* (1973), a film that did well at the box office.

Her career "break" came when she started recording for Chess Records in 1960. Her first album, *Moms Mabley, the Funniest Woman in the World*, sold over a million copies and became a Gold Record. She recorded a stag party hit, *Now Hear This*, in 1961 for Mercury Records. At that time she also appeared as a regular on the popular radio show *Swingtime at the Savoy*, and in several Broadway shows: *Swinging Dreams*, *Blackbirds*, and *Fasta and Foulos*. Her television debut came in 1967 in an all-black comedy produced by Harry Belafonte for ABC, entitled "A Time for Laughter." Later she performed on other television shows with Flip Wilson, Merv Griffin, the Smothers Brothers, Mike Douglas, and Bill Cosby. Once she refused to go on the Ed Sullivan Show to do a five-minute vignette because she said, "Honey, it takes Moms four minutes just to get on the stage." This wide exposure created a great demand. She played many white nightclubs and theaters such as the Copacabana in New York City and the Kennedy Cultural Center in Washington, DC.

Although never politically militant, she expressed opinions about current issues. She opposed war and abortion, supported the nonviolent civil rights movement, and held heroes as Adam Clayton Powell, John F. Kennedy, Robert Kennedy, and Martin Luther King, Jr. A member of the NAACP, Mabley condemned the rioters who looted following the assassination of Martin Luther King, Jr., as "looting people using the least excuse for their own selfish use."

Mabley's personal life reinforced her stage life. She was a devout Baptist, often listening to Oral Roberts on television. She was married twice, separated from her second husband, Ernest Scherer, for many years before his death in August 1974. She had three daughters and one son, six grandchildren, and seven great-grandchildren by 1975. Her final years were spent living with her youngest daughter, Bonnie, in Hartsdale, New York, suffering from arthritis, a bad knee, and a pacemaker after her heart attack. Here she lived a simple life of nature walks, playing checkers, and driving around in her Rolls Royce with a monogram license plate. She died May 23, 1975. Several years later, Ben Caldwell, a Harlem-born playwright, and Clarice Taylor, an actress, produced a play, *Moms*, based on the life of Jackie Mabley. The play won an Obie Award and played to sold-out audiences. The play was a fitting tribute to her memory.

—Nicholas C. Polos

Bibliography

For information about "Moms" Mabley's days in Harlem and New York, consult the Schomburg Center for Research in Black Culture, New York Public Library. For her entertainment career, several sources are helpful: Alain Locke, "The Negro and the American Stage," *Theater Arts 2* (February 1926): 112–120; Alain Locke, *The New Negro* (New York: Arno, 1968), p. 10; Le Roi Jones, *Blues People* (New York:

William Morrow, 1963); Donald Bogle, *Brown Sugar: Eighty Years of America's Black Female Superstars* (New York: Harmony Books, 1980); and Maryann Oshana, *Women of Color: A Filmography of Minority and Third World Women* (New York: Garland, 1985); and Eileen Southern, *Biographical Dictionary of Afro-American and African Musicians* (Westport, CT: Greenwood Press, 1982): 255. Her interviews in newspapers and periodicals are helpful for personal insights: M. Cardell Thompson, "Moms Mabley Raps about Old Women," *Jet* (January 3, 1974): 60–62; "Moms Mabley—Anybody That Comes to Me, I'll See 'Em," *Soul* (June 30, 1966): 2; *Ebony* (April 1974): 86; *New York Times* (August 19, 1987, and May 23, 1975); *Washington Post* (April 29, 1988, and October 4, 1974); *New York Post* (May 24, 1975, and July 31, 1974); New York *Daily News* (October 29, 1974, and October 12, 1983); *Newsday* (April 6, 1967, and May 13, 1973). For biographical information see *Biographical News* I (September 1974): 1048; *Current Biography* (January 1975).

McCLENDON, ROSE [SCOTT] (1884–1936), celebrated actress and community theater activist, was born Rosalie Virginia Scott in Greenville, South Carolina, on August 27, to Sandy and Tena (Jenkins) Scott. At age six, Rosalie Scott's family moved to New York City, where mother and father worked for a wealthy family as maid and coachman. There she attended Public School No. 40 and later married Dr. Henry Pruden McClendon, a chiropractor, on October 27, 1904.

McClendon's acting career began after she won a scholarship to the American Academy of Dramatic Art in 1916, where she studied with Frank Sargent. Upon completion of her studies there, she was cast in a minor role in John Galsworthy's *Justice*, performed by the Bramhall Players during the 1919–1920 season; she continued acting in *Roseanne* (1924). Her performance as Octavie in *Deep River* by Lawrence Stallings in 1926 catapulted her to a position of renown in theater. Subsequently, she was cast in almost every play that dealt with black life on the New York stage. McClendon continued to receive critical acclaim throughout the remainder of the 1920s and into the 1930s. She was in Paul Green's *In Abraham's Bosom*, the 1926 Pulitzer prize–winning play. She portrayed Serena in Dorothy and DuBose Heyward's critically acclaimed *Porgy*, staged by the Theatre Guild and directed by Reuben Mamoulian in 1928, which garnered extended runs in both New York and London. She was featured as Big Sue in *The House of Connelly* (1931) by Paul Green; in *Black Souls* (1932); as Mammy in *Never No More* (1932), a play about lynching produced by the Group Theatre; *Brain Sweat* (1934); *Roll Sweet Chariot* (1934); and Panic (1935). McClendon performed on radio in the "John Henry Sketches," during the 1933 season. McClendon's final performance before her death was in 1935, as Cora in Langston Hughes's *Mulatto*, which achieved the distinction of Broadway's longest-running play by a black author (October 1936–December 1939) prior to Lorraine Hansberry's *A Raisin in the Sun* (1959).

Offstage, McClendon was a theater activist who demanded that the actor's union provide additional theater opportunities for black performers. She established her own theater group to accomplish this goal. She was a financial benefactor as well as one of the directors of the Harlem Experimental Theatre. McClendon and Dick Campbell organized the Negro People's Theatre in 1935, for which she produced Clifford Odets's play *Waiting for Lefty* at the Rockland Palace the same year. (Campbell established the Rose McClendon Players in 1941.)

Shortly after this venture, and during the same year, Hallie Flanagen invited McClendon to take part in developing the Federal Theatre Project; McClendon immediately recommended that a Negro Wing of the project be established. She envisioned the function of this wing to be a training ground for blacks interested in becoming playwrights and a showcase for new works written by black playwrights. The Negro Theatre Unit eventually expanded into 16 units located in communities throughout the United States by 1936. They hired almost 1,000 blacks, produced approximately 75 plays, and at least 100 productions. McClendon recommended to Flanagen that, instead of placing inexperienced black people in charge of the unit, the FTP bring in experienced white directors who would educate blacks in theater, making it possible for them to assume administrative, directorial, technical, and playwright positions in theater. Toward this end, actor/director John Houseman was hired and, under the co-directorship of he and McClendon, the Negro Theatre Unit attempted to "discard the bandana and burnt cork casting to play a universal character."

Their administrative guidance spawned a series of national successes that began with *Walk Together Chillun* by Frank Wilson, succeeded by a rendition of *Macbeth* placed in Haiti, which was performed at the Lafayette Theatre in Harlem, followed by *Lysistrata* in Seattle; and *Mikado* in Chicago, among some of the most noted.

McClendon developed pleurisy while in the production of *Mulatto*, her final acting engagement, and died of pneumonia one year later on July 12, 1936.

—Elizabeth Hadley Freydberg

Bibliography

Reviews of Rose McClendon's performances can be found "In Abraham's Bosom," *Theatre Magazine* (August 1927); New York *Afro-American* (April 30, 1932); *Amsterdam News* (March 25, 1931 and March 24, 1934); and the *New York Daily Mirror* (April 10, 1934). Biographical information delineating her theater career are in Doris Abramson, *Negro Playwrights* (New York: Columbia University Press, 1969); Leonard C. Archer, *Black Images in the American Theatre* (Brooklyn: Pageant-Poseiden, 1973); Frederick Bond, *The Negro and the Drama* (College Park, MD: McGrath, 1940); Hallie Flanagan, *Arena: The Story of the Federal Theatre* (New York: B. Blom, 1940, reprinted by New York: Arno, 1985), DuBose Hayward, *Porgy* (Garden City, NY: Doubleday, 1929); James Haskins, *Black Theater in America* (New

York: Random House, 1982). *The Crisis* (April 1927): 55; Edith J.R. Isaacs, *The Negro in the American Theatre* (College Park, MD: McGrath, 1947); James Weldon Johnson, *Black Manhattan* (New York: Knopf, 1930); *Journal of Negro History* 22 (1937): 15–19; John O'Connor and Lorraine Brown, *Free, Adult, Uncensored: The Living History of the Federal Theatre Project* (Washington: New Republic, 1978); Lindsay Patterson, *Anthology of the American Negro in the Theatre: A Critical Approach* (New York: Publishers Company, 1968). Photographs of McClendon are included in Langston Hughes and Milton Meltzer, *Black Magic* (Englewood Cliffs, NJ: Prentice-Hall, 1967); McClendon's scrapbook and clippings are located in the Schomburg Collection at the 135th Street branch of the New York Public Library. Obituaries on McClendon are in the *Journal of Negro History* (January 1937), *Opportunity* (August 1936), *Amsterdam News* (July 18, 1936), and the *New York Times* (July 14, 1936). McClendon is included in Allen Woll, *Dictionary of the Black Theatre: Broadway, Off-Broadway, and Selected Harlem Theatre* (Westport, CT: Greenwood, 1983); *Notable Women in the American Theatre* (1989); Edward T. James, *Notable American Women* II (Cambridge: Belknap, 1971); David Lewis, "Harlem My Home," in *Harlem Renaissance* (New York: The Studio Museum of Harlem, 1987); and *The Oxford Companion to American Theatre* (New York: Oxford University Press, 1984).

McCOY, MINNIE ("MEMPHIS MINNIE") (1897–1973), blues performer, was born in Algiers, Louisiana, on June 3, the eldest of 13 children. When she was seven years old, the family moved to Walls, Mississippi, and later to Memphis, Tennessee. Described as a frisky child, she was nicknamed "Kid" by her parents. Her father is said to have bought her a banjo when she was a young child, and "Kid" apparently wasted no time in putting it to use. She played for neighborhood house parties, and by the time she was age 15, bought herself a guitar and entertained on Memphis street corners. Beginning in 1916 McCoy toured for several years with the Ringling Brothers Circus. Her recording career began in 1929 when she was discovered by a Columbia Records scout while performing in a Beale Street barbershop, along with her second husband, "Kansas Joe" McCoy. The scout renamed her "Memphis Minnie," and the duo went to New York, where they recorded as "Kansas Joe" and "Memphis Minnie."

McCoy married three times and recorded with each of her husbands, all of whom were blues musicians. Her first marriage was a common-law arrangement with Casey Bill Weldon beginning around 1925. He is credited with helping polish McCoy's style. Her second marriage in 1929 to singer-guitarist "Kansas Joe" McCoy was a musically productive one. The couple recorded over 125 solos and duets in New York and Memphis. They relocated to Chicago in 1930 and continued to perform and record individually and together until 1935, when they split up purportedly because "Memphis Minnie" had attained greater popularity and recognition than "Kansas Joe." She continued to record during the 1930s and 1940s, on some occasions accompanied by her first husband. In 1935, after her breakup with "Kansas Joe," she visited her hometown of Walls, Mississippi, where she met and married her third husband, singer-guitarist Ernest "Little Son Joe" Lawler. The couple moved to Chicago, where they performed and recorded. Again, McCoy was the most prolific of the pair and the majority of the recordings made were released under her name. "Little Son Joe" even recorded one title under the name "Mr. Memphis Minnie."

McCoy toured extensively during the 1940s and also appeared in Chicago clubs when not on tour. By this time her country blues style was taking on a more urban character, although the country sound was never totally absent. Her music reflected the impact of her urban experience in Chicago and the changing blues sound to electrical amplification, which was emerging in urban areas following World War II. It was also during this time (1940) that McCoy recorded her tribute to the woman known as the "Mother of the Blues," entitled "Ma Rainey Blues." She continued to record into the early 1950s on the Regal, J.O.B., and Checker labels; her next to last recording was on the J.O.B. label in 1954.

In 1957 "Little Son Joe" suffered a heart attack, and the couple returned to Memphis. She too suffered a heart attack shortly thereafter but recovered and continued to perform in Memphis, not wanting to leave her husband to travel. McCoy recorded for the last time in 1959 and suffered a stroke in 1960. Following the death of "Little Son Joe" in 1961 or 1962 (reports vary), McCoy entered a nursing home. Upon suffering another stroke, she returned to her younger sister's home and was cared for until her death on August 7, 1973.

—Adrianne Andrews

Bibliography

Several sources of information recount the life and music of Memphis Minnie McCoy. Selected printed sources are:

Aldin, Mary Katherine. "Memphis Minnie: Living the Country Blues," *Living Blues* 88 (September–October 1989): 37.

Garon, Paul and Beth. *Woman with a Guitar.* New York: DeCapo, 1992.

Hite, Richard James. *Moaning the Blues* (liner notes). MCA-1370, 1983.

La Vere, Steve. "Memphis Minnie," *Living Blues* 14 (Autumn 1973): 5.

Southern, Eileen. *Biographical Dictionary of Afro-American and African Musicians.* Westport, CT: Greenwood Press, 1982.

Welding, Peter. *I Ain't No Bad Gal* (liner notes). CBS Records, Inc., New York, 1988.
    Personal communication:

Garon, Paul. Personal (telephone) communication. Chicago, Illinois, June 5, 1991.

McCROREY, MARY [JACKSON] (1869–1944), educator and social activist, was born in Athens, Georgia. Her parents, Alfred and Louise Jackson, had been slaves of a professor at the University of Georgia, and Mary was their eighth child, the first born in freedom. McCrorey graduated from Atlanta University and did graduate work at Harvard University and the University of Chicago. In 1941 Benedict College bestowed on her the honorary degree of doctor of pedagogy.

She taught for four years in her home of Athens, served as principal of a large school in Orlando, Florida, for five years, and worked briefly at Atlanta University. In 1895 Lucy Laney, principal of Haines Institute in Augusta, Georgia, recruited her to be assistant principal of the school, where she served until 1916. In later life McCrorey taught at North Carolina Summer Normal Schools and at Johnson C. Smith University.

In 1916 she married Henry Lawrence McCrorey, president of Biddle University (later Johnson C. Smith University), in Charlotte, North Carolina. The couple had no children. Her marriage and subsequent retirement from full-time teaching enabled her to enter civic work. McCrorey helped establish one of the first black branches of the YWCA in the United States, and served as chairperson of the Phillis Wheatley branch from 1916 to 1929. On a local level she was president of the Associated Charity Auxiliary and of its successor, the Relief and Welfare Association, from 1916 until 1944. She was on the board of the Bethlehem Center in Charlotte.

McCrorey attended the first interracial women's meeting, between representatives of the YWCA and National Association of Colored Women's Clubs, in Memphis in 1920 and served on the Commission on Interracial Cooperation on the regional and state levels from 1920 to 1944. She was a member of the executive board of the North Carolina State Teachers Association and on the advisory board of the State Commission on Welfare and Public Charity from 1924 to 1944. Active in women's organizations, McCrorey was a member of the Federation of Women's Clubs and the Eastern Star, and was on the executive board of the National Council of Negro Women. She was corresponding secretary of the International Council of Women of the Darker Races from 1922 to 1944. She served the Presbyterian church as president of the Catawba Synodical Missionary Society of the Board of National Missions and the Board of Foreign Missions.

In 1937 McCrorey ran unsuccessfully as a candidate for the Charlotte City School Board, becoming one of the first African-American women in the South to run for elective public office. The press considered her a serious candidate, and she mounted a platform that called for educational fairness to all pupils.

Mary McCrorey died in a fire at her home in January 1944.

—Glenda Elizabeth Gilmore

Bibliography

Mary McCrorey's papers burned in the fire that took her life. Her correspondence appears in the papers of her associates Lugenia Burns Hope and Charlotte Hawkins Brown. The record of her life must be pieced together from newspaper accounts and correspondence. Since she was a member of the network of southern women leaders in interracial and YWCA work, several secondary works (listed below) mention McCrorey's work, including Jacquelyn Dowd Hall, *Revolt Against Chivalry*; Cynthia Neverdon-Morton, *Afro-American Women and the Advancement of the Race*; and Jacqueline Rouse, *Lugenia Burns Hope: Black Southern Reformer*. McCrorey's life awaits a biographer.

Primary Sources

Charlotte Hawkins Brown Collection, Arthur and Elizabeth Schlesinger Library, Radcliffe College, Cambridge, Massachusetts.
Neighborhood Union Collection, Woodruff Library, Atlanta University Center, Atlanta, Georgia.
North Carolina Commission on Interracial Cooperation Papers, Southern Historical Collection, Wilson Library, University of North Carolina at Chapel Hill.

Secondary Sources

Charlotte Observer (March 28, 1937): 13; (April 26, 1937): 1.
Gilmore, Glenda Elizabeth. "Black Women and Ballots in a 'Progressive' Southern State: North Carolina, 1898–1937." Paper delivered at the Southern Historical Association Meeting, 1989, in the author's possession.
Hall, Jacquelyn Dowd. *Revolt Against Chivalry: Jesse Daniel Ames and the Women's Campaign Against Lynching.* New York: Columbia University Press, 1974.
"In Memoriam." *76th Annual Commencement, Johnson C. Smith.* Charlotte, NC: Johnson C. Smith, January 13, 1944.
Lucas, Doris, Tom Parramore, and Earlie Thorpe, eds. *Paths Toward Freedom.* Raleigh: Center for Urban Affairs, North Carolina State University, 1976, p. 172.
Neverdon-Morton, Cynthia. *Afro-American Women of the South and the Advancement of the Race, 1895–1925.* Knoxville: University of Tennessee Press, 1989.
Parker, Inez Moore. *The Biddle-Johnson C. Smith University Story.* Charlotte: Charlotte Publishing, 1975.
Quarterly Review of Higher Education among Negroes 12:1 (January 1944): 52–54.
Rouse, Jacqueline Anne. *Lugenia Burns Hope: Black Southern Reformer.* Athens: University of Georgia Press, 1989.
"75th Anniversary, 1902–1977 Charlotte Y.W.C.A., Verticle Files, Charlotte Public Library, Charlotte, NC.
Yenser, Thomas, ed. *Who's Who in Colored America, 1941–1944.* New York: Thomas Yenser, 1944.

McDANIEL, HATTIE (1898–1952), a radio and film actress, the first black woman to win an Academy Award (Best Supporting Actress, *Gone with the Wind*, 1939), and the titled lead of the "Beulah" television series. Born in Wichita, Kansas, on June 10, 1898 (however, her brother Samuel gave 1895 as the year of birth on her death certificate), to Susan (Holbert) and Henry McDaniel, Hattie McDaniel started life as the thirteenth child in a religious family. Her father, a Baptist minister, had fought in the Civil War and had been a slave and a minstrel man. Her mother sang in the church choir, which influenced Hattie McDaniel to try vaudeville as a singer and dancer. The McDaniel family moved to Denver, Colorado, when she was a child. She sang on the radio as an amateur and then entered vaudeville professionally. Though she never studied formal acting, McDaniel received a gold medal for excellence in dramatic arts from the Women's Christian Temperance Union in Denver for her recital of "Convict Joe." She worked with her brother Otis on his tent tours, and performed in minstrel shows on the Shriner and Elks circuit. When acting parts were scarce, she accepted available work. When working as a restroom maid at Sam Pick's Suburban Inn, she won an audition singing "St. Louis Blues" and a starring spot in the club's show, a position she held for two years. By 1924 Hattie McDaniel was a headliner on the Pantages circuit.

By 1931 McDaniel found her way to Hollywood, where she worked as a maid and took in washing. She made her debut in *The Golden West* in 1932. In the next 17 years, she appeared in over sixty films including *Judge Priest*, *The Little Colonel*, *Showboat*, *Saratoga, and Nothing Sacred*. She was often praised for roles in such films as *Blonde Venus*, *Babbitt*, *Music Is Magic*, *They Died with Their Boots On*, and *Reap the Wild Wind*. She received recognition as the character "Mammy" in *Showboat*, with Paul Robeson. Some critics claimed that her role in *Gone with the Wind* was based on an interpretation of her former roles, yet McDaniel managed to create a series of characters that had their own integrity. After receiving the 1939 Academy Award, her career faded. She depended upon radio for her source of income in the roles of Hi-Hat Hattie and later of Beulah, a wise and comic maid.

Her personal life was less rewarding. Her first husband died young. Her later marriages to James Lloyd Crawford (1941), a Los Angeles real estate agent; Larry C. Williams, an interior decorator; and Nym Langford all ended in divorce. Hattie McDaniel, a big woman with a rich booming voice, boundless energy, and mobile face, had tragedy in these personal relationships, so during the 1940s, she turned to helping others. During World War II, McDaniel worked with the Hollywood Victory Committee as chairperson and helped to organize entertainment for the segregated black troops. She was likewise involved in fundraising for the education of black youth and in other community charity affairs. Not unaware of the color barriers faced by black artists, she made every effort to give her roles dignity and to open opportunities for more African Americans in radio, stage, and screen. She won plaudits and praise due to her honest and sincere interpretations of these roles. During the last two years of her life she suffered from cancer and died in October 1952 at the Motion Picture Home and Hospital, Los Angeles, California. She donated her Oscar from *Gone with the Wind* to Howard University.

—Nicholas C. Polos

Bibliography

The files on Hattie McDaniel at the Schomburg Center for Research in Black

Culture and the Lincoln Center Library and Museum of the New York Public Library have many interesting pieces of information on the subject, as does the Margaret Herrick Library, Academy of Motion Picture Arts and Sciences, in Beverly Hills, California.

Secondary sources placing McDaniel within the entertainment context include Peter Nobel, *The Negro in Films: Literature of the Cinema* (Port Washington, NY: Kennikat, 1970); Donald Bogle, *Toms, Coons, Mammies, Mulattoes and Bucks: An Interpretive History of Blacks in American Film* (New York: Continuum, 1989); Thomas Cripps, *Slow Fade to Black: The Negro in American Films, 1900–1942* (New York: Oxford University Press, 1977); Lena Horne, *Lena* (Garden City, NY: Doubleday, 1965); Susan Myrick, *White Columns in Hollywood: Reports from the "Gone with the Wind" Sets* (Macon, GA: Mercer University Press, 1982); and Roland Flamini, *Scarlett, Rhett, and a Cast of Thousands: The Filming of Gone with the Wind* (New York: Macmillan, 1975). Biographical information is in R.N. Logan, *The Dictionary of American Negro Biography* (New York: Norton, 1982); Edward Mapp, *A Directory of Blacks in the Performing Arts* (Metuchen, NJ: Scarecrow, 1978); *Current Biography* (September 1940); and *Photoplay* (June 1940): 80. Her obituaries provide information in the *New York Times* (October 27, 1952); *Variety* (October 29, 1952); *Amsterdam News* (November 1, 1952); and *Our World Magazine* (February 1952).

McKINNEY, NINA MAE (1912–1967), considered to be the first major black actress in the United States, was the only child born to Hal and Georgia McKinney in Lancaster, South Carolina. Her parents moved to New York City and left her in the care of her great aunt Mrs. Kelly Sanders of Lancaster. McKinney attended the Lancaster Training School until about the sixth grade. During this time she became interested in films and acting, probably as a result of her avid reading of film magazines. In fact, her favorite actress was Gloria Swanson.

McKinney eventually joined her parents in New York, where she became a performer at the Cotton Club in Harlem. In 1928 she appeared in the Lew Leslie musical revue *Blackbirds*. King Vidor, a leading motion picture producer, spotted her in *Blackbirds* and cast her as "Chick," the leading character in *Hallelujah*. This role would later cause her to be typecast as a "tragic mulatto" and "love goddess."

McKinney received rave reviews for her performance in *Hallelujah*. On the strength of her role, Metro Goldwyn Mayer signed her to a then unprecedented five-year contract. In spite of being called "one of the greatest discoveries of the age," opportunities for McKinney as a black leading lady fell short of her expectations. She was only able to get parts in minor films or in Oscar Micheaux's limited-release black films.

Within five years after *Hallelujah*, Nina Mae McKinney would be forgotten. In 1932 she left the United States and successfully toured Europe as the "Black Greta Garbo" with jazz pianist Garland Wilson. In 1935, while in England, she appeared with Paul Robeson in *Sanders of the River*. McKinney appeared in other movies, none of which matched the success of *Hallelujah*. Her last significant movie role was in the 1949 classic *Pinky*.

There is little known about McKinney's life after she appeared in *Pinky*. It seems that she remained in New York and performed primarily in theater productions. Her last known stage performance was as Sadie Thompson in a Brooklyn production of *Rain* in 1951. She died in 1967 in New York City, a year before her posthumous induction into the Black Filmmakers Hall of Fame. On the two hundredth anniversary of Lancaster, South Carolina, she was honored with a mural on the city's Wall of Fame.

—Frank W. Johnson

Bibliography

The information regarding Nina McKinney's early life came from a telephone interview conducted by Anthony L. Taylor, on August 6, 1991, with Mrs. Marjorie Clinton McMurray, a childhood friend. All of the secondary sources give a brief description of her discovery by Vidor and a list of her film appearances. There is little or no biographical information on her early life in these sources. These include Donald Bogle, *Blacks in American Films and Television* (New York: Garland, 1988); Charles Eugene Claghorn, *Biographical Dictionary of Jazz* (West Nyack, NY: Parker, 1982); Marianna W. Davis, *Contributions of Black Women to America* (Columbia, SC: Kenday, 1982); and Edward Mapp, *Directory of Blacks in the Performing Arts* (Metuchen, NJ: Scarecrow, 1990).

McQUEEN, THELMA ("BUTTERFLY") (b. 1911), actress, was born in

Tampa, Florida, on January 8. Her father was a stevedore on the Tampa docks and her mother worked as a domestic. McQueen finished high school in Babylon, New York, and attended nursing school in the Bronx, completing her training several years later at Georgia Medical College in Augusta. In 1946 McQueen began taking liberal arts courses at various institutions and completed the degree bachelor of arts in 1975 at the City University of New York.

McQueen's introduction to the theater came shortly after she finished high school, when she began to study ballet and voice. In 1935 she made her stage debut in New York as part of the Butterfly Ballet in an adaptation of *A Midsummer Night's Dream*. "Butterfly" became her stage name during this production and remained with her thereafter.

McQueen made her Broadway debut in 1937 in the George Abbott production of *Brown Sugar*. She received favorable reviews, and as a result she was cast in several other Abbott productions including *Brother Rat*, *Three Men on a Horse*, and *What a Life*.

In the late 1930s McQueen auditioned for the part of Prissy in the film *Gone with the Wind*. At first she was told that she was too fat, too dignified, and too old to play the part of a slave girl half her age. Producer David O. Selznick had other casting ideas, and he chose McQueen for the part. McQueen's famous line in

Gone with the Wind, "Lawsy, Miss Scarlet, Ah don' know nothin' 'bout birthin' babies!" has become her trademark.

McQueen's association with Gone with the Wind launched her film career. She accepted several other film roles but never to the acclaim of "Prissy." Her film credits include The Women, Affectionately Yours, Cabin in the Sky, I Dood It, Mildred Pierce, Flame of the Barbary Coast, and Killer Diller.

On and off the filming set, McQueen was known for her assertiveness and individualism. She resisted racial stereotyping, and protested rest room and transportation segregation. Eventually she refused to accept roles as servants or "handkerchief heads." It was a stand she admirably maintained with courage even though it cost her a number of film contracts in the 1950s and 1960s.

During her film boycott, she returned to the stage to play in such productions as The World's My Oyster, School for Wives, The Athenian Touch, Curley McDimple, The Wiz, and Showboat. She also produced her own musical revues including Butterfly McQueen and Friends in 1969, and Prissy in Person in 1976. In the 1970s she returned to films and appeared in The Phynx, Amazing Grace, Mosquito Coast, and Stiff.

The many honors bestowed upon McQueen include the Rosemary Award in 1973, the Black Filmmakers Hall of Fame Award in 1975, and an Emmy in 1979 for her role in the television production of The Seven Wishes of Joanna Peabody. She has remained unmarried, preferring to expend her energy instead working for racial equality, animal rights, environmental protection, and urban beautification. She maintains residences in Augusta and Harlem.

—Juanita Karpf

Bibliography

Among the most useful of secondary sources of information about Thelma McQueen are two books by Donald Bogle, Blacks in American Films and Television (New York: Garland, 1988) and Toms, Coons, Mulattoes, Mammies, and Bucks (New York: Continuum, 1989). Other valuable sources include two older works: Thomas Cripps, Slow Fade to Black (New York: Oxford University Press, 1977); and Daniel J. Leab, From Sambo to Superstar (Boston: Houghton Mifflin, 1975). Interesting, if chatty, inside information about the filming of Gone with the Wind can be obtained from Susan Myrick, White Columns in Hollywood: Reports from the "Gone with the Wind" Sets (Macon, GA: Mercer University Press, 1982). Most biographical information available on McQueen must be gleaned from newspaper and magazine clippings, a large file of which is located at the Hargrett Library of Rare Books and Special Collections, Main Library, University of Georgia, Athens. Fascinating details about McQueen and her first experiences in Hollywood are to be found in the correspondance files of Margaret Mitchell, housed in the Margaret Mitchell Marsh Collection, Hargrett Library of Rare Books and Special Collections, Main Library, University of Georgia, Athens.

McRAE, CARMEN (b. 1920), jazz singer, was born in Harlem on April 8, and, musically inclined as a toddler, she listened to and mimicked songs on the radio. The fourth child of Manhattan health club manager Oscar and Evadne McRae, she grew up in Brooklyn, where she took piano lessons but never pursued voice training. Her parents wanted her to become a classical pianist, but McRae was more interested in contemporary music, dreaming of becoming a jazz singer; she hid pages of popular music compositions intermixed with her classical sheet music. The highlight of her teenage years was meeting her idol Billie Holiday, whom she admitted intimidated her about her own abilities and potential for success.

McRae realized that she should use her piano playing to gain access to singing jobs as well as a means to earn income. She won a Wednesday night amateur contest at the Apollo Theatre, playing the piano, and attracted the attention of Irene Wilson Kitchings, who arranged an audition for McRae with Benny Goodman. He told her to get more experience, while McRae's parents urged her to pursue secretarial work.

She lived in Washington, DC, as a government employee for two years during World War II. McRae returned to Brooklyn in 1943 and compromised ambition with reality by working a daytime clerical position and then performing on piano at night in clubs. She accepted a variety of brief jobs that helped pay her bills and obtain musical experience, including being a chorus girl one summer in Atlantic City, New Jersey.

She moved to Chicago, the town she claimed established her as a singer, and between 1944 and 1947, McRae sang for the big bands of Benny Carter, Count Basie, and Mercer Ellington, with whom she made her record debut in 1946. Her initiation as a soloist was instigated by a Chicago friend who convinced her to audition for an available performance job. McRae succeeded in that position, which lasted for 17 weeks. During that time, she had little money, so her new employer loaned her the money to join the musicians union.

After her initial solo employment, McRae worked numerous brief engagements, while improving her piano skills to gain access to potential singing jobs. She initiated an intense study of music, hoping that this understanding would provide her a foundation to maintain a long-lasting musical career. In interviews, McRae stressed that her experiences in Chicago demonstrated her vocal potential.

Her parents invited McRae to move home, and after almost four years in Chicago, McRae returned to her family's New York City brownstone. In 1952 at the Harlem jazz club Minton's Play House, McRae performed as the intermission pianist. Within two years she had become the solo singer, while supplementing her income with clerical work. Finally, Decca Records offered her an album contract. Next, she signed a recording agreement with Bethlehem Records, a larger studio, which sparked her fame nationally.

In 1954 *Down Beat* magazine named her the Best New Female Singer, and she tied with Ella Fitzgerald in a 1955 *Metronome* poll for similar honors as Singer of the Year. In interviews, she summarized her philosophy of performance, stating that she placed priority on lyrics over melody and that singers should be inventive and original in their presentation of songs, noting, "If I don't have something new to offer in a song, well, I just won't sing it." She told Arthur Taylor, author of *Notes and Tones*, that her years as a pianist were valuable to her singing career because, she said, "Without it, I would perhaps not even be singing, or if I had become a singer, it might not be as impressive as whatever it is I do now."

Her albums contained original material as well as tributes to jazz singers she respected. She recorded an album honoring Billie Holiday in the 1960s, including her rendition of "Strange Fruit." She was friends with jazz singer Sarah Vaughan, to whom she dedicated a 1991 album; she also recorded songs done originally by Thelonious Monk, a composer and pianist she admired.

McRae married and divorced two husbands, drummer Kenny Clarke and pianist Ike Isaacs. As her singing career progressed, she moved to Manhattan, but has lived on the West Coast as well as traveled to Europe. She was especially popular in Japan and recorded an album of her Tokyo performances. She performed on the cruise Showboat 3, in jazz and musical festivals, and on television variety shows such as the "Tonight Show." In 1962 she appeared in *The Real Ambassadors* musical, singing opposite Louis Armstrong.

McRae actively pursues her career as a singer in the 1990s. She often sings at festivals in major cities such as Boston and Los Angeles and occasionally for charity programs and patrons who cannot afford the price of concert tickets. She realizes that the quality of her voice has changed with age, yet delights in acquainting new generations of listeners with her unique sound and interpretation of songs. McRae continues to call New York her home.

—Elizabeth D. Schafer

Bibliography

The Institute of Jazz Studies at Rutgers University contains collections and photographs of jazz performers, including McRae. Leonard Feather, *The Encyclopedia of Jazz in the '60s* (New York: Bonanza, 1966) and *The Encyclopedia of Jazz in the '70s* (New York: Horizon, 1976) lists her albums and accomplishments. Howard Reich, "Setting Standards," *Chicago Tribune* (March 13, 1990) is a recent depiction of McRae's talent and musical goals and in which she corrects her birthdate, which most sources list inaccurately as 1922. Two chapters in Leslie Gourse, one based on an interview with McRae's arranger and pianist, Norman Simmons, are in *Louis' Children: American Jazz Singers* (New York: Morrow, 1984). An in-depth, and often personal, interview exploring McRae's views of music, religion, and politics, among many topics, is in Arthur Taylor, *Notes and Tones* (New York: Coward, McCann, & Geoghegan, 1982). Ralph J. Gleason, *Celebrating the Duke, and Louis, Bessie, Billie, Bird, Carmen, Miles, Dizzy, and Other Heroes* (Boston: Little, Brown, 1975) devotes a chapter to McRae.

"Carmen McRae; New Singer Challenges Ella, Sarah for Jazz Supremacy," *Ebony* 11 (February 1956): 67–70; and James Howard, Sr., "Introducing Miss Carmen McRae," *Negro History Bulletin* 19 (March 1956): 125, are brief contemporary accounts of McRae's jazz singing. A bibliographical list of other periodical sources on McRae is included in JoAnn Skowronski, *Black Music in America: A Bibliography* (Metuchen, NJ: Scarecrow, 1981), pp. 404–409; Jervis Anderson, *This Was Harlem: A Cultural Portrait, 1900–1950* (New York: Harcourt Brace Jovanovich, 1982); Arnold Shaw, *52nd Street: The Street of Jazz* (New York: De Capo, 1977); Samuel B. Charters and Leonard Kunstadt, *Jazz: A History of the New York Scene* (Garden City, NY: Doubleday, 1962); Eileen Southern, *The Music of Black Americans, A History*, 2nd edition (New York: Norton, 1983); and Marshall Stearns, *The Story of Jazz* (New York: Oxford University Press, 1978) provide a historical context for McRae's career.

Numerous articles, most contemporary, addressing McRae's musical career can be located in *Down Beat, Metronome, Variety, Melody Maker, Saturday Review, Billboard, Jazz Magazine, Jazz Journal, Jazz Forum, Jazz Podium, Stereo Review, Nation*, as well as essays written in various languages in foreign publications issued by publishers in European, Asian, and Hispanic nations. American periodicals such as *Time, New York Sunday News*, and the *New York Post* reported on McRae's celebrity, and reviews of her albums and performances from the 1950s to the 1990s can be found in the *New York Times, Chicago Tribune, Boston Globe, Los Angeles Times, Washington Post*, and *Wall Street Journal*.

McRae's albums include *Alive!; The Art of Carmen McRae; Bittersweet; Carmen; Carmen Alone; Carmen-Billie; Carmen's Gold; Carmen McRae; Carmen McRae: Carmen Sings Monk; For Once in My Life; Great American Song Book; I Am Music; In Person; In Person, Carmen McRae; I Want You; In Person—San Francisco; It Takes a Whole Lot of Human Feelings; Just a Little Lovin'; Live and Doin' It; Live & Wailing; Live at Sugar Hill; Lover Man; Ms. Jazz; Portrait of Carmen; The Real Ambassadors; Sarah—Dedicated to You; Second to None—Haven't We Met?; Something Wonderful; Sound of Silence; Take Five; Woman Talk—Live at the Village Gate.*

MAHONEY, MARY (1845–1926), born in Dorchester, Massachusetts, on May 7, was the first black professional nurse in the United States. As the eldest of three children born to Charles and Mary Jane (Steward) Mahoney, Mary Eliza Mahoney grew up in Roxbury, Massachusetts, where she worked as an untrained nurse until the age of 33. When a group of women incorporated the New England Hospital for Women and Children on March 18, 1863, to provide health care to women by female physicians and to train nurses, Mahoney sought employment at the institution as a cook/cleaner. Her work impressed a female physician, who sought Mahoney's acceptance in the nursing program, although she was two years above the age limit of thirty-one. Thus, at age 33, Mary Mahoney started her training as a student nurse.

Of 42 students admitted in 1878, only 4 completed the grueling program of 16-hour days, 7-day weeks, and night duty to graduate in August 1879. Mary Eliza Mahoney's graduation made her the first black professional nurse in the United

States during a time when black women were not accepted in white schools of nursing and black schools of nursing had not yet emerged.

Her graduation did not mean acceptance without discrimination. She worked as a private-duty nurse after registering with the Nurses Directory at the Massachusetts Medical Library in Boston. Her manner, efficiency, and skills overcame the prejudices of many employers. As her reputation spread, she received nursing jobs in North Carolina, Washington, DC, and other states. When the Nurses Associated Alumnae of the United States and Canada was formed in 1896, she became one of the first black members of the ANA. After working in the field for several years, however, she, too, sought privileges given to white nurses. When the National Association of Colored Graduate Nurses (NACGN) was formed in 1908, Mahoney welcomed the organized attempt to improve the status and working conditions of black nurses. Invited by National Medical Association leader and prominent Roxbury physician John B. Hall to have their convention in Boston, the NACGN accepted and held their first convention in Boston in 1909, where Mahoney gave the welcoming address. By 1911 she received lifetime membership in the NACGN and became the chaplain responsible for the induction and training of new officers. During that same year, Mahoney relocated to Kings Park, Long Island, to administer the Howard Orphan Asylum for black children. In 1912, she retired.

Her retirement from employment did not mean retirement from community obligations. She worked diligently for women's rights, especially for women's suffrage. At age 76, she became the first woman in her city to register to vote after ratification of the Nineteenth Amendment. Never married, Mahoney developed family relationships with the families she had worked for and physicians she had worked with during the years, such as the Armes family and John B. Hall family. When she died in January 1926 of breast cancer, she was survived by Frederick Saunders, the grandson of her sister, Ellen Mahoney. She was buried at Woodlawn Cemetery in Everett, Massachusetts.

In her honor, several affiliates of the NACGN took her name, and in 1936, the organization established an award in her name to honor sister nurses who actively participated in organizations to improve the status of black nurses in the nursing profession. The award was continued after the NACGN merged with the American Nurses Association in 1951. In Roxbury, the former New England Hospital for Women and Children became the Dimock Community Health Center and houses a comprehensive Mary Mahoney Health Care Clinic to continue her commitment to the community. She was admitted to the Nursing Hall of Fame in 1976. In 1984 the nursing sorority Chi Eta Phi and the ANA organized a national pilgrimage to her grave in her honor.

—Beth Schneider

Bibliography

Information on Mary Mahoney is now readily available due to the recognition she has received from the professional nursing associations. The best complete source on black women in the nursing profession is Darlene Hine, *Black Women in White* (Bloomington: Indiana University Press, 1989), which has an extensive bibliography. Although this focuses on the time period 1890–1950, Hine provides background information about Mahoney and her significance to the profession. See also, M.E. Chayer, "Mary Eliza Mahoney," *American Journal of Nursing* 54 (April 1954): 429; P. and B. Kalisch, *The Advance of American Nursing* (Boston: Little, Brown, 1978); Mabel Staupers, *No Time for Prejudice* (New York: Macmillan, 1961); Adah B. Thoms, *Pathfinders* (New York: Kay Printing, 1929); and Althea T. Davis, "Mary Eliza Mahoney," in *American Nursing: A Biographical Dictionary*, edited by Vern Bullough, Olga Church, and Alice Stein (New York: Garland, 1988).

MARSHALL, PAULE [BURKE] (b. 1929), novelist and short story writer, was born in Brooklyn, New York. Her parents, both from Barbados, met with friends from the islands to discuss issues and weave stories in the lilting, lyrical English typical of the West Indies. These people and tales surrounded Paule Marshall's childhood and appear throughout her novels as linkages with her heritage. As she listened to the women talk about their employers, she developed the skill of characterization. They used language as an art; they created poetry. In addition to these women, she traveled to Barbados for connection to her mother's lineage. She spent a year in Barbados with her grandmother to "continue my grandmother's line." The Brooklyn environment provided her with political insights. Since her parents had come to New York in the post–World War I era, the influence of Marcus Garvey was ever present. The women were members of his Nurses Brigade, marchers in his parades, and politically involved role models.

Armed with her love of language and the written word, she attended school in Brooklyn and started writing poetry as a teenager. She entered Hunter College in 1948 to become a social worker, married her first husband in 1950, and had to leave college temporarily due to illness. With time on her hands, she started writing letters to friends, who suggested she think about a writing career. On her return to college, she changed her major to English literature and graduated from Brooklyn College as a Phi Beta Kappa.

She sought employment as a writer for newpapers or magazines, but received rejection. Eventually, she found employment with *Our World Magazine*, a small black publication, starting as a researcher and gradually assuming responsibilities for fashion/food sections, then feature stories. As the only female, she felt the men were waiting for her failure. So she struggled on to prevent their satisfaction.

At night she started to write as a creative outlet. *Brown Girl, Brownstones*, her first major novel about the painful awakening of a black girl, took shape over five years. In 1959 its publication brought together the threads of Marshall as child and woman. The book was both a popular and critical success. Ironically, her reluctance to go on the road for book promotion lessened the potential sales of the novel. Her next publication was a collection of four short stories set in Brazil, Barbados, British Guiana, and Brooklyn, and primarily described the experiences of men. *Soul Clap Hands and Sing* (1961) seemed easier to write, but was slowed by the birth of a baby. She used money from her first novel to hire babysitters so that she could write at a friend's apartment. This produced a strain in the husband-wife relationship. Her strong need to fulfill herself through her writing prevailed. After 13 years, her marriage ended. She became active in the Association of Artists for Freedom, an organization created after the church bombing in Birmingham in 1963. The group of writers and performers organized to promote active participation of the black community in the independence movement.

Her most ambitious undertaking took almost seven years to write. Published in 1969, *The Chosen Place, A Timeless People* details the rejection of "progress" by the island people of Bournehills, who struggle to keep their traditions despite the intrusion of well-meaning humanitarians. Her characters are strong black women who overcome obstacles and carry on the heritage.

Paule Marshall considered such pioneer writers as Dorothy West and Zora Neale Hurston her mentors. She goes beyond their vision to deal with themes of sexuality, oppression, relationships, history, independence, dependence, and revolution. She concentrates on writing novels, even though she has been periodically induced to enter other fields. Her adaptation of *Brown Girl, Brownstones* for the CBS Television Workshop enabled her to win a Ford Foundation grant for playwriting. She turns to outside funding sources for grants and to periodic teaching positions at Yale and Columbia universities to support her writing between books and to lessen the anxiety about bills. She remarried in 1970 to a Haitian businessman. Both retain their financial and lifestyle independence. Her receipt of the Guggenheim and Ford Foundation fellowships, the National Book Award, and other honors have not clouded her vision or dedication to continue to write about the triumphs of the human spirit. Her most recent books continue that theme in her fourth novel, *Praisesong for the Widow* (1982); a short story collection *Reena and Other Stories* (1984); and latest novel, *Daughters* (1991).

At age 59, she continues to do her writing throughout the year, except when she teaches fiction writing at Virginia Commonwealth University in Richmond, Virginia. During that semester, she becomes involved in her students' lives and their work. She feels that teaching draws upon the same energy as does writing; hence, her priorities are developed based upon her class schedule.

—Beth Schneider

Bibliography

Biographical information is included in several sources: Ronda Glikin, *Black American Women in Literature* (Jefferson, NC: McFarland, 1989); Carol Myers, et al.,

Black American Writers Past and Present (New York: Appleton-Century-Crofts, 1970); Ann L. Shockley, *Living Black American Authors* (New York: Bowker, 1973); and *Negro Almanac* (New York: Bellwether, 1976). Periodicals also provide much information about her and her work: *Black World* (August 1974): 10–18; *Book World* (December 28, 1969): 10; *CLA Journal* (September 1972): 49–71; *Ebony* (March 1970): 67 (August 1966): 149; *Negro Digest* (January 1970): 51; and *Essence* (May 1979): 70+. She describes her craft in "The Making of a Writer," in the *New York Times Book Review* on January 9, 1983. Her most recent interview with Nancy Connors, "Writer Explores Linkages with the Past," appeared in the Cleveland *Plain Dealer* on November 24, 1991.

MASON, BIDDY (1818–1891), philanthropist, businesswoman, and church founder, was born a slave in Hancock County, Georgia, on August 15. While still a child, she was sold to Robert Marion Smith and Rebecca (Crosby) Smith of Mississippi. While enduring the harshness of slavery on the Mississippi River, Biddy Mason gave birth to three daughters: Ellen (1838), Ann (1844), and Harriet (1847). Her master might have been the father of these children. During this time, she specialized as a midwife and nurse, having learned the skills of treatment and knowledge of herbs, roots, and foods from other slave specialists.

When her master converted to the Mormon faith in 1847, he decided to take his family and slaves to Utah in the spring of 1848. Biddy Mason was responsible for organizing the camp, which included 56 whites and 34 slaves and a caravan of 300 wagons. Once they arrived in Utah, she and the other slaves received bad treatment from the Mormon community, which believed in the inferiority of the African race. Since Smith's dreams had not been realized by 1851, he decided again to move to another Mormon colony in San Bernadino, California. Again, Biddy Mason organized the camps for this journey, moving slaves and white families to California in the fall of 1851.

Obviously, Smith was not aware that the California State Constitution forbade slavery and that its status as a free state (September 1850) became part of the Compromise of 1850. Upon arrival, Smith's knowledge about the tenuous status of his "property" led to plans for another move to Texas, where slavery was intact. Providence smiled on the family of Biddy Mason when a freeman, Charles Owens, fell in love with Biddy Mason's eldest daughter, Ellen. To prevent Smith from removing the Mason family from California, Charles Owens received the help of his father, Robert Owens, an influential black businessman from Los Angeles, to serve Smith with a writ of habeas corpus through the local sheriff. During court proceedings, Mason could not testify due to California's restrictions against blacks testifying against whites in court. Smith failed to appear in court (January 21, 1856); thus, the Mason family received legal manumission. Charles Owens married Ellen Mason, and they had two sons.

Biddy Mason and her daughters lived with the Robert Owens family while she established a nurse-midwife business in Los Angeles. Since her clients included many wealthy whites, she was able to become economically independent. Within ten years she had purchased land on Spring Street in Los Angeles. By 1884 she had moved onto this land, built a commercial building on another parcel, and had started a financial empire for her family. She told her daughters and their families never to sell or abandon the land, which provided her heirs with wealth and social standing. Ellen's son, Robert Curry Owens, became known as "the richest Negro in Los Angeles" through his development of real estate. He combined his business ventures with his career in politics.

As Biddy Mason acquired her wealth, she never forgot her responsibilities to community. She established with Charles Owens the First African Methodist Episcopal Church in Los Angeles in 1872. She contributed to charity concerns throughout her life to provide for the poor and homeless of all races. She regularly visited jails to serve the incarcerated. She donated land for the construction of schools, churches, and a nursing home.

With all the service she provided, it is curious that her death on January 15, 1891, earned her a grave that went unmarked for nearly a century in the Evergreen Cemetery in Los Angeles. On March 27, 1988, Mayor Tom Bradley and members of the First African Methodist Episcopal Church dedicated a tombstone to mark this grave. The following year, the Broadway Spring Center dedicated on Biddy Mason Day, November 16, 1989, a memorial highlighting Biddy Mason's life on a wall listing her chronological achievements for present and future generations to remember her legacy.

—Kelle S. Taha

Bibliography

Most of the information on Biddy Mason's life can be found in Delilah Beasley, *Negro Trailblazers in California* (Los Angeles: Times Mirror, 1919). Repetition of the information is found in Marianna Davis, *Contributions of Black Women to America* (Columbia, SC: Kenday, 1982): x. Recent historical research has expanded the information: Bobi Jackson, "Biddy Mason: Pioneer 1818–1891," an essay written for the Los Angeles Center for the Study of Women, University of California, 1985; and Dolores Hayden's article "Biddy Mason's Los Angeles, 1856–1891," *California History* 68 (Fall 1989): 86–99. Two articles in the *Los Angeles Times* provide additional details: Gregory Crouch, "Early Black Heroine of L.A. Finally Receives Her Due" (March 28, 1988); and Myrna Oliver, "A Lot of History" (November 17, 1989).

MATTHEWS, VICTORIA [EARLE] (1861–1907), the journalist, author, clubwoman, and social worker, was described by author I. Garland Penn as "the most popular writer of her day." Matthews was born Victoria Earle, one of nine children born to Caroline Smith, a slave at Fort Valley, Georgia, about twenty-five miles southwest of Macon. It was reported that her mother fled to New York

City to escape her master's cruel treatment, leaving Matthews and three other children in their white father's household. After the Civil War Caroline Smith returned to Georgia and gained custody of Matthews and her sister. After stopping in Norfolk and Richmond, Virginia, she moved them to New York City in 1873.

Considered to be a bright, happy, and studious child, Matthews attended Public School 48 until family hardships forced her to leave school to work as a domestic. She was able to continue her education by gaining access to the large library of the house in which she worked. In spite of her circumstances she matured into a self-educated and cultured black woman.

In 1879 she married William Matthews and settled in Brooklyn with the their son Lamartine. It was during this period when she began her career as a writer. She contributed childhood reminiscences to the *Brooklyn Eagle* and the *Waverly Magazine*. She was also a "sub" reporter for other New York papers such as the *Times, Herald, Mail and Express, Sunday Mercury, The Earth,* and the *Phonographic World.* She contributed articles to the leading black newspapers such as the *Boston Advocate, Washington Bee, Richmond Planet, Catholic Tribune, Cleveland Gazette, New York Globe, New York Age,* and the *New York Enterprise.* In 1893, under the name Victoria Earle, she published *Aunt Lindy: A Story Founded on Real Life.* It is the story of an aged ex-slave in postbellum Georgia who resists the temptation to murder her former master. At the urging of T. Thomas Fortune, editor of the *New York Age* (newspaper), she also edited *Black Belt Diamonds,* a collection of Booker T. Washington's speeches in 1898.

Besides her literary interests, Matthews was also quite active in the women's club movement. In 1892 she founded the Woman's Loyal Union of New York and Brooklyn to work for black women's rights. She also sponsored a successful testimonial fundraiser with Maritcha Lyons of Brooklyn at Lyric Hall on October 5, 1892. It was to assist Ida B. Wells in reestablishing *Free Speech,* her newspaper that was destroyed when she was forced to flee from Memphis. In 1893 Matthews participated in the Columbian World Exposition in Chicago by delivering a speech entitled "The Value of Race Literature." In 1895, with Josephine St. Pierre and others including Margaret Murray Washington and Elizabeth Carter, she helped found in Boston the National Federation of Afro-American Women. Matthews also served on the editorial board of its publication, *The Women's Era.* As chairperson of its executive committee, she was principal planner of the 1896 convention in Washington, DC, at which the federation merged with the National Colored Women's League to become the National Association of Colored Women (NACW).

After serving as national organizer for NACW from 1897 to 1899, Matthews began to devote her life to the growing social problems that plagued young blacks in urban centers. This was intensified by the death of her son at age 16. She was particularly concerned with the large numbers of young black women from the South who were being drawn into prostitution in New York City. After traveling as far as New Orleans, Matthews discovered that black women were lured into prostitution under the guise of so-called employment agencies' promises of work in the North. To combat this she opened the White Rose Industrial Association on February 11, 1897, in New York City. White Rose Mission, as it was commonly known, was a haven where newly arrived black women were befriended, counseled, and prepared for employment through courses in cooking, sewing, and housekeeping. It also provided shelter and classes for young black males who were homeless. The kindergarten provided care, and education was provided by leading clubwomen, including Alice Ruth Moore (Dunbar). Soon White Rose missionaries such as Grace H. Dodge were stationed at the piers in New York and Old Dominion, Virginia, making certain that the young migrants did not fall prey to corrupt individuals.

Originally located in an apartment that was provided rent free by a benevolent landlord, the White Rose Mission moved in 1900 to 217 East 86th Street. This, too, was made possible through the philanthropic gifts given to Matthews. The new larger quarters enabled Matthews to operate White Rose as a settlement house with mother's clubs, recreational activities, and a kindergarten. Matthews herself taught a class in black history and established a large library of books by and about African Americans. As black leaders came to the city, Matthews invited each to speak to the women at the White Rose Home, thus providing information and serving as role models of achievement.

Matthews operated the White Rose Mission until she died of tuberculosis at age 45. Her influence can be seen in the numerous auxiliaries that blossomed from the White Rose Mission. The most notable was the Victoria Earle Matthews Club in Brooklyn. All of these were later collected under an umbrella organization known as the National League for the Protection of Colored Women, which became one of the founding groups of the National Urban League. There is also a plaque commemorating Matthews's life in the White Rose Mission on West 136th Street in Harlem.

—Frank W. Johnson

Bibliography

For Victoria Matthews's early life and work with the White Rose Mission see Hallie Quinn Brown, *Homespun Heroines and Other Women of Distinction* (Xenia, OH: Aldine Press, 1926). I. Garland Penn describes her rich career as a journalist in his *Afro-American Press and Its Editors*, (1891, New York: Arno Press, reprint edition, 1969). Dorothy Salem's *To Better Our World: Black Women in Organized Reform, 1890-1920* (Brooklyn: Carlson, 1990) and Floris Cash's "Womanhood and Protest: The Club Movement among Black Women, 1892–1922" (unpublished dissertation, State University of New York at Stony Brook, 1986) are good sources for Matthews's club work. Other useful sources for Matthews are the New Muse Community Museum of Brooklyn's *An Introduction to the Black Contribution to the Development of Brooklyn* (n.d.) and Jean Blackwell Hutson's essay in *Notable American Women*, edited by Edward T. James, et al. (Cambridge: Harvard University Press, 1971).

MILLS, FLORENCE [WINFREY] (1895–1927), stage performer, vocalist, comedienne, and dancer, was born on January 25 in Washington, DC, the youngest of three daughters of John and Nellie (Simon) Winfrey. Her career in show business was launched at an early age when as "Baby Florence" she performed in the homes of Washington diplomats. Mills's first stage appearance was in Bert Williams and George Walker's *Sons of Ham* (1900) at age five, at the Bijou Theatre in Washington, DC. Billed as "Baby Florence Mills, an Extra Added Attraction?" she sang "Miss Hannah from Savannah." She received several encores for singing and dancing. By age six she had already won dancing awards for the cakewalk and the buck dance. Although her family moved to Harlem when Mills was eight years old, she continued to entertain, since New York abounded with performance opportunities.

Mills joined the Bonita Company soon after her debut with *Sons of Ham* and traveled with Lew Hern for several years as one of the "picks." After leaving this company around 1910, she joined her two sisters, Olivia and Maude, and traveled on the Theater Owner's Booking Association (TOBA) circuit as the Mills Sisters, touring the country in various vaudeville troupes. The trio eventually became a duo; Florence later teamed with Kinky Clark and entertained as Mills and Clark. By 1914 Mills was working with Ada "Bricktop" Smith and Cora Green in the Panama Trio for the Panama Club in Chicago. Bill "Bojangles" Robinson claimed to have taught Mills "a few dance steps" during this time. After Chicago, the trio traveled coast to coast for three years on the Pantages circuit. Around 1918 Mills married Ulysses S. ("Slow Kid") Thompson, then one of the leading comedians and dancers of the traveling troupe, Tennessee Ten. She performed with her husband on the Keith circuit in this show for four seasons.

Mills's career soared when Noble Sissle and Eubie Blake cast her as the lead in *Shuffle Along* in 1921, in which she enchanted audiences with the song "I'm Crazy for That Kind of Love." Bricktop exclaimed that during her first performance in *Shuffle Along*, Mills "had seventeen encores. Seventeen encores! She never looked back. After that, Florence Mills was a star." The show was so popular that there were traffic jams on Sixty-Third Street every night. Mills was affectionately known as "Little Twinks," because she was a small, delicate woman, described as "pixieish," "birdlike and beautiful." Poet and critic James Weldon Johnson said of her, "She could be whimsical, she could be almost grotesque; but she had the good taste that never allowed her to be coarse. She could be risque, she could be seductive; but it was impossible for her to be vulgar, for she possessed a naivete that was alchemic." A multitalented person, her repertoire included pantomime in addition to song, dance, and comedy. After rave reviews, she was in great demand by white Broadway producers. Mills later left the *Shuffle Along* company to star in Lew Leslie's *Plantation Revue* on Broadway, which included Paul Robeson.

Mills was in demand internationally almost at once, after the *Plantation Revue* troupe received critical acclaim in London. Mills performed in Paris and London in 1923 and 1924 in *From Dover to Dixie*. She returned to the United States in 1924, and opened on Broadway as the star of *From Dover to Dixie* on October 29. Her performance shattered the tradition that two male comedians as central characters constituted a black musical. Mills sang and danced with her friend "Bojangles" at the New York Hippodrome in late October 1925 after they both had become star attractions. Fresh from this triumph, she took the leading role in Lew Leslie's *Blackbirds* (1926), written especially for her, and which contained the song that became her trademark, "I'm Just a Blackbird Looking for a Bluebird." After an illustrious six-week engagement at the Alhambra Theatre in Harlem, Mills went with *Blackbirds* back to Paris and London. Her name and photograph were celebrated throughout Europe. The Prince of Wales was said to have seen her performance 16 times and to have pronounced her "ripping." There were dolls named for her, and a plethora of blackbird songs were penned. Mills left the show after its tour and returned home to rest, suffering from exhaustion; she had performed for a solid year without missing one of 300 performances.

Upon her return to Harlem in 1927, Mills checked into a hospital for an appendectomy that she had previously postponed; she died several days later on November 1, 1927, from a ruptured appendix. Her sudden death stunned theatergoers who had looked forward to seeing her *Blackbirds* performance. Her funeral was legendary. Five thousand people were packed in Mother Zion Church, while 150,000 waited outside for the funeral procession. "She was more their idol," said James Weldon Johnson, "than any other artist of the race." Mills was buried in a $5,000 bronze replica of Rudolph Valentino's coffin. A flock of blackbirds were released from an airplane as a funeral cortege slowly carried Mills on her final trip through Harlem.

It is difficult to measure her contribution, since there are no vocal recordings nor artists who point to Florence Mills as their teacher (she died at the age of 32), and since she excelled in a theatrical form not usually associated with lasting significance. Writers speak of an indefinable quality in Florence Mills, one for which the most carefully chosen words are unsuitable. What cannot fail to strike wonder is the sheer magnitude of the respect and love that she seemed to call forth from her audiences, both American and European.

—Elizabeth Hadley Freydberg

Bibliography

The most comprehensive background on Florence Mills is in James Weldon Johnson's *Black Manhattan* (New York: Knopf, 1968). Donald Bogle provides an overview of her life and lists her theater credits in "Florence Mills: Make Way for Little Twinks," in *Brown Sugar: Eighty Years of America's Black Female Superstars* (New York: Harmony, 1980); Jim Haskins, *Mr. Bojangles: The Biography of Bill Bojangles Robinson* (New York: William Morrow, 1988), provides information on Mills's relationship with Bojangles; Henry T. Sampson, *Blacks in Blackface: A Source Book on Early Black Musical Shows* (Metuchen, NJ: Scarecrow, 1980), has a listing of stage productions with cast and personnel in which Florence Mills participated. See also Langston Hughes and Milton Meltzer, *Black Magic: A Pictorial History of Black Entertainers in America* (Englewood Cliffs, NJ: Prentice-Hall, 1967); Loften Mitchell, *Black Drama: The Story of the American Negro in the Theatre* (New York: Hawthorne, 1967); and Lindsay Patterson, *International Library of Negro Life and History: Anthology of the American Negro in the Theatre* (Chicago: Johnson Publishing, 1968). See also Charles B. Cochran's memoirs, *The Secrets of a Showman* (New York: Henry Holt, 1926). Mills's obituary and other appreciative articles after her death appeared in the *New York Times* (November 2, 4, 7, 1927). There are clippings about Mills in the Harvard Theatre Collection, in the Schomburg Collection at the 135th Street branch of the New York Public Library, and in the Theatre Collection of the New York Public Library Performing Arts Research Center at Lincoln Center. There are biographical accounts of Florence Mills in *Who's Who in the Theatre* (Chicago: Marquis, 1925); Edward T. James, *Notable American Women* II (Cambridge: Belknap, 1971); *Who Was Who in the Theatre* III (Chicago: Marquis, 1978) and *The Oxford Companion to the American Theatre* (New York: Oxford University Press, 1984).

MITCHELL, ABBIE (1884–1960) was a singer, actress, and teacher whose career spanned more than half a century from star billing in turn-of-the-century musicals to featured roles on Broadway. Born on September 25 in the Lower East Side of New York City to an African-American mother and German Jewish father, both parents were involved with music. Abbie Mitchell was sent to school in Baltimore, where she lived with her maternal aunt, Alice Payne. She returned to New York in 1897. At age 13, she auditioned for a role in the musical comedy *Clorindy: The Origin of the Cakewalk*, a musical with lyrics by Paul Laurence Dunbar and music by Will Marion Cook, whom she married in 1899. Within a few years, their daughter, Marian Abigail (1900–1950) and son, Will Mercer (1903–1987), were born into this entertainment family. The family and career accomplishments enabled Mitchell to join the ranks of other such stars as Bert Williams, George Walker, and Harry T. Burleigh.

In the space of a few years, Abbie Mitchell developed into an accomplished actress and concert singer. She starred with Bert Williams and George Walker in the 1903 London command performance for King Edward VII of *In Dahomey*. In 1904 she appeared with Black Patti's (Matilda Jones) Troubadours, in *Jes Lik White Folks*, and *The Southerners*, both produced by her husband. In 1905–1906, she sang in New York City, toured Europe with the Memphis Students, and later starred in her husband's production of *Bandana Land* and *The Red Moon*, musicals by Bob Cole and J. Rosamond Johnson. In 1908 Mitchell divorced Will Marion Cook, but continued her musical association with him. She continued to perfect her vocal performances under the guidance of Harry T. Burleigh, Emilia Serrano, both of New York, and Jean de Reszke of Paris. Praised for her *lied* (German art song) interpretations in the concert halls of both Europe and the United States (New York, Atlanta, Chicago, and San Francisco), Mitchell graduated to operatic arias. From 1931 to 1934, she taught voice at Tuskegee Institute in Alabama and appeared on the NBC radio shows. By 1934 her progress led to her role as Santuzza in the opera *Cavalleria Rusticana*. One of her most critically acclaimed performances was as the original Clara in George Gershwin's *Porgy and Bess* in 1935. Although performing in the Metropolitan Opera was a goal of hers, the racial barrier was yet to be conquered during her career. An accomplished performer, Mitchell, though widely appreciated in Europe, was never totally accepted on the American stage or theater.

Her "other" career as a dramatic actress did not blossom until the late 1920s. She appeared with Rose McClendon in the Pulitzer Prize–winning play *In Abraham's Bosom* (1926), with Helen Hayes in *Coquette* (1927), and in Langston Hughes's *Mulatto* (1937), a play banned by the mayor of Philadelphia due to its racial theme. She returned to the stage in 1939 as Addie in Lillian Hellman's *Little Foxes*. Her activities in the theater led to her assumption of the role of executive secretary to the Negro Actors Guild of America.

As the 1940s approached, Mitchell felt concert performing too demanding. She turned to lecturing and teaching voice. Her students regarded her as an excellent teacher. These years brought personal loss. Will Marion Cook died in 1944, and her daughter Marian, in 1950. Her son, Will, became a professor at Howard University and, later, an ambassador to Niger and Senegal. One of her last performances was at Westport, Connecticut, in the 1947 summer production of *The Skull Boat*, with Fay Bainter. She refused the role of the mother in Lorraine Hansberry's *A Raisin in the Sun* (1959) due to poor eyesight. Her emphasis on excellence would not allow her to perform when not in shape. After a long illness, Abbie Mitchell died in Harlem Hospital on March 16, 1960.

—Nicholas C. Polos

Bibliography

A newpaper file on Abbie Mitchell is in the Schomburg Center for Research in Black Culture, New York Public Library. To place her within the context of the performing arts, refer to Edith Issac, *The Negro in the American Theater* (College Park, MD: McGrath, 1947); Tom Fletcher, *100 Years of the Negro in Show Business* (New York: De Capo, 1954); Maude Cuney-Hare, *Negro Musicians and Their Music* (New York: De Capo, 1936). For biographical information, consult Barbara Sicherman, Carol Hurd Green, et al., eds., *Notable American Women* (Cambridge, MA: Belknap Press, 1980); W.S. Robinson, *Historical Negro Biographies* (New York: International Library of Negro Life and History, 1967–1969): pp. 229–230; and newspaper clippings in the *Chicago Daily News* (October 22, 1930); *New York Sun* (April 22, 1927); *New York Daily News* (February 17, 1939); *Amsterdam News* (March 4, 1939); and *New York Times* (March 20, 1960).

MITCHELL, L. PEARL (1883–1974), civil rights advocate, humanitarian, and sorority leader, was born to Dr. and Mrs. Samuel T. Mitchell in Wilberforce, Ohio. Her family background reflected a tenacity that undoubtedly passed from generation to generation. Her grandfather, David Mitchell, was born a slave, but ran away from South Carolina to Indiana at age 18. He brought his family to Cleveland, where he opened a wheelwright shop on Ontario Street. The grandparents valued education, so their children excelled. The oldest son, John G. Mitchell, became one of the first graduates of Oberlin College and a founder of Wilberforce College. When David Mitchell died in 1856, John G. brought the family to Wilberforce to live. There, her father, Samuel T. Mitchell, received his BA and entered educational administration as principal of a Wilmington, Ohio, school, where her parents met and married. They traveled to Jefferson City, Missouri, where her father served as president of Lincoln College, before finally coming back to Wilberforce.

In Wilberforce, L. Pearl Mitchell grew up in the college community that offered her special opportunities. Her father became the president of African Methodist Episcopal–sponsored Wilberforce College at age 33. Her mother, a schoolteacher who graduated from a Quaker college near Harveysburg, Ohio, continued to teach in an elementary school near Wilberforce. Her father combined vocational education with academic preparation to afford the students the best possible job opportunities after graduation.

Into this environment, he placed his daughter. Although educated entirely in Wilberforce from elementary school to Wilberforce Academy to Wilberforce College, she nevertheless received a diverse education. At age 16, L. Pearl accompanied a group of African students attending Wilberforce on their tour throughout the United States to raise money for their education. Thus, exposed to higher education and to the Christian ideals of the African Methodist Episcopal (AME) church, L. Pearl Mitchell became energized to carry her privileges to the community.

When her father died at age 49, she sought employment to help her mother with financial obligations. Joining her brother Charles in Washington, DC, she quickly found a job as a typist at Howard University Law School. The money assisted her younger sister and two brothers in obtaining their education and allowed L. Pearl Mitchell to continue her own education.

From 1915 to 1923 she combined her teaching with her desire to serve the community. She taught school at Edward Waters College in Jacksonville, Florida, and later at an elementary school in the black town of Lovejoy, Illinois. During World War I she served as a record clerk for the ROTC stationed at Wilberforce and worked with the War Camp Community Service receiving training from Mary Church Terrell at Hampton Institute in Virginia. Her first assignment was at a recreational center near Camp Dodge (Iowa) as the girl's director. Her training and experience in these years led to a career in social work. For four years she served as the director of the Douglass Community Center in Kalamazoo, Michigan, moving in 1923 to Cleveland.

In Cleveland she immediately applied her skills to the Playhouse Settlement at 38th Street and Central, which later became Karamu House at 89th Street and Quincy. Her interest in music and drama led to her membership in the Gilpin Players, a forerunner of the Karamu Theatre Group. After taking a civil service test, she received the appointment as probation officer and investigator at the Cuyahoga County Juvenile Court, a position she held for over 20 years.

She served on many government committees, as people in power recognized her skills and commitment. Mayor Frank J. Lausche appointed her to the Woman and Manpower Commission to help blacks secure jobs in Cleveland's industrial plants. Her influence prevented government contracts until policies of segregation were changed. After formation of the Fair Employment Practices Commission, she served as the executive secretary of the Cleveland group.

When she retired for health reasons in the 1940s, a second career of community service emerged. She earned the title "Miss NAACP" during the next two decades. As the director of membership campaigns for the NAACP, L. Pearl Mitchell organized major drives in cities throughout the North and South. Under her direction, membership expanded greatly. In addition to her membership role, she served as a national vice president, a member of the board of directors, the director of youth work in Ohio, and on the NAACP National Committee of Life Memberships. Locally, her skills benefited the Cleveland branch as president and as executive secretary. During the war years, she worked on the NAACP Housing Committee to ensure the Central Area Housing Project's admission of all groups.

In addition to her work with the NAACP, L. Pearl Mitchell gained recognition as "Miss A.K.A." for her work with the sorority Alpha Kappa Alpha. She used her position within the sorority to encourage young women to continue their education and lend their services to the community. As the third "Supreme Basileus," she has held other elected offices as parlimentarian, Great Lakes regional director, and Basileus of the Alpha Omega chapter in Cleveland, Ohio. During her 50-year membership, she attended all but one national convention. By combining her interests, she was able to get the AKA contribution of $440,000 to the NAACP Life Membership Drive.

Her later years continued to demonstrate her spirit. Her membership on the Ohio Soldiers and Sailors Home Board led to conflict over segregation in the cottages, finally ended by Governor Michael DiSalle. During her career in public service she worked with the Mental Health Association, Consumers League, National Association of Colored Women's Clubs, National Council of Negro Women, African Culture Association, and her beloved Mount Zion Congregational United Church of Christ Church.

She received many honors for her service from the NAACP, Wilberforce College, National Negro Business and Professional Women's Clubs, Women's Medical Association, AKA, and other associations. Langston Hughes honored her in his poem "I Dream." She spent her remaining years living on Terrace Road in East Cleveland. She died on September 6, 1974.

—Dorothy Salem with Mark Heppner

Bibliography

The papers of L. Pearl Mitchell are located at the Western Reserve Historical Society in Cleveland, Ohio. Other sources to consult include the (Cleveland) *Plain Dealer*, the *Cleveland Press* and the *Call and Post* newpapers. Secondary sources that mention her are Kenneth Kusmer, *A Ghetto Takes Shape: Black Cleveland, 1870–1930* (Urbana: University of Illinois, 1978); David D. Van Tassell and John J. Grabowski, eds., *The Encyclopedia of Cleveland History* (Bloomington: Indiana University Press, 1987), p. 685; and Johnson Publishing, ed., *1000 Successful Blacks* (Nashville: Southwestern Press, 1973).

MITCHELL, LUCY MILLER (b. 1899), at age 90, looking back at her life, considered herself a pioneer. Her activities were always at the beginning of things—developing the foundations and helping to change oppressive conditions and establish standards in organizations. Born the youngest of four children, Lucy Miller spent her childhood in Daytona Beach, Florida, where her father was a businessman. She attended Mary McLeod Bethune's Daytona Normal and Industrial Institute for Girls from kindergarten through high school. In the spring of 1918, Miller attended a YWCA conference in Atlanta, conducted by the national YWCA secretary, Juliette Derricotte. Miller was persuaded to attend Talladega College, in Alabama, where she served as president of the college YWCA and graduated magna cum laude in 1922. She returned to teach for one year at Bethune's school before marrying Joseph Mitchell, graduate of Talladega College and Harvard Law School.

The couple moved to Boston, where Lucy Miller Mitchell began her community role while raising her son and daughter. She initially assisted Dr. Abigail Adams Eliot in her nursery training school. After receiving a certificate in early childhood education from the training school in 1934, she earned an MA in 1935 from Boston University. As the Robert Gould Shaw House in Roxbury, Massachusetts, developed a nursery school program, Mitchell served as the assistant director and then director of the program, a model and training site for students from area colleges. By 1951 this work and education pushed Mitchell into the forefront of efforts to establish higher standards for child care through use of comprehensive child care, health, and social services. She helped create a unified child care agency, the Associated Day Care Services of Metropolitan Boston, serving as executive director for 13 years.

Her work and that of Associated Day Care led to the passage of a state licensing law in 1962, which addressed the problems of overcrowding, poor materials, and inadequate education of caregivers. Also during this time, she worked at Wheelock College training Peace Corps workers to work with young children in Tunisia. Although in her sixties and planning to retire, Mitchell helped launch the new Head Start projects in Massachusetts in 1965, which required her to organize workshops and to consult and coordinate training programs throughout New England.

Mitchell served on many boards where her role as pioneer and catalyst was evident. During five years on the board of directors of the United Childcare Services Managing Board (UCSMB), Mitchell helped develop a child guidance clinic for preschool children. She served for seven years on the board of the Boston YWCA, during which time the organization became fully integrated. As part of a citizen group, she helped to establish Freedom House in Boston, a service organization and settlement house in the black community. Mitchell also served on the boards of Family Service Association of Metropolitan Boston, the Massachusetts Association of Mental Health, and the advisory committee of the Office for Children.

Lucy Miller Mitchell often relied upon black female networks such as the Alpha Kappa Alpha sorority and the Boston chapter of Links, Inc., a black women's social service organization. Mitchell's early mentor, Mary McLeod Bethune, inspired the perseverance needed for community organization, and the motto of the National Association of Colored Women, "Lifting as We Climb," reinforced her commitment to help others.

—Sharlene Voogd Cochrane

Bibliography

The interview with Lucy Mitchell is included in the Black Women Oral History Project, Schlesinger Library, Radcliffe College. In addition, see the following:

Cochrane, Sharlene Voogd. "And the Pressure Never Let Up: Black Women, White Women and the Boston YWCA, 1918–1948," *Black Women in United States History*, edited by Darlene Clark Hine, 1990.

Mitchell, Lucy M. "Raising Day Care Standards in Massachusetts," *The Journal of Nursery Education* 16 (November 1962).

MOORE, AUDLEY ("QUEEN MOTHER")

MOORE, AUDLEY ("QUEEN MOTHER") (b. 1898), political activist and organizer, was born in New Iberia, Louisiana. Her father, St. Cyr Moore, was a former deputy sheriff of Iberia Parish; her mother, Ella (Henry), had been raised and educated in a middle-class French Creole household. Her mother died when Audley was five years old; her father, a few years later. His death marked the end of her formal schooling, as she assumed the role of parent for her two younger sisters, Eloise (c. 1900–1963) and Lorita. During World War I, the sisters worked as activists in racial rights causes and for Republican candidates. By 1919 Moore had married into a black middle-class family. She, her sisters, and her husband all joined the Universal Negro Improvement Association (UNIA) after hearing its leader, Marcus Garvey, speak in New Orleans. The experience was transformative; Moore credits Garvey with changing her consciousness by introducing her to a strong identification with Africa and an intense pride in her rich African heritage.

Moore moved to Harlem in the early 1920s; her UNIA activism declined with Garvey's deportation in 1927. She became involved in organizing black domestic workers in New York City, particularly those involved in the Bronx labor market, and in the rental rights movement, organizing tenants in Sugar Hill. Jailed three times for her activities, she used the opportunity to organize fellow prisoners. By 1931 she had joined the International Labor Defense, and by 1933, the Communist Party (CP), backing the idea of a separate black republic in the southern United States. A master street agitator and orator, she worked on such issues as the Italo-Ethiopian war, economic boycotts, unionization, the Scottsboro case (a legal lynching of nine black boys during the Depression), racial gerrymandering, black political representation, the integration of the armed services and of major league baseball, and the depiction of blacks in films.

She was a member of the National Association of Colored Women and a founding member of the National Council of Negro Women. She was a CP candidate for the New York State Assembly in 1938, and in 1940, ran for alderman. She became executive secretary of the New York State branch of the CP in 1941 and was the campaign manager for Benjamin Davis's successful CP bid to succeed her close friend Adam Clayton Powell, Jr., on the New York City Council in the mid-1940s. She credits her time in the CP with developing a new level of analysis of the system under which blacks live in the United States. She left the CP in 1950. She founded the Universal Association of Ethiopian Women with her sister Eloise and worked in the South on welfare rights, prisoners' rights, and racial violence. Her political focus turned increasingly toward the idea of federal reparations to blacks, and in 1962–1963 she formed the Reparations Committee of Descendants of U.S. Slaves. She was lauded by the Black Power movement of the 1960s, including Malcolm X. In the early 1970s she made her first trip to Africa to attend Kwame Nkrumah's funeral in Guinea. Idi Amin invited her to Uganda to attend the Organization of African Unity; she also attended the 1972 meeting of the All African Women's Conference in Dar es Salaam, where she received the title "Queen Mother." Moore remains a noted figure in the Pan-African community.

—Barbara Bair

Bibliography

Oral histories with Queen Mother Moore are available at the Tamiment Library, New York University (part of the Oral History of the American Left Project) and at the Arthur and Elizabeth Schlesinger Library on the History of Women in America, Radcliffe College, Cambridge, Massachusetts (interview by Cheryl Townsend Gilkes, August 1978, as part of the Black Women Oral History Project). The transcript of the

Gilkes interview is also available at the Schomburg Center for Research in Black Culture, New York Public Library. Articles about and interviews with Queen Mother Moore have appeared in *The Black Scholar* (March–April 1973); *The New Afrikan* (Detroit) (December 18, 1983); and *Burning Spear* (San Francisco) (January–March 1987). Moore was among those photographed and profiled for Brian Lanker's exhibition and book *I Dream a World: Portraits of Black Women Who Changed America* (New York: Stewart, Tabori, and Chang, 1989), pp. 102–103. She is also the subject of a biographical profile by Muhammad Ahmad in *Encyclopedia of the American Left*, edited by Mari Jo Buhle, Paul Buhle, and Dan Georgakas (New York: Garland, 1990), pp. 486–487; and is discussed in Mark Naison, *Communists in Harlem During the Depression* (New York: Grove Press, 1983); in a profile by Raymond R. Somerville in *Notable Black American Women*, edited by Jessie Carney Smith (Detroit: Gale, 1992), pp. 764–767. She is featured in an exhibition of photographs by Judith Sedwick entitled *Women of Courage*, edited by Ruth Edmonds Hill (Radcliffe College, 1984), p. 59.

MORRISON, TONI [WOFFORD] (b. 1931), novelist, poet, editor, and playwright, was born Chloe Anthony Wofford on February 18 in Lorain, Ohio. She is the second of four children born to enterprising parents who migrated from Greenville, Alabama. Morrison's rich familial and cultural past strongly inform her work. Her mother, Ramah (Willis) Wofford, who sang a great deal of the time, was given a name selected randomly from the Bible as was Pilate in *Song of Solomon*. Her father, George Wofford, a shipyard welder, held three jobs for more than 17 years in order to support and educate his family. He was also a master storyteller who told black folktales and "scary" ghost stories, which provided Morrison with the strong sense of the supernatural, magic, and mystery that pervade her work. Morrison's maternal grandmother, Ardelia Willis, first introduced her to the supernatural in her childhood. Her grandfather, Solomon Willis, a carpenter and violinist, was, like the male ancestor, Jake Solomon, in *Song of Solomon*, cruelly divested of his land. His violin became his only possession, one that remained with the family wherever they moved.

Morrison's family moved to Lorain, Ohio, where she graduated with honors from the Lorain public schools in 1949. In 1953 she earned a bachelor's degree in English from Howard University. In 1955 she completed the master's in English from Cornell University with a thesis on Virginia Woolf and Faulkner. In 1957 Morrison married Jamaican architect Harold Morrison. They divorced eight years later in 1965. She is the mother of two sons, Harold Ford and Slade Kevin.

Morrison began her professional career as an instructor at Texas Southern University in Houston, Texas, from 1955 to 1957. From 1957 to 1964 she served as instructor of English at Howard University in Washington, DC. She credits her years of teaching at African-American universities with sharpening her conscious understanding of the black experience.

She then proceeded to combine professions serving as the associate editor at the L.W. Singer Publishing Company (1964–1967); as the senior editor with

Random House Publishing (1967–1984); as a visiting lecturer at Barnard and Yale universities (1975–1977); and as an associate professor at State University of New York (SUNY) at Purchase in 1979, the same year she also taught courses at Bard College in upstate New York. She served as the Albert Schweitzer Professor of Humanities, SUNY, Albany, from 1984 to 1989, followed by her appointment in 1989 as the Robert F. Goheen Professor (endowed chair) at Princeton University.

As editor at Random House, Morrison influenced the work of many contemporary writers, among them a number of African-American authors. According to Andrew Young, Morrison was one of the most important supporters of black writers. She encouraged the writings of fiction, nonfiction, and history by such authors as Toni Cade Bambara, Amiri Baraka, Angela Davis, Ivan Van Sertima, and Andrew Young.

In addition to her support for writers, Morrison is a leading contemporary American novelist. Her vision is stunning and original. Her characters are often the dispossessed as is Pecola in her first novel, *The Bluest Eye* (1970). Her great gifts as a storyteller allow her to treat both her heros/heroines and villains with sympathy. Her voice and language styles range from the biblical and incantatory to down home and street wise. Toni Morrison's vision has continued to expand with each novel. Her most recent novel, *Beloved* (1987) enlivens the past by utilizing as its central incident the story of Margaret Garner, an escaped African-American woman captive who was placed on trial for killing one of her four children and planning to kill the others to prevent their re-enslavement. *Beloved* and *Song of Solomon* (1977) explore myth and the supernatural at their best. Utilizing symbolism from African philosophy and Greek mythology, Morrison explores both women and men characters with facility. Her treatment of Milkman, a character in *Song of Solomon*, is undoubtedly one of the most effective renderings of a male character by a woman writer in American literature. Morrison's major themes focus on the importance of self awareness, community dynamics, women's friendships, male/female relations, the tragedy of social constraints such as social class and racism, the dynamics and complications of communal life, and the consequences of seeking or denying one's past or cultural roots.

Her professional excellence has resulted in many honors. She was nominated for the National Book Award for *Sula* (1974); won both the American Academy and Institute of Arts and Letters Award and the National Book Critics' Circle Award for Fiction for *Song of Solomon* (1977); was a finalist for the Ritz Hemingway Prize in Paris for *Beloved* (1987); became a finalist for the National Book Critics' Circle Award for *Beloved* (1987); received a Pulitzer Prize for Fiction for *Beloved* (1988); and was one of seven artists to receive the New York City Mayor's Award of Honor for Art and Culture (May 1988). She was elected to the American Institute of Arts and Letters in 1981. Her business address is through Random House in New York City.

—Margaret Wade-Lewis

Bibliography

As of 1991, Morrison has written the following novels and become the first African-American woman to have six novels published: *The Bluest Eye* (New York: Holt, Rinehart and Winston, 1970); *Sula* (New York: Alfred Knopf, 1973); *Song of Solomon* (New York: Alfred Knopf, 1977); *Tar Baby* (New York: Alfred Knopf, 1981); *Beloved* (New York: Alfred Knopf, 1987); and *Jazz* (New York: Alfred Knopf, 1992). She is also the author of *Dreaming Emmett*, a play about the life of Emmett Till, a 14-year-old youth murdered in Mississippi at the beginning of the civil rights movement in 1954. It was directed by Gilbert Moses and produced by the New York State Writers Institute at the Market Theatre in Albany, New York, beginning January 4, 1986. Among her other writing projects are the lyrics and story for the musical *New Orleans* (Storyville), a New York Public Theatre Workshop Production, and the screenplay for *Tar Baby*.

Among Morrison's best known essays are the following: "What Black Women Think of Women's Lib," *New York Times Magazine* (August 22, 1971); "Behind the Making of *The Black Book*," *Black World* 23 (February 1974): 86–90; "Rediscovering Black History," *New York Times Magazine* (August 11, 1974) 14ff.; "A Slow Walk of a Tree (as Grandmother Would Say), Hopeless (as Grandfather Would Say)," *New York Times Magazine* (July 4, 1976) 104ff.; "The Site of Memory," in *Inventing the Truth: The Art and Craft of Memoir*, edited by William Zinsser (Boston: Houghton Mifflin, 1987), pp. 103–124.

Secondary Sources

The best study of Morrison's life and work is Wilfred D. Samuels and Clenora Hudson-Weems, *Toni Morrison* (Boston: Twayne, 1990), which also contains one of the best annotated bibliographies of work by and about Morrison. A complete bibliography is David L. Middleton, *Toni Morrison: An Annotated Bibliography* (New York: Garland, 1987). Other important full-length sources are Robert Stepto, *From Behind the Veil: A Study of Afro-American Narrative* (Urbana: University of Illinois Press, 1979); Bessie W. Jones and Audrey L. Vinson, *The World of Toni Morrison: Explorations in Literary Criticism* (Dubuque, IA: Kendall Hunt Publishing, 1985); Karla Halloway and Stephanie Demetrakopoulous, *New Dimensions of Spirituality: A Biracial, Bicultural Reading of the Novels of Toni Morrison* (Westport, CT: Greenwood Press, 1987); and Nellie Y. McKay, *Critical Essays on Toni Morrison* (Boston: G.K. Hall and Company, 1988).

Among the important essays and interviews are Joan Bischoff, "The Novels of Toni Morrison: Studies in Thwarted Sensitivity," *Studies in Black Literature* 6 (Fall 1975): 21–23; Bettye J. Parker, "Complexity: Toni Morrison's Women—An Interview Essay," in *Sturdy Black Bridges: Visions of Back Women in Literature*, edited by Roseann Bell, Bettye J. Parker, and Beverly Guy-Sheftall (Garden City, NY: Doubleday, 1979), pp. 250–257; Michael Harper and Robert Stepto, eds., "Interview," *Chant of Saints* (Urbana: University of Illinois Press, 1979), pp. 213–229; Claudia Tate, ed., "Toni Morrison," *Black Women Writers at Work* (*Conversations with*) (New York: Continuum, 1983), pp. 117–181; Mari Evans, ed., "Toni Morrison" (two essays) in *Black Women Writers (1950–1980): A Critical Evaluation* (Garden City, NY: Doubleday, 1984), pp. 339–370. See also, Barbara Christian, "Community and Nature: The Novels of Toni Morrison," pp. 47–64; "Testing the Strength of the Black Cultural Bond: Review of Toni Morrison's *Tar Baby*," pp. 65–70; and "The Concept of Class in the Novels of Toni Morrison, all in *Black Feminist Criticism: Perspectives on Black Women Writers* (New York: Pergamon, 1985); Valerie Smith, "Toni Morrison's Narratives of Community," *Self Discovery and Authority in Afro-American Narrative* (Cambridge: Harvard University Press, 1987), pp. 122–153.

General commentaries of Morrison's work with useful biographical information are Laura B. Randolph, "The Magic of Toni Morrison," *Ebony* (July 1988): 100ff.; Thadeus Davis, ed., *Dictionary of Literary Biography of African American Writers after 1955* (Detroit: Gale, 1984); and Jean Strouse, "Toni Morrison's Black Magic," *Newsweek* (March 30, 1989): 52–57.

Morrison is referenced in Ann Evory, ed., *Contemporary Authors: A Bio-Bibliographical Guide to Current Authors and Their Works* (Detroit: Gale, 1972, 1978), p. 473; Harry A. Ploski and James Williams, eds., *The Negro Almanac: A Reference Work on the African American* (Detroit: Gale, 1989), pp. 1007–1008; and Mariana Davis, *Contributions of Black Women to America* (Columbia, SC: Kenday, 1982).

MORTON-JONES, VERINA [HARRIS] (1865–c. 1950), physician, clubwoman, civil rights activist, and suffragist, was born in Cleveland, Ohio, on January 28. She attended State Normal School in Columbia, South Carolina. Verina Harris married twice; the first time in 1890 to W.A. Morton, MD, who died in 1895, and the second time in 1901 to Emory Jones, who died in 1927. She had one child from her first marriage, Franklin W., who was born in 1892. Morton-Jones attended the Woman's Medical College of Pennsylvania in Philadelphia from 1884 to 1888, and received her MD in 1888.

Among the first African-American women in the United States to receive her degree in medicine, Morton-Jones practiced in Brooklyn and on Long Island, New York, during the Progressive era. She was the first African-American woman to practice medicine in Nassau County, Long Island, and took part in the Kings County Medical Society. Beginning in 1888 she also headed the Lincoln Settlement House in Brooklyn, an extension of white social reformer and nurse Lillian Wald's Henry Street Settlement House located on the Lower East Side of New York City. Through her directorship of Lincoln House, Morton-Jones implemented change in the lives of many Brooklyn African Americans. For example, Lincoln House boasted a clinic, lecture series on health and hygiene, and a day nursery to address the needs of working mothers.

Morton-Jones participated in a variety of organizations addressing both the political and the socioeconomic issues touching the race. She took part in the Equal Suffrage League of New York and in the female auxiliary of the Niagara movement, an organization formed to demand full justice for blacks, in 1905 and 1906. She also played an integral role in the Committee for Improving Industrial

Conditions of Negroes in New York City (founded in 1906), which in 1911 merged with two other social reform groups to become the National Urban League. Morton-Jones, active in the NAACP, served on its board in 1913 and worked on the executive committee until 1925. Mary White Ovington, a white social reformer and one of the founders of the NAACP, in her 1947 autobiography *The Walls Came Tumbling Down*, reminisced about a typical 1917 board meeting in which Morton-Jones was the only "colored woman." Morton-Jones also did volunteer work for the "Phillis Wheatley" YWCAs, most often the Brooklyn branch, and actively participated in conferences designed to improve the organization and operation of all YWCAs in their emphasis on health and hygiene for young women.

Morton-Jones was an Episcopalian and a Republican. She practiced medicine far into her old age, and died after 1944 (date unknown).

—Thea S. Arnold

Selected Bibliography

Information can be found on Verina Morton-Jones in the organizational papers of the National Board of the YWCA, New York City; the NAACP Papers and the National Urban League Papers, both in the Manuscript Division, Library of Congress, Washington, DC. Other sources in print include the following:

Aptheker, Herbert, ed. *The Correspondence of W.E.B. Du Bois*. (Amherst: University of Massachusetts Press, 1973.

Brooklyn Times (June 27, 1891).

Ovington, Mary White. *The Walls Came Tumbling Down*. New York: Harcourt, Brace and World, 1947.

Salem, Dorothy. *To Better Our World: Black Women in Organized Reform, 1890–1920*. Brooklyn: Carlson, 1990.

Scruggs, Lawson A. *Women of Distinction*. Raleigh, NC: L.A. Scruggs, 1892.

Who's Who in Colored America, 1941–44. New York: Who's Who in Colored America Corp., 1944.

MOSSELL, GERTRUDE BUSTILL (1855–1948) was a journalist, teacher, and poet, born July 3 to Charles H. and Emily R. Bustill, who were Quakers and later joined the Old School Presbyterian Church in Philadelphia. She was educated in the public schools of Philadelphia before attending the Institute of Colored Youth and the Robert Vaux Consolidated Schools in that city. Influenced by black evangelical Christianity and its demand for a disciplined person and a moral lifestyle, Mossell balanced her strong political views with an evangelical appeal to the spirit and Christian values.

Mossell taught in the public school systems of Philadelphia; Camden, New Jersey; and Frankfort, Kentucky. She wrote for the Philadelphia *Press*, the *Times*, and the *Inquirer*, the *Indianapolis Freeman*, the *Richmond Rankin Institute*, and *Our Women and Children*. On July 12, 1880, she married Nathan Francis Mossell, a physician and founder of the Frederick Douglass Memorial Hospital in Philadelphia and, after the birth of two daughters, Florence and Mary C., resumed her public career with syndicated columns in the *Philadelphia Echo*, the *Philadelphia Times*, the *Independent*, and the *Press Republican*. Mossell edited the "Women's Department" column of the *New York Age*, the *Indianapolis World*, and the *New York Freeman*. She also contributed to the *A.M.E. Church Review*.

Mossell is best remembered for her book *The Work of the Afro-American Woman* (1894). Mossell advocated that the home should be founded on right principles, morality, Christian living, heredity, and an environment that promised a good future. She deftly handled the social location of women in African-American culture while advocating for a wider range of possibilities for male and female interaction and roles. Mossell offered her wisdom to newly married women and exhorted her white sisters to join African-American women in their quest for the social and moral uplift of African Americans. She also published a children's book, *Little Dansie's One Day at Sabbath School* (1902).

After 1895 Mossell was a collector for the charity fund of the Frederick Douglass Hospital and served as president of its social service auxiliary. Mossell founded the Bustill Family Association and organized the Philadelphia branch of the Afro-American Council. She also served on the board of managers for the YWCA.

Mossell died on January 21, 1948, at the Frederick Douglass Hospital. She was buried in Eden Cemetery in Philadelphia. One of her nephews was Paul Robeson, and she was a cousin of Sarah Douglass.

—Emilie M. Townes

Bibliography

Giddings, Paula, *When and Where I Enter: The Impact of Black Women on Race and Sex in America*. New York: William Morrow, 1984.

Lerner, Gerda. *Black Women in White America: A Documentary History*. New York: Vintage, 1973.

Logan, Rayford W., and Winston, Michael R., ed., *The Dictionary of American Negro Biography*. New York: Norton, 1982.

Mather, Frank. *Who's Who of the Colored Race*. Chicago: n.p., 1915; Reprint. Detroit: Gale Research, 1976.

MOTLEY, CONSTANCE BAKER (b. 1921), civil rights lawyer, began
life as one of eight children. Born September 14 in New Haven, Connecticut, to Willoughby, a chef for a Yale fraternity, and Rachel Baker, Constance Baker demonstrated an intellectual curiosity and ability early in life. In her biracial Sunday school classes at the Episcopal church, she developed an early interest in black history from the integrated curriculum. Her West Indian father's emphasis on preparation and experience influenced Constance Baker's conduct. After attending high school, her parents could not afford to send her to college. She

received the opportunity after Clarence Blakeslee, a wealthy contractor, heard her speak at a public meeting. Her delivery impressed Blakeslee so much that he offered to pay for her college education. In 1941 she entered Fisk University to major in economics. Soon she transferred to New York University to complete her degree in economics from the Washington Square College at NYU in 1943. Her entrance in the Columbia University Law School brought her to Thurgood Marshall, chief counsel for the NAACP Legal Defense Fund. She worked for the Legal Defense Fund while earning her law degree from Columbia University (June 1946). During 1946 she married real estate broker Joel Wilson Motley, Jr., and became a full-time legal staff person for the Legal Defense Fund. Their marriage produced a son, Joel Wilson Motley III, to complete a supportive family structure.

Her legal career with the NAACP Legal Defense Fund brought her into the mainstream of the legal challenge to segregated education. She prepared the essential briefs for the *Sipuel* vs. *Oklahoma* and *Sweatt* vs. *Painter* Supreme Court decisions argued by Thurgood Marshall on segregation in higher education. She also played a major role in the legal preparation for the 1954 *Brown* vs. *Topeka Board of Education* case. She served as the chief legal counsel for James Meredith in his fight to enter the University of Mississippi and for other students fighting for entrance to segregated universities. For children denied admission, she served as counsel for children in southern cities—Atlanta, Pensacola, Jacksonville, Daytona Beach, Sarasota—and in northern cities—Hillsboro, Ohio; New Rochelle and Hempstead, New York; and Englewood, New Jersey.

She also became a leading defense lawyer for the students using direct action tactics to challenge discrimination. She won nine of ten civil rights cases argued before the Supreme Court from October 1961 to the end of 1964 on cases involving arrests and rights to counsel during Freedom Rides sit-in demonstrations.

With the passage of the 1964 Civil Rights Act, Motley gained national protections for student demonstrators and an entrance into a new career—politics. When a vacancy occurred in the New York State Senate, she decided to run in the special election. She won the right to represent her district in Manhattan. She served as the first woman senator in the state's history until another special election brought her to the position of borough president of Manhattan in February 1965. In citywide direct elections she won the endorsement of Democratic, Republican, and Liberal parties for a full term. The first woman and first black to serve in that elective office, Constance Baker Motley demonstrated the capabilities of black women. In September 1966 she received an appointment by President Lyndon B. Johnson to the United States District Court. The lifetime appointment as a judge is the culmination of a lifetime commitment to the law.

During her career in law and public service, she has received over 70 awards and 8 honorary degrees from universities. She continues to live and work in New York.

—Kelle S. Taha

Bibliography

Information on Constance Baker Motley's legal activities for the NAACP can be found in the NAACP Files, Manuscript Collection, Library of Congress. Her biographical information can be found in John D'Emilio, *The Civil Rights Struggle: Leaders in Profile* (New York: Facts on File, 1979); both volumes of The *Ebony* Success Library, *1000 Successful Blacks* and *Famous Blacks Give Secrets of Success* (Nashville: Southwestern, 1973); and Marianna W. Davis, ed., *Contributions of Black Women to America* II (Columbia, SC: Kenday, 1982). Motley has many articles that appear in accessible periodicals, including "Constitution: Key to Freedom," *Ebony* 18 (September 1963): 221–222+; "James Meredith in Perspective," *The Crisis* 70 (January 1963): 5–11; and "Madame Borough President: Constance Baker Motley," *The Crisis* 72 (April 1965): 224–225. Articles about her appear in *Sepia* 14 (May 1965): 71; 13 (May 1964): 35–39; 15 (November 1966): 70; in *Jet* 20 (July 20, 1961): 16–20; and A. Morrison, "Top Woman Civil Rights Lawyer," *Ebony* 18 (January 1963): 50–52.

MURRAY, PAULI (1910–1985), lawyer, civil rights activist, and priest, was born in Baltimore, Maryland, on November 20. Despite the fact that her generation was born too soon to take full advantage of the social advances achieved by the civil rights movement of the 1960s, Murray achieved success as a lawyer, teacher, and priest. She successfully combined the strengths of her mixed African, Native American, and southern planter ancestors.

Murray was the daughter of William H. Murray and Agnes (Fitzgerald) Murray. She described her Fitzgerald ancestors in *Proud Shoes: The Story of an American Family*. Her publication of this work in 1956 was a significant advance in black family history and genealogy, and it demonstrated that she came from a family of achievers. She graduated from Hunter College in January 1933, and she obtained her law degree from Howard University in 1944. She obtained additional graduate degrees in law from the University of California at Berkeley in 1945 and Yale University in 1965. She was admitted to practice in New York and California and before the U.S. Supreme Court.

Murray's legal career included civil rights activism, starting in her law school days. In addition to being a practicing attorney, she taught law at Brandeis University and in Ghana. A devoted Democrat, Murray admired Eleanor Roosevelt. She consistently urged Roosevelt to work for black civil rights. As an early black activist, she was imprisoned for her role resisting segregation on an interstate bus in 1940. In 1946 she served as the assistant attorney general in California, receiving national recognition as one of the Ten Outstanding Women of the Year. As the contemporary civil rights movement gained momentum during the 1950s, Murray was a vocal supporter of the various organizations and leaders.

Murray embraced the common threads of egalitarianism. Thus, as the women's movement emerged, she became a pioneer advocate of women's rights and founder of the National Organization for Women (NOW). She served on several national and international committees that focused on the themes of human rights and legal protections.

Murray's final career was as an Episcopal priest. After attending the General Theological Seminary, Murray was ordained as a priest on January 8, 1977, having been interested in feminist spirituality for many years. She celebrated all her identities throughout her life in the many forms of activism.

Having taught at many schools, including the Ghana School of Law, Murray understood the importance of education and knowledge of civil rights. She authored two books on law: *States' Laws on Race and Color* (1951) and *The Constitution and Government of Ghana* (1961). She served as the Stulberg Professor of Law and Politics at Brandeis University until her retirement. She died in Baltimore on July 1, 1985.

—Susan Stussy

Bibliography

Pauli Murray recorded her perspectives of her life in her autobiography *Pauli Murray: The Autobiography of a Black Activist, Feminist, Lawyer, Priest and Poet.* Knoxville: University of Tennessee Press, 1989. Her other books include the following:

Dark Testament and Other Poems. Norwalk, CT: Silvermine, 1970. This short collection of poems demonstrates Murray's multifaceted talent.

Proud Shoes: The Story of An American Family. New York: Harper & Row, 1956. Murray describes the trials and triumphs of her racially mixed Fitzgerald ancestors. She vividly portrays the psychological pain caused by racial discrimination and color tone differences among African Americans, and she also shows that determined and gifted achievers always manage significant personal and professional achievements against great odds.

Song in a Weary Throat: An American Pilgrimage. New York: Harper & Row, 1987. In this book, Murray describes her personal history and multiple careers. Throughout her life, she fought for racial justice for African Americans and equal rights for women in a reasoned and rational manner. Although her faith wavered at times, she was a dedicated Christian, and she was well qualified to preach a gospel of love and reconciliation.

Paul Murray's collection of papers is the largest belonging to an African-American woman in the Arthur and Elizabeth Schlesinger Library on the history of women in America, Radcliffe College.

Secondary Sources

Guzman, Jessie P. "The Social Contributions of the Negro Woman since 1940," *Negro History Bulletin* 10 (January 1948): 10.

Sanders, Charles L., ed. *1,000 Successful Blacks.* Nashville: Southwestern, 1973.

Shockley, Ann A. *Living Black American Authors.* New York: Bowker, 1973.

N

NAPIER, LETTIE [LANGSTON] (1861–1938), community activist, clubwoman, and home founder, was one of Nashville, Tennessee's most prominent citizens in the late nineteenth and early twentieth centuries. Lettie Langston Napier, the only daughter of attorney John Mercer Langston, was born on June 17 in Oberlin, Ohio. When she was nine years old, the family moved to Washington, DC, where she became a student at Howard University for one year. She returned to Oberlin to complete her education (1876–1878). In 1878 she married prominent Tennessee lawyer, banker, and political leader James Carroll Napier. The couple lived with her parents in Washington, DC, while James Napier completed law school at Howard University. They returned to Nashville after the election of President Grover Cleveland in 1885.

Napier spent her life developing organized approaches to community needs. Most of her work was devoted to problems affecting women and children. She founded the Day Homes Club, an organization concerned about the welfare of the children of working parents, and became the president of Nashville's Porter Homestead Day Home in 1907. She organized a convention in Nashville in February 1907, at which she stressed the importance of the day home concept and the need for providing quality care for the nation's abused and neglected children and children with working mothers. The couple adopted a daughter, Caroline Langston Napier.

She was instrumental in getting the National Association of Colored Women (NACW) to meet in Nashville in 1897, but did not become an active member until the Buffalo, New York, biennial in 1901. Thereafter, Napier became an active leader of the NACW, later becoming the president of the Douglass Memorial Fund. Napier was one of the many Nashville women who worked with the Phillis Wheatley Club, the New Idea Club, and the Nashville City Federation supporting the day home concept, poor relief, and other benevolent programs. Napier's pioneering work paved the way for significant reforms in the regulation of day homes. During World War I, Napier was selected by the white women of Nashville to cooperate as chair of a committee of African-American women in work with the Red Cross. She died in Nashville on September 27, 1938, and was buried in Greenwood Cemetery in Nashville.

—Regennia N. Williams

Bibliography

A short biographical sketch about Lettie Napier's club work appears in Elizabeth Davis, *Lifting as They Climb* (Washington, DC: NACW, 1933), pp. 222–224. Lester C. Lamon provides a detailed account of early twentieth-century life in Nashville's African-American community in *Black Tennesseans, 1900–1930* (Knoxville: University of Tennessee Press, 1977). For a short biographical sketch see the *Atlanta Daily World* (October 3, 1938) or H.P. Kletzing and William Crogman, *Progress of a Race: The Remarkable Advancement of the Afro-American Negro* (Chicago: J.L. Nichols, 1898). The papers of James Carroll Napier are housed at the Tennessee Historical Society, Nashville.

NASH, DIANE (b. 1938), civil rights activist and leader of the student movement for racial justice, was born on May 15. She grew up on Chicago's South Side. She left Chicago to attend first Howard University in Washington, DC, and then Fisk University in Nashville, Tennessee. As a northerner, Diane Judith Nash was initially shocked at the segregation of restaurants, water fountains, and public facilities in the South. The consistent exposure to racial injustice motivated Nash, a tiny, slim, Fisk beauty queen, to participate actively in efforts to improve the situation. In Nashville, her racial consciousness and commitment to black equality blossomed. Outraged at segregation and the apparent apathy of black students, Nash joined the nonviolent workshops offered by James Lawson, a divinity student at nearby Vanderbilt University.

In 1960 the beginning of student sit-ins moved Nash to prominent leadership as the chairperson of the Nashville student sit-in movement. The excitement generated by the student activism in the civil rights movement led to a meeting at Raleigh, North Carolina, over the Easter vacation break. Under the guidance of Ella Baker of the Southern Christian Leadership Conference (SCLC), the students formed the Student Nonviolent Coordinating Committee (SNCC). Nash left Fisk to devote full-time effort to the struggle for civil rights. In 1961 she married the Reverend James Bevel, a fellow student activist and leader in SCLC. Pregnant with her first child, Nash was jailed as part of the "Rock Hill Four" as SNCC tested the "jail no bail" strategy in Rock Hill, South Carolina. Nash became the first paid field staff member of SNCC and was the leading candidate for the election for chair of SNCC, but declined her name.

In addition to Nash's serving as the director of the youth organization of the Nashville Christian Leadership Council (NCLC), she assembled a second group of Freedom Riders to continue the journey to New Orleans after the initial group was dispersed through consistent racial harassment. Her determination in the coordination of the Freedom Rides resulted in the desegregation of southern interstate travel.

For the next four years (1961–1965), Nash served the SCLC in a variety of capacities including field staff person, organizer, and workshop instructor. Her unyielding commitment to racial equality culminated in her acceptance of SCLC's highest award for co-conceptualizing and directing the Selma Right-to-Vote movement, the catalyst for the Voting Rights Act of 1965.

Despite her many and distinguished contributions to the civil rights movement, Diane Nash has enjoyed limited recognition. While the civil rights movement is experiencing a renewed and reinvigorated history, information on

Nash remains scattered. Currently, Nash lives in Chicago, Illinois; she lectures at colleges and universities and has served in a number of administrative positions in local social service agencies. Diane Nash is the mother of two.

—Gina E. Beavers

Bibliography

Primary sources on Diane Nash's significance can be found in the Fisk University Archives; the Carl and Anne Braden Papers and the Students for a Democratic Society Papers (1960–1969), both in the State Historical Society of Wisconsin (Madison); and facsimile reproductions of the SNCC papers, *The Student Voice*, and *The Movement*, edited by Clayborne Carson (Westport, CT: Meckler, 1990). An interview of Nash is recorded on the third part of the PBS civil rights series "Eyes on the Prize," entitled "Ain't Scared of Your Jails." Nash talks about the reasons for her participation in the civil rights movement and chronicles a few of the extraordinary accomplishments of which she was a part. Nash's interview, however, is not published in the companion volume, *Eyes on the Prize*, edited by Juan Williams (New York: Viking Penguin, 1987). Nash's own article, "The Men Behind Martin Luther King," *Ebony* (1965), contradicts her role in the movement. She advocated a movement led by men in the SCLC, yet was a leader in her own right.

The published sources that include information about Nash are Paula Giddings, *When and Where I Enter* (New York: Morrow, 1984); Sara Evans, *Personal Politics* (New York: Random House, 1979); Anne Standley, "The Role of Black Women in the Civil Rights Movement," in *Women in the Civil Rights Movement: Trailblazers and Torchbearers, 1941–1965*, edited by Vicki Crawford, Jacqueline Rouse, and Barbara Woods (Brooklyn: Carlson, 1990), pp. 183–202; and Dianetta Gail Bryan, "Her-Story Unsilenced: Black Female Activists in the civil rights movement," *Sage* 5:2 (Fall 1988): 60–63. Patricia Shaw, "Biography of Diane Nash," an unpublished paper (1986) based on personal interviews conducted in Nashville with Diane Nash, provides a good chronology of Nash's involvement and major events in the civil rights movement. The paper can be found in the Fisk University Archives.

NORTON, ELEANOR HOLMES (b. 1938), congresswoman, attorney, human rights advocate, and educator, was born in Washington, DC, on April 8 to college-educated parents. She attended the prestigious all-black Dunbar High School. After graduation she attended Antioch College in Yellow Springs, Ohio, where she received her bachelor of arts degree. After completing her undergraduate studies, she enrolled in Yale University for postgraduate study, earning master of arts and juris doctor degrees in 1963 and 1964, respectively.

Norton is renowned for her work as an attorney and human rights advocate. In 1964 she worked as constitutional lawyer for the American Civil Liberties Union, a position that compelled her occasionally to take controversial stances. She demonstrated her commitment to the Constitution's First Amendment freedom of speech clause when she was called upon to defend the right of the segregationist former governor of Alabama George Wallace to articulate his racist views in a public forum in New York City. Despite her critics, Norton successfully defended him. In 1970 New York City mayor John Lindsay appointed Norton chair of the Human Rights Commission. As chair she traveled and lectured extensively and during an Atlanta address won the praise of Georgia governor Jimmy Carter.

Eleanor Holmes Norton has been involved in a number of projects designed to eradicate racism and sexism. She participated in the civil rights sit-in demonstrations during the 1960s and was the attorney that advised the Mississippi Freedom Democratic Party, the grassroots organization that challenged the legitimacy of the all-white delegation to be seated at the Democratic National Convention of 1964. In 1973 Eleanor Holmes Norton and others founded the National Black Feminist Organization, a group established to address racism, sexism, and economic exploitation. She also was an early supporter of the Free South Africa movement founded by Randall Robinson of Trans-Africa, United States Civil Rights Commissioner Mary Frances Berry, Congressman Walter Fauntroy, and political scientist Roger Wilkins.

President Jimmy Carter appointed Eleanor Norton chair of the Equal Employment Opportunity Commission (EEOC) in 1977. As chair she was responsible for enforcement of Title VII of the Civil Rights Act of 1964 and the Equal Employment Act of 1972. Norton remained at the EEOC until 1983, when she became a professor of law at the Georgetown University Law Center. Despite controversy over her failure to file District of Columbia tax returns for several years, residents of Washington, DC, elected Norton their nonvoting delegate to Congress in 1990, replacing Walter Fauntroy, who withdrew his candidacy to run for mayor of the city. Following the election, Norton announced that she and her attorney husband, Edward Norton, were separating. She is the mother of two children, John and Katherine.

—Lillian S. Williams

Bibliography

Primary Sources

Vertical File, Moorland-Spingarn Research Center, Howard University, Washington, DC.

Vertical File, Schomburg Center for Research in Black Culture, New York Public Library.

"The MacNeil-Lehrer Report Bakke Decision." New York: WNET/WETA, 1978.

"A Conversation with Eleanor Holmes Norton" (June 29, 1979), American Enterprise Institute for Public Policy Research, Washington, DC.

National Alliance of Black Feminists, Manuscript Collection, University of Illinois Library, Chicago.

Equal Employment Opportunity Commission Papers. Record Group 403. National Archives, Washington, DC.

Secondary Sources

Afro-American Encyclopedia 7. North Miami, FL: Educational Book Publishers, 1974, p. 3126.

Davis, Marianna W. *Contributions of Black Women to America* 1. Columbia, SC: Kenday, 1982, pp. 473–474.

"Eleanor Holmes Norton," *Current Biography* 37 (November 1976): 15–17.

"Eleanor Holmes Norton: A Tough New Sister at E.E.O.C," *Black Collegian* 8 (March–April 1978): 124–126.

"Eleanor Holmes Norton: From Human Rights to Equal Opportunity," *Encore* (June 20, 1977).

Gordon, Ed. "A Dialogue with Eleanor Holmes Norton," *Emerge* 1 (August 1990): 11–12.

Lamson, Peggy. "Eleanor Holmes Norton Reforms the Equal Employment Opportunity Commission," in James David Barber and Barbara Kellerman, eds., *Women Leaders in American Politics*. Englewood Cliffs, NJ: Prentice-Hall, 1986.

Lewis, Ida. "Conversation: Ida Lewis and Eleanor Holmes Norton," *Essence* 1 (July 1970): 46–51+.

Low, L. Augustus, and Virgil A. Clift, eds. *Encyclopedia of Black America*. New York: McGraw-Hill, 1981.

Partnow, Elaine, ed. *The Quotable Woman*. Los Angeles: Corwin Books, 1977.

"Reorganized Courts Reduce Strategies for Gaining Equity Professor Says," *Black Issues in Higher Education* 16 (July 6, 1989).

"Women in Government: A Slim Past But a Strong Future," *Ebony* 32 (August 1977): 89–92.

Wortman, Jacob. "EEOC: Has It Really Worked," *Black Enterprise* 8 (September 1977): 21–24.

Works authored or co-authored by Eleanor Holmes Norton

"For Sadie and Maude," in Robin Morgan, ed., *Sisterhood Is Powerful: An Anthology of Writings from the Women's Liberation Movement*. New York: Random House, 1970.

"Impact of the Equal Rights Amendment: A Symposium," *Human Rights* 3 (Summer) 1973): 125.

"Population Growth and the Future of Black Folk," *The Crisis* 80 (May 1973): 151–153.

After Integration: Problems of Race Relations in the High School Today: A Study of Madison High School with Recommendations for New York City Schools (as chair of the New York City Commission on Human Rights) New York: The Commission, 1974.

"Some People Derive Their Energy from Struggle" (conversation with A. Westin), *Civil Liberties Review* 2 (Winter 1975): 90.

"You and Me Brother: The Urban Ghettos Are Crueler Than the Countryside from which We Came," *Essence* 7 (July 1976): 53–55.

"Overhauling the EEOC." *Labor Law Journal* 28 (November, 1977): 683.

Guidelines for the Development of a Federal Recruitment Program to Implement 5 U.S.C. Section 7201, As Amended (as chair, United States Equal Employment Opportunity Commission. Washington, DC: U.S. EEOC, 1978.

"Employment of Black Males Declines," *The Crisis* 88 (October 1981): 400.

"Prologue," *EEOC Guidelines on Sexual Harassment, Capital University Law Review* 10. (Spring 1981): 471.

Fair Housing and Neighborhood Stabilization: A New Way to Look at an Old Problem. (transcript from Terence K. McCormack Memorial Lectureship at St. Louis University Law School) 3 PUB. L.F. 55 (1983).

"Public Assistance, Post-New Deal Bureaucracy, and the Law: Learning from Negative Models" (transcript in the symposium. "The Legacy of the New Deal: Problems and Possibilities in the Administrative State," *Yale Law Journal* 92 (June 1983): 1287.

"The Marion County Lawyer's Club: 1932 and the Black Lawyer," *Black Law Journal* 8 (Fall 1983): 170.

"The Role of Black Presidential Appointees," *Urban League Review* 9 (Summer 1985): 106–111.

P

PAINTER, NELL IRVIN (b. 1942), born August 2 in Houston, Texas, is an American historian specializing in the African-American experience, southern history, and the history of the Reconstruction and Progressive eras. She is known for her work on the "exodusters," blacks migrating to the West, and for her oral histories, one of which, Theodore Rosengarten, a reviewer, has called "a modern epic." Since 1988 she has been a professor of history at Princeton University.

Painter attended the University of California at Berkeley, where she received a BA degree in anthropology (1964). Later she received an MA from the University of California, Los Angeles (1967), and a PhD from Harvard University (1974). In addition, she attended the University of Bordeaux (1962–1963) and the University of Ghana (1965–1966). She has taught at the University of Pennsylvania (1974–1980), was a resident associate of Afro-American studies at the W.E.B. Du Bois Institute at Harvard University (1977–1978), and, prior to moving to Princeton, New Jersey, taught at the University of North Carolina at Chapel Hill (1980–1988).

Painter herself has said that she is more researcher than teacher. She became interested in history because she found inadequate treatment of race and race relations in the United States in American textbooks and wanted to correct that situation. Her books have been critically reviewed and include *Exodusters: Black Migration to Kansas after Reconstruction* (1977), *The Narrative of Hosea Hudson: His Life as a Negro Communist in the South* (1979), *The Progressive Era* (1984), and *Standing at Armageddon* (1987). She has been part of the recent discussion on multiculturalism on American campuses and has said that, if people remembered the past condition of college and university campuses, "they would hesitate before assailing the attempt to forge a pedagogy appropriate for newly diversified student bodies and faculties."

Painter is a member of the Organization of American Historians, the American Historical Association, the Association for the Study of Afro-American Life and History, the Berkshire Conference of Women Historians, and the Association of Black Women Historians. In 1969 she received the Coretta Scott King Award from the American Association of University Women.

Painter is married to Glenn R. Shafer and currently resides in Princeton, New Jersey.

—Nancy Elizabeth Fitch

Bibliography

As there is no book-length biography of Nell Irvin Painter, the critical sketch of her work in the New Revision Series by James G. Lesniak, *Contemporary Authors* 19 (Detroit: Gale, 1985) is very useful. Reviews on her landmark work, *The Exodusters*, and her historical style include Alden Whitman, "Kansas: Black Lodestone," *New York Times* (January 29, 1977): 17; and Theodore Rosengarten's review in the *New Republic* (February 12, 1977): 21–25. Painter's views on multiculturalism in higher education are included in the recent the *New York Times* forum "Opening Academia Without Closing It Down" (December 9, 1990): E5.

PARKERSON, MICHELLE (b. 1953) was born and raised in Washington, DC, mostly attending Catholic schools. She credits the 1960s television program "Black Journal" and early black filmmakers Madeline Anderson and St. Claire Bourne with sparking her interest in film. Following her dream, she graduated from Temple University, where she earned a BA in communications in 1974. Parkerson worked in Washington, DC, for eight years as a television engineer (NBC, 1975; Fox, 1976–1983).

Parkerson left television and began her own film/video production company in DC in 1978. The company is called Eye of the Storm because, for Parkerson, film represents "the clarifying agent amidst the turbulent historical period we [African Americans] find ourselves in the midst." Consequently, her creative cultural expression reflects a commitment to education and social activism.

Writing has always functioned as an important aspect in Parkerson's life. "I consider myself a writer; and I like to work in a variety of forms. I like to write poetry, short fiction, scripts, essays and scholarly papers. I loved writing even in grade school. Writing is the foundation of filmmaking." In 1983 she published a book of poetry and fiction entitled *Waiting Rooms*. She has also collaborated with Essex Hemphill to produce two theatrical pieces, *Voicescapes: An Urban Mouthpiece* (1986) and *Voicescapes II* (1987).

Parkerson's films examine personalities and explore issues relevant to African-American women. She explains:

> I think we [black women] tend to make productions about other black women first, which is thematic. We tend to turn the camera on ourselves first because our story hasn't been told. It's only been recently that black women have been making films; thus our story has only recently been told cinematically and realistically. There's a lot more humanity in the way we approach black and female subjects in films because we are that race and that gender.

Her films are: *Urban Odyssey*, 1991 (director/producer); *It's My Choice*, 1988 (associate producer); *Storme: The Lady of the Jewel Box*, 1987 (director/producer/editor); *I Remember Betty*, 1987 (director/editor); *Gotta Make This Journey: Sweet Honey in the Rock*, 1983 (producer); *But Then, She's Betty Carter*, 1980 (director/producer); and her first film, *Sojourn*, 1973 (director/producer).

Parkerson has several works in progress including a documentary on black lesbian writer and activist Audre Lorde, entitled *A Litany for Survival: The Audre Lorde Film Project* (with Ada Griffin), and a film on black women ministers entitled *Upon This Woman Rock: Black Women in the Ministry* (with Adrienne Seward).

Parkerson has taught at several universities, including Howard University (1987–1990), Temple University (1986), the Institute for Policy Studies (Washington, DC), and University of Delaware (1985). She has also lectured extensively. Parkerson has won numerous grants, fellowships, and awards. In 1989 she was selected as a delegate to the Black American Cinema Tour of India. Other awards include honoree, Gallery of Greats: Black Filmmakers Miller Brewing Company (1991); fellowship from American Film Institute Independent Filmmaker Program (1990); Delegate to PBS/Sundance Retreat for Women in Media (1988).

—Gloria J. Gibson-Hudson

Bibliography

"Michelle Parkerson *IS* the Eye of the Storm," *Black Film Review* 4:1 (Winter 1987–1988), is an in-depth interview with Michelle Parkerson. Greg Tate, "Cinematic Sisterhood," *Village Voice* (June 4, 1991) includes Parkerson in a brief overview article of black women independent filmmakers. Gloria J. Gibson-Hudson, "African American Literary Criticism as a Model for the Analysis of Films by African American Women," *Wide Angle* 13:3 (July/October 1991), analyzes Parkerson's work in relation to that of black women writers.

PARKS, ROSA [McCAULEY] (b. 1913), catalyst of the 1955 Montgomery bus boycott, was born on February 4 to James and Leona (Edwards) McCauley of Tuskegee, Alabama. When Rosa Louise McCauley was two years old, her father, a carpenter, wanted to seek greater opportunities in the North, a goal that led to their family's disintegration. Her mother, a teacher, returned to live with her parents, Rosa and Sylvester Edwards, in Pine Level, Alabama, the rural part of Montgomery County, where Rosa's brother, Sylvester James McCauley, was born on August 20, 1915. Until age 11, Rosa McCauley cared for her grandfather and attended school where her mother was the only teacher in a one-room schoolhouse.

To improve her educational opportunities, her mother sent her to live in Montgomery with a widowed aunt, Fanny Williamson, who worked at the Jewish country club. There she attended Montgomery Industrial School, a private girls' school partially supported by the Congregational church. The teachers, white women from the North, lived in a dormitory next to the school, separated from the white community. The black girls wore uniforms; received instruction in reading, writing, and mathematics; developed skills in home economics; and followed the strict discipline of the school's principal, Miss White. To pay for her tuition, young Rosa McCauley cleaned the schoolrooms in the evening before returning home, where more chores awaited her. In her limited leisure time, she returned to Pine Level, about 30 miles south of Montgomery, where she played baseball and went fishing with her grandfather, who died when she was ten years old. Although she never finished school, she had developed the foundation of a good education and had picked up skills in sewing and nursing that helped her through the years.

In 1932 at age 18, she married Raymond Parks in Pine Level. An orphan, Raymond Parks worked in the Atlas Barber Shop in Montgomery, where he discussed and worked for the release of the Scottsboro boys (nine black youths who were framed and convicted of rape during the Depression). A neat, thin, serious, light-skinned black man, Raymond Parks came from Randolph County, Alabama, a community of few black people. Since the colored school was too far away and his grandparents needed his help, Raymond Parks lacked much formal schooling until he moved in with a cousin and attended Tuskegee Institute at age 21. While working at different jobs, he picked up the barber trade. Introduced by a mutual friend, she was attracted to Raymond Parks because of their common hardships. She enjoyed listening to his discussions of race problems.

After their marriage, Rosa Parks did sewing at home to help with living expenses. She tried doing insurance work for the Metro Life Insurance Company, worked as a file clerk, and then served as the secretary of the Montgomery chapter of the NAACP during the war years. Working with E.D. Nixon, a leader in the Brotherhood of Sleeping Car Porters Union, Parks became well known in the community through her NAACP role and through her work with the African Methodist Episcopal church.

On December 1, 1955, Rosa Parks boarded the Cleveland Avenue bus on her way home. It had been a long and tiring day. She spent most of it on her feet at the downtown Montgomery department store where she worked as a seamstress. With hands clutched to a bag of groceries and weary feet, she boarded the bus, taking a seat in the section reserved "For Colored Only." She remained there until her arrest several hours later. For the most part, there was nothing significantly unusual about that day in December. Her refusal to give up her seat was the beginning of the precedent-setting civil rights case that changed the South and American history forever. It had become southern tradition—the way of life. The seats in the back were specifically designated "For Colored Only" while the first several rows were "For Whites Only." But according to Parks, each busdriver enforced the code individually. She recalled that, although the rules required black passengers to pay up front and then exit the bus to enter in the rear, she paid and continued on to the back. Many busdrivers did not make black passengers stand as the bus filled with whites—unless the white passengers insisted. On the day of her arrest, all of the seats in the white section had been taken. It was, therefore, legally permissible to demand that blacks give up their seats for whites in the "For Colored Only" section. Three of the blacks stood, but Parks remained seated. Determined to no longer be victimized by the system's archaic treatment of blacks, she remained in her seat. Shortly thereafter she was arrested and taken into custody.

Prior to her arrest, for several months the Montgomery chapter of the NAACP headed by E.D. Nixon had tried negotiating the bus rules with local officials, simply requesting that busdrivers treat all passengers with respect as they boarded the buses. Their cry for help went unattended. In many cases, drivers seemingly were more intolerant of the black passengers who rode the buses. Immediately upon her arrest, Parks telephoned Nixon, who mobilized the Women's Political Council (WPC), organized in 1946 by Mary Fair Burks and others. The WPC under the leadership of Jo Ann Robinson had been concentrating its efforts on correcting the abuses on the buses. A committee was organized, and within days flyers and brochures urging blacks not to ride the buses were circulated. Carpools and taxis that charged bus rates were organized to make way for the historic Montgomery bus boycott. The Montgomery Improvement Association, led by Dr. Martin Luther King, Jr., included Rosa Parks on the board of directors. In 1956 the U.S. Supreme Court banned bus segregation affirming that Alabama's state and local laws requiring segregation on buses were unconstitutional.

Shortly after refusing to give up her seat, Parks was fired from her seamstress job. Life was not easy. For awhile, Rosa Parks accepted a job at Hampton Institute in Hampton, Virginia, while her husband taught apprentice barbers in a barber school. She moved to Detroit, Michigan, the home of her brother, so that her mother could spend more time with both adult children. For 25 years, Rosa Parks worked as a special assistant to Michigan Congressman John Conyers, and continued to travel throughout the country as a symbol and speaker for civil rights. Parks currently resides in Michigan, where she is founder/president of the Rosa and Raymond Parks Institute for Self-Development.

—Dorothy C. Salem and Dorri Scott Eades

Bibliography

The 1978 oral history interview with Rosa Parks is part of the Black Women's Oral History Project, Radcliffe College. Information about Rosa Parks and her civil rights activities is found throughout *Women in the Civil Rights Movement*, edited by Vicki L. Crawford, Jacqueline Rouse, and Barbara Woods, Volume 16 of the series *Black Women in United States History*, edited by Darlene Clark Hine (Brooklyn: Carlson, 1990). Other sources include David Garrow, ed., *The Montgomery Bus Boycott and the Women Who Started It* (Knoxville: University of Tennessee Press, 1987); Martin Luther King, Jr., *Stride Toward Freedom* (New York: Harper & Row, 1958); Kai Friese, *Rosa Parks* (Englewood Cliffs, NJ: Silver-Burdett, 1990); Fiona Macdonald, *Working for Equality* (New York: Hampstead Press, 1988); and Janet Stevenson, *The Montgomery Bus Boycott, December, 1955* (New York: Franklin Watts, 1971).

PARSONS, LUCY [GATHINGS] (1853–1942) is historically one of the most ignored women of African-American descent. A recognized leader of the white male working-class movement in Chicago and co-worker with radical labor leader Mother Jones in the late nineteenth and early twentieth centuries, her

achievements as an adult have been cloaked in the obscurity and contradictions of her early years. Lucy Ella Parsons was a woman who fought fiercely against discrimination based on race, gender, and class, and yet denied her racial identity, behaved as a lady in daily life and operated a successful dressmaking business for middle- and upper-class women. Yet, she is best remembered for her tireless efforts to wage class warfare to overthrow the capitalistic system in the United States.

Many of these contradictions can be explained by the time and locations in which she lived. Due to the racial violence that penetrated the South following Reconstruction and due to her marriage to Albert Parsons, a white Radical Republican, a union that was clearly against the law in the South, Lucy Parsons often claimed she was of mixed Spanish and Indian heritage. Lucy claimed that Marie del Gather and John Waller, an Americanized Creek Indian, were her parents. On her son's birth certificate in 1879, she listed her maiden name as Carter, yet on her daughter's, her name is listed as Hull. On both children's birth certificates, Lucy listed Virginia as her birthplace, yet in interviews she always revealed her birthplace as Buffalo Creek, Texas. In her account of her husband's life given to the *Dictionary of American Biography*, she listed her maiden name as Gonzales. Her death certificate lists Pedro Diaz and Marie Gonzales as her parents. These origins can only be inferred from various records. Slave schedules suggest her birth around March, 1853, on a plantation belonging to the wealthy Gathings brothers of Hill County, Texas. When she met Albert Parsons, who was traveling for his brother's *Houston Daily Telegraph*, she was living with a former slave named Oliver Gathings. Since the May 6, 1886, issue of *Waco Day* insisted that hundreds of whites and blacks remembered Lucy Parsons, she was most likely a well-known Waco resident and was originally associated with the Gathings plantation. Although she denied her heritage for various reasons during most of her life, interviews with Katharine Parsons Russell acknowledged the family privately accepted their African heritage, an identity confirmed by the photographs of Lucy Parsons and by the identities assigned her children on their birth certificates.

Her identification with the radical labor movement started with her relationship to Albert Parsons. Though no records of their marriage have been located, both Lucy and Albert Parsons list 1871 as the year of their marriage in Austin, Texas. In 1873 Albert was elected to the Radical Republican convention in Travis County. He then worked as a journalist accepting a free train tour from the Missouri, Kansas and Texas Railway. Once settled in Philadelphia, he asked Lucy to join him, and then both came to Chicago in the winter of 1873–1874, as 10,000 workers and unemployed protested in front of city hall.

Albert Parsons joined the Typographical Union and worked as a printer at the *Times*. He joined organizations seeking to improve conditions for the working class. In the spring of 1876, he joined the Social Democratic Party of North America; by summer he belonged to the Knights of Labor, founding the first Knights of Labor Assembly in Chicago; and later that year, as the Social

Democratic Party dissolved, Parsons helped found the Workingmen's Party of the United States. Since the Chicago group met at the Parsons' house, Lucy Parsons gained experience with socialist politics and a socialist acceptance of her heritage. As economic conditions worsened in the cities throughout the nation in 1877, organized opposition of workers increased. Albert Parsons spoke at a rally drawing 25,000 to Market and Madison streets. The following day, he was arrested for starting the strikes, lost his employment at the *Times*, and became a popular leader of the growing Workingmen's Party. Lucy opened a dress and suit shop to earn money to support the family. By late 1877 the party's name had been changed to the Socialistic Labor Party, which supported total equality of rights for both sexes.

These events in Chicago shaped her awareness about the conflicts between capital and labor. Her first known literary effort, a parody of a Lord Byron poem, "A Parody," appeared in the *Socialist* during the peak of her husband's success as a labor organizer during the strikes and violence of 1877. She disregarded property rights for human rights, which were violated all around her. Between 1875 and 1886, she and her husband moved at least once a year. Her neighbors remembered her "well-bred" behavior that commanded respect, perhaps as a means to lessen potential racial discrimination. The moving was probably due to the homes being used as meeting places for the socialist gatherings. By the time the neighbors figured out what was going on, the couple moved on to another location. Her personal comfort and family needs were secondary to the struggle. Her view of history neglected the role of the individual, since she was movement oriented. Hence, while she was pregnant with her first child in 1879, she wrote for the *Socialist*, edited by her husband and Frank Hirth, and spoke for the Working Women's Union, a group formed in the 1870s by wageless women who worked for a suffrage plank in the Socialist Labor Party and for the concept of equal pay for equal work. When the Knights of Labor admitted women on the same basis as men, Lucy Parsons quickly joined their other female labor leaders, including Mother Jones.

Just as the labor movement gained adherents, internal divisions developed. One month after the *Socialist* folded, Lucy Parsons had her first child, Albert Richard Parsons, on September 14, 1879. Out of the political struggles of 1879–1881, Lucy Parsons emerged more militant than her husband, became the sole supporter of the family through her successful dress shop, and gave birth to a second child, Lulu Eda, born on April 20, 1881 (labeled a "nigger" on the birth certificate). While most labor leaders were becoming syndicalists by 1883, Lucy and her friend, Lizzie M. Swank, a widowed music teacher, became advocates of armed revolution, a position that earned them the anarchist label. In 1884, the International Working Peoples Association (IWPA) published *The Alarm*, an English language newspaper, with Albert Parsons as editor and Lizzie Swank as assistant editor. The first issue published the essay "To Tramps" by Lucy Parsons. She expressed anger over the numbers of hungry, homeless people dying due to lack of shelter and appropriate clothing during the cold Chicago winters. She preferred them to join the revolution and risk death in explosions rather than face a lingering death. On April 28, 1885, she and Lizzie Swank led a march on the Board of Trade Building, where the wealthy leaders of Chicago dined on $20-a-plate meals. As her husband continued his organizing in the IWPA, Lucy was left to push the struggle alone. She published articles against child labor, racial violence, industrial accidents, and sweatshop employment of women.

These efforts seemed successful. By May 1, 1886, many workers had gained the eight-hour day, the goal sought by Albert Parsons, and Lucy Parsons and Swank had successfully organized several hundred sewing women for better working conditions. Within a few days, however, one rally at the Haymarket Square in Chicago on May 4, where labor leaders spoke about the movement and goals, led to suppression of their activities, arrest of the staff of the *Alarm*, and pursuit of Albert Parsons as a fugitive. A bomb was thrown into a crowd of police long after the Parsons family and other leaders had departed. But their visual and vocal leadership of the labor movement in Chicago brought both into the center of legal persecution and prosecution. In June, the grand jury indicted 31 labor leaders on conspiracy charges that led to the bombing on Haymarket Square. Albert Parsons returned to Chicago to surrender voluntarily for trial with his "innocent comrades." The Parsons gave interviews with the press during his time in jail trying to deal with scathing attacks on Lucy Parson's virtue based on her relationship with Oliver Gathings, on her mixed heritage, and on the legitimacy of her marriage to Albert. The couple came up with a story that protected Lucy's background, but was most likely a creation of the imagination. By October 1886, the trial was completed, and eight leaders, including Albert Parsons, had been condemned to death by hanging on December 3.

As his lawyer sought appeals, Lucy placed her children in the care of others and went on a lecture and writing tour taking the injustice of this trial to Knights of Labor assemblies, to IWPA locals, and to other socialist, anarchist, and labor groups. Her daughter, Lulu, was sick much of this time with a glandular disease, at first diagnosed as scarlet fever, that eventually led to her death two years later. Lucy was arrested in March 1887 in Columbus, Ohio, where the mayor halted the speech of any anarchist. She used her arrest to publicize defense of free speech. Out on bail, she continued her speaking tour. Throughout this time, she brought radical ideals to thousands of people helping to keep the reform and radical movement alive to neutralize the disintegration and conservative effects of the Haymarket bombing on the American labor movement. Meanwhile, the conservative leadership of the labor movement undermined the credibility of Lucy Parsons by questioning the legality of her marriage.

As the higher courts upheld the verdict, Lucy Parsons continued to distribute literature and inform the public about the labor injustices. When Lucy made her final visit to the jail with her children, all were strip-searched by a matron and locked naked in a cell. Without seeing his family, Albert Parsons joined three other "conspirators" on the gallows on November 11, 1887. This final act of inhumanity branded her soul with hatred of the "system," which had sacrificed her husband on the altar of class hatred. With a stipend of $12 a week awarded the widows and children of the Haymarket martyrs by the Pioneer Aid and Support Association, Lucy Parsons continued proselytizing for class struggle. She edited and published her husbands writings: *Anarchism: Its Philosophy and Scientific Basis* and *The Life of Albert R. Parsons* in 1888–1889. In October 1888 she sailed for London to speak to the Socialist League. The English were enthralled with her eloquence.

In the years following her husband's execution, Lucy Parsons wore the mantle of widow-martyr at public gatherings. She criticized charities as "hush money to hide the blushes of the labor robbers," government and churches as "Siamese twins" promoting immoral suffering of the working people, and voting as ineffective. Her vision of a future society was labeled anarchist; it was actually syndicalist in nature, advocating a society of voluntary association in which members of trade unions would regulate the means of production and distribution. This type of idealistic vision was countered by tragedies in her personal life. Her eight-year-old daughter Lulu died on October 13, 1889, of lymphodenoma. In 1891 Lucy Parsons filed malicious mischief charges (threats were made against her life and property) against Martin Lacher, a fellow anarchist, who "boarded" at her home. This incident led to her being cast in the role of a sexually promiscuous woman who lived with a married man. Her moral integrity came into question again in the press.

These hardships did not dampen her revolutionary spirit. That same year, she began editing *Freedom, A Revolutionary Anarchist-Communist Monthly*. This paper, through Parsons's essays, continually criticized the racial violence and discrimination directed against African Americans. In 1893 she presided over the unveiling of a monument to the Haymarket martyrs in Waldheim Cemetery in Chicago. The following day, the jailed Haymarket conspirators were pardoned by Governor John Altgeld, who condemned the prejudicial evidence and judicial errors of the earlier trial.

The turn of the century did not bring great strides for the labor movement or for Lucy Parsons. The prosperity of the William McKinley era lessened the effects of working-class propaganda. When President McKinley was assassinated in September 1901, the Chicago press again sought out the radical Lucy Parsons for an interview. Parsons unpredictably praised the wounded President and claimed no knowledge of the assailant. *Free Society* folded in the wave of persecution following the McKinley assassination. Yet, these negative conditions led to the formation of a new industrial union formed secretly in Chicago in January 1905, the Industrial Workers of the World (IWW). Lucy Parsons sat on the platform with Mother Jones and radical trade unionist Eugene V. Debs listening to "Big Bill" Haywood call for "the emancipation of the working class from the slave bondage of capitalism." She addressed the crowds in attendance supporting the

IWW direct action and strike agenda. Through the columns of *The Liberator*, a new publication under the IWW label, Parsons again pushed her vision of an egalitarian society of working-class people. Within two years, the IWW split. Parsons concentrated on the history of the Haymarket riot and the legal aftermath in her writings and speeches. From Los Angeles to New York, she toured, selling over 10,000 *Famous Speeches* and *The Life of Albert R. Parsons* in 1911. She wrote articles for the IWW's *Industrial Worker* in 1912.

The economic crashes of 1914–1915 increased unemployment and hunger. Parsons focused her work on organizing the unemployed. She and a co-habiting friend, George Markstall, were arrested for distribution of literature without a license in 1913. Released until trial, she took part in the free speech movement in Seattle, Washington, and went down to San Francisco to continue organizing the unemployed in 1914, where she was arrested and rearrested several times. She returned to Chicago in 1915 to lead hunger demonstrations around Hull House. Jane Addams, Sophinisba Breckenridge, and Irwin St. John Tucker, an Epicopalian minister, helped to secure jury trials for the demonstrators. Parsons worked with the reformers to improve life for the hungry. In 1916, she went to the Mesabi Range in Minnesota to help the striking iron miners. War fever grew, when finally the United States went to war in April 1917. George Creel's Committee on Public Information controlled the news, while Congress passed the Espionage Act and the Sedition Act. When friend Cassius Cook was arrested for his work with the League of Humanity, Lucy Parsons put up her house to cover the last $7,000 of his bond. Within months, the leadership of the IWW and the Socialist Party had been indicted under the Espionage Act, radical publications had been denied access to the mails, and leaders were deported. Lucy Parsons lost her son in 1919, as the Palmer Raids smashed the leadership of the IWW and the government created a legal lynching of two Italian anarchists, Nicola Sacco and Bartolomeo Vanzetti.

The last decades of her life showed her continual commitment to the workers. She spoke and organized in the unreceptive atmosphere of the 1920s. She was a main speaker in the 1930 May Day celebration at the Ashland Auditorium in Chicago. She corresponded with Carl Nold, radical labor supporter, who was in Ann Arbor helping anarchist librarian Agnes Inglis develop the anarchist collection of which anarchist intellectual Joseph Labadie donated the core. Her eyesight was failing and she suffered from occasional bouts with pleurisy. She stopped in on meetings, often speaking at the Dill Pickle Club, a radical avant garde gathering place. She worked for famous legal cases of injustice such as the 1930s prosecution of communist Angelo Herndon and the Scottsboro boys, nine black youths framed and convicted of the rape of two white women in the South. Lucy had converted one of the bedrooms of her home into a library of at least 1,500 books on sex, socialism, and anarchy, including classical French socialists Voltaire, Rousseau, Marx, and Engels. Her last public appearances included a speech to the striking workers at International Harvester on February 23, 1941, and riding in the May Day parade as guest of honor on the Farm Equipment Workers' float. She died in a fire caused by her wood stove on March 7, 1942, while George Markstall was out buying groceries. He tried to save her when he returned, but was overcome by smoke inhalation. He died the following day in Belmont Hospital. Her library was damaged, but many volumes remained intact. When her friend, Irving Abrams, arrived at the house to retrieve the materials, he found only the most damaged books. The FBI had removed the good materials earlier that day, but denied any action. She left her home to the Pioneer Aid and Support Association to maintain the Haymarket monument, but even these wishes went unfulfilled because a bequest could not be made to a private monument. Although her material legacy could not survive, her spiritual leadership as a founder of the modern labor movement remained intact through the young workers and her historical role in preparing the ground for their growth.

—Dorothy C. Salem

Bibliography

The most complete study of Lucy Parsons is Carolyn Ashbaugh, *Lucy Parsons: American Revolutionary* (Chicago: Charles Kerr, 1976). Her research provides detail to the life of Lucy Parsons from the Waco-McLennan County Library; Chicago Historical Society; Albert R. Parsons Papers, State Historical Society of Wisconsin (Madison); Edward Clark Papers, University of Texas Archives, Austin; and the Labadie Collection, University of Michigan, Ann Arbor. For much of the early information on Lucy Parsons, Ashbaugh relied on the extensive research of Lucie C. Price on the careers of William and Albert Parsons, and on vital statistics documents (birth and death records), most of which conflict with other information.

Writings by Lucy Parsons include these titles, which are all self-published in Chicago: *The Life of Albert R. Parsons* (1889, 1903); *Altgeld's Reasons for Pardoning Fielden, Schwab, and Neebe* (1915); *The Principles of Anarchism* (n.d.); and *The Famous Speeches* (1909, 1910, 1912).

Details of the life of Lucy Parsons can best be found in published sources dealing with the Chicago and labor history topics, especially under anarchism. Most histories of the labor movements of syndicalism, anarchism, socialism, and the IWW leave out the role of women, thus, Lucy Parsons receives no mention. For those sources that provide brief mention or delineate the context in which to analyze Lucy Parsons, see Jane Addams, *Twenty Years at Hull House* (New York: Macmillan, 1945); William Adelman, *Haymarket Revisited* (Chicago: Illinois Labor History Society, 1976); Richard Boyer, *Labor's Untold Story* (New York: United Electrical, Radio and Machine Workers of America, 1974); Jeremy Brecher, *Strike!* (San Francisco: Straight Arrow Books, 1972); Alan Calmer, *Labor Agitator: The Story of Albert R. Parsons* (New York: International Publishers, 1937); Philip Foner, ed., *The Autobiographies of the Haymarket Martyrs* (New York: Humanities Press, 1969); Mary Harris Jones, *The Autobiography of Mother Jones*, 3rd ed. (Chicago: Charles Kerr, 1976); Roderick Kedward, *The Anarchists. The Men Who Shocked an Era* (New York: American Heritage Press, 1964); Patrick Renshaw, *The Wobblies* (Garden City, NY: Doubleday, 1967); and Paul Nursey-Bray, *Anarchist Thinkers and Thought: An Annotated Bibliog-*

raphy (New York: Greenwood Press, 1992). Michael J. Schank, *Anarchy and Anarchists: A History of the Red Terror and the Social Revolution in America and Europe* (Chicago: F.J. Schulte, 1889) is an account written by a contemporary of Lucy Parsons, a police captain, who presents a different perspective of the Haymarket Square incident and the role of Lucy Parsons in labor agitation.

PATTERSON, MARY JANE (1840–1894) is often cited as the first black female to earn a bachelor's degree in the United States; however, Grace A. Mapps achieved that distinction in the 1850s from New York Central College. Nevertheless, Patterson's educational achievements are noteworthy.

Born in Raleigh, North Carolina, Patterson had access to educational opportunities because her parents, Henry and Emeline Patterson, were free blacks who had relocated their family to Oberlin, Ohio, in the 1850s so that their children could attend quality educational facilities. Their efforts were rewarded with the graduation of four children from college. Their fifth child became an accomplished mason like his father.

Mary Jane Patterson enrolled at Oberlin College for five years. She devoted one year of study in the Preparatory Department and then matriculated to the college program. Patterson took Latin, Greek, and advanced mathematics courses in an intensive curriculum. She graduated with a BA in 1862. A professor described Patterson as "a superior scholar, a good singer, a faithful Christian, and a genteel lady."

Soon after graduation, Patterson moved east and taught in Philadelphia at the Institute for Colored Youths for seven years. In 1869 she transferred to Washington, DC, to accept a teaching position at the recently established Preparatory High School for Negroes (which became known as the M Street School and then Dunbar High School). Two of Patterson's sisters also became teachers in the capital city. In autumn 1871 she was appointed the first black principal of the school.

After one year as principal, Patterson was replaced by Richard T. Greener, the first black man to graduate from Harvard, and she served as assistant principal. He departed the school in 1873, and Patterson was reappointed as principal. The enthusiastic Patterson constantly tried to improve the school. During her tenure, the name Preparatory High School was discontinued, and the first commencement was held in 1877. Regarded as an energetic and empathetic teacher, Patterson wielded great influence on her students, encouraging them to attain high goals. Many of her pupils became distinguished in a variety of professional fields such as medicine, music, law, and education.

Patterson served as principal until 1884 when F.L. Cardozo, Sr., assumed that position. Sources explain this personnel change was due either to Patterson's ill health or to the administration's belief that a man could better manage the school's increased enrollment. Patterson continued to teach at the school and set high standards for her pupils.

Patterson participated in Washington life. She belonged to the Bethel Literary and Historical Association and was a charter member of the National Colored Women's League. She joined her sister, Chanie A. Patterson, in a debate promoting the advantages of professional education for blacks against two supporters of trade school training, Alexander Crummell and Robert Purvis. Patterson taught at the high school until her death in 1894.

—Elizabeth D. Schafer

Bibliography

Manuscripts concerning Mary Jane Patterson's collegiate activities are in the Patterson file of the alumni records at Oberlin College. The Bethel Literary and Historical Society Papers are kept at Howard University, and a file of records of the National League of Colored Women is in the Mary Church Terrell Papers at the Library of Congress.

Patterson's collegiate education is briefly mentioned in Ellen N. Lawson and Marlene Merrill, "Antebellum Black Coeds at Oberlin College," *Oberlin Alumni Magazine* (January–February 1980): 18–21; and Robert S. Fletcher, *A History of Oberlin College From Its Foundation Through the Civil War* (originally published in 1943; reprint edition, New York: Arno Press, 1971), which contains a photograph of Patterson. Sylvia G.L. Dannett, *Profiles of Negro Womanhood 1619–1900*, Volume 1 (Chicago: Educational Heritage, 1964) profiles Patterson's educational leadership. Frances Juliette Hosford, *Father Shipherd's Magna Charta: A Century of Coeducation in Oberlin College* (Boston: Marshall Jones Co., 1937) is a general history of coeducation at Oberlin and does not provide specific information about Patterson. W.E. Bigglestone, archivist at Oberlin College, wrote an article about postbellum education for blacks: "Oberlin College and the Negro Student," *Journal of Negro History* 56 (July 1971): 198–219.

Linda M. Perkins, *Fanny Jackson Coppin and the Institute for Colored Youths, 1865–1902* (New York: Garland, 1987) provides a historical account of the Institute for Colored Youths in Philadelphia. An essay by Linda Perkins, "The Institute for Colored Youth in Philadelphia: An Argument for the Race," appeared in *Blacks in Pennsylvania History: Research and Educational Perspectives*, edited by David McBride (Harrisburg, PA: Pennsylvania Historical & Museum Commission, 1983), pp. 18–33, which states that Patterson accompanied Fanny Coppin, a former Oberlin teacher, to Philadelphia. Two articles address the history of the Preparatory High School for Negroes in which Patterson taught: G. Smith Wormley, "Educators of the First Half Century of the Public Schools of the District of Columbia," *Journal of Negro History* 17 (April 1932): 124–140, and Mary Church Terrell, "History of the High School for Negroes in Washington," *Journal of Negro History* 2 (July 1917): 252–266. U.S. Department of the Interior, *Negro Education: A Study of the Private and Higher Schools for Colored People in the United States* (Washington, DC: U.S. Department of the Interior, 1969) is a contextual study of educational developments for black students and teachers.

Hallie Q. Brown, *Homespun Heroines and Other Women of Distinction* (Xenia, OH: Aldine Press, 1926) notes Patterson's achievements in education. Dorothy Salem, *To*

392   *Patterson, Mary Jane*

Better Our World: Black Women in Organized Reform, 1890–1920 (Brooklyn: Carlson, 1990) mentions Patterson's involvement in Washington, DC, organizations and notes, as does Dorothy Sterling, ed., *We Are Your Sisters: Black Women in the Nineteenth Century* (New York: Norton, 1984), that Patterson was not the first black female recipient of a bachelor's degree.

Constance M. Green, *The Secret City: A History of Race Relations in the Nation's Capital* (Princeton: Princeton University Press, 1967); and Helen A. Cook, "The Work of the Women's League of Washington, D.C.," in *Some Efforts of American Negroes for Their Own Social Betterment* 1, edited by W.E.B. Du Bois (Atlanta: Atlantic University Press, 1898), pp. 57–59, cite the work of organizations with which Patterson was affiliated. The Washington, DC, newspaper *Evening Sun* included items about Patterson's education and contemporary activities, including an obituary in 1894.

PAUL, SUSAN (1809–1841), abolitionist and educator, was born in Boston, Massachusetts. Her father the Reverend Thomas Paul, was an early abolitionist and the spiritual and political leader of Boston blacks during the first quarter of the nineteenth century. After acquiring an excellent education, she taught for most of her adult life in one of the city's primary schools for African-American children. She never married, but took on the responsibility of supporting her widowed mother and the four children of a deceased sister.

Paul was one of the first African-American women to gain renown in the antislavery movement. More of an activist than a theorist, she contributed to the formation and development of several antislavery organizations. She was a life member of the Massachusetts Anti-Slavery Society, an officer in the interracial Boston Female Anti-Slavery Society, and a key figure in the annual Boston antislavery fairs, which raised funds to sustain abolitionist speakers and the reform press. In 1838 Paul was elected a vice president of the second annual Anti-Slavery Convention of American Women in Philadelphia. She also formed and directed the Garrison Juvenile Choir, whose songs were a regular feature at local antislavery gatherings in the 1830s.

Paul was equally concerned about the injustices faced by women and free blacks. She became an outspoken advocate of the rights of women. Conscious of the close connection between slavery and racial discrimination, she attempted to persuade white abolitionists to make the struggle against prejudice a major component of their work. Paul believed that sobriety would aide African-American advancement, so, to further this end, she helped found the Boston Colored Female Temperance Society in 1833 and served as its secretary through the remainder of the decade. When Paul died of tuberculosis in Boston on April 19, 1841, a brief but promising reform career came to an untimely end.

—Roy E. Finkenbine

Bibliography

No biography of Susan Paul exists, but aspects of her life and career are noted in James O. Horton and Lois Horton, *Black Bostonians: Family Life and Community Struggle in the Antebellum North* (New York: Holmes & Meier, 1979); James O. Horton, "Generations of Protest: Black Families and Social Reform in Ante-Bellum Boston," *New England Quarterly* 49 (June 1976): 242–256; and J. Marcus Mitchell, "The Paul Family," *Old-Time New England* 63 (Winter 1973): 73–77.

There is information on Paul's reform work in several primary sources. She is regularly mentioned from 1833 to 1841 in *The Liberator* (Boston), the leading journal of the American antislavery movement; an obituary appears in the January 23, 1841, issue. Several Paul documents appear in the microfilm edition of *The Black Abolitionist Papers, 1830–1865*, edited by C. Peter Ripley and George E. Carter (New York: Microfilming Corporation of America, 1981). Her only known publication is an interesting tract entitled *Memoir of James Jackson* (Boston: James Loring, 1835), which enumerates the causes of racial prejudice.

PEAKE, MARY [KELSEY] (1823–1862), social reformer and educator, was born in Norfolk, Virginia, the daughter of a free black woman and a white Englishman. At age six, her mother sent Mary Smith Kelsey to live with an aunt, Mary Paine, in Alexandria so that she might attend school. While there she attended two different schools for blacks, the last being taught by an Englishman. She received an excellent education plus instruction in needlework and dressmaking. At age 16, she moved back to Norfolk.

Being a devout Christian, Peake worked with the poor and needy as a member of the First Baptist Church in Norfolk. When her mother married Thompson Walker in 1847, the family moved to Hampton, Virginia, where Peake supported herself as a seamstress. It was there that she formed the Daughters of Zion, a benevolent organization that ministered to the poor and sick. Peake taught black children and adults, both free and slave, at her home, but had to do so cautiously because slave law strictly forbade such activity.

In 1851 Mary Smith Kelsey married Thomas Peake, a former slave. They had one daughter, Hattie, who was affectionately called Daisy. After Hampton was burned during the Civil War, the family moved to Brown Cottage, located across the Hampton River in the vicinity of Fortress Monroe. On September 17, 1861, Brown Cottage became the site of the first school for freed slaves, sponsored by the American Missionary Association (AMA). Peake became the first teacher and held day classes for children and evening classes for adults in the front room of the first floor. This school was the first of many sponsored by the AMA that provided an education to all blacks who wished to attend.

Peake died of tuberculosis at her home in February 1862 at age 39. For her excellence as an educator and her work with freed slaves, she received the American Tract Society Medal of Praise. This was the first time the medal was given to an African American. As a September 1941 *New York Times* article reported, a housing project near her childhood home of Norfolk was named Peake Point in her honor.

—Linda Cannon-Huffman

Bibliography

The most interesting and authoritative account of Mary Peake's life was written by her friend and co-worker in the American Missionary Association, Lewis C. Lockwood. His book, *Mary S. Peake: The Colored Teacher at Fortress Monroe*, n.p. American Missionary Assocation, was originally published in 1863. Lockwood writes simply and lovingly about Peake's brief yet influential teaching career. A more concise history of Peake's life is listed in the *Dictionary of American Negro Biography*, edited by Rayford Logan and Michael Winston (New York: Norton, 1982). *The Negro in Virginia*, published as a part of the Virginia Writers' Project, mentions Peake and her teaching career in the context of her time. Other sources, such as *Noted Negro Women: Their Triumphs and Activities* by M.A. Majors (Chicago: Donohue & Henneberry, 1893), and the *Negro Year Book, 1914–15*, 3rd edition, have short entries emphasizing a few of the most important aspects of Peake's life.

Secondary Sources

Baskin, Wade, and Richard N. Rivers. *Dictionary of Black Culture*. New York: Philosophical Library, 1973.

Lerner, Gerda, ed. *Black Women in White America: A Documentary History*. New York: Pantheon Books, 1972.

PETRY, ANN [LANE] (b. 1911), novelist, short story writer, and journalist, was born October 12 to Peter C. and Bertha (James) Lane, a New England couple who managed their pharmacy businesses in Old Saybrook and Old Lyme, Connecticut. Although Ann Lane was born above her father's pharmacy store and received the college preparation for a career in pharmacy, she did not remain in her family's pharmacy business. Her grandfather, aunt, uncle, and parents were all pharmacists. She grew up in predominantly white Old Saybrook, Connecticut, attending the public schools. As a child, she enjoyed reading as entertainment to counter the small-town boredom. By adolescence, she had decided to become a writer. She wrote poetry and plays during high school. She graduated in 1929, went to the Connecticut College of Pharmacy until graduation in 1931, and worked in Old Saybrook's Pharmacist James' Pharmacy until 1938. Following her marriage to George David Petry on February 22, 1938, the young couple moved to New York, where a new life opened to Ann Petry.

In New York, Ann Petry gained employment at the *Amsterdam News*. From 1938 to 1941, she worked in the advertising department. She worked for another weekly paper, *People's Voice*, as the editor of the women's page and as a general reporter during World War II from 1941 to 1944. While she continued this employment, she continued her writing and increased her community activities. She worked to lessen the effects of segregation on children in the Harlem school system, took classes in creative writing at Columbia University, taught business classes at the YWCA, and participated in the American Negro Theatre. These experiences gave her material for her writing through varied short stories and novels.

Encouraged to submit her work, Petry eventually published her first piece, a short story entitled "On Saturday the Siren Sounds at Noon," in *The Crisis* in December 1943. She followed with "Olaf and His Girl Friend" and "Like a Winding Sheet" in the May and November 1945 issues. These articles won her an award (Best American Short Story, 1946) and the attention of an editor at Houghton Mifflin Publishers, who awarded her a fellowship in 1945 to complete a literary project uninterrupted. In January 1946 she published that project, *The Street*, a story about the life chances for an educated, ambitious, attractive black woman, Lutie Johnson, who becomes defeated by the squalor of the environment in which she lives. Due to the theme and style, her first novel was placed in the category of realist Richard Wright's novels. Such categorization led to Petry's consistent attempts to change and create something different.

Her following novels differed in themes and issues from her initial success with *The Street*, which sold over one million copies. In 1947 she published her second novel, *Country Place*. This story reflected the problems of social chaos on women during World War II in its depiction of a small Connecticut town that suffers a devastating hurricane and the breakdown of conventional morality by the displacements of wartime. The characters in this story were white, which led to some criticism from black critics. She published another story, "Harlem," in *Holiday* (April 1949) before she entered the field of children's books. She wrote her first children's book in 1949, *The Drugstore Cat*. Her next novel, *The Narrows*, published in 1953, focused on the pressures of an individual's past on the adult behaviors. She examines this issue in the relationship between a black man and a white woman in a small New England town. Although she received mixed reviews, the psychoanalytic characterizations endured.

To restore her interest in change, Petry began to do historical research for her next works in children's literature. To increase the student understanding of slavery, she published in 1955 *Harriet Tubman: Conductor on the Underground Railroad*. Interest in the Salem witchcraft trials led to another children's book, *Tituba of Salem Village*, in 1964. These fictional presentations of historical events and people led to research on South American slavery and on the Atlantic slave trade. She did not complete the books on these subjects because she felt limited by historical facts. In 1970 she published the stories of ten saints in *Legends of Saints*. Her final book appeared in 1971, *Miss Muriel and Other Stories*, a collection of her short stories. All these works demonstrate her achievement of variety among her topics, settings, and style.

Occasionally, Petry participates in conferences or lectures at colleges. She served as a professor of English at the University of Hawaii (1974–1975) and received honorary degrees from Suffolk University, the University of Connecticut, and Mount Holyoke College.

Petry has written extensively on the writing process, but remains guarded about her private life. Her marriage produced at least one daughter, Elizabeth Ann Petry. She moved back to Old Saybrook to write in a historically preserved home, where she enjoys simple interests in gardening, sewing, and cooking. She belongs to the professional writers' organizations PEN, the Authors Guild, and Authors League.

—Dorothy C. Salem

Bibliography

Ann Petry's letters are located at Boston University. She describes her work in James Ivy, "Ann Petry Talks about First Novel," *The Crisis* (February 1946): 48–49; and Marjorie Green, "Ann Petry Planned to Write," *Opportunity* 24 (1946): 78–79. Articles that describe her work include Vernon Lattin, "Ann Petry and the American Dream," *Black American Literary Forum* 12:2 (Summer 1978): 69–72; Margaret McDowell, "*The Narrows*: A Fuller View of Ann Petry," *Black American Literary Forum* 14:4 (Winter 1980): 135–141.

Her works are criticized in *Afro-American Literature—Fiction*, edited by William Adams (Boston: Houghton Mifflin, 1970); Robert Bone, *The Negro Novel in America* (New Haven: Yale University Press, 1968); David Littlejohn, *Black on White: A Critical Survey of Writing by American Negroes* (New York: Viking, 1966); Jeanne Noble, *Beautiful, Also, Are the Souls of My Black Sisters* (Englewood Cliffs, NJ: Prentice-Hall, 1978); Lina Mainiero, *American Women Writers* (New York: Ungar, 1982); Barbara White, *American Women Writers: An Annotated Bibliography of Criticism* (New York: Garland, 1977); Bernard Bell, *The Afro-American Novel and Its Tradition* (Amherst: University of Massachusetts, 1987); Linda Metzger, *Black Writers* (Detroit: Gale, 1989); and Michael Popkin, *Modern Black Writers* (New York: Ungar, 1978).

For biographical information or listings of her works see *Who's Who of American Women* (Chicago: Marquis, 1974); *Who's Who Among Black Americans* (Detroit: Gale, 1990); *Current Biography*, edited by Anna Rothe (New York: Wilson, 1947); *Contemporary Authors* NR-4, edited by Hal May and James Lesniak (Detroit: Gale, 1989): 478–480; Ann Shockley, *Living Black American Authors* (New York: Bowker, 1973); Ora Williams, *American Black Women in the Arts and Social Science* (Metuchen: Scarecrow, 1978); James Page, *Selected Black American Authors* (Boston: G.K. Hall, 1977); Wilhelmina Robinson, *Historical Negro Biographies* (New York: Publishers Company, 1968); Darwin Turner, *Afro-American Writers* (New York: Appleton-Century-Crofts, 1970); Tonda Glikin, *Black American Women in Literature* (Jefferson, NC: McFarland, 1989); Jessie Carney Smith, *Notable Black American Women* (Detroit: Gale, 1992).

PETTEY, SARAH [DUDLEY] (1869–1906) was an educator, journalist, woman's suffragist, and activist in the African Methodist Episcopal Zion church. Born in New Bern, North Carolina, Sarah E.C. Dudley was the daughter of Edward Richard Dudley, a state representative, and Caroline Dudley. She graduated from Scotia Seminary with honors in 1883. She became assistant principal of the New Bern graded school and taught in the New Bern State Normal School. In 1889 she married Charles Calvin Pettey, a bishop in the AME Zion church. The couple had five children, and Pettey raised two of her husband's children from his first marriage.

In 1896 Pettey began a six-year stint as a regular columnist for the *Star of Zion*, a national AME Zion publication. She used her forum to advocate women's rights, including the right of suffrage, and to promote the rights of African Americans. From 1895 to 1898, Pettey traveled throughout the United States, speaking for woman's equality and suffrage. During the 1890s the Petteys traveled to England and were presented at the Court of Saint James. In addition to her columns in the *Star of Zion*, Pettey wrote an article, "What Role Is the Educated Negro Woman to Play in the Uplifting of Her Race?," which appeared in *Twentieth Century Negro Literature*. She served as an officer of the Woman's Home and Foreign Missionary Society of the AME Zion church from 1892 to 1900. Widowed at age 31, Pettey died in 1906 at age 37. The place and circumstances of her death are unknown.

—Glenda Elizabeth Gilmore

Bibliography

Sarah Dudley Pettey's life is chronicled in the author's article "Gender and Jim Crow: Sarah Dudley Pettey's Vision of the New South" in the *North Carolina Historical Review* (July 1991). The *Star of Zion* and a full run of her columns is on microfilm, published by the Regenstein Library, University of Chicago.

Works by Sarah Dudley Pettey

"What Role Is the Educated Negro Woman to Play in the Uplifting of Her Race?" in D.W. Culp, ed., *Twentieth Century Negro Literature: Or, a Cyclopedia of Thought on the Vital Topics Relating to the American Negro*. Toronto: J.L. Nichols, 1902, pp. 182–185.
"Woman's Column," *Star of Zion* (1896–1902).

Secondary Sources

Culp, D.W. "Mrs. Sarah Dudley Pettey," *Twentieth Century Negro Literature: Or, a Cyclopedia of Thought on the Vital Topics Relating to the American Negro*. Toronto: J.L. Nichols, 1902.
Gilmore, Glenda Elizabeth. "Gender and Jim Crow: Sarah Dudley Pettey's Vision of the New South," *North Carolina Historical Review* (July 1991).

Hood, Bishop J.W. "Mrs. Sarah E.C. Dudley Pettey," in *One Hundred Years of the African Methodist Episcopal Zion Church*. New York: A.M.E. Zion Publishing House, 1895, pp. 538–539.

PINYON, JOSEPHINE [HOLMES] (1888–1943) is known for her work with the YWCA during World War I. She was also a teacher and, later in life, a government worker in employment services. Pinyon was born January 10 and lived in Washington, DC. She entered Cornell University in September 1906, where she majored in agricultural science, but it is unclear whether she graduated or merely attended classes there. She later attended Columbia University and the University of Chicago as well.

Pinyon began her career as a social worker, and then as a teacher. Initiating her important affiliation with the YWCA, she first worked as a student secretary, organizing black college students from September 1912 to 1916. In this capacity, she helped plan the first conference in Atlanta in 1916. Pinyon then left the Y to teach high school in Kansas City from 1916 to 1917. After this single year, she resumed employment with the Y.

When the United States entered World War I, the YWCA created services for black servicemen and their families, who faced massive discrimination relative to accommodations and leisure time activities available to them. African-American "hostess houses," predecessors to the USO, provided recreation centers for black troops and their visitors. Eight houses were established by 1918. The Y also created Girls' Reserves and Recreation Centers for black women who found jobs in war industries and needed housing. Pinyon became a "special war worker"; she played an instrumental role in creating and supervising some of the facilities noted above. A few of the sites she was responsible for include Petersburg, Virginia (1917); Houston, Texas (1917); and Des Moines, Iowa (1918).

In 1919 Pinyon assumed a different position in the YWCA. She reorganized the employment services for black women workers, finding employees for trades, industries, and domestic work. After World War I written evidence about Pinyon becomes scarce. She married, and by 1936 was working in the New York State Employment Office. She also taught school in Normal, Alabama, and Durham, North Carolina. Josephine Pinyon Holmes died November 26, 1943.

—Susan Borchert

Bibliography

Much information can be found in New York City in the YWCA, National Board Archives, Records Files Collection. Other sources include the following:

Cornell University, Registrar's Office, Ithaca, New York. The university has a record of her attending sporadically, from her initial matriculation in September 1906 to a summer session in 1910.

Neverdon-Morton, Cynthia. *Afro-American Women of the South and the Advancement of the Race, 1895–1925*. Knoxville: University of Tennessee Press, 1989. This work chronicles the efforts of black women in initiating social welfare, reform and racial uplift. It explains the role of the YWCA and Pinyon in establishing the facilities for black troops and war workers.

Olcott, Jane. *The Work of Colored Women*. New York: YWCA, Colored Work Committee, War Work Council, 1919. This brief work depicts the accomplishments of the black Y workers during this era. It is out of print and difficult to obtain.

Salem, Dorothy. *To Better Our World: Black Women in Organized Reform, 1890–1920*. Brooklyn: Carlson, 1990. This book places the work of the YWCA into the reform context.

PLEASANT, MARY ELLEN ("MAMMY")

(c. 1814–1904) was a California pioneer, a businesswoman, and an activist for civil rights, but due to contradictory sources, researchers will probably never be able to ascertain her origins and some of her adult activities. Nonetheless, "Mammy" Pleasant's life experiences form the core of an excellent novel. What cannot be determined is the motivation for her most noteworthy achievements—the source of that business income (prostitution?), her role in extortion, and her history before moving to California. As with many self-made leaders, she might have enjoyed creating herself in the various interviews completed during her lifetime. Few friends were privy to the details of her life, hence, the actual information will probably never be known.

She claimed to have been born in Philadelphia on August 19 to a free black mother and a Hawaiian father, Louis Alexander Williams, a merchant who imported silks. Other accounts say she was born a slave in either Georgia or Virginia. The later accounts of slave status were probably closer to the truth based upon her own words years later. She told a black friend that she had no respect for whites because of the ways she had been treated by whites as a slave. Delilah Beasley in *Negro Trailblazers of California* wrote that Mary's freedom was purchased by a planter named Price, who sent her to Boston for education. Most accounts say she lived in Boston. There, she lived with her first husband, Alexander Smith, a Cuban planter and supporter of antislavery reforms. In Boston, she became acquainted with William Lloyd Garrison, the leader of the moral suasionist wing of the abolition movement. When her husband died, leaving her with a substantial inheritance to be used for antislavery purposes, Mary took the money, remarried a man named John Pleasant (reputedly the overseer of her husband's plantation), and moved to California in 1849, the year of the Gold Rush. Some accounts say she fled to California to escape bounty hunters eager for the reward posited by planters trying to stop her role in the Underground Railroad.

The move to San Francisco opened opportunities to Mary Pleasant. She purchased a boardinghouse, which prospered due to her good cooking and hard work, and because accommodations were scarce in this area's booming growth. In this boardinghouse she met men who became California's political and business elites. Some say she provided wealthy (often married) men with attractive young women to accompany the traditional card-playing and drinking activities at the boardinghouse.

Most sources agree that Pleasant was the type of person who made the most of any opportunities that came her way. Some stories say she lent money at 10 percent interest. Others say she used her boardinghouse as a brothel to meet the needs of lonely men coming to California to seek fortune and adventure. Some records indicate she served as the executor of the estates of several black families. Heirs sued to regain the family monies, but failed to punish Pleasant for her unsuccessful investments. One clipping in the Schomburg files claims that she held the monopoly on black domestics in the state.

Most accounts support her civil rights advocacy and service to her race. Since California was declared a free state in 1850, many accounts attest to her rescue of slaves being held illegally in the state. In 1858 she traveled to Chatham, Canada, to purchase real estate. An account reported that this trip was used for a secret meeting with John Brown to finance his raid on Harpers Ferry. The biographers of John Brown have discounted this story, since John Brown had left Chatham months before Mary Pleasant's arrival and no other proof exists. A note found on John Brown signed W.E.P. was attributed to Mary Ellen Pleasant, but again that is unproven. What can be substantiated are her legal challenges in California that won rights for blacks in the courts. In 1863 she won the right of blacks to have their testimonies accepted in the state courts. In 1868 she sued the North Beach and Mission Railroad for refusing her passage. The California Supreme Court returned a damage action of $500 against the railroad for their discrimination. She sued another streetcar company that same year for a similar refusal of passage and won that case as well. What cannot be substantiated is the motivation for these suits. Since Pleasant seemed to be a person who cherished retribution, each could have been sweet revenge for personal slights. She also received satisfaction from helping members of her race. In addition to these legal gains brought to the race by Pleasant, she was also well known for acts of charity to black families and churches, for which she sought public recognition.

Following the Civil War, Pleasant moved into a mansion belonging to banker Thomas Bell on Octavia Street, and served as his housekeeper. Known as the "House of Mystery," the mansion became the center of her power and the source of her funds until Bell's death in 1892. Her greatest notoriety came when one of Bell's rivals, a William Sharon, was sued for divorce in 1881. Sharon, a former resident of Pleasant's boardinghouse, had moved to Nevada to seek his fortune in mining and had become a senator from that state. Sarah Althea Hill sued Sharon for divorce using a forged marriage contract to gain a division of his property.

Court records indicate that Hill had been introduced to Sharon by Mary Pleasant, who in fact had advised Hill on this scheme to gain Sharon's fortune. The federal judge disallowed Hill's claims and attributed the scheme to Mary Pleasant.

Pleasant's later years contrasted to her early rise in fortune and power. She was evicted from the Bell estate after a quarrel with Theresa Bell. In June 1899 Pleasant was declared financially insolvent in bankruptcy court. In frail health and hungry, Pleasant was visited by an old friend, Mrs. Lyman Sherwood, who moved Mary into their home. She died there on January 11, 1904 and was buried in the Sherwood burial lot in the Tulocay Cemetery in Napa, California. Before she died, Pleasant transferred her property to a friend, Samuel Post Davis, with the stipulation that the funds would be used to continue her lawsuits against the Bell estate. Again, legal revenge went beyond her death. Little is known about the outcome of those suits.

Mary "Mammy" Pleasant had no children, and few records exist about her husband after the couple's arrival in California. Her legacy details a rise to the heights of entrepreneurial acquisition and a descent into the depths of extortion and manipulation. Fact can be determined in only the legal cases. The remaining details are obscured. As a California pioneer, Mammy Pleasant's life reflects the variation of human behavior and legend of frontier settlement.

—Dorothy C. Salem

Bibliography

Although some material can be found in the Clipping File of the Schomburg Center for Research in Black Culture, New York Public Library, and in the Bancroft Library, University of California at Berkeley, the best sources exist in the press. Delilah Beasley examined many of these sources for her book detailing black female pioneers, *The Negro Trailblazers of California* (Los Angeles: Times Mirror Publishing, 1919). The legal cases can be found in *Reports of Cases Determined in the Supreme Court of the State of California, at the October Term, 1867 and January Term, 1868*, Vol. 34 (San Francisco: Bancroft-Whitney, 1887); and the *Hastings Law Journal* 17 (1965– 1966), Hastings College of Law, University of California. The newspapers to be consulted include the *San Francisco Examiner* (October 13, 1895; January 1, 1904); *Oakland Tribune* (September 3, 1916); *San Francisco Chronicle* (July 9, 1899; January 12, 1904); *Daily Alta Californian* (October 18, 1866); *San Francisco Call* (May 7, 1899); and *San Francisco Call-Bulletin* (October 30, 1933).

Biographical sketches include W. Sherman Savage, "Mary Ellen Pleasant," *Notable American Women* III, edited by Edward T. James, et al. (Cambridge: Belnap Press, 1971), pp. 75–77; and Helena Woodard, "Mary Ellen Pleasant "Mammy Pleasant," in *Notable Black American Women*, edited by Jessie Carney Smith (Detroit: Gale, 1992), pp. 858–862.

Secondary sources that often create the Pleasant legend include Charles C. Dobie, *San Francisco: A Pageant* (New York: Appleton-Century, 1939); Helen Holdredge, *Mammy Pleasant* (New York: Putnam, 1953); Sue Thurman, *Pioneers of Negro Origin in California* (San Francisco: Acme Publishing, 1952); John P. Young, *San Francisco:*

A History of the Pacific Coast Metropolis (San Francisco, Chicago: S.J. Clarke, 1912); Stephen J. Field, *Personal Reminiscences of Early Days in California* (Washington, DC: Author, 1893); and Samuel Post Davis, *Pandex of the Press* (San Francisco: n.p., 1902).

PORTER, DOROTHY [BURNETT] (b. 1905), curator, librarian, and researcher in the history of black women, was born on May 25 in Warrenton, Virginia, to Hayes Joseph Burnett, a physician, and Bertha (Ball), a professional tennis player. One of three daughters and a brother, Dorothy Burnett attended school in the middle-class suburb of Montclair, New Jersey. She came to Washington, DC, in 1923 to earn a teaching degree from Miner Normal School (1925). She worked as the librarian of Miner Teacher's College in 1925 and then worked as a cataloger with the responsibility to build a collection on the African American at the Carnegie Library of Howard University until 1930. At Howard University, she earned a BA degree by 1928 and then went on to Columbia University to gain the master of library science in 1932. She joined the Delta Sigma Theta sorority and remained an Episcopalian.

She married James Amos Porter, artist and faculty member of the Fine Arts Department at Howard University, in 1930. Her only child, Constance Burnett, was born in 1939. As her husband was becoming the head of the Fine Arts Department at Howard University, Dorothy Porter continued to develop the Library of Negro Life and History, soon called the Moorland-Spingarn Research Center, at Howard University. Walking the stacks of Howard University's library, beginning with the original gift in 1914 of Jesse E. Moorland's private library and the earlier gift of Lewis Tappan's antslavery materials, Porter isolated and organized approximately 3,000 items on African-Americana into a cohesive collection. The collection includes pioneering black newspapers, vertical file items, microfilms, prints, photographs, manuscript and oral history materials, and several three-dimensional memorabilia artifacts. By her retirement in 1973, the collection had grown to 180,000+ cataloged items in spite of years of controlled budgets, staffing problems, and reorganized support services. She received awards and fellowships to continue her efforts. In 1962–1964, she was a consultant to the National Library in Lagos, Nigeria, through a Ford Foundation grant.

The knowledge she acquired from these very collections became her richest resource. With ardor and intensity, she pursued every lead to acquire materials. Her contacts with book dealers, collectors, clubs, and organizations were efforts to create networks for the reconstruction of the African American past. By the time black studies gained acceptance as a recognized discipline in the 1960s, Dorothy Porter was a master of her craft and sought to teach others how to uncover the neglected history. She used these resources to compile several bibliographies and research aids. These include *Early Negro Writing* (1971), *North American Negro Poets* (1945), *Negro Protest Pamphlets* (1969), *The Negro in the United States* (1970), and *Afro-Braziliana, A Working Bibliography* (1978). Her other articles appeared in *Journal of Negro History, Howard Bulletin, Phylon, Journal of Negro Education, Bulletin of Negro History, Opportunity,* and *African Studies Bulletin.*

She continued her role despite the death of her husband in 1970. In 1971 she was awarded the honorary degree of doctor of letters from the University of Susquehanna, Pennsylvania. When she retired, Howard University dedicated a literary room on June 8, 1973, as the Dorothy B. Porter Room, Founders' Library. In 1979 she married Charles Harris Wesley, a historian of the African-American experience. After his death in 1987, she continued to receive honors: doctor of humane letters from Syracuse University (1989), visiting scholar at the W.E.B. Du Bois Institute at Harvard University (1988–1989), Olaudah Equino Award of Excellence for Pioneering Achievements from the University of Utah (1989), and honorary degree of humane letters from Radcliffe College (1990). She continues to reside in Washington, DC, reviewing her personal papers.

—Esme E. Bhan

Bibliography

The information on Dorothy Porter can be found in the vertical files at Howard University. Personal interviews with Dorothy Porter by Esme Bhan, archivist at the Moorland-Spingarn Collection, Howard University, have produced several papers. See "Dorothy Porter: Profile of a Collector," paper read by Esme E. Bhan at the seventy-fifth annual conference for the Study of African American Life and History, Chicago, October 1990.

For a listing of Porter's publications, consult Ora Williams, *American Black Women in Arts and Social Science: A Bibliographic Survey* (Metuchen, NJ: Scarecrow, 1978).

PRESTON, FRANCES E.L. (1844–1929) was a noted temperance lecturer

and civic organizer born in Richmond, Virginia to a free father and a slave mother. Because her mother was classified as a slave, Frances Preston was also a slave. When she was a child her family moved to Detroit, where she briefly attended a school for black children. Later, she learned how to play the piano and organ and taught music lessons. She was an organist for the Second Baptist Church of Detroit and a member of a concert group that performed in recital tours.

Preston was also interested in public speaking, so she enrolled in English classes at the Detroit Training School of Elocution and graduated at the top of her class in 1882. She returned to the school for more courses in elocution. Preston's interest in temperance and public speaking led to her activities as an organizer and lecturer for the National Women's Christian Temperance Union. Preston was active in other types of women's organizations. The first attempt to organize black women's clubs on a statewide basis occurred in 1898, when Preston and a group of Michigan clubwomen attending the annual meeting of the National Association of Colored Women in Chicago founded the Michigan

Federation of Colored Women's Clubs. Preston served as the president of the Michigan Federation for four years. Later in life, Preston became a Baptist teacher throughout the South. She taught at academies in Alabama, Florida, Georgia, Kentucky, Oklahoma, and Texas until her death in 1929.

—Julieanne Phillips

Bibliography

Few resources exist on the life of Frances E.L. Preston. Robin S. Peebles, "Detroit Black Women's Clubs," *Michigan History* 70 (January–February 1986): 48, places Preston within the club movement, as does Elizabeth Davis, ed., *Lifting as They Climb* (Washington, DC: National Association of Colored Women's Clubs, 1933). Sylvia G.L. Dannett's biographical portrait of Preston appears in her *Profiles of Negro Womanhood, 1619–1900, Volume I* (New York/Philadelphia: M.W. Lads, 1964). Another brief discussion of Preston's work in the temperance and club movements appears in Dorothy Salem's study of organized reform, *To Better Our World: Black Women in Organized Reform, 1890–1920* (Brooklyn: Carlson, 1990).

PRICE, LEONTYNE (b. 1927), grand opera diva, once ranked as one of the most celebrated sopranos of the contemporary era alongside Birgit Nilsson, Joan Sutherland, and Renata Tebaldi. A complex figure, Price emerged from her birth (February 10) in Laurel, Mississippi, to Kate (Baker) and James A. Price, to achieve international recognition for her musical skills. One of only a few African-American artists who had extensive formal schooling, Price received her BA from the College of Education and Industrial Arts (now Central State College) in Wilberforce, Ohio, in 1948. She received a scholarship to attend Julliard School of Music, where from 1949 to 1952, she studied with Florence Page Kimball. There, Virgil Thompson, the noted critic, saw Price in the student production of Verdi's *Falstaff*. He was so impressed by her ability that he chose her to sing in the revival of his *Four Saints in Three Acts*. She performed this role for two weeks on Broadway during 1952, married William Warfield on August 31, 1952, and then played the role of Bess in the revival of George Gershwin's *Porgy and Bess*. She played at the Metropolitan Museum in New York and at Constitution Hall in Washington, DC, where she introduced the works of Stravinsky, Henri Saquet, John La Montaine, and others. Under the auspices of the U.S. State Department, Price toured Vienna, Berlin, Paris, and London as one of the best ambassadors in cultural affairs that the United States had to offer. In between these tours, she was a recitalist and soloist with several international symphonies, one of which included an impressive tour in India.

By the mid-1950s Price had developed into a highly disciplined performer. A perfectionist, Price's voice improved with each performance. She made operatic history appearing in the title role of *Tosca* for the NBC-TV Opera Company. She also performed Mozart's *Magic Flute* (1956), *Dialogues of the Carmelites* (1957), and *Don Giovanni* (1960). A handsome woman with an imperial posture, she brought to each of her operatic roles a new dimension that did not fail to impress even the most critical of music critics. Recitals for the San Francisco Opera Company (1957–1959), the Vienna State Opera (1958–1961), and at the Brussels International Fair under the auspices of the U. S. State Department (1958) were followed by a lengthy recording career for RCA-Victor. The recording medium helped to enhance her reputation. She received a 42-minute ovation for her role as Leonora, as she debuted at the Metropolitan Opera House in *Il Trovatore.*

After this unique experience Leontyne Price had her first opening in the title role in Puccini's *The Girl of the Golden West.* In September 1966 she opened the Metropolitan Opera season in the role of Cleopatra in *Antony and Cleopatra,* an opera written by Samuel Barber. Barber and critics considered Leotyne Price's voice as the "perfect Verdi voice." When she sang at the opera house La Scala in Milan, Italy, she packed the house, convincing music critics that "some of the sweetest voices in the music world are Negro voices." She became a world traveler and soloist at the opera houses in Salzburg, Rome, Hamburg, and Buenos Aires, Argentina. Her honors and awards proliferated throughout the world.

She won Grammy Awards for classical performances, the Spingarn Medal from the NAACP, the National Medal of Arts (1985), Musician of the Year from *Music American* magazine (1961), the Spirit of Achievement Award from the Albert Einstein College of Medicine (1962), the Presidential Medal of Freedom from the U.S. State Department (1964), Schwann Catalog Award (1968), and the Decorated Order at Ment, Italy.

With such a busy career traveling around the world, Price did not neglect civic responsibilities. She served on the board of directors of the Campfire Girls, as honorary vice-chair of UNESCO, and as a trustee of the International House. She served as a fellow of the American Academy of Arts and Sciences and as a member of several organizations: American Federation of Television and Radio Artists (AFTRA), the American Guild Musicians and Artists, the Actor's Equity Association, and Sigma Alpha Iota and Delta Sigma Theta sororities. She has continued to record. Her records are considered classics in the world of opera. Her entire career represents an accomplished artist who has brought international fame and appreciation to African Americans for outstanding talent.

—Nicholas C. Polos

Bibliography

Leontyne Price has a file in the Schomburg Center for Research on Black Culture, New York Public Library, and in the Metropolitan Opera House Library. The biography by Hugh Lee Lyon, *Leontyne Price: Highlights of a Prima Donna* (New York: Vantage, 1973), provides an in-depth view of her life. For her place in the performing arts see Edith Isaac, *The Negro in the American Theater* (College Park, MD: McGrath, 1947); John P. Davis, *The American Negro Reference Book* (Englewood Cliffs, NJ:

Prentice-Hall, 1968). For further biographical information, see *Who's Who in Colored America* (Detroit: Gale, 1950); *Dictionary of American Negro Biography*, edited by Rayford Logan and Michael Winston (New York: Norton, 1982); Edward Mapp, *A Directory of Blacks in the Performing Arts* (Metuchen, NJ: Scarecrow, 1978); and Barbara Sicherman, et al., eds., *Notable American Women* (Cambridge: Belnap Press, 1982).

PRIMUS, PEARL (b. 1919), talented dancer, born in Trinidad on November 29, became one of the most well known interpreters of African heritage through choreography and dance on the American and international stage. Emily (Jackson) and Edward Primus brought their daughter to New York City to enhance her educational opportunities. She attended Hunter College High School and later Hunter College with the intention of becoming a doctor. Since she attended night classes, Pearl Primus needed to find a job during the day. Jobs were scarce during the Depression year of 1940, so she applied to the National Youth Administration (NYA). The agency found her the role as an understudy in a dance group. Primus had no formal training, but her natural abilities, vitality, and coordination helped her to master the medium of dance. In July 1941, on a challenge, she applied and won one of the scholarships offered by the New York City New Dance Group. When the NYA dance group was discontinued, Pearl took on a variety of jobs to make a living. She worked as a photographer, taught health education in the summers in Manhattan and Brooklyn, gave dance lessons at a camp, worked as a welder in a shipyard, served as a switchboard operator for the United Office and Professional Workers of America, and held many other factory jobs.

She had not given up her ambition to become a doctor, but her natural inquisitiveness led to her study of various dance techniques. She continued to work during the day and studied dance by night. Her debut took place at the New York City Young Men's Hebrew Association, a group that made their facilities available to young artists. Her performance with a group of four other dancers won rave reviews from the critics. John Martin of the *New York Times* urged her to form her own company. When, in the spring of 1943, she became a full-time entertainer with the Café Society Downtown, Primus finally decided to concentrate on her career in dance. She left Café Society in February 1944 to concentrate on her studies, recitals, canteen work, and teaching. To Primus, dance was a medium through which she could express ideas and views on the human condition. As she studied, she developed her own original techniques. By that fall, she applied her innovations in a ten-day run at the Belasco Theater with her troupe of four male dancers, a five-piece jazz band, a narrator, two drummers, two singers, and Josh White, a ballad singer, who sang "Hard Time Blues." She used the innovative technique of using a narrator to produce an overall portrait of the African-American experience. She introduced two new numbers, *Slave*

Market and *Rock Daniel.* Later that year, she played the Roxy Theater to present her *African Ceremonial* with 14 other dancers. Her "intellectualized choreography" depicted her ideas about democracy and African Americans. Her six groups of dances were based on the steps of the African and West Indian cultures and sought to express the dignity of her race. These dances evolved themes of social unrest, early racial experiences, the jazz and blues period, the "Negro problem," and democracy. She often used the technique of reciting poetry such as Langston Hughes's "The Negro Speaks of Rivers," and "Our Spring Will Come" with expressive dance. Her artistic range was wide and interpretive, so her audiences—white and black—were enthusiastic about her presentations. A strong sense of drama, fine sense of comedy, and the ability to communicate a story to the audience made her a "storyteller with rhythm."

Primus celebrated her cultural heritage, but felt African-American artists should be considered "regular" artists, not "racial" artists. Although she had offers to appear in motion pictures, she turned them down. Instead, she opened her own dance school in New York in 1947, spent a year touring the Gold Coast, Belgian Congo, French Equatorial Africa and Nigeria, where she took part in court and social dances and made a study of native rituals, which she later incorporated into her dances. One of the greatest figures in primitive dance, Pearl Primus received wide recognition for *Fanja* (1949), for which she was awarded the Star of Africa by the Liberian president, and *The Wedding* (1961). Her biggest fan was her husband, Percival Borde, who shared her love for the intricacies of dance. She served as the director of the Art Centre of Black African Culture in Nigeria, taught at Hunter College, and continues to lecture on dance.

—Nicholas C. Polos

Bibliography

For information on Pearl Primus or her career in dance, see *Who's Who in Colored America* (Detroit: Gale, 1950); *Dictionary of Women's Biography* (New York: Continuum, 1985); H.A. Ploski and R.C. Brown, *The Negro Almanac* (Detroit: Gale, 1967); Mariana Davis, *The Contributions of Black Women to America* II (Columbia, SC: Kenday, 1982); Edward Mapp, *A Directory of Blacks in the Performing Arts* (Metuchen, NJ: Scarecrow, 1978); Ora Williams, *American Black Women in Arts and Social Science* (Metuchen, NJ: Scarecrow, 1978).

PROCTOR, BARBARA GARDNER (b. 1933) is the founder, president, chief executive officer, and creative director of Proctor and Gardner Advertising Agency in Chicago, Illinois. To accomplish this task, she "rose from a ghetto to build a multi-million dollar advertising agency." Born on November 30 in Black Mountain, North Carolina, Barbara Gardner Proctor saw education as a tool of empowerment. She earned a BA in psychology, sociology, and English education from Talladega College in Alabama.

She moved to Chicago and worked in several advertising agencies before establishing her own agency in 1970, becoming the first black woman in Chicago to found an advertising agency. A firm believer that gender should not limit the amount of success a woman can achieve, Proctor proves her belief through her receipt of many awards and honors. She has received over 20 advertising industry awards for excellence, which include Clio Awards from the American Television Commercial Festival; Headline Award (1978); Charles A. Stevens International Organization of Women Executive Achievers Award (1978); and the Frederick Douglass Humanitarian Award (1975). In 1984 President Ronald Reagan named her one of the "Heroes for the 80's." She is also Blackbook Business Woman of the Year, Chicago Advertising Woman of the Year (1974–1975), and Small Business Woman of the Year (1978).

Proctor feels that even though she had so many strikes against her because she was black, a female, and over 30, she said that in most cases she made the obstacles into an advantage. As a result, Proctor is in constant demand in the business world and her diversified talent is reflected in her wide range of interests. She has served on the board of directors of Seaway National Bank; Northwestern Hospital; and Illinois Bell Telephone Company. She has also been associated in some capacity with the Chicago Better Business Bureau; Du Sable Museum of Black History; Girl Scouts of America; NAACP; Handicapped Organized Women in Charlotte, North Carolina; League of Black Women; Chicago Council of Fine Arts; and Lincoln Trustee, Office of the Governor.

Along with Proctor's outstanding achievements, she also maintains high standards in promoting family values in her business. Her firm refuses to accept cigarette and liquor accounts or accounts that portray negative stereotypes of women and blacks. She said, "Advertising is the single most important way of reaching everyone in America, and I feel a deep sense of responsibility for my work."

—Julieanne Phillips

Bibliography

Materials on Barbara Gardner Proctor can be found in Christa Brelin, ed., *Who's Who among Black Americans, 1992–93*, 7th ed. (Detroit: Gale, 1992); Thura R. Mack, "Barbara Proctor," in *Notable Black American Women*, edited by Jessie Carney Smith (Detroit: Gale, 1992); and Robert D. McFadden, "President's 5 Heroes for the 80's Seek to Share Their Spotlight," *New York Times* (January 27, 1984). Interviews with Proctor appear in Millie Ball, "Ad Whiz Was on Her Way with Her First SBA Loan," *New Orleans Times-Picayune* (April 30, 1984), and Richie L. Francke, "Proctor Takes a Gamble and Hits the Jackpot," *Working Woman* 4 (August 1979): 19.

PROPHET, (NANCY) ELIZABETH (1890–1960), sculptor and educator, was born on March 19 to William H. Prophet, an employee of the Rhode
Island Parks Department, and Rosa E. (Walker) Prophet, a homemaker. As the
middle child with a brother and sister, Elizabeth Prophet had to hide her drawing
because her family considered such activity impractical and frivolous. Few sources
consolidate her early life, as though her life "began" with her education in art.

In 1914 she entered the Rhode Island School of Design. Due to the "frivolity"
of the career she had chosen, she had to pay for her own education by working
as a housekeeper for a wealthy Providence family. In 1915 she married 34-year-
old Francis Ford, who had founded the Athletic Association and attended Brown
University. In 1918 she graduated with a degree in freehand drawing and
painting. She attempted portraiture to earn a living, entered art exhibitions, and
developed sculpting designs for wealthy patrons, but each activity led to racial or
artistic differences. Unhappy about the progress of her career and marriage,
Prophet went alone to Paris in 1922.

Nearly collapsing from nervous exhaustion, she rented a flat in Montparnasse
and began her sculpting. At one time she stole food from a dog's bowl to stave
off her hunger. She lived with artist Ellen Barrows in Versailles in 1923, but
moved several times over the next few years seeking inexpensive shelter. She
continued to sculpt. After studying with Victor Joseph Segoffin at L'Ecole
Nationale des Beaux Arts, she finished two busts. One patron provided money for
materials, which Prophet spent to create her first life-size statue, *Volunte*. She
tried to grow vegetables to provide for her own food, but she was nevertheless
admitted to the American Hospital in 1925 for malnutrition. While waiting for
a studio to be built and recovering her health, Prophet received a surprise visit
from her husband, who collapsed on her couch in a drunken stupor. With the
added burden of her husband, Prophet smashed the piece *Volunte* in 1926, vowing
to improve on the next attempt. She finally moved into her new studio in the
summer of 1926 to battle poverty and compulsion in new surroundings. She kept
up a rigorous work schedule and received showings in the Salon d'Automne. She
sent some of her works back to the Rhode Island School of Design and Boston
Independent Exposition for display in 1928.

Her models were always black subjects that reflected pride and humanity.
Because she lacked money to pay models, she would create sculptures of male
subjects in cafes, of performers, or from imagination. She worked mainly in wood
and marble, but also worked in bronze, granite, terra-cotta, and clay, and tried to
record all her works in black-and-white photographs. In 1929 she won the Otto
Kahn Prize for *Head of a Negro*, which was exhibited at the International House
in New York that year. She lived with the family of W.E.B. Du Bois while she
stayed in New York and was a celebrated guest of the social and intellectual
leaders in the area. Her wood sculpture *Discontent* received First Prize in the
Newport Art Association competition in 1930. Despite her success, she contin-

ued to experience economic deprivation. When she returned to Paris, she had $500 with which to begin her work anew.

Although she was unable to get financial help from African Americans during the Great Depression, she eventually found French patrons Edouard and Julia Champion. With their assistance, she began again. After living several months in solitary existence, she created a woman's head in marble, *Silence*, and a man's head of white marble, *Laughing Man*. She also created *Poise*, *Peace*, and *Congolaise*, all of which were displayed in the United States in 1932. *Discontent* won the Richard B. Greenough Grand Prize of $75 and *Congolaise*, her best known piece, with a warrior headdress, was purchased by the Whitney Museum in New York.

To share her knowledge with others, Prophet became the artist-in-residence at Atlanta University. Never escaping from her poverty nor her drive to produce artistic works, Prophet had to seek employment as a housekeeper during her later years, despite her bad health. She died of a heart attack in December 1960. A former employer raised the funds for her burial.

Leaving no will, Prophet left no records as to the location of her works. Less than ten are in collections; many seem to have disappeared, rotted outdoors, or been destroyed by Prophet herself due to her dissatisfaction. Their existence has been recorded only in the photographs she so wisely took.

—Kelle S. Taha

Bibliography

Much of Elizabeth Prophet's correspondence can be found in the W.E.B. Du Bois Papers, University of Massachusetts, Amherst. She was featured in several articles in *The Crisis* 38 (September 1931): 308; 39 (August 1932): 259; 39 (October 1932): 315; 36 (December 1929): 407, 427. See also, Countee Cullen, "Elizabeth Prophet," *Opportunity* 8 (July 1930): 204–205 (contains photos of her work); Blossom S. Kirschenbaum, "Nancy Elizabeth Prophet: Sculptor," *Sage* 4 (Spring 1987): 45–52 (contains photos of her work); Gary Reynolds, *Against the Odds: African American Artists and the Harmon Foundation* (Newark: Newark Museum, 1989) (contains photos of her work); and Marianna Davis, *The Contributions of Black Women to America* (Columbia, SC: Kenday, 1982).

PROSSER, NANCY ("NANNY")

PROSSER, NANCY ("NANNY") (c. 1770s–?) was a slave in Henrico County, Virginia, in the late eighteenth century. She was married to Gabriel Prosser, a slave coachman on the Thomas Prosser plantation in Henrico County and the leader of a conspiracy to revolt from the institution of slavery on August 30, 1800. Her involvement in the plot supports the contention that African-American women were regular and active participants with their men in the struggle for freedom.

While information is limited on Prosser, it is evident that she played a key role in the insurrection. Cooperating with her husband, his brothers, and other slaves, Prosser notified, informed, and recruited other African Americans for the cause.

On August 29, 1800, she informed a black colleague that her husband and 1,000 men were meeting near Prosser's Tavern the following night to be in their revolution. Afterward, the troops were to kill whites in the surrounding area and converge on Richmond with their stockpiled weapons. Her knowledge of the numbers of insurgents, location of the meeting, and strategies suggest that she was a well-informed, loyal, and active co-conspirator.

The conspiracy mission was foiled by torrential rains, two slave informants, and by the Governor James Monroe of Virginia, who upon hearing the news called out the militia. The insurrection heightened white fears in slave communities, and conspirators were quickly hunted, captured, tried, and punished. Little is known of Nanny Prosser's fate, but Gabriel Prosser was captured in late September 1800 and executed.

—Wanda A. Hendricks

Bibliography

Aptheker, Herbert. *American Negro Slave Revolts.* New York: International Publisher, 1943.

Marszalek, John F. "Battle for Freedom—Gabriel's Insurrection," *Negro History Bulletin* 39 (March 1976): 640–643.

Mullin, Gerald W. *Flight and Rebellion: Slave Resistance in Eighteenth-Century Virginia.* New York: Oxford University Press, 1972.

PURVIS, HARRIET FORTEN (1810–1875), abolitionist and women's rights activist, was born into the wealthy and socially prominent Forten family of Philadelphia. Harriet Forten was inspired to follow in her parents footsteps and work to end slavery. Her mother, Charlotte Forten (1785–1884), was a founder of the Philadelphia Female Anti-Slavery Society, and her father, James Forten (1766–1842), a freeborn businessman, was a well-known abolitionist. Together they worked to open their home to reformers and to provide a safe haven for antislavery crusaders. Harriet Forten Purvis followed her mother's example of raising a family and managing a household while still finding time to work as an antislavery crusader and social reformer.

The second of five children, Harriet Forten grew up the daughter of privilege and was tutored at home in music and languages. Her education instilled in her a love of literature and fondness for music, art, and literature, which led to her founding an African-American literary society, the Gilbert Lyceum.

On September 13, 1831, she married Robert Purvis, son of an English-born cotton merchant. By all accounts, their marriage was fulfilling, since both were committed to antislavery reform. Robert Purvis was president of the Pennsylvania Anti-Slavery Society and had established a branch of the Underground Railroad. Such an alliance allowed Harriet Forten Purvis the luxury of working closely with her husband in an age that discouraged women from working outside the home.

When not working with her husband, Harriet Forten Purvis continued abolitionist activities with family members. She attended the Anti-Slavery Convention of American Women in 1837 with her sisters, Margaretta and Sarah, and returned as a delegate in 1838 and 1839. Like her mother, she became involved in the Philadelphia Female Anti-Slavery Society and helped to organize fundraising fairs and bazaars, which raised over $30,000 by the outbreak of the Civil War. She joined the Free Produce Society in an effort to curtail profits from slave labor and toured with the antislavery lecture circuit as it traveled to the North.

In 1843 the couple settled in the township of Byberry, 15 miles outside of Philadelphia. There she entertained many noted reformers such as Sarah Parker Remond, Susan B. Anthony, and William Lloyd Garrison. Visitors described their style of entertaining as "uncommonly rich and elegant," and Harriet Purvis as "very lady-like in manners and conversation." Often their visitors were sheltered runaway slaves, hidden in a specially constructed room that could be reached only through a trap door. Purvis kept detailed records of the guests until the passage of the Fugitive Slave Act prompted the destruction of incriminating documents. Together, the Purvises helped thousands of fugitive slaves escape to freedom. At all times Harriet Forten Purvis received constant support and encouragement from her husband, for it was with him that she produced her finest work. Together with her husband, Harriet Forten Purvis found herself at the forefront of antislavery and Underground Railroad activities.

Unlike many of her white co-workers, Harriet Purvis knew that racial struggle did not end with emancipation. Therefore, she continued to work in the removal of barriers throughout the 1860s and 1870s in the American Equal Rights Association and the Pennsylvania Equal Rights League to gain the right to vote for African-American men and all women.

Her happy family life was clouded by the loss of three sons from her eight children: William, Joseph, Harriet, Charles, Henry, Robert, Granville Sharp, and Georgianna. Joseph died in 1852 at age 14; William, in 1857, died of tuberculosis, soon followed by Robert in 1862. Tuberculosis also claimed Harriet Forten Purvis on June 11, 1875. She was buried at the Friends Fair Hill Burial Ground in Germantown, Pennsylvania.

—Thea Gallo Becker and Julie Winch

Bibliography

The antislavery activities are chronicled in the records of the Philadelphia Female Anti-Slavery Society, Historical Society of Pennsylvania. Her reform work finds mention in such newspapers as *The Liberator*, *National Anti-Slavery Standard*, the *National Reformer*, and the *Colored American*. The journals of her niece, Charlotte Forten Grimké, are invaluable for understanding her life. See Brenda Stevenson, *The Journals of Charlotte Forten Grimké* (New York: Oxford University Press, 1988). The two best summary works on Harriet Purvis are by Janice Sumler-Lewis, "The Fortens of Philadelphia" (PhD dissertation, Georgetown University, 1978); and "The Forten-Purvis Women of Philadelphia and the American Anti-Slavery Crusade," *Journal of Negro History* 66 (Winter 1981): 281–288.

Harriet Purvis is mentioned only briefly in connection with her husband's abolitionist activities in the following:

Blockson, Charles G. *The Underground Railroad.* New York: Prentice-Hall, 1987.

Quarles, Benjamin. *Black Abolitionists.* New York: Oxford University Press, 1969.

Sterling, Dorothy. *We Are Your Sisters: Black Women in the Nineteenth Century.* New York: Norton, 1984. Contains information on the abolitionist activities of Purvis's daughter, Hattie Purvis.

PURVIS, SARAH FORTEN (c. 1814–c. 1898), the younger sister of Margaretta Forten, was a founding member of the Philadelphia Female Anti-Slavery Society and served on its board of managers. Sarah Louise was born to Charlotte (Vandine) and James Forten of Philadelphia. Around 1837–1838, she married James Purvis, the brother of wealthy abolitionist Robert Purvis. The two newlyweds moved to a country home near Byberry, near Philadelphia. That same year Sarah Louise Forten Purvis represented the Philadelphia Female Anti-Slavery Society at the Anti-Slavery Convention of American Women along with her sister Harriet, the wife of Robert Purvis.

Sarah Louise Forten Purvis demonstrated her literary skill through her letters on antislavery and women's rights issues. She also helped organize antislavery sewing circles and annual fairs. Under the pen names Ada and Magwasca, she published her poems in *The Liberator* from 1831 through 1837. She addressed issues of universal emancipation, equality of the sexes, racism in general, and racism among female reformers. Like the rest of her family Sarah Louise Forten Purvis believed that the contributions of blacks and women were invaluable to society. Therefore, she lost no opportunity to attack the vices of racism and sexism through her writings. Her most famous writings included her letters to Elizabeth Whittier, sister of the poet John Greenleaf Whittier (1835); her opening poem for the Anti-Slavery Convention of American Women (New York City, 1837); and her letters to the abolitionist Angelina Grimké (1837). Soon after the exchange of these letters, the Forten and Grimké families united through the marriage of Charlotte Forten to Francis J. Grimké in 1878. Sarah took over the household after the death of Margaretta Forten in 1875. No exact date exists for Sarah's death. She appears in the census for 1880, but is dead by 1898 when a relative is listed as the last surviving family member. She is buried in the cemetery adjoining the church, St. James the Less of Philadelphia.

—Jacqueline D. Carr-Hamilton

Bibliography

Most of the information on Sarah Louise Forten Purvis must be gathered through sources relating to her famous family or the antislavery movement. Some of the contributions of the Forten women can be found in the Grimké Family Papers in the Moorland-Spingarn Research Center, Howard University, Washington, DC.

Secondary Sources

Aptheker, Bettina. "Abolitionism, Woman's Rights and the Battle Over the Fifteenth Amendment," in *Woman's Legacy: Essays on Race, Sex and Class in American History*. Amherst: University of Massachusetts Press, 1982.

Billington, Ray Allen, ed. *The Journal of Charlotte L. Forten*. New York: The Dryden Press, 1953. Covers Forten's experiences from Salem, Massachusetts, through the St. Helena's Island period.

Birney, Catherine. *The Grimké Sisters: Sarah and Angelina Grimké: The First Women Advocates of Abolition and Woman's Rights*. Boston: Lee Sheppard, 1885. Refers to abolition and women's suffrage movements, papers, and speeches.

Douty, Esther Morris. *Forten the Sailmaker: Pioneer Champion of Negro Rights*. New York: Rand McNally, 1968. Provides the story of the Fortens for four generations.

Giddings, Paula. *When and Where I Enter: The Impact of Black Women on Race and Sex in America*. New York: Morrow, 1984. Highlights the contributions of the Forten women to abolitionist struggles.

Hull, Gloria, et. al., eds. *All the Women Are White, All the Blacks Are Men, But Some of Us Are Brave: Black Women's Studies*. Old Westbury, NY: Feminist Press, 1982.

Lerner, Gerda. *The Grimké Sisters from South Carolina: Rebels Against Slavery*. Boston: Houghton Mifflin, 1967. Highlights the abolition struggles of Sarah and Angelina Grimké.

Neverdon-Morton, Cynthia. *Afro-American Women of the South and the Advancement of the Race, 1895–1925*. Knoxville: University of Tennessee Press, 1989. Discusses contributions of African-American women's organizations.

Sterling, Dorothy, ed. *We Are Your Sisters: Black Women in the Nineteenth Century*. New York: Norton, 1984. Provides some detailed biographies of the Forten women.

Stevenson, Brenda, ed. *The Journals of Charlotte Forten Grimké*. New York: Oxford University Press, 1988 (five journals, 1854–1892).

R

RAINEY, GERTRUDE ("MA") [PRIDGETT] (1886–1939), blues singer,

born April 26, was one of five children of minstrel troupers Thomas Pridgett, Sr., and Ella (Allen). She was baptized in the First African Baptist Church of Columbus, Georgia, the town in which she was born and died. As the daughter of minstrel troupers, Gertrude Pridgett received exposure to the emerging blues tradition, a rather nascent development in American folk music. The blues, some say, were a deeper, more folk-rooted and spontaneous component of jazz. Apparently, there are no accounts of blues singing prior to the 1890s. Originally known as "one-verse songs" because of their repetition of a single line several times, the format gradually changed, and the songs became known as the blues. Experts have argued that these alterations may have been an attempt by African Americans to accommodate the requirements of guitar accompaniment within the strains of field cries and work songs. Nonetheless, the blues caught on quickly, first through tent show performances of vaudeville singers like Gertrude Rainey, the first great black female blues vocalist and teacher of the renowned blues singer Bessie Smith.

Rainey worked as both a singer and a dancer in the talent show A *Bunch of Blackberries* at the Springer Opera House in Columbus. She teamed with and then married William "Pa" Rainey in 1904 when they began to tour as a song and dance team working the cabaret, tent shows, and levee camps throughout the South. The Raineys had one adopted son, Danny, who worked in the family touring troupe during the 1920s. Gertrude Rainey's sister, Malissa Nix, was also a singer.

Rainey, while on circuit in 1902 in a small Missouri town, heard a woman sing "a blues." Rainey liked the song and incorporated it into her act, calling it simply "the blues." She went from there to become one of the most popular and famous of all blues singers. A craze for the blues mushroomed in the 1920s among African Americans. The craze affected both southern born and those recently uprooted and living in northern ghettos. Hungry for down-home music, this era featured the classic blues singers including, among the men, Huddie Ledbetter, Big Bill Broonzy, Blind Lemon Jefferson, Sleepy John Estes, and Peetie Wheatstraw. Their female counterparts were Bertha "Chippie" Hill, Mamie Smith, and, first and foremost, Gertrude "Ma" Rainey and her young protégé Bessie Smith. She recorded prolifically, most extensively for Paramount. Her entire output consisted of some 94 blues compositions, recorded between 1923 and 1928. Of those listed, 47 are regarded as her own. Twenty-six are definitely those of other songwriters. The 19 without listed composers are probably Rainey's.

Rainey, along with other female blues singers, created an expressive and bold professional style of expression often referred to as "classic blues." Her importance was only beginning to gain recognition at the time of her death in Columbus, Georgia, at age 73 of coronary heart disease on December 22, 1939.

—Donna Van Raaphorst

Bibliography

An excellent overall discussion of the blues and the place of Gertrude Rainey in the development of this art form is by David Evans, *Big Road Blues: Traditional Creativity in the Folk Blues* (Berkeley: University of California Press, 1982). For a sound foundation in black music consult Ortiz M. Walton, *Music: Black, White & Blue* (New York: William Morrow, 1972). Jazz promoter and teacher Grover Sales's *Jazz: America's Classical Music* (Englewood Cliffs, NJ: Prentice-Hall, 1984) is also instructive.

RAY, CHARLOTTE E. (1850–1911), lawyer and educator, was born in New York City on January 13, tracing ancestry to African, Indian, and European origins. Charlotte Ray was one of seven children born to the Reverend Charles Bennet Ray and to his second wife, Charlotte Augusta (Burroughs), a native of Savannah. Unlike many blacks in the United States during the mid-nineteenth century, Charlotte Ray came from a privileged home. Her parents could afford the luxuries of education and the arts. Ray's father was editor of the *Colored American*, pastor of the Bethesda Congregational Church in New York, and one of the most distinguished black leaders during his time. No doubt, Charlotte took her courage and strength from her father, who helped slaves escape by means of the Underground Railroad. This experience encouraged her to become a lawyer in order to combat the many problems associated with racism, sexism, and classism.

As a minority woman working in a profession dominated by white men, Charlotte personally faced these problems while pursuing education. Charlotte Ray attended the Myrtilla Miner's Institution for the Education of Colored Youth in Washington, DC. By 1869 she had completed high school and started teaching in the Normal and Preparatory Department at Howard University, where she studied law. She graduated from the Law Department in February 1872. Charlotte Ray was admitted to the District of Columbia bar. Because Washington, DC's legal code had been revised and the word "male" removed, her application did not cause commotion. Consequently, Charlotte Ray not only became the first African-American woman to obtain a law degree, but also the first woman admitted to the bar in the District of Columbia.

Charlotte Ray's failure to establish a substantive law practice was indicative of black's lack of economic resources to support her practice and racial and/or gender discrimination of whites to use her services. Ray, a lawyer with tremendous ability, vacated her practice for these reasons. Nevertheless, Charlotte Ray continued to fight for women's rights and racial justice. She became involved with the woman suffrage movement attending the annual convention of the

National Woman Suffrage Association in New York City in 1876. In 1879 she moved back to New York and taught school in Brooklyn.

Little is known of Ray's personal life. She was married sometime after 1866 to a man with the surname of Fraim. During the early 1900s, Charlotte Ray became very ill from bronchial problems. She died on January 4, 1911, from acute bronchitis. She was buried in the family's plot in Cypress Hills Cemetery in Brooklyn. Charlotte Ray's legacy is a testament of the pioneering roles women have played in American society.

—Valerie Grim

Bibliography

Alexander, Sadie T.M. "Women as Practitioners of Law in the United States," *National Bar Journal* 1 (July 1941): 56–64. This article discusses the role of women as lawyers in the United States, and analyzes women's ability to defend the laws of this country.

Hanaford, Phebe. *Daughters of America*. Augusta, ME: True and Company, 1882. This book describes the roles women have played and contributions they have made to the development of American society.

Howard University Catalogue, 1869–1872. Washington, DC: Howard University, 1869–1872. This catalogue shows the years Charlotte Ray taught classes and attended the law school at Howard University.

Logan, Rayford W. *Howard University: The First Hundred Years, 1867–1967*. New York: New York University Press, 1968. This research explains the evolution of higher education at one of America's historical black universities. It describes the roles and contributions of Charlotte Ray.

Ray, F.T. *Sketch of the Life of Rev. Charles B. Ray*. New York: Doubleday, 1887. This book describes the lifestyle and livelihood of the Ray family; it provides some valuable information about Charlotte Ray and those influences that helped to shape her personality.

Stanton, Elizabeth C. et al., eds. *History of Woman Suffrage*. New York: Source Book Press, 1970, Reprint. This historical work examines women's efforts to secure the ballot for themselves.

REED, ROSALIE A. (b. 1945?) was the first woman veterinarian employed by the Los Angeles Zoo, the third largest zoo in the United States in the 1970s, as well as the first woman veterinarian of a major American zoo. Born and raised in Mount Vernon, New York, the daughter of George and Rosa Lee Reed, Rosalie was interested in animals since she was a child, bringing home strays and caring for a menagerie of pets.

Reed entered Tuskegee Institute after high school graduation, working on campus as well as summer jobs in New York City, to finance her education. She participated in the rifle club, which later aided her when tranquilizing wild animals. While a sophomore in veterinary school, Reed became interested in exotic animals. She graduated in 1972 and was employed by several private practices on the East Coast. Friends at Tuskegee noticed an advertisement on a campus bulletin board for the position at the Los Angeles Zoo and encouraged her to apply. She took written and oral examinations and was hired in 1973.

Reed's daily responsibilities included maintaining good health among the zoo animals, performing surgery, and quarantining and examining new arrivals. Daily she determined the health status and dietary needs of the zoo's tenants, which at that time consisted of an assortment of approximately 3,000 mammals, birds, and reptiles. As part of her work, Reed aided in the rehabilitation of a California condor at the zoo. Afraid only of spiders, she housed a caged tarantula in her office to conquer her fear.

Reed, ardently interested in her African heritage, wore a turban while she made rounds at the zoo. Vivacious and outgoing, she interacted with the zoo staff and patrons, promoting the study of veterinary medicine and respect for animals. Despite her devotion to her zoo work, Reed admitted to interviewers that her salary was meager, especially considering the cost of living in California. Soon after she accepted the zoo position, she began study for a California veterinary license, planning to work in private practice in her spare time to supplement her income.

When criticized by a review panel that stated the zoo needed more experienced veterinarians, Reed refuted their charges with her observation that veterinary schools did not train students specifically for zoo careers; she also noted the zoo's lack of adequate funding and that the problems they cited were widespread in American and foreign zoos.

Reed promoted veterinarians as legitimate medical practitioners, noting that veterinarians studied equivalent courses as medical students in addition to specific courses devoted to techniques and practices unique to various animals. Also outstanding medical processes were frequently first experimented on animals. She considered veterinary training and practice as being more rigorous and demanding than medical work. Seeing herself as a role model for students at Tuskegee Institute, Reed enlisted more women and blacks to enter the veterinary field.

—Elizabeth D. Schafer

Bibliography

Bob Lucas, "Big Game Healer: Woman Is Chief Veterinarian at Los Angeles Zoo," *Ebony* (March 1974): 64+; and Joe Bingham, "Lady Veterinarian at Los Angeles Zoo," *Sepia* (October 1973): 36–41, profile Reed's veterinary career; Mike Goodman, "Experts Call for Major L.A. Zoo Reorganizing," *Los Angeles Times* (December 18, 1973) notes Reed's opinions of zoo conditions and her reaction to criticism of her veterinary techniques. *The American Veterinary Medical Association Directory* (Schaumburg, IL: AVMA, published annually) lists the geographic location as well as the professional activity of Reed.

The Tuskegee Veterinarian was published when Reed was a student, and William H. Waddell IV, *The Black Man in Veterinary Medicine* (Schaumburg, IL: AVMA, 1969) cites historical information about black veterinarians as well as female veterinarians and the development of veterinary education at Tuskegee Institute. J. Frederick Smithcors, *The Veterinarian in America, 1625–1975* (California: American Veterinary Publications, 1975) provides a national context, and Joseph M. Arburua, *Narrative of the Veterinary Profession in California* (San Francisco: by author, 1966), although predating Reed's arrival, discusses the practice of veterinary medicine on the West Coast.

REMOND, NANCY [LENOX] (1788–1867), her daughters, and her daughter-in-law belonged to a large and successful family in Salem, Massachusetts, and were part of the network of antebellum free blacks in northern cities. In addition to their contributions to their family's wealth, they were active in the abolitionist movement.

Nancy Lenox Remond was the daughter of free blacks Cornelius and Susanna (Perry) Lenox, who married in Boston in 1780; Cornelius Lenox, at the time, was serving in the Continental Army. Following the Revolutionary War her parents settled on land that Cornelius Lenox owned in Newtown, Massachusetts. As a young woman, Nancy Lenox studied and practiced the skill of baking and decorating fancy cakes.

On October 29, 1807, Nancy Lenox married John Remond at the African Baptist Church in Boston. Redmond was born in Curaçao, migrated to Salem in 1798 at age ten, and in adulthood established himself as a successful caterer. The couple had eight children. Education, hard work, and opposition to injustice were taught as essential family values. Daughters were also taught domestic skills. From 1835 to 1841, the family had a home in Newport, Rhode Island, to insure that the children would receive adequate education without the discrimination they encountered in Salem schools. Both black and white visitors, many of them abolitionists and/or members of other prominent free black families, frequented the family's home. Charles Lenox Remond (1810–1873) and Sarah Parker Remond (1824–1894), the Remond's best known children, both gained fame for their activities in the antislavery movement.

Thorough her culinary skills, Nancy Lenox Remond contributed to the family business and continued catering after her husband's retirement. Several of her daughters were also important in the development of the family's enterprises. The mother and daughters were also members and officers of the Salem Female Anti-Slavery Society, the Essex County Anti-Slavery Society, and the American Anti-Slavery Society, and contributed money and handmade goods to the New England Anti-Slavery Society and the Massachusetts Anti-Slavery Society.

—Marilyn Dell Brady

Bibliography

Dorothy Porter has described the Remond family and the context of their lives in Salem in "The Remonds of Salem, Massachusetts: A Nineteenth-Century Family Revisited," *American Antiquarian Society Proceedings* 95 (1985): 259–295. The activities of the Remond women and selected primary sources by and about them are included in Dorothy Sterling, ed., *We Are Your Sisters* (New York: Norton, 1984).

Articles on Sarah Remond also provide information on other family members. For example, see Dorothy Porter, "Sarah Remond, Abolitionist and Physician," *Journal of Negro History* 20 (July 1935): 287–293; and Ruth Bogin, "Sarah Parker Remond: Black Abolitionist from Salem," in *Essex Institute Historical Collections* 110 (1974): 120–150.

Primary sources that give information about the Remond women include directories and newspapers from Salem and writings and publications by various abolitionists. For example, Charlotte Forten (1837–1914) lived with the family and described them in her journals, and Maritcha Remond Lyons (1848–1929) mentions them in her letters.

REMOND, SARAH PARKER (1824–1894) was born on June 6, in Salem, Massachusetts, to pioneer black abolitionists Nancy and John Remond. She received her early education in the schools of Salem and Newport, Rhode Island, where the family lived between 1835 to 1841 to avoid the discriminatory practices found in the high schools of Salem. Her formal education was enhanced by contact with the reformers who frequented the Remond household. When she embraced antislavery work as a young woman, she was following a family tradition.

She expressed her growing abolitionist commitment through involvement in a host of reform organizations. Remond became a key figure in the Salem Anti-Slavery Society, the corresponding secretary of the Essex County Anti-Slavery Society, and a life member of the Massachusetts Anti-Slavery Society. On occasion after 1842, she toured with Charles Lenox Remond, her brother and one of the foremost speakers in the antislavery movement.

Appointed an agent for the American Anti-Slavery Society in 1856, she became one of the first African-American women to lecture regularly before antislavery audiences. During the next two years, she spoke throughout the northern United States and emerged as an effective advocate for the cause.

Remond saw in slavery a metaphor for the plight of her sex. As a result, she joined the women's rights movement and served as a delegate to the National Woman's Rights Convention in 1858. A frequent victim of racial prejudice, she also participated in the struggle for equal rights. Twice in 1853, Remond and her companions were thrown out of public places of entertainment because of their color. She successfully challenged such treatment through the courts.

In December 1858 Remond sailed to Britain to further her education and enlist British support for the American antislavery movement. Although she studied at the Bedford College for Ladies in London from 1859 to 1861, she also found time to deliver more than 45 lectures in cities and towns throughout England, Scotland, and Ireland. Remond, who was not hesitant to tell of the separation of slave families and the sexual abuse of slave women, became a favorite of English feminists and working-class audiences. With the coming of emancipation, she collected funds and clothing to aid the former slaves. In 1865 she published a tract for the London Emancipation Committee entitled *The Negroes and Anglo-Africans as Freedmen and Soldiers.*

Remond went to Florence, Italy, in 1866 to study medicine at Santa Maria Nuova Hospital. After receiving a diploma in 1871 certifying her for "professional medical practice," she established herself as a respected physician. Remond married Lazzaro Pintor, a native of Sardinia, on April 25, 1877. She died on December 13, 1894, in London and was buried in the Protestant Cemetery in Rome.

—Roy E. Finkenbine

Bibliography

Dorothy B. Porter has spent decades researching and writing about Sarah Parker Remond, but her fullest discussions of the subject are "The Remonds of Salem, Massachusetts: A Nineteenth-Century Family Revisited," *Proceedings of the American Antiquarian Society* 95 (1985): 259–295; and an article in Rayford W. Logan and Michael R. Winston, eds., *Dictionary of American Negro Biography* (New York: Norton, 1982). Remond's English years are traced in C. Peter Ripley, et al., eds., *The Black Abolitionist Papers: Volume 1, The British Isles, 1830–1865* (Chapel Hill, NC: University of North Carolina Press, 1985).

Most of Remond's known letters and speeches appear in the microfilm edition of *The Black Abolitionist Papers, 1830–1865*, edited by C. Peter Ripley and George E. Carter (New York: Microfilming Corporation of America, 1981). Her thoughts on the meaning of emancipation can be explored in her tract entitled *The Negro & Anglo-Africans as Freedmen and Soldiers* (London, England: Emily Faithfull, 1864).

RINGGOLD, FAITH [POSEY] (b. 1934), one of the leading Afro-femcentrist, painters, printers, quilt makers, and performance artists. She believes strongly in the liberation of black women. "My art is for everyone, but it is about me (my sisters)." Her belief in black women's liberation has never taken away from her commitment to the struggle for all black people. "As long as sixty percent (the female sector) of the Black population continues under its double oppression, Black people will not be free."

Ringgold was born October 8, and grew up in Harlem, the daughter of Andrew, a truck driver, and Willi (Jones) Posey, who became a dress designer. She attended City College, where she minored in education, since women were not allowed in the liberal arts program. While at City College, she married

Burdette Wallace and decided to become an artist, maintaining her professional name, Ringgold. She had two daughters, Michelle and Barbara Wallace.

In the 1960s, Ringgold used the civil rights and black liberation struggles as her subject. "Die," a 1967 mural depicting a bloody riot, shows abstracted blacks and whites bleeding against a grey sidewalk. Her Flag Series is notable for its searing social commentary, and her poster, *United States of Attica* has been widely reproduced.

In 1970 Ringgold was one of the first activists to challenge sexism in art exhibitions. When leading male artists withdrew their work at the Venice Biennale in protest against "racism, sexism, repression and war," Ringgold and her daughter, Michelle Wallace, organized a strike against the sexism of the very protesting artists. She helped organize an ad hoc committee that pressured museums to accept the work of women artists, and then an organization, Women Artists and Students for Black Liberation, ultimately resulted in an exhibition of a group of black women artists called "Where We At."

In 1971–1972 Ringgold was commissioned to paint a mural for the Woman's House of Detention at Riker's Island Prison in New York City. At that time, Ringgold was also involved in working with women prisoners who gave her ideas of what they wanted. "They wanted something stimulating to prove women could be rehabilitated." The mural uses African and Cubist motifs and depicts white, black, Latina, and Asian women as busdrivers, policewomen, doctors, basketball players, a Supreme Court judge, and a President of the United States. There is a white woman caring for a Latina child (in a reversal of tradition) and a woman being married by a female priest and given away by her mother. The mural is still in Riker's Island Prison. Unfortunately, in order to see it, one must either be an inmate or employee of the prison.

Ringgold's Slave Rape Series, also done in the 1970s, is a powerful group of paintings expressing the horror and brutality of slavery, while at the same time evoking great dignity and strength from pregnant woman about to be captured. These pieces are framed on gorgeous brocade designed by Willi Posey, Ringgold's mother, called *tankas*, inspired by Tibetan and Asian wall hangings.

Ringgold has taken her interest in African culture to produce female masks with beaded, fringed embroidery. She collaborates with her mother, who dresses them, and with her daughters, who write skits about the masks. She has produced many quilts dealing with the African-American experience using both rural and urban themes. Today Ringgold is represented by the Bernice Steinbaum Gallery in New York City and enjoys an international reputation as a spokesperson for black feminism and an artist with universal appeal. Since 1984, she has been a professor of art at the University of California—San Diego.

—Barbara Winslow

Bibliography

The most complete bibliography and catalog of Ringgold's work is found in Lynn

Moody Igoe with James Igoe, *250 Years of Afro-American Art: An Annotated Bibliography* (New York: Bowker, 1981). Several articles are devoted to Ringgold in "African-American Women Artists," a special edition of *Sage* 4:1 (Spring 1987). Other sources of information about the artist and her work include the following:

Bersson, Robert. *Worlds of Art.* Mountain View, CA: Mayfield, 1991.

Galligan, Gregory. "The Quilts of Faith Ringgold," *Arts Magazine*, LXI:7 (March 1987): 96.

Gouma Peterson, Thalia, "Faith Ringgold's Narrative Quilts," *Arts Magazine* LXI:5 (January 1987): 64–69.

Gill, Susan. "Faith Ringgold," *Arts Magazine* LXI:7 (March 1987): 96.

Lewis, Samella. *Art: African American.* New York: Harcourt Brace Jovanovich, 1969.

Lippard, Lucy. "Faith Ringgold's Black, Political, Feminist Art," in *From the Center: Feminist Essays on Women's Art.* New York: Dutton, 1976.

Nemett, Barry. *Images, Objects and Ideas.* Fort Worth, TX: Harcourt, Brace, Jovanovich, 1992.

Rubinstein, Charlotte Streifer. *American Women Artists,* New York: Avon, 1982.

Slotkin, Wendy. *The Voices of Women Artists.* Englewood Cliffs, NJ: Prentice-Hall, 1993.

Wheeler, Daniel. *Art Since Mid-Century: 1945–Present.* New York: Vendome, 1991.

ROBERSON, (MOTHER) LIZZIE WOODS (1860–1945), founder

of the Women's Department of the Church of God in Christ, was born a slave on April 5 in Phillips County, Arkansas. Reared in poverty by her widowed mother, she managed to obtain an elementary education, and by all accounts, she was a bright student, who at age eight was reading the Bible. Her earliest religious affiliation was with the Baptist church, an association that enabled her to complete her education at the Baptist Academy in Dermott, Arkansas, where she later became matron.

In 1911 Mother Roberson left the Baptists and joined the Church of God in Christ (COGIC). Founded in 1906 under the principal leadership of Bishop C.H. Mason, this group became the largest denomination of the Sanctified, or Holiness, church. Impressed with her piety and conscientiousness, Bishop Mason appointed her as "overseer" of women's work. Although COGIC refused to ordain or recognize women as elders, pastors, or bishops, Mason acknowledged that women were vital to the church and that they ought to be guided by other spiritually developed women. It was possible, he thought, for women to become important co-workers of elders, bishops, and church founders. Over the years, Mother Roberson created a powerful and well-organized Women's Department. Since the so-called Sanctified church was stereotyped as a church of the downtrodden and ignorant, many failed to realize that COGIC placed a premium on literacy and general uplift. Accordingly, Mother Roberson developed prayer and Bible bands for female members where general literacy, biblical literacy, professional achievement, and other skills were emphasized after one had achieved salvation and holiness. In a real sense, the clubs or study groups within the Women's Department closely resembled the clubs and seminar groups of the National Association of Colored Women.

Mother Roberson's contribution to COGIC was not solely limited to directing and coordinating women's affairs. In 1881 she married an Elder Roberson, and together they traveled as evangelists, preaching and establishing churches. Lizzie Roberson also worked diligently to raise funds for a national headquarters building for COGIC in Memphis.

She died in Memphis in November 1945 soon after she toured the newly constructed headquarters building.

—Betty Plummer

Bibliography

Cheryl Townsend Gilkes is the authority on women of the COGIC. Of special importance are "The Role of Women in the Sanctified Church," *Journal of Religious Thought* 43:1 (1986); "Together and in Harness: Women Traditions in the Sanctified Church," *Signs* 10:41 (1985); and her contribution on the women of COGIC in Rosemary Radford Ruether and Rosemary Skinner Keller, *Women & Religion in America*, Vol. 3, 1900–1968 (San Francisco: Harper & Row, 1990). Elder Felton Best, a historian at Ohio State University, is also researching women in COGIC. Another source for Roberson is *History and Formative Years of the Church of God in Christ with Excerpts from the Life and Works of Its Founder—Bishop C.H. Mason* (Memphis: Church of God in Christ Publishing House, 1969).

ROBERTS, LILLIAN [DAVIS] (b. 1928), union executive and organizer, was born in Chicago on January 2. She was the second of the five children born to Henry and Lillian Davis, Mississippians who had migrated to the North during the 1920s. Due to her father's poor health, Roberts's family was on welfare throughout much of her childhood. At age 14, she became a hospital aide. She continued her determination to complete her schooling. Lillian Davis graduated from high school with honors and attended the University of Illinois on a tuition scholarship, until financial problems forced her to leave.

In 1946 Roberts became a nurse's aide at the University of Chicago Lying-In Clinics, thus becoming the first black employed in that capacity. During the early 1950s her job became more and more demanding due to long hours and her having to perform additional duties without compensation. These conditions forced her to become involved in her union—the American Federation of State, County and Municipal Employees (AFSCME). Eventually, she became shop steward, and her aggressiveness brought her to the attention of an AFSCME organizer who persuaded her to leave the hospital and work for the union.

In 1965 Lillian Roberts left Chicago to work for the union in New York. She assisted with a social service workers strike and organized employees of 19 municipal hospitals. Organizing in New York was quite a challenge for Roberts, especially organizing workers on a statewide basis. Eventually, union officials agreed to strike to force New York's Governor Nelson Rockefeller to adhere to legislation permitting an election and certification of a union for state employees. Because of her involvement in this strike, Roberts was found guilty of violations under the Taylor Law, which prohibits walkouts by public employees. Her sentence of 30 days and a fine of $250 was the stiffest to date for violation of that law, forcing the NAACP to request a reduction of her sentence.

Over the years, she rose through the ranks of union hierarchy from shop steward, local official, representative, and organizer to international union staffer and, finally, 1967–1981 to associate director of New York City's 100,000-member District Council 37 of the AFSCME. She served as New York State's commissioner of labor (1980–1982). For these efforts, Roberts has received several awards: A. Philip Randolph Award, 1969; Woman of the Year, NAACP, New York branch, 1971; Sojourner Truth Loyalty Award, 1979; and Coalition of Black Trade Unionists, 1979. She was also awarded an honorary doctor of humane letters by the College of New Rochelle in 1973. She married a silkscreen operator and is the mother of three. Currently, she is the senior vice-president of Total Health Systems.

—Betty Plummer

Bibliography

An extensive oral interview with Lillian Roberts is contained in Carol Ruth Berkin and Mary Beth Norton, *Women of America: A History* (Boston: Houghton Mifflin, 1979). For a list of Roberts's awards and a brief biographical sketch, see *Who's Who in Black America*, 3rd edition, 1980–1981 (Northbrook, IL: Who's Who Among Black Americans Co., 1981; and *Who's Who among Black Americans 1990–1991*, 6th ed. (Detroit: Gale, 1991).

ROBINSON, IDA [BELL] (1891–1946), founder of the largest African-American Pentecostal denomination headed by a woman, was born in Hazelhurst, Georgia, on August 3. The seventh child of Annie and Robert Bell, Ida Bell spent most of her childhood in Florida. Known for her religious zeal, it was not surprising that she began her ministry as a teenager, conducting prayer services in various homes in Pensacola, Florida. In 1909 she married Oliver Robinson, and in 1917 the couple moved to Philadelphia, Pennsylvania. Robinson's enthusiasm for the ministry continued, and in 1919 she became the pastor of Mount Olive Holy Church, an affiliate of the United Holy church. Robinson's success as a pastor attracted many to her small congregation, especially women. By the early 1920s, women, who outnumbered male members two to one, were demanding a more active role in the United Holy church. However, the "threatened minority" prevailed, and the denomination ended public ordinations for women. Disturbed by male oppression, especially the restriction on female ordination, Ida Robinson embarked on a ten day period of fasting and prayer. After this, she separated herself from the United Holy church to found a denomination where women could be "loosed from the bondage of male domination." This new body, the Mount Sinai Holy Church of America, was chartered in Philadelphia in 1924. By all accounts Bishop Robinson was a great preacher. On Sundays, the church was filled to capacity with persons coming to hear her two- to three-hour sermons, which were interspersed with her vocal renditions of "What a Beautiful City," "Oh I Want to See Him," and other hymns.

Between 1924 and 1946 Bishop Robinson's denomination included 84 affiliate churches from New England to Florida. By 1946 she had ordained 163 ministers, 125 of them women. Moreover, she had established missions in Cuba and Guyana. Ida Robinson died on April 20, 1946, while visiting in Florida.

—Betty Plummer

Bibliography

Felton O. Best's paper "African American Women and Leadership in the Pentecostal Church: The Mount Sinai Example," which he read at the Annual Meeting of the Association for the Study of Afro-American Life History (Dayton, Ohio, 1989), is one of the best studies on Bishop Robinson. Professor Best has an ongoing interest in black women preachers in Pentecostal churches. The Fiftieth Annual Convocation Bulletin of the Mount Sinai Holy Church of America contains valuable biographical data on Ida B. Robinson and a historical sketch of the church. Charles Edwin Jones's *Black Holiness: A Guide to the Study of Black Participation in Wesleyan Perfectionist and Glossolalic Pentecostal Movements* (Metuchen, NJ: Scarecrow, 1987) contains biographical information on Bishop Robinson and the Mount Sinai Holy Church of America.

ROBINSON, JO ANN GIBSON (b. 1912), a principal organizer of the Montgomery bus boycott (1955–1956), was born in Culloden, Georgia. She was the youngest of the 12 children of Owen B. and Dollie Gibson. The Gibsons were prosperous farmers until 1912, when Owen died, forcing Dollie and her younger children, who could not manage the land, to move to Macon. There, Jo Ann Gibson was a serious student, graduating from the city's black high school as valedictorian. She later earned a bachelor's degree from Fort Valley State College, becoming the first of her family to receive a college degree. She secured a job teaching in the Macon public schools. She also married Wilbur Robinson and gave birth to one son whose childhood death left her embittered.

Later she moved to Atlanta, where she earned a master's degree in English at Atlanta University. In 1949 she accepted a position in the English Department at Alabama State College in Montgomery. Jo Ann Robinson recalled that Alabama State and Montgomery had many attractions for her. She became a member of the Dexter Avenue Baptist Church, pastored by Martin Luther King,

Jr., and whose membership included several of her colleagues. She also joined the Women's Political Council, a black woman's civic organization. Perhaps Robinson would not have become a prime mover in the boycott, had it not been for her personal experience on board a city bus. Soon after her arrival in Montgomery, she boarded a bus to the airport. Unfamiliar with the segregated coach and preoccupied with her own thoughts, she took a seat reserved for whites. She was shaken when the white driver stood over her and demanded that she move from the white section. She left the bus hastily and embarrassed and was never quite able to forget the incident.

Having learned that her experience was not unique, Jo Ann Robinson was convinced that the Women's Political Council should address the deplorable treatment accorded blacks on the city buses. Although members of the WPC met with the mayor, his advisors, and representatives of the transit company, they were generally dissatisfied and had considered the efficacy of a boycott. The arrest of Rosa Parks for refusing to yield her seat to a white passenger was the catalyst that moved them to concrete action.

Determined to see Parks vindicated, Robinson and members of the WPC ventured out at night, meeting at the college ostensibly to grade examinations. There, they drafted protest letters and coordinated plans for a bus boycott. On December 5, 1955, an estimated 50,000 blacks walked off city buses in protest. Approximately one year later, federal authorities ordered integration on Montgomery buses. The boycott was successful.

In 1987, when Robinson published her memoirs, she was retired and living in Los Angeles.

—Betty Plummer

Bibliography

The best available source on Jo Ann Gibson Robinson's life and work with the bus boycott is Jo Ann Gibson Robinson, *The Montgomery Bus Boycott and the Women Who Started It: Memoirs of Jo Ann Gibson Robinson*, edited by David J. Garrow (Knoxville: University of Tennessee Press, 1987). See also, *Women in the Civil Rights Movement: Trailblazers and Torchbearers, 1941–1965*, edited by Vicki L. Crawford, Jacqueline Rouse, and Barbara Woods (Brooklyn: Carlson, 1990); and Sara Evans, *Personal Politics: The Roots of Women's Liberation in the Civil Rights Movement and the New Left* (New York: Random House, 1979).

ROBINSON, RUBY(E) DORIS [SMITH] (1942–1967), one of the least known heroines of the civil rights struggle, was born in Atlanta, Georgia on April 25, the second of seven children to beautician Alice (Banks) and John T. Smith, a mover. She graduated from Price High School at age 16, entered Spelman College, but due to the interruptions of the social movement for civil rights, did not earn her bachelor's degree from Spelman College until 1965. Ruby Doris recalled that her interest in race issues began when she was rather young, since she had grown up in the Summerhill section of Atlanta—a neighborhood in transition, where sharp lines were drawn between blacks and whites. Moreover, she believed that the Montgomery bus boycott had left a lasting impression on her mind as she witnessed the "walkers" on television.

When the students conducted the sit-in at Greensboro, North Carolina, in February 1960, the impact of the direct action led her to join other students from the Atlanta University Center to become actively involved in the civil rights movement when she worked with the Atlanta student movement. In April 1960 she attended the meeting of college students at Shaw University in Raleigh, North Carolina, where the Student Nonviolent Coordinating Committee (SNCC) was formed under the guidance of Ella Baker. From 1960 through 1966 Ruby Smith participated in a variety of activities. In 1960 she protested against student arrests in Rock Hill, South Carolina, and as a result, she became one of the first people in the movement to serve a full sentence under the "jail no bail policy." This 30-day jail term left her with a stomach ailment that troubled her for the remainder of her life. She also became a Freedom Rider in Jackson, Mississippi, which resulted in a 45-day jail sentence in the Parchman Penitentiary, as she was charged with breaching the peace.

Although she spent most of her time working at the SNCC office in Atlanta, she also assisted the organization in several cities, including Charleston, Nashville, and McComb, Mississippi. Described as one of the hardest working people in the movement, she served as SNCC's personnel chief; performed various administrative duties, including keeping the accounts; was the key organizer of a summer voter registration project in Mississippi; and was the administrator of the Sojourner Truth motor fleet, which provided a pool of 100 cars for transporting civil rights workers in 8 states. In addition, in May 1966, she replaced James Forman as SNCC's executive secretary, a position she held until her death.

Forman believed that Ruby Smith was "far more, both to me and the organization, than just a vital prop in the administrative structure." She had some brilliant ideas, he thought, and was more politically sophisticated than the others in the movement. She married Clifford Robinson of Atlanta, the mechanic for the Sojourner motor fleet, in 1964. One son, Kenneth Toure, named after Sekou Toure, the president of Guinea, was born of this marriage. His birth, according to Robinson, restricted her activities, but she continued to do as much as she could for the struggle. When the call was raised for Black Power, she strongly supported the new direction.

In January 1967 she became seriously ill and died of leukemia in October of that year. Ruby Doris Smith Robinson's zeal for the civil rights movement earned her the respect of many persons who met her. Pulitzer Prize winner Alice Walker stated that Robinson provided "the germ" of her book *Meridian*. Walker noted, however, that her character Meridian was "but a sort of corner" of Robinson's life. Walker felt that Robinson had given all of her energy to SNCC and was treated "shabbily." She was remembered as a fighter, an organizer, and theorist of the student movement.

—Betty Plummer

Bibliography

James Forman, *The Making of Black Revolutionaries: A Personal Account* (New York: Macmillan, 1972); Howard Zinn, *The New Abolitionists* (Boston: Beacon Press, 1964); and August Meier and Elliot Rudwick, *CORE: A Study of the Civil Rights Movement, 1942–1968* (Urbana: University of Illinois Press, 1973) contain valuable insights into Robinson's motivation and involvement with the movement. Sara Evans, *Personal Politics: The Roots of Women's Liberation in the Civil Rights Movement and the New Left* (New York: Knopf, 1979); Jacqueline Jones, *Labor of Love, Labor of Sorrow* (New York: Basic Books, 1985); and Paula Giddings, *When and Where I Enter: The Impact of Black Women on Race and Sex in America* (New York: Morrow, 1984) place her career in the civil rights and feminist contexts. Her papers remain in the possession of her family. Articles also provide some additional insights and information on her role in the movement: "SNCC: Rebels with a Cause," *Ebony* 20:9 (September 1965); "Ruby Doris Smith Robinson," *Sage* (Student Supplement) (1988): 3; "Builders of a New South," *Ebony* 21 (October 1966): 10. Alice Walker's comments on Ruby Doris Smith Robinson and an excerpt from *Meridian* are contained in *Essence* 7:3 (July 1976). Her obituary in the *Atlanta Constitution* (October 11, 1967) and an article in the *Chicago Defender* (October 18, 1967) contain biographical information on Robinson. Her obituary appeared in the *New York Times* (October 10, 1967). She is featured in Bernice Johnson Reagon's biographical sketch in *Notable American Women: The Modern Period*, edited by Barbara Sicherman and Carol Hurd Green (Cambridge: Belnap, 1980).

ROSS, DIANA (b. 1944), entertainer, was born March 26 in Detroit, Michigan, to Fred Ross (a factory worker) and Ernestine Ross. Although she was raised in Detroit's Brewster-Douglass Housing Project with five siblings, often sleeping three to a bed, Ross was surrounded with musical influences and opportunities that eventually paved the road for her rise to international fame.

Ross was educated in Detroit's Balch Elementary School, Dwyer Junior High School, and Cass Technical High School (graduated 1960). In Cass Technical High School, Ross studied design, sewing, costume illustration, and cosmetology, and originally considered becoming a model or fashion designer.

Diana Ross grew up surrounded with music. Both her parents sang in Detroit's Olivet Baptist Church choir. Ross herself often sang at home and in school performances. Her most important musical influences, though, came from peers in Detroit who were singing and dancing on street corners in a time when Detroit was just emerging as a leader in the music business.

In high school, Ross and friends Mary Wilson, Florence Ballard, and Betty Anderson formed a girl's singing group named the Primettes (a sister group to the Primes, which later evolved into the Temptations). Betty Anderson left the group and was replaced by Barbara Martin, who also left the group. Although the Primettes were initially rejected by Berry Gordy at Hitsville Records (which later became Motown Records), they continued to perform at various local events and signed their first recording contract with LuPine Records.

After graduation from high school, the Primettes were signed with Hitsville Records. At first, the Primettes backed up other singers and groups, including Marvin Gaye, Martha (Reeves) and the Vandellas, and Mary Wells. They were then renamed the Supremes and were given further grooming by Motown Records. Their first album, *Meet the Supremes*, was only slightly successful.

In 1964 the Supremes were assigned new producers, Holland-Dozier-Holland. The new producers emphasized Ross's voice on the new recordings. The result was the Supreme's first million-selling record, "Where Did Our Love Go?" In the 1960s, the Supremes had 12 Number One hits and another 8 that reached the Top 10 in the pop charts.

In 1965 Berry Gordy gave the group further grooming. Diana Ross was not only groomed by Motown but also by the John Powers School for Grace. In 1967 the group was renamed Diana Ross and the Supremes. Florence Ballard left the group and was replaced with Cindy Birdsong. In 1970 Diana Ross left the group to pursue an independent career and was replaced with Jean Terrell.

Diana Ross's solo career blossomed into several different areas. Ross discovered the Jackson Five and encouraged their success. Ross's first solo single, "Reach Out and Touch Somebody's Hand," ensured her own success as a solo artist. Since then, she has had numerous solo releases and has been teamed with other singers, including Marvin Gaye, Stevie Wonder, Michael Jackson, Lionel Ritchie, and Julio Iglesias. In 1981 Ross left the Motown label in order to sign with RCA, but she returned to Motown in 1989 as a partner and an artist.

Ross also starred in several films in this period. Her first film role, as Billie Holiday in *Lady Sings the Blues* (1972), won her an Academy Award nomination. She later performed in *Mahogany* (1975) and *The Wiz* (1978), which were less successful.

Diana Ross has diversified into business as well. She began Diana Enterprises as a record production company and RTC Management Company in order to manage her own career and the careers of other new artists. Her other business ventures include Anaid Films; JFF (Just for Fun) Enterprises, which focuses on merchandising; Rosco, which is an advertising firm; and Rosstown and Rossville, which are publishing companies. Finally, the Diana Ross Foundation cares for charitable interests.

In 1971 Diana Ross married businessman Robert Silberstein. They had three daughters: Rhonda, Tracee, and Chudney. Ross and Silberstein divorced in 1977. Ross then married Norwegian shipping magnate Arne Naess in 1985. They have two sons: Ross and Evan.

Diana Ross's career has spanned four decades, and the singer has been recognized with many different awards including the NAACP Entertainer of the Year (1970), a Grammy (1970), and an award for the Best Television Special, "Diana" (1971). In 1972 Ross won a Golden Globe Award, the Golden Apple Award, the Cue Award for Entertainer of the Year, and the Gold Medal Award Photoplay. Ross was also nominated by for an Academy Award for her role in *Lady Sings the Blues*, and she won the Antoinette Perry (Tony) Award in 1977. Ross was inducted into the Rock and Roll Hall of Fame in 1988 and she has a star on the Hollywood Walk of Fame. Finally, Ross has been presented with citations from Vice President Hubert Humphrey for her contributions to President Lyndon B. Johnson's Youth Opportunity Program and from Coretta Scott King and the Reverend Ralph Abernathy for her contributions to the Southern Christian Leadership Conference.

—Lisa M. Reynolds Abu-Raad

Bibliography

The best interviews with Diana Ross include Pearl Cleague, "DIANA," *Essence* (October 1989: 70–72+); Susan L. Taylor, "Diana!," *Essence* (December 1985: 50–52+); and Louie Robinson, "Why Diana Ross Left the Supremes: Rumors Become Reality when Diana Goes Solo," *Ebony* (February 1970: 120–126).

Information on Diana Ross is also included in numerous reference works. The best of these articles include: John Futrell, ed., *The Illustrated Encyclopedia of Black Music* (New York: Harmony Books, 1983), Jessie Carney Smith, ed., *Notable Black American Women* (Detroit: Gale, 1992), Harry A. Ploski and James Williams, eds., *The Negro Almanac: A Reference Work on the Afro-American* (New York: Wiley, 1983); Donald Bogle, *Black Arts Annual 1988/89* (New York: Garland, 1990); *The Ebony Success Library: Famous Blacks Give Secrets of Success* (Nashville, TN: Southwestern Publishing, 1973); and *Who's Who in America*, 45th ed., 1988–1989 (Wilmette, IL: Marquis Who's Who, 1988).

J. Randy Taraborrelli, *Call Her Miss Ross* (New York: Birch Lane Press, 1989) is a fully researched but unauthorized biography of Diana Ross. Mary Wilson also wrote her own memoirs of the Supremes—*Dreamgirl—My Life as a Supreme* (New York: St. Martin's, 1986).

RUDOLPH, WILMA (b. 1940) is an internationally renowned field and track star and winner of three Gold Medals in the 100- and 200-meter dashes and in the 400-meter relay at the 1960 Rome Olympic Games, which earned her the nickname "Tennessee Tornado." This "fastest women on earth" started out as a sickly premature baby born June 23, the twentieth child in a family of 22, to Blanche and Ed Rudolph in Clarksville, Tennessee. In 1944 the town's only doctor concluded that Rudolph would never walk again, a result of polio, which rendered her left leg virtually useless. Her proud parents, who survived on a meager $1,200 per year, facing dismal poverty, humiliating Jim Crow laws, and scarce medical facilities, nursed Rudolph at home, refusing public assistance. Her mother, a housemaid and washwoman, undaunted and armed with deep Baptist faith, made homemade medicines and daily massaged Rudolph's leg in between weekly 50-mile bus rides to Nashville, where Rudolph received physical therapy. Her father, a railroad porter, hired private tutors to instruct Rudolph in the basics of reading, math, and writing during her long and painful convalescence.

At age seven, Rudolph expanded her circle of experience when she entered Cobb Elementary School. Shy and withdrawn, Rudolph was deeply affected by the often cruel jeering by her classmates, who thought her poverty and handicap shameful. Rudolph secretly vowed to pay them back by becoming someone so famous that they would someday have to respect her. In 1952, at age 12, Rudolph was finally able to walk unsupported on her own, closing one of the darkest chapters in her life. That same year Rudolph entered Burt High School, where basketball dominated her life, earning her the nickname "Skeeter," (short for mosquito) because of her quick savvy on the court. Rudolph often ran track, easily defeating her opponents. Though a great admirer of Jessie Owens, she considered track simply a fun diversion between basketball seasons.

The turning point came when her basketball coach, Ed Temple, invited her to train professionally at Tennessee State University. Ed Temple became a strong and important figure in Rudolph's life, encouraging her to strive to her highest potential. In 1956, Rudolph participated in her first professional meet at Tuskegee Institute; the beginnings of a brief but rewarding career in track had begun. That year Rudolph won a Bronze Medal at the Melborne Olympic meet and, after several conditioning triumphs, tied her own world record for the 60-yard dash. Throughout her remarkable career, Rudolph traveled widely and received numerous awards.

In 1962 Rudolph retired from track after a successful Soviet meet. Since her retirement, she has sponsored several inner-city sports projects and founded the Wilma Rudolph Foundation, a nonprofit organization dedicated to training young athletes and based in Indianapolis. She holds a degree in elementary education from Tennessee State University, and is co-author of *Wilma*, her autobiography. She married her childhood sweetheart, Robert Eldridge, had four children, and taught school in Clarksville, Tennessee, before the family finally settled in Detroit, Michigan. In 1981 she founded the Wilma Rudolph Foundation, an organization dedicated to training young athletes. She also serves as a consultant for health fitness programs and is an active member of Delta Sigma Theta sorority.

—Vivian Gartley-Hindrew

Bibliography

Rudolph, Wilma (with Martin Ralbovsky). *Wilma*. New York: New American Library, 1977.
Biracree, Tom. *Wilma Rudolph*. New York: Chelsea House, 1988.

Bontemps, Arna. *Famous Negro Athletes*. New York: Dodd, Mead, 1964.

Davis, Mariana. *Contributions of Black Women to America, I*. Columbia, SC: Kenday, 1982.

Gerber, Ellen W. *The American Woman in Sports*. Reading, MA: Addison-Wesley, 1974.

"Wilma Rudolph Changes Gold Medals to Dollars," *Jet* (January 12, 1978): 52.

RUFFIN, ADELE (c. 1880s–19?) is notable for her work with the YWCA as a field supervisor and a "special war worker" during World War I. From 1915 to 1917 Ruffin was the first executive secretary (organizer) for the Phillis Wheatley branch of the YWCA in Richmond, Virginia. In October 1917 she became a field supervisor for the southeastern district of the Y, stationed in Atlanta. This office covered South Carolina, Georgia, and Florida. She later became the field secretary for all black YWCA participants in the South.

Ruffin was an accomodationist; she pushed the rights of black women only as far as the white Y women would support. When black Y women were denied hotel accommodations at a convention in Des Moines in 1919, Ruffin did not protest this treatment. In contrast, Catharine Lealtad resigned her position as a Y secretary over this incident.

Unfortunately, other biographical information about Ruffin is not known.

—Susan Borchert

Bibliography

The best source of information for the activities of the YWCA women in the South is in the Archives of the National Board of the YWCA in New York City and in Lugenia Hope's correspondence in the Neighborhood Union Papers, Atlanta University Center, Woodruff Library, Atlanta, Georgia. Other sources that place these conflicts within a perspective include the following:

Morton, Cynthia Neverdon. *Afro-American Women of the South and the Advancement of the Race, 1895–1925*. Knoxville: University of Tennessee Press, 1989. In this text of black women's role in social reform and social welfare, Morton describes Ruffin's social work positions and tasks.

Salem, Dorothy. *To Better Our World*. Brooklyn: Carlson, 1990. Part of a series on black women, this book places the women in the larger context of social reform in the Progressive era. Salem discusses the above-mentioned controversy regarding the hotel accommodations.

RUFFIN, JOSEPHINE ST. PIERRE (1842–1924) was a leader in civil rights, the black women's club movement, and women's suffrage. She was born in Boston, Massachusetts, in August. Her father, John St. Pierre, was of full African and Indian descent; her mother, Eliza M (Menhenick), was a white woman from Cornwall, England.

Ruffin left the United States for England in 1859 shortly after her marriage to George L. Ruffin—who became a prominent legislator and judge. The couple parented five children. The Ruffins returned to Boston during the Civil War. Josephine Ruffin undertook volunteer work during the war with the Home Guard. She also mended and made clothes at the local Baptist church. After the war, she organized the Boston Kansas Relief Association (1879) to aid black migration to Kansas.

Ruffin founded and served as the first president of the Woman's New Era Club (1893) one of the member clubs of the National Association of Colored Women (NACW). In 1894 the New Era Club founded *The Woman's Era* newspaper, which Ruffin edited. She believed that the black women's club movement should be involved in temperance, morality, higher education, hygiene, and domesticity. Ruffin took great pains to make it clear that the black women's club movement was not racially segregated or exclusionary. For Ruffin, the club movement represented racial uplift, urban progressivism, and the crusade for women's rights. In 1895 Ruffin issued a call to black women's clubs to the First National Conference of Colored Women, which convened under her leadership. The various clubs met in Boston and formed the National Federation of Afro-American Women. This organization focused on the uplift of the black woman and the improvement of African-American family life. This organization merged with the National Colored Women's League to form the National Association of Colored Women in 1896.

The Ruffins were friends of both black and white leaders, who included such abolitionists as Frederick Douglass and William Lloyd Garrison. She served as a visitor for the Associated Charities of Boston and worked with Julia Ward Howe and Lucy Stanton on the Massachusetts Moral Education Association and the Massachusetts School Suffrage Association. When her husband died in 1886, Ruffin expanded her activism. She helped found the Association for the Promotion of Child Training in the South, the Boston branch of the National Association for the Advancement of Colored People, and the League of Women for Community Service. In 1902 she helped found the American Mount Coffee School Association and served as its vice president.

Ruffin was a member of several prestigious white clubs. She was the first black woman to become a member of New England Federation of Women's Clubs and was an active member of the Massachusetts Woman Suffrage Association.

Ruffin opposed the segregation of blacks at the Atlanta Exposition in 1895 and refused to participate in other segregated activities. She broke with Booker T. Washington in 1900 when he refused to use his influence or to take a stand when Ruffin and other clubwomen were refused admission to the Milwaukee Convention of the General Federation of Women's Clubs.

She continued to be active in club work until her death caused by nephritis on March 13, 1924. Her funeral was held in Trinity Episcopal Church in Boston, where she had been a member. She was buried in Mount Auburn Cemetery, Cambridge, Massachusetts.

—Emilie M. Townes

Bibliography

Some of the Ruffin Papers and incomplete files of the Woman's New Era Club are in the Moorland-Spingarn Research Center, Howard University, Washington, DC, and the Amistad Research Center, New Orleans. Published sources include the following:

Davis, Elizabeth Lindsay. *Lifting as They Climb.* Washington, DC: NACW, 1933.

Giddings, Paula. *When and Where I Enter: The Impact of Black Women on Race and Sex in America.* New York: Morrow, 1984.

Lerner, Gerda. *Black Women in White America: A Documentary History.* New York: Vintage, 1973.

Logan, Rayford W., and Michael R Winston, ed. *The Dictionary of American Negro Biography.* New York: Norton, 1982.

Moses, Wilson Jeremiah. *The Golden Age of Black Nationalism, 1850–1925.* New York: Oxford University Press, 1978.

S

SAAR, BETYE (b. 1926) is an artist who makes boxes, collages, and constructions of historical and social significance. Her work is filled with images of the occult, astrology, and nostalgia. Her best known work, a symbol of black militancy, is *The Liberation of Aunt Jemima* (1972).

Saar was born in Pasadena, California, on July 30, to Jefferson and Beatrice Brown, but grew up in Watts, where she watched the famous Watts (or Simon Rodia) Towers being built. The towers were built by Rodia, an Italian immigrant, who took pieces of junk—broken glass, bottle tops, and shards of crockery—and mounted them into cement. Saar believes that the towering spirals made a lasting impression on her artistic imagery. Another artistic influence was her mother, who was fascinated by the occult and believed that her daughter had special powers. Saar denies that she was a clairvoyant, but has remained interested in mysticism.

Saar did not make a decision to be an artist until she was in her thirties. She attended UCLA and earned her BA in 1949, married an artist, had three children, Lesley, Alison, and Tracye, and in 1956 returned to get teaching credentials. Instead, she became so interested in printmaking that she earned her master's degree in graphic design. At this time her marriage ended.

Saar's works such as *House of Tarot* (1966), *Window for Leo* (1966), *Black Girl's Window* (1969), and *Nine Mojo Secrets* (1971) include references to mysticism and the occult, as well as the use of tarot cards. In *Nine Mojo Secrets*, Saar uses astrological signs as well as African and Oceanic motifs.

Saar was very moved by the civil rights and black liberation struggles of the 1960s. She began to collect derogatory commercial images of blacks such as Darkie toothpaste, Black Crow licorice, and Old Black Joe Butter beans, in an attempt to expose their racist implications. *The Liberation of Aunt Jemima*, a mixed media piece, shows many images of the well-known symbol for pancake batter. One traditional "darkie" image has Aunt Jemima holding a broom and a gun. An inset shows a powerful grinning Aunt Jemima holding a white baby. A collage of pancake flour labels is the background. The symbolic image of "Mammy" became a warrior in the black liberation army. Saar transformed racist images by placing them in new militant contexts in the struggle to "free" Uncle Tom and Aunt Jemima.

Whitey's Way (1970) is a box full of white alligators and the sides are covered with American flags. This box is Saar's counter on the racist joke that blacks are "alligator food." Her concern with and sympathy for other people of color is shown in *My Last Buffalo* (1973), which memorialized the 1890 and 1973 incidents at Wounded Knee, Indian Reservation.

Saar's work, while clearly motivated by her African-American traditions and heritage, is universally recognized. At one show, an elderly Jewish woman told Saar how her boxes evoked memories of her Jewish childhood.

Saar's work explores many aspects of the religious and mystical. Her more occult pieces contain Christian, Moslem, and Jewish imagery. Saar was given a solo show at the Whitney Museum in 1975. In 1988 she had exhibitions in Tai Chung, Taiwan, and in Kuala Lumpur, Malaysia. She has continued to serve as a professor at Otis-Parsons Institute in Los Angeles, where she continues to live.

—Barbara Winslow

Bibliography

The most complete bibliography and catalogue of Saar's work is found in, Lynn Moody Igoe with James Igoe, *250 Years of Afro-American Art: An Annotated Bibliography* (New York: Bowker, 1981). Other information is provided in the following:

Cederholm, Theresa D. *Afro-American Artists: A Bibliographical Directory.* Boston: Trustees of the Boston Public Library, 1973.

Lewis, Samella. *Art: African American.* New York: Harcourt Brace Jovanovich, 1969. This book contains a short article on Betye Saar.

Matney, William, ed. *Who's Who among Black Americans 1990/1991.* Detroit: Gale, 1991.

Rubenstein, Charlotte Streifer. *American Woman Artists.* New York: Avon, 1982. This book contains the most up-to-date article on Saar, which places her in the context of the feminist art movement.

SANCHEZ, SONIA [DRIVER, KNIGHT] (b. 1934), activist poet and playwright, was born on September 9, to Wilson L. and Lena (Jones) Driver of Birmingham, Alabama. Her given name, Wilsonia Benita Driver, demonstrates her heritage, her first name taken from her father. She, along with a brother and sister, grew up in the most industrialized city of the South—Birmingham, Alabama.

She was placed in a context of social change. As the Supreme Court case *Brown* vs. *Board of Education, Topeka, Kansas,* was decided (1954), she was emerging from her teen years and completing college at Hunter College (1955) with a BA degree. She studied further at New York University in 1958. As her generation increasingly assumed leadership of the civil rights movement through the student sit-ins of 1960 and the Freedom Rides of 1961, she became an activist through poetry. Her Birmingham connection gave her a vantage point from which she evaluated the attacks of dogs on marchers in Birmingham (1963) and the murders of college students attempting to register voters in Philadelphia, Mississippi, during Freedom Summer (1964).

Poet Dudley Randall brought together young poets to express their rage through the black arts movement of the 1960s. Together with Don L. Lee, Nikki Giovanni, and Etheridge Knight, Wilsonia Driver formed the "Broadside Quartet," a group of militant poets, and became Sonia Sanchez, a name from her first marriage. Her poetry rejected the language of academia and took on the language of the streets, using lowercase letters, abbreviations, phonetic spellings, and hyphens. She responded to the frustration of the urban ghetto of the North, a region and people neglected by the southern civil rights movement and forgotten by white society. She married her friend and fellow revolutionary Etheridge Knight, produced a family of three children, joined the Nation of Islam, and absorbed the teachings of Malcolm X, the militant leader of the Harlem Mosque.

Her poetry reflected the cynicism of the youth of the urban North calling for "truth," raging against racial and economic oppression, and advocating revolution (total change). She took her message to universities as a lecturer and as a teacher. She served as an instructor at San Francisco State College (1966–1967) and at University of Pittsburgh (1968–1969). She became an assistant professor at Rutgers University (1969–1970). During this time she composed ballads, essays, and haikus filled with rich images of black life. Her writing was mystical, humorous, and militant in its discussion of manhood, womanhood, love, and family values. Her poetry demanded involvement and participation in social change. She captured ordinary people in her poetry, immortalizing domestic workers, laborers, numbers runners, and her father. She heralded the coming of new black leaders who spoke to issues as identity, pride, poverty, and compassion, such as Malcolm X, Jesse Jackson, and Margaret Walker.

Following the assassinations of Malcolm X (1965) and Dr. Martin Luther King, Jr. (1968), the government oppression of radical groups, and the emergence of conservatism, Sanchez left the quartet and became a single poet. She began to express the vision of a black woman and all the experiences that black women celebrate and endure. She continued to teach as the assistant professor of black literature and creative writing at Manhattan Community College (1971–1973); as creative writing instructor at City College of the City University of New York (1972); and as associate professor of English at Amherst College (1972–1973).

These years were prolific, producing published volumes of poetry and plays. Her play *The Bronx Is Next*, was published in the *Drama Review* in 1968. Her almost exclusive use of the one-act play form developed simplistic action combined with direct language to communicate the black experience to the audience. Due to the rich auditory quality of her work, she recorded her poems on audiotape that same year on *Sonia Sanchez* (Pacifica Tape Library 1968). Her anthology, *Homecoming Poems* (1969), was followed by two plays: *We a BaddDDD People* (1970) performed at Theatre Blac'd in New York City that same year, and *Sister Sonji* (1970). She published poetry anthologies, *Liberation Poems* (1970) and *It's a New Day: Poems for Young Brothas and Sistuhs* (1971), while recording *A Sun Lady for All Seasons Reads Her Poetry* (1971) and *Sonia Sanchez and Robert Bly*

(1971); publishing a short story, "After Saturday Night Comes Sunday," in *Black World* (March 1971); and publishing the play *Dirty Hearts*. Her membership in the Nation of Islam influenced two products of 1972: *Ima Talking about the Nation of Islam*, a poetry collection, and *Malcolm/Man Don't Live Here No Mo'*, a play produced at Black Theatre.

By 1972 Sanchez started to win recognition for her work with a monetary award of $1,000 by the American Academy of Arts and Letters and with the PEN Writing Award. In 1973 she received an honorary doctorate in fine arts from Wilberforce University and edited *We Be Word Sorcerers*, an anthology of works by black women writers. That same year she published collected works of poetry: *A Blues Book for Blue Black Magical Women, Love Poems*, and *The Adventures of Fathead, Smallhead and Squarehead*. Her play, *Uh, Huh: But How It Free Us?*, was published in *The New Lafayette Theatre Presents: Plays with Aesthetic Comments by Six Black Playwrights* (1974). The following year, she recorded a few of these poems on *Sonia Sanchez: Selected Poems, 1974* for Watershed Intermedia in 1975. In 1977–1978, she received the National Education Association Award, which carried a monetary gift to help her continue her creative work, and published *I've Been a Woman*, a collection of poems reflecting her gender issues and experiences.

By the 1980s Sonia Sanchez added more publications reflecting her creative growth and received further honors for her work. She published a book of poems, *A Sound Investment*, in 1980; *I've Been a Woman: New and Selected Poems* and *Crisis in Culture: Two Speeches by Sonia Sanchez*, in 1981. In 1982 she recorded *IDKT: Capturing Facts about the Heritage of Black Americans*, was named an Honorary Citizen of Atlanta, and received the Tribute to Black Womanhood Award from Smith College. She received both the Lucretia Mott Award from Women's Way and the National Education Association Award in 1984. Her collection *Homegirls and Handgrenades* (1985) won her the American Book Award in 1985. Completing another book of poems, *Under a Soprana Sky* (1987), Sanchez returned to teaching as the poet-in-residence at Spelman College (1988–1989) and has continued as professor of English and poet-in-residence at Temple University from then until the present. Her latest publications include *Shake Down Memory* and *Continuous Fire*, both collections of poetry published in 1992. Her other awards include Outstanding Arts Award from the Pennsylvania Coalition of 100 Black Women, and the Community Service Award from the National Black Caucus of State Legislatures. Her community and professional responsibilities continue through her service on the Pennsylvania Council on the Arts, her sponsorship of the Women's International League for Peace and Freedom, and her lectures to student groups, the latest of which was at Cleveland State University on October 31, 1992.

—Beth Schneider

Bibliography

The best sources of information about Sanchez apart from her own works are collections of literary criticism and reference sources on women writers.

Basel, Marilyn K. "Sonia Sanchez," *Black Writers*. Detroit: Gale, 1989.

Brooks, A. Russell. "Motif of Dynamic Change in Black Revolutionary Poetry," *CLA Journal* 15 (September 1971): 27–36.

Clarke, Sebastian. "Sonia Sanchez and Her Work," *Black World* (June 1971): 45–48, 96–97.

Contemporary Literary Criticism. Detroit: Gale, 1976.

Davis, Marianna W., ed. *Contributions of Black Women to America*. Columbia, SC: Kenday, 1982.

Evans, Mari. *Black Women Writers: A Critical Evaluation*. New York: Doubleday, 1984.

Lee, Donald L. "The Poets and Their Poetry," in *Dynamite Voices I: Black Poets of the 1960's*, edited by Don Lee. Detroit: Broadside Press, 1971.

Lesniak, James G. *Contemporary Authors*. Detroit: Gale, 1992.

Shockley, Ann A., and Sue P. Chandler, eds. *Living Black American Authors*. New York: Bowker, 1973.

Tate, Claudia. *Black Women Writers at Work*. New York: Continuum, 1983.

Wade-Gayles, Gloria. "Sonia Sanchez," in *Notable Black American Women*, edited by Jessie Carney Smith. Detroit: Gale, 1992.

Williams, Ora. *American Black Women in the Arts and Social Sciences: A Bibliographic Survey*. Metuchen, NJ: Scarecrow, 1973.

SCHUYLER, PHILIPPA DUKE (1931–1967), composer, pianist, and writer, was born in New York during the Depression to George Schuyler, controversial editor of the *Pittsburgh Courier*, and Josephine (Cogdell) Schuyler, a white artist. She began her career as a child prodigy and ended her career as an American journalist, dying in a helicopter crash in Vietnam on May 9, 1967. Both parents believed that the mixing of races could produce children of hybrid strength and intelligence. They met in 1927 when "Jody" Cogdell left her childhood mansion in west Texas to come to New York City to meet George Schuyler, a journalist of progressive ideas and exciting wit. She soon moved into Schuyler's apartment in Harlem, and they married. Their daughter Philippa, named after Philip of Macedonia and Philip Schuyler, a war hero of the American Revolution, became their experiment combining the best of nature and nurture.

Philippa's meals consisted of fresh, uncooked fruits and vegetables, steamed fish, and no red meat, sugar, sodas, nor artificial ingredients. She was taught to read and write as a toddler and to play the piano by age four. By five, she composed music, wrote poetry, and performed Mozart. Isolated from American prejudices and from other children her age, Philippa received most of her education from tutors and a brief stay at the Convent School near Manhattanville College in Harlem. She graduated from the eighth grade at Sacred Heart

Annunciation Girls School at age ten, at which time New York University tested her IQ at 185. Then she attended Father Young's High School.

So much had been achieved as a child. Performing by age five, profiled by the white press, featured by the National Guild of Piano Teachers, and highlighted by the New York World's Fair, Philippa Schuyler became the youngest member of the National Association of American Composers and Conductors at age ten. By 11, she had over 100 compositions written for the piano. At age 14, her entry, *Manhattan Nocturne*, in the young composer's contest at Detroit's Grinnell Foundation won two prizes: originality and technical skill. The piece was performed by the New York Philharmonic Symphony Orchestra, the Chicago Symphony, and the San Francisco Symphony. She made her first major New York appearance at age 15 performing Saint Saen's "Piano Concerto in G Minor" with the New York Philharmonic before a crowd of 12,000 at the Lewisohn Stadium. Although she had no time to attend college during her performance tours, her parents arranged for tutors to teach her languages, humanities, and social sciences. Not yet out of adolescence, Philippa Schuyler had become her parents' creation.

As she lost the image of child prodigy, Philippa Schuyler met personal and career barriers. Racial and sexual discrimination in the professional musical field lessened her performances to white audiences in the United States. She traveled to Latin America, Europe, Africa, and Asia, performing to audiences who appreciated her music and accepted her identity. She performed before Queen Elizabeth, the Malaysian prince, and King Kalonji of the Baluba tribe in Africa. She performed at the inauguration of three presidents in Haiti; at the Congo Independence Day celebration before Haile Selassie, Lumumba, and Kasavubu; at the Ghana independence celebration before President Nkrumah; and at the Lamberene leper colony before Albert Schweitzer. Although ranked as exceptional by American critics, she never performed for any American leader. Her career was an American tragedy. A total product of America, Philippa Schuyler had to leave the United States to survive in her field.

Her travels throughout the world became necessary to her career, yet travel expanded her interests beyond music. As performance fees lessened in 1960, she became a journalist and writer. She had the language skills and intelligence for these fields. She spoke French, Spanish, and Italian, and could read many others, including Arabic. During the last 10 years of her life, she performed, traveled, and wrote articles in over 80 countries. Syndicated by UPI and NANA, Philippa Schuyler wrote more than 100 newspaper and magazine articles for European and American journals for the 7 years of her journalistic career. She wrote four books during these years of constant travel. In 1960 her biographical profile, *Adventures in Black and White*, examined the triumphs and troubles of double identity. In 1962 she examined the results of Congo independence in *Who Killed the Congo?*

When she returned to the United States at the end of 1962, her conflict over racial identity became apparent. She chose to pass as white in South Africa, to perform for white audiences, and to further her concert career. She applied for her passport under the name Felipa Monterro y Schuyler, a name that reflected her Iberian-American heritage until 1966, when she dropped the Schuyler name and traveled as Felipa Monterro. Then, she could use her talents without being referred to as the daughter of the black journalist. As Monterro, she tried to regain a reputation as a concert pianist through an April 1963 debut in Switzerland, but she received poor reviews. Although separated from her controlling mother by thousands of miles, she dutifully wrote her mother daily. She struggled for an independence that was impossible due to her heritage from these two powerful parents.

She was a paradox. Of extremely high intelligence and training, she nevertheless consulted mediums and tarot cards before making decisions. Raised to hold liberal views of race and culture, she gradually moved to the right in her political opinions. Late in 1963, she offered her speaking services to the John Birch Society. She earned lecture fees from several speeches on "The Red Menace in Africa," after she proved that Felipa Monterro spoke flawless English. Ultra-conservative views mixed with her disciplined regimen forbidding smoking, drinking, and the consumption of meat or processed foods created a complex personality.

Her writing increasingly reflected these conflicts. Her unpublished fiction was autobiographical. The novel about a confused identity, *Appasionata*, was followed by an eighteenth-century novel about the problems of women, *Sophie Daw*. Her nonfictional publication *Jungle Saints* (1963) was her third book—a tribute to missionaries in Africa. Two years later, she collaborated with her mother in writing a scientific study of dream interpretations, *Kingdom of Dreams*, published in 1966.

These complexities again appeared in her final trip to Vietnam. She completed a book about the Vietnam War, *Good Men Die*, which reported on the overcrowded and undermanned hospitals, the carnage, and the suffering of soldiers and civilians. Published posthumously, the book provided an analysis of the political complexities, while describing the land and people. She also started a novel, *Dau Tranh*, the tragic story about an illegitimate, mixed-race young woman in Vietnam. While on assignment for the *Manchester Union Leader*, her helicopter crashed in Vietnam. She died on May 9, 1967. The perfect child prodigy of hybrid strength was denied the promise of independence and adulthood. She died an American journalist with an alternate identity in a foreign country.

—Beth Schneider

Bibliography

The life of Philippa Schuyler is filled with complexities. The Schomburg Center for Research in Black Culture has manuscripts, journals, letters, and papers on the Schuyler family. The George Arents Research Library at Syracuse University has primary materials on Philippa Schuyler.

Works by Philippa Schuyler

Adventures in Black and White. New York: Robert Speller, 1960.
Good Men Die. New York: Twin Circle, 1969.
Jungle Saints. Rome: Herder, 1963.
with Josephine Schuyler. *Kingdom of Dreams.* New York: Robert Speller, 1966.
Who Killed the Congo? New York: Devin Adair, 1962.

Works about Philippa Schuyler

Cherry, Gwendolyn. *Portraits in Color.* New York: Pageant, 1962.
Smith, Jessie Carney, ed. *Notable Black American Women.* Detroit: Gale, 1992.
Smythe, Mabel A. *The Black American Reference Book.* Englewood Cliffs, NJ: Prentice-Hall, 1966.
Spradling, Mary Mace. *In Black and White.* Detroit: Gale, 1985.
Williams, Ora. *American Black Women in Arts and Social Science: A Bibliographic Survey.* Metuchen, NJ: Scarecrow, 1978.

Contemporary coverage beyond that appearing in her father's newpaper, the *Pittsburgh Courier* includes the following: "Buenos Aires Series Re-Engages Pianist," *Musical America* 75:14 (February 1955); and "Town Hall Recital," *Musical America* 76:20 (November 15, 1956). She is featured in *Musical Courier* 149 (May 15, 1954): 28; 150 (October 1954): 30; 159 (April 1959): 18; in *The Crisis* 57 (May 1950): 276–333; 61 (April 1954): 207; 74 (June 1967): 248; 76 (May 1969): 207–210; and in *Time* 47 (March 25, 1946); 27 (June 22, 1936).

SCOTT, HAZEL (1920–1981), musician, performer and advocate for racial justice, reflected the careful guidance of family and community. Born on June 11, in Port-of-Spain, Trinidad, Hazel Dorothy Scott received educational encouragement from her father, R. Thomas Scott, a college professor from Liverpool, England, who came to teach English at St. Mary's College. The musical instruction came from her mother, Alma (Long) Scott, a pianist-saxophonist, whose mother had come to Trinidad from Venezuela. Considered a child prodigy due to her exceptional abilities playing by ear from age two, Hazel performed at a hometown debut at age three.

To provide greater access to professional instruction for their daughter, the family moved to New York in 1924. She attended Public School 81 in New York City. Her father was a follower of fellow West Indian Marcus Garvey. The nationalism of Garvey penetrated the Scott home as Hazel grew up proud and conscious of her African heritage. The five-year-old Scott made her debut in New York's Town Hall, an event that brought the child to the attention of American audiences. She had perfect pitch, could play piano with both hands, and could improvise at the piano. Although Julliard School of Music accepted students at a minimum age of 16, her music teacher, Paul Wagner, recognized her abilities and persuaded the school to take her in at age eight with a six-year scholarhip. When she was an adolescent, her father died, leaving her mother with the responsibility of providing for the family. She used her musical talents in the Harlem Harlicans, an all-female orchestra under the leadership of Lil Armstrong, the wife of Louis Armstrong. Hazel played saxophone with the all-female Louis Armstrong band. At age 14, Hazel Scott performed in her mother's band, the American Creolians Orchestra, playing trumpet and piano. The strain of going to school and working nights proved too great. During her senior year at Wadleigh High School, she collapsed and was hospitalized. Her mother obtained tutoring for her, and in 1936, she graduated with her class.

As young Scott gained experience and poise, she gained special recognition with her own radio program in 1936 on the Mutual Broadcasting System and with her Broadway debut with the Count Basie Orchestra. She appeared in the musical *Sing Out the News* in 1938, and made her first recording with the Rhythm Club of London in 1939. When Ida Cox became too ill for a performance at Barney Josephson's Café Society Downtown and Uptown in New York, Scott replaced Cox and performed for Josephson for six years. Audiences and critics enjoyed her showy style of playing and her blend of classics with jazz. She composed "Love Comes Softly" and "Nightmare Blues." Her albums sold well and included *Swinging the Classics, Ritual Fire Dance, Two Part Invention in A Minor, Prelude in C Sharp Minor*. Her music, a hybrid of classical, jazz, and boogie woogie, attracted widely diverse audiences. Arna Bontemps described the audience reaction in his book *We Have Tomorrow*: "She begins by playing the music very well indeed— in the manner the composer intended. Slowly, rather playfully, she lets strange notes and rhythms creep in and before the listener can catch his breath, he is under the spell, and Hazel is beating the keyboard 'into a rack of bones.'"

During the World War II era, she performed in *Priorities of 1942* on Broadway, toured the United States, and performed in films: *Something to Shout About, I Dood It, Tropicana*, and *The Heat's On* in 1943; *Broadway Rhythm* in 1944; and *Rhapsody in Blue* in 1945. These performances won her the Newspaper Guild of New York's Page One Award, yet when she tried to enter a Washington, DC, theater to view her own performance in *Rhapsody in Blue* in 1945, she was refused admission because of her racial identity. This incident coupled with a personal relationship with the race leader Adam Clayton Powell led to her evolution as an advocate for racial justice.

By the end of the war, Scott had appeared at Carnegie Hall and had married the newly elected Congressman Adam Clayton Powell, Jr. Their wedding, one of the year's social events, was an indication of their future relationship. They had one son, Adam Clayton Powell III, but domestic life was not the prevailing interest of the couple. Their social life became the subject of many pieces in both the black and white press. Powell, the pastor of the Abyssinian Baptist Church in Harlem, was a charismatic, powerful leader who dramatically challenged the American system of racial discrimination. During the McCarthy era, she was accused of being a communist sympathizer, a charge that led to the cancellation of her television show, a 15-minute program on the DuMont Network, in 1950.

As the first black woman to have a musical network television show and as the wife of the challenging Powell, Hazel Scott had to appear before the House Un-American Activities Committee to defend her views and actions. These incidents coupled with Powell's personal behavior led to separation and finally divorce in 1956.

Scott left the country, living in France and Switzerland until her return in 1967. She married Ezio Bedin and collected miniature pianos and old calypso songs. She reentered television by appearing in several soap operas and series such as "Julia," "The Diahann Carroll Show," and "CBS Playhouse 90." She performed in East Coast nightclubs to bolster her career. She appeared on several television shows during her last decade of life, including "Not for Women Only," "Sunday," "Pat Collins Show" (all in 1974), up to "Straight Talk," and "Midday" (in 1981). Inducted into the Black Filmmakers Hall of Fame in 1978, Scott continued as a performer until 1981, when ill health forced her retirement. She died later that year on October 2, 1981.

—Dorothy C. Salem

Bibliography

Few resources delineate the career of Hazel Scott. Much of her career appears in the columns of black newpapers and magazines, especially *Ebony, Encore, Essence, Jet, Ms.*, and *Negro Digest*. Some of these are included in the clippings file in Schomburg Center for Research in Black Culture, New York Public Library. Where Scott appears in a collection, analysis is lacking. For example, *Contributions of Black Women to America*, edited by Marianna W. Davis (Columbia, SC: Kenday, 1982) describes her as one of two superstars of the 1940s and then devotes half a sentence to describing that superstardom with Lena Horne, whose career is recounted in two pages. A limited biographical essay on Hazel Scott is included in the selections in Gwendolyn Cherry, *Portraits in Color* (New York: Pageant Press, 1962); and Arna Bontemps, *We Have Tomorrow* (Boston: Houghton, Mifflin, 1945). She is also delineated in Mildred Green's essay in *Notable Black American Women*, edited by Jessie Carney Smith (Detroit: Gale, 1992).

For more information about Scott, consult references on the musical/performing arts fields. Mention of Scott can be found in Eileen Southern, *Biographical Dictionary of Afro-American and African Musicians* (Westport, CT: Greenwood Press, 1982); George Hill, *Black Women in Television* (New York: Garland, 1990); D. Antoinette Handy, *Black Women in American Bands and Orchestras* (Metuchen, NJ: Scarecrow, 1981); Edward Mapp, *A Directory of Blacks in the Performing Arts* (Metuchen, NJ: Scarecrow, 1978); Donald Bogle, *Blacks in American Film and Television* (New York: Garland, 1988); Donald Bogle, *Toms, Coons, and Mulattoes* (New York: Continuum, 1989); Sally Placksin, *American Women in Jazz* (New York: Wideview Books, 1982); and Arnold Shaw, *Black Popular Music* (New York: Schirmer Books, 1986). Some information about her experience in film is in Phyllis Klotman, *Frame by Frame* (Bloomington: Indiana University Press, 1979), which provides reference to films in which blacks have performed. Biographical material can also be found in books written about her famous husband, Adam Clayton Powell, Jr. See Claude Lewis, *Adam Clayton Powell* (Greenwich, CT: Fawcett, 1963).

SCRUGGS, YVONNE (b. 1933) holds a worldview that is as savvy as it is socially conscious. With her extensive background in academia and a long career as an effective government administrator, she brings an original perspective to both the public and business worlds with which she has been identified. Born June 24 in Niagara Falls, New York, into a family of third-generation educators and health professionals, she is the oldest of the late Leonard A. and Geneva B. Scruggs's four children including two sisters and one brother. She was raised with high expectations, which placed graduation from college as the beginning of adulthood. From this family of overachievers she garnered her motivation and will to make a difference in this life.

Now in her early sixties Scruggs has achieved many "firsts" in her life: the first black female elected to a New York State Youth-in-Government office; the first Fulbright fellow selected from her hometown of Buffalo, New York, from her undergraduate school, North Carolina Central University and the first black Fulbright fellow from the state of North Carolina; the executive director of President Jimmy Carter's Task Force, which produced the first National Urban Policy for the United States in 1979; the first black ever appointed to the cabinet-level position of Housing Commissioner for New York State.

Scruggs currently directs the Urban Policy Institutes for a prestigious private black think tank in Washington, DC, the Joint Center for Political and Economic Studies. She also is completing work on two forthcoming books, *Women of Distinction: Activists and Change Agents* and *Consensus and Compromise: The National Urban Policy Process*. She makes her home with her husband, Edward V. Leftwich, in the eastern United States. They have four children—three daughters and one son.

A recent innovative business venture was a partnership with her husband through which they provided vitally needed financial services to an urban population that was largely without access to bank accounts or checkbooks. These "non-depository banks, located in dense, urban minority communities," provided bill payment services and other types of money transfers. Scruggs served as chair of the board and chief operating officer of the firms, which hired only local indigenous workers, many of whom were just entering the labor force after job-readiness training. A cover story about Scruggs in *Success Magazine* described her as a business renegade who, as the people's banker, catered to the working poor.

Formerly the deputy mayor of Philadelphia, where she managed 13 direct-service mayoral agencies, Yvonne Scruggs also managed a staff of over 1,000 in her capacity as New York State's Housing Commissioner. She has worked in every national program designed to improve the quality of urban life since her entry into the professional arena in 1959. She conducted community-based evaluations of urban renewal in conjunction with neighborhood leaders; formed neighborhood and community liaisons as the associate director of the Ford Foundation's Philadelphia Grey Areas Project; served as a national consultant to the Poverty Program's Office for Economic Opportunity and its Community Action Program. Scruggs served as Deputy Assistant Secretary of the U.S. Department of Housing and Urban Development during the Carter administration.

Through the Model Cities Program and as the coordinator of field services for the Wharton School's Human Resources Center, she trained both business and urban leaders in the skills of institutional change and grantsmanship in the 1960s and 1970s. Scruggs has written and published a number of professional papers, including several on the subjects of community-based organizations and university-community urban change models. She also has written on planning in minority communities and planning in small communities, and has delivered a variety of papers to national and international organizations on the role of women in a changing world. She was the Maricopa College (Arizona) Honors Series Lecturer in 1987 on the topic "Shaping the Quality of City Life: Reshaping the American Dream."

Yvonne Scruggs has traveled and lectured, under the auspices of the United States Information Service, in Ethiopia, Kenya, South Africa, Nigeria, and Ghana. She also has lectured throughout southern Germany on problems of immigrant laborers on invitation of the German office of Foreign Relations. She has headed the United States delegations to the Economic Commission for Europe (ECE) and to the Organization for Economic and Community Development (OECD). For all of these efforts, she has received numerous honors and awards.

In addition to her Fulbright fellowship to Berlin, Germany, Scruggs holds a bachelor's degree in political science cum laude from North Carolina Central University, a master's degree from the University of Minnesota and an advanced certificate from Freie Universitate Berlins, and she has completed her doctoral work at the University of Pennsylvania. She has been a professor at two graduate schools of the University of Pennsylvania, at the State University of New York at Buffalo, and at Howard University, where she also was graduate department chairperson. She has served as a national and international consultant on municipal finance, social and physical planning, and public policy. Her current work focuses on citizen-based urban policy strategies and on increasing the capacity of black leaders to compete effectively for top priority positions on the urban policy and urban resource allocation agendas. She is currently updating a biographical collection, *Women of Distinction*, to produce a sequel to a book of the same title completed by her grandfather, L.A. Scruggs, in 1893.

—Yvonne Scruggs

Bibliography

Christian, Charles M. "Exclusive Interview with Yvonne Scruggs Perry," *Urban Concerns Magazine* (February–March 1980).

"A Conversation with Yvonne Scruggs-Leftwich," *Real Estate Reporter* (January 1986).

Maren, Michael. "Renegades: They Destroyed the Old to Create the New: The People's Banker," *Success* (February 1991).

Watson, Judy. "An Interview with Yvonne Scruggs-Leftwich," *Empire State Report* (August 1984).

Yvonne Scruggs-Leftwich is also listed in *Who's Who in America, Who's Who in Black America, Who's Who among American Women, International Who's Who of Women,* and several other biographical collections.

SCUGG, MARY ELFRIEDA. *See* Williams, Mary Lou.

SHABAZZ, BETTY [SANDERS] (b. 1936), wife of Malcolm X and supporter of civil rights, was born in Detroit, Michigan, on May 28. The only child of adoptive, Methodist parents, Shabazz was educated in Detroit at Northern High School. She then attended Tuskegee Institute in Tuskegee, Alabama, but left due to racial tensions in the town. Shabazz then moved to New York to attend the Brooklyn State Hospital School of Nursing.

Shabazz's move to New York marked one of the major turning points in her life, for it was in New York in 1956 that she was introduced to the Prophet Elijah Muhammad's Nation of Islam (Black Muslim) religion. She quickly converted, changed her name to Sister Betty X, and adopted the Muslim diet and dress code for women. As Sister Betty X, Shabazz became a teacher in the Nation of Islam and eventually traveled throughout the United States in order to set up classes for women in the Nation of Islam's mosques. It was also through the Nation of Islam that Shabazz met her husband, Malcolm X, a revolutionary leader in the movement.

Shabazz and Malcolm X were married in Lansing, Michigan, January 12, 1958. With Malcolm X, she had six daughters: Attilah, Qubilah, Ilyasah, Amilah, and twins Malaak and Malikan, who were born seven months after Malcolm X's assassination. Shabazz has dedicated a great part of her life to raising these children according to her and her husband's Islamic principles.

In 1964 Malcolm X broke from the Nation of Islam and completed his obligatory pilgrimage (*hajj*) to the holy cities of Mecca and Medina in Saudi Arabia. While on *hajj*, he came into contact with other Muslims throughout the world. He and Shabazz then converted to the traditional Sunni version of Islam. He changed his name to El-Hajj Malik El-Shabazz and she, accordingly, became Mrs. Betty Shabazz.

The period from the break with the Nation of Islam and the assassination of Malcolm on February 21, 1965, was one of great change and anxiety for Betty Shabazz. First, she witnessed her husband's emergence in this period as one of the greatest black leaders. Second, she and her family were threatened due to the break with the Nation of Islam. Her home in Queens was firebombed as she, Malcolm X, and their children slept. Then she and her four children witnessed Malcolm X's assassination in New York's Audubon Ballroom.

The next ten years in Shabazz's life were ones of tremendous personal growth. One month after Malcolm's assassination, she made her pilgrimage to Mecca and Medina and refocused her life. She completed her BA in public health education and was certified as a school nurse at Jersey City State College. In 1975 she earned her PhD in school administration and curriculum development from the University of Massachusetts at Amherst.

Although Shabazz is essentially a private person who has described herself as a supporter, not a leader, she is involved in numerous community activities. Some of these include the Day Care Council of Westchester County and the Women's Service League. Shabazz has also served as the director of the African American Foundation, a trustee of National Housewives League, co-chairperson to the New York *Amsterdam News*, and a member of the advisory board to the Sickle Cell Telethon. She also hosted her own radio show on New York City's WBLS-FM radio station and made numerous public speaking appearances. She is currently the director of communications and public relations at Medgar Evers College in Brooklyn, New York. Her residence is in Mount Vernon, New York.

—Lisa M. Reynolds Abu-Raad

Bibliography

Betty Shabazz is essentially a private person. She rarely grants interviews, and when she does she usually speaks about her deceased husband. Some of the interviews in which she discusses herself appeared in "A Visit with the Widow of Malcolm X," interview by Fletcher Knebel, *Look* (March 4, 1969: 74–77); *Ebony* (June 1969: 172–174+); *Newsweek* (November 3, 1969: 16); "A Conversation with Dr. Betty Shabazz," interview by Joy Duckett Cain, *Essence* (February 1985: 12). Susan Taylor's interview with Betty Shabazz, "Remembering Malcolm X: Loving and Losing Him," *Essence* (February 1992: 50–52+) is undoubtedly the most recent and comprehensive treatment of Betty Shabazz.

Another brief view of Betty Shabazz can be obtained through Malcolm X, *The Autobiography of Malcolm X* as told to Alex Haley (New York: Ballantine Books, 1964); and in Bruce Perry's controversial treatment of Malcolm X in *Malcolm: The Life of a Man Who Changed Black America* (Barrytown, NY: Station Hill Press, 1991).

Other writings on Betty Shabazz include entries in *The Kaiser Index to Black Resources, 1948–1986* (Brooklyn: Carlson, 1992); William C. Matney, *Who's Who among Black Americans, 1975–1976* (Northbrook, IL: Who's Who Among Black Americans Publishing, 1976); and Harry A. Ploski and James Williams, eds., *The Negro Almanac: A Reference Work on the Afro-American* (New York: Wiley, 1983).

SHADD, MARY ANN (1823–1893),

orator, educator, and the first black female editor of a weekly newspaper in North America, fought for the integration of blacks into American society throughout her lifetime. As the oldest of 13 children born (October 9) to a well-to-do free black family in Wilmington, Delaware, Mary Ann followed the example of her parents, Abraham and Harriet Shadd. Abraham, a shoemaker by trade, had invested in property to sustain his family while he worked for racial justice and advancement through the National Convention for the Improvement of Free People of Color. An advocate of self-help, Abraham Shadd opened his home to fugitive slaves and moved his entire family to Pennsylvania when educational opportunities closed to his children. Mary Ann Shadd embodied her father's values. Exposure to diverse beliefs was evident in her childhood and education. She was raised as a Roman Catholic, educated in a Quaker school in West Chester, Pennsylvania, and later espoused African Methodism when she felt that assimilation was impossible. When she graduated from school at age 16, Shadd returned to Wilmington, Delaware, to open a school for black children. She taught the children of her race in Delaware, New York, and later in Pennsylvania. Education was the most important means for racial uplift.

After the passage of the Fugitive Slave Act in 1850, Shadd gave up her career in teaching to accompany her brother Isaac to Canada. She wrote a pamphlet in 1852 to inform fugitive slaves about the conditions in Canada. Both Shadd and her brother became schoolteachers in Windsor, Ontario, before she started her career in journalism in 1853. After meeting antislavery journalist Samuel Ringgold Ward, Shadd cooperatively launched one of the best fugitive slave weeklies, the staunchly integrationist *Provincial Freeman*. She married Thomas G. Cary in 1856, and afterward shared the editorship with her brother and H. Ford Douglass. They found it difficult to find consistent financial backing, and the paper ceased publication in 1858.

Following the death of her husband in 1860, Shadd reentered teaching at an interracial school in Chatham to support herself and her children. During the Civil War, she returned to the United States as a recruiter of "colored" volunteers for the Union Army in Indiana. Following the war, she went to Washington, DC, where she served as a public school principal, wrote for Frederick Douglass's *New National Era*, and entered Howard University to study for a law degree, becoming the first woman to do so. In addition to her journalistic work for racial betterment, Shadd was active in women's rights organizations. A member of the radical National Woman Suffrage Association, Shadd organized suffrage rallies, testified before the House Judiciary Committee, and spoke to audiences in churches and at the Bethel Literary and Historical Society. She participated in the founding years of the Washington Colored Woman's League, but her death in 1893 of rheumatism and cancer prevented her from witnessing the national club movement for black women's rights. Her life served as a model of achievement and commitment that black women as a group would reflect in the future.

—Beth Schneider

Bibliography

Most of the information about her career can be found in the Mary Ann Shadd Cary Papers, Howard University, Washington, DC.

Secondary Sources

Barden, James. *Shadd: The Life and Times of Mary Shadd Cary.* Toronto: N.C. Press, 1977.

Brown, Hallie Q. *Homespun Heroines and Other Women of Distinction.* Xenia, OH: Aldine Press, 1926.

Hancock, Harold B. "Mary Ann Shadd: Negro Editor, Educator, and Lawyer," *Delaware History* 15 (April 1973).

Murray, Alexander. "The Provincial Freeman: A New Source for the History of the Negro in Canada and the United States," *Journal of Negro History* 44 (April 1959).

Silverman, Jason H. "Mary Ann Shadd and the Search for Equality," in *Black Leaders of the Nineteenth Century*, edited by Leon Litwack and August Meier. Urbana: University of Illinois Press, 1988, pp. 87–100.

Sterling, Dorothy. *We Are Your Sisters: Black Women in the Nineteenth Century.* New York: Norton, 1984.

SHANGE, NTOZAKE

(b. 1948), poet, playwright, and dancer, was born Paulette L. Williams on October 18 in Trenton, New Jersey, to P.T. Williams, a doctor, and Eloise (Owens) Williams. Before age 13, she had moved from Trenton to upstate New York to Alabama, back to Trenton, then to St. Louis, and finally, back to Trenton. She attended the segregated Sumner High School at a time when entertainers such as Ike and Tina Turner, the Shirelles, Smokey Robinson, and Chuck Berry were the only blacks with "a public aura." This constant moving, combined with the international travels of her parents to Europe, the Caribbean, Mexico, the Philippines, India, Africa, and Togo, meant a constant influx of people from a variety of cultures and countries. Visits to her home by musicians such as Dizzy Gillespie, Sonny Til, and Chico Hamilton expanded her musical exposure, which enabled her to associate languages with music and cultural expression.

Her family encouraged this appreciation of the arts. Surrounded by visual art in prints, textiles, and sculpture, she remembered the Sunday afternoon variety shows that included her parents, two sisters, and a brother. Her father played the congas and did magic tricks; her mother read poetry; her sisters played cello, flute, and saxophone; and Paulette and her brother danced. As a child, she played the violin. This artistic collage shaped her perception of sound, rhythm, visual movement, color, and emotion. Her exploration of the ambiance of each region in which she lived and the exposure to international cultures provided her with a broad tapestry of lifestyles from which to create her poetic visions.

In the mid-1960s college experiences at Barnard College fashioned her poetry. Influenced by the spirit of Imamu Baraka (a.k.a. LeRoi Jones), the technical aspects of Ishmael Reed, the nostalgia of Dave Henderson, and the risk taking of Thulani, Ntozake Shange experimented with her writing. After receiving her BA in American studies from Barnard, she went to the University of Southern California for her graduate work in American studies. In the California environment of the 1960s she traveled around doing poetry readings at prisons, Poetry-in-the-Schools programs, the University Museum, San Francisco State University, Intersection, A Woman's Place, and the Coffee Gallery. She met and was influenced by Pedro Pietri, Victor Hernandez Cruz, Jessica Hagedorn, Elvia Marta, Rosalie Alphonso, J.J. Wilson, and others. During this time, she also studied with Raymond Sawyer, Halifu, Ed Mock, and Saundra M. McPherson of the Contemporary Afro-American Dance Company and Dianne McIntyre of the Sounds in Motion Dance Company. She wrote the dance-drama *Sassafrass* performed in 1975 as a result of this earlier collaboration.

As an adult, she has repeated the pattern of mobility that dominated her preteen years. Since 1969 the unmarried Shange has moved from Los Angeles to Boston to New York to San Francisco, living in 17 residences. To counteract the loss of friends from this transiency, she and other artists, poets, and musicians formed COMIC-DU-WOP-COMMUNE to provide a support network of similar transients in the arts. This group provides the professional criticism, the community connections, and the emotional foundation for its members. The Third World Women's Collective, International Women's Day Affairs, and Shameless Hussy Poets have helped her growth as a woman and as a poet.

Shange's professional career has produced drama, novels, essays, and poetry written in English, Spanish, and French. She has appeared on radio and television, but her main vehicle is the theater. She wrote and acted in *For Colored Girls Who Have Considered Suicide when the Rainbow Is Enuf* (O.B.) 1976, the year after the performance of the dance-drama *Sassafrass*. She published her poetry and essays in periodicals such as *Essence, Ms., Black Scholar, Radical America, Heresies, Mademoiselle,* and *Callaloo* during the late 1970s. In 1980 her adaptation of *Mother Courage* won an award. Her short plays, *Spell No, A Photograph: Lovers in Motion,* and *Boogie Woogie Landscapes,* were published as a collection in *Three Pieces* in 1981. *Sassafrass, Cypress, and Indigo: A Novel* (1982); *See No Evil: Prefaces, Essays, and Accounts, 1976–1983* (1984); *From Okra to Greens: Poems* (1984); and *Ridin' the Moon in Texas: Word Paintings* (1987) continue to show her philosophy that the written word "shd fill you up with something/cd make you swoon, stop in yr tracks, change yr mind, or make it up. a poem shd happen to you like cold water or a kiss."

Ntozake Shange taught humanities and women's studies at Sonoma College in California, and English at the University of Houston in Texas before moving to Philadelphia, where she currently lives with her daughter Savannah.

—Beth Schneider

Bibliography

To complete the extensive listing of Ntozake Shange's creative works consult Ronda Glikin, *Black American Women in Literature* (Jefferson, NC: McFarland, 1989); Edward Mapp, *A Directory of Blacks in the Performing Arts* (Metuchen, NJ: Scarecrow, 1978); Esther S. Arata and Nicholas Rotoli, *Black American Playwrights*, 2nd edition (Metuchen, NJ: Scarecrow, 1978); and James Page, *Selected Black American Authors* (Boston: G.K. Hall, 1977). For greater insight into the cultural collage of her early years, see "Ntozake Shange Interviews Herself," *Ms.* (December 1977): 34+.

SHEPPARD, ELLA (1851–1914), pianist for the world-acclaimed Jubilee Singers of Fisk and community organizer, was born in Nashville, Tennessee, into slavery on February 4. Her father, Simon Sheppard, had purchased his freedom and was attempting to earn the money to buy the freedom of Ella's mother, Sarah, when the slave owner refused to honor the agreement. After Sarah threatened to drown herself and her child, the two were sold separately to punish the act of defiance. Sarah was taken to Mississippi by her new owner, and Ella Sheppard was purchased by her father for $350 in 1854. Her father remarried another slave woman and quickly purchased her freedom to avoid any repetition of the tragedy that befell Ella's mother. As economic conditions and racial violence worsened for free blacks in Nashville, the family fled to Cincinnati, Ohio, to avoid being seized and sold into slavery.

In that southern Ohio city, Ella Sheppard received a rudimentary education at the colored school. Her demonstration of musical talent led to her father's purchase of a piano and music lessons. Her father's death in 1866 left the 15-year-old and her stepmother penniless. To provide for the family, Ella Sheppard worked as a domestic for a family. She also acquired a few poor music students and played at various social events to earn money. She gained further musical instruction from a local piano teacher. As the teacher's only black pupil, she had to come to his home after dark and enter through the back door.

Following the end of the Civil War, Ella left Cincinnati in 1868 to teach school in Gallatin, Tennessee. After only 5 months, she left for Fisk University with a mere $6 in her pocket and a trunk small enough to be called her "pie box." Fortunately, this amount paid room and board for three weeks. The school was very poor and food was scarce, so once again she taught a few music pupils to maintain herself. Three pupils paid $4 per month, but travel to the city meant that Ella Sheppard had to go without supper on her teaching days. She shivered through winter and spent spare time studying with George L. White, Fisk's treasurer.

In September 1871 her sacrifices seemed in vain. Fisk's financial problems caused the major funding agency, the American Missionary Association, to close the school. In a final attempt to alleviate the financial hardships, George L. White organized a group of singers on October 6, 1871. Eleven former slaves, nine singers, a pianist, and a teacher-chaperone performed to raise money for the school. Ella Sheppard was the pianist of this select group, called the Jubilee Singers. At first, the singers received only clothing and travel expenses for singing spirituals. However, during their European tours, they earned as much as $800. Cordially received by the kings and queens of Europe, the Jubilee Singers raised $150,000 in seven years. In July 1878 the Jubilee Singers disbanded. Their years abroad had transformed their lives through exposure to societies lacking racial prejudice. Many did not return to the South.

Ella Sheppard brought her experiences home to Nashville. Following her years with the Fisk Jubilee Singers, Sheppard married a minister, George W. Moore, superintendent of southern church work of the American Missionary Association, and raised three children. In 1896 she helped organize the National Association of Colored Women in Washington with other famous black women such as Alice Moore Dunbar, Ida Wells-Barnett, Charlotte Forten Grimké, and Mary Church Terrell. She spent her life helping her family and the community by organizing Jubilee choruses, studying conditions of her people, presiding over the Women's Missionary Society, and lecturing about her experiences. She died on June 9, 1914, a few days following her delivery of the commencement address at Trinity School in Athens, Alabama. Her memorial service was held in the Fisk Memorial Chapel, where friends paid tribute to her life of service.

—Terri L. Jewell

Bibliography

For information on Ella Sheppard Moore, Fisk University provides the most complete records in the university archives, aided by Ella Sheppard Moore's descendant, Special Collections librarian, Beth M. Howse. These records include copies of the *Fisk University News* (November 1914): 7–12; articles written by Ella Sheppard Moore in publications for the American Missionary Association; publications resulting from the 1987 Nashville Conference on Afro-American Culture and History; and the American Missionary Association Papers, Amistad Research Center.

Few secondary sources provide detail on her life. Those providing some information include Marianna W. Davis, *Contributions of Black Women to America* (Columbia, SC: Kenday, 1981); and Dorothy Sterling, *We Are Your Sisters: Black Women in the Nineteenth Century* (New York: Norton, 1984).

SHOCKLEY, ANN ALLEN (b. 1927), novelist, critic, and librarian, was born in Louisville, Kentucky, on June 21 to Henry and Bessie (Lucas) Allen. Her education includes a BA from Fisk University (1948) and an MS in library science from Case Western Reserve University (1959). She married William Shockley in 1949 and became a widow in 1965. They had two children: William Leslie, Jr., and Tamara Ann. From 1961 to the present she has resided in Nashville, Tennessee. Shockley is the recipient the National Short Story Award

(1962), the American Library Association Black Caucus Award, the Hatshepsut Award for Literature (1981), and the Martin Luther King Award for literary output (1982).

Shockley is an accomplished scholar-librarian, reviewer, and longtime journalist. Ann Allen Shockley's two novels and single collection of short fiction have served to elevate and denigrate her status as an African-American writer. Respectively, *Loving Her* (1974) *The Black and White of It* (1980), and *Say Jesus and Come to Me* (1982), largely written on black, feminist, and lesbian themes, these three works encountered hostile and dismissive criticism as a result of ethnocentric, racist, homophobic, and critically biased reviewers and scholars.

Shockley's significance is that she introduced feminist and lesbian themes long before her contemporaries Maya Angelou, Alice Walker, and Toni Morrison. Her characters and themes are starkly drawn against realistic contemporary scenes. They tend to deny critics little symbolic or metaphorical grist for the interpretative mill; yet, they offer easy target practice against her portraits of abusive men, women-loving women, and hypocritical icons of the African-American community. Although Shockley has garnered thoughtful critical consideration of such outstanding critics and scholars as Alice Walker, Louie Crew, Rita Dandridge, Susan Koppleman, Evelyn C. White, and J.R. Roberts, few critics have traced the evolution of Shockley's writing, which began in 1945 with an early fiction entitled "The Lord Is My Shepherd." Often, misapprehensions and misrepresentations regarding her entire purview have tended to retard the research on Shockley.

Four major themes recur in the fiction of Shockley—interracial relations, the lives of women, the psyches of men, and the effect of religion on the lives of her characters. She compounds and exaggerates these themes so that they approximate the compression and tension in twentieth-century American life. In Shockley's three main fictions there is a "Queen Bee" figure, a modern version of an archetypical woman-loving blues singer, who contrasts and confirms the same portraits in fictions by other American writers. This portrait reconstructs the presence of a figure many scholars have called "the invisible woman in American literature."

Shockley's work represents the decided transformation in the consciousness of black American writers from "double-consciousness" to that of "the Considered Whole" (or perspective of wholeness). Shockley has called for stories "that sweep the gamut of the black woman's image," and she says her black women, as well as those of her contemporaries, must become "larger than the sum total of roles and images created by others."

—SDiane Bogus

Bibliography

Works by Ann Allen Shockley

"Black Book Reviewing: A Case for Library Action." College and Research Libraries 35:1 (January 1974): 16–20. An essay written for black librarians, suggesting how to select quality African-American materials and castigates publications that do not review black works regularly.

Loving Her. 1974; reprint ed., New York: Avon, 1976; reprint ed. Tallahassee, FL: Naiad Press, 1987. A novel about a runaway abused black mother who finds love in the arms of a rich white lesbian writer but must face community homophobia, racism, and her own personal failings.

"The New Black Feminists." *Northwest Journal of African and Black American Studies* 2 (Winter 1974): 1–5. An essay that discusses the feminist identity of black women writers and thinkers in relationship to the women's liberation movement.

with E.J. Josey. *A Handbook on Black Librarianship.* Littleton, CO: Libraries Unlimited, 1977. A first book for librarians and teachers to offer criteria for selecting works and materials for African-American library collections.

"The Black Lesbian: Invisible Woman in American Literature." Paper delivered at SAMLA, Atlanta (November 1, 1979). Shockley reconstructs the lives of black lesbians whose histories have been hidden by scholars. Includes work on Gladys Bentley, Edmonia Lewis, and Mary Fields.

The Black and White of It. Tallahassee, FL: Naiad Press, 1980; reprint ed. 1987. A collection of short stories that focus on the lives of black women as housewives, politicians, singers, professors, and caregivers. Outstanding in the collection are "Holly Craft Is Not Gay," "Play It But Don't Say It," and "Women in a Southern Time."

Say Jesus and Come to Me. New York: Avon, 1982; reprint ed., Tallahassee, FL: Naiad Press, 1987. An incredulous satire about a southern black lesbian minister who helps to eradicate drugs and prostitution in the South by starting a multi-ethnic, multicultural church and organizing a feminist march.

"On Lesbian Feminist Book Reviewing," *Sojourner: The Women's Forum* (April 1984): 26. Shockley takes on her critics and offers a set of criteria by which feminists should consider all books by black women and lesbians.

Afro-American Women Writers: 1746–1933. Boston: G.K. Hall, 1988. A useful text that documents the lives of early African-American writers from Lucy Terry to Jessie Redmon Fauset. Divided into biographies, excerpts, and literary and historical periods.

Works about Ann Allen Shockley

Bogus, SDiane. *Theme and Portraiture in the Fiction of Ann Allen Shockley.* Dissertation, Miami University, Oxford, Ohio, 1988. Bogus analyzes the critical reception of Shockley and the characters and themes in her major fictions, and posits a thesis that Shockley has moved away from "double consciousness" to a "perspective of wholeness."

Dandridge, Rita. *Ann Allen Shockley: An Annotated Primary and Secondary Bibliography*. New York: Greenwood Press, 1987. A herculean work that provides first and most complete citations of Shockley's work. Includes four sections: Fiction Written by Shockley, Nonfiction Written by Shockley, Reviews of Shockley's Fiction and Nonfiction, and Shockley's Biography and Criticism.

————."Male Critics/Black Women's Novels," *CLA Journal* 23:1 (September 1979): 1–11. Dandridge revisits critics who have misapprehended the works of such writers as Zora Neale Hurston and Ann Allen Shockley.

————."Shockley, the Iconoclast," *Callaloo* 7:3 (Fall 1984): 160–164. An insightful discussion of Shockley's satire of church and church people in *Say Jesus and Come to Me*.

Koppelman, Susan. "Ann Allen Shockley," *Critical Survey of Short Fiction: Current Writers* 7, edited by Frank N. Magill. Englewood Cliffs, NJ: Salem Press, 1981, pp. 2814. Bio-literary notations on the work of Shockley, principally *The Black and White of It* and *Loving Her*. Applauds Shockley's view of the effects of racism and homophobia on the lives of her black characters.

Roberts, J.R. "Black Lesbians Before 1970: A Bibliographical Essay," in *Lesbian Studies: Present and Future*, edited by Margaret Cruikshank. Old Westbury, NY: Feminist Press, 1982, pp. 103–109. A historical first work that cites the lives and work of black lesbians and artists. Includes several notations on the work of Shockley.

Walker, Alice. "Review of *Loving Her* by Ann Allen Shockley," *Ms.* 3:10 (April 1975): 120–124. Walker praises the courage of the Shockley book but dismisses the possibility of many lesbian lives.

White, Evelyn C. "Comprehensive Oppression: Lesbians and Race in the Work of Ann Allen Shockley," *Backbone* 3 (1979): 38–40. Reviews *Loving Her* and *The Black and White of It* and discusses the themes of black oppression of homosexuals in Shockley's work.

SIMKINS, MODJESKA MONTEITH (1899-1992), educator, social reformer, and civil rights activist, was born December 5, the eldest of eight children of Henry Clarence and Rachel Evelyn (Hull) Monteith of Columbia, South Carolina. As the oldest sibling, Modjeska was expected to be responsible for the other children and to supervise their work on the farm. The Monteiths were members of Second Calvary Baptist Church, in which Modjeska grew up, although she was not baptized until adulthood.

Simkins attended Benedict College from grade one through the completion of the bachelor's degree in 1921. Shortly after graduation, she took courses at Columbia University and at Morehouse College during the summer sessions. During the 1930s, she completed graduate work in public health at the University of Michigan at Ann Arbor and at Michigan State Normal School (now Eastern Michigan University) in Ypsilanti.

She followed the career path of her mother and maternal aunts, teaching first in the Teacher Training Division of Benedict College and going the next year to teach at Booker T. Washington School, where she remained until her marriage in 1929 to Andrew Whitfield Simkins, a prosperous black businessman. The couple did not have children.

In 1931 she became director of Negro work for the South Carolina Tuberculosis Association, assisting in health education among blacks in South Carolina, until 1942, when she began a full-time public service career. In 1956 she accepted a position with the Victory Savings Bank of Columbia. Also, in 1942, she was elected state secretary of the South Carolina Conference of the NAACP, a position she held until 1957. During this period, Simkins participated in the major South Carolina NAACP projects, most of which were lawsuits defending black civil rights, equal salaries for black teachers, black voting rights, and desegregation in the nation's public schools. She also worked with the Southern Negro Youth Congress (national adult advisory board), the Southern Regional Council, the Southern Conference for Human Welfare, the Southern Conference Educational Fund, the Civil Rights Congress, and others.

In 1956 Modjeska Simkins returned to full-time employment at the Victory Savings Bank, the only black-owned bank in South Carolina, which was owned by her brother. Simkins began as head teller, and then became a branch manager and finally, director of public relations, until the 1980s when she retired. She and her husband also owned property and various small businesses.

After 1957 her projects in South Carolina were channeled mainly through the Richland County Citizens Committee, an offshoot of the South Carolina Citizens Committee. Two significant projects accomplished by this organization were the desegregation of the Columbia city schools and the improvement of living conditions for black mental health patients at South Carolina's state-supported hospital.

Simkins also sought to foster the development of real competition among political parties. In the late 1940s she began working to create a support base within the South Carolina Republican Party. However, when welcoming disaffected Democrats who opposed President Harry Truman's support of civil rights, she lent her support to the Democratic Party. Within the state, she worked closely with the Progressive Democratic Party (1940s) and the United Citizens Party (1970s) of which she was "honorary life time president." These third-party platforms made significant gains for black South Carolina, stimulating black political involvement and in the 1970s and the election of blacks to the South Carolina General Assembly.

In summary, Simkins, an astute political activist, has given much to the human rights struggle in her home state, in the South, and in the nation. The local media call her the "matriarch of the civil rights movement in South Carolina"; she is strong-willed, direct, outspoken, bold, independent-minded, nurturing, witty, and humorous.

Simkins lived in the same home since the 1930s, in Columbia, South Carolina. She spent most of her time organizing her personal papers from throughout her career, but illness slowed her pace and led to her death in 1992. Benedict College has named their research archives after Simkins to keep her memory alive.

—Barbara Woods

Bibliography

Most of the information about Modjeska Simkins can be found through organizational records and interviews. Oral histories can be found in the Southern Women's Oral History Project, University of North Carolina, Chapel Hill, Wilson Library, audiotapes; University Library, Winthrop College, Rock Hill, South Carolina; "The Quest for Human Rights: The Oral Recollections of Black South Carolinians," audiovisual tapes, Afro-American Studies Program, University of South Carolina (many interviews with Simkins's co-workers are also in this collection); and the extensive collections of videotaped interviews at South Carolina Educational Television Network (Columbia) and at the State Historical Society of Wisconsin, Madison (concerning civil rights, December 1966).

Her personal papers include limited collections at Winthrop College and at Benedict College, Columbia, South Carolina, and Caroliniana Special Collections Library, University of South Carolina, Columbia.

Newpapers relate her role. See the following: *The State* (Columbia Newspapers, Inc.), Columbia, and the *News and Courier*, Charleston.

For photographs, the Southern Women's Oral History Project, University of North Carolina, Chapel Hill, has two photos. One shows Simkins addressing the audience at the Bill of Rights Dinner program of the National Emergency Civil Liberties Committee (c. 1964), photo by Mildred Grossmer, New York. The second photo shows Modjeska Simkins speaking before the Columbia City Council (1975), photo by Bill Scroggins. Columbia Newspapers, Inc., has several photos over a few decades as does Caroliniana Special Collections Library, University of South Carolina, Columbia.

Secondary Sources

Aba-Mecha, Barbara Woods. "Black Woman Activist in Twentieth Century South Carolina: Modjeska Monteith Simkins." PhD dissertation, Emory University, 1978.

Crawford, Vicki L., Jacqueline A. Rouse, and Barbara Woods. *Women in the Civil Rights Movement: Trailblazers and Torchbearers, 1942–1965.* Brooklyn: Carlson, 1990.

Woods, Barbara. "Profile of a Black Woman Leader: Modjeska Monteith Simkins," in *Notable Black American Women*, edited by Jessie Carney Smith, Detroit: Gale, 1992.

SLOWE, LUCY DIGGS (1885–1937), professional tennis player, educator,

and educational administrator was born on July 4 in Berryville, Virginia. Her father, Henry Slowe, owned a hotel; her mother, Fannie (Porter) Slowe, was a homemaker. Slowe was the youngest child, as well as third daughter. When Slowe was nine months old her father died, and when she was six her mother died. At age seven, she went to live with her paternal aunt, Martha Slowe Price, in Lexington, Virginia. In 1898, the family moved to Baltimore. A student of Baltimore public schools, Slowe became the first female graduate of Baltimore Colored High and entered Howard University in 1904. Her high school class salutatorian, she was also the first black woman of the city to obtain a scholarship.

Slowe finished her BA at Howard in 1908. While attending Howard, she proved a well-rounded student, participating in musical, athletic, and literary endeavors. She served as vice president and secretary of the Alpha Phi Literary Society. She was also president of the Women's Tennis Club, sponsored by faculty member Professor G.M. Lightfoot. One of Slowe's most significant achievements as a Howard student was co-founding the first Greek letter sorority for black college women, Alpha Kappa Alpha.

Upon finishing her degree, Slowe first taught at her high school alma mater for seven years. Meanwhile, she was pursuing postgraduate work at Columbia University. She received her MA in English from Columbia in 1915. She studied further at Columbia in 1917, 1921, and 1930.

Under the auspices of the Monumental Tennis Club of Baltimore, she entered the 1917 national tennis championships, held in Baltimore. Beginning with this tournament, she suffered three successive defeats before winning her first championship in 1921. Eventually Slowe won 17 silver loving cups, proving her tennis prowess.

Slowe's next teaching position was as an English teacher at Armstrong High for four years, one year of which she served as dean of girls. In September 1919 Slowe organized Shaw Junior High, the first junior high school for blacks, in Washington, DC, of which she became the first principal. While working in the DC public school system, Slowe started an in-training service extension course in education through Columbia University, a course attended by black and white junior high school teachers.

Slowe remained at Shaw Junior High until June 1922, when she accepted a position as the first dean of women (and associate English professor) at Howard University. Slowe's appointment as dean of women followed in the wake of major administrative reorganization at Howard University during the new presidency of Dr. Durkee. Slowe also worked with Durkee's successor, Dr. Mordecai W. Johnson, a relationship that was not without controversy. Slowe and Johnson were constantly at odds regarding various issues such as the administrative responsibility for the use of university dorms, dining areas, and assembly rooms; Slowe's salary; university provision of living quarters for the dean of women; and budgetary matters. Slowe and Johnson's administrative difficulties culminated at the time of Slowe's fatal illness in October 1937, during which Johnson publicly was accused of writing Slowe a letter demanding that she return to work within 24 hours or her successor would be named.

To initiate herself successfully as dean of women, Slowe traveled to 12 accredited schools in the North and West. Dr. Romiett Stevans of Columbia University was a major influence on Slowe, having taught the first class for deans of women in the United States. Slowe introduced a similar class to Howard.

As dean of women, Slowe was actively involved in several campus committees, including the Student Affairs, Discipline, Faculty Education Discussions, Lecture Recitals, and Public Functions committees. Slowe was by no means satisfied with the role of dean of women as matron and worked persistently to change the role to one as specialist in the educating of women. She persuaded the Howard University Board of Trustees to establish a women's campus. The board conceded, and consequently women's dormitories were built on Fourth Street in Washington, DC.

Slowe did not allow her difficulties with Johnson to stop her from contributing significantly to Howard University or organizations outside the university. Slowe's lifelong musical interest and talent served her well when she managed the "Cultural Series" at Howard University, beginning in 1929. One of this series' accomplishments was a concert in 1932–1933 with musicians from Howard University and the National Symphony Orchestra, headquartered in Washington, DC. Slowe managed to present other performers on Howard's campus, including concert pianist Tourgee DeBose, lyric soprano Elizabeth Sinkford, poet Countee Cullen, the Howard Players (founded 1907), the Men's Glee Club (founded 1873), the Women's Glee Club, Marian Anderson, and Abbie Mitchell. Possessing notable singing talent (she sang contralto) allowed Slowe to perform with the Howard University Choir, organized by Miss Lulu V. Childers. Slowe also sang with the choirs at the St. Francis Catholic Church and her own church, the Madison Street Presbyterian Church, both in Baltimore.

Nationally, Slowe participated in numerous organizations and associations at a time when many black women were barred from such activities. She served on the Executive Committee of the National Student Council; as member of the Council of Colored Work of the National Board of the YWCA; as delegate for six years to the Conferences on the Cause and Cure of War; as president of the College Alumnae Club in Washington, DC; as first president of the National Association of College Women, patterned after the American Association of University Women of which Slowe was also a member; as president of the Columbia Teachers' Association in DC; as chair of the Association of Advisors to Women in Colored Schools; as counselor to the Race Relations Group of the North American Home Mission Congress; and as member of the National Association of Deans of Women, the National Education Association, the

National Association of Teachers in Colored Schools, the National Council of English Teachers, and the Women's International League for Peace and Freedom.

While president of the National Association of College Women, Slowe promoted a survey on the status of women students and faculty members in coeducational institutions of higher education. She lectured at Vassar and Oberlin colleges and served as college pastor at Talladega College. Mary McLeod Bethune and Slowe co-founded the National Council of Negro Women in 1935, and Slowe became its first secretary.

Slowe fell victim to a two-month illness, resulting from a combination of influenza and kidney disease, in the fall of 1937. This illness ended in her death on October 21 at her Washington, DC, home. Slowe is buried in Lincoln Cemetery in Suitland, Maryland, near Washington, DC. Many memorials were held in Slowe's honor. The Howard University Board of Trustees publicly praised her five days after her death for her important contributions as an educator of women on and off the campus of Howard University. In her memory, Howard University women dedicated a stained glass window at the University Chapel on November 7, 1943. Howard University also named a dormitory in her honor, Slowe Hall, located on Third Street, near the university, while the city of Washington named an elementary school after her.

—Faye A. Chadwell

Bibliography

Works by Lucy Diggs Slowe

Slowe authored several articles:

"What Contribution Can a Program of Social Activities Fostered by the Institution Make to the Moral and Social Development of Students in Negro Colleges?" *Quarterly Review of Higher Education among Negroes* 1:2 (April 1933): 11–13.

"Higher Education of Negro Women," *Journal of Negro Education* (July 1933): 352–360.

Secondary Sources

Henderson, Edwin Bancroft. *The Negro in Sports.* Rev. ed. Washington, DC: Association Publication, 1939.

Logan, Rayford W. *Howard University: The First Hundred Years.* New York: New York University Press, 1969.

———. "Lucy Diggs Slowe," in *Dictionary of American Negro Biography,* edited by Rayford W. Logan and Michael R. Winston. New York: Norton, 1982, pp. 559–560.

"Lucy D. Slowe," *Journal of Negro History* 23:1 (January 1938): 136–137.

Turner, Geneva C. "School Names: For Whom Is Your School Named?" *Negro History Bulletin* (January 1955): 90–91.

Wright, Marion Thompson. "Lucy Diggs Slowe," in *Notable American Women,* edited by Edward T. James (Cambridge: Belknap Press, 1971), pp. 299–300.

SMITH, ADA ("BRICKTOP") (1894–1984), entertainer and hostess, was born in Alderson, West Virginia, on August 14. Many names were given Smith to honor and placate well-meaning relatives and friends; in full, Ada Beatrice Queen Victoria Louise Virginia "Bricktop" Smith. She began using the name "Bricktop," a reference to her red hair and freckles, when she was 18 years old.

Smith made her stage debut as a child in Chicago in an adaptation of *Uncle Tom's Cabin*. In her teens she held minor parts in various productions at the Pekin Theatre and later toured with the Georgia Troubadours, the Crosby Trio, and the vaudeville comedy team of Miller and Lyles.

In 1924 Smith accepted an offer to travel to Paris to entertain in the Montmartre cafe Le Grand Duc. At that time there were fewer than a dozen black singers and entertainers in all of Paris. Le Grand Duc was an establishment that attracted a well-known clientele, including Fred Astaire, Josephine Baker, Zelda and F. Scott Fitzgerald, Ernest Hemingway, Elsa Maxwell, Pablo Picasso, Cole and Linda Porter, Man Ray, and John Steinbeck. Smith soon became a sought-after hostess and entertainer of these and other members of the Parisian artistic and elite society.

Only two years after arriving in Paris, Smith became the owner of her first cafe. In 1929 she and saxophonist Peter Duconge were married. It was an unhappy union, and the couple separated permanently in 1933. Their childless marriage was never legally dissolved.

With the onset of the Depression and World War II, the Parisian cafe business came to a virtual standstill. Smith tried her luck at entertaining in New York City, with only limited success. Undaunted, she set out for Mexico City, where she ran a successful nightclub for six years. In 1950 Smith returned to Paris, and later opened another cafe in Italy. Smith retired from the nightclub business in 1964, owing to advancing arthritis and a heart condition.

In 1943 Smith converted to Catholicism, and in her later years she devoted much of her time to Catholic charitable causes. She took advantage of her position as an internationally known hostess and entertainer to raise money for institutions serving the needs of orphaned and disadvantaged children.

Among the honors bestowed upon Smith was an honorary doctor of arts degree awarded in 1975 by Columbia College in Chicago. In 1983, New York City Mayor Edward Koch presented Smith with a seal of the city and a certificate of appreciation for her "extraordinary talent and indomitable spirit." Her autobiography, entitled *Bricktop*, written with the assistance of James Haskins, was published in 1983.

Smith died in her sleep in New York City on January 31, 1984.

—Juanita Karpf

Bibliography

The most thorough and informative source of information about Smith is her autobiography, written with the assistance of James Haskins, *Bricktop* (New York:

Atheneum, 1983). An important account of Parisian nightlife can be found in a biography of Cole Porter written by David Grafton, *Red, Hot and Rich* (Briarcliff Manor, NY: Stein & Day, 1987). Langston Hughes, in his autobiography *The Big Sea* (New York: Thunder's Mouth Press, 1986, reprint ed.), describes his first encounter with Smith in Paris. Other useful sources of information are Donald Bogle, *Brown Sugar: Eighty Years of America's Black Female Superstars* (New York: Harmony Books, 1980); Eileen Southern, *Biographical Dictionary of Afro-American and African Musicians* (Westport, CT: Greenwood Press, 1982); and the article about Smith in *Baker's Biographical Dictionary of Musicians*, edited by Nicolas Slonimsky, 7th ed. (New York: Schirmer Books, 1984). Articles about Smith and subjects related to her career have appeared in the *Chicago Defender, Chicago Tribune, The Crisis, Ebony, Jet, Our World, People, Newsweek, Amsterdam News, New York Daily News, New York Times, Sepia, The Black Perspective in Music, The New Yorker, Time,* and *Vogue*. Smith bequeathed all her personal papers to author James Haskins, who in turn donated them to the Schomburg Center for Research in Black Culture of the New York Public Library.

SMITH, AMANDA [BERRY, DEVINE] (1837–1915), religious leader and temperance worker, was born on January 23 near Long Green, Maryland. Her parents, Samuel and Mariam (Matthews) Berry, were slaves on adjoining plantations. Her father later bought the family's freedom and moved to York County, Pennsylvania, where his farm became a stop on the Underground Railroad. Although she received only a few months of formal schooling, her parents taught her to read and write at home.

In September 1854 she married Calvin M. Devine from nearby Columbia. They had two children—one died in infancy; the other, a daughter named Mazie, lived into her twenties. Her unhappy marriage was saved only by her religious conversion in March 1856. When her husband was killed fighting with the Union Army in 1863, she married James Smith of Philadelphia, a coachman and African Methodist Episcopal (AME) clergyman. This union produced three children, but none survived childhood. She worked throughout her marriages as a washerwoman and domestic servant.

Smith became increasingly attracted to the perfectionist teachings of Phoebe Palmer in the late 1860s. In September 1868, she had a second religious experience—sanctification—and felt a call to preach. With the death of her second husband and last child in 1869, she began speaking in black churches throughout New York City and northern New Jersey. Despite meeting some resistance from AME pastors, she abandoned domestic work to become a full-time evangelist in 1870. From that time until 1878, she was a familiar figure in the American holiness movement, preaching at camp meetings from Tennessee to Maine. Smith also thrilled British audiences with her inspired preaching in 1878 and again in 1889–1890. She did missionary work in India, Liberia, and Sierra Leone in the intervening decade.

Smith returned home to the United States in 1890 and again toured churches throughout the East. Then in October 1892, she moved to the temperance community of Harvey, a Chicago suburb, and began to write her memoirs. They were published one year later as *An Autobiography: The Story of the Lord's Dealings with Mrs. Amanda Smith the Colored Evangelist.* Smith devoted her final two decades to operating orphanages for African-American children—first in Harvey, then after 1912 in Sebring, Florida. By the time of her death on February 24, 1915, of a paralytic stroke, her efforts and example had broadened the role of women in the AME and Methodist denominations.

—Roy E. Finkenbine

Bibliography

The chief source of information on Amanda Smith's life and thought up to 1892 is Jualynne E. Dodson, ed., *An Autobiography: The Story of the Lord's Dealings with Mrs. Amanda Smith the Colored Evangelist* (New York: Oxford University Press, 1988), a volume in the Schomburg Library of Nineteenth-Century Black Women Writers. For Smith's later career, see M.H. Cadbury, *The Life of Amanda Smith: "The African Sybil, the Christian Saint"* (Birmingham, England: Cornish Bros. Ltd., 1916); and an obituary in the March 6, 1915, issue of the *Chicago Defender*, a black newspaper. A brief but reliable biographical overview by John H. Bracey, Jr., appears in Edward T. James, Janet Wilson James, and Paul S. Boyer, eds., *Notable American Women*, 3 vols. (Cambridge: Harvard University Press, 1971).

A folder of records on Smith's management of her Sebring, Florida, orphanage is in the Julius Rosenwald Papers at the University of Chicago Library.

SMITH, BESSIE (1894–1937), the "Empress of the Blues," was born Elizabeth Smith to William and Laura Smith in Chattanooga, Tennessee, on April 15. Elizabeth joined three sisters and one brother in poverty, which worsened after both parents died by the time Elizabeth was nine years old. Perhaps these conditions combined with her natural talents for singing to produce a child performer, who was discovered at a local talent show by the manager of the Ivory Theatre in Chattanooga. Around 1910, Gertrude "Ma" Rainey saw Smith perform and added her to the touring company managed by Rainey's husband, Will. In F.C. Woolcott's Rabbit-Foot Minstrel Group, Smith received instruction in country blues from the "Mother of Blues," Gertrude "Ma" Rainey. Bessie toured with Rainey and other groups, appearing in tent shows, carnivals, and theaters for several years in circuits taking her to Memphis, Atlanta, Birmingham, Richmond, and other southern cities. By 1920 she made her first recording, but it was never released.

Her career began to change in 1923, when she recorded under the direction of Frank Walter on the Columbia label. With an exclusive contract, stability returned. Her first singles, "Downhearted Blues" and "Gulf Coast Blues," sold sensationally. She moved to Philadelphia, purchased a house, brought her siblings to the city, and married a Philadelphia policeman, Jack Gee. With Gee as her manager, Bessie Smith toured the black vaudeville circuit in the South and continued to increase her performances in the North in cities such as New York, Boston, Philadelphia, and Chicago. In 1924 she appeared in Chicago to rave reviews of her "classic blues style." Her interpretations of "Chicago Bound," "Nobody's Blues But Mine," and "St. Louis Blues" demonstrated the dramatic ability of the southern charmer, who needed no microphone to capture the audiences with her rich contralto tones. She sang about loneliness, poverty, love, jealousy, disasters, and joys, identifying with the experiences of many members of her audience. She wrote many of her own songs that spoke to the migrants from the South who shared her background. Often displaying captivating costumes from headdress to satin gowns to sequins sparkling in the spotlights, Bessie Smith thrilled her audiences with sound and sight. From the year of her marriage in 1923 to 1930, when she separated from her husband, Bessie Smith had made 160 recordings, often selling over 100,000 records in one week.

Her career started to decline by the early 1930s. She seemed to influence different groups in various ways. Some called her coarse, argumentative, and unreasonable. Smith's increased consumption of alcohol led to fluctuations in body weight and to frequent outbursts of temper. Yet many recalled her warmth and self-sacrifice. At one time, she even canceled professional appearances to nurse Frank Walker's child back to health.

Due to the advent of radio and the Great Depression, the record market dwindled. Her last recording, produced by John Hammond in 1933, signaled the end of an era. When Columbia dropped her contract, Smith again joined the road show/nightclub circuit. By the late 1930s Smith was attracting white audiences, who began to share appreciation for the blues.

In September 1937, while traveling with a road show in Mississippi, Smith was injured in an automobile accident. Although aided by a Memphis physician who happened by the accident, until the ambulance arrived to transport her to a Clarksdale Hospital, she, nevertheless, died on September 26, 1937, either in transit or shortly after arrival. Many people attributed her death to delay in treatment, which, as in the Edward Albee play *The Death of Bessie Smith*, was due to rejection by a whites-only hospital. Eyewitnesses contradicted this view, which cannot be substantiated from those at the scene. Smith was buried in Philadelphia at the Mount Lawn Cemetery. Her style influenced the blues and jazz musicians of her day from Louis Armstrong to Billie Holiday. In 1972 Columbia Records released a five-volume set of her recordings (originally produced by John Hammond) entitled *Bessie Smith*.

—Beth Schneider

Bibliography

Bessie Smith has been the object of several biographical analyses. These include Chris Albertson, *Bessie* (Briarcliff Manor, NY: Stein & Day, 1972); and Paul Oliver,

Bessie Smith (New York: Chilton, 1961) has a brief analysis of Smith's career and musical style. Musicians remember Smith in Nat Shapiro and Nat Hentoff, eds., *Hear Me Talkin' to Ya* (New York: Dover, 1955) and *The Jazz Makers* (Westport, CT: Greenwood, 1975). Her death is discussed in the *Second Line* (July–August and September–October 1959).

Several sources place Smith in the musical context of blues and jazz. These works include Ortiz M. Walton, *Music: Black, White, and Blue* (New York: Morrow, 1972); David Evans, *Big Road Blues* (Berkeley: University of California, 1982); Berendt E. Joachim, *The Jazz Book* (Westport, CT: Lawrence, Hill, 1981); Dan Morgenstern, *Jazz People* (New York: Harry Abrams, 1976); Martin T. Williams, ed. *The Art of Jazz* (New York: Oxford, 1959); Marshall Stearns, *The Story of Jazz* (London: Oxford University Press, 1970); Martin T. Williams, *The Jazz Tradition* (New York: Oxford University Press, 1983), provides a brief discussion of Smith's influence on jazz greats Charlie Parker, Billie Holiday, and Bix Beiderbecke.

Short biographical sketches are in Elizabeth Coughlin, "Bessie Smith," in *Handbook of American Women's History*, edited by Angela H. Zophy and Frances Kavenik (New York: Garland, 1990); Eileen Southern, *Biographical Dictionary of African-American and African Musicians* (Westport, CT: Greenwood Press, 1981); Sally Placksin, *American Women in Jazz, 1900–Present* (Cleveland: Winderview, 1982); *Blues Who's Who* (New Rochelle: Arlington House, 1979); LeRoi Jones, *Blues People* (New York: Morrow, 1963); and Larry Gara, "Bessie Smith," in *Notable American Women*, edited by Edward T. James, et al. (Cambridge: Belknap, 1982).

SMITH, CATHERINE [HAYES] (b. 1923), born on June 25 in Washington, DC, developed her commitment to girls and families through a gradual extension of her own family into the larger family of the black community. As with many women of her generation, Smith belonged to religious and community organizations that include New York's Abyssinian Baptist Church, Delta Sigma Theta, Sex Education Coalition of Metropolitan Washington, National Urban League, NAACP, National Council of Negro Women, and the American Public Health Association. Married in 1949 to J. Clifton Smith in Florida, Smith's first concern was raising her seven children: Gwendolyn, Julian, Alva, Sonja, Shirley, Jeffery, and Donna. Certified to teach elementary, secondary, and special education, she taught school in Florida, New Jersey, and Georgia.

Divorced in 1962, Smith moved beyond serving family and teaching into community youth development and religious instruction. Smith returned to higher education in the 1970s and earned degrees from Rochester School of Divinity, (1974) and John Jay College of Criminal Justice (MPA, 1975).

Smith served as the director of religious education at the Florida Normal College, St. Augustine, Florida. She became the first minority female superintendent for Union County, New Jersey; Director of Youth Ministry, Riverside Church; headed the Comprehensive Sickle Cell Center, Harlem Hospital Center, New York City; and consulted for the National Council of Churches in

New York and Washington DC; Ebony Research Systems in Washington, DC; and the Girls Clubs of America, Inc. of New York City (1982–1991). She is the co-founder and current executive director of the Greater Harlem Guidance Center in New York City, through which she directs and develops philosophy, program objectives, training programs, and fundraising activities. She currently serves on the boards of the Comprehensive Sickle Cell Center, Harlem Hospital, Greater Harlem Guidance Center, Sex Information and Education Council of USA. She is an advisory committee member of Newark (New Jersey) Adolescent Pregnancy and Parenting.

Her publications emphasize her commitment to developing the potential of African-American youth. As a consultant to the Girls Club of America, she has served on committees concerning issues of family life, education for staff, board, and local affiliates. As family life director she was the writer of *Growing Together*, *Will Power/Won't Power*, an assertiveness-training program for girls (11–18), and *Health Bridge*, an educational guide to community based health services. "Tomorrow Partners, Tomorrow Parents," serves as a manual for family life education.

For her leadership to strengthen family life and adolescent health education, Smith has received honors and awards for the writing and research in prevention of teenage pregnancy from the Greater Harlem Comprehensive Guidance Center (Outstanding Leadership Award) and the Girls Club, Inc. (Award for Services Rendered to Girls Club, Inc.). She was honored for her work by the Texas Sickle Cell Anemia Association. She received the "Award of Excellence" from Mayor Tom Dunn of Elizabeth, New Jersey; and was honored an Honorary Citizen of Fort Worth, Texas by Mayor Words. She continues to write numerous publications, training manuals and academic curricula on adolescent health, sickle cell disease, and ethnic studies. As an Adjunct Professor at Lehman College and City College, City University of New York, she guided ethnic studies while teaching youth. She has traveled extensively in West and East Africa, and teaching at the University of Ibaden and researching at Lagos University. She continues her work in youth development as a member of the National Association for Sickle Cell Disease.

—Olivia Pearl Stokes

Bibliography

The author conducted three 90-minute interviews with Catherine Smith between March and May 1991, and one 2-hour interview with the Girls Club of America, Inc. Family members provided the author with a program entitled "Celebration of a New Beginning" on March 15, 1991, which provided additional details.

SMITH, PHYLLIS [EDWARDS, BURROWS] (1896–1990), educator, minister, and businesswoman, was born in Elliot, South Carolina, on December 22 to Thomas and Julia (McDonald) Edwards. As one of 14 children, she received her education in Lee County public schools and at Voorhees Institute (now a college) located in Denmark, South Carolina. After her graduation from Voorhees, she taught for three years in Seneca, South Carolina, before moving to New York City to live with her aunt and uncle. There she met Nelson Burrows, a student of the New York School of Dentistry (now the New York University School of Dentistry). They married and had two children, Vinie and George Nelson.

Following the death of her husband, she worked in the New York garment district as a finisher, a draper, and finally, an operator, and was an active member of the International Ladies Garment Workers Union. Her ambition to improve her family's life chances eventually led to her ownership of a dressmaking establishment in White Plains, New York, that catered to an exclusive clientele. In addition to the dress business and raising two children, she operated a hairdressing salon.

At an age when most business owners retire, Phyllis Burrows returned to school for more education. In 1971, at age 75, Smith took up residence in Barbados and enrolled in Codrington College, taking courses also at the University of the West Indies. Later, she enrolled in the New York Theological Seminary, and in 1981, at age 85, she graduated with a certificate in christian ministry. It was during this period that she met and married a childhood friend, William Smith of South Carolina. The couple took up residence in Philadelphia on West Olive Street.

The Reverend Phyllis Burrows Smith passed away on January 28, 1990, and is survived by her daughter Vinie Burrows (the internationally acclaimed actress, producer, writer, and civil rights activist); two grandchildren, Gregory Brian Harrison and Sojourner Aletha Harrison; and three great-grandchildren, Bryan Robinson and Adrienne and Nicole Harrison.

—Mary Ann Williams

Bibliography

Information was obtained by the author through interviews with Vinie Burrows during 1990–1991.

SNOW, VALAIDA (1905–1956), trumpet player, vocalist, violinist, pianist, bandleader, actress, dancer, occasional producer, and director was born June 2 in Chattanooga, Tennessee. Snow's family were all musicians. Although her father was an entertainer, it was her mother who taught music to all the children: Valaida, her three sisters, and a brother. Mrs. Snow (first name unknown) studied music at Howard University. The sisters, Lavaida, Alvaida, and Hattie, and the brother, Arthur Bush, were all professional singers. Mrs. Snow taught all of her children how to play several instruments, but Valaida's talent far exceeded the other children. She could play the cello, bass, violin, guitar, banjo, mandolin, harp, accordion, clarinet, saxophone, and trumpet. Valaida Snow began performing at age four, and by age fifteen, she had started to work professionally. She had already established herself as a vocalist, dancer, and trumpet player throughout the United States by the time she was 18 years old.

Snow debuted in the 1920s in Pennsylvania and Atlantic City, New Jersey, clubs, where the best black musicians and entertainers performed before World War I. An extended engagement at Barron Wilkin's Harlem cabaret in 1922 propelled her to stardom. After this engagement, she performed in the musical *Man from Bam* (1923); was featured with Blanche Calloway and Esther Bigeou in *Ramblin' Round*, a 1923 musical; and with comedian Billy Higgins (whom she later married) in Will Mastin's *Follow Me* (1923) revue. Snow made her Broadway debut as Manda in Noble Sissle and Eubie Blake's *Chocolate Dandies* (originally *In Bamville*) during 1924–1925, along with Josephine Baker, Lottie Gee, and Inez Clough. One critic applauded her as a "thrilling young woman" who "carried the female honors for the show." She traveled to England in 1926 with the cast of *Blackbirds*, as Florence Mills's understudy. In August of the same year she embarked upon a tour that took her to Shanghai, Hong Kong, Rangoon, Cairo, Bombay, and Tokyo.

By 1928 she was back in Chicago playing the Sunset Theatre, a show described by many as a "showstopper"; Snow danced in seven pairs of shoes representative of different cultures, including Dutch clogs, Chinese straw sandals, Turkish slippers, and, Russian boots, dancing in the cultural style of each pair of shoes. In addition to stints to Paris as a cast member of Lew Leslie's *Blackbirds* (1929), Snow continued to perform throughout the 1930s in clubs, the hotbeds for jazz during this period: the Grand Terrace and the Regal in Chicago, the Cotton Club in Culver City, California, and the Apollo Theatre in New York. Snow also performed with several of the top jazz bands of the era, including those of Earl Hines, Count Basie, and Fletcher Henderson. She also appeared in the theater productions *Shuffle Along* (1930 edition) and the hit musical *Rhapsody in Black* (1931), in which she was the bandleader and solo trumpet player.

Snow appeared in England in the musical *Blackbirds* of 1934. During this same period she was an acknowledged trumpet player, garnering recognition in England and gaining international prominence as a pioneer jazz artist and solo instrumentalist. Critics and musicians alike were fond of her and extolled her excellence in musicianship and stage presence, often referring to her as "Queen of the Trumpet" (dubbed by W.C. Handy), "Little Louis" (equating her with Armstrong), and "Miss Show Biz." Snow's trumpet playing has been variously hailed as possessing a "melodic" and "refined" style, and as "on the beat, swinging powerfully broad-toned and with a most unfeminine vibrato." By now it was also well known that Snow could play every instrument in an orchestra. Snow married dancer Ananais Berry of the famed Berry Brothers, in 1934, and returned to the United States to work with him in Los Angeles in 1935. She returned to London during the fall of 1936 and made over 50 recordings throughout Europe with various bands up until the middle of 1937. She also recorded in Stockholm in 1939 and in Copenhagen until October 1940.

Snow continued to tour, and managed to appear in three films during the remainder of the 1930s—*Take It From Me, Irresistible You, L'Alibi* (1938), a French fllm starring Erich von Stroheim and Sidney Bechet, and *Pieges* (1939). The United States entered World War II in 1941 while Snow was performing in an exclusive club in Paris with Maurice Chevalier. After she completed this engagement she continued on to Copenhagen, where she was arrested by the Nazis because she was "non-Aryan" and held in a Wester-Faengle Concentration Camp for 18 to 20 months, before she was finally released as an exchange prisoner. Her release was engineered by a Copenhagen police chief who was a jazz devotee and knew of Snow's musical accomplishments. An emaciated 68-pound, mentally fragile Snow returned to the United States in 1943.

Shortly after her return she married entertainer Earle Edwards, who nursed her back to health and became her personal manager, booking her on a national tour limited to Canada and the United States. She appeared at the Apollo Theatre, the Alhambra, Cafe Society, the Waldorf-Astoria, and several other clubs. Snow, assisted by an all-male choir, performed Gershwin, Arlen, and spirituals at New York Town Hall on May 20, 1949. She subsequently made vocal and instrumental recordings in Los Angeles, New York, and Chicago.

The talented, glamorous woman received a gold trumpet for a command performance from Queen Wihelmina of the Netherlands, spoke seven languages, could play all the instruments in a complete orchestra, could write down music while it was being played; could break up an audience with her rendition of "Brother, Can You Spare a Dime?" during the Depression; conducted male orchestras and bands; and owned a chauffeur-driven purple Mercedes during the Depression. This confident, charismatic, glamorous, generous, self-disciplined, and fun-loving performer suffered a cerebral hemorrhage after a performance at the Palace Theatre in New York on May 30, 1956, and died 21 days later on May 30, 1956, in Kings County Hospital. Snow was buried in the Evergreen Cemetery in Brooklyn on her birthday.

—Elizabeth Hadley Freydberg

Bibliography

Linda Dahl, *Stormy Weather: The Music and Lives of a Century of Jazz Women* (New York: Pantheon, 1984) provides history and analyses of jazz women in the United States. Stanley Dance, *The World of Earl Hines* (New York: Scribner, 1977) provides biographical information about Valaida Snow's personal relationship with him, her performances, and interactions with musicians and their commentary concerning her. Sally Placksin, *American Women in Jazz: 1900 to the Present, Their*

Words, Lives, and Music (New York: Seaview, 1982) presents social history and profiles of American jazz women. Rosetta Reitz, *Hot Snow: Valaida Snow, Queen of the Trumpet, Sings and Swings* (liner notes) (Rosetta Records, 1982) provides biographical information with photographs of Valaida Snow. Henry T. Sampson, *Blacks in Blackface: A Source Book on Early Black Musical Shows* (Metchuen, NJ: Scarecrow, 1980) has a listing of stage productions with cast and personnel.

SPENCER, ANNE [SCALES] (1882–1975), poet, librarian, and avid gardener, was born in Henry County, Virginia, on February 6. She married Edward Spencer in 1901 and had three children: Bethel, Alroy, and Chauncey.

Anne Spencer was a member of the Harlem Renaissance, known also as the New Negro movement, though she never lived in New York. She was discovered in Lynchburg, Virginia, by the executive secretary of the NAACP, James Weldon Johnson, who suggested she change her name from Annie to Anne, as he introduced her poetry to the world. Johnson had come to Lynchburg to establish an NAACP chapter and met Spencer, who subsequently founded the chapter herself.

Spencer attended Virginia Theological Seminary in Lynchburg and graduated from this all-black college in 1899. Edward Spencer built their home, which is now a Virginia Historic Landmark and is listed in the National Register of Historic Places. Behind the house stands a writing cottage named for both of them—"Edankraal"— where she did most of her writing in its one room. Spencer was known for her interest in gardening and nature, sentiments of which she more often than not, included in her poetry. The poet Sterling Allen Brown, who taught at the seminary from 1920 to 1923, wrote the poem "To a Certain Lady in Her Garden," which still hangs on the wall in Spencer's dining room.

Lynchburg, as were most southern cities prior to the 1960s, was a city with separate facilities for blacks and whites, so Anne Spencer became the first librarian of the black high school's branch of the Jones Memorial Library. Dunbar High School was very like its famous namesake in Washington, DC, graduating many students who went on to distinguish themselves. Due to her efforts, black residents of the city had access to reading materials, many of which were donated to the library from her own collection.

The Spencer home saw the comings and goings of important African Americans, including W.E.B. Du Bois, James Weldon Johnson, Adam Clayton Powell, Jr., Langston Hughes, Roland Hayes, and Dr. Martin Luther King, Jr.

Spencer was a fine lyric poet who viewed her poems as part of her living. Like her gardening, writing was an integral part of her day, so some of it was written on grocery lists, walls of her bedroom, or on random pieces of paper. As a result, some of her work is lost. The body of her extant work deals not with racial issues but with nature and humankind—conflicts with a neighbor, flowers in her garden, and her love of husband, family and friends. She said, "I write about things I love. I have no civilized articulation for the things I hate. I proudly love being a Negro Woman—it's so involved and interesting. We are the PROB-LEM—the great national game of TABOO." Anne Spencer died in Lynchburg on July 27, 1975.

—Nancy Elizabeth Fitch

Bibliography

Anne Spencer has often been lost on the roster of the Harlem Renaissance. J. Lee Greene, however, has begun rectifying that situation as her biographer. His "Anne Spencer of Lynchburg," *Virginia Cavalcade* (Spring 1978): 178–186; and the mono-graph "Time's Unfading Garden: Anne Spencer's Life and Poetry" provide informa-tion about the poet's life, and the latter book includes her known extant poetry, collected in one place for the first time. The Lynchburg newspaper, *The News*, in an editorial on February 23, 1977, entitled "Anne Spencer's Due," speaks about the contributions she made to her community as well as to the literary world. She is featured in Margaret Busby, *Daughters of Africa* (New York: Pantheon, 1992).

SPRAGUE, ROSETTA M. DOUGLASS (1839–1906) was the eldest of five children of Frederick Douglass and Anna (Murray) Douglass. As the daughter of the internationally renowned orator, journalist, and abolitionist, Rosetta Douglass was expected to emulate her father's career and take up the cause against slavery. While her own inclinations favored those of her mother, toward a domestic life rather than a professional life, Sprague did not remain entirely outside of public view.

Born in New Bedford, Massachusetts, in June (her exact birthdate is unknown; several sources cite 1841), Rosetta Douglass grew up as the daughter of privilege in a white culture. Although she remained illiterate, her mother made certain that her children were well educated. When the family moved in 1848 to Rochester, New York, Rosetta attended Seward Seminary, a fashionable girls' school. But even Frederick Douglass's daughter could not escape racist attitudes. As the only African-American student, Rosetta was taught alone in a room separate from the other students. Since the only other school available was a poorly equipped and poorly staffed black school, Douglass sent Rosetta to school in Albany for a couple of years, and in 1850 hired a white governess to tutor her. From 1854 to 1855 Rosetta attended the Preparatory Department at Oberlin College, where she took business courses with the expectation of someday helping her father in his life's work.

Returning home Rosetta Douglass continued in her role as the family secretary, answering her father's mail and keeping him informed of family business. In 1862 Rosetta secured a teaching position in Salem, Massachusetts. In 1863 Rosetta married Nathan Sprague, a former slave and Union soldier who was poorly educated and unskilled. The two could not have been more different, and the result was a stormy marriage. Nathan had difficulty finding and keeping a job and failed in one business venture after another. With six children to support, Rosetta went to work in various clerking positions and sought her father's help to keep the family together.

The Sprague marriage nearly ended when Nathan, who had landed a post office job with Frederick Douglass's help, went to prison for mail theft. Rosetta sold their home in Rochester and moved to her parents' home in Washington, DC. Although Nathan and Rosetta Sprague reconciled following his release, she remained the primary financial support for the family. In later years Rosetta busied herself with her family and with public appearances made on behalf of organizations seeking to end slavery and improve African-American education.

Following her father's death, Rosetta Sprague was increasingly called upon as a speaker and addressed numerous public gatherings. In 1896 she addressed the founding convention of the National Association of Colored Women, which she had helped to organize. Sprague's best remembered speech was one she delivered before the Women's Christian Temperance Union on May 10, 1900. Published posthumously as "Anna Murray-Douglass: My Mother as I Recall Her," it was a tribute to her mother's role in helping Frederick Douglass aspire to greatness. Rosetta M. Douglass Sprague died in 1906.

—Thea Gallo Becker

Bibliography

Blight, David W. *Frederick Douglass' Civil War*. Baton Rouge: Louisiana State University Press, 1989.

Foner, Philip S. *The Life and Writings of Frederick Douglass: Early Years, 1817–1849*. New York: International Publishers, 1950. Provides an outline of Anna Murray and Frederick Douglass's early years.

Quarles, Benjamin. *Frederick Douglass*. Washington, DC: Associate Publishers, 1948.

Render, Sylvia Lyons. "Afro-American Women: Outstanding and the Obscure," *Quarterly Journal of the Library of Congress* 32 (October 1975): 307–319. Reprinted in Darlene Clark Hine, *Black Women in United States History: Theory and Practice* 2 (Brooklyn: Carlson, 1990). More interpretive than factual; favorably portrays Anna Murray Douglass as one of the obscure who is deserving of her place in history.

Sprague, Rosetta Douglass. "Anna Murray Douglass—My Mother as I Recall Her," *Journal of Negro History* 8 (1923): 93–101. Cited most often by biographers, it highlights only the positive aspects of her mother's life.

Sterling, Dorothy. *We Are Your Sisters: Black Women in the Nineteenth Century*. New York: Norton, 1984. Includes letters from Rosetta Douglass Sprague to her father, Frederick Douglass.

STAUPERS, MABEL [DOYLE, KEATON] (1890–1989), health care professional, was born in Barbados, British West Indies, on February 27 to Thomas Clarence and Pauline (Lobo) Doyle. She moved to the United States in 1903 at age 13 and became a naturalized citizen in 1917. That same year, she married James Max Keaton, from whom she was later divorced. Staupers graduated with honors from Freedman's Hospital School of Nursing in Washington, DC, in 1917, and from the Henry Phipps Institute in Philadelphia in 1920.

Staupers worked as a private duty nurse in Washington, DC, and New York City and as a nurse in the tuberculosis clinics at Jefferson Hospital in Philadelphia. She helped organize the Booker T. Washington Sanatorium, the first inpatient clinic in Harlem for black tuberculosis patients, and was the superintendent from 1920 to 1922. Staupers organized the Harlem Committee of the New York Tuberculosis and Health Association and served as its first executive secretary from 1922 to 1934. She was married to Fritz C. Staupers from 1931 until his death in 1949. Staupers served as the first nurse-executive of the National Association for Colored Graduate Nurses (NACGN) from 1934 until 1949, when she became the president. She retained the office until 1951, when the NACGN merged with the American Nursing Association.

Staupers was ever active in pursuing educational advancement and professional opportunities for black nurses. In 1934 she used monies from the Julius Rosenwald Fund to establish a New York office to concentrate on increasing the number of black women in nursing, to assure scholarship programs for black nursing students, and to equalize job opportunities in the profession. Additionally, she was one of the key persons responsible for the commissioning of black nurses into the armed forces during World War II. In 1941 Staupers was chosen as a nursing consultant to Surgeon General James C. Magee. To chronicle the history of the black nursing profession, she wrote *No Time for Prejudice*, which was published in 1961. Also in that year she lectured at Howard University in the College of Nursing. Staupers received numerous awards and honors during her long career. In 1947 she was given the coveted Mary Mahoney Award by the National Association of Colored Graduate Nurses and the Sojourner Truth Award by the New York branch of the National Association of Negro Business and Professional Women. She received the Spingarn Medal from the National Association for the Advancement of Colored People in 1951, and the American Nursing Association Award in 1974. Other awards include the Women's League of Science and Medicine Award for Humanitarian Achievements in Health in 1961, the National Urban League Award in 1963, the Howard University Alumni Award in 1970, and the Living Legacy Award from the National Black Caucus in 1986.

Staupers was active in many organizations. She held a 44-year membership in the Young Women's Christian Association of New York. She was a founding member of the National Council of Negro Women in 1935 and sat on the boards of the St. Phillips Parish Home for the Aged and the Mt. Morris Park Hospital. Staupers died of pneumonia at her Washington home in 1989.

—Linda Cannon-Huffman

Bibliography

Works by Mabel Keaton Staupers

"Negro Nurses in America," *Opportunity* (1937).

No Time for Prejudice: A Story of the Integration of Negroes in Nursing in the United States. New York: Macmillan, 1961.

The details of Mabel Staupers' life and career are fully described in *Who's Who in Colored America*, 7th edition, edited by G. James Fleming and Christian E. Burckell (New York: Who's Who in Colored America Corp., 1937); and in *Who's Who among Black Americans*, 6th edition, edited by Iris Cloyd (Northbrook, IL: Who's Who Among Black Americans, 1948). Interesting but abbreviated accounts are given in the *Encyclopedia of Black America*, edited by W. Augustus Low and Virgil A. Clift (New York: McGraw-Hill, 1981); and *The Contributions of Black Women to America* II, edited by Marianna W. Davis (Columbia, SC: Kenday, 1982).

Secondary Sources

Carnegie, M.E. *The Path We Tread: Blacks in Nursing, 1854–1984.* Philadelphia: Lippincott, 1986.

Hine, Darlene Clark. "Mabel Keaton Staupers," in *American Nursing: A Biographical Dictionary,* edited by Vern Bullough, Olga Church, and Alice Stein. New York: Garland, 1988, pp. 295–297.

———. "Mabel Staupers and the Integration of Black Nurses into the Armed Forces," in *Black Leaders of the Twentieth Century,* edited by J.H. Franklin and A. Meier. Urbana: University of Illinois Press, 1982.

———, ed. *Black Women in American History: From Colonial Times Through the Nineteenth Century.* Brooklyn: Carlson, 1990.

———, ed. *Black Women in the Nursing Profession: A Documentary History.* New York: Garland, 1985.

The New York Times Biographical Service: A Compilation of Current Biographical Information of General Interest 20:7 (July 1989).

STEWARD, SUSAN [SMITH, MCKINNEY] (1847–1918), a pioneering leader in medicine, suffrage, and temperance reform, and civil rights, was the first black woman to graduate from a New York medical school, and only the third from a medical school in the United States. Born Susan Maria Smith in Brooklyn, New York, she was the daughter of Sylvanus and Anne Springsteel Smith. She studied at the New York Medical College for Women, graduated as valedictorian of her class in 1870, and then successfully established a medical practice in Brooklyn.

She married the Reverend William G. McKinney in 1871; they raised two children, a daughter, Anna, and a son, William. McKinney died in 1894, and she married the Reverend Theophilus G. Steward, a chaplain in the U.S. Army, in 1896. They moved to Montana, where she became licensed to practice medicine. In 1898 she accepted a position as resident physician and a member of the faculty at Wilberforce University in Ohio while her husband served in Cuba and the Philippines. From 1902 to 1906 they lived in Texas and Nebraska, and then both obtained positions at Wilberforce. Throughout her life she adeptly balanced multiple duties: social, familial, educational, racial, professional, religious, musical, and reformist.

Susan M. Steward was an active suffragist and reformer. She and her sister, Sarah S.T. Garnet(t), were key figures behind the Equal Suffrage League, and both attended a testimonial fundraising dinner in 1892 to honor the antilynching crusade of Ida B. Wells. Steward was a founder of the New York Women's Loyal Union. As a supporter of the temperance movement, she served as a New York local Women's Christian Temperance Union president and befriended a WCTU chapter when living in Nebraska. She served on the board of directors for the Brooklyn Home for Aged Colored People from 1892 to 1895, and was a founder of the Brooklyn Woman's Homeopathic Hospital. At the beginning of World War I, she worked with the Red Cross.

She maintained her professional and scholarly interests and delivered at least two medical papers during the 1880s. During the 1887 academic year she pursued postgraduate study at Long Island College Hospital. In 1911 Steward presented a paper, "Colored Women in America," before the Interracial Congress in London, England, and in 1914 she delivered another paper, "Women in Medicine," at a meeting of the National Association of Colored Women's Club at Wilberforce. The latter essay, in pamphlet form, was widely circulated.

Steward satisfied personal interests as well. An avid student of music, she learned to play the organ, and during the years she practiced medicine in Brooklyn became choir director and organist for the Bridge Street African Methodist Episcopal Church. She was supportive of her family, sometimes accommodating many of them in her home. She actively participated in the varied programs of the Brooklyn Literary Union. Susan M. Smith McKinney Steward died on March 7, 1918.

—Bruce A. Glasrud

Bibliography

Susan McKinney Steward's life has been the subject of many investigations. See Leslie L. Alexander, "Susan Smith McKinney, M.D., 1846–1918: First Afro-American Physician in New York State," *National Medical Association Journal* LXVII (March, 1975): 173–175; Bettina Aptheker, "Quest for Dignity: Black Women in the Professions, 1865–1900" (unpublished paper, Women's Studies, San Jose State University, February 1980); Marianna W. Davis, *Contributions of Black Women to*

America II (Columbia, SC: Kenday, 1982); Maritcha R. Lyons, "Dr. Susan S. (McKinney) Steward," *Homespun Heroines and Other Women of Distinction*, edited by Hallie Quinn Brown (New York: Oxford University Press, 1988), pp. 160–164; Herbert M. Morais, *The History of Afro-Americans in Medicine* (Cornell Heights, PA: The Publishers Agency, 1976); William Seraile, "Susan McKinney Steward: New York State's First African-American Woman Physician," in *Black Women in American History* IV, edited by Darlene Clark Hine (Brooklyn: Carlson, 1990), pp. 27–44; Dorothy Sterling, *We Are Your Sisters: Black Women in the Nineteenth Century* (New York: Norton, 1984); Sylvia Dannett, *Profiles of Negro Womanhood* (Yonkers, NY: Educational Heritage, 1964); and William S. McKinney, Jr., "Susan McKinney Steward," in *Notable American Women*, edited by Edward T. James, et al. (Cambridge: Belknap, 1971).

Steward's writings include "Marasmus Infantum," *Transaction of the Homeopathic Medical Society of the State of New York* (New York: New York Homeopathic Medical Society, 1887): 150; "Colored American Women," *The Crisis* III (November 1911): 33–34; *Women in Medicine* (Wilberforce, OH: privately printed, 1914); and Theophilus Gould Steward, *From 1864 to 1914: Fifty Years in the Gospel Ministry* (Philadelphia: A.M.E. Book Concern, 1921).

Obituaries were published in *The Guardian* (Boston) (March 30, 1918); *New York Age* (March 16, 1918); and *The Crisis* XVI (May 1918): 15.

STEWART, ELLA [PHILLIPS] (1893–1987), pioneer in pharmacy, club-woman, and renowned contributor to international affairs, was the first black graduate from the Pittsburgh University of Pharmacy and the first black woman to pass the Pennsylvania State Board of Pharmacy. Born March 6 in Berryville, Virginia, to sharecropper parents Eliza and Hamp Phillips, Stewart was an outstanding grade school pupil. She entered Storer College in Harpers Ferry, West Virginia, at age twelve, earning five major scholarship awards. She married classmate Charles Myers after graduation in 1910. They moved to Pittsburgh, where she became a member of the Women's Culture Club. They had a daughter, Virginia, who died at age two. Ella Myers became a bookkeeper and cashier of Lincoln Drug Company. There she became interested in pharmacy. Through the encouragement of a local physician and friends, she entered Pittsburgh University in 1914. She graduated with a PhD from the University of Pittsburgh in 1916, becoming the first black female graduate of the College of Pharmacy. Following her divorce, she began her career as a pharmacist. Wanting her own drug store, she borrowed money from an insurance company to make a down payment. But with the outbreak of World War I, she closed the store and worked as pharmacist at Braddock General Hospital. Two years later, she bought another drug store in Pittsburgh.

On May 1, 1920, Ella Phillips Myers married pharmacist William Wyatt Stewart, who had been a lieutenant in World War I. The couple moved to Toledo, Ohio, where they opened a drug store in 1922. The Stewarts lived above the pharmacy and worked from 8:00 A.M. until 11:00 P.M. at night through the war years until 1945. Since hotels would not accommodate blacks in these times, the Stewarts hosted such celebrities as National Association of Colored Women leader Mary McLeod Bethune, the noted artist/cartoonist E. Simms Campbell, and General Benjamin O. Davis.

Beginning in the 1930s, Ella Phillips Stewart performed many community duties and received vast recognition for her work. She belonged to a number of organizations ranging from the YWCA, the League of Women Voters, the Toledo Council of Churches, and the NAACP. She served as the national chairman of the Department of Negro Women in Industry for the NACW in order to encourage women to take advantage of the opportunities in business and industry. She served as the editor of the NACW's *National Notes*. Within a few years, she had moved on to become the National Treasurer for the National Association of Colored Women's Clubs (NACWC). In 1948 she was elected president of the NACWC and served for 4 years. For her years of service to the club movement, she received the Silver Platter Award. In 1951 the U.S. Department of Labor placed her on the Women's Advisory Committee on Defense Manpower. From 1954 to 1955 she served on a goodwill tour of the world for the U.S. Department of State as the goodwill ambassador to Asia. In 1955 she was named Toledo Woman of the Year.

Despite her accomplishments, she was affected by the racism of the times. On May 17, 1957, Virginia governor Thomas B. Stanley invited her as an honoree at a banquet in Richmond. After learning that she was black, he declared that a regrettable error had been made. Toledo residents responded by arranging a testimonial dinner for her that was attended by over 200 people. In 1959 she received a plaque from the University of Pittsburgh for her outstanding contribution to pharmacy, and the same year, she served on the White House Conference on Aging National Advisory Committee.

She continued to receive honors for her commitment to service. The Toledo B'nai Israel Centennial Award followed in 1961, when the Toledo Board of Education named a $3 million elementary school after her. She was also elected vice president of the Pan-Pacific Southeast Asia Women's Association in 1961. A museum was established within the school in 1974 to house her many plaques and citations. Also in 1974, she received the doctor of humane letters from the University of Toledo. In 1976 her husband died at age 83. Ella Phillips Stewart was the oldest living black woman pharmacist in the country until her death on November 27, 1987, in her beloved Toledo, Ohio.

—Terri L. Jewell

Bibliography

The best source of information on Ella Stewart exists in her hometown of Toledo, Ohio, at her museum supervised by the Toledo Board of Education and at the Local History and Geneology Department of the Toledo-Lucas County Public Library.

Other sources of information are available through the National Association of Colored Women's Clubs: Elizabeth L. Davis, *Lifting as We Climb* (Washington, DC: NACW, 1933); and Charles H. Wesley, *The History of the National Association of Colored Women's Clubs* (Washington, DC: NACWC, 1984). Obituaries and tributes in the Toledo *Blade* (November 28, 30, and December 5, 1987) provide detailed information and local stories of the Toledo humanitarian. Small amounts of information are in Marianna W. Davis, *Contributions of Black Women to America* (Columbia, SC: Kenday, 1981); and Dorothy M. Love, *Salute to Historic Black Women* (Chicago: Empak Enterprises, 1984).

STEWART, MARIA W. [MILLER] (1803–1879), the first black woman to break social convention by speaking from a public platform in the United States, was born in Hartford, Connecticut. Orphaned at an early age, she was bound out in the family of a white clergyman, with whom she spent her childhood. Although given no formal schooling, she struggled to obtain an education by attending Sunday schools and reading in the family library. On August 10, 1826, after working for several years as a domestic servant, she married James W. Stewart in Boston. Nearly 20 years her senior, he was a veteran of the War of 1812 and operated his own business outfitting whaling and fishing vessels that sailed out of the port of Boston. At his insistence, she adopted his middle initial and became known as Maria W. Stewart for the remainder of her life. When he died on December 17, 1829, she was stripped by the probate court of his substantial estate and left virtually penniless.

In continual sorrow after her husband's death, Stewart, already a member of Boston's African Baptist Church, underwent a profound religious conversion. This prompted her to embrace abolitionism, feminism, and the struggle for black rights as part of the gospel mandate. She soon embarked on a brief career as a pamphleteer, speaker, and social activist. Although Stewart worked closely with white antislavery advocates such as William Lloyd Garrison, she directed her message at an African-American audience. From 1831 until 1833, she labored to convince Boston blacks of the value of education, the inevitability of their liberation (even if by violence), the need for unity and collective action, and the responsibilities of women in the struggle.

Stewart broke social conventions with a series of four Boston lectures. These came at a time when no female, except Englishwoman Frances Wright, had the audacity to speak from a public platform before American audiences. She exhorted African Americans to educate themselves, pleaded with them to press for their rights, and openly opposed the domesticity that characterized antebellum American womanhood. Stewart was an early practitioner of what scholars have recently called the African-American jeremiad—a denunciation of America's racial ills coupled with a vision of redemptive change. Garrison published these four speeches in his *The Liberator* and later reprinted them, along with a series of her religious meditations and prayers, as *Productions of Mrs. Maria W. Stewart* (1835).

Stewart's unconventional behavior stirred such hostility that in 1833 she left Boston. After teaching for the next three decades in the black schools of New York City, Brooklyn, Baltimore, and Washington, DC, she spent her last years as matron of the Freedmen's Hospital in the nation's capital. In March 1879, under a law approved by the U.S. Congress the year before, Stewart obtained a federal pension as the widow of a veteran of the War of 1812. She used this income to finance a second edition of her speeches and writings entitled *Meditations from the Pen of Mrs. Maria W. Stewart* (1879). Stewart died in the Freedmen's Hospital in December of 1879.

—Roy E. Finkenbine

Bibliography

The introductory essays in Marilyn Richardson, ed., *Maria W. Stewart, America's First Black Woman Political Writer: Essays and Speeches* (Bloomington: Indiana University Press, 1987) provide the best secondary source of information on Maria W. Stewart's life. Richardson also reprints or cites virtually all of the relevant manuscripts. Another useful biography is the one by Eleanor Flexner in Edward T. James, Janet Wilson James, and Paul S. Boyer, eds., *Notable American Women*, 3 vols. (Cambridge: Harvard University Press, 1971).

Stewart's political speeches and writings are reprinted in the Richardson volume. Her religious meditations and prayers can be easily found in Sue E. Houchins, ed., *Spiritual Narratives* (New York: Oxford University Press, 1988), a volume in the Schomburg Library of Nineteenth-Century Black Women Writers.

STEWART, SALLIE [WYATT] (1881–1951) is best remembered for her numerous contributions to women's organizations and for her achievements in the black community. Born in Ensle, Tennessee, on January 4 to Armstead and Eliza (Jones) Wyatt, Stewart moved with her family to Evansville, Indiana, which became her lifetime home until her death in 1951. Stewart excelled in education, graduating as the class valedictorian from Evansville High School at age 16. She continued her education at the University of Chicago and the University of Indiana to prepare for a teaching career. She taught elementary school and high school English for 32 years in the Evansville public schools and became the dean of girls (1928–1951) at Lincoln High School in Evansville. Among her many accomplishments as an educator, Stewart was the first to hold high school classes in stenography, domestic science, mental hygiene, and parent education for her students.

In 1911 Stewart married a real estate dealer, Logan H. Stewart of Mt. Vernon, Indiana, who owned a thriving business. During these years, she worked as a matron of the Elizabeth chapter, Order of Eastern Star, and as an active member of Grace Lutheran Church. She continued to operate the real estate business after her husband's death, since they had no children of their own.

Beyond her careers as an educator and real estate broker, Stewart contributed to a variety of women's and racial advancement organizations. She was a charter member of the Evansville branch of the NAACP in 1915 and served as its first secretary. In 1918 she joined the National Association of Colored Women (NACW). Upon her return from the 1918 biennial NACW Convention in Denver, Colorado, Stewart joined with other black women in revitalizing the local black women's club. Soon Stewart rose in the national organization to become chair of the NACW Social Science Department, member of the executive board, vice president-at-large, and later, president of the NACW (1928–1933). Stewart was instrumental in establishing the organization's basic policies and procedures. During these same years, she founded the Evansville Federation of Colored Women and became the president of the Indiana Federation of Colored Women. During her tenure, she established the Day Nursery for Colored Children and the National Association of Colored Girls in 1930. She traveled to over 60 cities to speak about community reform.

Sallie Stewart was the first black woman to hold an office in the interracial National Council of Women (NCW). Her tenure as vice president of the organization enabled her to go to Vienna, Austria, in 1930 as one of ten delegates from the United States to the international meeting of the NCW. She continued her local reforms through membership on the Evansville Phillis Wheatley Association, Carver Community Organization Board, and Zeta Phi Beta. She authored two books in 1933: *The National Association of Colored Girls Guide* and *Ethiopia Lifts as She Climbs.*

Her last major endeavor was the conducting of a successfull $100,000 drive for the perpetual care of the Frederick Douglass Memorial and Historical Association in Washington, DC, in 1950. Although she suffered from a crippling illness that restricted her mobility, Stewart continued her activism and teaching career. She retired from teaching in June 1951. One month later she died in her Evansville home.

—Julieanne Phillips

Bibliography

Much of the information about Sallie Stewart's role in the club movement can be found in the Indiana Federation of Colored Women Papers, Gary, Indiana; and Elizabeth Davis, *Lifting as They Climb* (Washington, DC: NACW, 1933). Chapter 4 of Darlene Clark Hine, *When the Truth Is Told: A History of Black Women's Culture and Community in Indiana, 1875–1950* (Indianapolis: National Council of Negro Women, 1981) details the life of Stewart. Other sources include Sylvia G.L. Dannett, *Profiles of Negro Womanhood, 1619–1900, Volume I* (New York/Philadelphia: M.W. Lads, 1964), pp. 315; and an entry in *Who's Who in Colored America*, 7th edition, edited by James Fleming and C. Burckel (New York: Who's Who of Colored America Corp., 1950).

STOKES, OLIVIA PEARL (b. 1916), lecturer, author, and community leader, is best known as the co-founder and former executive director of the Greater Harlem Comprehensive Guidance Center (1974–1990). Stokes, born in Middlesex, North Carolina, to William Harmon and Bessie (Thomas) Stokes, came with her family to Harlem in 1925. There she pursued her education, receiving a BA in education from New York University in 1947; an MA in education, New York University, 1948; an EdD, Teachers College, Columbia University, 1952; and a certificate from Union Theological Seminary, 1952, during which time she served as the director of religious education at Baptist Education Center from 1941 to 1953. She has completed postdoctoral studies in human relations at Boston University. In 1986 she studied the Yoruba civilization at the University of Ife, Nigeria, West Africa, as a Fulbright fellow. She held a fellowship at the Mary Bunting Institute of Radcliffe/Harvard University, Cambridge, Massachusetts, in 1989–1990.

Her role as an educator brought her to such leadership positions as the co-director of the Baptist Educational Center in New York, 1941 to 1952. In 1955, 1960, and 1970, she was a leader in White House Conferences on Education. She led 20 graduate student seminars to West, Central, and East Africa from 1958 to 1981. From 1973 to 1976 Stokes was chairperson for the development of a multi-ethnic, multicultural teacher education program at City University of New York's Lehman College. During summer session she developed a graduate teacher education study abroad program in African ethnic heritage in five Nigerian universities. During these years she also did research on African family life and women's roles in 20 African countries. She currently serves as a consultant for the Citizens Committee for New York City.

As a religious educator and an ordained minister in the American Baptist Churches, she led the educational component of the National Council of Churches' ecumenical Caribbean studies in 1965. During 1966–1973, she developed the National Council of Churches in Christ Black Curriculum Resource Center. She served as an educational consultant and urban education for the National Council of Churches from 1966 to 1973. She was associate director of the Baptist Educational Center in New York City from 1941 to 1952. In 1975–1976, she was a consultant to the education and ministry division for the National Council of Churches. From 1975 to 1980, Stokes was a member of the World Council of Churches Ecumenical Study Program at Bossey, Switzerland.

Stokes is the author of *Why the Spider Lives in Corners* and *The Beauty of Being Black*, as well as articles and chapters in books. She has been an adjunct associate professor at New York University since 1978 and was an associate professor of education at Lehman College, City University of New York, from 1971 to 1976.

She co-founded the Greater Harlem Comprehensive Guidance Center, which began its operations in 1979. The philosophy of the Center is based on the belief that "there is a great future in every child." Its program serves to support minority adolescent students in their developing years. The foundation of the Center's philosophy is the deeply held belief in the uniqueness of each youth. Through one-to-one group counseling, career guidance, and educational/cultural enrichment experiences, the Center's counselors seek to nurture and develop that which is unique within each participant. Weekly, the Center serves 250 junior and senior high school students and 50 to 60 families through the Parent Power Council, walk-in counseling interviews, career clinics, and recreational, educational, and cultural activities.

Stokes is a member of Delta Sigma Delta, Pi Lambda Theta, the Religious Education Association USA, American Association of University Professors, American Association of University Women, African American Association for Study of Life and History, the African-American Institute's Educators to Africa Association, Friends of City University and Bronx Community College, and a life member of the NAACP, National Council of Negro Women. She is a member of Abyssinian Baptist Church in New York City.

In 1990 the Harlem branch of the YMCA awarded her its Dr. Leo B. Marsh Memorial Award. She has received the Justice Award from the National Association of Public Continuing Education (1975); the National Bethune Achievement Award from the National Council of Negro Women (1976) and the International Award from the Business and Professional Women's Association (1979). She was one of 55 black women profiled in the 1982 Radcliffe/Harvard book *Women of Courage*. In 1987 Marymount College awarded her an honorary doctor of humane letters.

—Olivia Pearl Stokes

Bibliography

The interview with Olivia Pearl Stokes is part of the Black Women's Oral History Collection, Radcliffe College.

Works by Olivia Pearl Stokes

The Beauty of Being Black and *Why the Spider Lives in Corners*. New York: Friendship Press, 1971.
with Olivia David, eds. *Listen to the Children*. New York: Carlton, 1955.

SUL-TE-WAN, MADAME [CONLEY, HOLT, EBENTHEUR] (1873–1959), actress, has many ambiguous and puzzling aspects in her life. But, one indisputable fact has endured the test of time: Madame Sul-Te-Wan was the first African-American woman to grace the silver screen in a major film production. Many other aspects concerning her life, however, have entered the realm of myth. There are scraps and pieces of her life history scattered in various places. Because of poor record keeping, crucial details of her life may remain unconfirmed or unknown for years to come.

Madame Sul-Te-Wan was born in Louisville, Kentucky. According to her obituary in the *Los Angeles Sentinel* (Thursday, February 5, 1959), she was the daughter of Silas Crawford Wan and Cleo de Londa. Her father, who was a Hindu minister, apparently died while Sul-Te-Wan was a girl. Her mother was forced to work as a washerwoman for various actresses, including Mary Anderson and Fanny Davenport, until she (Cleo de Londa) decided to become a professional singer.

As a child Sul-Te-Wan delivered washing to the theater and then lingered there for hours watching performances. Through her acute observations, she absorbed and mastered intricate dance steps. According to *The Negro Trail-blazers of California* (1919), Sul-Te-Wan began her career by entering a contest for the best "buck and wing dancer." After Sul-Te-Wan won first prize (a granite dishpan and spoon), she and her mother moved to Cincinnati, Ohio, where she pursued her career. In Cincinnati Sul-Te-Wan performed at the Dime Museum. She later formed her own stock companies, the Black Four Hundred and the Rair Back Minstrels.

The threads of Sul-Te-Wan's personal life are just as difficult to unravel as her professional life. As a young woman, she married an African American, Robert Reed Conley. This union brought forth eight children (only one is mentioned in Sul-Te-Wan's obituary as survivor, Ernest Conley). For reasons unknown, perhaps family size or the impact of poverty, Conley subsequently deserted his family. According to the article in *Our World*, Sul-Te-Wan's second husband, a German, Count William Holt, died right after their marriage.

In 1910 Sul-Te-Wan ventured to Los Angeles, hoping to become a "movie star." Her dream was realized when she was offered a role making three, then five dollars a day in D.W. Griffith's *The Clansman*, later titled *The Birth of a Nation* (1915). According to several sources, because Griffith was impressed by her talent, Sul-Te-Wan was featured in the film as a rich, beautifully dressed "colored lady." Censors subsequently cut these scenes, fearing their controversial nature. She appeared in several Griffith films and was on his payroll until at least 1917.

Sul-Te-Wan was not only talented, but also tenacious and courageous. She was fired from the Majestic Motion Picture Company, accused of stealing a book from the set of *The Birth of a Nation*, and of inciting "colored people" to protest the film. Rather than leave in humiliation, she asked a prominent lawyer, Edward Burton Ceruti, to assist her in clearing her name. Through his efforts, Sul-Te-Wan was exonerated. She and Griffith remained lifelong friends. (Bogle states in *Brown Sugar* that rumors suggested their relationship might have been more than a friendship.)

Incredibly, Sul-Te-Wan's film career spanned 44 years. In addition to *The Birth of a Nation*, she appeared in more than 30 films, including *Uncle Tom's Cabin* (1927), *In Old Chicago* (1938), and *Mighty Joe Young* (1949). Interestingly, she is rumored to be the grandmother of Dorothy Dandridge (see Anthony Slide, *The Kindergarten of the Movies*), possibly encouraged by the fact that she appears in several films with Dandridge including *Carmen Jones* (1954) and *Porgy and Bess* (1959). At age 70, Sul-Te-Wan married her third husband, a French interior designer, Anton Ebentheur. Her last film was *Porgy and Bess*. She died on February 1, 1959, before the film was released.

—Gloria J. Gibson-Hudson

Bibliography

The best information about Madame Sul-Te-Wan can be found through resources on the black theater. Donald Bogle, *Brown Sugar* (New York: Harmony Books, 1980), and *Blacks in American Films and Television* (New York: Garland, 1988); Phyllis Klotman, *Frame by Frame: A Black Filmography* (Bloomington: Indiana University Press, 1979 [filmography entry, see p. 679]); Edward Mapp, "Madame Sul-Te-Wan," in *Directory of Blacks in the Performing Arts*, 2nd ed. (Metuchen, NJ: Scarecrow, 1990); Henry Sampson, *Blacks in Black and White: A Sourcebook in Black Films* (Metuchen, NJ: Scarecrow, 1977); Daniel J. Leab, *From Sambo to Superstar* (Boston: Houghton Mifflin, 1975); Thomas Cripps, *Slow Fade to Black: The Negro in American Films, 1900–1942* (New York: Oxford University Press, 1977); James Haskins, *Black Theatre in America*)New York: Crowell, 1982); and Anthony Slide, "Madame Sul-Te-Wan," *The Kindergarten of the Movies* (Metuchen, NJ: Scarecrow Press, 1980), p. 159.

Materials relating to her career as an African-American woman in California include: Delilah L. Beasley, *The Negro Trail-Blazers of California* (Los Angeles: Times Mirror Publishing, 1919), pp. 237–241; "Madame Sul-Te-Wan," *Our World* 9 (February 1954): 80–82; Hazel La Marre, "Mourn Madame Sul-Te-Wan," *Los Angeles Sentinel* (Thursday, February 5, 1959, cover story).

Her biographical sketch by Robert L. Johns appears in Jessie Carney Smith, ed., *Notable Black American Women* (Detroit: Gale, 1992), pp. 1093–1094.

T

TALBERT, MARY [BURNETT] (1866–1923), educator, organizer, and human rights advocate, was born on September 17 in Oberlin, Ohio, the youngest of the eight surviving children of Cornelius J. Burnett and Caroline (Nichols) Burnett. Natives of North Carolina, her parents moved to Oberlin in 1860 to avail themselves of the educational opportunities the town offered. The Burnetts owned several business establishments that catered to an Oberlin College clientele. Their home frequently was the center of political activities. Cornelius Burnett was involved in state and local Republican politics, as well as the politics of the Christ Episcopal church and, later, the Second Congregational church.

In this environment, the seeds of Mary Morris Burnett's political activism germinated. She attended the public schools of Oberlin and upon graduation in 1883, at age 16, she enrolled in Oberlin College. Completing her training in three years Mary Burnett, in 1886, began her professional career when she accepted a position as liberal arts instructor in the segregated school system of Little Rock, Arkansas. In 1887 Mary Burnett became the first woman in the state to hold the position of assistant principal, the highest position to which any woman had acceded. One year later she became principal of the Union High School of Little Rock. Mary Burnett remained in Little Rock until her marriage in 1891 to William Herbert Talbert, a successful Buffalo, New York, city clerk and realtor. The following year she gave birth to their only child, a daughter, Sarah May. For the next few years, managing the extended Talbert household and church activities consumed most of her time.

Mary Talbert became a charter member of the Buffalo Phyllis Wheatley Club in 1899 and thereby began the activities that led to her national and international prominence. This club soon affiliated with the National Association of Colored Women (NACW) and provided an important forum for Talbert's national activities in both the NACW and the NAACP. Black women in New York State founded the Empire State Federation of Women's Clubs in 1911. Mary Talbert also was a charter member of this organization, and members elected her its second president, a position she held from 1912 to 1916.

During the pre–World War I era, Mary Talbert held several administrative positions in the NACW. By 1914 she was vice president, and in 1916 members elected her president; she served two terms (1916–1920). With Talbert at the helm the NACW achieved several new heights. It established national goals and priorities. Talbert was the club's first elected delegate to the quinquennial conference of the International Council of Women that met in Christiana, Norway, in 1920. As a member of the United States delegation she addressed the assembled representatives urging them to return to their homelands to fight for the rights of illegitimate children. She also spoke to audiences throughout Europe regarding the conditions that African Americans experienced in the United States. During her presidency, the NACW purchased the Anacostia, Washington, DC, residence of Frederick Douglass as a monument to the eminent statesman and as a potential national headquarters.

Talbert was a goodwill ambassador during the World War I era, when she served as YMCA secretary and Red Cross nurse in Romagne, France, in 1919. She offered classes for African-American soldiers and comforted them. Upon her return to the United States, she traveled under the auspices of the U.S. government and lectured to black women's groups on food preservation and conservation. She spearheaded the Liberty Bond Drive among African-American women that raised over $5 million. Talbert was one of the American women appointed to the League of Nations Committee on International Relations.

Ever mindful that the United States participation in the "war to make the world safe for democracy" did not alter the status of African Americans, Mary Talbert joined other NACW members in organizing the International Council of Women of the Darker Races to address the needs of people of color around the globe in 1922. Talbert served on the organization's Committee on Education. She also joined the 1921 delegation of prominent black spokespersons who petitioned President Warren Harding to grant clemency to the members of the 24th Black Regiment, which was falsely accused of inciting the Houston, Texas, racial riots of 1917.

Mary Talbert had served as NAACP vice president and as a board member from 1918 until her death in 1923. She reputedly was instrumental in involving the NAACP in an investigation of U.S. atrocities committed in Haiti in 1921. Talbert also was national director of the NAACP's Anti-Lynching Campaign that hoped to win support for the antilynching bill that Leonidas Dyer introduced into Congress in 1921. The NAACP awarded her the coveted Spingarn Medal in 1922 for her efforts in preserving the Douglass home and for her other human rights activities; she was the first woman to be honored in this manner by the organization.

After a lengthy illness, at age 57, she died of coronary thrombosis in Buffalo, New York, on October 8, 1923. She is buried in Forest Lawn Cemetery in Buffalo.
—Lillian S. Williams

Bibliography

Although there is no scholarly biography of Mary Burnett Talbert, she wrote extensive accounts of her activities and thoughts on contemporary issues, most of which have been lost. There is no extant body of her papers. So much of the data needed to document the lives of even prominent women like Talbert have not been placed in repositories, or so little significance has been placed on black women's accomplishments that their papers have been destroyed.

This author's experience investigating the life of Mary Talbert illustrates the complexities involved in researching black women's lives. While working as a visiting professor of history at SUNY Buffalo, a librarian informed me that a local antique dealer possessed a substantial cache of Mary Burnett Talbert papers and memorabilia. After canceling several of our appointments over a number of months, the antique dealer finally agreed to meet with me. I arrived full of enthusiasm, and shortly therafter he returned with a box of materials that included a huge stack of letters. I was elated and thought for the first time that I would be able to learn more about her personality and thoughts. Unfortunately, all of the personal letters were discarded and only the envelopes were kept for the valuable stamps. This businessman had sold the Talbert household furnishings, retained photographs due to the affluence of the family, and yet discarded "tons" of personal papers. I was amazed that it did not occur to him that the papers of this affluent family were also important and of interest to a manuscript dealer in the Buffalo area. The quest for her papers continues. Remaining correspondence exists in the Mary Church Terrell Papers at Howard University and the Library of Congress; the W.E.B. Du Bois Papers at the University of Massachusetts, Amherst; and the Charlotte Hawkins Brown Papers at the Schlesinger Library, Radcliffe College, Cambridge, Massachusetts.

One of her essays, "Did the Negro Make in the Nineteenth Century Achievements along the Lines of Wealth, Morality, Education, etc., Commensurate with His Opportunities? If So, What Achievements Did He Make?" appeared in Daniel Wallace Culp, *Twentieth Century Negro Literature* (New York: Arno and *New York Times*, 1969), pp. 17–21. She also was a contributing editor to *Woman's Voice* and *The Champion*. The most comprehensive biographical sketch of her is Lillian S. Williams, "Mary Morris Burnett Talbert," in *Notable Black American Women*, edited by Jessie Carney Smith (Detroit: Gale, 1992).

Brown, Hallie Q. *Homespun Heroines and Other Women of Distinction.* Xenia, OH: Aldine Press, 1926, pp. 216–219.

Buffalo Express (July 15, 1923).

Buffalo Enquirer (October 16, 1923).

The Crisis (February 1923); (December 1923).

National Notes (May 1926).

Oberlin Alumni Magazine (April 1917).

Dannett, Sylvia. *Profiles of Negro Womanhood* II. New York: National Heritage, 1966.

Logan, Rayford. "Talbert, Mary" in *The Dictionary of American Negro Biography*, edited by Rayford Logan and Michael Winston. New York: Norton, 1985, pp. 576–577.

Robinson, Wilhelmina S. *Historical Negro Biographies.* New York: Publishers Co., 1967, pp. 127–128.

Wesley, Charles. *The History of the National Association of Colored Women's Clubs, Inc.* Washington, DC: NACWC, 1984.

Williams, Lillian S. "Talbert, Mary Morris Burnett," in *Encyclopedia of World Biography* 16, edited by David Eggenberger. Palatine, IL: McGraw-Hill/Heraty Associates, 1990, pp. 396–398.

TAYLOR, SUSIE [BAKER, KING] (1848–1912), Civil War nurse, teacher, and author, was the eldest of nine children born to slave parents Hagar Ann (Reed) and Raymond Baker on August 6 on the Isle of Wight, about 35 miles

from Savannah, Georgia. Taylor and a younger sister and brother were given permission by their master, Valentine Grest, to live with their free grandmother, Dolly Reed, in Savannah when Taylor was seven years old. There she was clandestinely educated for five or six years and used that literacy to write (liberty) passes for her grandmother. In April 1862, Taylor went with her uncle and his family to St. Simons Island in response to Union Army major-general David Hunter's announcement that all slaves in the immediate vicinity of the now-captured Fort Pulaski were free. There she was in charge of a school for children during the day and taught adults at night. She married Edward King, a member of the First South Carolina Volunteers.

When the island was evacuated in October, Taylor became laundress, nurse, and teacher of the First South Carolina Volunteers (later known as the 33rd United States Colored Troops) at Camp Saxton (named after General Rufus Saxton) and later Camp Shaw (named after Colonel Robert Gould Shaw) near Beaufort, South Carolina. In 1863, two months after celebrating President Abraham Lincoln's Emancipation Proclamation, Taylor accompanied the First SC Volunteers when it occupied Jacksonville, Florida. The 6th Connecticut and 8th Maine regiments reinforced the group, the first time, according to Colonel Thomas Wentworth Higginson, that blacks and whites "had served together on regular duty." When the regiment returned to Camp Shaw, Taylor nursed the sick and wounded with Clara Barton. In February 1865 Taylor, despite the sneering and harassment of white citizens, assisted in the care of the sick and wounded in Charleston, which had been evacuated and burned by the Confederate Army.

When the regiment was mustered out (after having served without pay) in 1866, Taylor and her husband returned to Savannah, where she opened a school in her home on South Broad Street (later Oglethorpe Avenue). Her husband worked at the docks because black codes prevented him from using his carpentry skills in free labor. Edward King died on September 16, 1866, while his wife was pregnant. After the birth of their son, Taylor opened a school in Liberty County, Georgia, but, not liking country life, returned to Savannah a year later and opened a night school for adults. When that school closed in the fall of 1868, she engaged in domestic service in the South and in Boston and put in a claim for the $100 bounty owed her husband as a Union soldier.

In 1879 she married Russell L. Taylor in Boston. In 1886 Taylor helped organize Corps 67, Women's Relief Corps, an auxiliary of the Grand Army of the Republic, and subsequently served as guard, secretary, treasurer, and president. In February 1898 Taylor went to Shreveport, Louisiana, where her actor son was dying. He was too weak to travel except by sleeper, a privilege denied African Americans, so Taylor could not bring him back to Boston and remained in Shreveport to care for him. Her experiences during the months in Shreveport reminded her once again of the brutality she had witnessed toward slaves in her childhood and toward blacks during her adulthood. She assisted in relief work during the Spanish-American War, lamenting the prejudice against blacks in

Cuba despite the efforts of black men there "who fought for freedom and the right." Taylor recounted these experiences in her autobiography published in 1902. Taylor died in 1912.

—Rosalie Murphy Baum

Bibliography

    Susie King Taylor's autobiography, *Reminiscences of My Life in Camp: With the 33rd United States Colored Troops, Late 1st S.C. Volunteers*, was published in 1902 (reprint ed. New York: M. Weiner, 1988); Patricia W. Romero's edition, *A Black Woman's Civil War Memoirs*, was published in 1988 (New York: Oxford); and a reprint as part of the Schomburg Library of Nineteenth-Century Black Women Writers appeared in *Collected Black Women's Narratives* (New York: Oxford, 1988). Excerpts are included in *Growing Up Female in America*, edited by Eve Merriam (Boston: Beacon Press, 1973); a summary appears in *Profiles of Negro Womanhood* (1964–1966) by Sylvia G.L. Dannett (Chicago: Educational Heritage, 1964). Col. Thomas Wentworth Higginson of the 1st SC Volunteers wrote the "Introduction" to King's autobiography; his *Army Life in a Black Regiment* (New York: Norton, 1984) offers "a wholly different [but complementary] point of view" of those who served with the earliest of the African-American regiments.

TEER, BARBARA ANN (b. 1937), actress, playwright, and leader in the National Black Theatre, was born on June 18, to Fred L. and Lila (Benjamin) Teer, in East St. Louis, Illinois. She attended local public schools and received a bachelor's degree with highest honors in dance education from the University of Illinois in 1957. In college, Teer joined Delta Sigma Theta sorority. She pursued advanced studies at the University of Wisconsin and Connecticut College for Women, and danced in Paris, Berlin, and Switzerland, attending the Wigman School of Dance. Teer also studied drama with Sanford Meisner, Paul Mann, Phillip Burton, and Lloyd Richards, who was director of the Yale School of Drama.

Teer's Broadway debut was in *Kwamina* at the 54th Street Theatre in New York in October 1961. She was the dance captain for Agnes DeMille, who choreographed that musical. Teer won a Tony Award for her performance. She performed with Pearl Bailey in Las Vegas and was featured at the 1962 Newport Jazz Festival. During the early 1960s she taught dance and drama in the New York City public schools and was the cultural director of a teenage workshop at the Harlem School of the Arts. She co-founded and taught with actor Robert Hooks at the Group Theatre Workshop (later renamed the Negro Ensemble Company) in 1964. Teer also danced with the Henry St. Playhouse Dance Company, Alvin Ailey Dance Company, and Louis Johnson Dance Company.

Teer was an actress in New York City and Boston plays. She played Bella Belafunky in *Raisin' Hell in the Son* (1962) at the Provincetown Playhouse in New York. In the next year she appeared in *The Living Premise*. In 1964 she portrayed the character Violet in *Home Movies* and won the 1965 Vernon Rice Drama Desk Award for Best Actress for that performance. Teer's other theatrical roles included *Funnyhouse of a Negro* (1965), *Prodigal Son* (1965), *Happy Ending*, as Mary in *Day of Absence* (1965), as Clara in *Who's Got His Own?* (1966), *Does a Tiger Wear a Necktie?* (1967), as Jean Biggs in *The Experiment* (1967), in *Slaves* (1968), *Angel Levine* (1969), and *Where's Daddy?* (1969).

Teer played both leads and featured roles in several films. Her screen debut was in the 1964 motion picture *Gone Are the Days*. She also appeared in *The Pawnbroker* (1965), *The Group* (1966), and *The Slaves* (1969). Teer performed on numerous television programs, including *A Carol for Another Christmas*, *Camera Three*, *Kaleidoscope*, *The Ed Sullivan Show*, and *Black Journal*. She directed the off-Broadway play *The Believers* in 1967.

Although Teer had a good reputation as an actress, she decided that the roles available to her and the atmosphere of established theater were unsatisfactory and quit her acting career. She explained that she had been disillusioned by the Western theater establishment, which she did not think seriously regarded black artists and unfairly excluded them from productions. She believed directors had limited viewpoints, and she resented being typecast in roles that were not representative of real life. She explained, "No one could tell me what had to be done, because I know better than anyone else."

Discouraged by the dearth of realistic roles for black performers, especially women, Teer created a theater especially to express black culture. During the 1960s, Harlem experienced the black arts movement, and many blacks dropped their "slave" names for African names. Teer is also referred to as Roho Taji Taifu. Teer's theater in Harlem was named the National Black Theatre.

Prior to its founding in 1968, Teer had expressed her frustration with traditional theater forms based on a Western European culture by writing articles for the *New York Times*, *Black Theater Magazine*, *Negro Digest/Black World*, and *Black Power Revolt*. She believed black artists should celebrate both their African and American cultures and stressed the need for the solidarity of the race. Teer picketed and distributed pamphlets in New York, demanding that black actors be offered more realistic roles in order to debunk stereotypes and concepts and to present a better image with which black youths could identify and emulate. She believed that black actors had to deny their blackness and culture in order to win the few roles open to them in traditional theater and that these roles only reflected white values.

Teer insisted that black actors should build a black identity instead. She wanted black artists to be offered opportunities and success within the black culture. She realized that economic power determined many actors' decisions to accept demeaning roles but argued that black artists had to seek their own stage because whites would continue to exploit them. Teer also disliked that black males had more acting opportunities than women and demanded that black women and men should work together, rather than against each other to the detriment of the race.

Teer was angry that the casting system was unfair to black women, who rarely were offered major roles. Casting directors claimed that the public expected and accepted black women to be in stereotypical and usually inferior and demeaning roles that perpetuated myths and stereotypes. Aware that there were many talented black actresses like herself eager to play major roles, Teer wanted to advance beyond this unfair and restrictive environment.

She complained that "as a black actress, as long as this condition prevails, I can merely look forward to playing 'demanding' roles such as prostitutes, maids, and/ or every now and then, just for local color, of course, some form of exotic." Teer expressed a dislike for black playwrights who wrote unsympathetic and degrading roles for black women. She explained, "It's part of the total culture. Men don't know how to behave toward women, don't understand us as sensitive human beings. They're always portraying us as prostitutes, who slink ridiculously around the stage, or as hateful people. That's why I've created my own theater."

Teer believed that black artists concentrated too much energy on attempting to work with the white theater. Instead of wasting time trying to integrate the preexisting system, she thought that blacks needed their own platform for expression. She expressed her opinion that black actors compromised, even sacrificed, their culture and identity by being forced to accept and conform to the white theater's spiritual and moral values in order to survive economically. As a result, the black racial identity was being destroyed, and Teer insisted that a new separate black theater was needed to cease this form of racism.

She emphasized that black actors should not be assimilated in the present theater culture and imitate whites and that they had a responsibility to their race. Teer considered white theater to be condescending and paternalistic, acting culturally superior to black art forms. She believed that blacks who assimilated within the white theater hampered the liberation of oppressed African Americans. She wanted these artists to fight for freedom, power, and control to oppose what she considered to be cultural imperialism. She stressed that black actors should not think as individuals but rather collectively and represent the best interests of blacks.

In what she labeled a cultural revolution, Teer demanded that black artists work to present true images of their culture to black communities to unify and to spread political and social messages to audiences in order to rehabilitate black Americans and survive as a race. She explained, "Our culture is rich and beautiful; There is nothing like, or equal to, the black life style. It is uniquely and intimately our personal gift to the world." She wanted her own theater in order to have control to experiment within the black community and reenhance intellectual as well as cultural values and traditions.

In order to develop an art form relevant to the concerns of the black community, Teer's National Black Theatre explored rituals derived from black folklore and religious experiences. Acting as the theater's founder, executive director, composer, and resident playwright, Teer labeled the loft theater as "The

Temple of Liberation" and the acting troupe as "The Liberators," because of the energy released when renewing cultural ties during the ritual. In such communal art Teer said, "There is no such thing as a stage, nor such a thing as an audience; only liberators and participants." She elaborated that "in a ritual you mold, meet and merge into one. You feel, laugh, cry and experience life together." Teer and the National Black Theatre rejected traditional formal theatrical presentations.

Creating a new black art standard and theater form, Teer created "ritualistic revivals," also referred to as "blackenings," which were presented instead of formal scripted plays. They were based on West African and West Indies rituals and incorporated religion, dance, music, drums, chants, skits, costumes, and flags in traditional African colors of green, red, and black, and communal participation. Teer's main goal was to enlighten and reaffirm audience members of their spiritual potential. The emphasis was on religion from within and was influenced by the common worship tradition and fervor of black churches to teach love and unity to make positive changes despite differences in socioeconomic or national identities.

Teer was inspired by what she called "God-conscious art," which was an internal creative expression as opposed to European art, which was based on the self-centered, external acquisition of material things in order to be fulfilled. Teer stated, "The Western concepts are so surface they cannot fulfill the spiritual needs of our people." She explained, "I was tired of seeing us hate each other. . . . There was no love, no patience for one another." According to Teer, "God-conscious art has the possibility of totally transforming the thrust of western theater." Teer demanded that all performances in the National Black Theatre raise the audience's conscious level and pertain to political issues as well as educate, illuminate, and entertain. The main goal was not to entertain but to reeducate the black community and restore its cultural tradition so that blacks could reclaim their spiritual freedom and strengthen their minds.

Because of this focus, the National Black Theatre was more revolutionary and militant than previous or contemporary attempts at establishing black theater. Teer's teaching technique was known as the "Teer Technology of Soul." She stressed the importance of the group over individual effort and insisted that all members of the troupe participate in all facets of performing rituals, from painting sets and arranging lights to dancing and singing. Teer emphasized the acceptance of self and culture as well as the communal family and cooperation. The National Black Theatre paid low salaries because the community and theater family was considered more important than the individual.

Theatrical training included a deprogramming purification process called "decrudin" in which the black spirituality denied by society was restored within individuals to form a collective identity. The actor evolved into a liberator by comprehending and passing through the "Five Cycles of Evolution," ranging from materialistic and individualistic identities to the ultimate nonmaterialistic, spiritual nature. They learned to transform selfish behavior to communal impulses and to heal greed by sharing. Liberators were requested to go to churches and bars in Harlem to observe black lifestyles and to collect information representing each cycle to be placed in a workbook. Questionnaires were distributed to people in Harlem to examine how they felt about being black. These experiences provided much of the inspiration for National Black Theatre productions.

The "Five Cycles of Evolution" were represented by characters of the National Black Theatre stage. At performances, the audience was greeted by the performers and incorporated throughout the play, singing, clapping, and dancing with the liberators. There were no restrictions on participation, and performances became so emotional and enthusiastic that one man asked for his son to be baptized. Performances portrayed common themes in black society. The goal was to preserve the beauty and spirit of black lifestyles and celebrate life.

Teer wanted to transform the lives of the audience so that they could experience their individual self as being creative, powerful, and wholesome while understanding that they were a vital component of the community. By invoking the force of ancestral spirits, liberators revealed in the ritual how the black community had been oppressed and taught them how to live together and develop their potential for positive change. Audience members discovered their individual and group African culture and character but were not forced to accept it. This new-found cultural energy could be redirected to eliminate negative attitudes and self-destructive patterns.

In one performance about the negative ramifications of illegal drugs, the emphasis was on how blacks could reinstate positive values in society by morally supporting each other. The stage depicted a normal Harlem street scene. The liberators, conversing and even sitting with the audience, told them facts about black financial power and encouraged them to patronize black and community businesses for consumer control. This purchasing behavior could change society positively through spirituality. Liberators thanked the audience for attending and asked them to tell as many people as possible about the performances and the message of positive change. By the end of the performance, the audience members were no longer strangers but could identify with each other.

Acts were referred to as spaces, and the only traditional theatrical custom utilized was the intercession. At the National Black Theatre, the liberators did not go behind the stage at intermission to change costumes but instead interacted with the audience, distributing refreshments and discussing ideas represented on stage. As a noncommercial, noncompetitive organization, Teer and her troupe were not interested in publicity or critical reviews, especially in the white press. They did not seek external funding because that would mean compromising their philosophy because traditional theatrical funding sources were primarily from white groups. Instead theirs subsisted on a low budget funded by the Harlem community according to its desire for such reeducation.

Teer insisted that she not be called a director but rather a creator or priestess because "I don't use people, tell them to move from here to there." She elaborated that "I don't direct people, I help them to liberate themselves, to free their creative powers through ritual, through dance, music, and poetry. And along the way, we help to liberate our audiences." Performers were encouraged to embrace positive thoughts, meditation, and fasting, and to respect and interact with the community as well as reflect it on the stage.

Teer emphasized that the theater served the community and that "the black artist must remember that it is the people that give him light and clarity of vision and who reinforce his sensibilities." Sunday symposiums of scholars and artists as well as a creative center for children, adult workshops, and a touring program were implemented to involve more blacks in the ritual experience. Lectures, concerts, poetry readings, and films were exhibited, and workshops to discuss problems encountered in society were established.

Year-round performances were scheduled for evenings from Thursday to Saturday with matinees on Sunday. The National Black Theatre's premiere production was *Ritual* in 1971. In July 1971 *Change! Love Together! Organize! A Revival*, which Teer wrote, including music and lyrics, with Charlie Russell, was presented, evolving with each performance. She wrote and co-produced the film *Rise: A Love Song for a Love People* in 1975 based on Malcolm X's life. She had previously written *Tribute to Brother Malcolm*, a historical documentary in the late 1960s that portrayed his life and assassination. This play was performed by the National Black Theatre in the late 1960s. She also wrote *We Sing a New Song* and *Softly Comes a Whirlwind, Whispering in Your Ear*, which her Theatre performed in 1978. With Nabii Faison she wrote *Soul Fusion*, which was performed in 1980.

Off-Broadway, in Boston, Chicago, and New York, she directed *Five on the Black Hand Side* in 1970 as well as *The Spook Who Sat by the Door, The Beauty of Blackness*, and *Me and My Song*. Teer appeared on television in "The Rural" and *Soul* and directed the Black Heritage Series for CBS in 1973 as well as serving as the series' guest director, lecturing on contemporary black art. She was also a guest lecturer on *Positively Black* in 1976.

In 1972 Teer received a Ford Foundation Fellowship to visit seven African nations and spent four months in Nigeria learning about the Yoruba culture and religion. In Nigeria, Teer realized that theater was the celebration of universal life, and she raised money for the theater company to go to Nigeria and work with native artists. She has returned annually to Nigeria to continue her studies of the secrets of the soul, considering that country as her second home. With the traveling troupe of the National Black Theatre, she has also traveled to South America, the West Indies, and Africa, as well as to churches, theaters, and colleges in the United States.

While traveling, Teer and her company researched native cultures and religions to understand the peoples' spirit and soul. Teer participated on the Theatre Committee for the second International Black and African Festival of Arts and Culture (FESTAC) at Lagos, Nigeria, in 1975. At FESTAC '77, the National Black Theatre presented *Souljourney into Truth*, written especially for that festival and based on their experiences with Nigerian culture. It was received with great acclaim and excitement from audiences. The musical evolved as a theatrical collage of impressions, which Teer wrote, directed, and choreographed with intense audience participation. One reviewer called it a "warm spiritual experience" that resembled a Baptist revival. It was also performed at the National Black Theatre in 1975 and as a theatrical tour in Caribbean countries.

Teer's memberships include serving on the Delta Sigma Theta Commission on Arts, the Black Theatre Collective Uptown Chamber of Commerce in Harlem, the Black Theatre Alliance, the Harlem Philharmonic Society, and on the board of directors of the Theatre Communications Group. She has received numerous awards for her leadership in black theater. To celebrate Martin Luther King, Jr.'s birthday, the Black Agency Executives, a group of black directors of social service agencies, presented Teer a 1992 award for leadership in a nonprofit agency. *Essence* magazine listed her in "Legends in Our Time" in 1990.

The Harlem Women's Committee presented her the Sojourner Truth Award, and the Hamilton Arts Center honored her with the National Black Treasure Award. East St. Louis, Illinois (Teer's hometown) Community Schools awarded her a Token of Esteem Award in 1973. Ten years later the National Council for Culture and Art bestowed Teer with the Monarch Merit Award for Outstanding Contributions to the Performing and Visual Arts.

At the National Association of Media Women's Black Film Festival, *Rise* was designated the best film. The National Black Theatre won the first annual AUDELCO Awards in 1973 for best musical, actress, actor, and music director for *The Legacy*. Costumer Larry Le Gaspi won an AUDELCO award in 1976 for *Souljourney into Truth*. New York City mayor Edward Koch and the New York State Government named May 7, 1979, as National Black Theatre Day because of Teer's and her Theatre's cultural contributions to the community. The National Black Theatre has been highly regarded by actors as well as the public as being successful in providing a platform for honoring and respecting black culture. By 1981 annual attendance reached 250,000.

The original National Black Theatre was razed by a fire in 1983. A new theater was built at the corner of 5th Avenue and 125th Street. Teer bought Harlem brownstones to house the Theatre's staff and artists as well as the property for the new Theatre's site. In addition to the performing Theatre, she established the National Black Institute of Communication Through Theatre Arts. The new Theatre is the first black theater that generates revenue because it rents commercial, retail, and office space in addition to the theater activity. The Theatre has 288 seats as well as workshop space and is the first mixed-use cultural facility built in Harlem.

Teer and Theatre members arranged a $5.7 million loan package to finance construction. As chief executive officer, Teer contracted with Nigerian craftsmen to design the Theatre's interior with a Nigerian sculpture mounted on the Theatre's aluminum and glass facade. Teer emphasized, "We want it to be a conversation piece in New York." New York governor Mario M. Cuomo, referring to Harlem's artistic history, lauded that the new Theatre "set the stage for a new phase in that splendid tradition."

Teer is divorced from comedian Godfrey Cambridge. She has two children, a son, Omi, and daughter, Folashade. Teer currently lives in New York City, where she is an active leader in the National Black Theatre. Following her philosophy that no one in the Theatre has a specific task, Teer has been depicted as fulfilling many roles: executive producer, writer, director, actress, educator, cultural leader, entrepreneur, philosopher, and real estate developer.

—Elizabeth D. Schafer

Bibliography

Biographical sketches of Teer, listing her complete awards, are included in Allen Woll, *Dictionary of the Black Theatre: Broadway, Off-Broadway, and Selected Harlem Theatre* (Westport, CT: Greenwood Press, 1983, p. 251); Bernard L. Peterson, *Contemporary Black American Playwrights and Their Plays: A Biographical Directory and Dramatic Index* (Westport, CT: Greenwood Press, 1988, pp. 443–445); Iris Cloyd, ed., *Who's Who among Black Americans, 1990–91* (Detroit: Gale, 1990, p. 1235); Walter L. Hawkins, *African American Biographies: Profiles of 558 Current Men and Women* (Jefferson, NC: McFarland, 1992, pp. 405–407); Monica M. O'Donnell, ed., *Contemporary Theatre, Film, and Television* , Vol. 1 (Detroit: Gale, 1984, pp. 491–492); and *Notable Names in the American Theatre* (Clifton, New Jersey: James T. White, 1976, p. 1175).

Teer wrote several drama articles: "The Black Woman: She Does Exist," *New York Times* (May 14, 1967: D15); "The Great White Way Is Not Our Way—Not Yet," *Negro Digest (Black World)* (April 1968): 25; "We Can Be What We Were Born to Be," *New York Times* (July 7, 1968, section 2, pp. 1, 3); "Needed—A New Image," in Floyd B. Barbour, ed., *The Black Power Revolt: A Collection of Essays* (Boston: Extending Horizons Books, 1968, pp. 219–223); and "Who's Gonna Run the Show?" *New York Times* (February 2, 1969: p. 2:9). Reaction to Teer's ideas can be located in letters to the editor in the *New York Times* (July 21, 1968: D5, D12). See also Teer, "The National Black Theatre as It Relates to Western Theaters," unpublished manuscript located at the National Black Theatre. An interview with Teer, January 3, 1973, is in the Hatch-Billops Collection, Archives of Black Cultural History, New York City. Teer is quoted in *Encore* (April 21, 1975).

Articles about Teer and her professional accomplishments include Paulette Williams, "Barbara Ann Teer: Producer," *Ebony* (August 1977: 138); George Gent, "Black Women Take Roles as Directors," *New York Times* (November 17, 1971: 40); Thomas A. Johnson, "On Harlem Stage, A Spiritual Journey," *New York Times* (May 11, 1971: 44); Mel Tapley, "Barbara Ann Teer Revisits Africa," *Amsterdam News* (December 1980); Marvine Howe, "Honoring Dr. King's Memory by Celebrating Excellence," *New York Times* (January 16, 1992, p. B7). Photographs of Teer are in Paul Carter Harrison and Bert Andrews, *In the Shadow of the Great White Way: Images from the Black Theatre*, introduction by Cicely Tyson (New York: Thunder's Mouth Press, 1989). Teer's awards are noted in the May 1990 *Essence*.

Works mentioning Teer include Mabel M. Smythe, *The Black American Reference Book* (Englewood Cliffs: New Jersey: Prentice-Hall, 1976); Genevieve Fabre, *Drumbeats, Masks and Metaphor: Contemporary Afro-American Theatre*, translated by Melvin Dixon, (Cambridge, MA: Harvard University Press, 1983), who quotes Teer on her philosophy of ritual theater; Mance Williams, *Black Theatre in the 1960s and 1970s: A Historical-Critical Analysis of the Movement* (Westport, CT: Greenwood Press, 1985), which examines Teer's philosophy and the development of her Theatre; Paul Carter Harrison, *The Drama of Nommo* (New York: Grove Press, 1972), who describes Teer performing with the National Black Theatre; and Marianna W. Davis, ed., *Contributions of Black Women to America*, 2 volumes (Columbia, SC: Kenday, 1981), in which Volume 1 discusses black women in the arts, including Teer. A review of *Souljourney into Truth* is in *Black World* (April 1976): 56.

Archival material about black theater can be located in the Archives, Theatre and Music Collection, Museum of the City of New York; Clipping Files, New York Public Library for the Performing Arts, Lincoln Center; and Clipping Files New York Public Library, Schomburg Center for Research in Black Culture. *Black Theatre Magazine* as well as *Drama Review* and *Encore* provide contemporary reviews and information about Teer and her Theatre.

Errol Hill, ed., *The Theater of Black Americans*, 2 volumes (Englewood Cliffs, NJ: Prentice-Hall, 1980), contains critical essays about the historical development of the black theater movement as does Larry Neal, "The Black Arts Movement," *The Drama Review* 12 (Summer 1968): 29–39; Samuel A. Hay, "African-American Drama, 1950–1970," *Negro History Bulletin* 36 (January 1973): 5–8; James Haskins, *Black Theater in America* (New York: Crowell, 1982); Woodie King., Jr., *Black Theatre: Present Condition* (New York: National Black Theatre Touring Circuit, 1981); and Evelyn Quita Craig, *Black Drama of the Federal Theatre Era: Beyond the Formal Horizons* (Amherst: University of Massachusetts Press, 1980), who explains Teer's use of the term "liberators."

Information specifically about the National Black Theatre can be located in Jessica B. Harris, "The National Black Theatre: The Sun People of 125th Street," *The Drama Review* 16 (December 1972): 39–45; "The National Black Theatre," in Laura Ross, ed., *Theatre Profiles 5* (New York: Theatre Communications Group, 1982), pp. 86–87; "The National Black Theatre," *Essence* (March 1971): 50; Don Heckman, "Black Theater Unit Combines Ritual, Dance, Song," *New York Times* (July 24, 1972, p. 35); "Audelco Awards Given for Black Theater," *New York Times* (November 26, 1987, p. C19); and Gerald Fraser, "Harlem Ground Is Broken for National Black Theater," *New York Times* (May 21, 1989, section 1, p. 67).

TERBORG-PENN, ROSALYN M. (b. 1941), teacher, historian, consultant, and editor, was born in Brooklyn, New York, on October 22 to Jacque Terborg, Sr., and Jeanne (Van Dorn) Terborg. She has one daughter, Jeanna Penn.

Rosalyn Terborg-Penn grew up in a household expecting educational excellence. She was a member of Phi Alpha Theta, the history honor society, at

Queens College (CUNY), from which she graduated in 1963. She received a Phi Alpha Theta Graduate History Scholarship for the academic year 1964–1965, which helped her attend graduate school at George Washington University in Washington, DC. As a graduate student, she participated in an organized attack on campus discrimination. She was active in the NAACP and the Northern Student Movement, picketing Woolworth's and tutoring inner-city youth as evidence of her idealism. She received her MA from George Washington University in 1967. She continued her pursuit of knowledge by entering the doctoral program at Howard University. She received the Howard University Department of History Graduate Fellowship for the academic year 1973–1974 and was a member of the Phi Delta Kappa Honor Society in 1975. During this time, she served as a co-editor with Thomas Holt and Cassandra Smith Parker on *A Special Mission: The Story of Freedman's Hospital, 1862–1962* (1975). Her dissertation reflected the combined interests of feminism and activism, "Afro-Americans in the Struggle for Women's Suffrage, 1830–1920." She received the PhD in American history in 1977 from Howard University.

With her many scholastic honors and research interest in black women's history, Terborg-Penn became an educator at Howard Community College and at the University of Maryland, College Park. She combined her interests with a fellow student at Howard University, Sharon Harley. The two women co-founded in 1978, the Association of Black Women Historians (ABWH). During that same year, the two women co-edited an anthology of writings about black women, *The Afro-American Woman: Struggles and Images.* A decade later, the women again co-edited a volume, *Women in Africa and the African Diaspora* (1989).

While Rosalyn Terborg-Penn serves as a professor of history at Morgan State University, she continues her professional roles serving on the editorial boards of ABWH's newsletter, *Truth, Feminist Studies, Maryland Historical Magazine,* and *Sage.* She is featured in *Who's Who Among Black Americans* (1980–1981, 1985–1986); *Who's Who of American Women* (1983); and *The World's Who's Who of Women* (1984).

—Regennia N. Williams

Bibliography

For information on Rosalyn Terborg-Penn see the biographical citations in the cited years of *Who's Who among Black Americans, Who's Who of American Women,* and *The World's Who's Who of Women.* Her contribution to black women's history is cited in August Meier and Elliott Rudwick, *Black History and the Historical Profession, 1915–1980* (Urbana: University of Illinois Press, 1986). Her co-edited books include:
with Thomas Holt and Cassandra Smith, eds. *A Special Mission: The Story of Freedman's Hospital, 1862–1962.* Washington, DC: Howard University Press, 1975.

with Sharon Harley. *The Afro-American Woman: Struggles and Images*. Port Washington, NY: Kennikat, 1978.

with Sharon Harley and Andrea Benton Rushing. *Women in Africa and the African Diaspora*. Washington, DC: Howard University Press, 1987.

Her articles appear in the series *Black Women in American History*, edited by Darlene Clark Hine (Brooklyn: Carlson, 1990):

"Black Women Freedom Fighters in Early 19th Century Maryland."

"Discontented Black Feminists: Prelude and Postscript to the Passage of the Nineteenth Amendment."

"Historical Treatment of Afro-Americans in the Women's Movement, 1890–1920: A Bibliographic Essay."

"Teaching the History of Black Women: A Bibliographic Essay."

TERRELL, MARY CHURCH (1863–1954) was born on September 23 in Memphis, Tennessee. She was the daughter of Robert R. Church (speculated to have been the first black millionaire in the South) and Louisa (Ayers) Church (owner of a fashionable hair salon). Because her parents thought that the schools in Memphis were not academically strong, Mary Eliza Church was educated in Ohio. She received her early education at the Model School associated with Antioch College and in the public schools of Yellow Springs and later attended Oberlin High and Oberlin College in Oberlin. After earning her BA degree from Oberlin in 1884, she taught at Wilberforce University and the Preparatory School for Colored Youth (later the M Street High School) in Washington, DC. Taking a leave of absence from the high school (1888–1890), she traveled and studied abroad in England, Belgium, Switzerland, France, and Germany. She received an MA degree from Oberlin during this time and was offered the position of registrar, which she declined in order to marry Robert H. Terrell.

Upon returning from her travel and study abroad, she rejoined the teaching faculty of the M Street High School and shortly thereafter married the principal, Robert H. Terrell, who was later appointed a municipal judge in the District of Columbia. As Mary Church Terrell, she began an active public career as a lecturer in this country and abroad, often appearing on the Chautauqua circuit, an organized tour of lectures by specific speakers on current topics. Terrell also served in many leadership roles, such as appointee to the Washington, DC, Board of Education (1895–1901/1906–1911), the first female president of the Bethel Literary and Historical Society of DC (1892–1893), a member of John Milholland's Constitution League, a founder and member of the NAACP Executive Committee, a founder of the Washington Colored Women's League, the first president of the National Association of Colored Women (NACW), a founder of Delta Sigma Theta, and the second vice president of the Council of Women of the Darker Races. During this active career, Terrell raised two daughters, Mary

Terrell (Tancil Beaupreu) and Phyllis Terrell (Langston), and remained active in Republican politics.

Mary Church Terrell was in one writer's words a "genteel militant" who was active in social reform efforts to overcome racism and sexism in this country. She was a member of many women's groups seeking suffrage, rights, and peace: the National American Women Suffrage Association, the Women's International League for Peace and Freedom, the National Woman's Party, and the Association of Collegiate Alumnae (later the American Association of University Women [AAUW]). She helped prepare for demobilization during World War I through the War Camp Community Service. Always concerned about her race's role in peace efforts, she served as a delegate to the International Peace Congress held in Zurich in May 1919 and at the World Fellowship of Faith in London in 1937.

She received honorary degrees from Oberlin College, Wilberforce University, and Howard University for her years of community commitment, which did not lessen with the years. At age 86, she launched a 3-year battle for membership in the Washington chapter of the AAUW to challenge its racial exclusionary policies. As she won that battle, she assumed leadership of the Enforcement of the District of Columbia Anti-Discrimination Laws Coordinating Committee. She participated in protest marches until her death at age 90 on July 24, 1954. She is interred at Lincoln Memorial Cemetery, Suitland, Maryland.

                                                            —Marcia Y. Riggs

Bibliography

Biographical profiles of Mary Church Terrell may be found in John P. Davis, ed., *The American Negro Reference Book* (Englewood Cliffs, NJ: Prentice-Hall, 1966); Kali Herman, *Women in Particular: An Index to American Women* (Phoenix, AZ: Oryx Press, 1984); Allen Johnson, ed., *Dictionary of American Biography, 1927–1957* (New York: Scribner. [Supp. v.5]); W. Augustus Low, ed., *Encyclopedia of Black America* (New York: McGraw-Hill, 1981); *The National Cyclopedia of American Biography* (Ann Arbor, MI: University Microfilms, Xerox Co., 1967, originally published, New York: James White & Co., 1898, 1899, 1921); Wilhelmina Robinson, *Historical Negro Biographies: International Library of Negro Life and History* (New York: Publishers Co., 1967); J.A. Rogers, *World's Great Men of Color* (New York: Macmillan, 1947; Dorothy Salem, "Mary Terrell," in *Handbook of American Women's History*, edited by Angela H. Zophy and Frances M. Kavenik (New York: Garland, 1990); and David G. Roller, and Robert W. Twyman, eds., *Encyclopedia of Southern History* (Baton Rouge: Louisiana State University Press, 1979). More extensive descriptions and interpretations of her life and work can be found in Sharon Harley, "Beyond the Classroom: Organized Lives of Black Female Educators, 1890–1930," *Journal of Negro Education* 51 (Summer 1982) and "Mary Church Terrell: Genteel Militant" in *Black Leaders of the Nineteenth Century*, edited by Leon Litwack and August Meier (Chicago:

University of Illinois Press, 1988); Endesha Ida Mae Holland, *The Autobiography of a Parader Without a Permit*, PhD dissertation, University of Minnesota (1986); Beverly Washington Jones, *Quest for Equality: The Life of Mary Eliza Church Terrell, 1863–1954*, PhD dissertation, University of North Carolina at Chapel Hill (1980); Dorothy Sterling, *Black Foremothers, Three Lives* (New York: Feminist Press, 1979); and Dorothy Sterling and Benjamin Quarles, *Lift Every Voice* (Garden City, NY: Doubleday, 1965).

For sociohistorical background and information regarding Terrell's leadership in and the work of the National Association of Colored Women, consult the following works: Floris Loretta Barnett Cash, "Womanhood and Protest: The Club Movement among Black Women, 1892–1922," PhD dissertation, State University of New York at Stony Brook (1986); Elizabeth L. Davis, *Lifting as They Climb* (Washington, DC: NACW, 1933); Dorothy Salem, *To Better Our World: Black Women in Organized Reform, 1890–1920* (Brooklyn: Carlson, 1990); Paula Giddings, *When and Where I Enter: The Impact of Black Women on Race and Sex in America* (New York: Bantam Books, 1984); Angela Davis, *Women, Race, and Class* (New York: Random House, 1981); Gerda Lerner, "Early Community Work of Black Club Women," *Journal of Negro History* 59 (April 1974); Cynthia Neverdon-Morton, *Afro-American Women of the South and the Advancement of the Race, 1895–1925* (Knoxville: University of Tennessee Press, 1989); Charles Harris Wesley, *The History of the National Association of Colored Women's Clubs: A Legacy of Service* (Washington, DC: Mercury Press, 1984); and Fannie B. Williams, "The Club Movement among Colored Women of America," in *A New Negro for a New Century*, edited by Booker T. Washington (originally published 1900; reprint ed., New York: Arno, 1968).

The best collection of primary sources (correspondence, diaries, addresses, writings [covering her college and later years], some early minutes of the National Association of Colored Women, and various nineteenth-century documents) can be found in the Mary Church Terrell Papers, Library of Congress, Washington, DC. Microfilm of the Terrell Papers are available in other centers such as the Schomburg Center, New York Public Library. Also, some primary documents can be found in the Manuscript Collection of the Howard University Research Center in Washington, DC.

Mary Church Terrell was a prolific writer, and many of her writings can be found in magazines, newspapers, and journals of the late nineteenth and early twentieth centuries, such as *The Nineteenth Century*, *The Voice of the Negro*, and *A.M.E. Church Review*. A representative sample of some of her writings are as follows: "Lynching from a Negro's Point of View," *North American Review* 178 (July 1904): 853–898; "The Progress of Colored Women," *The Voice of the Negro* (July 1904): 291–294; "The International Congress of Women," *The Voice of the Negro* (December 1904): 454–461; "The Club Work of Colored Women," *The Southern Workman* 30 (August 1901); and "The History of the Club Women's Movement," *The Aframerican Woman's Journal* 1 (Summer/Fall 1940). Her autobiography is *A Colored Woman in a White World* (Washington, DC: Randell, Inc., 1940).

TERRY, LUCY (c. 1730–1821) is reputed to be the first poet of African descent in the American colonies. Her poem preceded by a decade the writings of Jupiter Hammon, a New York slave, often called the first African-American poet. The record of her life is rather sparce. She was thought to have been stolen from Africa as a small child and brought to Deerfield, Massachusetts, from Rhode Island by Ebenezer Wells. In 1744 she was admitted to the fellowship of the church in Deerfield and was identified as the servant of Ebenezer Wells. She lived in Deerfield, a tiny hamlet on the frontier between British and French colonies, often under siege from native tribes allied with these nations. In 1746 Lucy Terry then 16 years old, wrote a poem about an Indian raid during King George's War (1742–1748). The poem, "Bar's Fight," recreated what was hailed by some historians as the most authentic account of the Indian massacre. Written in the tradition of Terence of Rome, Seneca, and Epictetus, the poem was originally published in Josiah Holland's *History of Western Massachusetts* in 1855.

Lucy Terry (also called Luce Bijah) gained a reputation as a storyteller and an eloquent speaker without formal training or organized schooling. On May 17, 1756, Lucy Terry married Abijah Prince, a free black man who had become a successful businessman. Although no records confirm the transaction, it seems that Prince purchased Lucy Terry's freedom after their marriage. Prince acquired some gifts of land, and expanded his holdings in Guilford and Sunderland by 1764. The couple settled in Vermont on the Batten Kill not far from Ethan Allen's home. There they raised six children, two of whom fought in the American Revolution.

This pastoral life was marred by conflict with their nearest neighbor, Eli Bronson, who claimed part of Prince's farm and enclosed the disputed land with his own fencing. Several lawsuits followed and brought the matter to the U.S. Supreme Court, where Lucy Terry acquired a national reputation for her brilliant argumentation. Isaac Ticknor, later the governor of Vermont, handled the case for the Princes. Bronson employed two leading lawyers, Stephen R. Bradley and Royal Tyler, the latter of the two became the chief justice of the state. When Lucy Terry became dissatisfied with the way her lawyer was handling her case, she rose and argued it herself. The presiding judge, Samuel Chase of Maryland, remarked that her plea "surpassed that of any Vermont lawyers he had ever heard."

Lucy Terry fought for racial justice and against racial hatred. When a neighbor tore down her fences and set her haystacks on fire, she carried her protest to Vermont's Governor's Council. Once again, Lucy Terry Prince was victorious. When her youngest son, Abijah Prince, Jr., was rejected by Williams College, Lucy Terry protested their decision and emphasized their obligation to accept all students regardless of color. She quoted law and the Gospel in vain. These public disputes brought her into the public eye as a spokesperson for her people.

The couple spent their last days on their 100-acre farm at Guilford. Abijah died January 19, 1794, at age 88. In 1803 Lucy Terry returned to Sunderland, where she died at age 91 in 1821. Although she lived a long life dedicated to racial justice, she is remembered for her poem "Bar's Fight," which made her a forerunner of African-American poets.

—Nicholas C. Polos

Bibliography

To obtain information about Lucy Terry, consult regional histories, poetry collections, and biographical sources. The regional histories include Josiah Holland, *History of Western Massachusetts* II (Springfield, MA: S. Bowles, 1855), p. 360; George Sheldon, *History of Deerfield, Massachusetts* (Greenfield, MA: Munsell, 1895–1896); Sheldon, "Negro Slavery in Old Deerfield," *New England Magazine* (March 1893): 850; Lorenzo J. Greene, *The Negro in Colonial New England, 1620–1776* (New York: Knopf, 1942), p. 248; and Sidney Kaplan, *The Black Presence in the Era of the American Revolution* (Amherst: University of Massachusetts, 1989), pp. 209–211. For poetry sources, see Pattie Cowell, *Women Poets in Pre-Revolutionary America, 1650–1775* (Troy, NY: Whitson, 1981); Dudley Randall, *The Black Poets* (New York: Bantam, 1971); William H. Robinson, *Early Black American Poets* (Dubuque, IA: W.C. Brown, 1969), pp. 3–4; Margaret Busby, *Daughters of Africa* (New York: Pantheon, 1992); and Langston Hughes, *The Poetry of the Negro, 1746–1970* (Garden City, NY: Doubleday, 1970), p. 3.

For biographical information see Sylvia G. Dannett, *Profiles of Negro Womanhood*, Vol. I, 1619–1900 (Chicago: Educational Press, 1964); John P. Davis, *The American Negro Reference Book* (Englewood Cliffs, NJ: Prentice-Hall, 1969), p. 850; and Bernard Katz, "A Second Version of Lucy Terry's Early Ballad?" in *Negro History Bulletin* 29 (Fall 1966): 183–184.

THOMAS, BETTYE [COLLIER] (b. 1943), museum director, historian, and educator,

was born in Macon, Georgia, on January 21. She earned a bachelor's degree from Allen University in Columbia, South Carolina. In 1966 she was awarded a master's degree from Atlanta University, and in 1974 she received her PhD in history from George Washington University in Washington, DC. Thomas began her professional career as a college teacher during the 1960s and taught for approximately ten years.

In 1977 she left the classroom to become director of the Bethune Historical Development Project (National Council of Negro Women) in Washington, DC. From 1982 to 1989 she served as founding executive director of the Bethune Museum and Archives, National Historical Site. During her tenure at the Bethune Museum, Bettye Thomas developed the nation's first museum and archives devoted exclusively to black women's history. In addition, in 1977 she coordinated the first national scholarly research conference on black women's history. In 1980 Thomas coordinated and directed the first national black museum conference. As a consultant to the National Endowment for the Humanities, she also developed the agency's first program of technical assistance to African-American museums and historical organizations. In 1989 she left the Bethune Museum to become the first director of the Center for African-American History and Culture and associate professor of history at Temple University in Philadelphia, a position she continues to hold.

—Betty Plummer

Bibliography

Good sources for biographical information on Bettye Collier Thomas are *Legacy*, Bethune Museum and Archives, Inc., Vol. 1 (Winter 1988); *Museum News* (February 1985); and *Heritage, A Newsletter of the Center for African American History and Culture*, 1:1 (Summer 1991). See also *Who's Who in Black America* (Detroit: Gale, 1980).

THOMPSON, ERA BELL (1905–1986), journalist and author, worked with Johnson Publishing Company and *Ebony* magazine for over 30 years. She served as both the associate and international editor, which brought her to many areas of the world and expanded her awareness of racial identity.

Born to Stewart C. and Mary V. (Logan) Thompson on August 10, Era Bell Thompson began life in Des Moines, Iowa. She attended Chesterfield Elementary School. Her father had held many jobs from chef to coal miner when his brother persuaded the family with three sons, Hobart, Stewart, and Carl, to move to a farm in Driscoll, North Dakota. Surrounded by German and Scandinavian farmers, Era Bell Thompson, the youngest and only daughter, grew up in that farming community and attended Sterling School. When she was age 12, her mother died in her presence, an event that frightened her and blocked out many early memories of her mother. The family relocated to Bismarck, where her father had a job as a messenger for the governor of North Dakota. There she attended Bismarck High School, where she competed in athletic events and continued her love of writing.

Her father, the dominant influence in her life, was the son of a slavemaster and a slave cook. His white half-brothers taught him to read and write. This outgoing, vibrant man gave her the love of learning and never denied her anything she needed. At age 70, he learned to type. His blind belief in her writing ability and his storytelling skills influenced her to write her first article, which was published in *Physical Culture* magazine. She completed high school in Bismarck, while writing articles in Dewey Jones's column for the *Chicago Defender*.

After her father's death, the 22-year-old aspiring writer tried to manage her father's store. Soon she went to live with an uncle who had a furniture store in Bismarck. She read all of her uncle's brochures on the furniture and bedding, which led to her winning a bedspring-naming contest sponsored by the United States Bedding Company of Minneapolis and the University of North Dakota. She used the "King-Koil" prize money to travel to Grand Forks, North Dakota, home of the University of North Dakota. At the university, she competed in intercollegiate sporting events, breaking five state records in one track meet. She wrote for the college paper doing a humor column and wrote sports articles for the local newspaper. She worked for room and board with a Jewish family until she became ill with pleurisy in 1931. Unable to continue her classes and continue to work, she went to live with the family of Robert E. O'Brian, pastor of the First Methodist Church. Their initial meeting was in his office on a rainy day. The paper in her shoes left puddles of standing water on the floor. Dr. O'Brien felt that anybody who wanted an education that much was worthy of his help. A rebel, Phi Beta Kappa, and dominant presence in his home, Dr. O'Brien thought of making Era Bell Thompson part of his family. When he accepted the presidency of Morningside College in Sioux City, Iowa, she transferred her credits and moved with the family.

In 1933 at the height of the Depression, she graduated with a bachelor's degree in English and left for Chicago to find employment. In Chicago she struggled to find jobs, even from employers who lacked college educations. At first, she worked as a domestic for a doctor. The doctor's wife made her wear a uniform, an attire that nearly "killed" Era Bell Thompson and led to her seeking other employment. After taking the civil service examination, she became a senior interviewer for the United States Employment Service. There she started a newspaper, the *Giggle Sheet*. Although the paper portrayed the supervisor in an unflattering way, she tried to help Thompson get on the Federal Writer's Project, where she could use her skills. She continued to write. She worked for a small black magazine, *Pulse*. After receiving a Rockefeller Fellowship from the Newberry Library in 1945, she published her recollections of her childhood in North Dakota in *American Daughter*, published in 1946.

She started working for *Ebony* magazine in 1947 as a journalist and an editor. She was sent to the South because her employer felt she did not know anything about black people. Her long assignment of 20 stories took her through the South and taught her about southern black culture. Covering Africa, Brazil, Australia, and the United States, Thompson became acutely aware of common problems facing those of African heritage throughout the world. Then, too, these experiences heightened her awareness of gender. She remembered instances where dignitaries refused to meet her plane because she was a woman and other situations where leaders expected her to be a white man. These travels produced books depicting an enhanced racial consciousness. In 1954 the account of her first impressions about Africa appeared in *Africa, Land of My Fathers*. In 1963 she co-edited *White on Black*.

Journalism was her career. She never married. She felt her constant travel would have been restricted by marriage. Her dislike for teas and socials did not restrict her social interactions with such prominent people as Elizabeth Kata, author of *A Patch of Blue*. She also remembered her community responsibilities. As a survivor of breast cancer, she volunteered in the Reach to Recovery program. Critical of class biases among black leaders, Thompson never forgot being blackballed by the University Women's Club for her lack of social background. She considered herself as "not much of a joiner, " yet she held memberships in the Association for the Study of Afro-American Life and History, the American Cancer Society, Society of Midland Authors, and she was one of the first black members of Zonta International. She served on the boards of Hull House and the Metropolitan YWCA.

Thompson has received numerous awards and honors during her decades as a journalist. The Capital Press Club honored her for journalism. The University of North Dakota and Morningside College gave her honorary degrees. She is an honorary member of Sigma Gamma Rho, and Iota Phi Lambda named her Outstanding Woman of the Year in 1965. Her portrait hangs in the North Dakota Hall of Fame. She died on December 30, 1986.

—Dorothy C. Salem

Bibliography

Interviews with Era Bell Thompson are included in the Archives, North Dakota Oral History Project, State Historical Society of North Dakota, Bismarck; and in the Black Women Oral History Project, Schlesinger Library, Radcliffe College. Files on her career can be found in the records of *Ebony* magazine at Johnson Publishing, Chicago. See James de T. Abajian, comp., *Blacks in Selected Newspapers, Censuses and Other Sources: An Index to Names and Subjects*, 3 vols. (Boston: G.K. Hall, 1977) for further information on her journalistic products. Her own account of her life is in Era Bell Thompson, *American Daughter* (Chicago: University of Chicago Press, 1946) and *Africa: Land of My Fathers* (New York: Doubleday, 1954). Biographical information can be found in articles, which include a selective citation of Thompson's best writings: Kathie Ryckman Anderson, "Era Bell Thompson," *North Dakota History* 49 (Fall 1982): 11–18; and Glenda Riley, "American Daughters: Black Women in the West," *Montana: The Magazine of Western History* 38 (Spring 1988): 14–27.

THOMS, ADAH [SAMUELS] (1870–1943), a founder of the National Association of Colored Graduate Nurses, was born January 12 to Harry and Melvina Samuels of Virginia. She attended school in Richmond and taught there before choosing a career in nursing. In the 1890s Adah Belle Samuels moved to Harlem and took courses in public speaking and elocution at Cooper Union. Several years later she enrolled at the Woman's Infirmary and School of Therapeutic Massage. She graduated in 1900 and worked as a nurse in New York City and then at St. Agnes Hospital in Raleigh, North Carolina, where she was a head nurse. At some point, she married a Dr. Thoms, about whom very little is known. The exact date of their marriage is not available. Her husband died after their return to New York City.

To improve her skills, Thoms entered the School of Nursing at Lincoln Hospital in New York City in 1903 and graduated two years later. Upon graduating she remained as an operating room nurse and as the supervisor of the Surgical Division. In addition, Thoms served as acting director of the Nursing School from 1908 to 1923. She attended the International Council of Nurses in Cologne, Germany, in 1912.

In 1908, as president of the Lincoln Nurses Alumnae, Thoms hosted a group interested in organizing an association for black nurses. This meeting resulted in the formation of the National Association of Colored Graduate Nurses (NACGN). Thoms was elected to serve as the first treasurer and later as the president from 1916 to 1923. She worked for better jobs and higher admission standards for black nursing schools. She opposed a merger with the National Medical Association, the organization for black physicians, so that NACGN could remain free for a more advantageous merger with the American Nurses Association.

Recognizing the importance of public health, Thoms added a public health course to the Lincoln Hospital's curriculum and enrolled herself in the first class. Thoms emphasized the importance of continuing education and completed courses at the School of Philanthropy, Hunter College, and the New School of Social Research. During World War I, Thoms successfully worked to obtain for black nurses the opportunity to serve with the American Red Cross. This was necessary to gain entry into the U.S. Army Nurses Corps.

Thoms retired from Lincoln Hospital in 1923. She married Henry Smith, who died within a year. Once again the details of the man and the marriage are missing. To chronicle the history of black nursing, Thoms wrote her only book, *Pathfinders: A History of the Progress of Colored Graduate Nurses*, published in 1929. In 1936 she became the first recipient of the Mary Mahoney Medal given by the NACGN.

Throughout her career Thoms was active in numerous organizations. In addition to the NACGN, the American Nursing Association, and the National Organization of Public Health Nurses, she was a member of the Harlem branch of the YWCA, the Harlem Committee of the New York Tuberculosis and Health Association, the New York Urban League, the Urban League Center of the Henry Street Nursing Committee, and St. Mark's Methodist Episcopal Church. She was also actively involved with the Hope Day Nursery, which was the only facility offering day care for the children of working black mothers.

Thoms died in 1943 from arteriosclerotic heart disease and diabetic complications. She is buried in Woodlawn Cemetery in New York City. In 1976 she was inducted into the prestigious Nursing Hall of Fame in recognition of her outstanding accomplishments and countless contributions to the field of nursing.

—Linda Cannon-Huffman

Bibliography

Adah Thoms produced one book, *Pathfinders: A History of the Progress of Colored Graduate Nurses* (New York: Kay Printing House, 1929). She wrote an article with C.E. Bullock, "Development of Facilities for Colored Nurse Education," *Trained Nurse and Hospital Review* 80 (1928): 722–723.

An excellent overview of Thoms's life and career is presented in *American Nursing: A Biographical Dictionary*, by Vern Bullough, Olga Church, and Alice Stern (New York: Garland, 1988). In *No Time for Prejudice* by Mabel Keaton Staupers (New York: Macmillan, 1961), her name is interwoven throughout as the book presents the history of the integration of blacks into nursing. Other important accounts are given in Edward T. James, ed., *Notable American Women, 1607–1950*, Volume III (Cambridge: Belknap, 1971); and *Makers of Nursing History*, edited by Meta Rutter Pennock (New York: Lakeside Publishing, 1940). See also Rayford W. Logan, and Michael R. Winston, eds., *Dictionary of American Negro Biography* (New York: Norton, 1982).

TROTTER, GERALDINE [PINDELL] (1872–1918) was born in Boston on October 3 to lawyer Charles Edward and Mary Frances Pindell. The Pindell family had a long tradition of activism, and Geraldine Pindell was taught that her privileged status placed upon her an obligation to serve her community.

The Pindells sent their daughter to public schools in Everett, Massachusetts, and then to a business college to learn bookkeeping and stenography. At this age, W.E.B. Du Bois, one of her closest friends, described her as "a fine forthright woman, blonde, blue-eyed and fragile."

On June 27, 1899, Geraldine Pindell married William Monroe Trotter. The Harvard-educated Trotter was the son of James Trotter, an affluent realtor. The couple bought a home in the Dorchester neighborhood of Boston, and Trotter followed his father into the real estate business.

In 1901 Trotter and a friend began publishing *The Guardian*. Like other members of Boston's African-American intelligentsia, Trotter distrusted Booker T. Washington, and he used *The Guardian* to attack "the Wizard of Tuskegee." After Trotter's arrest in the "Boston Riot" of 1903, Geraldine Trotter rallied to his support. Determined that *The Guardian* would not be silenced, she published the newspaper while Trotter was in jail.

Alarmed by the turn of events, Trotter's co-editor resigned, and Geraldine Trotter became *The Guardian*'s associate editor. She also took charge of *The Guardian*'s business ledgers. Despite her efforts, the paper lost money. To pay their mounting debts the Trotters were forced to sell their home, as Trotter's real estate business dwindled away to nothing.

Her husband's differences with fellow activists lost Geraldine Trotter many friends. Over the years she followed Du Bois's work with interest. When he published his *Credo*, she wrote him to describe the pride of the Boston women in his concern for the welfare of the race and to request his permission for reprinting and selling his work as a means for funding race work. He told her to use his work as she thought fit. The Du Bois family visited the Trotters every summer. The two families eventually became estranged, since Trotter and Du Bois disagreed over the policies of the Niagara movement, formed in 1905 as an organized attempt to gain racial justice during the era of leadership by accommodationist Booker T. Washington.

Apart from editing *The Guardian* during her husband's frequent absences from Boston, Geraldine Pindell devoted time to other causes. She raised funds for St. Monica's Home, an Episcopalian refuge for African-American women and children in Roxbury. She also promoted the welfare of African-American troops during World War I. Her sense of duty to her community was expressed in a speech given in 1905 on the centenary of William Lloyd Garrison's birth. She urged those like herself, who had the advantages of education, to willingly make sacrifices for the race.

Geraldine Trotter died of influenza on October 8, 1918. Du Bois praised her for working with Trotter "in utter devotion" to advance the cause of racial justice. "It was a magnificent partnership, and she died to pay for it." William Trotter never recovered from her death, and until his own death, *The Guardian* always carried a tribute to his "fallen Comrade" who gave her life "For the rights of her race."

—Julie Winch

Bibliography

The materials on Geraldine Pindell Trotter are scanty. The best source is obviously the files of *The Guardian*. Her funeral received coverage in the *Boston Post* (October 13, 1918); and *The Crisis* (December 1918): 75. In terms of secondary works, Stephen R. Fox's biography of her husband, *The Guardian of Boston: William Monroe Trotter* (New York: Atheneum, 1970); and John Daniels, *In Freedom's Birthplace: A Study of Boston Negroes* (Boston: Houghton-Mifflin, 1914) does include an assessment of Geraldine Trotter's contribution to his life and work. Her own life has not yet been studied in a biography.

TRUTH, SOJOURNER [ISABELLA BAUMFREE] (1797–1883), a nationally known speaker on human rights for slaves and women, was born a slave in Ulster County in Hurley, New York. Named Isabella, called Belle, she was one of twelve children born to Baumfree and Mau Mau Brett. Their home was a damp cellar under the main house on the farm of Colonel Charles Hardenbergh, a Dutchman. The family spoke with a Dutch brogue. With the death of Hardenbergh, Truth's parents were set free only to have their children sold at an auction. Truth was purchased by John Neally for $100 to do housework. Speaking only Dutch, she had difficulties communicating and was treated cruelly by her master. Truth's father encouraged a fisherman, Martin Schryver, to purchase Truth for $105 to remove her from the cruel circumstances. She worked in his tavern near the

Hudson River, and her English skills improved. With her increased skills, Truth's value increased. She was sold by Schryver to John Dumont, a wealthy plantation owner, for $300.

As a slave on the Dumont plantation, she experienced the problems of female slaves. Truth fell in love with Bob, a slave from a nearby plantation, but marriage was denied them by Mr. Dumont. Instead, Truth was given permission to marry fellow slave Thomas. She had five daughters, and then had one son, fathered by Mr. Dumont. Mrs. Dumont, upset over the circumstances, created conflicts that led to cruel whippings of Truth. Truth turned inward and found solace by speaking to God. She spoke aloud, and the frequency of these personal spiritual encounters enabled her to develop a strong speaking voice. After suffering from the sadistic cruelties of Mrs. Dumont, Truth sought peace in a cove lined with willows, where she could pour out her troubles to God.

When Dumont broke his promise to manumit her, she ran away in 1826, one year before the scheduled emancipation guaranteed by the New York Emancipation Law. With only her baby daughter Sophia, she found refuge with a Quaker family, the Van Wageners. Isaac Van Wagener paid Dumont $25 to satisfy Dumont's monetary claim to Truth. Truth adopted Van Wagener as her last name. Upon receiving the news that her son Peter had been sold to a neighbor and then illegally sold to a platation owner in Alabama, Truth successfully sued for his return. In New York, she was working as a domestic when she had a deep personal religious experience, even though she had never attended a formal church service nor received any formal religious education in Christianity. She discovered Jesus and saw Him as a friend that stood between man and God.

Following this experience she moved to New York City in 1829 with her son Peter and became a member of the African Methodist Episcopal Zion Church. She became the housekeeper of Elijah Pierson, a wealthy widower and religious zealot, who believed he was Elias Tishbite ordered to bring together the members of Israel. Truth and Pierson met Robert Matthews, an obsessed religious fanatic who convinced them, along with several prominent businessmen, in 1853 to form a community and live on a country estate called "The Kingdom," also known as "Zion Hill," at Sing Sing, New York. Scandal beset the utopian community after the death of Pierson. His relatives requested an autopsy, which revealed traces of arsenic, suggesting Pierson had been murdered. The utopian community was immediately disbanded. Matthews was arrested, but he was acquitted of the charges. Truth was implicated in the scandal, and vicious rumors were spread. Courageously, Truth fought the falsehoods aimed at her. With the aid of newspaperman Gilbert Vale, Truth used letters from former employers attesting to the integrity of her character to file a slander suit against the Folgers, the couple responsible for the rumors. Truth won the case and was found innocent. The jury awarded her a small sum of money.

Tragedy soon led her in a new direction. Disturbed by her son's minor encounters with the law, Truth allowed him to go to sea with friends. When he disappeared without a trace, Truth was devastated. Truth decided to throw off her name and old identity by taking the name Sojourner Truth, so chosen to signify her new role as a traveler speaking the truth about the institution of slavery. She left on June 1, 1843, and walked for miles headed in a northeasterly direction with 25¢ in her pocket. Truth's destination was New England, at God's calling. She rested from her travels only when she found lodging offered by either rich or poor. Occasionally she found work and accepted only what she needed in payment. She attended religious meetings. As her confidence in her spirituality grew, she began to hold religious meetings that were known to bring audiences to tears. As she logged mile after mile, her fame grew and her reputation preceded her. She had children read the Bible passages to her to avoid adult interpretations. She settled in Northhampton, Massachusetts, after having traveled through Long Island, New York, and Connecticut. Truth remained illiterate, yet her interpretations of the Bible and of constitutional law continued to bewilder seminarians and lawyers. She would tell them, "You read books but God himself talks to me." In 1850 she walked in a different direction, this time westward. She set up headquarters in Ohio and made trips to Indiana, Missouri, and Kansas. Her speeches often began with the phrase "Children, I talk to God and God talks to me." She became so popular and well known that she often shared the platform with Frederick Douglass.

Truth stands out as a spokesperson and vanguard of human rights. She was a moving and captivating speaker on the issue of women's rights, a cause she took on after attending the Worcester, Massachusetts, Convention in 1850. Harriet Beecher Stowe called her a Libyan Sybil. She moved audiences with her abolitionist and women's rights speeches and wisdom. She delivered her often-quoted "And Ain't I a Woman?" speech at the women's rights convention in Akron, Ohio, in 1851.

Her popularity was enhanced by her autobiography written by the abolitionist Olive Gilbert, with a preface written by William Lloyd Garrison. An edition published after the Civil War contained a preface written by Harriet Beecher Stowe. Her popularity won her an invitation to the White House in 1864, when President Abraham Lincoln personally received her. This trip to the nation's capital exposed her to the plight of homeless ex-slaves, the contraband of war. Thus, she turned her energies to helping them. She was a proponent for using western lands for the settlement of freedmen and worked to see a just period of Reconstruction, demanding a good education and the right for her people to earn a decent living. She served as a counselor for the National Freedman's Relief Association. Before the official end of Reconstruction, she retired in 1875 to Battle Creek, Michigan, the site of her family settlement 20 years earlier. She died on November 26, 1883. She was buried at Oak Hill Cemetery in Battle Creek.

—Mary Hovanec

Bibliography

The biography that made Sojourner Truth famous was Gilbert Olive's *Narrative of Sojourner Truth* (1850 and 1878) reprinted by Johnson Publishing (Chicago: Johnson, 1970). The biography by Arthur Fauset, *Sojourner Truth* (Chapel Hill, NC: University of North Carolina Press, 1938), has a fuller biographical narrative than Olive's. Hertha E. Pauli's *Her Name was Sojourner Truth* (New York: Appleton-Century-Crofts, 1967) provides a descriptive narrative within the nineteenth-century reform context. Jacqueline Bernard's *Journey Toward Freedom* (New York: Norton, 1967) places Truth into the antislavery movement. She is highlighted in Benjamin Brawley's *Negro Builders and Heroes* (Chapel Hill: University of North Carolina Press, 1937). She is featured in the book by Peter Krass, *Sojourner Truth: Antislavery Activist* (New York: Chelsea House, 1988). Saunders Redding has a sketch of Truth in *Notable American Women*, edited by Edward T. James, et al. (Cambridge: Harvard University Press, 1971).

For contemporary accounts of Truth's involvements in religious and reform activities see Gilbert Vale, *Fanaticism, Its Source and Influence: Illustrated by the Simple Narrative of Isabella* (New York: G. Vale, 1835); Elizabeth C. Stanton et al., *History of Woman Suffrage* I–III (New York: Arno Press, 1881–1886); and the Salem, Ohio, *Antislavery Bugle* (microfilm in Ohio Historical Society, Columbus, Ohio).

TUBMAN, HARRIET [ROSS] (c. 1821–1913), the famous leader of the Underground Railroad, became a legend during her lifetime. Heralded as the "Moses" of her people, conductor Tubman led approximately 300 slaves to freedom during the decade (1850–1860) of freedom work, carrying her into the South at least 15 times. One of 11 children born to Benjamin and Harriet (Green) Ross, on a plantation in Bucktown near Cambridge, Maryland, she was called Araminta (nicknamed Minty) Ross after her father. She chose the name of her mother, Harriet, when she reached her early teens. She traced her lineage from the Ashanti tribe in Africa through her grandmother, who had been forced into slavery. The family home was a one-room cabin on the plantation of Edward Brodas.

Denied any real childhood or formal education, Tubman was a full-time housekeeper and babysitter by age five. Hired out frequently, she labored in physically demanding jobs as a woodcutter, a field hand, and in lifting and loading barrels of flour. She was happiest when plowing fields and harvesting corn alongside the adults. Although she had heard of kind masters, she never experienced one. From masters, mistresses, and overseers, she endured mistreatment and numerous beatings. At age 13, she stepped between a slave trying to escape and an overseer. The overseer picked up a two-pound weight from a scale and threw it at the escaping slave, hitting Tubman instead. The force of the blow pushed a portion of her skull against her brain causing her to suffer from narcolepsy, recurring seizures of deep, sudden sleep, for the remainder of her life. Thereafter, she wore a turban to conceal the deep scar on her head. As she regained her strength, she continued to do manual labor equal to male slaves even though she was a woman of slight build.

Exposed to the injustices and horrors of slavery and motivated by a desire for freedom, she vowed from an early age that she would strive to emancipate her people. Hired out to John Steward, a shipbuilder and timber operator, her awareness expanded through tales of slaves who had successfully made it to freedom along an "Underground Railroad." Her parents, regular churchgoers, attended a church for slaves, where she learned Bible verses, religious songs, and a simple religious faith. She loved to sing and used song as her means of communication on her many trips to bring slaves to their freedom. "Go Down, Moses" became a very powerful song of rebellion and part of the slave rescue apparatus used by Tubman to maintain control of her charges. Her profound religious faith motivated fugitives to follow her because they believed her to be in direct communication with God.

At age 24, in 1844, she married John Tubman, a freeman whose parents had been manumitted by their master. He lacked her commitment to freeing the slaves. When her master died, two of Harriet's sisters were prepared for sale. Knowing that it was only a matter of time before she and her two brothers would meet the same fate, in the summer of 1849, she decided to make her escape. At the last minute, her brothers and husband refused to leave with her, so she set out by herself with only the North Star to serve as her guide. With the help of several Quaker families, in Maryland and Delaware, including Thomas Garrett, a well-known abolitionist, Tubman made her way to freedom in Pennsylvania.

She prepared for her return to the South to carry out her mission. Knowing she would need money, she went to work in Philadelphia, struggling in several part-time jobs to earn the necessary funds. A year later, she returned to Baltimore to rescue her sister, Mary Ann Bowley, and her two children. She carried a rifle both for protection and to intimidate her fearful runaways. Risking her own safety, Tubman guided others to their freedom. Travel became more dangerous with the passage of the Fugitive Slave Law. Inquiring of any place where slaves could be safe, she found that the laws of Canada protected runaway slaves. Thereafter, her destination was St. Catherine's in Canada. Clever, resourceful, and an expert at disguises, Tubman was not deterred, despite rewards offered by slaveowners for her capture, which totaled $40,000. Her most famous trip in 1857 brought her elderly parents to safety.

She worked closely with the integrated forces of the Underground Railroad. Black leader William Still, head of the General Vigilance Committee, and white Quaker Thomas Garrett of Wilmington, Delaware, provided economic support and risked personal safety, since Delaware was a slave state. She held abolitionist John Brown in high esteem. Only an illness prevented Tubman from accompanying Brown in his raid of Harpers Ferry in 1859. In Troy, New York, in 1860, she was a leader of a crowd that forced officers to release a fugitive slave, who was then assisted to escape to Canada.

Known foremost for her abolitionist activities, Tubman dedicated her entire life to helping others. Her heroism was further highlighted by her activities during the Civil War between 1862 and 1865. She served as a liaison between federal troops and freemen in Beaufort, South Carolina. Governor John Andrew of Massachusetts sent her to the South to serve as a spy and a scout for the Union Army. Her gift for directions and knowledge of geography remained an asset as she explored the countryside in search of Confederate fortifications. She accompanied Colonel James Montgomery on several raids in South Carolina and Georgia. When needed, she was employed as a hospital nurse and cook. Although she received official commendation from Union officers, she was never paid for the services she rendered the Union forces or to the government.

After the Civil War, she returned to Auburn, New York, where she had settled her parents in 1857. She worked to establish a home for indigent aged blacks of the community and began taking in both orphans and the elderly. Lack of sufficient funds prompted her to convert her own home to this purpose. She called it the John Brown Home in honor of the abolitionist leader, whom she admired. The people of Auburn came to her support and established the Harriet Tubman Home for Aged and Indigent Colored People. In 1869 she married her second husband, Nelson Davis, a Union soldier. She became involved in a number of causes, including the women's suffrage movement and became an eloquent speaker on women's rights. The women's groups fought for 20 years for her right to receive a pension for her service during the Civil War. Failing in this, they won a government pension for Tubman in 1890 as the widow of Nelson Davis, who died in 1888. The Woman's State Association of New York honored Tubman in December 1896, while the New England Woman Suffrage Association honored her in April 1987. She was the oldest delegate to the first annual convention of the National Federation of Afro-American Women in Washington, DC, in the summer of 1896. Black clubwomen continued to show concern for her. When the Empire State Federation heard in 1911 that she was in need, a major fundraising drive provided goods and money to help her. When she died on March 19, 1913, from complications of pneumonia, at age 90, the New York clubwomen paid for her funeral and the marble headstone.

Her death brought obituaries that demonstrated her fame not only throughout the United States but also in Europe. She was buried with military rites and with a military funeral. The city of Auburn closed down for one day as a memorial tribute to her one year later. Booker T. Washington served as a featured speaker. A tablet was dedicated in her honor, as a campaign was launched to collect funds for a monument in her name for the town square. To this day, the African Methodist Episcopal Zion church maintains her home as a monument. Today both remain as a symbol of her service and dedication to the service of others. During World War II, a liberty ship was christened the SS *Harriet Tubman*. In 1974 her Auburn home became a National Historic Landmark, and in 1980, a commemorative stamp became the first in the U.S. Postal Service's "Black Heritage U.S.A. Series." Her memory lives on.

—Mary Hovanec

Bibliography

There is a wealth of information available including legendary and many fictionalized accounts. Because of her illiteracy, she had no personal records, but she received correspondence from many important people. Her accounts of activities were recorded by others as with Henry Louis Gates, Jr., ed., *Four Fugitive Slave Narratives* (Reading, MA: Mentor-Penguin, 1969). Her activities can be found in the pages of *The Liberator, The Woman's Journal, The Commonwealth* and Elizabeth Stanton, ed., *History of Woman Suffrage*. The 1881–1886 Frederick Douglass Papers at the Library of Congress and Moorland-Spingarn Research Center, Howard University, Washington, DC, have accounts of her life in the abolition movement.

Two nonfiction biographies exist, the first written in 1866 by Sarah Bradford, *Scenes in the Life of Harriet Tubman* (Auburn, NY: Corinth, 1869) and the later expanded version *Harriet Tubman: The Moses of Her People* (Auburn, NY: Corinth, 1886). This account is based on interviews the author had with Harriet Tubman. The second biographical text was written by Earl Conrad, who grew up in Auburn, New York, *Harriet Tubman* (Washington, DC: Erickson, 1943). Dorothy Sterling's *Freedom Train* (Garden City, NY: Doubleday, 1961) also relates a fairly accurate account of Harriet Tubman's life as does M.W. Taylor's *Harriet Tubman* (New York: Chelsea House, 1988). Tubman's role in the Underground Railroad is discussed in William Still's *The Underground Railroad* (Philadelphia: W. Still, 1872) and James A. McGowan's *Station Master of the Underground Railroad: The Life and Letters of Thomas Garrett* (Moylan, PA: Whimsie Press, 1977). Her relationship with the Zion Methodists is discussed in William J. Walls, *The African Methodist Zion Church* (Charlotte, NC: AME Zion Publishing, 1974). Other books about Tubman or the Underground Railroad include Robert W. Taylor, *Harriet Tubman: The Heroine in Ebony* (Boston: Little, Brown, 1901); Ann Petry, *Harriet Tubman* (New York: Crowell, 1955); William Siebert, *The Underground Railroad from Slavery to Freedom* (New York: Macmillan, 1899); Larry Gara, *Liberty Line* (Lexington, KY: University of Kentucky Press, 1961); R.C. Smedley, *History of the Underground Railroad in Chester and Neighboring Counties of Pennsylvania* (Lancaster, PA: Office of the Journal, 1883); Priscilla Thompson, "Harriet Tubman, Thomas Garrett, and the Underground Railroad," *Delaware History* 22 (Spring/Summer 1986): 1–21; Benjamin Quarles, "Harriet Tubman's Unlikely Leadership," in *Black Leaders of the Nineteenth Century*, edited by Leon Litwack and August Meier (Urbana: University of Illinois, 1988), pp. 43–57; Earl Conrad, "I Bring You General Tubman," *The Black Scholar* (January/ February 1970): 2–7; and John Hope Franklin, "Harriet Tubman," in *Notable American Women* III, edited by Edward T. James (Cambridge: Harvard University Press, 1971), pp. 481–483. Newspaper accounts with lengthy praises of Tubman's achievements include *Afro-American Ledger* (March 15, 1913); and *The Weekly Anglo-African* (May 12, 1860). Transcripts of interviews conducted by Earl Conrad are in the Schomburg Collection of the New York Public Library. Primary material on the subject is also to be found in the Blockson Afro-American Collection at Temple University in Philadelphia. Letters dictated by Harriet are also available.

TUCKER, ROSINA [HARVEY, CORROTHERS] (1881–1987) was best known as an organizer for the Brotherhood of Sleeping Car Porters and as the international secretary-treasurer of the ladies auxiliary of the Brotherhood of Sleeping Car Porters. Born Rosina Budd Harvey on November 4 in Washington, DC, she began her formal education at the old Banneker School Building on Third Street, NW. She recalled, however, that her father—"a truly remarkable man"—had taught all of his children to read and write before they entered the public schools. In addition, he was musically talented and had given them music lessons before sending them to professional teachers. After completing the eighth grade, Rosina entered the old M Street High School (later Dunbar High School), the only black secondary school in DC and one of the finest schools established during the era of segregation. While visiting an aunt in Yonkers, New York, in 1897 Rosina taught Sunday school at the Colored Baptist Church, where she caught the attention of a guest preacher. James D. Corrothers, also a writer, poet, and early black graduate of Northwestern University, was impressed with her definition of the word "exodus." So impressed was he that Corrothers married her shortly before her seventeenth birthday. One son, Henry Harvey Corrothers, was born of this marriage on December 2, 1899. During the course of their marriage, the Corrothers lived first in New York City and then in South Haven, Michigan, where James had spent his childhood. There she taught music to about 30 students, the majority of whom were white, while her husband pastored a church and wrote a few poems for *Criterion* and the *Voice of the Negro*. In 1904 they moved to Washington, DC, where she became the organist for the Liberty Baptist Church in Foggy Bottom and James became the assistant secretary for the educational board of the National Baptist Convention. In 1906, "Poet," as Rosina Corrothers affectionately called her husband, became the pastor of the First Baptist Church in Lexington, Virginia. There the couple frequently presented concerts in the churches—he recited his poems and told original stories, while she played classical favorites at the piano. It was around this time that she composed a piece called "The Rio Grande Waltz," which she later published and sold.

Following the death of her husband in 1917, Rosina Corrothers took a job in the federal government as a file clerk. In 1918 she married Berthea J. Tucker, a Pullman car porter. This marriage was a turning point in her life, as she moved from a world where the church, literature, and music dominated her life to a world where racism and labor problems attracted much of her attention. Although black sleeping car porters often enjoyed steady employment, there were problems inherent in their job. The arbitrary attitude of white bosses, inadequate wages, and excessive hours were but a few of their woes. For this reason, concerned men formed the Brotherhood of Sleeping Car Porters in 1925.

Believing that the wife was her husband's helpmate, it was almost inevitable that she would become involved in whatever affected her husband. Eventually, she became a moving force in the ladies auxiliary of the Brotherhood of Sleeping Car Porters, an organization that grew from the the union's economic councils (the first of which was organized by the Brotherhood in 1925). As perceived by A. Philip Randolph, longtime president of the Brotherhood, these women assisted the union by raising funds and disseminating information. At its first international meeting held in Chicago in September 1938, Rosina Tucker was elected as international secretary-treasurer. She was also very active as president of Washington's local chapter of the auxiliary.

Rosina Tucker recalled that the porters' wives could work behind the scenes, thereby limiting unfavorable actions against their husbands who could not openly express themselves. In this role, the women formed the backbone of the organization. Her chapter sponsored teas, flea markets, and dances in an effort to raise money. She collected union dues, circulated information about the union, and even held what the union's critics called "secret meetings" at her home. Through her work with the auxiliary, Tucker developed rapport with A. Philip Randolph, holding strategic meetings in her home whenever he came to Washington.

In addition to having worked enthusiastically with the Brotherhood, Rosina Tucker was a civic activist. In 1983 she received a humanitarian award from the Leadership Conference on Civil Rights and the Candace Award for leadership from the Coalition of 100 Black Women's Clubs.

Rosina Tucker died at age 105, on March 3, 1987, in Washington, DC.

—Betty Plummer

Bibliography

The best source on Rosina C. Tucker is her unpublished autobiographical sketch, "Life as I Have Lived It." James D. Corrothers's *In Spite of the Handicap* (Salem, NH: Ayer, reprint of 1916 edition) also provides interesting insights on Tucker's activities. Jack Santino's *Miles of Smiles, Years of Struggle* (Urbana: University of Illinois Press, 1989) contains interviews in which Tucker talks about her work with the auxiliary and the porters in general. Brailsford R. Brazeal's *The Brotherhood of Sleeping Car Porters: Its Origin and Development* (New York: Harper & Row, 1946) recounts the founding of the ladies auxiliary and includes photographs of the international officers. Two articles contain valuable biographical data—*Washington Post* (November 3, 1986) and "Obituary," *Washington Post* (March 5, 1987).

TYSON, CICELY (b. 1939), film, stage, and television actress, brought the dignity of black women to movie and television. She was born on December 19 in East Harlem, New York, to William and Theodosia Tyson, immigrants from Nevis, a small island in the Caribbean. She grew up in poverty, selling shopping

bags on street corners at age nine. Her parents divorced when she was 11, and Tyson's mother focused her children's social life around religion. Cicely Tyson sang, played the piano and organ, and taught Sunday school at Saint John's Episcopal Church. Tyson was educated in Public School 121, Margaret Knox Junior High School, and Charles Evans High School in Manhattan.

After high school, Tyson worked as a secretary for the American Red Cross. She eventually studied modeling at the Barbara Watson Modeling School and appeared in high fashion magazines including *Harper's Bazaar* and *Vogue*. Earning up to $65 an hour, Tyson became one of the foremost models in the United States, but she tired of modeling because it became too mechanical.

From modeling, Tyson moved into acting. She studied acting in New York University and at the Actors' Studio. Her first appearance in a film was in 1957 in *Twelve Angry Men* and in 1959 she appeared in *Odds Against Tomorrow*. From there, Tyson's career spread out into the stage and television.

Tyson made her stage debut in *Talent '59* and quickly made her name in the theater by winning two Vernon Rice Awards. The first one was in 1961 for her role in the Off-Broadway play *The Blacks*. In 1962 she won her second Vernon Rice Award for her role in *Moon on a Rainbow Shawl*, another Off-Broadway production.

Since then, Tyson has appeared in numerous films, plays, and television programs. She is especially distinguished for her refusal to participate in films that would exploit or degrade black people. Her moral choice often resulted in sporadic work, but her persistence paid off as more films, plays, and television scripts portrayed black people more positively.

Tyson's other films include *The Last Angry Man* (1959), *A Man Called Adam* (1966), *The Comedians* (1967), *The Heart Is a Lonely Hunter* (1968), *The Blue Bird* (1976), *The River Niger* (1976), *A Hero Ain't Nothin' But a Sandwich* (1978), *The Concorde—Airport '79* (1979), *The Marva Collins Story* (1981), and *Benny's Place* (1982). Tyson's performance in *Sounder* (1972) is her most critically acclaimed film performance. She was named best actress by the Atlanta Film Festival and the National Society of Film Critics. This role also won Tyson an Academy Award nomination for Best Actress in 1972.

Tyson has appeared in other plays as well. These include *Trumpets of the Lord* (1963 and 1968), *A Hand Is on the Gate* (1968), and *Carry Me Back to Morningside Heights* (1968). Tyson also participated in *To Be Young, Gifted and Black*, which was a series of readings of Lorainne Hansberry's works.

Tyson has worked extensively in the television medium. Her first television appearance was in *Brown Girl, Brown Stones* (1960). She then appeared in *Between Yesterday and Today* and *Americans: A Portrait in Verse* before performing in *East Side/West Side*, her first major television role, in 1963. Tyson's other television appearances include *Naked City*, *The Nurses*, *To Tell the Truth*, *I Spy*, and *The Bill Cosby Show*.

The Autobiography of Miss Jane Pittman, though, is undoubtedly Tyson's most rewarding television role both artistically and personally. In *The Autobiography of Miss Jane Pittman*, Tyson played the title role and portrayed Miss Pittman from her youth to her death at 110 years of age. Not only did Tyson uphold her morals and play a positive role, she won an Academy Award as Best Actress and the drama won the Academy Award for the Best Drama Special. Since then, Tyson has played the role of Coretta Scott King in the television drama, *King* (1977), the role of Harriet Tubman in *A Woman Called Moses*, and also acted in Alex Haley's *Roots* (1977).

To encourage other young people, Tyson co-founded the Dance Theatre of Harlem and spends much time there. In 1981 Tyson married but later divorced jazz trumpeter Miles Davis.

Tyson has won numerous other awards from the NAACP, the National Council of Negro Women, the American Film Institute, the Human Family Institute, and Urban Gateways. She also won the Capitol Press Award.

—Lisa M. Reynolds Abu-Raad

Bibliography

Although willing to talk about her roles, ideals, and values, Cicely Tyson is a very private person and rarely reveals information about her private life. Her date of birth is "a well-kept secret" according to *The Ebony Success Library Vol. II* and most other sources that cite her birthdates ranging from 1935–1942 with her admission only to the day, December 19, although entertainment sources agree on the 1939 date. Some of the best personal information on Tyson is found in Kalamu ya Salaam's interview with Tyson, "Cicely Tyson: A Communicator of Pride," *The Black Collegian* (November/December 1978: 52–54, 86–91); and Charles L. Sanders's interview with the actress, "Cicely Tyson: She Can Smile Again after a Three Year Ordeal," *Ebony* (January 1979: 27–36).

Additional information about Tyson may be found in *Who's Who in America*, 45th ed., 1988–1989 (Wilmette, IL: Marquis Who's Who, 1988); *The Ebony Success Library Vol. II: Famous Blacks Give Secrets of Success* (Nashville, TN: Southwestern Publishing, 1973); Donald Bogle, *Black Arts Annual 1988/89* (New York: Garland, 1990); Harry A. Ploski and James Williams, eds., *The Negro Almanac: A Reference Work on the Afro-American* (New York: Wiley, 1983); Jessie Carney Smith, ed., *Notable Black American Women* (Detroit: Gale, 1992), *Who's Who among Black Americans*, 6th ed. (Detroit: Gale, 1990); and *Current Biography Yearbook* (New York: Wilson, 1975).

V

VAUGHAN, SARAH (1924–1990), whose place in the pantheon of influential African-American female vocalists is forever fixed, was once described by Murray Kempton (a reviewer of the *New York Times*), as one of the peaks sitting below Bessie Smith, along with Billie Holiday and Ella Fitzgerald.

Born on March 27, Vaughan, like many black singers, had her earliest training in a local church choir—the Mt. Zion Baptist Church choir in Harlem. Encouraged by Jabbo Smith, an artist who played in Newark while Vaughan was growing up, she tried out for the Apollo Theatre amateur contest in 1942. She won the show and was awarded the $25 dollar prize and a week billing at the Apollo for $40. Her rendition of "Body and Soul" that night impressed another singer in the audience— Billy Eckstine. Eckstine, the vocalist in Earl "Fatha" Hines's band, urged that she be hired. Hines signed her and hired her as a vocalist in his band. Later, in June 1944, Vaughan's professional mentor and now personal friend, Eckstine, formed his own band, and Vaughan became his vocalist. Among their many collaborative efforts of the 1940s were "Dedicated to You" and Cole Porter's "I Love You." It was during the early 1940s, in fact, that Sarah Vaughan became the first woman vocalist to adapt bebop to a popular ballad style. By 1949 Vaughan was earning a reported $2,500 at the Apollo and was considered the premier bebop vocalist.

Often described as an adventurous singer, Vaughan was never particularly concerned with lyrics. She took a physical delight in the act of singing. Sassy, as Vaughan was frequently called, was the vocalist of the Parker-Gillespie generation, but in the mid-1950s she was singing in a style labeled pop as well as jazz. Throughout her long career, which ended with her death of cancer in 1990, Vaughan worked with every important jazz musician of the times.

Although the demands and pressures of stardom and its concurrent lifestyle never seemed to take its toll on Vaughan musically, it appears to have done so personally. Four of her marriages ended in divorce. Marriage, according to some observers, was a subsidiary to her career. Like many famous and accomplished women, her husbands seemed to have taken the role of "Mr. Sarah Vaughan." Vaughan died on April 3, 1990, and is survived by an adopted daughter, Deborah.

—Donna Van Raaphorst

Bibliography

The ageless dancer, actor, comic, and emcee Ralph Cooper and Steve Dougherty provide the reader with a vivid picture of American music history within the framework of amateur night at the Apollo Theatre in *Amateur Night at the Apollo: Ralph Cooper Presents Five Decades of Great Entertainment* (New York: Harper Collins, 1990). Jazz promoter and teacher Grover Sales provides a fine introduction to the music and its artists in *Jazz: America's Classical Music* (Englewood Cliffs, NJ: Prentice-

Hall, 1984). An excellent discussion of Vaughan's career and contributions to American music can be found in Leslie Gourse, *Louis' Children: American Jazz Singers* (New York: Morrow, 1984). Jazz critic for London's *The Observer* provides brief, but helpful, profiles of jazz greats in *The Giants of Jazz* (New York: Macmillan, 1986). A moving tribute to Vaughan can be found by Murray Kempton, "On Sarah Vaughan," *New York Review of Books* (May 17, 1990): 42.

WALKER, A'LELIA (1885–1931), entrepreneur and patron of the arts, was the daughter of the famous inventor/entrepreneur Madam C.J. Walker, and heir to the bulk of her million dollar estate. She was affectionately referred to by Langston Hughes as the "joy goddess," of the Harlem Renaissance, and renowned for her business acumen, lavish parties, philanthropy, and devout support of the arts.

Walker, named Lelia Walker at birth, was the only child born to Sarah (Breedlove) Walker and Moses McWilliams in segregated Vicksburg, Mississippi, in 1885. She lived with her parents in extreme poverty, with no running water, indoor toilets, windows, tiled floors, or heat, and few prospects. At age two, Walker's father was reportedly killed by a lynch mob. Shortly thereafter, mother and daughter resettled in Saint Louis, Missouri, to live with relatives. After a series of menial jobs, Sarah Breedlove Walker began inventing and marketing her own Wonder Hair Grower products in the basement of her home.

A'Lelia Walker attended public schools, and after graduating from Knoxville College, a private black college located in Knoxville, Tennessee, in 1906, obtained a job supervising the mail-order operations of her mother's expanding business. She soon became indispensable to her mother and the business. In 1908 the Walkers moved to Pittsburgh, Pennsylvania, and opened their first beauty school, Lelia College, where they trained cosmetologists in the famous Walker method. There, A'Lelia Walker managed the manufacture of hair products. In 1913 she opened another Lelia College in New York, while her mother set up main headquarters in Indianapolis.

After the death of her mother in 1919, Walker became president of the company. She committed herself wholeheartedly to the running of the business, and left an indelible mark upon it and the community. In 1928 she built the Walker Building at 617 Indiana Avenue in Indianapolis, which contained the Walker College of Beauty Culture, a barbershop, salon, grocery store, pharmacy, professional offices, and the Majestic Walker Theater. The Walker Building became the first black-owned and -operated building of its kind in the country.

Walker changed her name to A'Lelia Robinson, carrying the last name of her first husband. She later adopted a daughter, and made her home in the magnificent mansion, Villa Lewaro, built by her mother on the Hudson River in Irvington, New York. This neo-Palladian-style structure was designed by the first registered black architect, Vetner Woodson Tandy, and became a symbol of racial success in business. She also remodeled her own townhouse on 136th Street, naming it "The Dark Tower," which was also the title of a poem by Langston Hughes. Between these lavish estates, Walker entertained and played hostess to hundreds of the world's most famous avant garde writers, poets, and artists. She used her wealth to give generous support to young black artists.

Her success at business was not matched in her marital life. Shortly after her divorce, Walker married Wiley Wilson. When that marriage failed, she married James Arthur Kennedy. All told, Walker was married four times.

A'Lelia Walker died unexpectedly in August 1931, at the home of friends in Long Branch, New Jersey. She was eulogized in a private ceremony presided over by Adam Clayton Powell, Sr., of the Abyssinian Baptist Church. Langston Hughes lamented that A'Lelia Walker's death "was really the end of the gay times of the New Negro era in Harlem." In death, she continued to put her wealth into the black community. She bequeathed her entire estate to the NAACP. When this organization needed money due to the Depression, the NAACP sold the building to a fraternal organization, the Companions of the Forest in America. In 1976 the building was listed on the National Register of Historic Places. A'Lelia Perry Bundles, the granddaughter of A'Lelia Walker's adopted daughter, is currently leading a movement to safeguard the building as the site of a museum honoring her female forebears.

—Vivian Gartley-Hindrew

Bibliography

Papers, photographs, and other memorabilia of A'Lelia Walker are in possession of A'Lelia Bundles of Washington DC, the Walker Urban Life Center, and the Indiana Historical Society in Indianapolis. Photographs are available in many publications, including David L. Lewis, *When Harlem Was in Vogue* (New York: Knopf, 1981). The most lively descriptions of her life come through the writings of her contemporaries as Langston Hughes, *The Big Sea: An Autobiography* (New York: Thunder's Mouth Press, 1940). Articles in periodicals provide detail as in Douglas C. Lyons, *"History's Children: Descendants of Legendary Figures Continue the Tradition,"* *Ebony* (February 1988): 33–37; and the articles by her great granddaughter, A'Lelia Bundles, "Madame C.J. Walker to Her Daughter A'Lelia Walker—The Last Letter," *Sage 1* (Fall 1984): 34–35; and "Madame C.J. Walker: Cosmetics Tycoon," *Ms.* 12 (July 1983): 91–94. The fate of the mansion is discussed in *The Plain Dealer*, February 29, 1992. A limited biographical sketch is included in Jessie C. Smith, ed., *Notable Black American Women* (Detroit: Gale, 1992).

WALKER, ALICE

WALKER, ALICE (b. 1944), born in Eatonton, Georgia, was the eighth and last child of Willie Lee Walker and Minnie Tallulah (Grant) Walker, a domestic worker. At age eight her older brothers shot her with a BB gun, and she lost the sight in one eye. It was at that time she began to write poetry, which she kept in a notebook. Books became her world, and education was important to her and her family. Her mother was a great influence.

Walker experienced racism at an early age, but in spite of the oppression, she had many excellent teachers, who she respected and admired. Alice Walker received an excellent education at college, first attending Spelman College from

1961 to 1963 and later leaving the South as had her siblings for a better chance in the North. Within a few years, Walker received a BA from Sarah Lawrence College.

Walker, a committed advocate for civil rights, worked on voter registration while in Georgia. She married white human rights lawyer Mel Leventhal, and had a daughter, Rebecca. The family moved to Mississippi in 1967, a time when an interracial marriage was considered dangerous and illegal. There Walker worked with the Head Start program. The family then moved to New York City, where Walker worked on the staff of the Welfare Department. In 1968–1969 she worked at Jackson State College as writer-in-residence and teacher of black studies. After working at other colleges and universities Alice Walker began to write. Her first novel, *The Third Life of Grange Copeland* (1970), was written from her awareness of the pervasiveness of the violent racist system of the South and its impact on the black family.

Most of her writings have autobiographical content describing and analyzing the plight of African Americans through her extended family. Walker's writings have been published separately and in collections. Her poetry includes *Revolutionary Petunias and Other Poems* (1973), "Horses Make a Landscape Look More Beautiful," *Once* (1968), and *Good Night Willie Lee, I'll See You in the Morning* (1979). Her essays include "Living by the Word" and *In Search of Our Mothers' Gardens* (1983). Walker's short story collections include *In Love and Trouble: Stories of Black Women* (1973) and *You Can't Keep a Good Woman Down*. Alice Walker's novels include *The Third Life of Grange Copeland* (1970); *The Color Purple*, which won her the Pulitzer Prize in 1983; *Meridian* (1976); and *Temple of My Familiar*. She has written a biography of Langston Hughes and has also edited a Zora Neale Hurston reader. Walker's essay "In Search of Zora Neale Hurston" in *Ms.* magazine sparked the contemporary interest in Hurston. In addition to these major works, Walker was an editor and frequent contributor to *Ms.* magazine. Her interviews and articles have appeared in *Essence*, the *Black Scholar*, the *New York Times*, *Mother Jones*, and other periodicals. Her autobiographical essay, "Beauty: When the Other Dancer Is the Self," is included in *Bearing Witness* (1991), edited by Henry Louis Gates, Jr. For children, Walker edited a short story illustrated reader entitled *To Hell with Dying*. Her sequel to *The Color Purple* is *Possessing the Secret of Joy*, published in 1992.

Walker now lives and works in California.

—LaVerne Nickson

Bibliography

Alice Walker materials abound. Information about her and her work can be found in John O'Brien's *Interviews with Black Writers* (New York: Liverwright, 1973). A selected bibliography of Walker's writings and interviews and two essays on Walker and her writings are included in *Sturdy Black Bridges*, edited by Roseann P. Bell, Bettye J. Parker, and Beverly Guy-Sheftall (Garden City, NY: Anchor, 1979), pp. 133–156 and 402–413. Walker receives critical treatment in McDowell's article "The Black Woman as Artist and Critic: Four Versions" *Kentucky Review* 7 (Spring 1987): 19–41. Walker's own vision of her role is evident in her article included in "The Negro Woman in American Literature," *Freedomways* 6 (Winter 1966): 8–25. For background on the context in which Walker writes see, *Black Writers of America*, edited by Richard Barksdale and Kenneth Kinnamon (New York: Macmillan, 1972). For biographical detail see, *Who's Who among Black Americans*, 6th edition (Detroit: Gale, 1990–1991); "Afro-American Fiction Writers after 1955," in *Dictionary of Literary Biography* 33 (Detroit: Gale, 1984), pp. 258–269; Carol Myers, et al., *Black American Writers: Past and Present* (Metuchen, NJ: Scarecrow, 1975); James Page, *Selected Black American Authors* (Boston: G.K. Hall, 1977); Claudia Tate, *Black Women Writers at Work* (New York: Continuum, 1983); Ann A. Shockley, *Living Black American Authors* (New York: Bowker, 1973); Ronda Glikin, *Black American Women in Literature* (Jefferson, NC: McFarland, 1989); Jessie Carney Smith, ed., *Notable Black American Women* (Detroit: Gale, 1992); Ora Williams, *American Black Women in Arts and Social Science* (Metuchen, NJ: Scarecrow, 1978); and the jackets of Walker's books.

WALKER, MAGGIE [MITCHELL] (1867–1934), the nation's first female bank president, clubwoman, civic leader, and feminist, came from humble origins to gain prestige and power in finance and in racial advancement organizations. Born on July 15 to former slaves Elizabeth (Draper) and William Mitchell, Maggie Lena Mitchell benefited from the privileges afforded the servants at the Van Lew mansion in Richmond, Virginia. Her mother, Lizzie, was a cook's helper; her father, William, was the butler to the Van Lew family. The estate on Church Hill, outside the city of Richmond, had a colorful heritage as a station on the Underground Railroad. The Van Lews provided service as Union spies and harboring Union soldiers during the Civil War. Growing up on the Van Lew estate provided young Maggie Lena with good role models and an excellent education.

To gain a greater sense of community, her parents left the Van Lew estate and moved to two rented clapboard houses in an alley in downtown Richmond. Her father gained employment at the St. Charles Hotel as a head waiter. Her mother took in laundry and raised the children, Maggie and Johnnie. After her father's death, probably due to a robbery, her mother increased her laundry business. A strict disciplinarian, her mother used Maggie as her delivery person and babysitter.

While working side by side with her mother, Maggie Lena received her education in the segregated public schools of Richmond. She attended old Lancaster School across from the jail and received an education in cursing from the inmates. This formal education was supplemented with the spiritual instruction in the Thursday night Sunday school at the Old First Baptist Church and the financial education gained through participation in the black insurance business connected with the fraternal organization, the Independent Order of St. Luke (IOSL), which she joined at age 14. Within two years, she served as an elected delegate to the annual convention at Petersburg, Virginia.

The same drive that was evidenced in her family work and community involvements was rewarded in education. She finished at the head of her class at Armstrong Normal and High School in 1883. For the graduation ceremonies, she led her senior class in requesting to join their white counterparts at the school auditorium, rather than accept their diplomas separately in the church hall. The school administration allowed the joint ceremony only if it respected the Jim Crow norms requiring segregated seating of students and audience. The students rejected that choice; the program awarded diplomas in the school auditorium, respecting Jim Crow norms.

Following graduation, she carried this spirit into the classroom by teaching three years at the Lancaster School and by taking classes in accounting and business management, skills put to use through the IOSL. Marriage in 1886 to Armstead Walker, a young contractor active in her church, redirected her energies from teaching into her community organizations, especially the IOSL. Their life on East Leigh Street, referred to as "the Fifth Avenue of Negro Society," provided privileges she never had as a child. After the birth of their first son, Russell, Maggie Lena Walker entrusted his care with household servants and ascended in the IOSL. Within 10 years she moved from executive secretary to grand secretary-treasurer, a position held for 35 years. By the time her second son, Melvin DeWitt, was born in 1897, she had drafted the governing laws for administering Juvenile Circles, had formed the Juvenile Branch of the Order, and had accepted the secretaryship of the St. Luke Endowment Department.

When she assumed the secretary-treasurer position in 1899 at the salary of $100 a year, the IOSL had inadequate staff, no property, no reserve funds, and only 3,400 members, of whom only 1,080 were paying members. The treasury contained only $36.61 and unpaid bills amounting to over $400. She immediately created a fraternal newspaper, the *Saint Luke Herald*, to establish communication and to market the services. Within 25 years, the financial status had improved, having collected nearly $3.5 million. Their membership had climbed to over 100,000 with a cash reserve of $70,000, an office building worth $100,000, and a staff of 55 with 145 field agents covering 24 states. She achieved these great benefits by moving the organization from its initial goals to provide funeral/burial services and assistance for ill and aged, to savings and investments.

Her early religious training was demonstrated in the IOSL's slogan of "Love, Purity, and Charity," and in the organization's "fraternal kindness." A person had to declare belief in the Supreme Being before receipt of coverage, but could purchase a $100 policy without a physical examination. Her vision produced many changes. In 1902 she suggested an idea to the Grand Council for a penny savings bank. In 1903 the St. Luke Penny Savings Bank became the St. Luke Bank and Trust Company. She started a short-lived department store venture, the St. Luke Emporium.

While she established the financial empire, she also was a leader in the National Association of Colored Women. She founded the Richmond Council of Colored Women in 1912. She helped organize the 1,400 members to raise money to buy the land for a reformatory for delinquent girls headed by Janie Porter Barrett. She became a member of the board of trustees of the Virginia School for Girls and the Virginia Manual Labor School in Hanover County. Her club fundraising helped the tuberculosis sanitorium in Burkeville and a community center and a nursing home in Richmond.

Professional achievements were marred by personal misfortune. Her son, Russell, an accountant, was given a position at the bank. Said to be spoiled by his life of privilege, young Russell created tragedy for Maggie Lena Walker. In 1915 her husband was shot to death by her son, who said he thought his father was a burglar. Since the story of an accidental shooting seemed implausible, Russell was arrested, brought to trial, and, after much anguished testimony, acquitted. Her enemies tried to remove her from her IOSL post to "safeguard" the Order from scandal. She fought the removal during this time of personal tragedy by enumerating her achievements. She continued in her position.

As one of the wealthiest African-American women of her day, she contributed to many charitable and educational projects. She established the St. Luke Educational Fund to continue helping black youth receive an education. She served as a trustee of the National Training School for Girls in Washington, DC, as both a national director and a vice president of the Richmond branch of the NAACP, as a board member of the National Urban League, and as the trustee of Hartshorn College.

The 1920s brought honors and a series of personal losses. Her beloved mother died in 1922 followed closely by her son, Russell, in 1923. Virginia Union University awarded her an honorary degree in 1925. On the eve of the Depression, her financial organization absorbed other black banks to become the Consolidated Bank and Trust Company with Maggie Lena Walker as the board chair.

Ill health during the Depression led to decreased activities. Already confined to a wheelchair as a result of complications from a 1907 fall that shattered her knee cap, she could barely get around as the years complicated her injuries. Upon her retirement from the IOSL, she was succeeded by Hattie N. Walker, the widow of her eldest son. The city of Richmond praised her in a quarto-centennial service celebration at the city auditorium and also named a street, a high school, and a theater in her honor. The month of October 1934 was declared Maggie L. Walker Month by African-American organizations throughout the nation as a tribute to her life. Walker died a few months later on December 15, 1934, of diabetes gangrene. She was buried in her family's section in Evergreen Cemetery in Richmond.

—Dorothy C. Salem

Bibliography

The United States Park Service has established the Maggie Walker National Historic Site in Richmond, Virginia, where her papers, diaries, and photographs can be found. The newspapers of her city carry many references to her in *Richmond News Leader* and *Richmond Times Dispatch*. A biography of her life was written by her childhood friend, Wendell Dabney, *Maggie L. Walker and I.O of St. Luke* (Cincinnati: Dabney, 1927).

Articles examine various facets of Walker's life and leadership. Many of the older resources contain inaccuracies in dates and other information. For material on Walker and the organizations see Caroline Bird, "The Innovators: Maggie Walker, Kate Gleason," *Enterprising Women* (New York: Norton, 1976); Pam White, "Famous Grandma Walker was 'Full of Fun,'" *Richmond News Leader* (July 16, 1979); Clement Richardson, *The National Cyclopedia of the Colored Race* (Montgomery, AL: National Publishing, 1919).

Biographical sketches of Walker abound. Written by her contemporaries until the present time, these biographical vignettes include much of the same information with occasional variation. These include Elsa Barkley Brown, "Maggie Lena Walker," in *Encyclopedia of Southern Culture*, edited by Charles Wilson and William Ferris (Chapel Hill: University of North Carolina Press, 1989); Sadie Daniel, *Women Builders* (Washington, DC: Associated Publishers, 1931); Elizabeth L. Davis, *Lifting as They Climb* (Washington, DC: National Association of Colored Women, 1933); Benjamin Brawley, *Negro Builders and Heroes* (Chapel Hill: University of North Carolina Press, 1937); Mary White Ovington, *Portraits in Color* (New York: Viking Press, 1927); John Gibson, *Progress of a Race* (Naperville, IL: J.L. Nichols, 1920); Sylvia Dannett, *Profiles of Negro Womanhood* (Chicago: Educational Heritage Press, 1964); Rayford Logan, *Dictionary of Negro Biography* (New York: Norton, 1968); Edward T. James, ed., *Notable American Women, 1607–1950* (Cambridge: Belknap, 1971); and Jessie Carney Smith, ed., *Notable Black American Women* (Detroit: Gale, 1992).

WALKER, MARGARET (b. 1915), poet, novelist, teacher, and writer, was born July 7 to a Methodist minister, the Reverend Sigismund C. Walker, and Marion (Dozier) Walker, a musician/teacher in Birmingham, Alabama. Later, when Walker was still a child, her parents moved from Birmingham to New Orleans, where they taught at New Orleans University.

Walker spent a culturally rich southern childhood that influenced her poetic and artistic vision. She grew up enmeshed in both folklore and traditional art. Her father, a scholar and lover of literature, instilled in his daughter a love of American classics, the Bible, English classics, and poetry. Her mother played music, especially ragtime, and read poetry from Paul Laurence Dunbar, John Greenleaf Whittier, the Bible, and Shakespeare. As she grew older, Walker chose her own poets, showing a particular attraction for the poetry of Langston Hughes and Countee Cullen. The family household included her maternal grandmother, who told the children folktales and stories. One story especially impressed Walker, the one of her grandmother's own mother who had been a slave in Georgia. This story stayed in Walker's consciousness and became the story of Vyry in Walker's famous novel *Jubilee*. Walker's love of art, poetry, and music continued through high school and college. Before she graduated from Northwestern University in Evanston, Illinois, Walker had heard the poet James Weldon Johnson read "God's Trombones" and the singers Marian Anderson and Roland Hayes perform in New Orleans.

The Depression served as the context for the publication in 1934 of her first poem in *The Crisis*, the journal of the NAACP. Walker's association with the Works Progress Administration (WPA) started in 1934 while she was a senior at Northwestern living on the North Side of Chicago. She started at WPA as a volunteer in recreation projects and then in 1936 became a full-time employee in the WPA Writer's Project as a junior writer. Her experience at the WPA was enriched by her contact with other writers and artists, who included Nelson Algre, Jacob Scher, James Phelan, Sam Ross, Katherine Dunham, Willard Motley, Frank Yerby, Fenton Johnson, and Richard Wright.

Walker had met Wright earlier, when Langston Hughes had introduced them, but the WPA Writer's Project cemented their friendship. Sadly, three years later, Wright broke off the friendship when he heard rumors that Walker was spreading gossip against him. Although Wright refused to identify the informer, Wright ignored Walker's protestations and declared the friendship over while Walker was in New York attending the League of American Writers Convention in June 1939. Walker never saw Wright again. Although Wright wrote to her some years later, for Walker the friendship had ended. Walker wrote about her friendship with Wright in her recently published book, *Richard Wright: Daemonic Genius: A Portrait of the Man; a Critical Look at His Work*, and in an essay titled "Richard Wright." She also examined the friendship in *A Poetic Equation: Conversations Between Nikki Giovanni and Margaret Walker*. In each of these publications, Walker stated that their relationship was literary and intellectual. Others have noted Walker's contribution and support of Wright during his writing of *Native Son*.

Walker finished her first novel, *Goose Island*, in 1939, but it was never published. Also in 1939, she left the WPA's Federal Writer's Project following the implementation of a congressional law requiring employees who had worked longer than 18 months to leave. Although Walker could have returned after an interim period, she chose instead to further her career in another way. Walker elected to pursue a graduate degree in writing. She planned to combine writing with a full-time teaching career. She enrolled in the Writer's Workshop at the University of Iowa in Iowa City and in 1941, and under the direction of Paul Engle, completed her master's thesis "For My People." This collection of poetry revealed her rekindled love and affinity for folk material. When Yale University Press published the collection in 1942, it won the Yale University Younger Poet's

Award. Walker's publication was the first book of poetry by a black woman to be published since Georgia Douglas Johnson's *The Heart of a Woman and Other Poems* (1918).

Armed with her MA degree and a prestigious poetry award, Walker began teaching in 1941. In 1943 Walker married Firnist James Alexander, and over the course of their marriage, gave birth to four children. In addition to teaching and raising a family during the 1940s, Walker also resumed research on her Civil War novel, the story of her great-grandmother, which received a Rosenwald fellowship in 1944. She continued her research off and on throughout the following decade, and in 1962 when she returned to the University of Iowa's Writer's Workshop to begin work on a PhD in English, she had already envisioned a novel as a dissertation project. Paul Engle, her advisor, helped her plan a graduate program around the project. *Jubilee* was published as a novel in 1966. Though it initially received mixed reviews, it has become a mainstay in the African-American literary canon. Walker's book *How I Wrote Jubilee* was published in 1972 to explain the evolution of the novel from her grandmother's oral history and her response to criticism of the novel.

Her long career spanned teaching at Livingstone College in North Carolina, West Virginia State College, and Jackson State University. In 1979 she retired from Jackson State, where she was director of the Institute for the Study of History, Life, and Culture of Black People. *Jubilee* was Walker's only published novel. Among her nonfictional works are *Richard Wright: Daemonic Genius* and *A Poetic Equation*. Walker returned to writing poetry, publishing *Prophets for a New Day* in 1970, *October Journey* in 1973, and *This is My Century, New and Collected Poems* in 1988.

Since her retirement from teaching, Walker has continued to write and has undertaken rigorous speaking tours, a practice started in 1943 when Arthur P. Davis invited her to read *For My People* at Virginia Union University in Richmond, Virginia.

—Mary Frances Stubbs

Bibliography

Margaret Walker Alexander's best known works are *For My People* (New Haven: Yale University Press, 1942) and *Jubilee* (Boston: Houghton Mifflin, 1966). Additional poetry collections are *Prophets for a New Day* (Detroit: Broadside Press, 1970); *October Journey* (Detroit: Broadside Press, 1973); and *This Is My Century: New and Collected Poems* (Athens: University of Georgia Press, 1988). Other selected important works are *A Poetic Equation: Conversations Between Nikki Giovanni and Margaret Walker*, by Walker and Nikki Giovanni (Washington, DC: Howard University Press, 1974) and *Richard Wright: Daemonic Genius: A Portrait of the Man, a Critical Look at His Work* (New York: Warner Armistad, 1989); "On Being Female, Black and Free," in *The Writer and Her Work*, edited by Janet Sternberg (New York: Norton, 1980); "Richard Wright," in *Richard Wright: Impressions and Perspectives*, edited by David Ray and Robert M. Farnsworth (Ann Arbor: University of Michigan Press, 1973); "Some Aspects of the Black Aesthetic," *Freedomways* 16 (Winter 1976); and *"The Humanistic Tradition of Afro-American Literature,"* (American Libraries, October 1, 1970).

The interview with Walker is in the Black Women Oral History Project, Schlesinger Library, Radcliffe College. Her archives are in the Margaret Walker Archival Collection in the Harry T. Sampson Library at Jackson State University. Discussions of Margaret Walker Alexander and her work have appeared in many reference works including Marianna Davis, *Contributions of Black Women to America I* (Columbia, SC: Kenday, 1982); *Dictionary of Literary Biography Vol. 6* (Detroit: Gale, 1984); *Contemporary Literary Criticism*, Vol. 1 (Detroit: Gale, 1973); *Black Women Writers at Work*, edited by Claudia Tate (New York: Continuum, 1983); *Women Poets of the World*, edited by Joanna Bankier and D. Lashgari (New York: Macmillan, 1983); and *Black Women Writers, 1950–1980: A Critical Evaluation*, edited by Mari Evans (New York: Doubleday, 1984).

WALKER, SARAH (MADAM C.J.) [BREEDLOVE] (1867–1919), although she was the daughter of slaves, became the first black female millionaire. She was respected in her own day for the substantial fortune she made in cosmetics and for helping to instill racial pride in her customers and salespeople. She still provides a significant role model for black entrepreneurs.

Madam C.J. Walker was born Sarah Breedlove on December 23 in Delta, Louisiana, on the Burney family plantation, where her parents had been slaves. She was orphaned at age seven, and she was raised by her sister, Louvenia, in Vicksburg, Mississippi. As a result of this impoverished background, she had only very limited formal education.

At age 14, Walker married a man named McWilliams, and her daughter A'Lelia was born in 1885. After she became a widow at age 20 in 1887, Walker moved to St. Louis. While in St. Louis, Walker started a cosmetics business when she began to lose her hair. After a prayer for God to save her hair, she claimed to receive a unique hair growth formula based on the inspiration of a dream. She soon demonstrated excellent marketing skills in selling hair products.

In July 1905 Walker moved to Denver. Six months later, she married newspaperman C.J. Walker, whose name she used long after business differences ended the marriage.

In 1910 Walker made Indianapolis the headquarters of her cosmetic and hair business, Walker College of Hair Culture and Walker Manufacturing Company (whose headquarters are currently in Tuskegee, Alabama). In 1906 she had turned over her mail order business to her daughter, who used Pittsburgh, Pennsylvania, as a headquarters for Walker College, which trained "hair culturists." In 1912 the businesses moved to Harlem, the capital of black America. Throughout the South and East, Walker enjoyed great success as a traveling salesperson. As a result, she acquired agents wherever black women lived, and she organized state and national clubs for them.

A generous donor to black charities, Walker encouraged her agents to support black philanthropic work. She made the single largest donation to the successful 1918 effort by the National Association of Colored Women to buy the home of Frederick Douglass. At the annual convention of Walker agents, she always donated to the most generous local affiliate.

Walker made particularly generous gifts to significant educational institutions such as Mary McLeod Bethune's Daytona Normal and Industrial Institute for Negro Girls. She was highly regarded by Bethune, who considered her a racial model.

Madam Walker died on May 25, 1919, of kidney failure and hypertension at her lavish estate, Villa Lewaro, located on the Hudson River in Irvington, New York. Despite her impoverished beginnings, Madam Walker achieved notable business success. Several generations of her family continued the business she established. In addition, she supported all the efforts of her generation to cope with Jim Crow laws and secure greater opportunities for education and self-improvement.

The estate went to A'Lelia Walker Robinson Wilson, who bequeathed the estate to the NAACP following her death in 1931. To raise money for the organization, which was hit hard by the Depression, the NAACP sold the building in 1932 to a fraternal organization, the Companians of the Forest in America. In 1976, Villa Lewaro, a neo-Palladian-style structure designed by the first registered black architect, Vetner Woodson Tandy, was listed on the National Register of Historic Places. Today, A'Lelia Perry Bundles, a producer with "ABC World News Tonight" and great-great-granddaughter of Madam Walker, is leading a movement to safeguard the building for establishment of a museum.

—Susan Stussy

Bibliography

The most helpful primary source materials are the Schomburg Center for Research in Black Culture, New York Public Library and the Moorland-Spingarn Collection at Howard University. Obituaries appeared on May 26, 1919, in the *New York Times*, *Indianapolis News*, and *St. Louis Post Dispatch*. Other sources include the following:

Adams, Michael Henry, "1918 Villa Built as Showplace for Blacks," *The Cleveland Plain Dealer* (February 29, 1992).

Bundles, A'Lelia P. "Madam C.J. Walker to Her Daughter A'Lelia Walker—The Last Letter," *Sage* 1 (1984): 34–35. Contains a brief biography and text of letter.

———. "Madame C.J. Walker: Cosmetics Tycoon," *Ms.* 12 (July 1983): 91–94. Provides a good popular article for a feminist magazine. Her byline identifies her as the grandaughter of Walker's adopted grandaughter.

Davis, Elizabeth L. *Lifting as They Climb*. Washington, DC: NACW, 1933. Relates the importance of Walker's philanthropic work to racial uplift.

Doyle, Kathleen. "Madam C.J. Walker: First Black Woman Millionaire," *American History Illustrated* 24 (1989): 24–25. A brief treatment for a popular history magazine.

Fisher, Walter. "Sarah Breedlove Walker," in *Notable American Women*, edited by Edward T. James, et al. (Cambridge: Harvard University Press, 1971), pp. 533–535.

Nelson, J. "Fortune That Madame Built," *Essence* 14 (June 1983): 84–86. Nelson provides a brief sketch about the business.

WASHINGTON, DINAH (1924–1963), born Ruth Jones in Tuscaloosa, Alabama, on August 29, to Alice (Williams) and Ollie Jones and had a brother named Harold and two sisters. She became one of the pioneers of the music known as rhythm and blues.

When Ruth Jones was about three years old, the family decided to move to Chicago in search of work and a better life. They settled on the South Side in the housing projects. Since these were the years of the Great Depression, they were very poor. Ollie Jones, a small-time gambler, was away from home for weeks at a time. Alice Jones worked as a domestic, a job that kept her away from home during the day.

As a child, she was chubby and had bad skin, an appearance that got her the nickname "Alligator." When Ollie Jones left home, he kept in contact with the family but could not be counted on for financial or emotional support. For extra money, Alice Jones played the piano at the Saint Luke's Baptist Church. Through this role, Alice Jones taught her daughter to play the piano and provided the environment through which people learned that her daughter had a good singing voice. Pushed by her mother, young Ruth Jones started singing gospel songs in the local churches. She was hired as an accompanist to Sallie Martin, a gospel singer, through which she gained entry to the gospel performance field which included Mahalia Jackson and Roberta Martin.

She attended Wendell Phillips High, where she was exposed to other types of music. Billie Holiday was her idol, but her mother was very religious and would not allow her daughter to sing anything but gospel songs. Without her mother's knowledge, Ruth Jones at age 15 entered a talent contest at the Regal Theater singing "I Can't Face the Music." She won the contest, and as a result local club owners took notice of her. She then began to sing in the local clubs as the Garrick Stage Lounge and was noticed by big band leader Lionel Hampton, who decided Ruth Jones was not the best name for her; her name was then changed to Dinah Washington.

Dinah Washington's career took off once she sang with Lionel Hampton and his band in 1943. She stayed with the band for almost three years traveling on the road. After leaving Hampton, Washington worked as a solo performer and did some recording for Keynote Records. She was touted as the first eligible successor to Bessie Smith. Such songs as "Blow Top Blues" and "I Love You, Yes I Do" were a credit to Washington's career. She captured audiences with her blues-tinged renditions of pop tunes like "What a Difference a Day Makes" and her album *Dinah Washington: The Jazz Sides* (EmArcy) highlighted her jazz-influenced vocals. She married seven times to John Young, Robert Grayson, George Jenkins, Walter Buchanan, Eddie Chamblee, Rafael Campos, and Richard "Night Train" Lane. She had two sons: Robert Grayson, Jr., and George Jenkins, Jr. During her career she recorded for Apollo, ABC, Grand Award, Parrot, Decca, and Mercury Records. Her songs regularly appeared on *Billboard*'s R & B charts. Remaining close to family, she moved to Detroit with her two sons and new husband, Dick Lane, in 1963.

Dinah Washington ran her own booking agency, Queen Attractions. Although her life was successful, it was short-lived. On December 14, 1963, Washington died in her home in Detroit from an accidental overdose of sleeping pills and diet pills.

—LaVerne Nickson

Bibliography

Most of the information about Dinah Washington must be obtained through the musical references. See *Blues Who's Who: A Biographical Dictionary of Blues Singers* (New Rochelle, NY: Arlington House, 1979); Sally Placksin, *American Women in Jazz, 1900 to Present, Their Words, Lives and Music* (Cleveland: Windeview, 1982); Dempsey J. Travis, *An Autobiography of Black Jazz* (Chicago: Urban Research Institute, 1983); Eileen Southern, *Biographical Dictionary of Afro-American and African Musicians* (Westport, CT: Greenwood Press, 1981); Edward Mapp, *A Directory of Blacks in the Performing Arts* (Metuchen, NJ: Scarecrow, 1978); Paul Oliver, *The Story of the Blues* (New York: Chilton, 1969); Ora Williams, *American Black Women in Arts and Social Science* (Metuchen, NJ: Scarecrow, 1978); and Jim Haskins, *Queen of the Blues* (New York: Morrow, 1985).

WASHINGTON, MARGARET JAMES [MURRAY] (1865–1925),

educator, club organizer, and advocate for women's and civil rights, was born on March 9, several months before the ratification of the Thirteenth Amendment, which abolished slavery and freed approximately 4.5 million slaves. Washington, a mulatto with reddish-brown hair, gray hazel eyes, and a large commanding figure, escaped the cruelties of that peculiar institution. As one of ten children born to her sharecropper parents in rural Macon, Mississippi, Washington understood hardship and privileges. Her mother, Lucy Murray, was a washerwoman; her father was an Irish immigrant. The sharecropping system implemented immediately after the Civil War kept blacks uneducated and on the plantation. But, unlike many of her peers who were doomed to a life of economic peonage, Washington rose above such obstacles and carved for herself a niche in United States history.

Her father died when Margaret was only seven years old, which led to her moving into the household of her Quaker teachers, who further enlightened her. At age 14, she embarked upon a teaching career that she maintained throughout most of her adult life. Recognizing the deficiencies in her education, she enrolled in 1881 at Fisk University, and worked to pay her expenses. Because of these influences she refused to accept restrictions caused by race, sex, and class. At Fisk University, a Freedmen's Bureau school started in 1866 in Tennessee and often referred to as the Black Harvard of the South, she suffered from poor health, but her ambitious spirits and iron will kept her there until graduation in 1889. Attending with such peers as W.E.B. Du Bois, she and another female were the only women in this predominantly male graduating class. She typified the struggle of ex-slaves who attempted to rise from humble origins through individual merit and pioneering endeavors during the Reconstruction era.

Before graduation, Washington applied to several institutions for a teaching position, including Prarie View Normal and Industrial Institute in Texas and Tuskegee Institute in Alabama. Prarie View offered her a post, but she declined in favor of Tuskegee after consulting with the school's director-founder, Booker T. Washington, who attended the commencement exercises at Fisk University in June 1889. She forged a bond with Tuskegee that she never regretted.

She came to Tuskegee Normal and Industrial Institute as a teacher of English literature. After one year of employment and in recognition of her strength of mind and disciplinary power, the board of trustees promoted and appointed her as the lady principal and dean of women. From these positions, she attempted to break down the barriers of racism, sexism, and pauperism, examining Booker T. Washington's policy of economic independence and nationalism and considering it the right solution to the race's problems. Thus, she nurtured and modified her female charges' personalities and behaviors by teaching the necessity and importance of self-help, race pride, and racial solidarity and uplift. When they left Tuskegee, they wore the crowns of strength and dignity, adorned themselves with the enduring grace of intellectual attainment, and committed themselves to racial uplift. In essence, they were equipped to deal with the challenges of a Jim Crow South. Murray instilled in them the Protestant ethic of hard work, thrift, and saving, which enabled them to invest in community and build institutions. This parallelism constituted an integral part of Booker T. Washington's economic nationalism that led to self-reliance, wealth accumulation, and racial uplift.

Washington turned her dormitory charges into acceptable southern ladies who epitomized the Talented Tenth that W.E.B. Du Bois later described in his work *The Souls of Black Folks*. These poor but proud students worked diligently to acquire the traits and intelligence that their mentor taught them. In so doing, they negated the stereotypical images of the plantation mammy associated with rural African-American females residing in the South. Washington was their surrogate mother, and taught them about the requirements of being a good wife and mother. Each acquired skills in the culinary arts, child care, and housekeeping, the prerequisitives for marriage and motherhood. With few jobs available in teaching and low wages common in the South, many young women opted for the security of marriage and home, as did Washington, their teacher.

Alone since the death in 1889 of his second wife, Booker T. Washington needed a wife to help him raise his three children and a co-partner he could rely upon for the management of Tuskegee. On October 12, 1892, Margaret Murray married Washington. Mutual respect, love, and admiration as co-partners in the workplace and as friends in the home kept their marriage intact until Booker T. Washington's death in 1915. As the third wife of Booker T. Washington, Margaret Washington's ambition or influence did not diminish. She combined professionalism with domesticity and provided a happy and loving home for his three children, Portia, a daughter of Fannie Smith Washington, and two sons of Olivia Davidson, the second wife. Her relationship with the boys progressed, but the relationship between Murray and Portia was always estranged.

Neither motherhood nor illiness impeded Margaret Washington's career. She suffered from ill health yet engaged in fundraising activities to keep Tuskegee financially solvent. To relieve Booker T. of some of the mundane and exhaustive tasks that kept him fatigued, Margaret Washington volunteered to tour and solicit financial support from northern philanthropists.

In reality, she stood next to Booker T. in power and in position whether in the home, on the job, or in public. Their lives were intertwined, and frequently the public failed to separate the careers and aspirations of these two individuals. Whenever business matters took Booker T. away from Tuskegee, she monitored the operation of the institute, and through a steady flow of correspondence, she recorded and detailed every incident, especially those that compromised the integrity and reputation of the female students.

Her concern for educating women was likewise evident in the formation of Mother's Meetings. In February 1892, when the first Negro Convention was held in Alabama, she wanted to correct the imbalanced sex ratio and ensure the participation of women by inviting women from the town. Approximately six women came, listened, and approved of Margaret Washington's plan to improve their lives. Out of this conference of dedicated females, the Mother's Meeting developed and flourished. The membership increased from 6 in 1892 to 300 by 1904. As the organization's membership increased, so did its publications. The organization printed numerous booklets and pamphlets, including one entitled "Your Need," which stressed the urgency for more race pride and self-respect. Other booklets contained information regarding recipes, home remedies, and members' addresses. A myriad of topics ranging from "Morals among Young Girls" to "Fruit Canning and Poultry Raising" were discussed. As the the facilities expanded, so did the services rendered by the group. These included child care for working mothers, educational skills for youths, and reading/learning facilities such as libraries that were designed to aid in the campaign against illiteracy. All of these projects had the indelible imprint of Margaret Washington's design of racial and gender liberation.

From these local roots grew the national black women's club movement. Washington's group emphasized racial solidarity and history. The Tuskegee Women's Club established by Washington and composed of wives and women associated with the institute "studied Black History and literature, kept the oral tradition alive and honored the surviving veterans of the abolitionist struggles." They also supported the scholarly work of famous men such as Carter Goodwin Woodson, historian, author, father of black history, and the founder of the Association for the Study of Negro Life and History, the *Journal of Negro History*, and the *Negro History Bulletin*; W.E.B. Du Bois, sociologist-historian, Pan-Africanist, and co-founder of the National Association for the Advancement of Colored People and the editor of that organization's official publication, *The Crisis*; and Charles S. Johnson, sociologist and renowned author of scientific research on race relations. The women of the Tuskegee Club transmitted racial pride for generations. In a letter to Lugenia Hope, wife of the president of Atlanta University (September 15, 1922), Margaret Washington wrote,

> The first thing we are doing is trying to get into every school, private, public or otherwise, Negro literature and history. We are not trying to displace any other literature or history, but trying to get all children of the country acquainted with the Negro. . . . I think you will be surprised to know how many schools, North and South, even our own schools where our children are taught nothing except literature of the Caucasian race. We are not fighting any race, we are simply looking for our own. The first law of nature is Self-preservation.

The club movement generated research on women and exposed the unfair treatment of African-American women in the literature. Due to the incorrectness of the analysis and not the paucity of the evidence, historians placed too much emphasis upon the passivity, mythical stereotypes, and pseudo-scientific arguments to dismiss the southern nonwhite woman as insignificant except as a domestic or farmworker void of intellect and aspiration. Margaret Washington and her cohorts through journalistic efforts and women clubs set the record straight.

In 1895 she founded the National Federation of Afro-American Women and served as its first president. In addition, she co-founded the National Association of Colored Women, which consisted of a merger of several women clubs, such as the National Federation of Afro-American Women and the National Colored Women's League. With the formation of the National Association of Colored Women's Clubs at the Nineteenth Street Baptist Church on July 21, 1896, in Washington, DC, African-American women had a means of improving their own conditions and that of the race. The leadership of the organization, Mary Church Terrell, Washington, and Josephine St. Pierre Ruffin, recognized the handicaps of all women in industrial and educational opportunities and "recognized the need for uplift work in all levels of community life," so they concerned themselves with existing social evils: woman's suffrage; equal pay for equal work; day care for working women; personal hygiene; shelter for single women; homes for wayward boys and girls, unwed mothers, the elderly and orphans; schools for the blind; centers for the insane; recreational facilities; and summer camps for youth. Their constitution pledged members "to participate in and support all causes working in the interest of the advancement of the Negro population as a whole and of women in particular." To publicize the accomplishments of the organization and to document the contributions of African American women."

As the organization's fifth president, Margaret Washington founded and edited its official publication, the *National Notes*, in 1906. Washington utilized the *National Notes* from 1914 to 1918 to propagandize the plight of the African-American race in general and the African-American woman specifically. As a journalist and clubwoman, she promoted interracial cooperation, sought improvement of the condition of African-American women, and spread the philosophy of Booker T. Washington from a regional setting to a national scene.

The club movement unified African-American women and provided a vehicle for political empowerment and civic reform. They worked for a federal suffrage bill so that there would be "an equal chance for all women as well as men to express their preference through their votes." Within the National Association of Colored Women's Clubs, they created a Department of Suffrage to conduct training classes in the reading and interpretation of the Constitution and to study governmental affairs so that women could handle the vote intelligently and wisely. Margaret Washington saw this as an opportunity for women to overcome the obstacles set by the literacy and understanding clauses that were specifically designed to disfranchise African Americans.

Together, she and Booker T. met the challenges of racism and suffered the consequences of their actions. In 1895, when Booker T. delivered his speech on the progress of the African American at the Atlanta Cotton Exposition and offered suggestions on racial problems, he and Margaret Washington gained overnight notoriety, anxiety, and success. His remarks earned both of them the wrath of the black intelligentsia and integrationists, the approval of southern racists, and the relief of northern liberals who no longer wanted to resolve the race issue. The bond forged during the marriage grew stronger in the face of adversity and political criticism.

The Washingtons endured the barbs and criticism. Margaret Washington retaliated when attacked. In 1899, when members attending the annual convention of the National Afro-American Council called Booker T. a "traitor, trimmer and coward" for not attending the meeting, Margaret Washington requested that her name be removed from the program. Although Washington had explained that he could not attend because of prior commitments, the delegation led by the Reverend Reverdy C. Ransom of Chicago and B.T. Thornton of Indiana denounced the Washingtons for being in Chicago and not finding the time to attend. In defense of the couple, Bishop Alexander Walter, president of the Council, asserted that "Washington's relations with African Americans and whites in the North and South" made it impractical for him to connect himself with the discussion of an organization which might be radical in its utterances to the destruction of his "usefulness in connection with many causes." Consequently, the Council adopted a resolution and applauded Washington for his "noble efforts." In 1899 she ran afoul of Charles Henry Smith (a.k.a. Bill Arp), racist columnist for the *Atlanta Constitution* in her scalding attacks upon the convict-lease system and pleaded that African-American women prisoners should not be locked nightly in the same cells or cell blocks with male prisoners. Arp refuted the allegations and reported that never in the history of the state of Georgia were such deeds done. Moreover, he held Booker T. as well as his wife accountable for "malignant slanders." Other southern newspapers reprinted the accusations and editorials. The media blitz prompted D.W. Iver of the *Montgomery Advertiser* to write Booker T. Washington to say that "his faith had been shaken by Mrs. Washington's charges, since he did not believe that male and female prisoner's were ever locked up together in any southern states." T. Thomas Fortune, the co-founder of the Afro-American League/Council in 1890, came to the Washingtons' defense. Later he became founder and editor of the militant *New York Age*, which fought for equality of opportunity for African Americans and equal protection under the law. With such a powerful friend, the Washingtons sustained the barrage of attacks.

Again in 1920, Margaret Washington found herself on the cutting edge of razor sharp criticisms following a speech at the annual meeting of the Commission for Interracial Cooperation. On October 27, 1920, she praised white women for serving as examples and role models for African-American women. In addition, she lauded them for their assistance in helping elderly females. Because of these comments, many of her critics labeled her an accomodationist with a conservative race policy.

Despite the criticisms, Washington remained one of the most respected individuals of her day. After the death of her husband in 1915, she participated in the club movement's work to pass a federal antilynching bill. The women helped mold sentiment against lynching. Their specific goal was to demonstrate that African-American and Caucasian women could forge alliances and work toward common goals, such as the condemnation of violence and lynching. Unfortunately, nothing changed during Margaret Washington's lifetime to end the wholesale slaughtering of innocent African Americans or to improve the political plight and quality of life of most African-American females. Repeatedly, Ida B. Wells, the NAACP, and Tuskegee's Research Department proved that political participation and competition for jobs and wealth sparked controversy and lynching and not the rape of white women as claimed by lynch mobs. Whites used Negrophobia and the ravishing and rape of white women to disguise their anxiety over the few economic gains, academic achievements, and better standards of living of African Americans to impede their progress. Sadistic mobs and vigilante groups invoked racial demagoguery to maintain the status quo. In a petition signed by members in all branches of the National Council of Negro Women, the organization called upon President Woodrow Wilson to stop lynching through federal intervention, but to no avail. They urged him to speak out against the lawlessness perpetrated against African-American women, men, and children, but still, he refused to act, stating that this was a state matter and did not fall within federal jurisdiction.

Despite Wilson's unwillingness to make democracy a reality at home, the NAACP supported the President's war effort. During World War I this group boosted the morale of the soldiers, supported greater recognition of African-American participation, and sold war bonds. They also purchased over $5 million worth of Third Liberty Bonds to show their loyalty and to help in the battle to make the world safe for democracy.

When the Congress passed the Nineteenth Amendment in 1920, Margaret Washington and the other loyal female patriots could not cast a ballot or participate in politics. Whites kept them from the polling places by the extralegal and discriminatory laws that were enforced by southern officials. White feminists and suffragists reaped and enjoyed the benefits of the women's suffrage movement.

In 1920 Washington joined with other black women in forming the International Council of Women of the Darker Races to spread knowledge about people of color throughout the world. They held their first meeting in Chicago in 1924. Due to the multiple activities of most of these women trying to improve housing, health, unemployment, illiteracy, discrimination, and juvenile delinquency through education, philanthropy, and organization, the international organization did not last long. These women supported all causes of the NAACP, the NACW, and the National Urban League, "working in the interest of the advancement of the African American population as a whole and that of women in particular." Margaret Washington gave directions and set attainable goals for African-American women. She emerged as a striver and an achiever within the physical, economic, and cultural confines of the American South and the Tuskegee community from the late 1890s until her death on June 4, 1925.

Unlike some hidden figures in history, Margaret Washington's death did not mark the end of an era, rather it served as a renewal of commitment to racial equality, freedom, and justice. She did not remain in the shadow of her husband, Booker T. Washington. A.L. Jackson of the *Chicago Defender* eulogized her:

> She took her place in the front rank not merely by the accident of being the wife and helpmate of a great man, but because by her own personality and effort she constantly proved her ability to lead others as well as to help them. In her work at Tuskegee Institute she had long been an indispensable

factor and her position in various organizations throughout the country was recognized as strong and helpful.

This outstanding woman should be evaluated by her talent as a teacher, administrator, fundraiser, domestic engineer, and club organizer. She left her mark on the society of her time.

—Margaret L. Dwight

Bibliography

The best source of information on Margaret Murray Washington can be found in the Washington Papers at Tuskegee Institute and through her correspondence in the National Association of Colored Women. Information can be found in the National Association of Colored Women's Clubs, Newspaper Clipping Files, Washington, DC, and in the Peabody Room, Hampton Institute Library, Hampton, Virginia. See also *The Booker T. Washington Papers*, 13 vols., edited by Louis R. Harlan (Urbana: University of Illinois, 1972–1984). She was the most recognized wife of Booker T. Washington.

Contemporary accounts by her and sister clubwomen include Margaret Washington, "The Tuskegee Woman's Club," *The Southern Workman* 49 (August, 1920): 365–367; Elizabeth Ross Haynes, "Margaret Murray Washington," *Opportunity* (July 25, 1925): 207–209; Mary McLeod Bethune, "Margaret Murray Washington," *The Tuskegee Messenger* 1 (August 1, 1925): 3; Jennie B. Moton, "Margaret M. Washington," in Hallie Q. Brown, *Homespun Heroines and Other Women of Distinction* (Xenia, OH: Aldine Press, 1926); and Elizabeth Davis, *Lifting as They Climb* (Washington, DC: NACW, 1933).

Other contemporary accounts emphasize her achievements and leadership. These include *Tuskegee Alumni Bulletin* (August 1925): 7; J.W. Gibson, *Progress of a Race* (Naperville, IL: J.L. Nichols, 1920); Brawley Benjamin, *Negro Builders and Heroes*, (Chapel Hill: University of North Carolina Press, 1937); Emmett Scott, *Builders of a Civilization* (New York: Doubleday, 1917); and Booker T. Washington, *Up from Slavery*, reprint ed. (New York: Airmont, 1967).

For secondary sources that describe Washington's influence and the movements she touched, consult Eleanor Flexner, *Century of Struggle* (New York: Atheneum, 1972); Louis R. Harlan, *Booker T. Washington: The Making of a Black Leader,1856–1901* (London: Oxford University Press, 1972); "The 3 Wives of Booker T. Washington," *Ebony* 37 (September 1972): 29–30+, reprinted in (February 1991): 36+; *Ebony* (June 1972): 76–78; *Jet* (March 16, 1972): 10; Wilma King Hunter, "Three Women at Tuskegee, 1825–1925: The Wives of Booker T. Washington," *Journal of Ethnic Studies* III (September 1976): 76–89; Eleanor Hoytt, "International Council of Women of the Darker Races," *Sage* (Fall 1986): 54–55; Jessie Carney Smith, ed., *Notable Black American Women* (Detroit: Gale, 1992); Cynthia Neverdon-Morton, "The Black Woman's Struggle for Equality in the South," in *The Afro-American Woman*, edited by Sharon Harley and Rosalyn Terborg-Penn (New York: Kennikat, 1978); George Sewell and Margaret L. Dwight, *Mississippi Black History Makers* (Jackson: University Press of Mississippi, 1984); Geneva B. White and Eva

Bishop, eds., *Mississippi Black Women* (Jackson: Mississippi Bicentennial Commission, 1976); Rosalyn M. Terborg-Penn, "Afro-Americans in the Struggle for Women Suffrage Movement," PhD dissertation, Department of History, Howard University, Washington, DC (1978)

WASHINGTON, OLIVIA [DAVIDSON] (1854–1889), co-founder with

Booker T. Washington of Tuskegee Institute, was born free in Virginia on June 11. Her parents, Elias, a former slave of Joseph Davidson, and Eliza (Webb), a free woman, moved to Ironton, Ohio, so that their children could benefit from the public school education in the North. Following the death of her husband, Eliza Davidson brought her children to Albany, Ohio, a community of antislavery sentiments. Her older sisters served as role models; Margaret Davidson was a teacher in the Albany schools, while Mary Davidson, married to Dr. Noah Elliott, operated a dressmaking/millinery business.

After graduation from the Albany Enterprise Academy, Davidson felt a strong obligation to serve her people, so she returned to the South to teach in the rural areas of Mississippi for five years. She then taught in Memphis, when, in 1878, the yellow fever epidemic caused her to volunteer as a nurse. Always described as frail, delicate, and of poor health, Davidson was turned down as too weak for the service. Her constant contact with common diseases such as tuberculosis, influenza, and diptheria in the dilapidated surroundings in which she taught stressed her resistance.

Not one to sit back, she then decided to attend Hampton Institute to prepare herself as a professional teacher. In 1879, she graduated with honors. Her talents gained recognition from Mrs. Augustus Hemenway of Boston, who helped finance her study at Framingham Normal School in Massachusetts, an experience that placed Davidson in contact with some of the best families of Boston. She physically collapsed at her graduation in 1881, but was spiritually buoyed by an invitation to join Booker T. Washington at Tuskegee the month after it opened in July 1881.

As the assistant principal and teacher at Tuskegee, Olivia Davidson started in August 1881 to tackle the problems caused by lack of money. The rain poured in through the roof of the shanty school building in which she taught classes; students could not earn enough money to support themselves through the nine-month program; and no "program" had been developed for the under-prepared students. The purchase of a nearby plantation provided an opportunity to solve the interrelated problems. The students could earn their board; food could be raised, making the school self-sufficient; and agriculture could become the foundation for the vocational training of the Institute. The purchase required money, however. Davidson's delicate health did not stop her from organizing fairs, festivals, and bazaars, getting black and white families to contribute food, home products, and other goods, as well as money, and from inventing fundraising schemes to keep Tuskegee alive. She was so successful that Tuskegee received the deed to the land in five months.

Eventually, expansion required more than pies and cakes. Olivia Davidson turned to the North for financial support. She not only raised money on her own, but provided an entree to influential families to Booker T. Washington. During the first two years, their combined efforts raised more than $11,000, most of which went into buildings. The educational programs expanded as resources and needs appeared. Discovery of clay deposits on the plantation led to the development of a brickmaking program, which provided bricks for the school buildings and the town of Tuskegee. Soon carpentry, mattress making, cabinet making, metalworking, and other programs emerged to serve the growing campus and the community.

Following the death of his wife, Fanny Smith Washington, on May 4, 1884, Booker T. Washington faced domestic responsibility for his 11-month-old daughter and continued obligations of Tuskegee. Soon, the professional relationship between Davidson and Washington became personal. On August 11, 1886, Olivia Davidson, the noble aristocrat, married Booker T. Washington at the home of her sister in Athens, Ohio. Through correspondence and visits to the North, Davidson continued her fundraising by interesting sponsors through visits to the school. Although she often suffered from exhaustion, she continued her work at Tuskegee as principal and teacher. For the community of Tuskegee, she developed services for the elderly of her race. In addition to these roles, she taught Sunday school classes and gave birth to two boys, Baker Taliaferro and E. Davidson Washington, who joined their half-sister, Portia, in the Washington home. With the building program going so well, with over 400 students in attendance, the farm expanded from the original 100 acres to 540 acres; Washington honored his wife's efforts by naming a building Olivia Davidson Hall.

All this success came to an abrupt end in 1889. While Washington was in the North raising money and Davidson was recuperating from the difficult birth of her second son, a fire at the Washington house caused Olivia Davidson Washington to suffer from "severe strain and exposure." Her inability to recuperate from what was later diagnosed as laryngeal tuberculosis led to Washington taking his wife to Massachusetts General Hospital in Boston in April 1889. Her death on May 9, 1889, was a turning point in the life of the rising leader. He took her body back to Tuskegee, where she was buried in the Tuskegee Institute Cemetery. Her tombstone reads, "She lived to the truth," a memorial to her dedication to the school and to life. Following her death, Washington shaved off his drooping mustache and, without the joy that characterized his life with Olivia Davidson, continued to pursue their common goals for Tuskegee and the race.

—Dorothy C. Salem

Bibliography

The correspondence of Olivia Davidson and Booker T. Washington can be found in the Booker T. Washington Papers, Library of Congress, and are published in *The Booker T. Washington Papers*, Vol. I and II, edited by Louis R. Harlan and John Blassingame (Urbana: University of Illinois Press, 1972). Information about Olivia Davidson is included in research done by Ann E. Garrett Robinson cited in "The 3 Wives of Booker T. Washington," *Ebony* (February 1991): 36–42; and two articles by Carolyn A. Dorsey, "Despite Poor Health: Olivia Davidson Washington's Story," *Sage* II:2 (Fall 1985): 69–72; and "The Pre-Hampton Years of Olivia A. Davidson," *Hampton Review* 14:1 (Fall 1988): 44–52. Her influence on Washington is described in Samuel R. Spencer, Jr., *Booker T. Washington and the Negro's Place in American Life* (Boston: Little, Brown, 1955); Louis T. Harlan, *Booker T. Washington: The Making of a Black Leader* (New York: Oxford University Press, 1980); and by Washington himself in *Up from Slavery* in Louis R. Harlan, ed., *Booker T. Washington Papers* I, pp. 281, 290, and 525.

WATERS, ETHEL (1896–1977), actress, dancer, and singer (a.k.a. Ethel Perry, Mamie Jones, Martha Pryor, and in her early singing career, "Sweet Mama Stringbean"), was born in October in Chester, Pennsylvania. The date of her birth has often been given as 1900, but that was a falsehood she perpetuated until her second autobiography, *To Me It's Wonderful*, where she explained the use of the latter date as an attempt to assist a friend trying to get group life insurance. Waters was married twice, first to Merritt Purnsley and then to Edward Mallory.

Ethel Waters was the consummate entertainer, though best known as a blues/jazz singer and dancer and dramatic actress. She was also a vaudevillian, a comedienne, and an actress in musical theater on Broadway. As a singer she produced albums for the famed Jazz Masters, Black Swan label, the first black-owned record label. She recorded with, among others, the Duke Ellington Orchestra, the Dorsey Brothers, Fletcher Henderson, and was part of Irving Berlin's revue "As Thousands Cheer." She was also the first woman to perform W.C. Handy's "St. Louis Blues" and is especially known for her renditions of such standards as "Dinah," "Am I Blue?," and "Stormy Weather." Her signature song, however, was "His Eyes Are on the Sparrow," the hymn that her grandmother, who raised her, loved so much. It is also the title of her first autobiography.

Waters was the "first" African-American woman in many areas: the first to star as a single act at the Palace Theater in New York City; the first to star in a commercial network radio program; the first to star on Broadway in a dramatic play, Dorothy and DuBose Heyward's *Mamba's Daughter*; and the first to appear in a dialogue color motion picture, *On with the Show*.

Ethel Waters received a lot of attention for her role as Berenice Sadie Brown in the play and movie *The Member of the Wedding*. She was nominated in 1953 for an Oscar for Best Supporting Actress in the movie and was also nominated, in 1949, for her supporting role in the film *Pinky*. Waters also performed in stage and movie productions of *Cabin in the Sky*. In 1953, she starred in the "Beulah" television series.

A turning point in Ethel Water's life occurred when she joined evangelist Billy Graham as a member of the choir for his 1957 Youth for Christ Crusade. She and the Graham family remained close friends until her death, and she was a featured member of his Christian crusades up to a year before she died. In 1971 she performed at a Sunday worship service at the White House for President and Mrs. Richard M. Nixon, with whom she was also friendly.

Ethel Waters had been a member of the executive council of Actors' Equity Association and vice president of the Negro Actors Guild of America. Her awards included the Negro Actors Guild of America plaque for dramatic achievement (1949), the Boston Chamber of Commerce Twenty Most Distinguished Women of Achievement in 1951, the Tamiment Institute Award for Outstanding Literary Work for *His Eye Is on the Sparrow* (1951), and the 1951 St. Genesius Medal of the American Theater and Academy. Also, on several occasions, days were named in her honor.

Ethel Waters died in Chatsworth, California, on September 1, 1977.

—Nancy Elizabeth Fitch

Bibliography

Ethel Waters's second autobiography, *To Me It's Wonderful* (New York: Harper & Row, 1972) is more reliable, in terms of her early life, than her first, *His Eyes Are on the Sparrow: An Autobiography by Ethel Waters with Charles Samuels* (Garden City, NY: Doubleday, 1951). In the latter, for example, she clarifies the discrepancy about her age. In that book also, she talks about rediscovering God and the impact that incident had on her life. In fact, *To Me It's Wonderful* is dedicated to her good friend the Reverend Billy Graham, with whom she performed at Christian Crusades. In *His Eyes Are on the Sparrow*, we see her childhood and early harrowing life and the motivation she exhibited to excel in her work.

Sheldon Harris's essay "Ethel Waters" in *Blues Who's Who: A Biographical Dictionary of Blues Singers* (New Rochelle NY: Arlington House, 1979), pp. 538–544, is most informative on all aspects of her career—the music as well as the acting and the acclaim she earned in both.

Editor's note: Other works that feature information about her career are Edward Mapp, *A Directory of Blacks in the Performing Arts* (Metuchen, NJ: Scarecrow, 1978); Ora Williams, *American Black Women in Arts and Social Science* (Metuchen, NJ: Scarecrow, 1978); Gwendolyn Cherry, *Portraits in Color* (New York: Pageant, 1962); and Marianna Davis, *Contributions of Black Women to America* (Columbia, SC: Kenday, 1982).

Her obituary, "Ethel Waters Is Dead at 80," written by C. Gerald Fraser, in the *New York Times* (September 2, 1977): A1+, should be consulted as well.

WEBB, ALFREDA [JOHNSON] (b. 1923), one of the first two black women veterinary graduates and a renowned anatomist, graduated from Tuskegee Institute Veterinary School in 1949. In that same year Jane Hinton received a DVM from the University of Pennsylvania. Johnson was the only woman in a graduating class of five seniors.

Born in Mobile, Alabama, on February 21, Johnson earned a BS from Tuskegee Institute in 1943. In that year the Tuskegee Institute Veterinary School was established as the only veterinary school created especially to train black veterinarians. The college's president, Frederick D. Patterson, had earned a veterinary degree at Iowa State College. The medical facilities for animals, including a staff veterinarian, had existed since the college's early years when George Washington Carver instructed anatomy classes. The first veterinary class began studies in 1945.

Entrance requirements for the professional veterinary school included one year of preprofessional work with students enrolling in a four-year curriculum. The courses were based on a system of theory and lectures supplemented with access to practical, hands-on experiences in the profession; free clinics were offered weekly for nearby residents and farmers to bring in animals to be examined and treated.

After graduation Johnson received an MS from Michigan State University in 1951 and returned to Tuskegee Institute as a teacher and researcher in the veterinary school. She was first an instructor and then became an associate professor of anatomy at Tuskegee Institute from 1950 to 1959. She then served as professor of biology at North Carolina A & T State University, Greensboro, North Carolina, until 1978, when she became a professor of laboratory animal science.

Her research focuses on histology, embryology, and cytology. She is a member of the American Association of Veterinary Anatomists, the American Veterinary Medical Association, and Sigma Xi. Webb is married, has three children, and resides in Greensboro.

—Elizabeth D. Schafer

Bibliography

A biographical profile of Alfreda Webb is in *American Men and Women of Science* (New York: R.R. Bowker, 1990). "Most Veterinarian Schools Do Not Maintain Color Line," *Ebony* 5 (August 1949): 42, notes her pioneering status as a black female veterinarian. A picture of Webb examining a feline patient with other senior veterinary students accompanies the article "Tuskegee's Vet School Holds Open House in November," *Negro Farmer* (December 1948). The *American Veterinary Medical Association Directory* (Schaumburg, IL: AVMA, published annually), lists the geographic location as well as professional activity of Webb.

The Tuskegee Veterinarian was published while Webb taught at Tuskegee. L. Albert Scipio II, *Pre-War Days at Tuskegee: Historical Essay on Tuskegee Institute (1881–1943)*

(Silver Springs, MD: Roman Publications, 1987) contains photographs of early veterinary facilities and student life at Tuskegee; and William H. Waddell IV, *People Are the Funniest Animals* (Philadelphia: Dorrance & Co., 1978) discusses his role in developing the veterinary school at Tuskegee Institute. Waddell's *The Black Man in Veterinary Medicine* (Schaumburg, IL: AVMA, 1982) provides information about pioneer black veterinarians and includes a brief statement about women entering the veterinary profession as does Bert W. Bierer, *American Veterinary History* (Fort Dodge: IA: National Museum of Veterinary Medicine, 1940).

J. Frederick Smithcors, *The Veterinarian in America, 1625–1975* (Santa Barbara, CA: American Veterinary Publications, 1975) is a national view; and Elizabeth D. Schafer, "Reveille for Professionalism: Alabama Veterinary Medical Association, 1907–1952," MA thesis, Auburn University (1988), provides a historical context for the practice of veterinary medicine in Alabama, especially at the beginning of Webb's career. Also see Charles C. Morrill, *Veterinary Medicine in Michigan: An Illustrated History* (East Lansing: Michigan State University College of Veterinary Medicine, 1979); and William Moore, L.J. Faulhaber, and J.H. Brown, *A Veterinary History of North Carolina* (New Bern: Owen G. Dunn Co., 1946) for information pertaining to veterinary medicine in those states.

WELLS-BARNETT, IDA B. (1862–1931), antilynching leader, suffragist, community activist, journalist, and speaker, was born on July 16 in Holly Springs, Mississippi, to Lizzie Warrenton, a slave cook, and Jim Wells, a slave carpenter. As the eldest of eight children, Wells at age sixteen took over the family responsibilities of raising her siblings after the death of her parents and nine-month-old sibling in a small pox epidemic (1878). With the help of the black community, Wells attended Rust College, and found employment as a teacher first in Holly Springs and then in Memphis, Tennessee.

In May 1884 Wells sued and won a case against the Chesapeake and Ohio Railroad Company for forcefully removing her from a segregated ladies' coach. Victory was bittersweet, however, because the state supreme court reversed the ruling of the lower court. The incident served as a catalyst to a more militant Wells and pushed her to investigate and report other incidences of racism. As part owner and editor of the *Memphis Free Speech and Headlight*, she spent much of her time writing about the poor conditions for black children in local schools, leading to her dismissal in 1891 by the Memphis School Board. After the 1892 lynching of three of her friends, she was diligent in her antilynching and anti-accomodation crusade. In May 1892, following speaking engagements in Philadelphia and New York, her printing press at the *Free Speech* was destroyed and threats were made on her life. Exiled from her home, she continued her exposés on lynchings in the *New York Age*. In 1892 her thorough investigative research culminated in *Southern Horrors: Lynch Law in All Its Phases*. Speaking tours in England and Scotland on lynching and the plight of African Americans guaranteed her message an international platform.

In 1893 Wells carried her fight for equality to the Chicago World's Fair. She solicited funds and published 20,000 copies of a protest pamphlet, *The Reason Why the Colored American Is Not in the Columbian Exposition.* She remained in Chicago and helped spawn the growth of numerous black female and reform organizations: the Ida B. Wells Club, the Negro Fellowship League, the National Association of Colored Women, and the Alpha Suffrage Club. Wells marched in the 1913 suffrage parade in Washington, DC, with the all-white Illinois contingent and was one of two African-American women to sign the call for the formation of the National Association for the Advancement of Colored People. Her anti–Booker T. Washington stance and alliance with T. Thomas Fortune, W.E.B. Du Bois, and Marcus Garvey often placed her at odds with her peers.

She married Ferdinand Barnett, owner of the *Chicago Conservator,* in 1895. Ferdinand Barnett brought two children from a previous marriage into this union, which produced four others: Charles Aked, Herman Kahlssat, Ida B. Wells, Jr., and Alfreda M. Domestic life did not keep Wells from speaking and writing about racial injustices. She reported on several riots, including the one in East St. Louis in July 1917. Wells-Barnett often linked the oppression and exploitation of African Americans to white economic opportunity. Wells-Barnett continued her "crusade for justice" until her death of uremia in Chicago in 1931.

—Wanda A. Hendricks

Bibliography

The Ida B. Wells Papers are in the J. Regenstein Library, University of Chicago. Some information on Wells-Barnett can be found in the NAACP Collection, Manuscript Division, Library of Congress; Mary Church Terrell Papers in the Library of Congress; and in the Moorland-Spingarn Collection, Howard University. Her own autobiography was published by her daughter Alfreda Duster, ed., *Crusade for Justice: The Autobiography of Ida B. Wells* (Chicago: University of Chicago Press, 1970).

Secondary Sources

Davis, Elizabeth Lindsay. *Lifting as They Climb.* Washington, DC: National Association of Colored Women, 1933.

———. *The Story of the Illinois Federation of Colored Women's Clubs.* Chicago: 1992.

Holt, Thomas. "The Lonely Warrior: Ida B. Wells-Barnett and the Struggle for Black Leadership." In *Black Leaders of the Twentieth Century,* edited by John Hope Franklin and August Meier. Urbana: University of Illinois, 1982, pp. 39–61.

Thompson, Mildred. "Ida B. Wells-Barnett: An Exploratory Study of An American Woman, 1893–1930." PhD dissertation, George Washington University, 1979.

WEST, DOROTHY (b. 1907), noted writer of short stories, critic, and editor, was born in Boston on June 2 to Isaac Christopher and Rachel (Benson) West. She had experienced a great deal of attention from an extended kinship network of aunts, uncles, and cousins, since her half-white mother was one of 22

children. A younger sister died when Dorothy West was ten years old, which left her the only child. Her father, though born a slave and freed at age seven, became a successful businessman in Boston. He owned a restaurant and wholesale produce business, which led to his being called the "Black Banana King of Boston." She remembered visits to her home by William Monroe Trotter, a family friend.

She attended school in the Mission Hill district of Boston, where at age six she received dancing lessons with forty of Boston's finest children. After elementary school, she went to the Girls' Latin School, where she lost her accent and became familiar with students having New England names, servants, and chauffeurs. After her graduation in 1923, she took courses at Boston University and the Columbia School of Journalism.

Dorothy West wrote her first story at age seven. Her father was so proud of the story that he put it in his pocket to show others. Soon he lost the story, which Dorothy West attributed to male lack of attention. She remembers that her father "allowed" her to write, since he made a good living in the produce business. By age ten she had won prizes in the *Boston Post*. Her cousin, Helen Johnson, and Dorothy West entered their writings in a contest for *Opportunity* magazine. "The Typewriter," the short story written by 17-year-old Dorothy West, tied for second prize with the story by 25-year-old Zora Neale Hurston, who became a close friend. West's autobiographical sketch appeared in the June 1926 issue of *Opportunity*.

When she moved to New York in the 1920s, she became part of the Harlem Renaissance. Her friends included Wallace Thurman, Langston Hughes, Claude McKay, Countee Cullen, and others. Fannie Hurst helped her gain the support of literary agent George Bye, who helped her publish in several New York magazines.

During the 1930s she traveled to Russia to make a movie about the life of African Americans with the help of Henry Moon, her potential suitor. During those years, she also edited two black quarterlies: *Challenge* and *New Challenge*. She worked as an actress and helped to organize social workers making $23 dollars a week, an experience that developed a sociological perspective in her work. Her contact with author Richard Wright drew her into the ideas of communism for a brief time. Working 18 months with the Federal Writers Project raised her awareness of economic problems.

Best known for her novel *The Living Is Easy*, published in 1948, Dorothy West's literary career spans three decades of the black novel. She is recognized for her use of verbal irony and for her work's reflection of typical Renaissance themes.

For the past two decades, West has lived on Martha's Vineyard, Massachusetts, working summers as a cashier in the Harborside Restaurant and writing a weekly column and occasional interviews with prominent visitors to Martha's Vineyard for the *Vineyard Gazette*. In 1984–1985, she toured several cities promoting

Women of Courage: An Exhibition of Photographs by Judith Sedwick, based on the Black Women Oral History Project at Radcliffe College.

—Kelle S. Taha

Bibliography

No major biography has been published on Dorothy West. Her oral history interview is part of the Black Women Oral History Project, Schlesinger Library, Radcliffe College. She is featured in such works about the Harlem Renaissance as *The Harlem Renaissance Remembered*, edited by Arna Bontemps (New York: Dodd, Mead, 1972); Darwin Turner, *Afro-American Writers* (New York: Appleton-Century-Crofts, 1970); Ronda Glikin, *Black American Women in Literature* (Jefferson, NC: McFarland, 1989); and Ann Shockley, *Living Black American Authors* (New York: Bowker, 1973). For West's own writings see issues of *Opportunity*, the *Boston Post*, the *Saturday Evening Quill*, and "Elephant's Dance," in *Black World* XX:1 (November 1970): 77–80. Her novel is analyzed in Robert Bone's *The Negro Novel in America* (New Haven: Yale University Press, 1958).

WHEATLEY, PHILLIS (c. 1754–1784), colonial poet, was born in Senegambia, West Africa. Carried into slavery after kidnapping in 1761, she arrived in Boston on the ship *Phillis*, from which she took her name. Despite the traumatic impact of slavery and exile from her homeland, Wheatley adjusted well to her new surroundings. She was fortunate to be purchased by John and Susannah Wheatley, a sympathetic Quaker couple, who recognized her unusual aptitude for scholarship and her poetic gifts. Phillis Wheatley received competent tutoring and mastered both English and Latin as well as becoming a devout Christian. She was given light housework, ate with the family, and had her own room. Her favorite author was Alexander Pope, whose neoclassical style influenced her writings. During the 1760s and 1770s, she gained attention for her poetry, which was used to demonstrate the benefit of education for her race. When visitors came to the Wheatley home, they were impressed with her poetry and with her poised demeanor.

With the support of the Wheatley family, Phillis Wheatley visited England in 1773, after receiving advice from a physician that rest and sea air would improve the health of the young woman. She stayed in England as the guest of the Countess of Huntington, to whom she dedicated her first book of poems, *Poems on Various Subjects, Religious and Moral*, published later that year in London to critical acclaim. Although she was to be presented at court, Phillis had to return to America when news of Mrs. Wheatley's illness reached her. Returning in September 1773, Phillis cared for her mistress until her death in 1774. With the daughter Mary Wheatley married (1771), the son John living abroad, and the death of Mr. Wheatley, the tight-knit family support was lost.

Freed in 1778, Wheatley married John Peters, a persuasive free businessman, in April of that year. John Peters failed to provide a stable home for Wheatley, so she had to work in a boardinghouse to support herself and her one child. Wheatley and her child died from hunger and exposure on December 5, 1784. They were buried in unmarked graves before admirers read of her death and provided posthumous recognition.

Although she never enjoyed financial or personal security, Wheatley was fortunate in being more kindly treated than most colonial slaves. She met many of the leading figures of her day, including George Washington, and she provided an excellent model of positive black potential that helped make it difficult to justify slavery by claims of black inferiority.

—Susan Stussy

Bibliography

For information on Phillis Wheatley, see Margretta Odell (distant relative of the Wheatleys), *Memoir and Poems of Phillis Wheatley* (1843). Other sources include the following:

Redding, Saunders. "Phillis Wheatley," in *Notable American Women*, edited by Edward T. James, et al. Cambridge: Belknap, 1971.

Richmond, Merle. *Phillis Wheatley, Poet.* New York: Chelsea House, 1988. Richmond has written an excellent introduction for young readers.

Robinson, William H. *Critical Essays on Phillis Wheatley.* Boston, MA: G.K. Hall, 1982. Robinson provides an exhaustive survey of critical reaction to Wheatley from her own day to the present.

———. *Phillis Wheatley: A Bio-Bibliography.* Boston: G.K. Hall, 1981. This scholarly annotated reference work is required reading for all students of Wheatley's life and writings.

———. *Phillis Wheatley and Her Writings.* New York: Garland, 1984. This collection of writings by and about Wheatley also includes biographical information.

———. *Phillis Wheatley in the Black American Beginnings.* Detroit: Broadside Press, 1975. Robinson states, "Phillis Wheatley not only belongs squarely in the Black American literary tradition; she, almost singlehandedly created that tradition" (p. 73).

Wheatley, Phillis. *The Collected Works of Phillis Wheatley*, edited with an Introduction by John C. Shields. New York: Oxford University Press, 1988. This volume reprints Wheatley's *Poems on Various Subjects, Religious and Moral* of 1773 plus additional poems.

WILLIAMS, FANNIE [BARRIER] (1855–1944), clubwoman, lecturer, and community activist, was born February 12 to Mr. and Mrs. A.J. Barrier, one of the most esteemed families of Brockport, New York. Because of the social prominence and economic stability of her family, she was able to follow a propitious educational course, attending the public schools and Collegiate Institute of

Brockport, the New England Conservatory of Music, and the School of Fine Arts in Washington, DC.

Fannie Barrier taught in the public schools of Washington, DC, for about ten years until her marriage to S. Laing Williams, graduate of the University of Michigan and the Columbian Law School (now George Washington Law School) in Washington, DC. The couple moved to Chicago, where S. Laing Williams started a law practice; they became especially active in the political, social, and cultural affairs of Chicago's black elite. They had no children.

Her involvement in the sociopolitical life of Chicago was accomplished primarily through her women's club work, lecturing, and articles in the black press. The subjects of her lectures and articles included the nature of religious duty, suffrage rights, the relationship between the black elite and the black masses, the race problem, and much more. It seems that philosophically Fannie Barrier Williams had "strong integrationist sentiments" as evidenced by her successful protest to have African Americans included in the 1893 World's Columbian Exposition and her membership in the white Chicago Woman's Club. She was the only black speaker at the eulogy ceremonies of Susan B. Anthony at the 1907 convention of the National American Woman Suffrage Association. Some of Williams's other activities included president of the Illinois Federation of Colored Women's Clubs and a correspondent for and member of the editorial board of the *Woman's Era* (the first newspaper published by black women in this country). She succeeded in persuading many employers to hire qualified black women as clerical and stenographic employees.

Perhaps as a result of her concern for employment opportunities or in pursuit of political appointments for her husband, Williams supported the educational practices of Booker T. Washington. Elected corresponding secretary of the Afro-American Council in 1902, she courted Booker T. Washington's favor in return for the appointment in 1908 of S. Laing Williams as the federal assistant district attorney in Chicago, a position soon lost under the administration of President Woodrow Wilson. She and her husband were also active members of the All Souls Unitarian Church and the Prudence Crandall Study Club.

Fannie Barrier Williams was a prolific writer, prominent lecturer, and ardent social reformer. She became less active following the death of her husband in 1921. She served as the first of her race and gender on the Library Board of the city of Chicago from 1924 to 1926. She lived with a sister until her death in 1944 from arteriosclerosis. She is buried in the family plot in Brockport High Street Cemetery.

—Marcia Y. Riggs

Bibliography

There are several secondary references that offer biographical and bibliographic profiles of Fannie Barrier Williams: Sylvia G.L. Dannett, *Profiles of Negro Womanhood* 1 (New York: M.W. Lads, 1964); Kali Herman, *Women in Particular: An Index to*

American Women (Phoenix, AZ: Oryx Press, 1984); Edward T. James, *Notable American Women, 1607–1950: A Biographical Dictionary* (Cambridge: Harvard University Press, Belknap Press, 1973). [Supplementary volume edited by Barbara Sickerman and Carol Hurd Green]; Johnson, Allen, ed., *Dictionary of American Biography, 1927–1957*, (Supp. v. 3) (New York: Scribner); Charlotte Elizabeth Martin, *The Story of Brockport for One Hundred Years* (Brockport, NY: n.p., 1929); Obituary, *New York Times* (March 8, 1944), 19:1; Mrs. N.F. Mossell, *The Work of the Afro-American Woman* (New York: Oxford University Press, 1988); and Marilyn Richardson, "Three Women in the Black Church: An Introduction," *Black Women and Religion: A Bibliography* (Boston: G.K. Hall, 1980).

Also, these secondary sources are particularly helpful because they provide sociohistorical background and interpretation of the life and thought of Williams: Barbara Hilkert Andolsen, *Daughters of Jefferson, Daughters of Bootblacks* (Macon, GA: Mercer University Press, 1986); Elizabeth Lindsay Davis, ed., *Lifting as They Climb* (Washington, DC: NACW, 1933); Allan H. Spear, *Black Chicago: The Making of a Negro Ghetto, 1890–1920* (Chicago: University of Chicago, 1967); Wilson J. Moses, *The Golden Age of Black Nationalism, 1850–1925* (New York: Oxford University Press, 1978); and Cynthia Neverdon-Morton, *Afro-American Women of the South and the Advancement of the Race, 1895–1925* (Knoxville: University of Tennessee Press, 1989).

A couple of Fannie Barrier Williams's writings are found in James Bert Lowenberg and Ruth Bogin, eds., *Black Women in Nineteenth-Century American Life: Their Words, Their Thoughts, Their Feelings* (University Park: Pennsylvania State University, 1976). A majority of her writings are found in books and black newspapers of the late nineteenth and early twentieth centuries (some of which have now been reprinted in the *New York Times* Arno Press Series). Some representative works by Williams are as follows: Williams Fannie Barrier, address, "The Intellectual Progress of the Colored Women of the United States since the Emancipation Proclamation," in *World's Congress of Representative Women*, edited by May Wright Sewall (Chicago: n.p., 1893); "The Club Movement among Colored Women of America," in *A New Negro for a New Century* (reprint of 1900 edition); (New York: Arno Press, 1969); "The Club Movement among the Colored Women," *The Voice of the Negro* 1 (1904): 101; "Club Movement among Negro Women," in *Progress of a Race*, edited by J. Nichols and W. Crogman (Atlanta: J.L. Nichols, 1903); Fannie B. Williams, "The Colored Girl," *The Voice of the Negro* (June 1905): 400–403; "The Colored Woman and Her Part in Race Regeneration," in *A New Negro for a New Century* (Chicago, 1900); "The Negro and Public Opinion," *The Voice of the Negro* (January 1904): 31–32; and *The Present Status and Intellectual Progress of Colored Women* (Chicago, 1893).

WILLIAMS, MARY LOU [MARY ELFRIEDA SCUGG] (1910–1981),

also known before her marriage as Mary Lou Burleigh, was born in Atlanta, Georgia, on May 8 and was raised in Pittsburgh, Pennsylvania. Williams was a premiere jazz pianist and composer, and one of the very few female jazz instrumentalists. She was married twice, first to saxophonist John Williams in the late 1920s and then to Harold Baker, a trumpet player who performed with her in the Andy Kirk band. Williams, who had performed in the band with her first husband, was with Kirk for 12 years in a variety of roles, the first as band arranger and subsequently as pianist. Prior to joining her husband with the Kirk Band, she had taken over his band as director.

As a teenager, Williams's talent was recognized by her elders, including Fats Waller and Art Tatum. She was an important instrumentalist and composer/arranger during the swing era and graced the bebop movement, which was a seminal period in jazz history commencing in the 1940s. Williams performed with, and wrote scores for, such other jazz greats as Duke Ellington, Benny Goodman, Dizzie Gillespie, Cab Calloway, Tommy and Jimmy Dorsey, and Louis Armstrong. Her first major large piece, entitled "The Zodiac Suite," was performed with the New York Philharmonic Orchestra. It was one of the first times jazz was recognized as serious music by a symphony orchestra. Mary Lou Williams, throughout her career, however, never forgot what her music owed to the blues.

During the 1950s Mary Lou Williams traveled and performed in Europe, but in 1954 she halted her career after experiencing a spiritual epiphany that changed her life and the direction of her work. Before she returned to jazz and performing, she converted to Roman Catholicism and founded, in 1957, the Bel Canto Foundation to assist jazz artists in rehabilitation from drug and alcohol abuse. In part to support that charitable work, she founded her own record company, Mary Records, as well as a thrift shop.

Shortly thereafter, Williams had written only the first of her sacred works plus three masses when, in 1967, she was commissioned by the Vatican to write a mass. It was originally called "Music for Peace" but later became known as "Mary Lou's Mass." Alvin Ailey choreographed a work to accompany the mass, which was sung, in 1975, at St. Patrick's Cathedral in New York City. Over 3,000 congregants heard the mass, the first time a jazz performance had been held in the cathedral. For the occasion, Williams called it a "Mass for the Young or the Young Thinking," as four Catholic school choirs performed. She said at the time that jazz was "spiritual and healing to the soul. It's the only true art in the world." "Mary Lou's Mass" was later sung in Rome and in churches throughout the United States.

In 1971 Williams, along with 30 other African-American musicians, received the Ellington Medal from Yale University. She was the only woman instrumentalist to be so honored. Though she died in Durham, North Carolina, on May 28, 1981, she was entered into *Down Beat* magazine's Hall of Fame in 1990, again the first woman instrumentalist. Williams received several honorary degrees from American colleges and universities. In her career she taught in public and parochial schools and at several universities, including the University of Massachusetts in Amherst from 1975 to 1977 and finally, until her death, Duke University.

—Nancy Elizabeth Fitch

Bibliography

Whitney Balliett, in "Profiles: Out Here Again, Mary Lou Williams," *New Yorker* 40 (May 2, 1964): 52+, writes a stunning essay on Williams and her position as a woman instrumentalist and composer within the jazz movement. It is in-depth and celebratory. In February 1975, Williams performed her mass at St. Patrick's Cathedral in New York City. The *New York Times* had two articles that day, both written by John S. Wilson: "Mary Lou Takes Her Jazz Mass to Church" (February 19, 1975): D20, and "Mary Lou Williams, at Piano, Leads Her Own Jazz Mass at St. Patrick's" (February 19, 1975): 37. *Down Beat* magazine, in honoring Mary Lou Williams, discussed her unique position in the music world as a black woman and inducted her posthumously into *Down Beat*'s Hall of Fame. At her death, John Wilson wrote the obituary for the *New York Times* (May 30, 1981): 21.

WILSON, HALENA (1897–1975), longtime president of the Ladies' Auxiliary to the Brotherhood of Sleeping Car Porters (BSCP), displayed organizational abilities that led to the Auxiliary's success and to the Brotherhood's survival. Black labor unions, more so than white labor unions, found female auxiliaries indispensable. Since the porters had to be organized in secret to avoid reprisals by the Pullman Company, women played roles as recruiters, as well as morale boosters and fundraisers. As one of these leaders, Halena Wilson rendered service to the emerging unionization of black workers.

Wilson seemed destined to help her people. From the scanty information about her early life, researchers have determined that she was born on February 25 and received her early education in the public schools in Denver, Colorado. She admitted to having little formal schooling, but felt that life experiences had provided her with an excellent education. She described herself as being troubled most of the time as a young girl, wanting to do good and experiencing relief only upon praying for guidance. When grown, she again felt disturbed and burdened, suffering from "the feeling of being useless, of living an utterly aimless and unproductive life." The feeling persisted and grew to such proportions that she was no longer content in her surroundings. She moved to Chicago, where she married porter Benjamin Wilson. At first the new environment eased her burdens. Soon she realized "that she had run away from her surroundings, but that she had not been able to run away from herself or from an aimless existence." Remembering her childhood, she turned to prayer and joined the women supporters of the Brotherhood of Sleeping Car Porters Union, an organization that sought to empower her exploited people. Through the women's group, Wilson gained the abilities and wisdom to better serve her fellowmen.

Wilson's leadership career with the Ladies' Auxiliary began in 1931 with her election as president of the Chicago Division Women's Economic Council following a series of unsuccessful presidents. From the time of her election until the enactment of the amended Railway Labor Act in 1934, the Chicago Council, like the union itself, fought a grim, but determined, battle to remain alive. The group sponsored innumerable activities to raise funds and hold the interest of the few active members. Under Wilson's leadership, the Council became involved in affairs outside the purview of the union, fighting to improve the situation of the race as a whole.

Following official recognition from the Pullman Company in 1937, A. Philip Randolph, the head of the Brotherhood of Sleeping Car Porters Union, requested a national meeting of the women's groups. The Colored Women's Economic Councils met in Chicago in September 1938 and combined into a national organization, the Ladies' Auxiliary to the Brotherhood of Sleeping Car Porters. Randolph personally chose Wilson for leadership of the Auxiliary, which followed the same organizational divisions as the Brotherhood. Its purpose was to support the Brotherhood, to protect and improve the jobs of the porters, and to promote the general well-being of their homes as well as the progress of all African-American working women.

The Ladies' Auxiliary fell within the tradition of African-American women's clubs, which sought to improve the image of black womanhood, to uplift the race, to fight segregation and mob violence, and to cope with poverty. Unlike contemporary married white female reformers, the porters' wives worked outside the home and enjoyed middle-class status in the black community. Wilson viewed herself as an educator because very little was known in the black community about trade unions or the Ladies' Auxiliary. She took on the responsibility to translate terms like "economic security," "cooperation," and "collective bargaining" into language that had meaning for women, stressing the effects of such phrases upon the lives of the workers and their families. She sought to begin education about economic organizations early. With the support of A. Philip Randolph, Wilson encouraged young people to join the Junior Auxiliary to mold their minds and train them for community service. At the same time, Wilson tried to broaden the women's interests from such trade union issues as higher wages and better working conditions to larger civil rights issues.

For her efforts, Wilson became a member of the executive board of the Chicago Women's Trade Union League, the only African-American woman to be so honored. Most of Wilson's time, however, was devoted to the Ladies' Auxiliary. "The Ladies' Auxiliary is my life," she said, "and I don't want any other and I have no desire to serve in any other capacity in any way, shape or form." Although so much of her life was spent in work outside of her home, Wilson preferred to consider herself a housewife despite her career as a paid professional receiving a salary from the Auxiliary, which the Brotherhood augmented.

Restricted by a tight budget, Wilson still managed to travel extensively throughout the United States and Canada instructing existing auxiliaries and organizing new ones. She sent a continual stream of written messages to the locals. Although not actively engaged in church work, she served for several years as a trustee of her church.

Ironically, as the modern civil rights movement gained momentum, both the BSCP and the Ladies' Auxiliary declined as a result of the faltering railroad industry and the aging membership and leadership of the union and its auxiliary. As the active members aged, the number of new recruits proved insufficient to replace the veterans as they retired or died. Wilson's later years followed the pattern of the organization she served. She became ill from an apparent stroke in November 1951. While she was recovering her husband underwent several operations and died in January 1955. She turned to religion for solace and continued in her role as president of the International Auxiliary until 1965. Wilson suffered from heart disease and was confined to a wheelchair during her last years. She died April 16, 1975. Despite her front page obituary picture in the *Chicago Defender*, the woman described by one porter as "one of the greatest women of our race whom I can never forget" is virtually unknown today.

The Ladies' Auxiliary limped along for a few years after her death, but her historical significance lived on in the younger generation. Under Wilson's leadership the Ladies' Auxiliary fulfilled an important function for its members. On one level the Auxiliary women remained subservient to the male union officers; on another they insisted on running their own organization. As they fought for the good of the BSCP they also struggled to enhance their own station in their homes, in the union, and in their communities, seeking to improve the social and economic status of the race. In the process they found their own internal satisfaction. Perhaps the most important contribution of Wilson and the Auxiliary, however, lay in conveying the idea of mass action to the younger generation. Equal to Randolph and the porters, the women, through their influence, "laid the foundation for the civil rights movement in this country" and "inspired black people by proving that they could organize and get results."

—Paula F. Pfeffer

Bibliography

Halena Wilson's papers are filed with the Chicago Division of the BSCP Papers at the Chicago Historical Society. These sources provide little about her early life or her maiden name. A check of birth records in Denver likewise revealed nothing. Much of this information has come from Wilson's remembrances or from her contemporaries. There has not been much written about either Wilson or the Ladies' Auxiliary to the BSCP until now, but Paula Pfeffer's article "The Women Behind the Union: Halena Wilson, Rosina Tucker, and the Ladies' Auxiliary to the Brotherhood of Sleeping Car Porters" has been submitted for inclusion in *Southern Women: Histories and Identities*, forthcoming from University of Missouri Press. A second woman, Melinda Chateauvert, has studied Wilson through her dissertation research on the Ladies' Auxiliary at the University of Pennsylvania. Some information about the Auxiliary can be found in Brailsford Reese Brazeal, *The Brotherhood of Sleeping Car Porters: Its Origin and Development* (New York: Harper & Bros., 1946).

WINFREY, OPRAH (b. 1954), actress, television host, producer, and busi-
ness woman, Oprah Winfrey has ascended the ladder in the difficult entertainment
field to become the most publicized black woman on television and the first woman
to own and host her own television show. Her beginnings did not predict her
success. She was born Oprah Gail Winfrey in Koscuisko, Mississippi, on January 29.
Named after the biblical figure Orpah, her name was misspelled on the birth
certificate. Her father, Vernon Winfrey, was home on furlough from Fort Rucker
in Alabama when Oprah was conceived. He did not know he had become a father
until Oprah's mother, Vernita Lee, sent him a card with the birth announcement.
They never married. Shortly after Oprah's birth, Vernita Lee moved to Milwaukee
in search of better-paying work as a domestic. She left Oprah with Vernon
Winfrey's mother, a disciplined, churchgoing woman.

Within this secure, supportive environment in rural Mississippi, Oprah
Winfrey gained the love and structure to shape her future. Winfrey looked back
on this childhood for the television special "Successful Lives" and recounted that
her grandmother did not stifle her abilities. Her isolation on her grandmother's
two-acre farm stimulated her creativity. She always felt she had a higher purpose
in life and could accomplish anything she wanted to attain. She remembered
always being told she was "too fast and too adult," from the groups of
churchwomen surrounding her grandmother. She could read before entering
school and displayed early rhetorical abilities. At age three, she recited in church
and remembered looking down at the chickens underneath the flooring of the
church with the fanning churchwomen telling her grandmother that "this child
is gifted." When she went to kindergarten, she wrote to her teacher explaining
that she belonged in first grade. When she returned to school the next day, she
was moved into the first grade. Her fourth-grade teacher also provided a
prominent influence on her childhood development, encouraging young Oprah
to accomplish anything she wanted. Since all these influences made the child feel
secure and special, Oprah never felt she was less of a person.

She was a demanding child who needed greater challenges than Mississippi
could afford. She went to live with her mother in Milwaukee, where they lived
in a rented room in a woman's home. The low wages of a domestic combined with
welfare payments proved insufficient income for the two. Her mother was not
skilled in providing parental supervision or guidance to the increasingly unruly
child, so Oprah was again shuffled to another relative—her father, Vernon
Winfrey.

In 1962 she joined her father and his wife in Nashville, Tennessee, where he
had settled after completing military service. The spirited child found discipline
and support in this new household. Her stepmother helped her with math skills,
while her father continued inculcating the religious values of the church. She
accompanied her father to services at Progressive Baptist Church, where she
performed in pageants and choral presentations. She was returned to her mother
for a summertime visit, a decision that led to problems.

Although her mother had married a man with whom she had had a relationship for several years, the new family, which included his two children, did not provide the support and discipline needed by young Oprah. She was again neglected by a family that did not place importance on intellectual activities or skills and placed value on light-skinned beauty as that of her stepsister. She became increasingly isolated, introspective, and abused during this period. Sexual abuse by an uncle and other family acquaintances further aggravated her isolation and withdrawal. School, however, became her only pleasant outlet. A teacher, Gene Abrams, recognized her abilities and helped her obtain a scholarship to the junior high school in suburban Fox Point. This experience was not enough to balance the five years in her mother's dysfunctional home life, so again she was returned to her father's home in Nashville. She again adjusted to his high standards and discipline, enrolled in East High School, and participated in extracurricular activities that further developed her speaking and performance skills. She became a participant in the 1970 White House Conference on Youth held in Washington, went to Los Angeles as a church speaker, toured Hollywood, won titles of Miss Black Tennessee and Miss Fire Prevention. Structure and support had produced fruit.

The local black-owned Nashville radio station WVOL gave her the chance to enter the media world. She worked as a news announcer while attending Tennessee State University in Nashville on a scholarship won through an Elks-sponsored oratorical contest. Her performance led to employment at a major radio station, WLAC, as a reporter-anchor. Her earnings and performance in college did not lessen her father's restrictions. A few months before graduation from college, Oprah Winfrey accepted a position as a reporter at a television station in Baltimore, Maryland, in 1976. Put through an intensive makeover to improve her television presence, Oprah was placed as a co-host on a local morning show, *People Are Talking*. Her personality and rhetorical abilities paid off. She sent tapes to other markets to further her career. When the co-producer left Baltimore for a position in Chicago, she used these tapes to convince the station manager at WLS-TV, a ABC-TV affiliate, to hire Oprah for the *A.M. Chicago* program. Taking over the show in 1984, Winfrey soon gathered ratings that competed with and outdistanced the popular *Phil Donahue Show*. In 1985, he moved his show to New York, leaving Oprah as the Queen of Chicago talk shows.

Oprah Winfrey was never satisfied with achievement in one field. She campaigned for the role as Sofia in the 1985 film production of *The Color Purple*. She took leave from her Chicago talk-show host job to go South to study for the role, for which she won a Golden Globe Award and was nominated for an Academy Award (1986). Next, she appeared as the mother in the motion picture *Native Son* in 1986. She was selected as one of *Playgirl* magazine's Ten Most Admired Women in 1986. During this time, her *A.M. Chicago* became the *Oprah Winfrey Show*, and went into syndication. She received a portion of the syndication contract that led to her becoming the highest-paid performer in show business in 1987–1988. She received the Outstanding Talk/Service Host Award in 1987, and her program won the award in 1987 and 1988. She gained the Broadcaster of the Year Award from the International Radio and Television Society in 1988. In addition to all her awards, she continued to appear in special roles in the National Black Theatre Festival in Winston-Salem, North Carolina, in August 1988.

Her success did not confuse her. Although she felt that society often confuses fame with greatness, she evaluated success by the way she treats people and herself. Although her five-year contract carried her through the 1990–1991 season, she formed her own production company, Harpo Productions, which assumed ownership and production of the *Oprah Winfrey Show* in 1988. The production company formed from her name spelled backward was renamed Harpo Studios in November 1988. The company brought forth productions of social and spiritual meaning as "The Women of Brewster Place," in which Winfrey starred in the miniseries, a ratings winner. Her sexual abuse as a child has led to her production of shows on children and sexual abuse. Her business interests also include partnership in a Chicago restaurant.

Winfrey now uses her power to make a difference in people's lives. Referred to as a "Roadmaker" by author Maya Angelou, Winfrey gives motivational lectures to groups of students emphasizing the importance of self-esteem and discipline. She started a minority training program in early 1989 to bring more people of color into the film and television industry as producers. She has "adopted" a group of black girls in Chicago to serve as their mentor and guide through adolescence. Her experiences have created concern for black women, children, and education. In 1988 she returned to Tennessee State University to receive a deferred reward, her college diploma in recognition of her achievements. She established a scholarship in her name to cover expenses for ten students each year, a select group of students who maintain a personal relationship with their patron during and after their college years. In 1989 she was one of Ms. magazine's Women of the Year. In 1990 she was recognized by *Ladies Home Journal* as one of America's Fifty Most Powerful Women. She continues to balance her career with a long-term relationship with Stedman Graham. She plans to produce feature films from Toni Morrison's *Beloved*; Mark Mathabane's autobiography of his African youth under apartheid, *Kaffir Boy*; and Zora Neale Hurston's *Their Eyes Were Watching God*. Oprah Winfrey has proved those church ladies correct. She is truly gifted and has made sure that her gifts are being shared with others.

—Beth Schneider

Bibliography

Oprah Winfrey has received much coverage in the contemporary press. Interviews abound covering her television, film, and business careers: Marcia Gillespie, "Winfrey Talks All," *Ms.* 17 (November 1988): 50; Maya Angelou, "Oprah Winfrey, Woman of the Year," *Ms.* 17 (January/February 1989): 88; T. Chapelle, "The Reigning Queen of TV Talk Oprah!!" *Black Collegian* 21 (November/December 1990): 136; "Oprah Opens Up," *TV Guide* 38 (May 5–11 1990): 4–6+; "Oprah Winfrew Tells Why Blacks Who Bash Blacks Tick Her Off," *Jet* 78 (September 17, 1990): 60–62; "Cutting Out the Middlemen," *Forbes* 146 (October 1, 1990): 166; "Morehouse College Names Seven Oprah Winfrey Scholars," *Jet* 79 (December 3, 1990): 12; E. Sherman, "Oprah's Wonder Year," *Ladies Home Journal* 107 (May 1990): 157–159+; W. Brashler, "Next on Oprah," *Ladies Home Journal* 108 (August 1991): 94–96; "Oprah Wins Two Daytime Emmies," *Jet* 82 (July 13, 1992): 54; Audrey Edwards, "Stealing the Show," *Essence* 17 (October 1986): 50–52+; Pearl Cleage, "Walking in the Light," *Essence* 22 (June 1991): 46–48; F. Goodman, "Madonna and Oprah: The Companies They Keep," *Working Women* 16 (December 1991): 52–55; C. Anderson, "Meet Oprah Winfrey," *Good Housekeeping* 208 (August 1986): 56–58; A. Ebert, "Oprah Winfrey Talks Openly About Oprah," *Good Housekeeping* 213 (September 1991): 62–64; M. Farrell, "Oprah's Crusade," *People Weekly* 36 (December 2, 1991): 68–69; "Winfrey Asks Congress to Start Child Abuse Registry," *Jet* 81 (December 2, 1991): 34.

Her biographical sketch appears in Jessie Carney Smith, ed., *Notable Black American Women* (Detroit: Gale, 1992); *Who's Who among Black Americans 1990/ 1991* (Northbrook, IL: Who's Who among Black Americans, 1992); *Who's Who in Entertainment 1992/1993* (Chicago: Marquis, 1992); and *Current Biography* (New York: Wilson, 1992). Her career in entertainment is followed in Donald Bogle, *Black Arts Annual 1988/89* (New York: Garland, 1990); and George Hill, *Black Women in Television* (New York: Garland, 1990).

WYATT, ADDIE L. (b. 1924),

successful union executive, was born in Brookhaven, Mississippi, on March 8. She moved to Chicago as a youngster and at age 17 applied for a typing job at Armour and Company. However, due to her race, she was denied a clerical job and was instead hired to put lids on army stew. There, she became a member of the United Packinghouse Workers Union (now merged with the Amalgamated Meat Cutters and Butchers) and subsequently realized that, as a union member, she was making more money than a typist.

In 1954 Wyatt became the first woman president of a packinghouse local. She later served as one of the Amalgamated Meat Cutter's five international representatives. In 1974 she organized the Coalition of Labor Union Women and was elected vice president of that group. That same year, she was also appointed director of the Women's Affairs Department of the Amalgamated Meat Cutters and Butcher Workmen of North America. As a unionist, Wyatt persuaded the industry to promote women to more demanding, higher paying, previously all-male jobs. At the same time, she assured many doubtful women that they could handle these positions. By the mid 1970s, she proudly pointed to women who were beef luggers, journeyman butchers, hamboners, and forklift operators. In 1975 *Time* magazine cited Addie L. Wyatt as one of its 12 Women of the Year, describing her as a "bold unionist." Two years later, *Ladies Home Journal* chose her as one of its nine Women of the Year, representing the area of business and economy. In addition, Wyatt has received numerous other awards and has served as member-at-large of the Democratic National Committee.

In 1940 she married Claude S. Wyatt, Jr., a clergyman and current pastor of the Vernon Park Church of God in Chicago, where she is minister of music and delivers an occasional sermon. The Wyatts have two sons.

—Betty Plummer

Bibliography

An interesting sketch on Addie L. Wyatt appeared in *Time* (January 5, 1975). Another brief, but informative, sketch of Addie L. Wyatt appeared in *Ladies Home Journal* XCIV:6 (June 1977). Biographical information, including a listing of her awards, is included in *Who's Who among Black Americans*, 3d edition, 1980–1981 (Northbrook, IL: Who's Who Among Black Americans Publishing Company, 1981). A shorter listing of her awards appears in *Who's Who in American Politics*, 10th edition (New York: Bowker, 1985).

Y

YATES, JOSEPHINE [SILONE] (1859–1912), club leader, educator, and writer, was born on November 15 in Suffolk County, New York. She was the daughter of Alexander Silone and Parthenia (Reeve); they were the third generation of prominent families in Southhold who were believed to have descended from African slaves who gained their freedom when the ship transporting them wrecked on the coast of New England.

At an early age, Josephine Silone was taught by her mother reading, writing, and arithmetic, and was quite advanced when she entered the local district school. At age 11, she went to live with her uncle, the Reverend J.B. Reeve, in Philadelphia so that she could attend the School for Colored Youth operated by Fannie Jackson Coppin. A year later her uncle moved, and Josephine returned to New York. At age 14, she went to live with an aunt, Mrs. Francis L. Girard, in Newport, Rhode Island. In Newport, she completed the highest grade of the grammar school and attended Rogers High School. She was the only "colored" student in the graduating class of 1877, of which she was the valedictorian. In 1879 the final phase of her formal education was completed when she graduated from Rhode Island State Normal School.

In the 1880s Silone began a teaching career at Lincoln Institute in Jefferson City, Missouri, where she became head of the Department of Science. She taught at Lincoln until her marriage in 1889 to William Ward Yates, principal of the Wendell Phillips School, of Kansas City, Missouri.

After her marriage, Silone Yates wrote for newspapers and became active in the women's club movement combining her duties as wife and mother. She wrote both prose and poetry on a wide range of topics under the pseudonym R.K. Potter. She wrote for the first national magazine for black women, *The Woman's Era*. Silone Yates and three other women initiated the first black women's club in Kansas City, Missouri, in 1893, one of the first three black women's clubs in the country. Her club work was on the local, state, and national levels. She was elected the second president of the National Association of Colored Women, serving two terms from 1901 to 1906, and was state president of the Missouri Association of Colored Women's Clubs in 1909. During Silone Yates's national presidency, the National Association was incorporated under the laws of Missouri.

Throughout her life, Josephine Silone Yates was an ardent educator, clubworker, wife and mother. She died on September 3, 1912, in Kansas City after a brief illness.

—Marcia Y. Riggs

Bibliography

Among the best secondary references for biographical profiles of Josephine Silone-Yates are Sylvia G.L. Dannett, *Profiles of Negro Womanhood* 1 (New York: M.W. Lads, 1964); Kali Herman, *Women in Particular: An Index to American Women* (Phoenix, AZ: Onyx Press, 1984); Norma Olin Ireland, *Index to Women of the World from Ancient to Modern Times: Biographies and Portraits* (Westwood, MA: F.W. Faxon, 1970); and Harry A. Ploski and Warren Marr II, eds., *The Negro Almanac: A Reference Work on the Afro-American* (New York: Bellweather, 1976).

More extensive essays and commentary on the life and work of Silone-Yates are found in Lawson Scruggs, *Women of Distinction* (Raleigh, NC: L.A. Scruggs, 1893); Hallie Q. Brown, *Homespun Heroines and Other Women of Disctinction*, reprint edition (New York: Oxford University Press, 1988); Charles Harris Wesley, *The History of the National Association of Colored Women's Clubs: A Legacy of Service* (Washington, DC: Mercury Press, 1984); and Frances J. Wilson "Josephine Silone-Yates: Early Years of the Black Women's Club Movement in Missouri," *The Lincoln University Journal on Ethnic Studies* 1:1 (Summer 1982).

Other works that place Silone-Yates sociohistorically as well as chronicle the work of the black women's club movement are also important secondary sources, for example, Elizabeth L. Davis, *Lifting as They Climb* (Washington, DC: NACW, 1933); Wilson J. Moses, *The Golden Age of Black Nationalism* (New York: Oxford University Press, 1978); Tullia K. Brown Hamilton, "The National Association of Colored Women, 1896 to 1920," PhD dissertation, Emory University (1978); Floris L. Cash, "Womanhood and Protest: The Club Movement among Black Women, 1892–1922," PhD dissertation, State University of New York at Stony Brook (1986); Dorothy C. Salem, *To Better Our World: Black Women in Organized Reform, 1890–1920* (Brooklyn: Carlson, 1990); and Paula Giddings, *When and Where I Enter: The Impact of Black Women on Race and Sex in America* (New York: Morrow, 1984). A couple of articles by Josephine Silone-Yates are "The National Association of Colored Women," *The Voice of the Negro* 1 (July 1904): 238; and "Women's World," *Colored American* (May 8, 1902): 2; other writings by her may be found in *The Rising Sun* (a column entitled "Lincoln Notes") and other black newspapers of the late nineteenth century.

Contributors

Lisa M. Reynolds Abu-Raad
Graduate Student
History Department
Cleveland State University

Adrianne Andrews
Afro-American Studies Department
Smith College

F. Michael Angelo
Archives and Special Collections on
  Women in Medicine
Medical College of Pennsylvania

Thea S. Arnold
Doctoral Candidate
History Department
State University of New York—
  Binghamton

Barbara Bair
African Studies Center
University of California—
  Los Angeles

Rosalie Murphy Baum
English Department
University of South Florida

Roland M. Baumann
Oberlin College Archives
Oberlin College

Gina Beavers
Doctoral Candidate
University of Massachusetts

Thea Becker
Attorney and Historian
Cleveland, Ohio

Esme E. Bhan
Research Associate
Moorland-Spingarn Center
Howard University

SDiane A. Bogus
American Literature and Rhetoric
  Department
DeAnza College

Susan Borchert
Sociology Department
Lake Erie College

Marilyn Dell Brady
History Department
Virginia Wesleyan College

Lauretta Byars
Vice-Chancellor for Minority Affairs
University of Kentucky

Debra Calhoun
Pan-African Studies Department
Kent State University

Linda Cannon-Huffman
Thomas Cooper Library
University of South Carolina

Jacqueline D. Carr-Hamilton
Religion Department
Virginia Polytechnic Institute
 and State University

Faye A. Chadwell
Thomas Cooper Library
University of South Carolina

Robin Chandler
African-American Studies
Northeastern University

Sharlene Voogd Cochrane
Liberal Studies and Adult
 Learning Division
Lesley College

Margaret L. Dwight
Black Studies Department
Ohio State University

Dorri Scott Eades
Storyteller
Leawood, Kansas

Roy E. Finkenbine
History Department
Florida State University

Nancy Elizabeth Fitch
History Department
Temple University

Elizabeth Hadley Freydberg
Department of African-American
 Studies
Northeastern University

Vivian Gartley-Hindrew
Augusta College Library
Martinez, Georgia

Gloria J. Gibson-Hudson
Afro-American Studies Department
Indiana University

Glenda Elizabeth Gilmore
History Department
Queens College
Charlotte, North Carolina

Bruce A. Glasrud
History Department
California State University—
 Hayward

Valerie Grim
Afro-American Studies Department
Indiana University

Wanda A. Hendricks
Department of History
University of North Carolina-
 Charlotte

Lisa Beth Hill
Doctoral Candidate
History Department
Emory University

Gerald Horne
Black Studies Department
University of California—
 Santa Barbara

Mary Hovanec
History Department
Cuyahoga Community College

Terri L. Jewell
Freelance Writer
Lansing, Michigan

Frank W. Johnson
Anthropology Department
Temple University

Adrienne Lash Jones
Black Studies Department
Oberlin College

Juanita Karpf
Music and Women's Studies
  Department
University of Georgia

Ann M. Lindell
Librarian
Queens College
Charlotte, North Carolina

Heather Martin
Graduate Student
  English & Library Science
University of South Carolina—
  Columbia

Jimmy E.W. Meyer
Doctoral Candidate
Social Policy History
Case-Western Reserve University

Janet Miller
Archives and Special Collections on
  Women in Medicine
Women's Medical College of
  Pennsylvania

LaVerne Nickson
National Assembly of Religious
  Women
Chicago, Illinois

Lucille O'Connell
History Department
Bridgewater State College

Janet Owens
Librarian
University of South Carolina—
  Columbia

Linda M. Perkins
Department of Educational Policy
  Studies
University of Illinois—
  Urbana-Champaign

Paula F. Pfeffer
History Department
Loyola University

Julieanne Phillips
History Department
University of Dayton

Betty Plummer
History Department
University of Tennessee

Nicholas C. Polos
History Department
University of La Verne

Rama Ramakrishna
Historical Consultant
National Conference of State
  Historic Preservation Officers

Jane Rhodes
School of Journalism
Indiana University

Marcia Y. Riggs
Columbia Theological Seminary
Decatur, Georgia

Elizabeth D. Schafer
Doctoral Candidate
History of Technology
Auburn University

Beth Schneider
Freelance Writer
Lorain, Ohio

Debra L. Schultz
Assistant Director
National Council for Research on
  Women

Susan Shifrin
Doctoral Candidate
Bryn Mawr College

Yvonne Scruggs
Urban Policy Institute
Joint Center for Political and
  Economic Studies

Olivia Pearl Stokes
Executive Director
Greater Harlem Comprehensive
  Guidance Center

Mary Frances Stubbs
Trotter Institute
University of Massachusetts

Susan Stussy
Law Student
Washburn University

Kelle S. Taha
Educator
Amman, Jordan

Ula Y. Taylor
Doctoral Candidate
History Department
University of California—
  Santa Barbara

Emilie M. Townes
Christian Social Ethics Department
Saint Paul School of Theology
Kansas City, Missouri

Donna Van Raaphorst
History Department
Cuyahoga Community College

Margaret Wade-Lewis
Black Studies Department
State University of New York—
  New Paltz

Christopher D. White
History Department
Purdue University

Lillian S. Williams
Women's Studies/African Studies
State University of New York—
  Albany

Mary Ann Williams
Department of Black Studies
Ohio State University

Regennia N. Williams
Doctoral Candidate
Case-Western Reserve University

Julie Winch
Department of Black Studies
University of Massachusetts—Boston

Barbara Winslow
Women's Studies Department
Hunter College

Barbara Woods
Institute for Southern Studies
University of South Carolina

Jean Fagan Yellin
English Department
Pace University

Patricia A. Young
English Department
Western Illinois University

Entries by Career Category

AVIATION
Bates, Daisy
Brown, Jill
Coleman, Bessie
Jemison, Mae (astronaut)

BUSINESS AND COMMERCE
*philanthropist
Brown, Clara
Burton, Annie
Cass, Melnea
Ferguson, Catherine
Forten, Charlotte
Hopkins, Pauline
Johnson, Pamela
Keckley, Elizabeth
Mason, Biddy*
Pleasant, Mary Ellen ("Mammy")*
Proctor, Barbara
Remond, Nancy Lenox
Ross, Diana
Simkins, Modjeska Monteith
Smith, Phyllis
Stewart, Ella
Stewart, Sallie
Teer, Barbara Ann
Waklee, A'Lelia
Walker, Sarah (Madam C.J.)*
Walker, Maggie Lena

CIVIL RIGHTS ACTIVIST
Adair, Christia
Baker, Ella
Bates, Daisy
Berry, Mary

Burks, Mary Fair
Clark, Septima
Clifford, Carrie
Craft, Juanita
Davis, Angela
Davis, Henrietta Vinton
Dee, Ruby
Dozier-Crenshaw, Doris
Du Bois, Shirley Graham
Edelman, Marian
Fleming, Lethia
Garvey, Amy Jacques
Hamer, Fannie Lou
Height, Dorothy
Hunton, Addie Waites
King, Coretta Scott
Kofey, Laura
Lampkin, Daisy
Lealtad, Catherine
Mitchell, L. Pearl
Morton-Jones, Verina
Motely, Constance Baker
Murray, Pauli
Nash, Diane
Parks, Rosa
Pleasant, Mary Ellen
Robinson, Jo Ann
Robinson, Ruby(e) Doris
Shabazz, Betty
Simkins, Modjeska Monteith
Stewart, Sallie
Talbert, Mary
Terrell, Mary Church
Walker, Alice
Walker, Sarah (Madam C.J.)

575

CLUBWOMAN

National Association of Colored Women

Albrier, Frances
Allensworth, Josephine
Barrett, Janie
Bethune, Mary McLeod
Bowser, Rosa
Branch, Mary Elizabeth
Brown, Hallie Quinn
Bruce, Josephine
Carter-Brooks, Elizabeth
Cass, Melnea
Clifford, Carrie
Cook, Coralie
Dunbar-Nelson, Alice
Fleming, Lethia
Garnet, Sarah
Hope, Lugenia Burns
Hunt, Ida Gibbs
Hunter, Jane Edna
Hunton, Addie Waites
Jackson, Eliza Belle
Lampkin, Daisy
Logan, Adella
Matthews, Victoria
McCrorey, Mary
Moore, Audley "Queen Mother"
Mitchell, L. Pearl
Morton-Jones, Verina
Mossell, Gertrude
Napier, Lettie
Preston, Frances E.L.
Ruffin, Josephine St. Pierre
Sprague, Rosetta M. Douglass
Steward, Susan
Stewart, Ella
Stewart, Sallie
Talbert, Mary
Terrell, Mary Church
Trotter, Geraldine
Walker, Maggie
Washington, Margaret James
Williams, Fannie
Yates, Josephine

National Council of Negro Women

Bethune, Mary McLeod
Ferebee, Dorothy
Height, Dorothy
Hunter, Jane Edna
Kemp, Maida
Mitchell, L. Pearl
Moore, Audley "Queen Mother"
Slowe, Lucy Diggs
Staupers, Mabel

EDUCATION

Historian

Beasley, Delilah
Berry, Mary Frances
Brown, Hallie Quinn
Edmonds, Helen
Harley, Sharon
Hine, Darlene Clark
Painter, Nell Irvin
Porter, Dorothy
Thomas, Bettye

Librarian

Lorde, Audre
Porter, Dorothy
Shockley, Ann Allen
Spencer, Anne

Linguist

Bailey, Beryl

Schoolteacher

*school founder; †school administrator

Adair, Christia
Allensworth, Josephine
Baldwin, Maria†
Bethune, Mary McLeod*
Bishop, Anna†
Bowser, Rosa
Branch, Mary
Brown, Charlotte Hawkins*
Brown, Emma*
Brown, Hallie Quinn
Bruce, Josephine Beall
Burks, Mary Fair
Burroughs, Nannie*
Butcher, Margaret
Carter-Brooks, Elizabeth
Chisholm, Shirley Anita
Clark, Septima
Coleman, N. Juanita
Cook, Coralie
Cooper, Anna†
Cobb, Jewel Plummer†
Coppin, Fannie†
Craft, Ellen*
Davis, Angela
Derricotte, Juliette†
Douglass, Grace Bustill*
Douglass, Sarah Mapps*
Dunbar-Nelson, Alice
Dunham, Katherine
Early, Sarah
Edmonds, Helen
Fauset, Jessie Redmon
Ferguson, Catherine*
Forten, Margaretta
Garnet, Sarah
George, Zelma
Grimké, Charlotte L. Forten
Harris, Blanche
Haynes, Elizabeth Ross

Hunt, Ida Gibbs
Johnson, Pamela
Joseph-Gaudet, Frances*
Laney, Lucy*
Logan, Adella Hunt
McCrorey, Mary
Mitchell, Lucy Miller
Mossell, Gertrude
Norton, Eleanor Holmes
Patterson, Mary Jane†
Peake, Mary
Petry Ann
Pinyon, Josephine
Robinson, Jo Ann
Shadd, Mary Ann*
Slowe, Lucy Diggs†
Stewart, Maria
Stewart, Sallie
Stokes, Olivia Pearl
Talbert, Mary
Taylor, Susie
Terrell, Mary Church
Walker, Margaret
Washington, Margaret†
Washington, Olivia*†
Wells-Barnett, Ida B.
Yates, Josephine†

INVENTOR
Walker, Sarah (Madam C.J.)

LITERARY ARTS
Journalist/Editor

Bass, Charlotta
Bates, Daisy
Beasley, Delilah
Bruce, Josephine
Clifford, Carrie
Cook, Coralie
Dunbar-Nelson, Alice
Fauset, Jessie Redmon

Garvey, Amy Jacques
Giddings, Paula
Harper, Frances E.
Hopkins, Pauline
Johnson, Georgia Douglas
Johnson, Pamela
Jones, Claudia
Lampkin, Daisy
Matthews, Victoria
Mossell, Gertrude
Parsons, Lucy
Petry, Ann
Pettey, Sarah
Ruffin, Josephine St. Pierre
Schuyler, Philippa Duke
Shadd, Mary Ann
Shockley, Ann Allen
Stewart, Maria
Terrell, Mary Church
Thompson, Era Bell
Trotter, Geraldine Pindell
Washington, Margaret James
Washington, Olivia
Wells-Barnett, Ida B.
West, Dorothy
Yates, Josephine

Novelist

Angelou, Maya
Childress, Alice
Fauset, Jessie Redmon
Hopkins, Pauline
Hurston, Zora Neale
Marshall, Paule
Morrison, Toni
Murray, Pauli
Petry, Ann
Schuyler, Philippa Duke
Shockley, Ann Allen
Walker, Alice
Walker, Margaret
West, Dorothy

Playwright

Angelou, Maya
Burrill, Mary Powell
Childress, Alice
Collins, Kathleen
Cuney Hare, Maud
Delany, Clarissa
Du Bois, Shirley Graham
Fauset, Jessie Redmon
Grimké, Angelina Weld
Hansberry, Lorraine
Hopkins, Pauline
Johnson, Georgia Douglas
Kennedy, Adrienne
Morrison, Toni
Sanchez, Sonia
Shange, Ntozake
Teer, Barbara Ann

Poet

Angelou, Maya
Bishop, Anna
Brooks, Gwendolyn E.
Clifford, Carrie
Cuney Hare, Maud
Delany, Clarissa
Du Bois, Shirley Graham
Fauset, Jessie Redmon
Giovanni, Nikki
Grimké, Angelina Weld
Harper, Frances E.
Johnson, Georgia Douglas
Lorde, Audre
Morrison, Toni
Murray, Pauli
Sanchez, Sonia
Shange, Ntozake
Spencer, Anne
Terry, Lucy
Walker, Alice
Walker, Margaret
Wheatley, Phillis

Writer (general)

Butcher, Margaret
Childress, Alice
Clifford, Carrie
Collins, Kathleen
Cooper, Anna
Cuney Hare, Maud
Delaney, Lucy A.
Du Bois, Shirley Graham
Dunbar-Nelson, Alice
Fauset, Jessie Redmon
Giddings, Paula
Goldberg, Whoopi
Hopkins, Pauline
Hunton, Addie Waites
Hurston, Zora Neale
Johnson, Georgia Douglas
Lorde, Audre
Marshall, Paule
Matthews, Victoria
Mossell, Gertrude
Petry, Ann
Pleasant, Mary Ellen
Terrell, Mary Church
Thompson, Era Bell

MISCELLANEOUS

Craft, Ellen (fugitive slave)
Hemings, Sally
   (slave of Thomas Jefferson)
Keckley, Elizabeth
   (seamstress to Mary Todd Lincoln)

PERFORMING ARTS
Actress

Allen, Debbie
Avery, Margaret
Bailey, Pearl
Baker, Josephine
Beavers, Louise
Burrows, Vinie
Bush, Anita
Carroll, Diahann
Carter, Nell
Cash, Rosalind
Childress, Alice
Cox, Ida
Dandridge, Dorothy
Dandridge, Ruby
Davis, Henrietta Vinton
Dee, Ruby
Dobson, Tamara
George, Zelma
Goldberg, Whoopi
Holiday, Billie
Horne, Lena
McClendon, Rose
McDaniel, Hattie
McKinney, Nina Mae
McQueen, Thelma "Butterfly"
Mills, Florence
Mitchell, Abbie
Ross, Diana
Scott, Hazel
Shange, Ntozake
Sul-Te-Wan, Madame
Snow, Valaida
Teer, Barbara Ann
Tyson, Cicely
Waters, Ethel
Winfrey, Oprah

Comedienne

Goldberg, Whoopi
Mabley, Jackie "Moms"
Mills, Florence
Waters, Ethel

Dance/Choreography

Allen, Debbie
Angelou, Maya
Baker, Josephine

Chenzira, Ayoka
Dandridge, Dorothy
Dunham, Katherine
Jamison, Judith
Mills, Florence
Primus, Pearl
Shange, Ntozake
Snow, Valaida
Teer, Barbara Ann
Waters, Ethel

Instrumentalist/Composer

Austin, Lovey
Cox, Ida
Cuney Hare, Maud
Chinn, May
Du Bois, Shirley
Evanti, Madame Lillian
Fitzgerald, Ella
Hackley, Emma
Hopkins, Pauline
Hunter, Alberta
McCoy, Minnie "Memphis Minnie"
McRae, Carmen
Schuyler, Philippa Duke
Sheppard, Ella
Scott, Hazel
Snow, Valaida
Williams, Mary Lou

Vocalist

Anderson, Marian
Austin, Lovey
Bailey, Pearl
Baker, Josephine
Carroll, Diahann
Carter, Nell
Cox, Ida
Dandridge, Dorothy
Davis, Henrietta Vinton
Evanti, Madame Lillian
Fitzgerald, Ella

Franklin, Aretha
George, Zelma
Greenfield, Elizabeth
Hackley, Emma
Holiday, Billie
Horne, Lena
Hunter, Alberta
Jackson, Mahalia
Jones, Pearl Williams
Jones, M. Sissieretta
McCoy, Minnie "Memphis Minnie"
McRae, Carmen
Mills, Florence
Mitchell, Abbie
Price, Leontyne
Rainey, Gertrude "Ma"
Ross, Diana
Sheppard, Ella
Smith, Ada "Bricktop"
Smith, Bessie
Snow, Valaida
Vaughan, Sarah
Washington, Dinah
Waters, Ethel
Williams, Mary Lou

PIONEER
Brown, Clara
Mason, Biddie
Pleasant, Mary Ellen ("Mammy")

POLITICS, GOVERNMENT, LAW

Alternative Politics

Albrier, Frances
Bass, Charlotta
Davis, Angela
Davis, Henrietta Vinton
Garvey, Amy Jacques
Jones, Claudia
Kofey, Laura

Moore, Audley "Queen Mother"
Parsons, Lucy
Simkins, Modjeska Monteith

Democratic/Republican

Berry, Mary
Bethune, Mary McLeod
Brown, Willa
Burke, Yvonne Brathwaite
Burrows, Vinie
Chisholm, Shirley Anita
Craig, Ellen
Fauset, Crystal Dreda Bird
Fleming, Lethia (UN Delegate)
George, Zelma
Hamer, Fannie Lou
Harris, Patricia Burrows
Haynes, Elizabeth R.
Jordan, Barbara
Motley, Constance Baker
Norton, Eleanor Holmes
Scruggs, Yvonne
Simkins, Modjeska Monteith
Wells-Barnet, Ida B.Lawyer
Alexander, Sadie
Berry, Mary
Burke, Yvonne Brathwaite
Edelman, Marian
Harris, Patricia
Hunter, Jane
Jordan, Barbara
Kennedy, Flo
Motley, Constance Baker
Norton, Eleanor Holmes
Ray, Charlotte
Shadd, Mary Ann

Probation Officer/ Reformatory Matron

Barrett, Janie
Dunbar-Nelson, Alice
George, Zelma

Joseph-Gaudet, Frances
Mitchell, L. Pearl
Wells-Barnett, Ida B.

REFORMER
Abolitionist

Craft, Ellen
Douglass, Anna Murray
Douglass, Grace
Douglass, Sarah Mapps
Early, Sarah
Forten, Charlotte
Forten, Margaretta
Grimké, Charlotte L. Forten
Harper, Frances E.
Harris, Blance
Jacobs, Harriet
Paul, Susan
Pleasant, Mary Ellen
Prosser, Nancy
Purvis, Harriet Forten
Purvis, Sarah Forten
Remond, Nancy L.
Remond, Sarah Parker
Shadd, Mary Ann
Sprague, Rosetta M. Douglass
Stewart, Maria W.
Truth, Sojourner
Tubman, Harriet

Antilynching

Burrill, Mary Powell
Dunbar-Nelson, Alice
Grimké, Angelina Weld
Johnson, Georgia Douglas
Talbert, Mary
Wells-Barnett, Ida B.

Community/Civic Activist

*founder of settlement house/community home for the elderly

Allensworth, Josephine
Avery, Byllye Y.
Barrett, Janie*
Brown, Clara
Bryant, Eliza*
Carter-Brooks, Elizabeth*
Cass, Melnea
Coffey, Lillian
Craft, Juanita
Delaney, Lucy A.
Dunbar, Mathilda
Ferebee, Dorothy*
Ferguson, Catherine
Fleming, Lethia
George, Zelma
Hope, Lugenia Burns*
Hunter, Jane Edna*
Jackson, Eliza Belle*
Joseph-Gaudet, Frances
Keckley, Elizabeth
Matthews, Victoria*
Mitchell, L. Pearl
Mitchell, Lucy Miller
Moore, Audley "Queen Mother"
Napier, Lettie
Patterson, Mary Jane
Preston, Frances E.L.
Ruffin, Josephine St. Pierre
Shabazz, Betty
Simkins, Modjeska Monteith
Smith, Amanda
Smith, Catherine
Stewart, Ella
Stewart, Sallie
Stokes, Olivia Pearl
Talbert, Mary
Terrell, Mary Church
Trotter, Geraldine
Washington, Margaret James
Wells-Barnett, Ida B.
Williams, Fannie

Feminist/Women's Rights

Burrows, Vinie
Forten, Margaretta
Grimké, Charlotte L. Forten
Harper, Frances E.
Kennedy, Flo
Murray, Pauli
Paul, Susan
Pettey, Sarah
Purvis, Harriet Forten
Purvis, Sarah Forten
Ray, Charlotte E.
Remond, Nancy
Remond, Sarah Parker
Shadd, Mary Ann
Sprague, Rosetta M. Douglass
Steward, Susan
Stewart, Maria W.
Truth, Sojourner
Tubman, Harriet
Walker, Alice

Lesbian

Dunbar-Nelson, Alice
Grimké, Angelina Weld
Lorde, Audre
Shockley, Ann Allen
Slowe, Lucy Diggs

Peace

Adair, Christia
Alexander, Virginia
Bass, Charlotta
Beasley, Delilah
Burroughs, Nannie
Burrows, Vinie
Du Bois, Shirley Graham
Dunbar-Nelson, Alice
Fauset, Crystal Dreda Bird

Hunt, Ida
Talbert, Mary
Terrell, Mary Church

Temperance

Brown, Hallie Q.
Cook, Coralie
Early, Sarah
Harper, Frances E.
Harris, Blanche
Jacobs, Harriet
Joseph-Gaudet, Frances
Paul, Susan
Preston, Frances E.L.
Smith, Amanda
Steward, Susan

Woman's Suffrage

Adair, Christia
Clifford, Carrie
Cook, Coralie
Dunbar-Nelson, Alice
Garnet, Sarah
Harper, Frances E.
Hunton, Addie Waites
Logan, Adella
Pettey, Sarah
Ray, Charlotte E.
Ruffin, Josephine St. Pierre
Stewart, Maria W.
Talbert, Mary
Terrell, Mary Church
Wells-Barnett, Ida B.

RELIGIOUS LEADER

Burroughs, Nannie
Coffey, Lillian
Elaw, Zilpha
Ferguson, Catherine
Harris, Barbara
Harris, Blanche V.

Hedgeman, Anna Arnold
Jackson, Rebecca
Kelly, Leontine
Lee, Jarena
Mason, Biddy
Murray, Pauli
Peake, Mary
Pettey, Sarah
Roberson, Lizzie Woods
Robinson, Ida
Smith, Amanda
Smith, Phyllis
Stokes, Olivia Pearl
Truth, Sojourner

SCIENCE/MEDICINE

Anthropologist

Dunham, Katherine
Hurston, Zora Neale

Nurse

Adair, Christia
Albrier, Frances
Hinton, Jane
Hunter, Alberta
Hunter, Jane Edna
Mason, Biddy (midwife)
Mahoney, Mary
Staupers, Mabel
Taylor, Susie
Thoms, Adah
Tubman, Harriet

Pharmacist

Stewart, Ella

Physician

Alexander, Virginia
Chinn, May Edward

Epps, Roselyn
Evans, Matilda (Dentist)
Ferebee, Dorothy
Gray, Ida (Dentist)
Grier, Eliza
Jemison, Mae
Johnson, Halle
Lealtad, Catherine
Lee, Rebecca
Morton-Jones, Verina
Remond, Sarah Parker
Steward, Susan

Public Health Researcher

Alexander, Virginia M.
Avery, Byllye
Chinn, May Edward
Epps, Roselyn
Ferebee, Dorothy
Lealtad, Catherine
Smith, Catherine

Scientist

Cobb, Jewel Plummer
Jemison, Mae

Veterinarian

Reed, Rosalie A.
Webb, Alfreda

SPORTS

Ashford, Evelyn
Brisco-Hooks, Valerie
Devers, Gail
Gibson, Althea
Joyner, Florence Griffith
Joyner-Kersee, Jackie
Rudolph, Wilma
Slowe, Lucy Diggs

UNION ORGANIZER

Adair, Christia
Hedgeman, Anna Arnold
Kemp, Maida
Moore, Audley "Queen Mother"
Parsons, Lucy
Roberts, Lillian
Tucker, Rosina
Wilson, Halena
Wyatt, Addie

UNITED NATIONS DELEGATES

Burrows, Vinie
George, Zelma

VISUAL ARTS

Filmmaker/Producer/Director

Allen, Debbie
Anderson, Madeline
Chenzira, Ayoka
Collins, Kathleen
Dash, Julie
Parkerson, Michelle
Snow, Valaida
Winfrey, Oprah

Painter/Printmaker/Designer

Catlett, Elizabeth
Hunter, Clementine
Jones, Lois Mailou
Lewis, Edmonia
Ringgold, Faith

Sculptor

Catlett, Elizabeth
Fuller, Meta Warrick
Jackson, May Howard
Lewis, Edmonia
Prophet, Nancy Elizabeth

Ringgold, Faith
Saar, Betye

YWCA
Bowles, Eva D.
Derricotte, Juliette
Fauset, Crystal Dreda Bird
Haynes, Elizabeth Ross

Hedgeman, Anna Arnold
Height, Dorothy
Hunt, Ida Gibbs
Hunter, Jane Edna
Hunton, Addie Waites
Lealtad, Catherine
Pinyon, Josephine
Ruffin, Adele St. Pierre

Index